D0848733

Comparative Labour Law and Industrial Relations in Industrialized Market Economies

Comparative Labour Law and Industrial Relations in Industrialized Market Economies

Editors:
R. Blanpain
and
C. Engels

G. Bamber
R. Ben-Israel
M. Biagi
R. Blanpain
G. Cella
B. Creighton
C. Engels
D. France
M. Franzen
F. Gamillscheg
A. Gladstone
A. Goldman
F. Hendrickx
S. Jackson
A. Jacobs
S. Pursey
J. Rojot
L. Salas
R. Schuler
J. M. Servais
P. Sheldon
L. Swepston
T. Treu
M. Vranken
J. Windmuller

VIIth and revised edition 2001

WITHDRAWN
IOWA STATE UNIVERSITY LIBRARY

Kluwer Law International
The Hague – London Boston

Published by Kluwer Law International
P.O. Box 85889
2508 CN The Hague, The Netherlands

Sold and distributed in North, Central and South America by
Kluwer Law International
101 Philip Drive
Norwell, MA 02061, USA

Sold and distributed in all other countries by
Kluwer Law International
Distribution Centre
P.O Box 322
3300 AH Dordrecht, The Netherlands

A C.I.P. Catalogue record for this book is available from the Library of Congress

Printed on acid-free paper

ISBN 90-411-1565-X Hardback

ISBN 90-411-1565-8 Softcover

© 2001 Kluwer Law International

Kluwer Law International incorporates the publishing programmes of Graham & Trotman Ltd,
Kluwer Law and Taxation Publishers and Martinus Nijhoff Publishers

This publication is protected by internatinal copyright law
All rights reserved. No part of this publication may be reproduced, stored in a retrieval
system, or transmitted in any form or by any form by any means, electronic, mechanical,
photocopying, recording or otherwise, without the prior permission of the publisher.

Printed and bound in Great Britain by Antony Rowe Limited.

Table of Contents

EXTENDED TABLE OF CONTENTS

Notes on Contributors

Greg J. Bamber is Professor and Director of the Graduate School of Management at Griffith University, Brisbane (Australia); His (joint) publications include: *Employment Relations in the Asia Pacific* (Thomson, 2000); and *International and Comparative Employment Relations* (Sage, 1998). (g.bamber@mailbox.gu.edu.au)

Ruth Ben-Israel, Professor of Labour Law, The Alain Poher Chair in Labour Law, Tel-Aviv University, Faculty of Law (Israel). (benisral@post.tau.ac.il)

Marco Biagi is Professor of Labour Law at the University of Modena and Adjunct Professor of Comparative Industrial Relations at the Johns Hopkins University School of Advanced International Studies, Bologna Centre (Italy). (biagi@unimo.it)

Roger Blanpain is Professor of Belgian and European Labour Law and Comparative, Labour Law at the Catholic University of Leuven (Belgium). He is also President of the International Society for Labour Law and Social Security. (roger.blanpain@cer-leuven.be)

Gian Primo Cella is Professor of Economic Sociology at the University of Brescia (Italy).

Breen Creighton is a partner in a large Australian law firm, and is a Professorial Fellow at The University of Melbourne. He practices in the field of labour law and labour relations. He is a former official in the Freedom of Association Branch of the ILO. (breen_creighton@corrs.com.au)

Chris Engels is a Professor at the School of Law and School of Economics of the Catholic University of Leuven, a lawyer at the Brussels bar, and a partner in the law firm Claeys & Engels (Belgium). (chris.engels@claeysengels.be)

Deborah France is currently Deputy Secretary General with the International Organisation of Employers (IOE), the Geneva based organization which represents employers on labour and social affairs at world level. (france@ioe-emp.org)

Martin Franzen is Professor of Civil Law and Labour Law at the University of Constance (Germany). (martin.franzen@uni-konstanz.de)

Franz Gamillscheg is Professor of Labour and International Private Law at the University of Goettingen (Germany).

Alan Gladstone is a former Director of the Labour and Industrial Relations Department of the ILO as well as Secretary-General of the International Industrial Relations Association (Switzerland). (glad@freesurf.ch)

Alvin Goldman is Professor of Law at the University of Kentucky (USA). (agoldman@pop.uky.edu)

Frank Hendrickx is Professor of European labour law at the University of Brabant, Tilburg (The Netherlands) and Postdoctoral Research Fellow – Fund for Scientific Research Flanders, University of Leuven (Belgium). (frank.hendrickx@law.kuleuven.ac.be)

Susan E. Jackson is a Professor of Human Resource Management and Director of the Doctoral Program at the School of Management and Labor Relations, Rutgers University (USA). (sjacksox@rci.rutgers.edu)

Antoine Jacobs is a Professor of Law of the Catholic University of Brabant, Tilburg (The Netherlands). (a.t.j.m.Jacobs@kub.nl)

Stephen Pursey was Head of the Economic and Social Policy Department of the ICFTU and is currently a Senior Economic Policy Advisor at the ILO. (pursey@ilo.org)

Jacques Rojot is a Professor at the University of Paris I, Panthéon Sorbonne (France). (j.rojot@univ-paris1.fr)

Lisa M. Salas is attorney at law, admitted to the bar of the State of Florida, USA. Senior Officer Employment Law Network for Landwell, correspondent law firm of PricewaterhouseCoopers. (lisa.salas@be.pwcglobal.com)

Randall S. Schuler is a Professor of Strategic and International Human Resource Management at Rutgers University, New Jersey (USA). (schuler@rci.rutgers.edu)

Jean-Michel Servais is Research Coordinator at the International Institute for Labour Studies (ILO), Secretary-General of the International Society for Labour Law and Social Security and visiting Professor at the Faculty of Law of the University of Liège (Belgium). (servais@ilo.org)

Peter Sheldon is Associate Professor in the Graduate School of Business and Professional Development, University of Wollongong, NSW, Australia. Currently, his main research areas are employer association policy and behaviour and industrial relations history. (peter_sheldon@uow.edu.au)

Lee Swepston is Chief of the Equality and Employment Branch of the ILO. (swepston@ilo.org)

Tiziano Treu is former Minister of Labour and Professor ordinarius of Labour Law at the Catholic University of Milan (Italy).

Martin N.A. Vranken is Associate Professor at the Faculty of Law, the University of Melbourne (Australia). (m.vranken@law.unimelb.edu.au)

John Windmuller is a former Martin P. Chaterwood Professor in the New York State School of Industrial and Labour Relations at Cornell University since 1951, specializing in international and comparative labour relations (USA).

Editor's Preface

Comparativism is no longer a purely academic exercise but has increasingly become and urgent necessity for industrial relations and legal practitioners due to the growth of multinational enterprises and the impact of international and regional organizations aspiring to harmonize rules. The growing need for comprehensive, up-to-date and readily available information on labour law and industrial relations in different countries led to the publication of the *International Encyclopaedia for Labour Law and Industrial Relations*, in which almost 60 international and national monographs have thus far been published.

This book, *Comparative Labour Law and Industrial Relations in Industrialized market Economies*, goes a step further than the *Encyclopaedia* in as much as most of the chapters provide comparative and integrated thematic treatment. Our aim is to describe the salient characteristics and trends in labour law and industrial relations in the contemporary world. Our book is obviously not exhaustive, with respect to the coverage of countries and topics. We limit ourselves mainly to the industrialized market economies.

The book is divided in three main parts: an **introduction** relating to methodology, and documentation, including the use of Internet. The second part concerns **international actors**, like the International Employer's Organisations and the International Trade Union Movement, as well Human Resources Management. The third concerns the **sources of regulation**, concentrating on International and European Labour Law, as well as on Codes of Conduct for Multinational Enterprises and describes also the rules in case of conflict of laws. The last part deals with **international developments and comparative studies** in not less than 15 chapters.

Encouraged by the warm reception of the first six editions, we hope that also the VIIth edition will serve as a textbook and reference work to facilitate the task of teachers and students of comparative labour law and industrial relatoins. We hope, too, that the book will provide labour lawyers with the necessary insights to cope with a world which is increasingly international.

R.B and C.E
Leuven, 31 December 2000

List of Abbreviations

AB	Nederlandse Jurisprudentie/Administratiefrechtelijke Beslissingen
ACAA	Australian Conciliation and Arbitration Act
ACAC	Australian Conciliation and Arbitration Commission
ACAS	Advisory, Conciliation and Arbitration Service (UK)
ACSPA	Australian Council of Salaried and Professional Associations
ACTU	Australian Council of Trade Unions
AFL	American Federation of Labor
AFL-CIO	American Federation of Labor-Congress of Industrial Organizations
AIFLD	American Institute for Free Labor Development (AFL-CIO)
ALMPS	Active Labour Market Policies
ASAP	Association of Petrochemical Plants (Italy)
ASEAN	Association of South East Asian Nations
AUCCTU	All Union Central Council of Trade Unions (USSR)
AUEW	Amalgamated Union of Engineering Workers (UK)
BATCO	British American Tobacco Company
BATU	Brotherhood of Asian Trade Unionists (WCL)
BDA	Bundesvereinigung der Deutschen Arbeitgeberverbände
BDI	Bundesverband der Deutschen Industrie
BIAC	Business and Industry Advisory Committee (OECD)
BIM	British Institute of Management
CAC	Central Arbitration Committee (UK)
CCO	Confederación de Comisiones Obreras (Spain)
CEEP	Centre Européen des Entreprises Publiques
CFA	Committee on Freedom of Association
CFDT	Confédération Française Démocratique du Travail
CFTC	Confédération Française des Travailleurs Chrétiens
CGC	Confédération Générale des Cadres (France)
CGD	Christlicher Gewerkschaftsbund Deutschlands
CGIL	Confederazione Generale Italiana del Lavoro
CGT	Confédération Générale du Travail (France)
CIFE	Counseil Industriel des Fédérations Européennes
CIME	Committee for International Investment and Multinational Enterprises
CIO	Congress of Industrial Organizations (USA)
CISC	Confédération Internationale des Syndicats Chrétiens
CISL	Confederázione Italiana Sindacati Lavoratori
CNPF	Conseil National du Patronat Français
CNV	Christelijk Nationaal Vakverbond (The Netherlands)
COCCEE	Comité des Organisations Commerciales de la Communauté Econoimique Européenne
COGECA	Comité Général de Cooopératives Agricoles (EC)
COPA	Comité des Organisations Professionnelles Agricoles (EC)

COPE	Committee for Political Education (AFL-CIO)
CRE	Commission of Racial Equality
CSC	Confédération des Syndicats Chrétiens (Belgium)
DAG	Deutsche Angestelltengewerkschaft
DBB	Deutscher Beambtenbund
DGB	Deutscher Gewerkschaftsbund
DOMEI	Japanese Confederation of Labour
EAT	Employment Appeal Tribunal (UK)
EC	European Communities
ed.	editor
ECJ	European Court of Justice
EEOC	Equal Employment Opportunity Commission (USA)
EES	European Employment Strategy
EFA	European Federation of Agricultural Workers
EIRO	European Industrial Relations Observer
EIRR	European Industrial Relations Review
ELC	Employers' Liaison Committee (UNICE)
EMF	European Metalworkers' Federation
EO	European Organisation (WCL)
EP	European Parliament
EPCA	Employment Protection (Consolidation) Act (UK)'
EPD	Employment Discrimination
ERO	European Regional Organisation (ICFTU)
ESC	Economic and Social Committee (EC)
ETUC	European Trade Union Confederation
ETUI	European Trade Union Institute
EWC	European Works Council
FCA	Federal Court of Australia
FFCC	Fact-Finding and Conciliation Commission on Freedom of Association
FMCS	Federal Mediation and Conciliation Service (USA)
FNV	Federatie Nederlandse Vakbeweging (The Netherlands)
GDP	Gross Domestic Product
GLs	Guidelines
GS	General Survey
HTML	Hypertext Mark up Language
ICC	International Chamber of Commerce
ICCPR	International Covenant on Civil and Political Rights
ICEF	International Federation of Chemical, Energy and General Workers Unions
ICESR	International Covenant on Economic, Social and Cultural Rights
ICFTU	International Confederation of Free Trade Unions
id.	idem
IDS	Incomes Data Services
IELL	International Encyclopaedia for Labour Law and Industrial Relations
IFTU	International Federation of Trade Unions
ILO	International Labour Organisation

IME	Committee on International Investment and Multinational Enterprises (OECD)
IMFJC	International Metalworkers Federation – Japanese Council of Metal Workers Unions
IOE	International Organisation of Employers
IPEC	International Programme for the Elimination of Child Labour
ISP	Internet Service Provider
ITS	International Trade Secretariat
ITT	International Telephone and Telegraph Corporation
JTT	Journal des Tribunaux de Travail
LO	Landsorganisationen (Denmark, Norway, Sweden) (Central Confederation of Employees)
MNE	Multinational Enterprise
NAFTA	North American Free Trade Association
NAP	National Action Plan
NGO	Non-Governmental Organisations
NLRB	National Labor Relations Board (USA)
NJ	Nederlandse Jurisprudentie
NPC	National Contact Point
NVV	Federation of Dutch Unions (The Netherlands)
OECD	Organisation for Economic Cooperation and Development
OEEC	Organisation for European Economic Cooperation
OR	Official Bulletin (ILO)
OJ	Official Journal (EC)
ORIT	Interamerican Regional Organization of Workers (ICFTU)
PDF	Portable Document Format
PES	Public Employment Services
PERS	Private Employment Services
QWL	Quality of Working Life
RILU	Red International of Labour Unions
SAF	Svenska Arbetsgivareföreningen (Swedish Employers' Confederation)
SE	Societas Europeae
SNB	Special Negotiating Body
SOHYO	General Council of Trade Unions of Japan
TAR	Tijdschrift voor Ambtenarenrecht
TCO	Tjänstemanns Centralorganization (Sweden)(Central Organization of Salaried Employees)
TCP/IP	Transmission Control Protocol/Internet Provider
TECS	Training and Enterprise Councils
TGWU	Transport and General Workers' Union (UK)
TUAC	Trade Union Advisory Committee (OECD)
TUC	Trade Union Congress (UK)
TUI	Trade Union International (WFTU)
UAW	United Automobile Workers (USA)
UIL	Unione Italiana del Lavoro
UIMM	Union des Industries Métallurgiques et Minières (France)
ULA	Union der Leitenden Angestellten (Germany)
UN	United Nations

UNCTAD   UN Conference on Trade and and Development
UNIAPAC International Christian Union of Business Executives
UNICE   Union of Industrial and Employers' Confederations of Europe
URL   Universal Resources Locator
WAP   Wireless Application Protocol
WCL   World Confederation of Labour
WFTU   World Federation of Trade Unions
WTO   World Trade Organisation
ZFA   Zeitschrift Für Arbeitsrecht
WWW   World Wide Web

METHODOLOGY

Chapter 1. Comparativism in Labour Law and Industrial Relations

R. Blanpain

'The use of the comparative method requires a knowledge not only of the foreign law, but also of its social, and above all its political context. The use of comparative law for practical purposes becomes an abuse only if it is informed by a legalistic spirit, which ignores this context of the law.' O. Kahn-Freund, 'On Uses and Misuses of Comparative Law', *The Modern Law Review*, 1974, p. 27.

Professor Folke Schmidt said: A person who embarks upon comparative research is very akin to a visitor to a foreign country. By this I mean that at the outset of his journey he will be in his home country, with knowledge of the substance of that country's laws and of how those laws are administered. In addition, he will have, as part of his general education, some concept of how things should be – or what is good and what is bad. In other words, he will share some basic values with the people around him. These may not be explicit, and, indeed, he will often not even be aware of them.[1]

I. IN SEARCH OF A DEFINITION

1. 'In every country, North and South', Schregle points out, 'workers, employers, and governments have both common and divergent interests, short term and long term. The divergent interests must be accommodated and reconciled .... The way in which such interests are expressed and reconciled is the subject of industrial relations. It will of necessity vary from country to country. International comparison must bring out and explain the differences and similarities of national industrial relations systems'.[2] Schregle's statement, which obviously also applies to labour law, brings us to the two schools of thought concerning the development of comparative

---

1. A. Neal, 'Comparative Labour Law and Industrial Relations: Major Discipline? – Who cares?', in *Labour Law and Industrial Relations at the Turn of the Century. Liber Amicorum in Honour of Prof. Dr. R. Blanpain*, Kluwer, The Hague, 1998, p. 69.
2. J. Schregle, 'Comparative Industrial Relation: Pitfalls and Potential', *International Labour Review*, 1981, p. 27.

labour relations. One is the *convergence* school, which holds that the spread of industrialization would gradually bring labour relations systems closer to one another. This view was first expounded by Dunlop in his classic book on *Industrial Relations Systems*[3] and further elaborated by other American scholars such as Harbison, Coleman, and Kerr. The other school of thought, the *divergence* school, maintained that labour relations are a subsystem of political systems and mostly reflect prevailing national conditions and cultural values. This view has gained momentum in recent years as a result of the efforts made by developing countries to depart from Western systems, inherited from colonial times and to mould their own labour relations system in the light of their own development requirements.

2.   Referring to Schregle's point, one can consequently say that comparing labour law and industrial relations consists of the study of the labour laws and industrial relations systems of different countries. As Valticos puts it: 'The basic aim of comparative labour law can be said to be essentially *scientific* in nature – namely to gain a *more extensive knowledge of the law of nations*'.[4] This is to say that it involves, first, a scientific analysis of law and practice in order to set them side by side, and doing so note the similarities and the differences; secondly, an attempt to explain those similarities and differences; and thirdly, an effort to perceive eventual trends and overall developments, which operate across national boundaries.

II.   Uses of the Comparative Method

3.   It goes without saying that the knowledge gained by this examination on a comparative basis can serve several purposes which do not exclude each other but on the contrary may very well – and do indeed – go together.

A.   *Better Insight into One's Own National System*

4.   Comparative law is undoubtedly an excellent tool of education. It has thereby often been stressed that the analysis of foreign systems entails the enormous benefit of putting one's own national experience into perspective; that when studying other systems one often experiences a (cultural) shock in discovering that a similar problem is resolved in another country in a completely different way, such that one cannot help but initiate the analysis and evaluation of one's own system again, but now from another angle, from an enriched point of view, from a new insight.

Comparativism consequently contributes to the better perception of one's own national system; besides, it 'enriches one's own approach to and understanding of industrial relations, and improves one's own skills in analysing a variety of industrial relations'.[5]

---

3.   J. Dunlop, *Industrial Relations Systems*, New York, 1958.
4.   'Comparative Law and the International Labour Organisation', *Comparative Labour Law*, 1977, p. 274.
5.   Schregle, *op. cit.*, p. 24.

5. Comparativism may also facilitate the penetration of the national system through the sapping of the 'interpretations' as advanced in foreign doctrines, which can be a source of renewed intellectual stimulation.

We must, however, recognize that comparing the labour law of different countries is for many, if not most, lawyers of no explicit practical value for their daily work. No doubt there are many labour lawyers, extremely busy and successful, for whom national law and developments are plentiful and more than sufficient. Most lawyers have rarely or never been exposed to another legal system, except perhaps when travelling as a tourist and experiencing the legal procedures involved in a car accident, loss of luggage and the like. Many lawyers, if so asked, would certainly argue that they see no compelling reasons to engage in comparative work and that they are more than busy keeping up with national developments.

The fact is that many national systems are more or less mature and capable of resolving the cases, with which the legal profession in a given country has to deal.

6. Except for dramatic circumstances, as a consequence of wars, or drastic revolutions, massive transfers of legal systems do no longer take place. Rarely are there, in actual times, such dramatic legal gaps in given country, that a wholesale transfer is needed, advocated and carried through, although this may partially occur e.g. as in *Spain*, when during the post-Franco period the *Italian* Statute of Workers' Rights of 1970 was often referred to in the elaboration of the Spanish Estatuto de los Trabajadores of 1980.

Those occasions currently being rare, references to a foreign system are in many countries not frequent for purposes of day to day practice.

There are however very important exceptions: for example in *Austria* and *Switzerland* where the influence of German doctrine is reported to be overwhelming, given *inter alia* the fact of a common language and also arising from the fact that the evolution of German labour law is more advanced in Germany than in Switzerland.

In *judgments* themselves, comparison plays a role only in exceptional cases, although e.g. in *Germany* the comparative method is recognized as a valid method of interpretation.

It is only when countries have a common problem – e.g. when a labour relationship transcends national boundaries, or when a given organization has an international, supranational or multinational jurisdiction – that the knowledge of more systems becomes mandatory.

B. International Private Labour Law

7. Knowledge of another legal system is obviously required in the application of *international private labour law*. There is no need to expand on this, except for saying that due to the growing internationalization of business and the expanding free movement of labour across national boundaries, as e.g. in the European Union (EU), the phenomenon of employees involving different national jurisdictions has become a normal fact of life. One should recognize, however, that judges, when confronted with international private labour law problems, may tend to apply their own national system and that lawyers confronted with those problems frequently rely on a report given by a foreign colleague, without themselves striving to discover the foreign solution.

5

C. Multinational Enterprises and International Unions

8.   *Multinational enterprises*, which by their very nature operate – in a more or less centralized way – in different countries, clearly have more than a vested interest in studying and comparing the labour law of the home country and of actual or potential host countries.

Labour relations are in essence national in the multinational enterprise in the sense that subsidiaries have to follow national rules and practice,[6] at least up to a certain point, since a national system may have a lot of manoeuvring space for multinational input; national labour law and practice may constitute an important factor in deciding where to invest and disinvest.[7] In central and regional headquarters specialists attentively follow developments in the different countries in which operations take place, or might take place as well as developments in international organizations, like the ILO, the OECD and the EU.

One can foresee that the growing development of international labour relations, namely relations between headquarters in one country and employees in one or more other countries, on issues such as the co-responsibility of the parent for the debts of the daughter or the 'access to real decision makers', will grow in importance in the years to come.

In *international trade unions*, the same interest exists in comparing and following developments in different countries. This is obviously in order to defend the interests of workers, especially those employed in multinational enterprises. Some unions also closely follow collective bargaining developments in different countries, in order to advise their members and coordinate certain actions.

D.   Forecast of Further Developments

9.   Moreover, if comparative analysis allows us to acknowledge certain trends and developments, then the exercise will enable the comparative scholar 'to find out to *what extent our own national system is synchronized with such trends*, or whether it precedes them, lags behind them or even moves in a different direction. This opens up fascinating prospects'.[8]

By the same token, comparativism may help to forecast future developments as ideas and concepts do indeed, more than before, due to the growing internationalization of our world, cross national and regional boundaries; and what may happen to us may already be inscribed in the labour relations in other countries.

---

6.   Paragraph 7 of the Introduction of the OECD Guidelines for Multinational Enterprises (1976). A similar principle is laid down in the Tripartite Declaration of Principles Concerning Multinational Enterprises and Social Policy of the ILO, 1977, No. 8.

7.   R. Blanpain, *The OECD Guidelines for Multinational Enterprises and Labour Relations 1976–1979*, Deventer, 1980, pp. 15–16. Review of the OECD Guidelines for Multinational Enterprises: Possible revisions to the chapter on employment and industrial relations, in *Multinational Enterprises and the Social Challenges of the XXIst Century, Bulletin of Comparative Labour Relations*, No. 37, pp. 18–29.

8.   Schregle, *op. cit.*, p. 24.

E. To Guide or Promote Social Change at Home – Assistance

10. Another use of comparativism is to promote at home a social change which foreign law of practice is designed either to express or to produce,[9] which obviously involves difficulties of transplantability to be discussed below.

11. Many examples could be given to illustrate this use. When 'temporary work' was introduced in Europe and national legislators were taking measures to regulate this new social phenomenon, national measures were, in many countries, inspired by regulations elaborated in other countries.[10]

12. Other examples can be given, showing that this is not without problems. Thus, one may cite the Spanish case, where due to the fact that the workers' statute (Statuto de los Trabajadores) was close in name and apparent content to the Italian Statuto dei Lavaratori (1970), it raised expectations with Spanish workers that, to some extent, could not be met. In some Latin American countries, the use of the Labour Code of a more advanced country (e.g. the influence of the Colombian Labour Code on Honduran legislation) also entailed some difficulties of implementation.

Another example can be found in the adoption of the Australian system of compulsory arbitration by some developing countries, like Singapore, which resulted in the establishment of an Industrial Court vested with relatively wide powers.

13. A distinction may be made between developing countries and developed countries. In the former, transplantation has been used as a tool of modernization or industrialization. Here, too, there are two sides to the coin. The positive side is the easiness in the introduction of industrial change; less advantageous is the fact that those countries may suffer from inconsistencies between the system introduced and the social context of that country.

14. Another use for comparativism lies in the area of advice and assistance given to specific countries, either by international organizations or in a bilateral framework.

F. As an Instrument in the Formulation and the Application of International Labour Standards: Horizontal and Vertical Comparison

15. Valticos rightly underlines that the formulation of international minimum standards or international labour law is often quoted as one area where the use of the comparative method has been the most extensive.[11] Here naturally come to mind not only the international labour conventions and recommendations elaborated in the framework of the ILO, but also the European Social Charter as the harmonization of social standards in the Member States of the Council of Europe, next to United

---

9. O. Kahn-Freund, 'On Uses and Misuses of Comparative Law', *op. cit.*, p. 2.
10. R. Blanpain (ed.), *Temporary Work and Labour Law of the European Community and the Member States*, Deventer, 1993.
11. *Op. cit.*, p. 273.

Nations Instruments and the European Human Rights Convention, to name only the most important.

In addition, mention should be made of the Charter of Social Rights, adopted by the *Organization of American States* in 1948 (Bogota), and the Conventions adopted by the *Arab Labour Organization*.

1. The International Labour Organisation (ILO)

16. The ILO Conventions are, by far, the main source of international labour law. This is due not only to their number, ratifications by numerous countries, but also to their detailed character and the increasingly broad field they cover.[12]

17. It is self-evident that the first step in the formulation of international legislation and practice is to collect information on national legislation and practice: international standards are indeed not created out of the blue, but should relate as much as possible to national experience. It is, therefore, only natural that before the governing body of the ILO decides to place an item on the agenda of the International Labour Conference with the aim of adopting an international instrument, the office must place before it 'a concise statement of the existing laws and practice in the various countries relative to that item'.

18. Valticos describes the formulation process as follows:

'Once it has conducted this general survey of the state of current legislation throughout the world, the Governing Body decides whether or not to place the item on the agenda of the Conference. If the item is placed on the agenda, a second, more detailed comparative study must be carried out. The ILO prepares "a preliminary report setting out the law and practice in the different countries" and any other useful information. The report draws attention to generally accepted guiding principles in the field concerned, usually under several headings, and to the various national regulations on the subject…

Together with this comparative survey of law and practice, the ILO sends governments a questionnaire with the request that they should give reasons for their replies. On the basis of the replies from governments, the ILO prepares a further report indicating the principal questions which require consideration by the Conference so as to be able to reach conclusions as to the general, or at least the majority, view. This report forms the basis of an initial discussion by the Conference. Following this first discussion, which leads to the adoption of conclusions with a view to an international instrument, a second series of consultations is carried out by the ILO, which then drafts one or more Conventions or Recommendations on which governments are invited to comment, whereupon the matter is again placed before the Conference, which adopts the final texts'.[13]

---

12. N. Valticos, 'International Labour Law', in *International Encyclopedia for Labour Law and Industrial Relations*, pp. 43, 229; *see* Chapter 5.
13. 'Comparative Law and the International Labour Organisation', *Comparative Labour Law*, 1977, pp. 279–280.

19. The comparative method is also used for the examination of the application of the international minimum standards. 'In the context', Valticos indicates, 'it generally takes the form of a comparison between the international standard and the national legislation of countries that have ratified the Convention concerned – though also sometimes of countries which have not ratified it. At times, too, the international standards may even be compared with all known national laws on the subject'.[14]

2. The Council of Europe and the European Communities

20. Mention should obviously also be made of the *European Social Charter*, promulgated by the *Council of Europe* in 1961, as revised (1996). The supervision of the application of the Charter is mainly in the hands of a Committee of Experts, which examines the reports the governments are required to submit.[15]

Equally important are certain Articles (4–10–11) of the *European Convention of Human Rights and Fundamental Freedoms*, adopted in 1950.

21. Comparativism is also at the heart of the harmonization of labour laws which takes place within the framework of the *European Union*. One of the goals of he Community consists of the development of a social policy aiming to promote improvement in the living and working conditions of labourers so as to permit the equalization of such conditions in an upward direction. This development, the EU treaty indicates, 'will result not only from the functioning of the Common Market, which will form the harmonization of social systems, but also from the approximation of (legislative and administrative) provisions' (Article 136). Harmonization of labour laws is, however, not a goal of the EC. It is only where 'different, territorially limited, legal systems disturb the realisation of the goals of the treaty' that the *Community* is entitled to propose a measure favouring harmonization.[16]

22. *Jörn Pipkorn*, a civil servant at the European Communities, gives a clear description of the use of the comparative method in the drafting of harmonized EC rules.

'When an action for harmonizing social and labour law is envisaged under those circumstances, the competent service of the Commission (for example, the Directorate General for Social Affairs) asks qualified experts in all the Member States (in most cases professors of social and labour law) to prepare reports on the legal situation in the respective Member State as to the subject to be covered by the envisaged harmonization. One such expert is entrusted with summarizing these reports and evaluating their findings with a view to indicating possible trends towards harmonization. This general rapporteur has to ensure, in cooperation with the competent officials of the EC Commission, that the national reports have a common structure and a coherent approach to the relevant problems, as is necessary for the comparative study. To these ends, the general

---

14. *Ibid.*, pp. 284–286.
15. O. Kahn-Freund, 'The European Charter' in F.G. Jacobs (ed.), *European Law and the Individual*, Amsterdam, 1976, pp. 181–211.
16. J. Pipkorn, 'Comparative Labour Law in the Harmonization of Social Standards in the European Community', *Comparative Labour Law*, 1977, p. 263.

rapporteur and the EC officials prepare a questionnaire which is then discussed with the national rapporteurs before it serves as a basis for their reports. Those reports, as well as the draft synthetic report of the general rapporteur, are discussed among all rapporteurs, in order to clarify the relevant problems.'

23. If the problems to be solved do not appear so difficult to the competent EC officials, they may, however, simplify the preparatory work, entrusting one or two experts with the comparative research for all the Member States.

Whether one or more experts do the comparative research, the result will inevitably reflect certain inconsistencies or some overemphasis due to the personality of the author. But those imperfections are revealed, in both cases, in the subsequent stages of the procedure.

When the synthetic report is ready, the responsible Directorate General of the Commission sends it to the employer and union organizations, UNICE, CEEP and ETUC. These organizations send the report to their affiliated organizations in all the Member States and prepare a paper reflecting the joint opinion of their affiliates. Both organizations send their papers to the Commission and discuss them with the responsible service.

The responsible service of the Commission then convenes a working party of experts nominated by the governments of the Member States to discuss the synthetic report and possible measures of harmonization. The governments normally send to this working party officials of their competent departments. Those officials are generally the same persons who will subsequently represent their governments on the working party of the Council when the Commission eventually submits its proposal to that body. But at this earlier stage of the process, the officials are not meant to express the views of their governments but to give a reasoned opinion as experts. The responsible services of the Commission then prepare a draft proposal of a directive or a regulation embodying the envisaged harmonization measure on the basis of the Article of the Treaty of Rome relevant to this measure. This draft proposal is discussed in the same way as the synthetic report before it is finalized and formally adopted by the Commission. One and another may lead to a European collective agreement, which may be rendered binding by a Council Directive.

24. The proposal of the Commission is submitted to the Council, the Community's main legislative body. Self-evidently also the European Parliament (EP) and the Economic and Social Committee (ESC), as provided for in the respective Articles of the Treaty, are involved.

The crucial and decisive stage is reached when the Council discusses the proposal of the Commission.

The discussion within the Council has of course much 'feed-back' with the national employer and labour organizations and their legal and socio-economic framework. This process offers the maximum guarantees for making available all arguments of comparative law for the political discussion.[17]

---

17. *Op. cit.*, pp. 264–267; for a description of the decision-making procedure and the involvement of the social partners also in relation to the Treaty of Amsterdam (1997), *see* R. Blanpain, *European Labour Law*, 7th and revised ed., Kluwer, The Hague, 2000.

G. As an Instrument for Theory Formulation

25. The important contribution to comparativism of theory formulation and theorizing in industrial relations reveals another area of the possible uses of comparativism in industrial relations.

Professor John Dunlop, in his seminal work *Industrial Relations Systems*, was one of the first to articulate the need to adopt a comparative approach in order to acquire theoretical insight in industrial relations. As he and others[18] have explained, comparativism could and should be used as an instrument to verify *a priori* hypotheses or to produce abstract generalizations derived from research findings in a variety of national contexts.[19]

As Walker rightly points out, however, comparativism used for such purposes should transcend the descriptive approach to foreign industrial relations systems, and concentrate upon the explanation of the functioning of industrial relations systems, in order to identify the role, importance and interaction of the different factors shaping and influencing industrial relations systems in a variety of national contexts.

26. One of the most prominent examples of theoretical studies, where comparativism was the main underpinning method, is the research project known as 'the Inter-university Study of Labour Problems in Economic Development', from which originated major works such as *Industrialism and Industrial Man, Labour in Developing Economies*.[20]

A further review of the industrial relations literature provides us with many other examples, where comparativism appears as a vital instrument for theory formulation.

We refer in this context to a number of theoretical contributions, which cover the various subfields of the industrial relations discipline, and which fruitfully used comparativism for the study and theoretical explanation of industrial relations problems such as strike trends and industrial conflict, collective bargaining, trade-unionism, etc.

Ross and Hartmann,[21] for example, used the comparative method to confirm the famous 'withering away' hypothesis; they also contributed to theory formulation by identifying the different factors which explained the (decreasing) level of strikes, caused by factors such as the development of labour parties with close trade union affiliations, the growing importance of the State as the major institution influencing workers' welfare, changing employers' policies etc.

27. Finally, it might be of interest to note that comparativism has retained much of its prominence as a research method for theory formulation in industrial relations,

---

18. J. Porter, 'Quelques observations sur les études comparées', in *Bulletin International Institute for Labour Studies*, 1967, p. 97. *See also* M. Shalev, 'Industrial Relations theory and the comparative study of industrial relations and industrial conflict', BJIR, Vol. XVIII, March 1980, p. 26.

19. K. Walker, 'L'étude comparée des relations professionalles', in *Bulletin International*, Institute for Labour Law Studies, 1967, No. 3, p. 213. *See also* T.A. Kochan, 'The Need for New Industrial Relations Institutions', in *Labour Law and Industrial Relations at the Turn of the Century. Liber Amicorum in Honour of Prof. Dr. R. Blanpain*, Kluwer, The Hague, 1998, pp. 41–54.

20. C. Kerr, J. Dunlop, F. Harbison, C. Meyers, *Industrialism and Industrial Man*, London, 1962. W. Galenson (ed.), *Labour and Economic Development*, New York, 1959.

21. A. Ross and P. Hartmann, *Changing Patterns of Industrial Conflict*, New York, 1960.

as is illustrated by the International Institute for Labour Studies, a Geneva programme for comparative industry studies. Some of the research objectives of this project also provided us with a good example of the possible use of comparativism for theory formulation. They were defined as follows: (a) to use the international variations in the strength of certain factors to assess the manner and extent of the influence of those factors upon industrial relations in the industry under study; (b) to establish which characteristics of industrial relations in a particular industry are sufficiently powerful to withstand the pressure of national industrial relations systems in the countries compared, thus helping to identify and clarify the role of certain strategic factors in industry-level industrial relations systems; (c) to advance, through the comparison of a number of industries across a number of countries, an understanding of the operation of strategic factors in industrial relations systems, as a further step towards the development of a general theory of industrial relations.[22]

III. WHAT AND HOW TO COMPARE?

A. Comparison of Functions rather than Institutions

28. In order to compare what is in fact comparable, one needs to compare the functions institutions perform, rather than institutions themselves. Indeed similar institutions, e.g. works councils, labour courts, union delegations, may perform different functions in different countries. One is interested in what is going on, thus in the functions rather than in institutions as such. Schregle illustrates this point by considering three examples: labour courts and labour disputes, collective agreements and collective bargaining, and workers' participation. Let us limit ourselves to Schregle's third example: worker's participation.

'There is much confusion and disagreement over this term. Whatever the expression "workers' participation" may mean in the terminology and context of a given country, I propose to use it here in its wide sense as encompassing various arrangements by which workers and their representatives have a say in the decision-making process at the enterprise level ... Again we must guard against falling into the trap of a purely institutional comparison. A tabular listing of the respective rights of, say, the *French* works council, the *Austrian*, or *German* works council, the *Belgian* or *Dutch* works council, may be of some informative usefulness but it does not permit any meaningful evaluative comparison. It is certainly interesting to see what the respective rights of such bodies are, as regards, for instance, management decisions on personnel questions, social and welfare matters, terms and conditions of employment, as well as in the fields of production, marketing, finance and investment ... Such charts or tabular listings do not allow a comparative evaluation of the respective degree of workers' influence on management decisions in different countries. At first sight, it might appear that in the German highly institutionalized system of

---

22. M. Derber, 'Strategic Factors in Industrial Relations Systems, the metal working industry', *Labour and Society*, 1976, p. 18.

works councils with far-reaching statutory co-determination rights, workers' influence would be greater than in a country where there are no such bodies. However, it may well be that in fact the influence that workers can exercise on management decisions is much stronger under a system of enterprise-level collective bargaining, as is the case in the United States.

Here again – and this cannot be repeated too often – we must compare functions and not institutions. Whether the worker's representatives on the supervisory boards of the Volkswagen Company who help to take important investment decisions in the boardroom really have a greater or lesser influence on management than the trade unions in Italy, which as a matter of principle and policy reject the very idea of workers' representation on company boards but have secured agreement on large-scale FIAT investments in the south of Italy through collective bargaining with the management in Turin, would be an interesting subject for comparative industrial relations research.'[23]

B. Comparison of What is 'Going on'

29. From what has been said thus far concerning the comparison of functions, it clearly follows that the comparative scholar should try to find out what is 'going on', look for 'reality'. It is therefore not sufficient to compare the text of the legislation of different countries, one should also look at collective agreements, work rules in the enterprise, tacit understandings, customs and past practice. It is above all important to find out whether and how laws are applied and how institutions function in practice. Is it not interesting to know whether the Belgian works councils do in fact get the abundant information they are by legislation entitled to? A recent investigation showed that the implementation that legislation is far from adequate.

30. It is, to give another example, equally relevant not only to examine the law on trade-union freedom, but also to know whether there are trade unions in a given country, what rights they enjoy in reality, how they are structured and the like. It is certainly interesting to know that the Belgian labour courts, in practice, deal almost exclusively with individual disputes of dismissed employees; this raises challenging questions such as why this is so and what happens to grievances of employees still at work.

C. Looking for 'Models'

31. One of the best means of obtaining the benefits of the comparative method is the comparison of 'models', a model being a distinctive way of approaching a given problem, and by illustrating how a given 'model' functions in one or more countries. Such a method enables us to get a panoramic view of the different ways in which similar problems are solved, how one's system relates to these models, and to note differences, similarities and trends.

---

23. Schregle, *op. cit.*, pp. 22–23.

32. Let us illustrate how this might be done in the field of job security. One can obviously distinguish different systems or models for promoting job security, e.g.:

- through lifetime employment;
- government action: permission by a government official, e.g. a director of the employment office, is needed before an employer can dismiss an employee;
- through workers' representatives (e.g. a works council) who may oppose dismissal;
- through legal obligation upon the employer to respect a term of notice;
- through the application of various criteria for selection for redundancy such as: last hired – first hired (the seniority system);
- by means of the rule that employment may not be terminated unless there is a valid reason connected with the capacity or the conduct of the employee or based on the operational requirements of the enterprise, establishment or service ...

33. These different systems of securing employment could then be illustrated by referring to experience in one or more countries where one or more models are in operation. The lifetime employment model is obviously to be represented by the Japanese practice; while the role of the government could be depicted by e.g. the Dutch or the French experience; for the evaluation of the role of the representatives of employees one could refer to the competence of the works council in Germany or of the local union (union delegates) in Sweden. The obligation to respect a term of notice could be best illustrated by the Belgian example of the (rather long) terms of notice to be given in the case of a dismissal of a white-collar employee. Seniority could be depicted on the basis of the American system, as it is elaborated in collective agreements, while the justification of dismissal could be illustrated by a number of countries, which follow the widely applied ILO Recommendation (No. 119) of 1963 as further elaborated by Convention No. 154 of 1981 on the same subject concerning the Termination of Employment at the Initiative of the Employer.

34. One could further look for models in the area of the remedies designed to achieve employment security, namely compensation, reinstatement, (penal) sanctions, then again look for countries where such models are in operation.

35. Another example can be easily found in the area of workers' participation, used in the sense of the influence by labour on management decision-making. Here the models (functions) are obvious: information, consultation, co-decision making, possibly self-government for certain issues. The question is whether and how these functions are fulfilled in different countries by examining the role of collective bargaining, of representative bodies of employees in the enterprise (works councils, union delegates, shop stewards, committees for hygiene, ...); the role of employees sitting on company boards, the effect of job enrichment schemes, semi-autonomous work groups and the like.

D. An Integrated and Global Approach

36. This heading covers different points. It goes without saying that if comparativism aims not only at the discovery of similarities and differences of common or opposing trends, but also at explaining why different systems operate the way they do in a given country, one can study a given problem only within the overall context of the industrial relations' system, or even the society taken as a whole, both in its contemporary and in its historic dimension. In order to understand and appreciate the role of a labour director (an employee sitting on the management board of a company) in Germany one has to relate this form of workers' participation not only to the works council(s) – which are established also at plant level and at enterprise or company level –; to the economic committee; also to the '*Vertrauensleute*' (trusted men) at enterprise level (in the metal-working industry); as well to collective bargaining, which takes place at the industrial level of the different states. This leads us in turn to consider the role of German trade unions, which are not active at the level of the plant or the enterprise. Just as one needs insight into this unique German character of order and discipline, one has to know that workers' participation started long before the Second World War, and that it is the outcome of a long and evolutionary process, brutally interrupted by the Nazis and first reintroduced in the coal, iron and steel industries by Allied Command after the Second World War. This is obviously not an easy task.

37. It is clear, then, that comparing labour laws and industrial relations' systems involves much more than setting side by side summaries of legislation from different countries on a given number of subjects. This is only part of the material needed. What is necessary is a thorough knowledge of the different industrial relations' systems, seen within a wider societal framework, i.e. a knowledge of what is going on and why this is so. The real comparative work starts when one writes on 'one subject, comparing and contrasting the law and practice' in all countries covered. This I would call the *integrated approach*: not county reports in succession, but a concentration on issues across national boundaries. It is obvious that this constitutes an ideal which can only be fully obtained in rather exceptional circumstances, namely, within the framework of collective scholarship.

E.   Group Collaboration

38. The best way to reap the full benefits of the comparative method as a tool for research is obviously the group approach used e.g. by the European Communities as mentioned earlier; namely, to start with national reports, written by national experts, prepared on the basis of a common outline; then on the basis of those reports a comparative report is written. Both the national reports as well as the general report are discussed by the members of the expert group. In doing so, one develops a framework guaranteeing the best use of national expertise and insight, ensuring that the reports are clear and understood by the different members of the group and that the general report is a true reflection of similarities, differences, trends and explains the nature of and reasons for particular developments.

39. This method is used, at least in part, by a number of international societies, such as the International Society for Labour Law and Social Security. The collective method was also used by the Comparative Labour Law Group, now no longer in existence, which involved six professors from Britain, France, Italy, Sweden,

the USA, and Germany. In his personal appraisal of their work, Aaron writes:

> 'The strongest single conviction produced by my participation in the work of the Comparative Labour Law Group is that our various methods of conducting our research represent a unique and lasting contribution to comparative research. I knew at the start that no one person could learn within a reasonable time, if ever, as such about the system in any other country as was already known by a competent scholar from the country. Hence, we began with the national reports. But preparing a series of national reports is really not comparative research; it may sometimes be essential, but it is never sufficient. Accordingly, we moved to the next step: each member writing on one subject but comparing and contrasting the law and practice in all six countries. This was the real thing.'[24]

F. Educational Visits

40. Of course, this does not imply that individual scholars cannot effectively engage in comparative work, but this obviously should not, except for purely technical issues, be limited to a 'desk study'. It is especially necessary, in the case of individual research involving foreign countries, to make frequent visits to the countries in question and to inquire, with the aid of extensive interviews with local scholars and practitioners (lawyers, employers, trade unionists), about the realities of the situation.

IV. THE TRAPS

A. Language and Terminology

41. One of the main difficulties, which presents a real pitfall for the comparative scholar, is the fact that identical words in different languages may have different meanings, while the corresponding terms may embrace wholly different realities.

42. Examples are easy to find. Let's limit ourselves to an *English–French* interchange and start with the word 'eventually', in French 'éventuellement'. Although both words are identical, they convey a different, almost opposite meaning: 'eventually' means 'ultimately', while the French 'éventuellement' means 'possibly'. I must, to my shame, confess that I have used the English 'eventually' for more than ten years with the French meaning in mind.

Another example is constituted by the word 'arbitration' – in French 'arbitrage'. To my great surprise, I learned when participating in an EEC Working Group on 'The Prevention and Settlement of Industrial Disputes' as general reporter,[25] that the

---

24. 'The Comparative Labour Law Group: A Personal Appraisal', *Comparative Labour Law*, 1977, p. 235.
25. *See* 'Settlement of Industrial Disputes in the EEC Countries', *Bulletin of the Industrial Law Society*, 1979, pp. 10–24.

word 'arbitration' (arbitrage), which usually means a binding decision by an impartial umpire, signifies in Luxemburg a recommendation by a government conciliator to the conflicting parties.

When discussing the competence of works councils in different European countries with *Goldman*, and more specifically the 'economic' and 'social' competence of the councils, we found that the words 'economic' and 'social' carry different meanings in the American and European contexts: in the USA, wages and benefits are looked upon from the financial side and are consequently classified under the heading 'economic' competence, while in Europe wages and benefits relate to the social conditions of the employee and are by that logic filed under the heading 'social competence'. Another example concerns the American 'public company' and the French 'enterprise publique'. The latter is a state-owned enterprise while the American public company is a private company, the shares of which are however publicly listed ... The list is endless.

43. The traps set by language are minor compared to those which arise in connection with terminology. Schregle rightly points out that 'comparative industrial relations faces a tremendous problem of terminology ... as concepts, expressed in words, are laden with values, emotions, past experiences and future expectations',[26] which make comparativism almost a mission impossible. He recalls that Hanami, in his book on *Labour Relations in Japan Today* (1979) pointed out that 'applying Western terminology to Japanese phenomena ... has led to confusion'.

B.   Parochialism and Ideological Hangovers

44. A major danger for comparativism lies undoubtedly in the possibility that the researcher may be overly influenced by the system in his/her own country. He may attempt to analyse another country's system by continuously identifying, assimilating and evaluating practices there with local familiar experiences. 'Comparative industrial relations must liberate us from emotions and prejudices inherent in our own national systems and from the idea that our own system should be a model for others.'[27]

45. A second threat is constituted by ideological hangovers, which can hamper exchanges of ideas, and consequently comparative work. One example may suffice to illustrate this point. The debate on workers' participation has been extremely confused, since those involved in the debate depart from different ideologies and expectations.

Some see workers' participation or industrial democracy as a fundamental political goal and want, by introducing more democratic schemes, fundamentally to change the socio-economic system of society, striving, for example, towards self-government by workers on the former Yugoslav model. Others refuse to discuss the possibility of having employees on supervisory boards of companies, since this

---

26.   Schregle, *op. cit.*, p. 26.
27.   *Ibid.*

conflicts with their theories of class struggle because it promotes the 'integration of the working class in neo-capitalist society'. Still others view workers' participation in terms of efficiency and point out that certain participatory devices are necessary to engage the enthusiastic participation of employees in furthering the goals of the company. A number of others see workers' participation in terms of the humanization of the workplace and think, *inter alia*, in terms of job-enrichment schemes (advocated by some to keep unions out) and semi-autonomous work groups. Still others think of 'participation' in terms of profit-sharing, which was one of General De Gaulle's approaches to the 'participation' problem. Thus, ideological perceptions provide a serious obstacle to fruitful comparative analysis.

46. It is only when one tackles the problem of workers' participation independent from ideology by simply stating that whatever system or model of workers' participation is considered, it entails greater power for labour to influence managerial decision-making, that comparativism becomes possible.

Obviously, ideology cannot be ignored – on the contrary – for ideology will, *inter alia*, help us to find out why things evolve in a certain way. It is also crucial since at the end of the day each individual will have to decide what sort of participative society is desirable. But again, ideology *should not* hinder us from taking reality as it stands or from engaging in open discussion.

V. The Transplantability Issue

47. In his unforgettable 'Uses and Misuses of Comparative Law',[28] *Kahn-Freund* formulated and analysed the transplantability issue in a few pages, which everyone engaged in comparative work must read. Kahn-Freund in his unique, penetrating and all-embracing way, said it all in a way no one can match. Kahn-Freund makes the following point: 'we cannot take for granted that rules or institutions are transplantable ...; any attempt to use a pattern of law outside the environment of its origin continues to entail the wish of rejection'.[29] Indeed, 'labour law is a part of a system, and the consequences of change in one aspect of the system depends upon the relationship between all elements of the system. Since those relationships may not be similar between the two societies, the effects of similar legislation may differ significantly as between the two differing settings'.[30]

This does not however mean that we cannot adopt solutions that have proved successful in other countries, nor that there is no case for introducing riles that will not be rejected, but integrated. There are indeed 'degrees of transferability'.[31]

48. The degree of (non-)transplantability depends largely on the relationship to the distribution of power in society. In considering this, one must constantly bear in mind that labour relations are, in essence, power relations; that, in any labour relations

---

28. *The Modern Law Review*, 1974, pp. 1–27.
29. *Op. cit.*, p. 27.
30. Meyers, *op. cit.*, p. 243.
31. Kahn-Freund, *op. cit.*, p. 6.

system, the main question is, who has the power to take decisions. It is obvious that the answer to that question has to do with the political system of the country involved: whether one lives in a pluralist system, where different groups share power, or in a country where considerable power is concentrated in the hands of one group – e.g. a political party. It is obvious that the role of trade unions, of collective bargaining (the autonomy of labour-management), of the right to strike, let alone the influence of labour on management decision-making, fundamentally differ according to the type of political system. This is clearly demonstrated by the Polish experience and the development of the free trade union 'Solidarity'. It is also obvious that independent trade unions sharing power did not fit into now defunct socialist model of the eastern European countries. The political arrangements in a given country are a determining factor affecting the transfer of rules which might have an impact on the power relations in that country.

49. This is so even in countries which share more or less the same social, economic, political structures as do, for example, the Member Countries of the EU. In a given country, the balance of power – however evolving between all organized groups, not only business, trade unions, farmers, the self-employed, political parties, but also cultural groups, consumer organizations, religious groups, universities, and the like – is indeed so delicate that any change affecting that package will be most cautiously considered and runs a high chance of being rejected.

50. This is why the proposed directive providing for more workers' participation in the EU Member Countries, the so-called proposed V Directive, although already put forward in 1972 is still not on the books: it affects the power relationship in the enterprises. The same is true for the European Company Statute. This is why a real battle has taken place, both in the European capitals and in the European headquarters of Brussels and Strasbourg (the European Parliament), concerning the proposed (1980) directive on information and consultation of employees in transnational enterprises and in enterprises with a complex structure: multinational enterprises fear that trade unions may find in that directive a platform for international collective bargaining and thus affect the overall managerial flexibility multinational headquarters enjoy at international level. The outcome of that battle meant that the establishment of EWCs was facilitated by the great amount of flexibility enterprises and employees' representatives enjoy in concluding information and consultation agreements, which suit their proper needs. The conclusion is clear: rules relating to the power relations in the industrial relations systems and also in society as a whole will be the most difficult to transplant. Even if transplanted under dramatic circumstances, as with the transfer of the American collective bargaining (plant-enterprise bargaining) model to Japan after World War II, the foreign model will be completely absorbed and transformed into a new and unique system as the Japanese experience so abundantly illustrates.

51. This point becomes crystal clear if one analyses the success of the ratification of the ILO Conventions and the impact of its Recommendations, which, as Kahn-Freund puts it, constitute a 'gigantic enterprise of transplantation'. The fact is that the bulk of ILO instruments do not relate to elements of power in the industrial relations systems but to protection standards, such as industrial safety and hygiene,

holidays, forced labour, discrimination in employment, employment policies, general conditions of work (hours of work, weekly rest, paid leave) women's work, children, older workers, migrant labour, and the like. The conventions relating to trade union freedom and collective bargaining, although extremely important, constitute exceptions. They are, moreover, drafted in very cautious and flexible terms: the obligation to promote collective bargaining, to be implemented by 'measures appropriate to national conditions' and only 'where necessary'.[32]

52.   To put it otherwise, collective labour law (trade union freedom, workers' participation including collective bargaining, the right to strike and the rules concerning lock-out, as well as the procedures concerning settlement of industrial disputes – conciliation and arbitration) is resistant to transplantation, while individual labour law (categories of contracts, rules on leave, hours, sickness, discrimination, job security, and the like) lends itself much more easily to transplantation.[33]

VI.   THE STATUS OF THE 'ACADEMIC ART'

53.   Academia curricula are usually not in the forefront of legal developments. Rather they develop with caution, moderation and a certain element of conservatism. This may be one of the reasons why comparativism in general and comparative labour law specifically are not yet prominent in the list of obligatory or even optional courses for law students in a number of countries; why a comparative touch is mostly lacking when national labour law is taught. In certain countries, we might recall, (national) labour law is not even part of the obligatory curriculum.

In a number of countries there are, however, encouraging signs and a noticeable growing interest.

In *Italy*, for example, nine universities provide courses in comparative labour law, focusing on trade unions, collective bargaining, industrial relations systems, and the like.

In *Belgium*, every law school is obliged to have a number of optional comparative courses in its programme, among which are included comparative labour law, and each student has to choose one comparative course.

In other countries comparative teaching seems less widespread. In *Switzerland*, the University of Geneva has had a comparative labour law course since 1963; in *Germany* there are some optional courses, *inter alia* at Göttingen. In the *Netherlands* there is a regular course in Tilburg. There are comparative courses on labour law in the *Nordic Countries*.

54.   Encouraging signs can also be reported in the area of *research*. Besides studies by the international organizations, like the ILO, the OECD and the EU as reported by Vranken, there are a number of non-governmental groups that engage in interesting comparative work, such as the International Society for Labour Law and

---

32.   *Ibid.*, p. 72.
33.   *Ibid.*, p. 21.

Social Security, or the International Industrial Relations Association, where, in fact, the main comparative task is performed by the general reporters.

It is also interesting that many *Ph.D.s in labour law* have a comparative aspect and that in *Switzerland*, to give an example, each Ph.D. must testify to comparative work.

VII. *DE COMPARATIONE FERANDE*: GUIDELINES

55. Where does all this lead us to?

There is no doubt that comparativism is an excellent tool for education and research, for the understanding and better solving of problems. One the other hand, we see, even from our sketchy 'state of the art', that the role of comparativism can be improved upon in teaching, research and also problem solving. Here, the International Society for Labour Law and Social Security could contribute by setting some guidelines for the promotion of comparativism in labour law, which I submit for consideration.

A. *Teaching*

(1) Each labour law course should provide some comparative insights on certain topical issues, in order to open the students' minds toward comparative thinking.
(2) Each law school should provide an 'optional course' or 'seminar' of comparative labour law.
(3) Each law library should have a minimum of comparative labour law materials.

B. *Research*

(1) Doctoral theses should, whenever possible and appropriate, make use of the comparative method.
(2) The International Societies should favour the creation of *informal working groups*, which should be able to present the result of their comparative work at the regional and worldwide congresses.

CONCLUSIONS

56. There is no doubt that the need for comparativism is growing, as our world becomes more and more our village, as people and ideas cross boundaries as easily as they do due to the ever-expanding communications and information technology, as international cooperation develops and multinational investment and free movement of labour increases, for all entail enormous cross-fertilization.

57. Comparativism is, however, a very demanding discipline. The comparative student not only needs to know about labour law and industrial practice, he also needs an insight into the history, the culture, the political system, and the prevailing values of a society in order to be able to grasp the essentials of any industrial relations

system. There are the necessary skills of knowledge of languages, as well as an awareness of the traps and pitfalls.

58. For many this may raise the question of whether comparativism is not reversed for a happy few, the international civil servants, the jet-setting professors, constantly travelling and exposed to foreign experience, with ample time and money. The answer to that question is a resounding and categoric no! Otherwise it would be like saying that tennis is reserved for professionals, for the Sampras and the Hingins; not taking into account that even those with much less physical, psychological and time facilities do enjoy and benefit from a (good) game of tennis. This does not alter the fact that comparativism requires long practice and experience, perhaps more so than in other branches of law and industrial relations. Moreover comparativism remains even for the professionals an ideal which can only partly be realized. For all of us, comparativism is finally an exercise in modesty as we are constantly and overwhelmingly confronted with the richness and diversity of so many different cultures.

SELECT BIBLIOGRAPHY

B. Aaron, 'The Comparative Labour Law Group: A Personal Appraisal', *Comparative Labour Law*, 1977, pp. 228–237.

R. Adams (ed.), *Comparative Industrial Relations: Research and Theory*, London, 1991.

R. Adams, 'Contemporary Research and Theory', in *Comparative Industrial Relations*, London, Harper-Collins, 1991.

G.J. Bamber and R.D. Lansbury, *International and Comparative Industrial Relations: A Study of Developed Market Economies*, London, 1992.

G.J. Bamber and R.D. Lansbury (eds) *International and Comparative Industrial Relations*, 2nd ed., Sydney/London, Allen and Unwin, 1992.

R. Bean, *An Introduction to Cross-national Perspectives*, 2nd ed., London, Routledge, 1994.

B. Hepple, *The Making of Labour Law in Europe. A Comparative Study of Nine Countries up to 1945*, London/New York, 1986.

P. Legrand, 'European Legal Systems Are Not Converging', *International and Comparative Law Quarterly*, Vol. 45, 1996, pp. 52–81.

F. Meyers, 'The Study of Foreign Labour and Industrial Relations', in S. Barkin et al. (eds.), *International Labour Law*, New York, 1967.

A. Neal, 'Comparative Labour Law and Industrial Relations: Major Discipline? – Who cares?', in *Labour Law and Industrial Relations at the Turn of the Century. Liber Amicorum in Honour of Prof. Dr. R. Blanpain*, Kluwer, The Hague, 1998, pp. 55–71.

M. Paole, 'Industrial Relations: Theory and Managerial Strategies', *The International Journal of Comparative Labour Law and Industrial Relations*, Vol. 4, 1988, No. 1, pp. 11–24.

J. Pipkorn, 'Comparative Labour Law in the Harmonisation of Social Standards in the European Community', *Comparative Labour Law*, 1977, pp. 260–272.

J. Rojot, 'Industrial Relations in Europe: Recent Changes and Trends', *The International Journal of Comparative Labour Law and International Relations*, Vol. 4, 1988, No. 2, pp. 61–70.

J. Schregle, 'Comparative Industrial Relations: Pitfalls and Potential', *International Labour Law*, 1977, pp. 15–30.

N. Valticos, 'International Labour Law', *International Encyclopaedia for Labour Law and Industrial Relations*, I, Deventer, Kluwer, 1995.

Chapter 2.   Documentation

M. Vranken

1.   DOCUMENTATION

1.   The study of comparative labour law and industrial relations is a relatively new discipline. Ultimately, it must be seen in the broader context of the emergence of labour law itself. The subject which is now generally called 'labour law' is indeed of recent origin: in most countries it became recognized as a distinct division of law only after the Second World War.[1]

Even so, a rich body of documentary material has gradually become available over the years, and any attempt to draw up a fully comprehensive list would almost certainly fail. The text below sets out to give an overview of the main sources only. Specifically, the focus will be on publications which offer an international and/or comparative perspective to labour issues. For this reason studies with a purely national outlook generally will not feature in this survey, even though they may occasionally involve internal comparisons as between States (e.g. Australia or the USA) or between provinces (e.g. Canada). Of course, it must always be appreciated that national research often provides the necessary building stones for the work undertaken by comparative scholars.

This chapter has been prepared with a readership that is familiar with the English language in mind. Hence, the emphasis is primarily on publications in English.

It is by no means implied, though, that interesting material in other languages would not be available. A good example may be the various contributions to the Zeitschrift *fur ausländisches und internationales Arbeits-und Sozialrecht* published by the Institut für Arbeitsrecht und Arbeitsbeziehungen in der Europaischen Gemeinschaft and the Max-Planck-Institut für auslandisches und internationales Sozialrecht.

A.   *ILO Publications*

2.   Most important of all are the materials produced by the *International Labour Organisation (ILO)*. The *International Labour Office* is the Organization's permanent secretariat, its operational headquarters, research body and publishing house.

---

1. B. Hepple, 'Introduction', in B. Hepple (ed.), *The Making of Labour Law in Europe. A Comparative Study of Nine Countries up to 1945*, London/New York, 1986, p. 6.

The oldest and widely read of the periodical and non-periodical publications issued by the Office is the *International Labour Review*. It contains articles based on recent ILO and other research into economic and social topics of international interest. The *International Labour Review* appears six times per year. Its editorial staff recently prepared *Freedom of Association. An annotated Bibliography* (1999) in English, French, and Spanish.

3. Selected statutes and regulations enacted throughout the world on labour law and social security are published in the *Labour Law Documents* (formerly: *Legislative Series*). As the various ILO publications have been available in the three official languages (English, French, and Spanish) ever since 1945, the reader thus gains access to foreign laws which would otherwise be out of reach due to the language barrier. *Labour Law Documents* also comprises an international section, containing the texts of important international instruments including new ILO Conventions and Recommendations. Three issues are published each year.

4. The preparatory work for the Annual General Meetings of the ILO yields a wide range of materials. Typically, the adoption of Conventions and Recommendations by the International Labour Conference is preceded by the preparation of preliminary reports. These reports, which are the responsibility of the International Labour Office, set out the law and practice in different countries on the questions at issue. They are followed by subsequent reports containing government responses to ILO questionnaires together with research undertaken by officials of the ILO and others.[2] The wealth of the material thus produced can hardly be exaggerated. And the various countries concerned self-evidently make careful checks to ensure that their legal systems are correctly reported. Hence, the accuracy of the provided information is generally guaranteed.

The supervisory role of the ILO is at the basis of yet another rich source of documentation. Reference can be made here to the voluminous *Reports on the Application of Conventions and Recommendations*. These reports are published annually for discussion by the Tripartite Committee on the Application of Conventions and Recommendations. They contain very detailed information on national legislation and practice, including the most recent changes and developments.

More generally, *Series A* of the Official *Bulletin* provides information on the activities of the ILO, texts adopted by the International Labour Conference and other official documents. *Series B* of the Bulletin contains the reports by the Committee on Freedom of Association and related material. Three issues of each Series are published every *year. Two* or three issues of the *Judgements of the Administrative Tribunal of the* ILO are published yearly as well.

5. A quarterly journal, the *Social and Labour Bulletin*, contains short reports on world developments. Its information is derived from a variety of sources, including newspapers. Also published on a quarterly basis is *Labour Education*. As the title

---

2. A description of the procedure for the adoption of ILO Conventions and Recommendations can be found in N. Valticos and G. von Potobsky (1994) IELL (*International Labour Law*).

may suggest it is designed to promote the educational activities of trade unions and other workers' education bodies. *Women at Work* is a half-yearly news bulletin exclusively devoted to questions concerning the economic and social contribution of women to society.

6.   *The Year Book of Labour Statistics* contains a comprehensive survey of annual data from all parts of the world relating to, in particular, active population, employment, unemployment, hours of work, wages, labour cost, industrial disputes, occupational injuries, and consumer prices. Current statistical figures feature in the *Bulletin of Labour Statistics*. Four main issues of the Bulletin appear each year. The Bulletin also comprises articles on methodology and special topics.

7.   Industrial safety issues once constituted a primary topic of ILO publications. More recently, collective labour law has become the main focus of interest.[3] The special *Labour–Management Relations Series* can be mentioned in this context. It provides occasional monographs and reports on labour law and labour–management relations. This series is not to be confused with the *Management Development Series* in which monographs dealing with specialized management subjects and management development methods are recorded.

8.   In addition to its periodicals, reports, and special series, the International Labour Office also publishes a number of books on a variety of subjects related to labour matters. A recent example is *Negotiating Flexibility. The role of the social partners and the state* edited by M. Ozaki (1999). This book discusses the extent to which the labour market is becoming more flexible. It evaluates collective bargaining in promoting this flexibility. Specifically, it contains information from 22 countries, both industrialized and developing nations across western Europe, North and South America, and Asia. The introduction of flexibility in 4 areas analysed are: contracts of employment, pay, working time, and work organization. Noteworthy is also a 1993 publication authored by W. Blenk entitled *European Labour Courts: Industrial Action and Procedural Aspects*.

9.   All of the publications referred to above can be found in the library of the International Labour Office. This library arguably contains more books on labour law than any other library in the world. Its acquisitions are reported in the monthly *International Labour Documentation*, an abstracting bulletin produced from the database LABORDOC. The Documentation does not merely contain a catalogue of titles; it also provides headings indicating the contents of the various publications.

10.   Closely connected with the International Labour Office is the *International Institute for Labour Studies*. Founded in *1960* and based in Geneva, this research institute remains relatively unknown. Among its main publications are *Labour and Society,* a quarterly journal with articles on social and labour problems as well as

---

3.   This information is derived from the chapter on Documentation by F. Gamillscheg in an earlier edition of the book.

accounts of current educational and research activities carried out by the Institute. Moreover, monographs reflecting the results and findings of research projects undertaken by the Institute are published in a Research *Series*. The main headings are strategic factors in industrial relations systems: quality of working life; women, work, and society; workers' participation in management; multinational enterprises and labour; industrial relations and the political process. In support of its research programs the Institute additionally publishes bibliographies in a *Bibliography Series*. Finally, a *Directory of Institutes for Labour Studies* lists several hundreds of institutes worldwide. The Directory includes entries in English, French, or Spanish. It provides information on aims, administrative structure, staff size, programmes and activities, and publications and facilities. The entries are updated and new entries added regularly.

B. Other International Sources

11. The various institutions of the *European Union* produce an abundance of materials in all sorts of monographs, series, bibliographies, periodicals, information papers, etc. Most of these publications are recorded in an annual polyglot catalogue. Their informational value from a comparative labour law perspective is often limited, though. An obvious explanation may be that, unlike the ILO the European Community (EC) was not perceived initially as an instrument of social harmonization. Even so, in more recent years the EC Treaty has been understood to provide (limited) authority for the organs of the Community as regards social policy. To the extent that the achievement of the economic goals of the Common Market depends upon the solution of social problems, economic and social issues are indeed inevitably linked.

12. The most visible presence of the EC in the field of labour law consists in the creation of a uniform, or at least a harmonized, social law through the adoption of supra- national legislation. In labour law, the practical possibilities of harmonization by means of Directives generally outweigh those of Regulations.

All European legislation is published in the Official *Journal of the European Communities*. The Official Journal appears almost daily. It is available in each of the official languages of the Communities, including English. The Journal is published in two series: one is devoted to legislation (the 'L' series); the other contains non-normative communications and information about drafts of legislation, opinions of the EC bodies during the legislative process, activity programs, etc. (the 'C' series).

One should also mention here the '*Directory of Community Legislation in Force, and other Acts of the Community Institutions*'. The Directory gives, as its title suggests, an overview of all Community acts in force on a given date. The Directory is published in all the official Community languages and is re-published every six months.

13. The *Bulletin of the European Communities* is published by the Commission in periodical parts. Its main emphasis is on giving a monthly account of current activities and developments, *Supplements* to the Bulletin appear in a separate series and at irregular intervals. The Supplements contain the texts of important reports and proposals for legislation, communications to the Council of Ministers, programs, etc.

Each year the Commission prepares a *General Report on the Activities of the European Communities*. The Report is presented to the European Parliament. It provides a general picture of Community activities over the previous year. Published in conjunction with the General Report is a *Report on Social Developments*.

14. The text of the judgments by the European Court of Justice as well as the opinions of the Advocates-General are published by the Court in each of the official languages of the Communities. The English is entitled *European Court Reports*.

15. The Commission occasionally sponsors private research which contributes to the European debate. The role of the industrial parties in the EC integration process is acknowledged as well. The European organizations of trade unions and employers' associations are the European Trade Union Confederation (ETUC) and the Union of Industries of the European Community (UNICE), respectively. Both organizations have a membership which reaches beyond the EC. In 1978 ETUC established a separate European Trade Union Institute (ETUI). ETUI is the research, information, documentation, and educational instrument of the European trade union movement. Several of its research projects have been published.

16. *The Organisation for Economic Co-operation and Development* (OECD) has produced a considerable number of comparative studies of industrial relations, particularly on economic aspects. Its publications are generally available in English and French. The OECD has also done work in connection with its Guidelines on Multinational Enterprises.

C. *Private Collections*

17. An indispensable reference work and arguably the most comprehensive project ever undertaken in the field is the *International Encyclopaedia for Labour Law and Industrial Relations*. Edited by R. Blanpain, the work now comprises some twenty-nine volumes, covering labour law and industrial relations in sixty countries. The various national reports are set in a common framework so as to make it easier for the reader to find his or her way.

Typically, each national monograph contains three parts. The introductory part gives general background information about the country at issue, the second part covers various aspects of the individual employment relationship, and part three discusses collective labour relations. The national reports are supplemented by the text of the most important labour laws and regulations in each country. Furthermore, the Encyclopaedia comprises several international monographs on, among other things, Guidelines for Multinational Enterprises, International Employers' Organizations, and the International Trade Union Movement. Published as separate binders are, moreover, an international labour law Codex and a volume on international Case Law. Both the Codex and Case Law volumes distinguish between worldwide and regional organizations. The Encyclopaedia is loose-leaf and updated regularly. It is now a part of the much wider *International Encyclopaedia of Laws*, again with R. Blanpain as its general editor.

18. Mention should also be made of the *International Encyclopaedia of Comparative Law*. This Encyclopaedia is edited under the auspices of the International Association of Legal Science. Volume XV of the Encyclopaedia is devoted to labour law with B.A. Hepple as the chief editor. Its integrated treatment of selective topics makes it a welcome addition to Blanpain's Encyclopaedia on labour law. There are chapters on Collective Agreements and Collective Bargaining by F. Schmidt and A.C. Neal, Labour Courts and Organs of Arbitration by B. Aaron, Equality of Treatment in Employment and Representation of the Employees at Plant and Enterprises Level by R. Blanpain.

D. Books and Periodicals

19. Even today comprehensive books offering an integrated treatment on comparative labour law and/or industrial relations are quite rare. *Comparative Labour Law and Industrial Relations in Industrialised Market Economies* clearly fills an important gap in this respect. An introduction to cross-national perspectives is also provided by R. Bean in *Comparative Industrial Relations* (1994). The stated aim of the latter publication is to review the broad domain of comparative industrial relations via a survey and a drawing- together of the recent, analytic literature. The book thereby offers some varied perspectives on the current state of knowledge as regards a number of mainstream topics within the field.

20. More popular because more manageable are regional projects. Representative publications are, for Europe, *European Labour Law* by R. Blanpain, now in its 7th edition (2000), and, for South-East Asia, *Facing the Challenge in the Asia Pacific Region. Contemporary Themes and Issues in Labour Law* by R. Mitchell and J.M.A. Wu (eds) (1997). The far-reaching regulatory changes introduced in Australia and, in particular, New Zealand also warrant the mentioning of a book edited by American academic Dennis R. Nolan on *The Australasian Labour Law Reforms. Australia and New Zealand at the end of the Twentieth Century* (1998).

21. Special occasions may trigger special publications. Pride of place takes the recent *Festschrift* in honour of Prof. Dr. R. Blanpain: *Labour Law and Industrial Relations at the Turn of the Century* (1998). This *Liber Amicorum* comprises some 40 contributions on a very diverse range of topics. There is also *Fifty Years of Labour Law and Social Security* (1986) by M.G. Rood (ed.), published on the occasion of the fiftieth anniversary of the chair in labour law and social security at the University of Leyden, the Netherlands. It was in Leyden that the founding father of modern labour law, Hugo Sinzheimer, gave his inaugural address in 1936.[4] An excellent treatment of questions as to the origins of labour law can also be found in B.A. Hepple (ed.) *The Making of Labour Law in Europe. A Comparative Study of Nine Countries up to 1945* (1986).

---

4. O. Kahn-Freund singled out H. Sinzheimer as the one to whom belongs 'the conception of labour law as a unified, independent legal discipline'. See O. Kahn-Freund, *Labour Law and Politics in the Weimar Republic*, Oxford, Basil Blackwell, 1981, p. 75. Kahn-Freund was Sinzheimer's brilliant pupil.

22. Specific topics in the area of labour law and industrial relations feature in a variety of periodicals. Special reference can be made here to the *Bulletin of Comparative Labour Relations* of which several dozen issues have been published. Issue no. 39 addresses the Council of Europe and the Social Challenges of the XXI century, edited by R. Blanpain (2000).

23. Relatively brief but up-to-date information on recent developments can be found in the monthly *European Industrial Relations* Review, a publication of the Industrial Relations Services, London, England. This journal carries national features as well as comparative surveys on such themes as, for instance, fixed-term contracts of employment and bipartite/tripartite consultation. It has, moreover, a 'Documents' section in which important collective agreements, official reports, and EC documents are reprinted.

24. A*cademic journals* that are truly comparative and international in terms of both content and source include *Comparative Labor Law & Policy Journal* and *The International Journal of Comparative Labour Law and Industrial Relations.* Both Journals underwent changes in recent years. The former is the result of a 1997 revamp of the *Comparative Labor Law Journal.* Still a publication of the US national branch of the International Society for Labour Law and Social Security, it is now based at the University of Illinois College of Law instead of the Wharton School/Law School of the University of Pennsylvania. New general editors are Matthew W. Finkin, Harno Professor of Law (Illinois), and Sanford M. Jacoby, Professor of History, Management and Policy Studies at the University of California at Los Angeles. J.R. Bellace and C.W. Summers remain on the editorial board as senior editors. L. Betten, editor in chief of *The International Journal of Comparative Labour Law and Industrial Relations* handed over the day-to-day management of the Journal to Professor Marco Biagi from Modena University where it is in very capable hands.

There is also the *Zeitschrift für ausländisches und internationales Arbeits-und Sozialrecht,* under the auspices of the Institute for Labour Law and Labour Relations in the European Community and the Max-Planck Institute. The first volume dates from 1987. While its title may suggest otherwise, this journal contains contributions in English as well as in German.

25. At the outset of this chapter it was stressed that the emphasis would be on publications with an international and/or comparative focus only. Several national journals exist, however, which occasionally contain articles on developments abroad. For example, European topics are increasingly dealt with in British periodicals. A good illustration is the *Industrial Law Journal* or, with respect to industrial relations, the *British Journal of Industrial Relations.* A similar tendency appears to exist elsewhere, and useful commentaries on foreign developments may be found in, e.g. the French *Droit social et intersocial,* the German *Recht der Arbeit,* and the Italian *Giornale di Diritto del Lavoro e delle Relazioni Industriali.* A further addition to this illustratory list is the *Australian Journal of Labour Law*, the first issue of which appeared in May 1988. While its founding editor, R. Mitchell from Melbourne University, anticipated that the primary focus would be on Australian labour law, it was also stressed that contributions on overseas developments are considered for publication where they are of wide general interest or of relevance to the national situation. His statement of intent may then be representative for the approach taken in a growing number of, *prima facie*, national periodicals.

The above-noted trend arguably constitutes a direct reflection of the growing internationalization of our world. While laudable as such, it does not necessarily facilitate the scholar's search for comparative material. His or her task is complicated further by the consideration that even general legal periodicals publish (most interesting) articles every so often. Apart from University Law Reviews, both the *Modern Law Review* and *Current Legal Problems* warrant a special mention in this respect. The consultation of general legal periodicals (the *Revue Trimestrielle de Droit* Civil or the Archiv für Civ. Praxis to give some further examples) may be advisable, in particular, where issues of labour law touch upon aspects of general law.

II. INTERNATIONAL SOCIETIES AND MEETINGS

26. Comparative law could not possibly flourish without personal contacts at conferences or colloquia. Labour law is no exception to this general rule. *The International Academy for Comparative Law* has paid some attention to labour law topics in the past. But such general congresses do not constitute a sound base. A truly representative association of labour and social lawyers is the *International Society for Labour Law and Social Security* (ISLLSS). It was established at a 1958 Conference in Brussels as the product of an amalgamation of the International Association for Social Law and the International Congress for Labour Law. The ISLLSS is made up of national representative committees and private members. World congresses are held on average every three years. Intermittently, regional conferences are organized which cover Europe, Africa, Asia, and the Americas.

Conferences provide regular opportunities for labour lawyers to meet and discuss topical issues in an informal atmosphere. The official aspect of these conferences reveals a fixed pattern, though. First, a special committee decides on three main themes, one of which always relates to social security law. The participating countries are invited to submit national reports, which are processed by a General Reporter and then put before the assembled congress in summary form. Typically, the proceedings of the conference are published. In this way they can become available to a wide audience. Themes of past conferences include, among others, collective bargaining at the enterprise level, atypical employment relationships, worker participation, employment termination, and the position of women in labour law and social security.

27. The leading international association in the area of industrial relations is the *International Industrial Relations Association* (IIRA). Founded in 1966, it is an international gathering of 29 national industrial relations associations, 37 academic or professional institutions, and some 1,000 individuals. To date the IIRA has held many world conferences and various regional congresses. Papers and communications submitted to IIRA meetings are available from its Secretariat in Geneva. The Association publishes an IIRA *Bulletin* with information on past and forthcoming activities.

28. Less institutionalized scholarly cooperation takes place at various levels and in varying degrees. An early example is the *Comparative Labour Law Group.* Following up a suggestion by Kahn-Freund, B. Aaron secured the services of a number of scholars in different countries. Aaron's initiative has led to several joint contributions during the 1960s and 1970s.[5] More recently, the (American) Committee on International Studies of the National Academy of Arbitrators has published multiple nation studies on The Neutral and Public Interests in Resolving Disputes (1992) and Worker Privacy (1995). Both studies were published in the *Comparative Labor Law Journal.*

In between the official conferences of the IIRA, on-going research is carried out in various IIRA study groups. Five such study groups have been formed to date. Together they cover a wide range of topics which include industrial relations as a field and industrial relations theory, technological change, equality in pay and employment, worker participation, industrial conflict, trilateral concertation, urban labour markets in developing countries, and since 1987, the rights of employees and industrial justice.

SELECT BIIBLIOGRAPHY

ILO Publications

W. Blenk, *European Labour Courts: Industrial Action and Procedural Aspects,* Geneva, 1993.
Bulletin of Labour Statistics, Geneva (four main issues per year).
Freedom of Association. An Annotated Bibliography, Geneva (1999).
International Labour Documentation, Geneva (twelve issues per year).
International Labour Review, Geneva (six issues per year).
Judgments of the Administrative Tribunal of the ILO, Geneva (two or three issues per year).
Labour Education, Geneva (four issues per year).
Labour Law Documents (formerly: Legislative Series), Geneva (three issues per year).
Labour–Management Relations Series, Geneva (occasional monographs).
Management Development Series, Geneva (occasional monographs).
M. Ozaki, *Negotiating Flexibility. The Role of the Social Partners and the State,* Geneva, 1999.
Official *Bulletin, Series A,* Geneva (three issues per year); *Series B,* Geneva (three issues per year).
Reports on the Application of Conventions and Recommendations (annually).
Social and Labour Bulletin, Geneva (four issues per year plus annual index).
Women at Work, Geneva (two issues per year).
Year Book of Labour Statistics, Geneva (annually).

International Institute for Labour Studies

Bibliography Series, Geneva (occasional publication).
Directory of Institutes for Labour Studies, Geneva (updated annually).

---

5. *See* B. Aaron, 'The Comparative Labor Law Group: A Personal Appraisal', *Comparative Labor Law,* 1977, Vol. 2, pp. 228–237.

Labour and Society, Geneva (four issues per year).
Research Series, Geneva (occasional monographs).

European Communities

Bulletin of the European Communities, Luxembourg (twelve issues per year plus supplements).
Directory of Community Legislation in Force, and other Acts of the Community Institutions, Luxembourg (published every six months).
European Court Reports, Luxembourg (eleven issues per year plus index).
General Report on the Activities of the European Communities, Luxembourg (annually).
Official Journal of the European Communities, Series L; *Series* C.
Report on Social Developments (annually).

Private Collections

R. Blanpain (ed.), *International Encyclopaedia for Labour Law and Industrial Relations*, The Hague, Kluwer, s.d. (loose-leaf).
R. Blanpain (ed.), *International Encyclopaedia of Laws*, The Hague, Kluwer, s.d. (loose-leaf).
B.A. Hepple (ed.), *Labour Law*, Vol. XV of the *International Encyclopaedia of Comparative Law*, Tübingen (J.C.B. Mohr) and Dordrecht (M. Nijhoff Publishers).

Books

G. Bamber and R. Lansbury (eds), *International and Comparative Industrial Relations*, 3rd ed., Sydney and London, Allen and Unwin, 1998.
R. Bean, *Comparative Industrial Relations. An Introduction to Cross-National Perspectives*, 2nd ed., London, Routledge, 1994.
R. Blanpain, *European Labour Law,* The Hague, 7th and revised ed. Kluwer, 2000.
J.S. Bradley (ed.), *International Handbook on Contracts of Employment*, Deventer, Kluwer, 1988 (loose-leaf).
C. Engels and M. Weiss (eds), *Labour Law and Industrial Relations at the Turn of the Century. Liber Amicorum in Honour of Prof. Dr. R. Blanpain*, The Hague, Kluwer, 1998.
B.A. Hepple (ed.), *The Making of Labour Law in Europe. A Comparative Study of Nine Countries up to 1945,* London, Mansell, 1986.
W. Kolvenbach and P. Hanau (eds), *Handbook on European Employee Co-Management*, Deventer, Kluwer, 1987 (loose-leaf).
R. Mitchell and J.M.A.Wu (eds), *Facing the Challenge in the Asia Pacific Region. Contemporary Themes and Issues in Labour Law*, Melbourne, Centre for Employment and Labour Relations Law, 1997.
D.R. Nolan, *The Australasian Labour Law Reforms. Australia and New Zealand at the End of the Twentieth Century*, Sydney, Federation Press, 1998.
M.G. Rood (ed.), *Fifty Years of Labour Law and Social Security*, Deventer, Kluwer, 1986.

Periodicals

Australian Journal of Labour Law, Butterworths (three issues per year).

British Journal of Industrial Relations, Basil Blackwell for the London School of Economics (three issues per year).

Bulletin of Comparative Labour Relations, Kluwer for the Institute for Labour Relations, Catholic University of Leuven (annually).

Comparative Labor Law & Policy Journal, University of Illinois (four issues per year).

Current Legal Problems, Stevens & Sons for the Faculty of Laws, University College London (annually).

Droit social et intersocial, Editions Techniques et Economiques (Paris) (ten issues per year).

European Industrial Relations Review, Industrial Relations Services (London) (twelve issues per year).

Giornale di Diritto del Lavoro e delle Relazioni Industriali, Milano.

Industrial Law Journal, Sweet & Maxwell for the Industrial Law Society (four issues per year).

International Journal of Comparative Labour Law and Industrial Relations, The Hague, Kluwer (four issues per year).

Journal of Industrial Relations, Industrial Relations Society of Australia (four issues per volume).

Modern Law Review, Stevens & Sons, London (six issues per year).

Recht der Arbeit, C.H. Beck-Verlag (Munchen) (six issues per year).

Zeitschrift fur ausldndisches und internationales Arbeits- und Sozialrecht, C.F. Muller Heidelberg (four issues per year).

Chapter 3. Comparative Research in Labour Law using the Internet

L. Salas

I. INTRODUCTION

1. In the early days of the Internet, it was mostly used by academics to exchange ideas and communicate with each other. They used e-mail and bulletin boards extensively to advance their theories and push towards new discoveries using a faster and cheaper media. In 1993, the University of Illinois invented the Mosaic browser and released it to the public,[1] hence began the era of surfing the World Wide Web (WWW). At that point the Internet consisted largely of university sites, self-made web pages and eccentric collections of little known facts. It was only in 1995 that the business community latched on to what until that point had mostly been the realm of computer geeks and academics.

2. Since then, the Internet has become an ubiquitous feature of modern life. We can use it to order groceries, book our vacations or find audience appropriate jokes for our next public speech. But the hallmark of the Internet, which is its geographic and temporal autonomy, and its self-regulating nature, is what makes it the perfect tool for conducting comparative research. However, these same characteristics which make the Internet so attractive to everyone, present novel challenges for researchers in labour law. This chapter will present some practical advice for approaching the incredible behemoth that is the Internet. One caveat to this, and almost any guide to the Internet, is that almost as fast as I hit the final enter-key, this chapter will already be out of date. But such is the nature of the information super highway, which is moving at the speed of light.

II. WHAT IS THE NET?

3. Perhaps a more important first question should be 'why'? Why is it relevant for researchers and practitioners to know how to use the Internet? After all we have

---

1. *The Economic and Social Impact of Electronic Commerce*, OECD Report, 1998.

books, legal journals, periodicals and can barely keep up with all the information that is in print. There are two very good reasons why every researcher should know how to use the Internet: (1) availability of timely information; and (2) no geographic boundaries. Any university library, no matter how extensive, is limited by space as to the amount of books and paper it can hold. Thus, a researcher is limited to accessing that which is available to her locally. The Internet, on the other hand, is literally limitless, both in content and geography. So a researcher in England can access information on trade union activity in Peru, which may otherwise be very difficult for her to locate at the libraries in her area. The other reason is the availability of timely information. A reference has already been made to the fact that as we read this article it is already out of date because information is constantly streaming onto the Internet. It is possible to find the very latest update to employment law regulations in various countries around the world, or access United States Supreme Court decisions 30 minutes after they have been handed down.[2]

4. The Internet is a complex system of networks, which connects millions of servers around the world. A server is basically a computer, or a software package that provides a specific kind of service to client software running on other computers. The term can refer to a particular piece of software, such as a WWW server, or to the machine on which the software is running.[3] Information on the Internet is available at a comparatively low cost, and access at most universities is free. The private user usually has to pay only the subscription fees to his Internet Service Provider (ISP), perhaps the cost of a telephone call, and in an increasing number of cases, for the right to view or download substantive information available on a web site.

5. One vital factor which has made the Internet so attractive to people who wish to post things on the Web (i.e. web pages, web sites) is the non-proprietary nature of the technology. Anyone can use and have access to the technology necessary to make a web page or a site. Hypertext mark up language (HTML) is the coding language used to create documents for use on the WWW and Transmission Control Protocol/Internet Protocol (TCP/IP) is the suite of protocols that defines the Internet.[4] This software is available for every major kind of computer operating system, hence the ease with which anyone can make information available on the Net. The next wave of technology is X-HTML and Wireless Application Protocol (WAP), the latter of which promises to bring information from the Net onto mobile telephones or other wireless devices. All of these things combined have lead to the ubiquitous nature of the Net.

But perhaps the most significant and troublesome characteristic for a researcher wanting to use the Net is the fact that there are no standards of quality. The Net has been referred to as the ultimate anarchistic media, resulting in valuable, well-documented material appearing along side useless information. This will require the researcher to be especially vigilant and well informed before relying on information taken from the Web.

---

2. *See www.supremecourtus.gov* – the official web-site of the United States Supreme Court.
3. E. Matisse *Glossary of Internet Terms*, www.matisse.net/files.glosasary.html
4. *Ibid.*

III. TIPS FOR SURFING

6. When conducting research on the Net, different kinds of research skills are necessary than when researching in print media. There is an increased need to maintain one's focus because it is very easy to get lost in the sea of information on the Net. Most web sites contain links to other sites, and this linking up to different sites is almost endless. With one or two clicks of the mouse the researcher who started out at a legal web site could end up at a site about travel without knowing how to return to the original legal site. The positive side to the connectivity of the Net is that one web site may lead to very useful information elsewhere that you did not know existed. Therefore, it is imperative that when doing research on the Net, the researcher takes notes of what pages she is currently viewing and to note the web address. A good practice is to make full use of bookmarks which is a feature available on all browsers that stores the full address (called a URL = universal resources locator) of web pages selected. Another feature to trace back the path visited while surfing across multiple sites, is the 'history' function. Most web browsers, such as Microsoft Explorer, will have an icon on the menu bar that says 'History'. Clicking on the icon will open up another frame on the screen with the URL of all pages visited over a specified period of time, even going back days or weeks (depending on the programmed settings).

7. Unlike doing research using traditional print media, one cannot view different sources at once, like laying different books or articles on the desk in front of you. It is also not possible to make notes directly on your source, since it appears on your computer screen. Again, this highlights the need to take good notes while doing research. Of course, the upside is the ease with which one can print out the full text of what appears on the screen and also the ability to download it onto one's computer for future use or incorporation into other documents.

8. When conducting research on the Net, one should follow a triangular model, which consists of the following factors to consider: the types of sources available, the economics of the sources, and the validity of these sources.[5] The types of sources refer to the traditional sources that you would also use when conducting research in print media: primary legislation, secondary (case law), and tertiary sources. The second factor is the economics of the sources. Generally speaking, the Net is free, however one must look to the format in which it is presented and the ease of using it afterwards. Is the information in a format that is easy to download, such as .html? Or is it a PDF file, which normally cannot be edited nor changes made to it (unless you have the complete Acrobat software package)? And also the availability of the information. As portals are increasingly appearing on the Net, many offer information at a price which with some good research, could be found for free in print media. The final, and for the researcher most important factor, is the validity of the sources. How reliable and accurate is the information that you would like to use. Legal researchers are familiar with the reputation of law journals or treatises on labour law. But,

---

5. J. D. Blackman, D. Jank, *The Internet Fact Finder for Lawyers: How to Find Anything on the Internet*, by American Bar Association publications, 1999.

because anyone can post information on the Net, some material may not be as reliable or persuasive as that from a trusted source. Many of the sites listed later on in this chapter are among the more reliable sources currently available.

A. Trouble-shooting

9.   When one starts effectively looking on the Internet, problems often arise in accessing sites. When this happens, it is necessary to determine where the problem lies before proceeding. The problem may be with the local service provider where perhaps lines are busy or there is some sort of network maintenance happening (i.e. the server is down). In that case, it is best to just try again later. There may be a problem with the target source being accessed, in which case some sort of message will be generated such as: *'ABC.com is currently experiencing a temporary fault. We are working to bring the site back to you as soon as possible.'* Again, the only solution is to try again later. There could be a problem with the hardware being used (is the modem working? Try calling your mobile phone or other nearby number to see if it is working) or with the software being used (are you using an outdated version of your web browser to view high-graphics pages or pages with lots of Java content?). It is important to keep in mind that just because one may have a high performance computer or modem, this does not always result in faster access. This is because data travels through many links and gateways which may be travelling at slower speeds before it finally reaches your computer.

10.   A few practical suggestions for surfing include the following. Use mirrored web sites to get around Net traffic congestion. These are sites which are duplicated in full on one or more servers throughout the world. Although the site may be an American site, there may be mirrored sites on servers physically located closer to the researcher. Whether a site has a mirrored site will always be indicated on the home page itself and the researcher should select the site that is geographically closest. If no mirrored site is available try to avoid peak hours when Americans are surfing on the Net, since the USA has the largest population of people using the Internet. Also, refrain from downloading large data files during peak times and do not access high graphical sites with low performance computers or modems. Generally speaking, most legal sites are not high graphic sites with lots of pictures and animation. There are many sites that give you the option of viewing a text-only version of a document.

B. Web site vs. Portal

11.   The last year or so has seen the dramatic rise of the portal. A portal is meant to be an Internet user's main point of entry to the Web and is often geared towards a certain topic or theme (i.e. sports, world news, law, etc.), although sites such as Yahoo and MSN offer more general interest portals. A portal often contains information plus tools for the user, such as calendars, search engines, e-mail accounts, bulletin boards, etc. They are content filtered to the specific user's needs or interests. On many web sites you may see something which says 'My Yahoo' or 'My MSN' just to give an example. The user fills out a sort of on-line questionnaire which will

then allow the portal to feed the individual tailored information (i.e. stock performance of stock owned by the user, weather reports for your locality, tax updates for your country, etc.). A portal also gathers data about usage for further site development and further customization and it also often involves users in a community of peers and experts, such as chat rooms or bulletin boards (for instance, a chat room focused on sports or politics).

C. Starting Points

12. An excellent starting point for doing comparative legal research on the Net is the university library homepage. Law librarians have long realized the great value of the Internet for doing research and many have very well organized sites listing numerous valuable links. The librarians have often previewed sites before making links to them, so the researcher has some indication of quality and reliability. The library sites also often group links together by the type of information, such as primary legislation (i.e. on-line civil codes or homepages of parliaments or legislative bodies), secondary law (i.e. sites which have case law or links directly to the courts themselves), and tertiary sites (e.g. on-line law journals, homepages of the social partners or trade unions). Most university sites will have links to the most important national sources, including government institutions, which can be a very rich source of statistical data. When looking for reliable information about a foreign jurisdiction, a well-known university library web site in that country is a good starting point. A directory of universities worldwide can be found at geowww.uibk.ac.at/univ/index.html. An example of an excellent university law library web site is the Catholic University of Leuven, Belgium at www.law.kuleuven.ac.be/lib/.

D. Search Engines

13. Another starting point for surfing the Web is a search engine. This is a web site or portal which acts as a searchable directory of web sites and pages on the Net. It is a sort of telephone book to the Net. Search engines categorize sites by topic such as 'Arts & Humanities', 'Entertainment', 'Government', 'Reference', etc., with further sub-categories. There is also a search bar (a blank box usually appearing at the top of the web page) where one can type in a word or phrase to be searched. There is even a search engine for search engines which lists general interest as well as special interest search engines, see: Searchenginewatch.com. Many search engines have developed national sites which are in the local language, for instance the popular Yahoo search engine now has sites for Denmark, France, Norway, Spain, etc. Some of the more popular general search engines are:

– Yahoo
– Alta-Vista
– Web Crawler
– InfoSeek
– Excite
– Lycos.

While general search engines may yield valuable results, there are also special interest search engines that are focused on legal sources available on the Net. The most well known are LawCrawler, FindLaw, Heiros Gamos, and the Legal Information Institute. LawCrawler International allows you to specify the country or origin of the sources you are searching for and can be found at www.lawcrawler.com. FindLaw has a structure very similar to Yahoo that organizes sources by category, such as Legal Subject Index, Law School, Foreign & Int'l, Law Firms & Lawyers. FindLaw can be found at www.findlaw.com. Another is Heiros Gamos which describes itself as 'The Comprehensive Law and Government Portal'. Heiros Gamos is available in several languages, including Spanish, German, Italian, and French and tends to have a more international focus. It can be found at www.hg.org. Catalaw (www.catalaw.com) is a catalogue of worldwide legal sources on the Net. It lists all web sites by country, region, and subject. It is a meta index, which means that it is an index of indexes on the Net regarding law-related sites. Its stated goal is to be the single point of entry for all legal and government sites. A search of the topic 'labor and employment law' will yield a list of web sites dedicated to this topic listed by region and country.

14. A highly recommended starting point for research is the Legal Information Institute of Cornell University Law School (hereafter LII), which can be found at www.law.cornell.edu. This site is one of the first and most developed legal sites to appear on the Web. It provides brief introductions to various fields of American law,

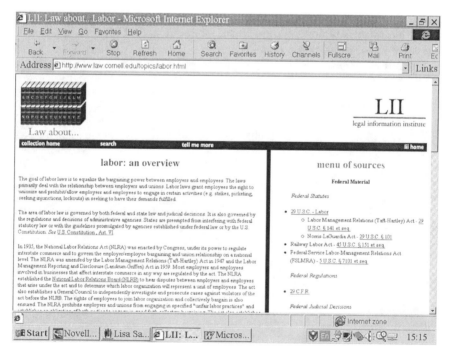

Figure 1. Illustration of http://www.law.cornell.edu/topics/labor.html.

including a primer on US labour law which explains the general features and structure of the labour and industrial relations system in the US. This series is called 'Law About' and covers topics such as administrative law, banking law, criminal law, divorce, and employment, to mention only a few. One frame provides a brief overview of the area of law and the other frame has a menu of sources (see Figure 1).

IV. KIND OF MATERIAL BEING SOUGHT

15. Most traditional legal research starts with identifying the kind of material being sought. This should remain the same for research on the Net. Primary sources are where one can find legislation. Secondary sources consist of case law, court decisions, and also government regulatory sources. Tertiary sources include such sources as law reviews, law journals, reports, and studies by international organizations and the social partners. Generally speaking, web sites where you can find primary and secondary sources are very reliable as these are often official government sites. Tertiary sites vary more in terms of their quality and reliability. Sites that are sponsored by well-known organizations, such as the OECD and the ILO also provide very trustworthy material. There is an increasing amount of commercial sites, which offer more practically oriented material, such as guides on how to draft employment contracts. Quite often, the more practically oriented or the more in-depth the legal analysis, the more likely that this information will be accessible for a fee. As for law journals, many well known journals have web sites which contain mostly bibliographic information.[6] If a journal is available in print at a price or subscription, one should not expect to find this for free on-line. There are on-line legal journals, but many of these are also for pay.

A. *Primary*

16. Primary sources will contain the laws, civil codes and legislation of a jurisdiction. Most United States laws (all federal and most state) are available on-line, as well as other Anglo-Saxon countries (Australia) and most European countries also. Some South American countries have links to their civil codes, in part or whole. One should keep in mind that many of these will be in the language of the country. The ILO web site has some English translations available, but these are only translations of national laws implementing ILO conventions. The official journals or official gazette of many countries are also available on line. The US Code can be found on line through the Cornell Legal Information Institute at www4.law.cornell.edu/uscode/. The LII also has links to state law sources. The LII is also an excellent source for links around the world including legislation, official journals, case law, and/or official court sites. These international links can be found under the section entitled 'Law from around the world'. It is often indicated if the site is in a language other than English. One example of an official journal is the Belgian Official Journal, available in Dutch and French at www.staatsblad.be. French legislation (in French) can be found at

---

6. *See* the web site of the European Law Journal at *www.iue.it.*

www.legifrance.gouv.fr/ citoyen/index.ow. Another good source for finding primary law in the Australian – South Pacific region is the Australasian Legal Information Institute at www.austlii.edu.au. Here links can be found to Australian codes, the laws of New Zealand and other South Pacific jurisdictions. The Australian Federal Government maintains a very useful site which can serve as a gateway to various kinds of sources on Australian law at www.fed.gov.au.

B. Secondary Sources

17. Secondary sources refer to cases and jurisprudence. The importance of case law will vary depending on whether the jurisdiction is a common law or civil law country. Generally speaking, common law countries such as the USA, United Kingdom and Australia, all have very reliable sources on the Internet where one can find case law. Another valuable source of secondary law is regulatory and government agencies. The most relevant institutions for labour law will be the labour courts (in countries that have them), ministries of labour and employment, national labour councils, and other specialized agencies, such as equal employment agencies. As with primary law sources many of these sites may also be in the local language of the country.

For the USA, the highest law of the land comes from the US Supreme Court. The Supreme Court decisions can be found at the Cornell LII site, which relies on different projects and universities to gather both historic court decisions and recent decisions.[7] The US Supreme Court official site was recently established in April 2000 and can be found at *www.supremecourtus.gov*. The site has the opinions for the current term, often within 30 minutes of the opinions being released, and calendars for arguments and hearings. Attorneys will find it a convenient reference for rules, bar admission forms and instructions. Students and the public can learn about court traditions, caseload, and biographies. The site also displays excellent photographs of the Supreme Court and the two prior chambers.[8] However, some commentators feel that the official site is a bit confusing to use and the decisions are in PDF format, which requires the use of Acrobat reader software.[9] The important courts of other countries can also be found on-line. A few examples include the United Kingdom's House of Lords at www.parliament.the stationery-office.co.uk/, which publishes

---

7. The Legal Information Institute offers Supreme Court opinions under the auspices of Project Hermes, the court's electronic-dissemination project. This archive contains nearly all opinions of the court issued since May of 1990. Other collections of decisions prior to 1990 are available on the Net, in a variety of formats. FedWorld provides pointers to various uses of the FLITE database, including one at Villanova University; FLITE only covers the period from 1937 to 1975, but does so comprehensively. The FindLaw collection also reaching back to 1937 is comprehensive without the post-1975 gap. The fee-based USSC+ service has full coverage from 1922, and leading opinions reaching back to 1793. Finally, the fee-based Lexis, Westlaw, services provide full coverage of all the court's decisions. There are other sources for the opinions; this is not a comprehensive list. Another interesting collection is Northwestern University's collection of oral arguments, delivered via streaming audio.
8. M. Pruner, 'Lawyers and Technology: A "Supreme" Web Site for the Supremes,' *The National Law Journal*, June 14, 2000, www.law.com.
9. *Ibid.*

decisions only from 14 November 1996; and the Italian Constitutional court at www.corteconstituzionale.it (in Italian).

18. Government agencies play a very important role in the labour and industrial relations of many countries. Before searching on the Web for information about these institutions, it is useful to know something about the particular country you are researching. This presents a bit of a chicken-and-the-egg situation, where a researcher may want to know more about a particular country's labour relations system, but you need to know something about the country's labour relationships system before you can dive full speed into the Internet. As most researchers in the area know, the major players are government, trade unions, and business/management. Knowing this basic structure will lead one to the right sources on the Net. The competencies for labour and employment in most governments will be housed in some specialized agencies, be it a ministry, a secretariat, labour courts or a national labour council. The connectivity of the Net, with sites offering links to other useful sites, will often guide the researcher along to the most relevant institutions within a country.

19. In the USA, the most relevant government institutions are the Department of Labor, whose web site is a wealth of statistical data (see www.dol.gov), the National Labor Relations Board (see www.nlrb.gov) and the Equal Employment Opportunities Commission (see www.eeoc.gov). These are official government sites and thus provide accurate and trustworthy information. In other countries, such as Belgium, the National Labor Council provides a site in English, Dutch, French, and German, although many working documents are only in Dutch or French (see www.cnt-nar.be). For Australia, the Australian Industrial Relations Commission is a valuable source of information and it includes decisions rendered in hearings, see www.airc.gov.au.

V.   EUROPEAN LAW SOURCES

20. The law of the European Union (EU) (directives, regulations, decisions, and case law) is very well documented and widely available on the Net. In addition to legal material, many other kinds of information are available such as press releases, commissioner's speeches, white and green papers. The EU web sites are very well organized, user friendly and multi-lingual, with most official documents available in all languages of the EU. The starting point for research into EU materials is the official EU site at europa.eu.int (Figure 2).

21. The EU site is searchable by subject matter, but this may produce an inordinate amount of documents. The institutions of the EU maintain their own sections as do the various DG's. Narrowing your search by the type of document which is being sought (press releases, white papers, directives, case law) will yield more manageable results, or else searching by institutions. The institutions, namely the parliament, the commission, the courts and the council, all have organized materials that are searchable and can be downloaded. The Official Journal, both L and C series, is also available in both PDF and .html format. The site of the European Court of

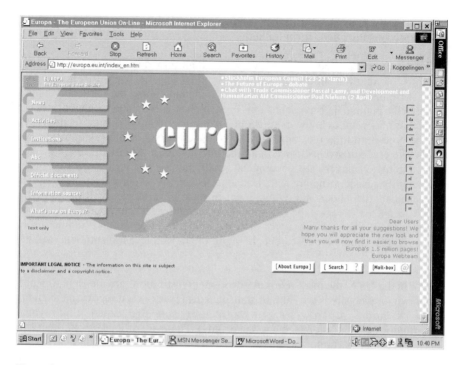

Figure 2.

Justice provides all cases as from June 17, 1997 only.[10] In order to access cases on-line from before 1997, it is necessary to access the Celex database which is available for a fee, otherwise, the Celex CD-ROM, which many libraries have available. But this is an example of where one can find this information in print for free in the C-series of the EU Official Journal, if it is available at a local library. The EU site allows research along several parameters, including institutional sources, date, legislation, court decision, press releases, and others. When searching for law, it is advisable to look in the Eur-Lex[11] section, which breaks down the law into the following categories:

– Official Journal
– Treaties
– Legislation
– Community preparatory acts
– Case Law.

Eur-Lex also provides a directory of EU legislation in force that gives an analytical structure with subject words to help define the search. This allows the researcher to

---

10. *See* curia.eu.int. There is a link to the European Court of Justice from the main EU web site also.
11. europa.eu.int/eur-lex/.

narrow the search so as to yield the best results and avoid getting hundreds of documents back.

22. Directorate General V on Employment and Social Affairs is a good starting place for information on labour, employment, and industrial relations in the European Union. Subject areas include employment and the European Social Fund, equality between men and women, social security and social integration, key documents and publications, just to name a few. It also contains some statistical data about employment in the EU. The DGV site contains links to Member State labour law sites, including the employment/ labour ministries of all Member States. The DGV section also has a list of important EU directives and references to the national implementing laws. Note that the texts themselves of the national implementing laws are not available from the EU site, for that it is necessary to go to the individual country's legislation. The 'Key Documents' section contains links to many studies and white papers, such as the following (as examples)

- The Impact of Eastern Enlargement on Employment Labour Markets in the EU Member States.
- National Employment Action Plans 2000
- Strategies for Jobs in the Information Society
- Proposals for a Council Directive implementing the principle of equal treatment between persons irrespective of racial or ethnic origin.

Most of these are available in PDF format and in various languages.

VI. TERTIARY SOURCES: THE SOCIAL PARTNERS & INTERNATIONAL ORGANIZATIONS

23. When searching for tertiary sources a bit more caution needs to be exercised, as well as creativity on where to look. Specialized legal search engines will be helpful to locate tertiary sources. It is also more likely that access to some tertiary information is available at a price. A good initial point of reference is an international organization, as well as trade union sites.

A. *International Organizations*

24. Information from recognized international organizations is very reliable. Many organizations provide information on-line that is also available in print. Other more extensive reports by organizations may be available for a price or otherwise can be ordered on-line. Many sites also have links to national government sites. The International Labour Organisation web site can be found at www.ilo.org. It has its own search engine which is quite straightforward. There is a separate section that lists all ILO conventions, thus making them very easy to locate. Documents are also easy to download. The ILO provides links to national labour sites, usually to the ministries of labour. The ILO has mirrored sites for researchers located outside of Europe and it has an excellent site map (which is a sort of road map to the organization of a web site) making the site very easy to use.

25. Another recommended international organization web site is that of the Organization for Economic Cooperation & Development at www.oecd.org. Some publications on this site are available only through an on-line ordering form for a price, but there are valuable statistics and studies which can be downloaded for free. One excellent example is the study on the Social and Employment Impact of Electronic Commerce, which is a fundamental source of information on this topic. The OECD site (Figure 3) also has economic indicators, such as inflation rates and industrial output of OECD member countries.

The European Industrial Relations Observer (here after EIRO) provides information on industrial relations in the member states of the EU. It is the web site associated with the European Foundation for the Improvement of Living and Working Conditions. This site also has a very useful site map which shows information by time (month by month) or level (EU level or national level). EIRO produces comparative studies focusing on current issues, such as, working time developments, the 'Europeanisation' of collective bargaining, and these are all available for free and can be downloaded. The site is an invaluable source of information for industrial relations developments in the member states of the EU and can be found at www.eiro.eurofound.ie.

A special project of the EIRO deals with European Works Council agreements and can be found at www.eurofound.ie/ewc. The welcome screen explains the contents

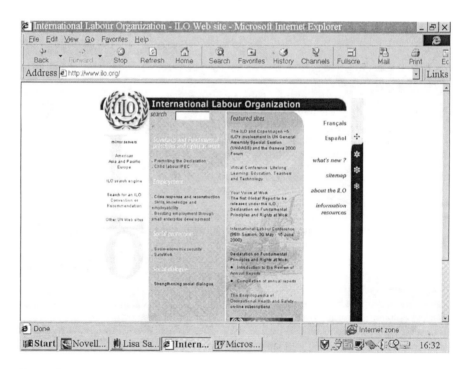

Figure 3.

of the site:

> This database contains information on the provisions of agreements establishing European Works Councils (EWCs), including 386 agreements concluded under Article 13 of the Directive on EWCs and 63 agreements concluded under Article 6. It is not a complete collection of all existing EWC agreements, though we are continuing to collect agreements and will update the database. Some agreements not available here may be included in the CD-ROM produced by the European Trade Union Institute.

B. Social Partners

26. The other two sides of the industrial relations triad, besides government, are the trade unions and employers. Trade unions have recognized the enormous potential that the Net offers as a medium to communicate with their members. Trade unions at all levels have well developed web sites, including the European Trade Union Confederation (at www.etuc.org) and the European Trade Union Institute (at www.etuc.org/ETUI/) which is the research arm of the ETUC. Many national trade unions, national confederations, and local level unions also have web sites, many of them in the national language. Trade union web sites can be a source of information regarding current events in a certain region. Many of the higher level associations have interesting responses to proposed legislation or in-depth of analysis of new legislation, which is often found on the ETUC site. The trade union sites are far too numerous to mention, but the ILO has a very extensive list (a few examples: the Mississippi Association of Educators (USA) at www.ms.nea.org; Sindicato dos Bancarios da Bahia (Brazil) at www.svn.com.br/sbba; the Belgian socialist trade union at www.abvv.be (multi-lingual)). Another valuable link is that to LaborNet whose stated mission is to be the 'global online communication for a democratic, independent labor movement' (see www.labornet.org). The LaborNet offers a lot of information on the labor movements in developing countries and the struggle for worker's rights throughout the world.

27. On the employers side, the Union of Industrial & Employers' Confederations of Europe (UNICE) arrived rather late on the web. The web site can be found at www.unice.org and is available in English or French. It provides information on European developments, European law and its own studies, such as the recent study on benchmarking entitled: 'Stimulating creativity and innovation in Europe: the UNICE benchmarking report 2000'. This report is available for free to be downloaded from the web site. The UNICE also has an extensive list of other employer organizations, categorized by industry. The Federation of European employers can be found at www.euen.co.uk.

Other tertiary sources can be found at universities and specialized research institutes such as the Canadian International Labor Network which is a collaborative research venture between the Social Sciences and Humanities Research Council (SSHRC) and McMaster University. It can be found at labour.ciln.mcmaster.ca. The Cornell School of Industrial and Labor Relations (USA) is also a site to consult at www.ilr.cornell.edu; and also the Informationsstelle für Europäisches from Saarbrucken University (Germany) at http://www.jura.uni-sb.de/.

VII. The Legal Profession

28. The Internet is many things to many people, a research library, a shopping center, a place to meet new people. The Internet is the ultimate marketplace of ideas and marketplace period. Its importance as a marketing tool has rendered the Net 'the place to be' for many businesses, including law firms and the legal profession. The last several years have witnessed a dramatic rise in commercial sites (starting generally in 1995 when Amazon.com began selling books online), many of which offer services on-line. While the offering of legal services is still in a nascent stage, the legal profession has definitely latched onto the Net's potential for marketing and many law firms, large and small, as well as solo practitioners, have web sites. Some of the more developed sites can also be a source of information, although they are generally more limited in the substantive content they provide. Obviously, lawyering is also a profession for profit and they do not want to give too much away for free, but many firm web sites have legal bulletins or updates which give brief descriptions or analysis of current legal issues. The Net can be a source of information about the profession itself (i.e. bar rules, ethics rules, disciplinary proceedings against US attorneys), to find a lawyer or law firm, or to search for employment. The Net has become a primary resource for job seekers. In the United States, a firm which is well known for representing management in employment law is Seyfarth, Shaw, Fairweather & Geraldson (see www.seyfarth.com/home.html). This web site has a section entitled 'News' and contains several articles on recent developments in American labour law and employee benefits law. Recent topics included a congressional proposal to increase the US minimum wage and major Supreme Court decisions that set new tests for punitive damages and definitions of disability. The web site of the British firm, Freshfields, has a section entitled 'Knowledge' which contains information and articles on recent developments in British law, including such things as commentary on decisions from the House of Lords on issues of labour law. The site can be found at www.freshfields.com.

29. Sites that are aimed at the legal profession in general are also worthy of consultation. In the United States, the stated mission of *Law.com* is to be the single, comprehensive destination for legal information, e-law services and legal products on the Web.[12] *Law.com* breaks down its information into the legal profession, law students, business and the public. The site offers everything from articles on recent Supreme Court decisions, to features on well-known American attorneys, to on-line ordering of reference books, and other practical tools for lawyers. The section entitled 'public' offers references and links to the public who want to handle simple legal matters themselves. European and British sites on the legal profession include Law Money International (www.lawmoney.com) and The Lawyer (www.the-lawyer.co.uk).

Conclusion

30. For almost all features and characteristics of the Internet there is a plus side and a negative side. The connectivity of the Net is what makes it so voluminous and

---

12. *See* www.law.com

seemingly endless. Almost all sites have links to other sites, and back to their original site which can lead to very interesting information which the researcher did not know existed, but can just as easily result in an endless waste of time. Therefore, it is imperative that the researcher be focused in her research. However, it is that much easier to embark on a great fishing expedition for information in the vast ocean of the Net.

Aside from the vastness of the Net, one should also be mindful of the regional differences affecting the development of the Net. Asian and African sites are not very prevalent on the Net for several reasons ranging from lower access to the hardware, less well developed telecommunications networks and language issues. The language of the Net started out being English, and only in the last year or two has it been possible to produce the symbols and writing of Asian and middle-eastern languages.

The Internet has significantly contributed to the world becoming a global village (to use a hackneyed expression). The Net has knocked down geographic barriers in a way that no other media has done. It allows academics and professionals from all over the world to communicate with each other, share each other's knowledge and bring forth new ideas. The Net is a very powerful tool that can further enhance comparativism. It is an indispensable research tool which all professionals must learn to use in order to say they have fully researched any issue.

LIST OF USEFUL WEB SITES

Academic/University Sites

Universities World-wide (search engine): *geowww.uibk.ac.at/univ/index.html*
Catholic University of Leuven, law library: *www.law.kuleuven.ac.be/lib/*
Canadian International Labor Network: *labour.ciln.mcmaster.ca*
Cornell School of Industrial & Labor Relations (USA): www.ilr.cornell.edu
Cornell Law School Legal Information Institute: *www.law.cornell.edu*

General Search Engines

www.yahoo.com
www.lycos.com
www.altavista.com
infoseek.go.com

Legal Search Engines

CataLaw: *www.catalaw.com*
FindLaw: *www.findlaw.com*
Hieros Gamos: *www.hg.org*

USA – Useful Sites

Department of Labor: *www.dol.gov*
Equal Employment Opportunities Commission: *www.eeoc.gov*

National Labor Relations Board: *www.nlrb.gov*
United States Supreme Court: *www.supremecourtus.gov*

Miscellaneous European & International Sites

Belgian National Labour Council: *www.cnt-nar.be*
Australian Industrial Relations Commission: *www.airc.gov.au*
European Union: *europa.eu.int*
European Court of Justice: *curia.eu.int*
European Foundation for the Improvement of Living & Working Conditions:
   www.eurofound.ie
EuroFound European Works Council site: *www.eurofound.ie/ewc*
United Kingdom House of Lords: *www.parliament.the-stationery-office.co.uk*
French legislation: *www.legifrance.gouv.fr/citoyen/index.ow*

International Organizations

International Labour Organization: *www.ilo.org*
Organization for Economic Cooperation & Development: *www.oecd.org*
European Trade Union Confederation: *www.etuc.org*
LaborNet: *www.labornet.org*
Union of Industrial & Employer's Confederations of Europe: *www.unice.org*
The Federation of European Employers: *www.euen.co.uk*
Juristisches Internetprojekt Saarbrücken [Germany]: *www.jura.uni-sb.de*

Commercial sites, companies, law firms

Law.Com (USA): *www.law.com*
Seyfarth, Shaw, Fairweather & Geraldson [USA law firm]: *www.seyfarth.com/
home.html*
Freshfields (UK law firm) : *www.freshfields.com*
Landwell (correspondent law firms of PricewaterhouseCoopers): www.landwell-
   global.com
LawMoney.com (UK) : www.lawmoney.com
The Lawyer (UK): *www.the-lawyer.co.uk*
International Law Office: *www.internationallawoffice.com*

ACTORS

Chapter 4. International Employers' Organizations

D. France

I. INTRODUCTION: DEFINITION

1.   In this chapter employers' organizations are defined as formal groups of employers set up to defend, represent or advise affiliated employers and to strengthen their position in society at large with respect to labour and social matters as distinct from economic matters (usually chambers of commerce or trade associations). Many employers' organizations conclude collective agreements with trade unions but this is by no means always the case and therefore this cannot be an element included in their definition. Unlike trade unions that are composed of individual persons, employers' organizations are composed of enterprises.

2.   The concept of employer organization does not imply a particular legal identity or form and the term 'employers' associations' is avoided for this reason. Most legal definitions of a trade union can also apply to employer organizations: they are organizations whose principle object is to regulate the relations between employees and employers (British definition) and they are associations for the defence of economic interests (French definition). Employers' organizations may also choose other legal personalities, or none at all to suit their purposes and/or depending on national law and practice. Employers' organizations have no common history: some evolved out of bodies created for another purpose, for instance a chamber of commerce. In this chapter we will give a brief history of the origins of employers' organizations and their evolution as a result of historical developments and varying cultures and traditions. We will then look at the various structures of employers' organizations and highlight some current challenges facing them.

II. HISTORICAL DEVELOPMENT: FROM GUILDS TO EMPLOYERS' ORGANIZATIONS

3.   It is often said that employers' organizations were established as a reaction to trade union power and therefore are a much more recent phenomenon than workers' organizations. However, this is not strictly the case if we accept that employers' organizations are to some extent the successors to the guilds of the Middle Ages. Nevertheless, there are some differences of course: contrary to Guilds, employers' organizations are usually freely constituted organizations, representing enterprises usually in free competition with one another and dealing on an equal footing with workers' organizations, especially for the establishment of the 'price' of labour.

4. A market economy, a liberal economy and the political and social structure were initially regarded as incompatible with the guild system. For example in France the Le Chapelier Act of 14–17 June 1791 forbade members of the same trade to form associations in defence of their 'so-called common interests'. This is because the logic of the market economy leads an employer to consider other employers as rivals or competitors. Workers very soon realized that competition between fellow workers was a weakness and an advantage for the other party i.e. employers. Adam Smith observed in 1776 that 'we rarely hear … of the combination of masters, through frequently of those of workmen. But whoever imagines, upon this account that masters rarely combine, is as ignorant of the world as of the subject. Masters are always and everywhere in a sort of tacit, but constant and uniform combination, not to raise the wages of labour above their actual rate'.

5. Certainly entrepreneurs, individualists by nature and by function, are less inclined to associate than other social groups. This could be because they do not easily accept a discipline that may interfere with their technical or commercial operations. Freedom of action is regarded as an essential element of production. Any restriction on this freedom has therefore to be justified. The first associations of industrialists or tradesmen were therefore more like clubs or social institutions and were used mostly for exchanging views or opinions. Their members were no doubt divided on questions of manufacturing policy or foreign trade, while labour questions simply did not arise. The situation only began to change at the turn of the last century.

6. At the end of the 19th century came the end of 'laissez-faire' policies, i.e. of a certain neutrality of the state in respect of economic and labour questions. The first element was the emergence and recognition of trade unionism and the legitimacy of industrial action that led to labour unrest and the first serious strikes. In addition, and partly as a response, employers began to experiment with the development of labour legislation. Today what was proposed, for example on health and safety and working hours may appear benign, but at the time it was considered as an intolerable encroachment on freedom of enterprise.

7. Many sectoral employers' federations were therefore created in the period before the First World War. This was followed by a number of central employers' confederations, for example in the Nordic countries (Denmark 1896, Norway 1900, Sweden 1901, and Finland 1905), as well as in Germany where two organizations merged in 1913 to form an organization not so dissimilar to the present organization, despite the interruption of the Nazi regime. For most of the last century, these organizations remained organizations specializing in labour matters and distinct from the economic organizations. However, this distinction is now increasingly under review with the Norwegian employers joining with the industry federation and forming the NHO in the early 1990s. At the time of writing, the Swedish business community is also contemplating a merger of its employer and economic organizations. In other European countries central organizations were a later development. In France such an organization, which ultimately became the Conseil National du Patronat Francais was founded in 1920. In 1998 it changed name again to become the Mouvement des Enterprises de France (MEDEF). In the United Kingdom the present Confederation of British Industry was founded in 1965 as a result of a merger between three organizations, one of which was the British Employers' Confederation. In these two countries therefore the employers' organization also deals with economic and trade matters.

8.   In non-European countries, there are also some examples of employers' organizations with a long history: for instance the Union Industrial Argentina was founded in 1887. Many of these organizations, particularly in the Americas, were not established initially to deal with industrial relations matters but mainly to deal with such questions as fiscal legislation or foreign trade. They assumed the functions of an employers' organization *stricto sensu* over time when it became necessary to respond to a particular government policy or to the development of the trade union movement. In some Latin American countries business organizations were set up in the thirties with compulsory membership. Others were free associations. In other parts of the world, newly independent nations followed the pattern of their former colonial power: for instance 'employers' federations' based on the British model of the time proliferated in English speaking African and Asian states. The main problem of organizations in developing countries has been the difficulty of integrating a very heterogeneous membership and of securing the means necessary to enable them to play a significant role as representative of the productive sector of the economy.

9.   In countries which were submitted to central planning (such as the former USSR), the concept of an employers' organization did not really exist, as there were no contractual relations between an employer and an employee. A few functions of an employers' organization were assumed by the chambers of commerce but they had no responsibility for labour and social matters and their activities were strictly controlled. Since the collapse of Communism in central and eastern Europe, employers' organizations have been set up in most countries and some are recognized internationally but their growth is still in initial stages. They are part of the new tripartite structures that are being put in place as part of the democratization process. The main challenge facing these new organizations is the heterogeneity of their membership that consists of former state enterprises, employing the majority of the workforce and managed by their former directors, privatized companies and the emerging purely private small enterprises. For the moment the two last categories represent a minority but are an essential part of the transition towards a market economy.

III.   FUNCTIONS OF EMPLOYERS' ORGANIZATIONS

A.   *Defence and Promotion*

10.   Employers' organizations began to emerge therefore at the same time as trade unions. However, at that time they did not try to defend their members by direct dialogue with the emerging workers' unions but rather by approaching government leaders. In early times discrete representations to political authorities, politicians or

senior civil servants was all that was necessary. However, like all interest groups, employers' organizations gradually began to find their place in the democratic decision-making process. Employers' organizations are not mass membership organizations and therefore are not in a privileged position in a modern society based on mass institutions. They are, however, influential by virtue of their economic control and because they influence – or appear to be able to influence – society at large. On the whole employer representatives are not usually directly represented in parliaments. There are no political parties formally linked with an employers' organization in the way that the Labour party is linked with the British trade union movement, for example. The more informal relationships which exist between most socialist parties and trade unions are also not replicated by relationships between employer organizations and conservative parties. Most employer organizations are openly apolitical bodies, as they need to influence and lobby on behalf of their members whatever party happens to be the government of the day. Employer's influence on parliaments, political parties, and civil servants can sometimes be considerable but the reasons why this is so are difficult to analyse. The influence is probably based less on formal structures than on informal contacts and the technical of expertise of the particular organization on a given subject.

11. This traditional way of protecting members' interests, i.e. by representations to government is still of value but is now considered as insufficient. The main reason for a new approach is that public opinion is becoming better informed and more sophisticated and employers have a role to play informing public opinion on certain issues. Relying on influencing the political process is no longer sufficient. Today, the groups employer organizations try to influence have extended from their members to other opinion formers, to consumers and wider society at large often through the media.

12. Employers' organizations are also increasingly being expected to involve themselves in social policy issues as a whole rather than just react to specific industrial relations and workplace issues. This no doubt mirrors the evolution of the trade union movement which is moving away from the defence of employed persons (trade union members) and into wider offering services and a lobby group for society as a whole.

B. Function of Representation

1. Representative Function in the Political Structure

13. A government department may take the initiative to seek the advice of a particular interest group before taking action on a policy proposal. This is usually done when it is felt necessary to gauge the likely reaction of a particular group before taking the final decision on any action to be taken. If an organization is consulted in this way this usually implies some recognition of its technical expertise and representative character. This system developed at the beginning of the 20th Century as a necessary corollary to the growing state intervention in social and economic questions. In Switzerland this concept was recognized in the Federal Constitution in 1947.

Article 32, al. 3 states that 'interested economic groups shall be consulted in the preparation of implementing regulations'.

14. When governments take such action they must make a choice of organizations to be consulted. In some countries this choice is straightforward. In others the choice is not clear and this may enable the authorities to choose the organization which will most likely give the response they are looking for. An important condition for the credibility of an employers' organization is therefore to be representative in order to be recognized as the voice of its membership. Judging the representative character of employer organizations is often more difficult than for other groups: members of employers' organizations are not individual persons but enterprises of different sizes and natures. The simple arithmetic of adding up units is not enough. Representation has therefore to be judged by considering the final result: is the organization able to present the real views of those who will have to live with the results of any policy decision taken?

15. The representative function of employer organizations assumed a new dimension when consultation became formalized in tripartite or bipartite institutions. The International Labour Organisation (ILO), created in 1919 is a unique illustration of tripartism with its structure associating employers' and workers' delegates on an equal footing with representatives of governments. Before and mainly during the First World War, some form of tripartite machinery was established in the UK, France, and Germany, especially to guide the management of the war economy. The ILO and its tripartite structure have had an influence on many countries, especially developing nations that have benefited from its technical cooperation measures. In most countries governments deal with employers' representatives and other partners usually in a consultative capacity. This consultation does not often lead to direct participation in the decision making process itself however.

16. Economic and Social Councils were also a response to the need for economic and social interests to be represented. These exist in a number of countries e.g. France and the Netherlands and also large parts of French speaking Africa and Latin America.

17. Employers are also represented in other bodies such as consultative bodies concerned with specific policy issues such as health and safety. In some developing countries that have a single party system, employers' organizations sometimes have a relationship association with the ruling party together with other 'national' organizations. Tripartism is often also applied to the management of social security systems established by legislation. Some of these schemes were established by collective agreement and are run on a tripartite basis by employers' and workers' organizations.

2. Representative Function in the Industrial Relations System

18. The representative character of employers' organizations is perhaps seen most through their role in collective bargaining arrangements. However, in many countries employers' organizations do not bargain directly with trade unions. There are various models, although the distinguishing features between these various models are now becoming blurred. The first model is or was typical of the Nordic countries, where negotiations are undertaken at the national level. This does not mean that agreement is always achieved at this level: negotiations are then continued at branch or sectoral level to apply the centrally agreed provisions. Of course such a system implies a strong centralized employers' organization as for agreements to be accepted at sectoral or enterprise level, the national organization has to be structured in a way that enables the negotiators to be fully aware of the needs of all of its members. Such as system relies on discipline between members based on an acceptance that individual members will not suffer from a decision taken at central level. A mutual strike insurance system has therefore been an important element of this system. Recently the 'Nordic model' has been criticized for imposing rigidities on the labour market, which affect the competitiveness of enterprises. The trend in these countries has therefore been towards a decentralization of negotiations towards branch and enterprise level. In Sweden for example, the Swedish employers have withdrawn from all tripartite structures.

19. At the other end of the scale some employer organizations play no role in collective bargaining at all and negotiations take place almost exclusively at enterprise level. This does not mean however that the employers' organization plays no role in industrial relations. In the case of Japan for example, the Japanese Federation of Employers' Associations (Nikkeiren) does not negotiate but considers one of its main missions to be the formulation of guidelines for employers in the bargaining process. These are drawn up by its policy-making bodies in which major corporations are represented and is prepared by extensive research by economists on the staff. In North America, negotiations are generally at enterprise level, employers' groups are numerous and well organized but the two main associations, the National Association of Manufacturers and the Chamber of Commerce of the United States, whilst being active in political and legislative affairs, do not intervene in collective bargaining.

20. Another model, which may be called the German model, is based on negotiations at the level of national branches of industry. There are no other levels of negotiation. The German models of works councils which involve participation and consultation in the enterprise is not collective bargaining in its strict sense and it does not embrace items dealt with in collective agreements. Relations between the peak organizations of employers and workers are limited to common participation in various tripartite national bodies and to informal contacts. As a rule no formal agreements are concluded between them. The central organization therefore has the function of coordinating the policy of its members and to ensure a common approach based on internal consultation and research. This model demands well organized branch organizations able to assume the bargaining function.

21. The last model, typical for example of France, Belgium, or Italy, is different from the last three ones mentioned because it is based on negotiation at several levels. The emphasis is still on branch level negotiations but it does not exclude the conclusion of agreements at the national multisectoral level. These agreements may consist more of broad statements on general policy or they may deal with more specific problems such as hours of work, wage indexation etc. Frequently these agreements set out general principles that have to be further implemented at the branch or enterprise level. Such a system based on a chain of negotiations is difficult to monitor. The structure of the employers' organizations as a whole has to be based on frequent liaison between all levels involved in the negotiating process.

C. Internal Functions of Employers' Organizations

22. It is not always easy to draw a line between activities supporting the functions described above and those undertaken for members in their direct interest. Research for instance is necessary before action is taken to influence government or public opinion or to furnish negotiators with sound arguments. However, enterprises also need research. For this reason most employer organizations undertake various types of enquiries and surveys on issues such as wages or benefits, health and safety, equal opportunities, etc. At a time when management principles and techniques are increasingly under the spotlight, employers' organizations provide a forum for the discussion of new approaches. Many new concepts such as participative management, communications policies, continuous training and lifelong learning have been developed in this way. Consultation and discussion with members is also necessary to gauge the business response to general issues such as workers' participation, income policies, the role of trade unions in collective bargaining, etc.

23. Employers' organizations are also becoming training institutions. At a basic level they develop an awareness of the need to raise the skills of the workforce and contribute to drawing up the business approach. The largest organizations have established management development centres. These activities are growing as the concept of lifelong learning takes hold.

24. Employers' organizations are also sometimes active in wider social projects. For instance the provision of housing for workers' was often initiated by employers. In France, family allowances were introduced during the First World War by employers and the schemes (compulsory from 1932) continued to be administered until 1945 by equalisation funds set up by employers. Most of these functions were finally taken over by social security institutions, but some still remain.

25. Enterprises also expect direct services from their organization. They ask for information and advice to guide them through the labyrinth of legal obligations deriving from laws and agreements. This function is growing especially where regional organizations such as the EU, add to the legislative framework. In some countries employers' organization assist employers before labour courts and provide mediation/conciliation services. Advice on methods to improve management and productivity is also sought, particularly in developing countries.

IV. STRUCTURE OF EMPLOYERS' ORGANIZATIONS

26. It is not fruitful to study the structure of employers' organizations in isolation. For example, how does one compare a local trade association with a confederation? Variations from country to country will depend on the relative importance given to its different functions and especially on the degree of centralization of the industrial relations system as a whole. In this respect there are some parallels between employers' and workers' organizations. Other variations are due to factors external to the industrial relations system, such as the size of the country and its form of government. The employers' structures in India are different for example from the ones prevailing in Mauritius. A federal state leads normally, but not always, to a decentralized employers' organization. The degree of economic development of a particular country also has to be taken into account. A diversified industry based on small and medium sized enterprises calls for a different type of organization than an economy based on one or few basic sectors. However, one of the main reasons for the differences between employer organizations comes as a result of history. The slow and peaceful development of a country leads to a more complex and less rational structure of employer organizations than that of a country which has been rebuilt after complete collapse, such as Germany or Japan.

A.   Unity of the Central Organization at National Level

1. Economic and Social Organizations

27.   As well as employers' organizations which represent enterprises in social and labour affairs, enterprises also group together to defend their interests in other policy areas such as the regulation of domestic and foreign trade, customs policies, company taxation or investment promotion. In the Nordic countries, Germany, Switzerland, Ireland, and in most countries which experienced British colonization, these functions were traditionally assumed by separate organizations. Many of them had the word 'industry' in their titles or in English-speaking parts of the world were called Federations or Chambers of Industry and/or Commerce. (In French-speaking and continental European countries chambers of commerce are public establishments, often with compulsory membership, run by organs elected by all.) In other countries, especially Belgium, France, Italy, and some Latin American countries, the two groups of functions are assumed by a single organization called a Federation of Industry, of Enterprises or, in France, 'Patronat'. The British themselves joined this camp when the Confederation of British Industry came into being in 1965. In the Netherlands the Federation of Dutch Enterprises (VNO) replaced two organizations previously responsible in the social field and the economic field respectively. There is now a definite trend for the merger of 'economic' and 'social' organizations. This has happened recently in Norway, Finland and Ireland, and the issue is a subject of debate in other countries.

28.   Of course it is sometimes rather difficult to make a clear-cut division between 'social' and 'economic' questions. Tax laws or investment inducements may have implications for wage or employment policies. This intermingling of policies can make it difficult to justify the on-going existence of separate organizations. Participation in national planning and global economic and social policy implies an integrated approach to economic and labour issues. However, in countries where the dual structure has been maintained, employers justify it, indicating that it is easier to maintain cohesion in labour matters than in the economic field where the opposition of interests is greater. Whatever structure is chosen, however, there is now a need for closer cooperation between organizations representing business.

2. Coverage of the Central Organization

29. The coverage of the central or national organization varies very much from country to country. It is difficult to propose criteria but it seems that wide coverage is easier to achieve in an organization specialized in labour matters. In one group of countries (UK, New Zealand, etc.) only a single organization exists, open to all sectors of the economy including agriculture. In another group the central employers' organization covers all sectors, except agriculture where there is a special organization (France and Tunisia). In a larger group of countries, the central organization embraces a sizeable number of groups in the secondary sector – mostly manufacturing – while the tertiary sector – and sometimes also building, transport, or mining – form different separate organizations. It is often difficult to bring together manufacturing and commerce in the same organization. In Switzerland, membership of the central organization extends to cover banks, insurance companies, and the large department stores but not the wholesale and retail trade. In Belgium, however, it has been possible to merge the organization for industry and for tertiary sector. The coverage question represents a real challenge for organizations in their search for greater representativity.

3. Parallel Organizations

30. In some countries, there is more than one employers' organization with some overlapping among them. This is the case in the United States with the National Association of Manufacturers and the Chamber of Commerce of the US, both with very similar functions. In India, one organization is mainly composed of large enterprises including multinationals, while another exists for smaller national businesses and still another for the public sector. In the two cases, the duality is explained by history and has no rational justification. In India, a joint Council has been established by three bodies, particularly for international representation. In Australia, a very complex situation has led to the creation of an apex body, the Australian Chamber of Commerce and Industry. In the Netherlands, there were also two organizations, both covering almost all sectors, one non-denominational and another Christian (resulting from the merger of a Catholic and a Protestant organization) but they merged in 1995.

31. Associations of Christian employers also exist in other countries, forming the national sections of International Christian Union of Business Executives (UNIAPAC). Their purpose is more to define a certain approach to social problems than to act as representatives of employers. Their members are persons acting as individuals, and not as enterprises. Therefore they are not employers' organizations. Organizations also exist which provide a forum for debate on given topics, e.g. corporate social responsibility, equal opportunities, etc. Companies are often members of these organizations and the relevant national employers' organization at the same time. These organizations, whilst providing an important channel for debate and developing ideas, are not employers' organizations because they lack any representative character.

B. Membership of Employers' Organizations

1. Small and Medium-sized Enterprises

32. The concept of small and medium-sized enterprises is widely accepted but difficult to define in quantitative terms. Normally it refers to an enterprise where the manager is normally the owner of the majority or a large part of the capital and maintains direct and permanent relations with the employees. The climate of industrial relations is sometimes quite different. SMEs often lack expert staff and need more advice from their relevant employer organization. These enterprises have specific technical needs. The question is often asked whether those needs are best met by the creation of special SME organizations or by SMEs joining the main employers' organization? The great majority of central employers' organizations are open to all undertakings, irrespective of their size. Restrictions, where they exist, apply to very small firms. However, employer organizations often do not reach out enough to SMEs and SME companies are less active in the various decision-making bodies of employer organizations. Central organizations usually try to encourage a large membership of small enterprises to ensure more political influence and to avoid the creation of splinter groups but this demands implies an effort to involve them in decision making, to increase the direct services to members and to adapt the scale of contributions.

33. Parallel organizations catering solely for smaller undertakings are to be found in some countries. A typical example is France where a General Confederation of Small and Medium Sized Enterprises' has been in existence since 1946 and is considered as representative of the category. It has at times been a member of the CNPF (now MEDEF) but is now separate. Most of its members are nevertheless still represented in the central organization through the branch trade associations in which they remain members and they are covered by collective agreements concluded at the branch level. In Spain, the Confederation of Small Enterprises is a member of the General Confederation, the CEOE, and its President is one of the Vice-Presidents of the latter, ensuring the autonomy and the co-operation of these organizations. In Britain the CBI has a special SME Council.

2. Public Sector Enterprises

34. As the promotion of free enterprise is at the core of employers' organizations, the principle of membership of enterprises in the public sector sometimes raises a difficult issue. In some countries the State is the largest employer and employers' organizations have taken a pragmatic attitude to membership of these companies. In very few countries – such as the United States and Switzerland – the employers' organizations are closed to public enterprises, but these are typically countries where this sector is very small indeed.

35. The general attitude of employers' organizations towards public sector undertakings is that of limiting membership to publicly-owned companies largely run on the same economic principles as private companies. This would normally exclude state monopoly sectors like postal, telegraph and telephone services, radio and television, rail transport, or less frequently, coal mines and electricity providers. A characteristic of these undertakings is that the price of their products does not result from a competitive market but is determined by the government. The result of this situation makes the position of management in the collective bargaining process quite different. Another criterion might be the degree of autonomy of the management in relation to government authorities. Public sector undertakings may be not very different from ministerial departments without even a special budget, or companies with state participation may have practically the same freedom of action as private groups. This situation varies from country to country. This debate has become quite important in the countries in transition where employers' organizations are needed to help their members manage the transition from public to private enterprise.

36. Sometimes, the State prohibits public sector undertakings from joining employers' federations. For instance, in Italy, an Act of 1956 prohibits companies in which the State has a direct or indirect interest from joining trade or regional associations affiliated to the General Confederation of Italian Industry.

C. *Employers' Organizations at the Sectoral and Regional Levels*

37. In very small countries, it is possible to have a single employers' organization to which individual employers or enterprises are directly affiliated. However, this is of course impracticable in most countries. Usually individual firms are grouped under trade and/or regional associations with the latter directly affiliated to the central organization. In one group of countries, including the Nordic countries, Belgium, the Netherlands, and a few others, trade associations alone are affiliated. This is typical of medium-sized centralized countries with an industrial relations system based on an emphasis on negotiation at branch level. In a few federal countries, with negotiation at enterprise level, member associations are all regional. In a larger group trade and regional associations are members and most firms are themselves affiliated both to a trade and a regional unit (with possibility of any form of intermediary groups). The number of direct members in an organization may therefore vary between a dozen and a few hundred.

38. In most organizations, the branch structure has more weight than the regional one due to the fact that major labour questions are dealt with at the branch level. But the general trend is towards the reinforcement of regional structures. This is linked with the need to maintain closer contacts with smaller firms who often do not have headquarters in the capital city, but also to the need to facilitate the drawing up of employers' policy on regional issues. This new stress on regions is sometimes accompanied by a reinforcement of regional associations or by the establishment of regional offices and a decentralization of activities (for instance in organizing important meetings in different parts of the country). A regional policy is an essential means of preserving the cohesion of the institution.

39. These intermediate structures contribute to the decision-making process. Employers' organizations sometimes have specific problems compared with most other associations. As stated above, members of employer organizations are not physical persons but entities. Enterprises are of different sizes. A simple application of the democratic principle – one man, one vote – would not be very practicable and ultimately not very democratic.

40. Employer organizations therefore give more weight to larger enterprises but at the same time, have to try not to reduce to a minimum the influence of small enterprises. This is sometimes a difficult balancing act.

41. Formalizing the structure of employer organizations through sectoral and regional organizations can lead to the central organization being remote from actual enterprises. One way to address this has been to admit individual firms as members of the central organization along with sectoral or branch associations. This is for instance the rule in the Confederation of British Industry. A potential drawback of this approach is that it may lead to a weakening of the branch organizations and a certain imbalance in so far as it can give more weight to the opinion of large firms.

D. *Means and Resources*

42. Employer organizations need resources to fulfil all of the functions mentioned above. They need expertise that can be given by a permanent staff of lawyers, economists, public relations specialists, statisticians, political scientists but also experts in the running of employers' organizations. Many employers' organizations have set up special institutions for the training of their staff and organize career development for their personnel. But to be truly strong, an employers' organization also needs a real contribution from its actual members. Usually presidents and chairmen of committees are honorary functionaries. It is often difficult to find company representatives willing and able to spare their time. The running of an employers' organization is based on close cooperation between elected chairmen and professional staff members. Costs are usually covered by contributions paid by enterprises either directly or though the branch or regional organizations. In a very centralized system (for instance the Nordic countries), the contributions are paid directly to the central body which returns a fraction of it to the branch federations, but this is the exception rather than the rule. Contributions are based on the wage bill (or sometimes on the number of employees). For 'economic and social' organizations, account is also taken of such data as turnover, sales, value added, etc.

E. *Future Challenges for Employer Organizations*

43. Governments nationally, regionally and globally are seeking to develop closer relationships with the world's largest companies. At the same time, the world's largest organizations are establishing direct relationships with those they seek to influence either individually or by developing powerful network groups. A survey recently carried out by the Bureau for Employer Activities of the ILO revealed that around a quarter of employer organizations have no direct contact with enterprises, membership in the large company category is an area of net membership decline in the developed country employer organizations and employers' organizations in the developing countries and in eastern Europe need to attract into membership the subsidiaries of major multinational businesses.

44. In most countries a range of employer organizations exist nationally, sectorally, by specific business interest or regionally. Current relationships are described in many countries as 'competitive' and 'overlapping' in responsibilities. Employers' organizations, primarily in eastern Europe, have concerns about the representativeness of their organizations. A large number of employer organizations describe chambers of commerce as major competitors and are planning alliances and/or mergers.

45. Lobbying activities or service provision continues to be seen as a primarily national activity. Governments are increasingly working globally or in regional groupings and companies are increasingly multinational either through direct ownership, alliances or joint ventures, or through their supply chains. Major consultancies and law firms are building international competence to deal with the international demands of their existing and potential future clients.

46. The most important issue facing employers' organizations in the less developed countries and in eastern Europe is the generation of additional income; these concerns are also shared; though perhaps to a lesser extent by organizations in developed countries. Organizations are considering what they can do to increase simultaneously both membership and member subscriptions. Employers' organizations in developed countries are asking whether they have the potential for cost savings or whether they offer a level of service genuinely demanded by their members. More generally organizations are asking whether they need to broaden their income stream beyond the almost total reliance on subscription income.

V.   INTERNATIONAL EMPLOYERS' ORGANIZATIONS

A.   *Historical Development*

47. The first international meeting of representatives of central employers' federations, as understood here, was held in 1912 in Turin on the occasion of a World Labour Exhibition. It recommended the creation and promotion of employers' associations in their own countries and the study of the possibility of establishing an international group. It was in fact the first ILO Conference in 1919 that provided a new opportunity for a gathering of employers' representatives at international level. In 1920, the 'International Organisation of Industrial Employers' was created with its headquarters in Brussels. After the Second World War, the organization changed its name to the 'International Organisation of Employers' (IOE).

48. Between the two World Wars, the IOE remained active almost solely within the framework of the ILO. The development of international federations of trade unions in the twenties had no real counterpart on the employers' side. After 1945, the development of the specialised agencies within the United Nations system led to a reinforcement of the IOE, whose headquarters were moved from Brussels to Geneva in 1964.

B. *International Employers' Organizations at the World Level*

1. General Description

49. As in many national situations, there are two organizations representing the interests of employers at international level, one in charge of the so-called social questions, IOE, and one specialised in economic questions, the International Chamber of Commerce (ICC). An agreement exists between the two organizations establishing a division of work. It is a fact, however, that the borderline between the two types of questions is becoming blurred, for instance in the current debate on the linkages between trade and labour standards for example.

50. Other groups aim at representing special categories of enterprises. For instance, an International Association of Crafts and Small and Medium-Sized Enterprises was founded in 1947 and has members in 22 countries. Other organizations have been set up at sectoral level, such as the International Shipping Federation. National federations of building and civil engineering employers are grouped in three regional federations that set up a 'Confederation of International Contractors Associations' in 1973. These associations are rather active in labour matters, especially in the context of the ILO. Other sectoral Organizations, such as the Road Transport Union, the International Iron and Steel Institute, the International Textile Manufacturers' Federation, deal mainly with scientific or technical issues and only occasionally with labour matters. As the trade union movement begins to strengthen at international sectoral and regional level and begins to push for international social dialogue, employers will need to consider their own response.

2. The International Organisation of Employers (IOE)

51. The members of the IOE, 134 in 130 countries, are 'central employers' federations'. This means that companies cannot be in direct membership even if they are multinational enterprises. It should also be noted that members are national multiindustry groups – normally one per country –, in practice the most representative organization called upon to nominate the employers' delegate to the International Labour Conference in accordance with the ILO Constitution. International sectoral organizations cannot be members but working arrangements have been concluded.

52. IOE members also have to fulfil certain conditions. They have 'to be composed exclusively of employers' or employers' organizations, to stand for and defend the principles of free enterprise and to be a free independent organization, not subject to control or interference of any kind from any governmental authority or any outside body'. However, 'free enterprise' is not a synonym for private enterprise. Many IOE members include public corporations as mentioned above when this type of membership does not appear to affect the independence of the overall organization. The breakdown of communist systems in countries called now 'in transition' has led to a growing membership in the IOE of new employers' organizations who are engaged in the process of privatization and restoration of the market economy.

53. The internal structure of the IOE is based on a General Council, where all members are represented, a Management Board, a President, an Executive Vice-President and a permanent Secretary-General. The Executive Vice-President is the employers' Vice-Chairman of the ILO Governing Body and as such, the political leader of the employers at major ILO meetings, including the General Conference.

54. This symbiotic relationship between the IOE and the Employers' Group of ILO illustrates the fact that the ILO remains one of the main concerns of the IOE. The international trade union federations also organize the Workers' Group but their other activities are more extensive or better known to the public. The IOE is now developing cooperation with other international institutions, such as the World Bank and the World Trade Organisation. The IOE also provides a forum for members to share information on labour issues and discussion of topics of special interest. The IOE also provides technical assistance to employers in developing countries, for instance by organizing seminars or by sending experts to help them with organizational problems, often with the help of the ILO.

55. The IOE is one of the organizations enjoying full consultative status with the ILO (as well as with the UN). But its main function, in an organization where employers' (and workers') delegates are able to express directly the point of view of enterprises, is to maintain the cohesion of the Employers' Group and to make sure that the delegates are well briefed on the substance of the issues. Through the employers' delegates, the IOE contributes to the process of drawing up of ILO instruments and to the development of technical cooperation. As the majority of IOE members come from developing countries they are particularly interested in general training, management training and industrial safety. The ILO has now introduced a programme of assistance to employers' organizations, which is operated in close liaison with the IOE.

C. *Regional Organizations*

56. The number of regional employers' associations is increasing. For instance, presidents of central employers' federations in Asia and in Latin America now meet regularly under the auspices of the IOE. A Pan-African Employers' Confederation was established in Cairo in October 1986 with strong links to the IOE, most of its members being members of the latter organization. Its headquarters are in Nairobi. The Confederation enjoys consultative status with the ILO and is also active within the framework of the OAU, especially its Commission of Ministers of Labour. Other employers' organizations *stricto sensu* have been constituted at the sub-regional level, for instance in the Caribbean and in southeast Asia (ASEAN group). The development of the Arab Labour Organization has induced the General Union of Chambers of Commerce, Industry and Agriculture for Arab Countries to establish a standing Committee for Social Affairs. This trend will grow as the number of regional trading blocs, each promoting a social dimension, increases.

57. The tendency to establish employers' organizations to represent the views of enterprises to intergovernmental institutions is perhaps most developed in Europe. Thus the Council of European Industrial Federations (CIFE) was created in 1949 to make possible direct consultations with the Organisation for European Economic Co-operation (OEEC). When the latter disappeared in 1961 and was replaced by the OECD, most activities of the CIFE were taken over by the Business and Industrial Advisory Committee (BIAC). In the early phases of the development of the European Union, employers' affairs were taken care of in the framework of CIFE but a 'Union of Industries of the European Community' (UNICE) was formally created in 1958 by the national employers' federations of the then six member countries.

58. The CIFE had as a matter of fact a wider representation than did the OEEC, since Spain and Finland were members in spite of the fact that, in the beginning, their governments had remained outside of the intergovernmental organization. In UNICE, the same situation arose: the Federation of Greek Industry was associated with its work as early as 1962. In 1972–1973, the employers' organizations of the three new EEC Member States, the UK, Denmark, and Ireland, joined UNICE and a little later employers' organizations from European countries remaining outside the Community decided also to become associate members. UNICE is now not only an organization of EU employers but also an organization of European employers. It has presently members in 27 countries including in eastern Europe.

59. UNICE, like BIAC, is competent both in the social and in the economic field, as its new name: 'Union of Industrial and Employers' Confederations of Europe' indicates. It members represent a wide variety of membership structures from 'economic', 'social', or 'mixed'. Industry has also to be understood in a broad sense as including the tertiary sector, although initially the organization's sphere of competence was limited to the industrial sector. Agriculture is still organized separately, as is the public sector through the European Centre for Public Enterprises (CEEP). This is rather paradoxical, because most members of UNICE are open to the public sector and there is no special organization covering this sector only except in Italy. UNICE membership is not open to organizations representing a particular sector of activity at national or European level. However, it services the European Employers' Network that brings together the European level sectoral organizations.

60. UNICE's structure is characterised by the daily involvement of its members and the relative importance of the services provided. This is due to the growing influence of the EU and its policies. The organization is headed by a President elected by the Council of Presidents (of the member federations), an Executive Committee composed of the Directors-General of Member Federations and a Committee of Permanent Delegates which is in constant contact with the Secretary-General.

61. The cooperation between UNICE and the EU institutions is often informal but regular. In addition, the EU structure includes an Economic and Social Committee made up of persons representing employers, workers and other groups. The members are appointed in a personal capacity and do not necessarily reflect the views of UNICE, which, however, provides them with experts and documentation.

62. UNICE meets European workers' organizations represented in the European Trade Union Confederation (ETUC) and also has direct relations with them. In the 1980's UNICE began participating in the so-called 'Social Dialogue' with the European Confederation of Trade Unions under the auspices of the EU Commission. The 'Joint Opinions' agreed upon by the parties were not collective agreements. However, the Maastrict and Amsterdam Treaties gave new powers to the social partners at European level. As the EU has increased its competence in the social affairs field, it also made social dialogue a part of the 'acquis communautaire' and introduced the requirement that the social partners be consulted on EU initiatives in the social affairs field. The social partners, through UNICE and the ETUC also have the opportunity to negotiate at European level and for these agreements to be implemented through Community legislation. To date this process has resulted in UNICE/ETUC agreements which have been turned into Directives on parental leave, part-time work and fixed term contracts. Employment was brought into the Treaty as a 'common objective' and also incorporates the role expected of the social partners. UNICE has therefore participated with the ETUC in the macro-economic dialogue with the European Central Bank.

63. UNICE is a regional employers' organization which is becoming more like a national federation. As such the decision-making process is sometimes difficult given the different political frameworks and industrial relations structures which exist in Europe. However, as European integration continues and as, particularly in social affairs the EU takes on more powers of legislative initiative, its structure will need to adapt accordingly.

SELECT BIBLIOGRAPHY

J.J. Oechslin, 'Employers' Organisations: Current Trends and Social Responsibilties', *International Labour Review*, Vol. 121, September–October, 1982.

J.P. Windmuller and A. Gladstone (eds), *Employers' Associations and Industrial Relations – A comparative study*, Oxford, 1984.

ILO Labour Relations Series

No. 39 – *Role of Employers' Organisations in Asian Countries*, Geneva, 1971.

No. 42 – *Role of Employers' Organisations in English Speaking African Countries*, Geneva, 1973.

No. 53 – *Role of Employers' Organisations in English Speaking Caribbean Countries*, Geneva, 1977.

No. 46 – *Role des organizations d'employeurs dans les pays d'Afrique francophone*, Geneva, 1975.

No. 54 – *Role des organizations d'employeurs dans les pays arabes*, Geneva, 1978.

No. 51 – *Papel de las organizaciones de empleadores en America Latina*, Geneva, 1976.

D. Sadowski and O. Jacobi (eds), *Employers' Associations in Europe*, Baden, 1991.

M. Upham, *Employers' Organisations of the World*, London, 1990.

S.R. de Silva, *Managing an Employers' Organization*, ILO, Bangkok, 1993.

Bureau for Employers' Activities, ILO, *The Future of Employer' Organisations: Issues, Challenges and Responses*, Geneva, 1999.

Chapter 5.   The International Trade Union Movement

J.P. Windmuller and S.K. Pursey

I.   HISTORICAL OVERVIEW

A.   *To 1914*

1.   The international trade union movement is built on the foundations of millions of local unions. Trade unions form, develop and pursue their primary tasks of defending and improving the conditions of life and work of their members mainly within national systems of industrial relations. Yet for well over a century trade unions have also had international interests and commitments many of which they have expressed through international trade union organizations. The purpose of this chapter is to briefly recall this history so that the emerging new features of international unionism can be seen in perspective.[1]

2.   Two different types of international trade union organizations established themselves securely in the last decades of the nineteenth century and the first decade of the twentieth century. One was based on an identity of interests among individual national unions for specific crafts, trades, and industries in various countries and resulted in the formation of what are known as International Trade Secretariats. The other type was of a broader character, for its members consisted of the central federations of trade unions, also called national centres.

3.   International Trade Secretariats (often abbreviated as Secretariats or ITSs) first became established in 1889 with the creation of international federations of typographers and printers, hatters, cigar makers, and tobacco workers, and boot and shoe operatives. Their constituent bodies were unions of workers engaged in manufacturing in several European countries. Organizations composed of unions in other trades and industries followed the example in the next few years, including those for miners (1890), clothing workers (1893), metal workers (1890), textile workers (1894), transport workers (1896), and many others. By 1914 28 ITSs existed. While

---

1.   Carew, Dreyfus, Van Goethem, Gumbrell-McCormick and van der Linden 2000 (Peter Lang), *The International Confederation of Free Trade Unions* provides a comprehensive history of both the first fifty years of the ICFTU and of its precursors from 1902.

acknowledging their support of long-range socialist aims, their main efforts were devoted to such practical tasks as disseminating trade information, helping travelling journeymen, and discouraging the international transport of strike-breakers.

4.   The second type of international trade union organization, composed of central trade union federations, emerged from conferences in Copenhagen (1901), Stuttgart (1902), and Dublin (1903). First known as the International Secretariat of Trade Union Centres, the organization called itself the International Federation of Trade Unions (IFTU) from 1913 on. Before the outbreak of war put an end to its activities, it claimed as affiliates about 20 central trade union federations with some 7,700,000 individual members, mostly from Europe, but also including the American Federation of Labor (AFL).[2]

B.   From 1914 to 1939

5.   After the war the IFTU reorganized itself in 1919 under a new constitution at a meeting held in Amsterdam, while many ITSs, too, re-established their organizations.[3] Another important development at this time was the establishment of two new organizations: the Red International of Labour Unions (RILU) and the International Federation of Christian Trade Unions (French initials: CISC). The RILU came into existence in 1921 when the leaders of the Communist Party in the Soviet Union decided to create a competing worldwide trade union international, often also called the Profintern. The formation of the so-called Popular Front in 1935 put an end to the activities of the RILU. At that time Communist parties and trade unions throughout the world were ordered by Moscow to cooperate with and join democratic political and trade union organizations to stem the advance of Nazi and fascist movements and build-up their presence within the mainstream trade unions. The formal dissolution of the RILU, however, occurred only in 1943 when the Comintern was disbanded.

6.   The creation of a separate Christian trade union international (CISC) in 1920 was the culmination of many years of organizational work among Christian workers in several European nations, particularly Germany, Italy, France, and the Low Countries. First organized at local or regional and then at national levels, the Christian trade unions offered an organizational and philosophical alternative to those believing Catholic and Protestant workers for whom membership in socialist unions, with their anti-clerical and even anti-religious sentiments, was unacceptable.

7.   Of the three international federations – IFTU, RILU, and CISC – the IFTU was the largest and certainly the most representative, even though its membership fluctuated from a peak of well over 20,000,000 in the immediate post-World War I period to fewer than 10,000,000 after the destruction of the German unions by the Nazi regime. When World War II broke out in 1939, the IFTU's affiliates claimed a total of about 14,000,000 members, including the AFL.

---

2.   *See* Dreyfus, *ICFTU, op. cit.*
3.   *See* Van Goethem, *ICFTU, op. cit.*

C.   After 1939

8.   World War II did more than merely disrupt the functioning of international trade union organizations. It also created the opportunity to reconsider fundamentally the international trade union structure. For many organizations, post-war labour unity in place of pre-war division became a key objective. A world labour conference, meeting in London in February 1945, decided to disband the IFTU and establish a new and all-encompassing world labour organization, the World Federation of Trade Unions (WFTU). Its principal initiators were the British Trade Union Congress (TUC), the Soviet All Union Central Council of Trade Unions (AUC-CTU), and the American Congress of Industrial Organizations (CIO). The founding congress was held in Paris in October 1945. The most important absentee was the AFL which as a matter of principle refused to be associated with unions controlled by governments or political parties, specifically with unions in Communist countries and more generally with Communist-dominated unions anywhere.[4]

9.   Other organizations that declined to join the WFTU were the affiliates of the Christian international labour federation (CISC). That rather small body re-established itself after the war on a scale even smaller than before 1939, due to the loss of important affiliates in Germany and Italy where post-war drives favouring labour unity had led to the formation of all-encompassing trade unions. In the ensuing decades the CISC gradually loosened its traditional ties to the Church and adopted a more secular programme. In 1968 it adopted the name of the World Confederation of Labor (WCL).

10.   In the WFTU the co-existence of organizations representing entirely different conceptions of the role of trade unions in society was of relatively short duration. When disagreements over the Marshall Plan and over other political and trade union issues, notably the role and independence of the sectoral internationals (ITSs), became unbridgeable, unions from Western countries severed their ties with the WFTU in 1949. Later in the same year they launched a new organization: the International Confederation of Free Trade Unions (ICFTU). In this endeavour the AFL joined the unions that disaffiliated from the WFTU. (The AFL and the CIO merged in 1955.)

11.   The divisions that came about in the early post-war years have been maintained, although since 1989 important changes have occurred, and are still in process, which have dramatically changed the overall shape of international union activity. There still exist currently three international trade union federations: the ICFTU, the WFTU, and the WCL. Given their worldwide scope, the three may be referred to as global internationals although as will be explained this does require some qualification regarding the WFTU and the WCL which are considerably smaller than the ICFTU. In addition, there are other international trade unions serving specific regional or industrial interests, some of which are of considerable importance.

---

4.   *See* MacShane, *International Labour and the Origins of the Cold War*, Oxford, 1992 and Carew *ICFTU, op. cit.*

The structures of the world of international labour are profuse, and the relationships between the various parts are complex. Consequently one of the main objectives of the account that follows is to establish a certain measure of clarity in what can appear a confusing plethora of acronyms.

II. THE INTERNATIONAL CONFEDERATION OF FREE TRADE UNIONS

12. By any measure the ICFTU is the most representative of the three global trade union internationals, especially since the American AFL-CIO decided to rejoin it in 1981, after an absence of 12 years, and a rapid growth of affiliations in the late 1980s and 1990s. Not only are the ICFTU's affiliates the largest trade union organizations in almost every Western European country as well as in North America, Japan, and Australasia, but the ICFTU also has sizeable membership in Asia and Latin America. In Africa, for reasons to be explained, it was sparsely represented until recently, but now counts a significant number of important affiliates (see para. 24). In the Communist countries of Eastern Europe and elsewhere (Cuba, Vietnam, North Korea, the PR of China) it had no members at all until 1986, when the Polish Solidarity trade union became an ICFTU affiliate while at the same time it joined the Christian international WCL. With the collapse of the old Soviet system, a number of trade unions emerged and several established organizations began a process of internal reform. As of April 2000, when the ICFTU held its Seventeenth World Congress in Durban, South Africa, it had affiliates in the following former Communist countries: Bulgaria, Croatia, the Czech Republic, Estonia, Hungary, Latvia, Lithuania, Moldova, Mongolia, Poland, Romania, the Slovak Republic, and Yugoslavia. The ICFTU is open to trade unions of various views including those with close ties to socialist and social-democratic parties, and also those who take a pragmatic stance on party political matters. Its Constitution stipulates that the affiliated organization be free from domination by governments, political parties, or other external forces and accept the Confederation's aim of developing democratic trade unionism. The range of members in terms of their countries' level of economic development is extensive. The ranks of the ICFTU include unions from the most highly industrialized countries and from the developing world.[5]

A. *Aims and Activities*

1. Overall Goals

13. Because of the diversity of its membership the ICFTU has always taken care to formulate its basic aims in fairly general terms and to avoid taking sides on issues likely to be divisive, such as the nationalization of basic industries or the transformation of society from capitalism to socialism. Instead it emphasizes those beliefs and values that are shared by the largest possible number of constituents, including the defence of human and trade union rights, firm opposition to totalitarian regimes,

---

5. *Report to the Seventeenth World Congress*, ICFTU, Brussels.

support for all genuine efforts to safeguard world peace, endorsement of the struggle for social justice, and demands for the fair distribution of wealth and incomes at national and international levels. Within these basic aims there is room for more specific objectives whose formulation and priority are to some extent subject to changing circumstances. For example, calls for employment-creating measures have been given strong emphasis in recent years as a result of the economic crisis in developing, transition, and industrialized countries. The demand for the inclusion of provisions linking the observance of core labour standards to trade in the rules of the World Trade Organization is one of its major current ongoing campaigns.

2. Representational and Organizational Work

14. Most ICFTU activities can be divided into one of two categories: representation and organization. Representational work consists of the use of public forums, reports, statements, and similar means to express concerns and protests on a wide range of issues, from restrictions on freedom of association to the plight of migrant workers. A major current preoccupation is the structural adjustment policies of the IMF and World Bank, that affect directly unions and their members in developing and transition countries. The ICFTU thus acts as a voice of international labour campaigning against injustices committed by governments or employers and appealing to the international community to exert moral authority and political and economic pressure on behalf of a particular principle, policy, cause, organization, or individual, as in the case of an unjustly imprisoned trade union leader. In this representational work, the ICFTU relies on its affiliates to lobby governments in support of agreed international policies that the ICFTU itself presents to the appropriate UN or other international agency.

15. The organizational work of the ICFTU is directed chiefly to the promotion and strengthening of trade unionism in areas where unions are weak and vulnerable, thus mostly in countries of the developing world. The object is to strengthen those organizations that share the philosophy of trade unionism represented by the ICFTU. Assistance is mainly in the form of training programmes for union officials. Direct financial subsidies are now usually avoided although occasional gifts of equipment are offered. Although the organizational work is a key activity, it is limited by available resources and must be coordinated with parallel activities conducted bilaterally by certain national trade union federations, including the American AFL-CIO, the German DGB, the Swedish LO, and several others. There is, however, some important cooperation and coordination among those affiliates. Since the ICFTU Congress in 1996, much of the work in this area has been de-centralized and is carried out by ICFTU Regional Organizations. The ICFTU also works closely with the ITSs and is increasingly involved in campaigns regarding disputes with individual transnational corporations.

16. The ICFTU is frequently engaged in various types of campaigning which cut across neat categorizations. For example, it undertook a long-standing campaign with the independent black trade unions of South Africa against apartheid which has involved representations to governments and the UN, training programmes in South

Africa, financial assistance for court cases, disinvestment efforts, and the coordination of action against individual TNCs in disputes with unions. In recent years the ICFTU has organized numerous regional conferences on the themes of democracy and development that have sought to highlight and build support for increased international assistance to developing countries that respect trade union rights.

B. *Structure and Government*

1. Membership and Finances

17. The ICFTU is mainly composed of national trade union centres. In some instances, two or more national centres of similar scope, but separated by political or philosophical differences, have been accepted into membership. Italy (CGIL, CISL, and UIL), India (INTUC and HMS), France (CGT-FO and CFDT), and Brazil (CGT, Força Sindical, CUT) are apt examples. In other instances, dual affiliation stems from the existence of separate organizations for blue and white collar workers, as in the case of Sweden (LO, SACO, and TCO) and Denmark, (LO, FTF, and AKAVA). Individual unions are not generally eligible for membership, but some exceptions have been made.

18. ICFTU membership figures, at the time of its 2000 Congress, totalled of 215 affiliates in 145 countries and territories with an overall individual membership of about 125 million, of whom approximately one third are women. The ICFTU Report on Activities in 1995–1998 (Brussels, 2000), provides a detailed listing of affiliations and also of the Confederation's work. By comparison with earlier periods the continuing strength of its West European membership is increasingly counterbalanced by large and representative affiliates in all regions of the world. Even in the Arab countries where most governments discourage or prohibit independent unions, the ICFTU now has members in Algeria, Jordan, the Lebanon, Morocco, and Tunisia. The major gaps are Russia and the CIS countries, China (although Hong Kong and Taiwanese unions are members) and Indonesia. (Four small Indonesian centres are still recorded in the affiliates list but their rights and privileges have been held in abeyance for many years.)

19. To support its core activities, the ICFTU depends essentially on two sources of income: regular affiliation fees from all members and voluntary contributions from the more affluent ones. In 1998, regular affiliation fees made up about 90 per cent of the total, roughly US$10 million out of US$11.1 million. (Fees, which are fixed in Belgian francs, were $160 at prevailing exchange rates in 2000 per 1000 members per year for organizations in countries with an annual per capita GNP of over $10,000.) This means that an organization with about 7 million members, such as the British TUC, would be paying well over $1 million in regular annual contributions.) Three reduced rate affiliation fee bands apply for middle and lower income country members. In 1998, 25 per cent of affiliates paid Band 1 fees and accounted for nearly 90 per cent of dues income. Voluntary payments have averaged about $1.0–$1.5 million per year recently, but are well below the levels of the late 1980s. They serve to maintain the Confederation's International Solidarity Fund.

20. In the last three decades a third source of income has become available which has greatly eased the ICFTU's financial position: the so-called extra-budgetary funds. These funds represent in the main grants made from the treasuries of various national governments, especially the Netherlands, the Scandinavian countries, and Japan. As part of their aid programmes to less developed countries these governments have consented to support certain ICFTU-administered development programmes by making allocations to their own central trade union federations which, in turn, then pass on all or part of the amount to the ICFTU, and increasingly direct to its regional organizations. The ICFTU has also received funds from the UN, the ILO, and the European Commission. (In several instances, extra-budgetary funds have also been made available to support the development work of the International Trade Secretariats that are discussed below.) Recently, the ICFTU's central income from extra-budgetary funds has declined from an average of US$9.0 million annually in the early 1990s to US$2.0 million in 1998 reflecting the regionalization of aid flows, but still a sizeable amount relative to the income contributed by affiliated organizations. In fact, because the availability of such large sums from government sources may create a variety of problems, the ICFTU has deemed it wise to adopt a special set of rules governing the acceptance and use of extra-budgetary funds.

2. Governing Bodies and Secretariat

21. Policy-making responsibilities in the ICFTU are divided among several bodies. Supreme authority is vested in a Congress that meets every four years. Because of their relatively large size and the long intervals between meetings, the Congresses set overall policy guidelines. More detailed decision taking is vested in the Executive Board and certain committees of the Board. The membership of the Board currently consists of 53 titular representatives and an equal number of first and second substitutes, all chosen so as to ensure the widest possible geographic distribution. The Board also includes five women members nominated by the Confederation's Women's Committee and a youth member nominated by the General Secretary following consultation with the Youth Committee. The General Secretary is a Board member *ex officio*, and the International Trade Secretariats are all entitled to be represented as non-voting members. Normally the full Board meets once a year. Urgent matters arising between Board sessions are placed before a Steering Committee of members, which also has a broad mandate for allocating ICFTU resources, which are of course a key item in decision-making.

22. Day-to-day ICFTU activities are the responsibility of a secretariat headed by a general secretary, who is elected by the Congress. Currently the position is held by Bill Jordan, who was formerly President of the British Amalgamated Engineering Union and active in the International Metalworkers Federation. Of the six general secretaries who have held that office since 1949, all have been men from Europe.

3. Regional Organizations

23. The ICFTU was the first international trade union body to foster the formation of regional organizations. This innovative idea was designed both to create a mechanism through which trade unions could join forces to cope with problems spe-cific to their area of the world and also to avoid an excessive concentration of author-ity at ICFTU headquarters. The implementation of the idea, however, has been quite divergent. The ICFTU's regional organizations in Asia and the Western Hemisphere – known respectively as APRO and ORIT – have, in the course of time, become largely self-standing organizations, due largely to the presence, in their areas, of important large, well-financed national trade union federations able to provide leadership direc-tion and financial support. To be sure, their efforts to develop a set of independent regional activities have not always proceeded smoothly, largely because their aspira-tions to regional autonomy have, on occasion, clashed with the central body's insis-tence on its own ultimate authority. But this is probably an inevitable problem, one that involves conflicting interests and priorities. For example, in the late 1970s the ICFTU Executive Board refused to approve a new constitution adopted by ORIT, the regional organization for the inter-American region, because practically all references to ORIT's status as an ICFTU regional body had been dropped from the document, as had the references to the ultimate authority of the ICFTU Executive Board. A revised and acceptable version did ultimately secure approval.[6] Similar examples could be cited to show the existence of occasional tensions between ICFTU head-quarters and APRO, the regional organization for Asia and the Pacific.

24. The experience in Africa has been somewhat different. Until recently, the ICFTU's regional organization (AFRO) could not develop sufficient momentum, nor had it ever had the resources to become even a moderately autonomous body. A key obstacle to its development had been the opposition of most African governments to a regional trade union organization under non-African authority, that is, one whose resources would depend largely on funds contributed from outside the African area. Following the establishment of the OAU in 1970, many governments barred affilia-tion to international bodies and supported the Organization of African Trade Union Unity (OATUU) which itself constitutionally barred members from joining the ICFTU. Most likely governments feared that such a body would encourage a degree of independence and claims-making ability among trade unions that would go well beyond the point that the governments were willing to tolerate at that time. However, since 1990, organizations from many African countries affiliated or rejoined the ICFTU. This development which was closely related to the trend towards greater democracy and multipartyism in the continent, enabled the ICFTU to launch a fully-fledged regional organization for Africa in 1993 headquartered in Nairobi.

25. Experience with regional organizations in Europe has taken still another course. Although it was in this area, where the ICFTU established its first regional organization, European Regional Organization (ERO), and although ERO easily had the potential for becoming a powerful body, its national trade union constituents decided to support the establishment of an even more widely based European trade union federation, one that would be open both to ICFTU affiliates and non-affiliates, but also therefore necessarily separate from the ICFTU. As a result of this decision,

---

6. *Report of the ICFTU 12th World Congress 1979* (Brussels, 1979), p. 196.

made in the early 1970s, ERO was dissolved and a nearly all-inclusive European Trade Union Confederation (ETUC) put in its place. Because the ETUC is constitutionally independent from the ICFTU, despite having a preponderant number of the same affiliates, it belongs to a separate section of this account.

III.   The World Federation of Trade Unions

26. From 1949 until 1989, a substantial portion of the WFTU's principal constituents was the labour organizations in countries that were governed by Communist parties. In addition, the WFTU contained a substantial number of labour organizations from non-communist countries, although most of these groups are of only secondary importance on their home grounds. One could, therefore, characterize the WFTU as being largely the international trade union body of the Soviet Bloc. With the collapse of Soviet-model Communism, first in Central and Eastern Europe and then in the USSR itself, the WFTU has been brought to the verge of collapse. Although successor national organizations to former WFTU affiliates continue to exist in most of the former Soviet bloc, all left the WFTU between 1989 and 1992. Its only remaining significant affiliates in Europe, the General Confederation of Labour (CGT) of France and the All Poland Alliance of Trade Unions (OPZZ), withdrew in 1995 and 1997. The Syrian General Federation Of Trade Unions and a number of Arab country organizations together with the Central de Trabajadores de Cuba (CTC) of Cuba, the Vietnam Federation of Trade Unions (VFTU), the All India Trades Union Congress (AITUC) and a few other members are left struggling to keep the organization afloat. Its headquarters remain in Prague.

A.   *Aims and Activities*

27. Under the terms of its constitution, the WFTU's overall aim was and is 'to improve the living and working conditions of the people of all lands'. This is to be achieved by the organization and unity of the world's working class, assistance to unions in less developed countries, opposition to war, and an unremitting struggle against fascism. Despite this very broad mandate, the inability of trade unions in Communist countries to play an adversary role in domestic affairs severely circumscribed the field of action of the WFTU inside the old Soviet Bloc. That explained why the WFTU agenda was concerned to a very large extent with events and situations outside the Soviet orbit. Belatedly, during the period of perestroika and glasnost, the WFTU tried to change its image, as was indicated by the unprecedented appearance in the WFTU's official journal, World Trade Union Movement, of articles severely critical of the meagre role of trade unions in Eastern Bloc countries, especially the USSR. However, with the collapse of Soviet power its affiliates rapidly left what was the symbolic apex of a system of party control over labour activities. Many of these organizations are gradually emerging from extensive internal reforms to adapt to a new role in a more democratic society and a market-oriented economy. Those that do successfully change will no doubt survive; others will probably decline into insignificance. However, it seems rather unlikely that the WFTU in anything like its previous form will recover.

28.   A foremost but not admitted WFTU objective had always been firm support for the foreign policy goals of the Soviet Union. The lone and almost inexplicable exception was the WFTU secretariat's rebuke of the 1968 invasion of Czechoslovakia by the Warsaw Pact powers, but that singular deviation was quickly redressed and those responsible for it removed from their official positions. More characteristic were the uniformly optimistic accounts in WFTU publications of working conditions and trade union activities in the Soviet Union and other Communist countries, together with exposures of brutal violations of trade union freedoms and human rights in Western countries and a carefully selected group of Third World countries. An important WFTU activity, conducted in cooperation with certain affiliates, consisted of training programmes for trade union leaders and activists from less developed countries. Considerable importance was also attached to the WFTU presence at United Nations headquarters and in the specialized UN agencies, especially the International Labour Office (ILO).

29.   Soviet trade unions were from the beginning the dominant, not to say determining, force within the WFTU. The death knell for the organization was therefore the attempted coup d'état in the Soviet Union in August 1991. One of the figure heads of the junta which attempted to replace Mikhail Gorbachev as President of the USSR was the former General Secretary of the AUCCTU Gennady Yanaev, and it appeared that the coup leaders expected the Soviet trade unions, along with the Red Army, to rally in support of its attempt to reverse Gorbachev's reforms. Street rallies in Moscow, newly emerging unions and even the recently created official unions of the Russian Republic backed Yeltsin's stand against the coup. In the aftermath of the coup, the General Confederation of Trade Unions (VKP), the renamed (AUCCTU) of the USSR, froze its membership of the WFTU citing the tardy and weak response of the WFTU to the challenge to constitutional rule and democracy. In April 1992 the VKP transformed itself into a regional organization for CIS countries and announced that it would not be affiliated to any existing world body.

B.   Structure and Government

1. Membership and Finances

30.   In 1986 the WFTU's approximately 90 affiliates contained a total of somewhere between 200 and 250 million members. Whatever the precise figure might have been, the Soviet labour federation (AUCCTU) alone accounted for over half of the total. It should be noted, of course, that union membership in Communist countries was usually close to the total non-agricultural labour force, if only because social benefits and various entitlements (access to vacation resorts, social insurance, etc.) were often administered by the unions. In other words, union membership conferred such important advantages and non-membership such serious dangers of discrimination, that the price of not belonging was too high to be countenanced by all but the most committed dissidents. More recent figures are not available but are certainly considerably reduced, and if counted in terms of paid-up membership may be negligible.

31. Not all Communist-led countries were represented in the WFTU. Yugoslavia's unions were expelled in 1950 after Tito rejected Soviet hegemony. They were later invited to return but declined, although they had sent observers to WFTU congresses and exchanged trade union delegations with Soviet Bloc countries for many years. The break-up of Yugoslavia has now also led to a multiplicity of centres in each newly independent State, some of which are newly established while others are the successors to the republic-level bodies of the old Confederation of Trade Unions of Yugoslavia. The Albania Union Federation left in the mid-1960s. After the democratic revolution in that country it changed its name and constitution and new independent unions were also established. The All China Federation of Trade Unions exited in the mid-1960s, after the Chinese government's break with the USSR became irreparable.

32. Very little is known about the WFTU's finances. Some years ago, a budget figure of $1.6 million for 1976 was very exceptionally made public. This would have been considerably higher by 1989. However, at the present time its income from members is probably very little and investment income and grants from friendly governments are probably its main means of survival. One of the resolutions adopted at the 14th WFTU Congress was a starkly worded appeal for affiliates to pay their dues and take immediate steps to maintain the Federation's structures. It included a request to 'progressive governments, national, regional and international institutions and foundations to make grants and other such regular contributions to the WFTU and especially its Solidarity fund ...'.

2. Governing Bodies and Secretariats

33. Supreme authority is vested in a Congress convened most recently in New Delhi in March 2000 and prior to that in Damascus in 1994. The WFTU does not publish membership figures but does record the sum total of the unions 'represented' at the Congress by participants many of whom are individual sympathisers or observers rather than delegates of dues paying members. The New Delhi Congress ratified the election of a 20 member Presidential Council elected by the General Council, which in turn, is made up of delegates of affiliates attending the Congress. The current President is K.L. Mahendra, General secretary of the All India Trade Union Congress. Finally there is the secretariat that consists of a General Secretary – Alexander Zharikov, a national of Russia and six deputy general secretaries.

3. Trade Union Internationals

34. To serve the industrial interests of its membership the WFTU established eleven Trade Union Internationals (TUI) for individual economic sectors such as mining, metals, and transport. Whether the TUIs actually performed conventional industrial functions is uncertain, for in countries governed by Communist parties the main tasks assigned to trade unions at least until very recently were production-oriented. Only secondarily were the unions concerned with protective and claims-making activities. The tenuous industrial role of the TUIs was once acknowledged

by the head of the TUI for the textile industry who wrote in the WFTU's own journal, the World Trade Union Movement in 1981: 'The question of the relationship
between the political and trade interests of the TUIs is often the subject of study.
Various discussions are underway to see if the political problems and general
resolutions are not predominant in the work of the TUIs, with matters relating to the
particular branches of industry relegated to a back-seat position.'

35. TUI policies and activities were controlled, at least in a general sense, by the
WFTU, for the TUIs are not autonomous bodies. They report to the WFTU and are
financed by allocations from the WFTU rather than by dues collected directly from
their own member unions. Like the WFTU itself, the TUIs have lost many of their
affiliates since 1989 and show few signs of activity.

IV. THE WORLD CONFEDERATION OF LABOUR

A. *Membership*

36. In 1968, at the 16th Congress in Luxembourg, the International Federation of
Christian Trade Unions transformed itself into the WCL. A new Declaration of
Principles was adopted stipulated that the WCL was guided by 'either a spiritual concept based on the conviction that man and universe are created by God, or other concepts that lead together with it to a common effort to build a human community united
in freedom, dignity, justice and brotherhood'. The WCL adopted a programme based
on a mixture of humanist, socialist, and syndicalist ideas. It also sought to alter the
traditional balance of its programme and the composition of its membership by
enlarging its activities in the less developed countries. At the time these key decisions
were made, the core of the WCL's dues paying membership consisted of a few affiliates in Belgium, the Netherlands, and France. Other affiliated organizations were
scattered mostly among Third World countries where they usually ranked far below
the affiliates of the ICFTU and the WFTU in terms of membership.

37. Since then, the already small nucleus of dues-paying European organizations
with a significant membership has shrunk even further. The French CFDT, an important trade union federation in its own country, left the WCL's ranks in 1978. It joined
the ICFTU in 1989. One of the two Dutch affiliates, the Catholic NKV, departed in
1980 as a result of its merger with the ICFTU-affiliated Socialist federation NKV.
The joint organization (FNV) is affiliated only with the ICFTU. Both the CFDT and
the NKV had unsuccessfully urged the WCL to engage in serious merger negotiations with the ICFTU. Some allowance should be made, however, for the decision
by the Polish Solidarity union to affiliate simultaneously with the ICFTU and WCL;
an almost unprecedented arrangement. (The ELA-STV of the Basque Country
became a dual affiliate in the Franco days and remains in both organizations for the
same reasons; to support an embattled and illegal organization in its struggle.) The
WCL has also actively sought affiliations in Central and Eastern Europe and the
developing world, although in general its members consist of smaller unions or
groups of union activists within larger organizations.

38. The WCL claimed in 2000, a worldwide membership of 26 million in 113 countries. Its biggest members are the Confederation of Christian Trade Unions (CSC) of Belgium with 1.1 million members and Solidarnosc of Poland with 2 million. Since the WCL does not publish a detailed breakdown of its affiliates' membership, it is unclear how total claimed membership is derived. In 1996, it recorded its Latin American organization as having 7.7 million members, the African and Asian groups with 1.9 million and 3.6 million, respectively and 8.8 million in Europe and North America. It is possible that some affiliates count supporters of Catholic workers' organizations, which do not perform the same type of bargaining and representational work as unions. In addition, the WCL has relations with factions within centres affiliated to the ICFTU and it is unclear how this is recorded. It may be assumed that many affiliates, especially outside Europe, pay no dues or only nominal dues. Extra-budgetary project funds, especially from the Dutch and Belgian governments and the European Union, probably constitute a significant portion of its income and help to account for the remarkable survival powers of what is, all things considered, a rather small and weak organization.

B. Aims and Activities

39. Since its transformation in the 1960s, the WCL has sought to emphasize its status as an ideological alternative both to the Marxist–Leninist materialism of the WFTU and the social–democratic welfare orientation of the ICFTU. In place of either it propagates a system based on democratic planning, worker participation in decision making, and trade union independence from any form of external control. It describes itself as based on a humanist and spiritual conception of unionism inherited from its Christian origins with a strong commitment to union pluralism. It also describes its positions as a 'Third Worldist'. This contrasts with what might be described as the centrist Christian Democratic tradition of its core European affiliates.

40. WCL activities focus on educational and social programs in the less developed and transition countries. The organization is represented at most major ILO meetings, and in recent years, as a result of an agreement with the ICFTU, secured representation amongst the worker delegates on the ILO Governing Body. Its remaining European affiliates participate in the work of relevant EU agencies and European trade union bodies, including the ETUC.

C. Organization and Structure

41. The WCL's arrangements for internal government and administration follow a conventional four-tiered structure: a Congress, which meets quadrennially, a Confederal Board of 38 members, an executive committee of nine members, and the secretariat. The present general secretary, Willy Thys, has held his office since 1996. Also attached to the WCL are nine International Occupational Federations that represent the industrial and occupational interests of the WCL's membership. Two members of the WCL secretariat service them.

42. Regional WCL organizations exist for Latin America (CLAT), Asia (BATU) and Africa (DOAWTU). The European regional body (EO) was dissolved in 1974 when the WCL's European affiliates joined the new European trade union body, the ETUC, although the European members continue to meet regularly. CLAT is militantly anti-establishment, anti-capitalist, and anti-American, and has concentrated its efforts particularly among peasants and agricultural workers in Latin America.

V. INDEPENDENT REGIONAL FEDERATIONS AND RELATED BODIES

43. The three international confederations reviewed in the preceding sections seek to attract eligible members in almost all parts of the world and for that reason may be referred to as global organizations. A more limited territory is claimed by an increasing number of regional and subregional trade union bodies functioning not as affiliates of one of the global organizations but as independent entities. Of special importance are the European Trade Union Confederation (ETUC), the OATUU, the Trade Union Advisory Committee to the Organization for Economic Co-operation and Development (TUAC-OECD), and the Council of Nordic Trade Unions. Mention should also be made of the International Confederation of Arab Trade Unions (ICATU), which is an essentially political rather than trade union body, the Commonwealth Trade Union Council, the Council of Trade Unions linked to the ASEAN area (Association of South East Asian Nations), the Union Syndicale des Travailleurs du Mahgreb Arabe (USTMA) and the Southern African Trade Union Coordination Council (SATUCC). The South Pacific and Oceanic Council of Trade Unions (SPOCTU) and the Caribbean Congress of Labour (CCL) are important regional bodies that act independently but are essentially part of the ICFTU structure, as is the Asia Pacific Labour Network (APLN), which consists of ICFTU and ITS members in the APEC countries.

44. Regional organizations owe their existence to a multiplicity of reasons. In the fifties and sixties, most were founded to express, in the domain of labour, the regional hegemonic aspirations of a particular country or ruler or to propagate a particular ideology, perhaps even both. More recently, others came into existence mainly to articulate the joint economic interests of trade unions in a particular region or to meet a need for bringing the special concerns of workers to the attention of a regional intergovernmental entity such as the European Union.

A. *The European Trade Union Confederation*

45. Currently, by far the most important trade union body at European regional level is the ETUC. It came into being in 1973, but had several forerunners that cannot be reviewed here.[7] The ETUC currently has 65 affiliates in 28 countries, plus 14 industrial federations, with a total membership of over 59 million. Headquarters are

---

7. *See* J.P. Windmuller, 'European Regionalism: A New Factor in International Labour', *Industrial Relations Journal*, Vol. 7, No. 2 (Summer 1976), pp. 35–48.

in the same building as the ICFTU in Brussels, where most European agencies of concern to the ETUC have their central offices. Congresses are held every four years. The current General Secretary is the Italian Emilio Gabaglio.

46. The ETUC is an entirely independent body, organizationally and financially. Its membership includes almost all trade union federations in Western European countries (with a few exceptions noted below) and an increasing number of union centres in Central and Eastern Europe, and most of its activities are centred on the defence of joint trade union interests in the European Union and other European-wide bodies. Most ETUC affiliates belong simultaneously either to the ICFTU or the WCL, and relations with the ICFTU in particular are very close. For example, it has become customary for each organization, i.e. ETUC and ICFTU (or ETUC and WCL), to participate in the executive board meetings of the other organization, and there are frequent informal contacts at the staff level.

47. ETUC policies and activities reflect the primary concerns of its members. Insofar as the European Union has developed its policies on a Single Market and Economic and Monetary Union leading to an increased coordination of economic and social policies, the ETUC seeks to ensure that labour's priorities are taken into account. The ETUC thus largely acts as a lobby in the context of a supranational agency, supplementing and – to a certain extent – harmonizing the separate national efforts of its member organizations. It has also recently started to bargain with its counterpart employers' organization, UNICE, and in some cases has concluded agreements, on issues such as part-time work, fixed term contracts and private employment agencies. Areas of recent concern to the ETUC have included unacceptably high levels of unemployment and the need for more employment-oriented economic policies, the Social Charter and the Social Chapter of the Maastricht Treaty, the extension of industrial democracy throughout the Single Market and in particular the creation of European Works Councils in large multinational companies, the adoption of integrated energy policies, proposals to improve the work environment, and efforts to eliminate discriminatory treatment of the weaker segments of the labour force (women, young workers, migrants, the handicapped, etc.). The ETUC has received funding from the Commission for some of its activities and has established the European Trade Union Institute (ETUI)[8] for research, the Trade Union Technical Bureau for safety standards and the European Trade Union College for trade union training. The Commission also funds trade union participation in a wide range of consultative meetings.

48. Political issues have generally been of secondary importance in ETUC activities, though the organization regularly adopts formal resolutions expressing its support of political freedom, democratic forms of government, strict observance of human and trade union rights, peaceful coexistence, and negotiated steps toward disarmament. If differences on some of these issues exist, they tend to be matters of emphasis rather than principle and can usually be overcome by judicious formulations.

---

8. The ETUI's many publications are an invaluable resource on the policies and structure of the European trade unions and the ETUC. *See*, for example, the *ETUC Yearbook*, 1998 edited by Emilio Gabaglio and Rainer Hoffman.

49. One long-running but now largely resolved controversy involved the eligibility for ETUC membership of Communist-led trade union organizations in Italy, France, Spain, and Portugal. Here the views of key ETUC affiliates diverged quite sharply. One group, led by the British TUC, considered all-inclusiveness to be more important than ideological compatibility and has favoured their admission, while another group, headed by the German DGB, has opposed admission on grounds of principle, i.e. that the ETUC's doors should not be open to trade unions whose commitment to democracy is less than wholehearted. However, as the European Communist parties broke away from their historic ties to Moscow, a parallel process of internal reform in the unions occurred. The Italian CGIL was taken in at an early date in the seventies, and CCOO of Spain and CGT of Portugal in the early nineties. (CGIL and CCOO are now also members of the ICFTU.) The CGT of France was admitted into membership in 1998 after many years during which its requests were deferred.

50. To round out its structure, the ETUC has promoted the establishment of individual industry committees to represent the European-wide interests of workers and their unions in particular economic sectors, as for example, in metals, mining, agriculture, and communications. The industry committees currently act as lobbies and pressure groups *vis-à-vis* European institutions but are gradually becoming bargaining agents for their constituents within an emerging European-wide system of industrial relations stimulated by the creation of European Works Councils. They are recognized as members of the Confederation in their own right.

51. The relationship of the ETUC's European industry committees to the International Trade Secretariats has raised certain jurisdictional problems. Some industry committees operate with a high degree of independence, while others are linked more closely to the ITSs in their particular economic sector, and in fact even depend on them for vital services. The conflicting pulls and the competitive channels of authority as between the ETUC and the ITSs, created by the ETUC's decision to have both national centres and international sectoral organizations as affiliates, have been a source of tension.

B. The Organization of African Trade Union Unity

52. Trade unionism in most African countries began during the colonial era and was often closely linked to the independence movement. Several regional organizations for Africa have already appeared and then disappeared, some oriented toward Western conceptions of trade unionism, others more compatible with the WFTU trade union model. During the era of one-party states and dictatorship most African governments showed little tolerance for trade union pluralism or for trade unions independent of government control, and with their support the intergovernmental Organization of African Unity (OAU) in 1973 established a regional trade union organization – the OATUU – that was intended to be an all-inclusive and unitary regional trade union body for Africa. But in recent years the OATUU's claim to exercise a regional monopoly has received several setbacks, and an increasing number of African trade unions have affiliated mainly with the ICFTU, but also with the WCL.

The OATUU claims a membership of 73 affiliates in 53 African countries with about 30 million individual union members. The General Secretary is the Nigerian Hassan Sunmono.

53. Despite its exclusionary mandate, the OATUU maintains working relations with the ICFTU, WFTU, and WCL and cooperates with them in various activities such as labour education programmes. But prior to the democratization wave in Africa in the nineties, it also followed closely the political and ideological positions adopted by the OAU and still reflects to a certain extent pan-Africanist ideas and a deference to control by undemocratic governments of trade unions. On the other hand, AFRO now has a recognized status with the OAU. Consequently the OATUU adopted a position of so-called 'positive neutrality' in world affairs and proclaimed itself to be an anti-capitalist, anti-imperialist, anti-colonialist, and anti-Zionist organization. The major targets of its criticism were forces external to the region, in particular multinational corporations and their governments in Western countries. By contrast, African governments and their sometimes very harsh labour and social policies were treated with much circumspection. Of the obscure financial arrangements in the OATUU it can be said with confidence only that the organization is not supported solely or even chiefly by contributions from its own affiliates and that government subsidies from Libya and perhaps elsewhere were and probably still are of considerable importance in balancing the accounts. The OATUU in the late 1990s is going through a period of considerable internal debate, as it searches for a new role, identity and means of financial support.

C. The Trade Union Advisory Committee to the OECD (TUAC-OECD)

54. When the Marshall Plan for European economic recovery from the ravages of World War II neared completion in the early 1960s, the participating governments in Europe and North America decided to maintain certain supranational structures that had played a key role in the administration of the programme. From its inception in 1948 trade unions had been closely associated with this work in an advisory capacity and when the Organization for Economic Co-operation and Development (OECD) came into existence in 1960, the Trade Union Advisory Committee (TUAC-OECD) and the Business and Industry Advisory Committee, were formed and accorded consultative privileges that remain an exceptional example amongst inter-governmental organization of openness to the views of social partners.[9]

55. TUAC now represents some 65 trade union federations from 29 OECD member countries in the European area, North America, and Japan, with a total membership of 70 million. Virtually all TUAC members are affiliates of the ICFTU or the WCL, but no affiliates of the WFTU have ever been admitted to membership. Its affiliates meet twice a year in plenary sessions. The current General Secretary is John Evans, a British national.

---

9. *See* P. Gaskell, *TUAC Marks 50 Years* 'TUAC 1948–1998: Proceedings of the 50th Anniversary symposium'.

56. Because the OECD itself is basically a research-oriented, idea-producing, and consensus-seeking organization in key areas of economic policies rather than an action agency, TUAC's foremost objective is to ensure that adequate consideration is given to trade union viewpoints in the preparation of OECD reports, studies, and policy recommendations to member governments. In recent years, OECD agenda items of chief interest to TUAC have included employment creation, manpower, and human resource development programmes, trade and tariff issues, and the development and supervision of international guidelines for the conduct of multinational companies, an area in which the OECD has done pioneering work.[10] An important role is played by TUAC in preparing trade union submissions to the annual summits of the Group of Seven, the OECD Ministerial Council and in preparatory work on issues such as the revision of the OECD's Guidelines on Multinational Enterpreises, its anti-corruption convention and corporate governance.

D. Subregional Bodies

57. Regional coalitions of countries often lead, sooner or later, to the emergence of parallel coalitions of trade unions. That tendency applies not only to genuine regional alliances, as in the case of the European Union, but also to interregional and sub-regional groupings. For example, the existence of the Commonwealth (formerly called the British Commonwealth of Nations), which is a loose association of states based chiefly on a shared historical attachment to the former British Empire, led in 1980 to the formation of a Commonwealth Trade Union Council whose declared purpose it is was to ensure that 'trade union views are taken into account by Commonwealth governments and institutions.' A similar organization is the ASEAN Council of Trade Unions, an alliance of trade union federations in the member countries of the ASEAN.

58. Another group of this kind is the Council of Nordic Trade Unions (NFS), a sub-regional association of trade union federations in the five Nordic countries (Sweden, Norway, Denmark, Finland, Iceland), founded in 1972, whose membership is expressly limited to organizations affiliated both with the ICFTU and ETUC. The NFS now includes federations representing the special interests of professional and managerial employees, which have all recently joined the ICFTU, ETUC, and TUAC. The Nordic Council coordinates the policies of its member organizations on socio-economic and labour market issues pending before the Nordic governments, such as labour mobility, social welfare, social insurance, and international trade; prepares research papers and policy positions on these matters; and serves as a device for reaching an identity of views among Nordic trade unions participating in international labour bodies. By acting as a unified bloc in the ICFTU, ETUC, TUAC, ILO, and similar organizations, the unions of the Nordic countries increase their weight by a considerable margin. Moreover, their joint views carry great force in bilateral contacts with sister or organizations elsewhere, such as the British, German, and American labour federations.

---

10. *See* Windmuller *op. cit.*

VI. INTERNATIONAL TRADE SECRETARIATS

59. The organizations to be reviewed in this section, the ITSs, differ from those in the preceding sections in that they are composed of individual national unions grouped according to major sectors of industry or occupation. Their mandate is primarily economic or industrial, and their focus is on developments and problems in particular economic or industrial sectors. Consequently they are sometimes referred to as industrial internationals. They maintain close ties with the ICFTU and are non-voting members of its Executive Board.

A.   *Organization and Structure*

1. Relations with Global Internationals

60. The ITSs are autonomous and self-governing organizations. Collectively their relationship to the ICFTU is based on the so-called Milan Agreement of 1951 (most recently revised in 1990) under which the ITSs follow the ICFTU's lead on broad policy issues, while the ICFTU recognizes the General Conference of the ITSs as the joint representative of ITS interests and grants non-voting representation to the ITSs in all ICFTU governing organs.

61. The principle of autonomy determines not only the relations between the ITSs and the ICFTU but also among the ITSs themselves. Their formal link is a General Conference, a loosely structured body that meets once or twice a year for a review of common problems and interests. Informal contacts are, of course, far more extensive, both among top ITS officials and between them and the ICFTU leadership. They are, after all, constituent parts of the same general labour movement, sharing identical or at least very similar values and conceptions with regard to the position of trade unions in society.

2. Membership and Finances

62. There are 11 ITSs. The number has reduced in recent years as a result of a series of mergers, but their total membership has increased substantially. Although Western Europe and North America account for the bulk of ITS membership most ITSs contain affiliates from almost all parts of the world (Table 1).

63. Each ITS has its own source of income. Average current dues are probably about $0.75 per individual member per year, but each ITS has a dues structure of its own. For those ITSs that are engaged in particularly extensive activities in Third World countries, special levies and supplemental outside funding constitute important sources of extra income. Special grants for educational and union-building programmes have been made available by the ICFTU, the ILO and through the respective national centres and unions from the foreign aid agencies of European and North American governments.

Table 1. The International Trade Secretariats (2000)

	Total members (millions)	Affiliates	Countries
Education International (EI)	24	296	153
International Metalworkers Federation (IMF)	23	193	101
International Federation of Chemical, Energy, Mine and General Workers' Unions (ICEM)	20	404	113
Public Services International (PSI)	20	500	140
Union Network International (UNI)	15.5	900	140
International Federation of Building and Wood Workers	11	296	153
International Textile, Garment and Leather Workers' Federation	10	225	110
International Union of Food, Agricultural, Hotel, Restaurant, Catering, Tobacco and Allied Workers' Association (IUF)	10	326	118
International Transport Workers' Federation (ITF)	4.74	571	135
International Federation of Journalists (IFJ)	0.45	140	103
Universal Alliance of Diamond Workers (UADW)	0.06	22	18

3. Governing Bodies and Trade Groups

64. Although each ITS operates under its own system of internal government, a fairly common pattern prevails which usually includes a general assembly or Congress, an executive board, and the elected officers and staff. The Congresses set the broad policy guidelines and are useful occasions to cement the ties between the ITS and its affiliated organizations, particularly those affiliates which are not sufficiently large and important to hold a seat on the executive board. A key role in each ITS is played by its top full-time official, the general secretary.

65. When the ITSs were first established toward the end of the nineteenth century and the beginning of the twentieth, many covered only a single occupation or a limited industrial sector. That is no longer the case. Mergers and the rise of new industries, coupled with the effect of union mergers aimed at financial consolidation and the improvement of services, have transformed most ITSs into multiindustrial or multioccupational bodies whose component sub-units sometimes face entirely different challenges in their spheres of activity. To cope with this internal diversification, several ITSs have established special industrial sectors. The Metalworkers ITS, for example, whose industrial jurisdiction includes automotive manufacturing, basic steel, mechanical engineering, electrical and electronic products, shipbuilding and several other sectors, has established a number of so-called trade groups to meet the varying needs of its affiliated unions, especially in countries where the structure of unionism is relatively fragmented and specialized, as in Britain, the United States, and Canada. Changes in technology and the emergence of large cross-sector conglomerate transnational companies are an additional factor. In addition, in some sectors the historical reasons for the existence of competing internationals have become of diminished importance. For example, the International Federation of Free Teachers Union (IFFTU) and the World Confederation of Organizations in the Teaching Profession merged in February 1993 to form a new ICFTU-linked ITS, the Education International. In 2000, the Union Network International formed from the white collar ITS (FIET), Communication International (CI), the International Graphical Workers' Federation (IGF) and the international committee of Media and Entertainment Unions (MEI). It has 12 sectors and 3 interprofessional groups.

B. Aims and Activities

66. Advancing the joint interests of their constituents, and particularly their economic interests, remains the principal aim of the ITSs. They do, of course, also declare their support of the search for a more just social order, the protection of human and trade union rights, the extension of democratic forms of government, and the maintenance of peace with freedom. But their traditional orientation and their structural make-up leads them to stress practical trade union work, and this they perform in a variety of ways.[11]

1. Solidarity and Organizational Work

67. Mobilizing international support on behalf of an affiliated organization involved in a major domestic conflict is one such activity. Support may be expressed in various forms: moral encouragement, appeals to member organizations to extend financial assistance (the ITSs usually do not maintain strike funds of their own), coordination of international actions against employers, or public condemnation of a government for particularly harsh anti-union measures.

68. A major portion of ITS activities since the early 1950s has been organizational work in Third World countries. The aim is the establishment or reinforcement of individual unions to the point where they can effectively represent the interests of their members and at the same time contribute to the development and modernization of their societies.

---

11. For an ITS engaged in a broad range of activities on behalf of employee interests *see* H.R. Northrup and R.L. Rowan, *The International Transport Workers and Flag of Convenience Shipping* (Philadelphia: The Wharton School, University of Pennsylvania) 1983.

2. Information and Research

69. Disseminating information about economic conditions and terms of employment in particular industrial sectors has long been one of the most useful services that the ITSs provide to their members. Some of the larger ITSs have recently begun to compile and computerize data on the financial condition and terms of employment of large individual firms, particularly multinational firms, so as to be able to make this information readily available to affiliates for use in collective bargaining. Some ITSs have initiated research on the long-term economic outlook for the industries in which they operate, with special attention to prospective changes in the volume and structure of employment. Increasingly, too, several ITSs are attending to problems of occupational health and safety in their sectors.

70. As long as collective bargaining remains primarily a national rather than an international activity, the influence that the ITSs can exert on the outcome will be a relatively modest one. However, the expansion of multinational companies during the past few decades, the adoption by the OECD and other international bodies of international codes of conduct for employers, and the extension of the Single European Market in 1993 raise the possibility that international bargaining structures may emerge in which the ITSs could become key participants on the employee side. Some initial steps in that direction have already been taken. The Metalworkers' ITS, for instance, has established several so-called company councils for a substantial number of multinational companies (General Motors, Ford, etc.) to facilitate bargaining coordination among unions in different countries whose members are employed by the subsidiaries of these corporations. Of particular importance is the rapidly expanding system of European Works Councils brought into effect under the first employer/trade union agreement under the Social Chapter of the Maastricht Treaty. This provides for regular European-wide information and consultation meetings between management and worker representatives, who are generally coordinated by the European Industry Committees linked to ITS. As this system takes root it may evolve into a vehicle for bargaining on some cross-country issues and broaden to include union representatives from non-EU member countries. A further recent development is the negotiation of global framework agreements with individual multinational companies on basic labour rights and information and consultation. Examples include IFBWW/IKEA, ICEM/Statoil, IUF/Danone, and UNI/Telefonica. The ITF has also negotiated with the International Maritime Employers Committee on employment conditions on IMEC ships registered in flag of convenience states.

VII. CONCLUSIONS

71. Although trade unions must generally operate within national economic, social, political, and legal contexts, they have nevertheless established a complex even if fragmented network of international associations. To some extent the fragmentation is caused by the functional distinctions between the broad political concerns of national trade union federations and the more specific industrial concerns of individual national unions. But that is only a partial explanation. Political commitments and regional attachments have been important determinants of international union structures. Following the major changes in the political map of the world in the late 1980s and 1990s, and the far-reaching challenges posed by the process of continuing technogical change coupled with trade and investment liberalization, often termed globalization, international union structures are evolving rapidly.

72. In retrospect the turning point in international trade union affairs was the emergence of the free Polish trade union Solidarnosc in 1980. It will be re-called that the strikes of August 1980 were resolved by the Gdansk agreements that accorded recognition to Solidarnosc as a trade union independent of control by the ruling Polish Communist Party. This was anathema to the Leninist conception of the role of trade unions as a conveyor belt for the Party to the workers. When in 1981 the Polish government was replaced by that of General Jaruzelski, who imposed martial law, the failure of the communist model of the workers' state became transparent. Martial law did not restore the old system nor end the challenge of Solidarnosc, which re-emerged forcefully in the strikes of 1988. The crisis was only resolved by the creation of a Round Table through which Solidarnosc effectively negotiated a new Constitution, breaking the control of the Party/military monopoly on government.

73. It is important to note that the starting point for the Round Table discussions in Poland was the implementation of the 1984 ILO Committee of Experts' report on Freedom of Association in Poland that originated from a complaint by the ICFTU concerning the dissolution of Solidarnosc in December 1981. The confrontation within the international trade union movement between the Leninist conception of the dictatorship of the proletariat and the vanguard role of the Party and the social democratic/liberal view that 'workers ... have the right to establish and join organizations of their own choosing without previous authorization' (Article 2 of ILO Convention 87) which began in 1919 and was the ideological frontline in the division of Europe in the post-war period, was decisively resolved in favour of the ICFTU. The consequence of this breakthrough sent shockwaves not just through the Soviet-dominated countries of Central and Eastern Europe but throughout the world. In many developing countries, governments had adapted the Communist ideas of Party control of unions using nationalism as a form of self-legitimation. The bankruptcy of the state planning model of economic development and its concomitant justification of Party control over unions has effectively ended the often fierce battle of ideas between the WFTU and the ICFTU.

74. The possibilities for strengthening international trade union cooperation on the basis of a shared belief in freedom of association have enlarged considerably in terms both of the relations between national centres and also between industrial or occupational unions. However, while the ICFTU, the ITS and their member organizations, and also the WCL, have always regarded freedom of association as a collective right for workers generally, another strand of liberal or neo-conservative political philosophy holds that it is an individual right. This line of thinking, often submerged during the post-war era, re-emerged strongly in the 1980s and has led a number of governments to introduce or amend laws to sharply circumscribe the ability of unions to organize collectively and to create the counterbalance to the power of employers which lay at the heart of the welfare state and the social market economy. Coupled with the challenge to national industrial relations and social security

systems posed by the emergence of powerful international market forces, this political trend is obliging unions to work out new approaches to organization and to the means for achieving their social and economic goals.

75.   This debate came to the fore at the ICFTU's Sixteenth World Congress in June 1996 in Brussels. Under the theme 'The Global Market – Trade Unionism's Greatest Challenge', union leaders from all over the world discussed how unions needed to adapt themselves and their international union structures to the rapidly changing economic, social, and political environment. Few argued for a reversal of the trend towards reduced barriers to trade and investment, but most highlighted the increased insecurity and inequality that their members were struggling to deal with. In essence the conclusion was that unions needed to develop much stronger means for influencing the pattern of international development both through the policies of intergovernmental institutions like the International Monetary Fund, the World Bank, and the World Trade Organization and directly with the major global companies. Ensuring the universal observance of the ILO's core labour standards on freedom of association, equality of opportunity, forced and child labour was a persistent demand and was focused particularly on proposals for a formal linkage of the WTO's agenda for trade and investment liberalization and a strengthening of the ILO's supervisory machinery.[12] With unions all over the world, but particularly in Europe and North America, facing the need to shift resources into efforts to organize to counteract the effects of a steady decline in employment in traditionally strong unionized sectors of manufacturing industry, the ICFTU and the ITS were under pressure to do more with less.

76.   These issues remained at the centre of both the ICFTU's Fiftieth Anniversary Executive Board meeting in Seattle in November 1999 and the Seventeenth World Congress in Durban, South Africa, in April 2000. The locations of the two meetings were not accidental and illustrate two important elements of the new challenges facing the international labour movement. The ICFTU and the AFL-CIO as hosts decided to link the Executive Board meeting to a major lobbying effort at the 3rd WTO Ministerial Meeting being hosted by the US government. With a special conference attended by the Director-Generals of the WTO and the ILO and a number of Ministers and a peaceful rally of some 50,000 American trade unionists led by several hundred international visitors, the ICFTU was a very visible presence in and around the Ministerial meeting with clear proposals on the need to start serious discussions on the connections between trade liberalization and core labour standards. The Ministers failed to launch a new round of trade negotiations in part because they could not agree on how to respond to the ICFTU's pressure.

77.   The Seattle Meetings were the culmination of over a year's lower key lobbying of governments in capitals all over the world in which particular attention was paid to democratic developing countries that the ICFTU believes are threatened by competition from countries of similar levels of development that do not respect basic

12.   See ICFTU, *The Global Market – Trade Unionism's Greatest Challenge* and *the Report of the Proceedings of the 16th World Congress*, Brussels, 1996.

labour rights. The trade and international labour standards campaign was very much a joint effort of the ICFTU, ITS, TUAC, and the ETUC with a substantial input from the ICFTU's regional organizations. Making extensive use of information and communication technologies, it demonstrated the extraordinary reach of the international labour movement when it is able to mobilize all or nearly all of its national affiliates behind a single cause.

78. The ANC government of South Africa, with its strong links to the labour movement and particularly COSATU, which affiliated to the ICFTU in 1997, was seen as key potential ally. In addition, the ICFTU also wished to demonstrate its continuing support for its South African affiliates in their efforts with the government to overcome the legacy of Apartheid. The invitation to hold its Millennial Congress in South Africa was thus readily accepted by the ICFTU leadership also because it would show the growing strength of the organization in Africa. The theme of the Durban Congress, 'Globalising Social Justice' was a launching pad for a policy programme aimed to convince those who criticized the ICFTU as being protectionist of industrial country union jobs, that its goal was to shape the rules of the global market to ensure a narrowing of the social divides within and between countries through the strengthening of democracy and international cooperation. Core labour standards were central to both these objectives along side debt relief, increased aid, a re-orientation of structural adjustment programmes and open markets.[13] The ILO as the 'social pillar' within the multilateral system was urged to make itself a stronger force in the shaping of globalization; a challenge readily taken up by its new Director-General Juan Somavia in his keynote address to the Congress.[14]

79. If the main message the ICFTU wanted to send out from the Durban Congress was that it intended to be a major player on the stage of international policy-making, the main message it wanted delegates to take home was that to sustain the effort required would need major changes in the international labour movement. The Congress debates showed that the need for change in the methods, strategies and even structures of the international trade union movement was widely understood. In a concluding statement, the Congress instructed 'the Executive Board, Steering Committee and General Secretary to organize a wide-ranging review of the ICFTU's structural relationships and means of co-operation, both within our own structures and with other international trade union organizations.'

80. The now dominant free trade unions in the ICFTU, the ITS, TUAC, and the ETUC are having to work out new methods to ensure that common global interests and the priorities of different regions and industry groupings are articulated and heard in intergovernmental bodies and the board rooms of the multinationals. The WCL is faced with the same challenges but remains determined to retain its distance from the main stream of the international labour movement. If the development of governmental regional cooperation continues to move ahead more rapidly than the

---

13. *Globalising Social Justice: Report to the Seventeenth World Congress*, ICFTU, Brussels, 2000.
14. Text available on *www.icftu.org* along with full documentation on the 17th Congress.

painstakingly slow changes to global institutions, unions will naturally tend to focus limited resources on regional bodies. This is especially noticeable in Europe, where the pace of change in recent years as a result of the Single Market, Economic and Monetary Union, and Enlargement has immediate consequences for unions who as a result put a great deal of time and energy into the work of the ETUC and its industry committees. Although the ICFTU and the ITS are now much less reliant on the core of strong unions in Western Europe, with powerful new unions growing in South Africa, Brazil, and Korea for example, nevertheless they still need a solid financial and political commitment from their European members. Similarly US and Canadian unions, historically the second main pillar of the ICFTU and ITS, are also heavily preoccupied with a difficult domestic agenda and new initiatives in regional integration such as the North American Free Trade Area. Increasingly they view their international relations through the prism of the contribution they make to struggles at home. The same can be said in varying degrees for the powerful Japanese and other Asian unions and, indeed, most unions.

81. By comparison with the decades of ideological confrontation, which were often fought most fiercely within the international trade union movement, global labour politics is no longer a specialist activity of small rather separate international departments of unions but more an added dimension of the broad union agenda driven by the pressing needs of members. The union internationals themselves are changing to meet the new priorities of affiliates and are increasingly adept in the use of the new information technologies and the public presentation of their activities and policies to the media; a process which is itself forcing change.[15]

82. Both the supporters and critics of international trade unionism sometimes exaggerate its importance, but the debates within the movement about policies and activities have often proved to be a significant bellwether of trends in the role of trade unions. In both the industrialized, developing and transition countries, international activities are an increasingly integral part of national trade union strategies. This has been true in Europe for some time but is now a noticeable feature of most unions in the 1990s. Although struggles to defend unions under attack from hostile regimes is still a core activity for the movement, a number of unions in Asia, Latin America and Africa are now looking for support in furthering their wider social and economic aims. In turn, long established unions in Europe and North America now call for support from other regions in their efforts to obtain recognition and collective agreements with multinational companies. Modern international trade unionism is increasingly multifaceted and multidimensional. Yet it is often faced with the difficult task of mobilizing significant resources to address new issues of considerable importance to the future of unions from national organizations that themselves are undergoing difficult and costly internal reforms. The 1990s have seen a major turning point in the way unions look at their international relations and the structures they developed in the past. The new century is likely to see many further changes, but they will take place on a canvass that has many layers of experience that should

---

15. *See www.global-unions.org* a jointly owned web site of the 11 ITS, ICFTU, TUAC, and the ETUC.

not be neglected. The purpose of this brief review is to provide some perspective to those who will study the new patterns of international trade unionism by explaining at least some of its rich history.

SELECT BIBLIOGRAPHY

B. Barnouin, *The European Labour Movement and European Integration*, London, 1986.

B. Bendiner, *International Labour Affairs*, 1987.

R. Blanpain (ed.), *International Encyclopaedia for Labour Law and Industrial Relations*; *International Trade Union Movements* by J.P. Windmuller, 1991.

A. Carew, M. Dreyfus, G. Van Goethem, R, Gumbrell-McCormick, M van der Linden (ed.), *The International Confederation of Free Trade Unions*, 2000.

A.P. Coldrick and P. Jones, *The International Directory of the Trade Union Movement*, London and New York, 1979.

P. Gaskell, *TUAC Marks 50 Years in TUAC 1948–1998. Proceedings of the 50th Anniversary Symposium*, Paris, TUAC, 1998.

K. Johansson and J.-E. Norling, *Building the Future: One Hundred Years of International Cooperation, a History*, Geneva, IFBWW, 1995.

E. Lee, *the Labour Movement and the Internet: The New Internationalism. London*, *1997*.

L.L. Lorwin, *The International Labour Movement. History, Policies, Outlook*, New York, 1953.

D. MacShane, *International Labour and the Origins of the Cold War*, Oxford, 1992.

S. Mielke (ed.), *Internationales Gewerkschaftshandbuch*, Opladen, 1983.

R. Miotto, *Les Syndicats Multinationaux, Rome*, Instituto per l'Economia Europa, 1976.

R. Neuhaus, *International Trade Secretariats: Objectives, Organization, Activities*, Bonn, Friedrich Ebert Stiftung, 1982.

E. Piehl, *Multinationale Konzerne und Internationale Gewerkschaftsbewegung*, Frankfurt, 1973.

B. Reinalda, (ed.), *The International Transport Workers Federation 1914–45: The Edo Fimmen Era*, Amsterdam 1997.

R.L. Rowan et al., *Multinational Union Organizations in the White-Collar, Service and Communications Industries*, Philadelphia, 1983.

R. Rowan et al., *Multinational Union Organizations in the Manufacturing Industries*, Philadelphia, 1980.

J.P. Windmuller, *The International Trade Union Movement*, Deventer, 1987.

J.P. Windmuller, *International Trade Secretariats: The Industrial Trade Union Internationals*, Washington D.C., 1991.

LIST OF INTERNATIONAL UNION WEB SITES

Global Unions (ICFTU, ITS, *www.global-unions.org*
 TUAC, ETUC)
ICFTU *www.icftu.org*

TUAC	*www.tuac.org*
ETUC	*www.etuc.org*
WCL	*www.cmt-wcl.org*
WFTU	*www.wftu.cz*
OATUU	*www.ecouncil.ac.cr/ngoexch/oatuu2.htm*
CTUC	*www.commonwealthtuc.org*
EI	*www.ei-ie.org*
IFBWW	*www.ifbww.org*
ICEM	*www.icem.org*
IFJ	*www.ifj.org*
IMF	*www.imfmetal.org*
ITF	*www.itf.org.uk*
IUF	*www.iuf.org*
PSI	*www.world-psi.org*
UNI	*www.union-network.org*
ITGLWF	*www.itglwf.org*

Chapter 6. Human Resource Management: Past, Present, Future

R.S. Schuler and S.E. Jackson

1. INTRODUCTION

1. The focus and context of human resource management, both in its practice within organizations and its study within academia, is in the midst of a significant change. In part, this change reflects the dramatic changes that began to occur during the 1980s. For example, during that period, the focus of business shifted from domestic to multinational to global; the speed at which business is conducted increased; organizations recognized that labour costs and labour must be viewed from a worldwide perspective; and organizations realized that competitive advantage can be seized and sustained through the wise utilization of human resources.[1] As a consequence, human resource (HR) departments in businesses throughout the world today are being viewed not only as acquirers and motivators of resources previously not thought of as competitive weapons, but also as resources of sufficient significance to play a role in the making of major decisions regarding business strategy.[2]

2. These changes in focus, context and their consequences have themselves been coming at a very rapid pace. This chapter gives us a chance to pause to put them into perspective. In order to provide this perspective from our vantage point in the United States, we will examine both the changes and the consequences of those changes in terms of both the focus of and the context for human resource management. Throughout our examination, we refer to both the professionals and the department of human resource management (e.g. human resource professionals and the HR department) and the function of managing people (i.e. the human resources) in organizations. The importance of these distinctions becomes more evident as the

---

1. R.M. Kanter, 'Change in the global economy: An interview with Rosabeth Moss Kanter', *European Management Journal*, Vol. 12, No. 1, 1994; C.K. Prahalad, 'New view of strategy', *European Management Journal*, Vol. 13, No. 2, 1995.
2. S.E. Jackson and R.S. Schuler, *Managing Human Resource: A Partnership Perspective* 7th ed., Cincinnati, Ohio: South-Western, 2000; M. Poole (ed.) *Human Resource Management*, Vols I, II, and III, London: Routledge, 1999; J. Storey, *Human Resource Management: A critical test*, London: ITL, 2000.

chapter develops. As the chapter unfolds, two major phenomena in human resource management – strategic human resource management and international human resource management – are described. In addition to these large, macro-developments in human resource management, this chapter also discusses major contemporary issues and topics, such as workforce flexibility, diversity, and the question 'Is there one best way? The academic side of all that is happening in human resource management is revealed in the discussions of theoretical frameworks now being used in the field as well as in the discussion of the stakeholder model. Both the academic and practitioner sides of the changes in the focus and context of human resource management and their consequences are combined in the discussion of the activities now considered to be the essentials of human resource management.

II. WHAT IS HUMAN RESOURCE MANAGEMENT AND HOW DOES IT OPERATE?

A. *What are the Activities that HR Entails?*

1. Strategic Analysis

3.   Today, human resource management, in playing a greater role in the strategy of the organization, includes scanning the environment and looking at such things as competitors' activities, legal conditions, economic trends, and workforce demographics. Human resource management also requires keeping tabs on the environmental elements inside the organization such as its goals, competitive strategy, technology, culture, structure, and workforce characteristics.[3] Once this external and internal environmental scanning takes place, human resource planning begins to identify the firm's short-term and long-term human resource requirements.[4] In part, the determination of how to staff these requirements depends on the results of an analysis of jobs, which determines the sets of skills, abilities, and competencies needed, as well as the numbers of people needed with each different set.[5] To this point, human resource management has identified the business needs of the organization and their broad implications for human resource management. In part, this assessment of the needs of the organization promulgates in a view of the human resource management function and the people within the organization as sources of competitive advantage.[6]

2. Strategic Implementation

4.   After having identified the needs of the organization, the HR department is typically responsible for the creation and execution of a recruitment, selection and

---

3. R.S. Schuler, 'Human resource management: Domestic to global', in Warner, M. (ed.), *International Encyclopedia of Business and Management,* London: Routledge, 1994.
4. Schuler, *op. cit.*
5. Schuler, *op. cit.*
6. Jackson and Schuler, *op. cit.*; J. Pfeffer, *Competitive Advantage Through People*, Boston: Harvard Business School Press, 1994; J. Pfeffer, *The Human Equation*, Boston: Harvard Business School Press, 1998.

socialization program. This program must also take into account the external environmental conditions found during the environmental scan.[7]

a. Selection

5.　The selection process entails both the selection of the appropriate employees and the selection of the appropriate means for identification and recruitment of future employees. Socialization of the new employees into the way in which the company does business (e.g. 'the IBM way') includes both an element of job training for the position and an element of familiarization with and perhaps indoctrination into the culture of the company.[8] Both elements of the socialization process may be used to align the skills of the employees with the goals of the organization.[9] Training is not limited to new employees.[10] Rather, it is used for skill enhancement in all levels of employees.

b. Environmental improvements

6.　As an employee's tenure with the organization increases, the HR department often uses improvement of the workplace environment to create organizational commitment within employees.[11] Environmental improvements are a means of increasing the satisfaction of an organization's employees, potentially resulting in increased organizational commitment and in helping the firm achieve its strategic goals[12] Environmental improvements can take the form of the introduction of new types of technology, changes in the level of quality of the product or service, and an increase in the development opportunities available to the employees.

c. Empowerment

7.　Another action in the furtherance of the strategic objectives of the organization is the empowerment of the employees.[13] Empowerment results from a change in the culture of the organization which gives employees a greater opportunity to ' affect both their working conditions and the way in which they perform their jobs. Empowerment is an important human resource management objective, particularly in organizations that are attempting to implement total quality management programmes, which rely heavily on the empowerment of employees.

3. Updated Role

8.　The view that the HR department is a strategic partner assumes greater integration of that department into the activities of the organization than the traditional view of human resource management. Nevertheless, the more traditional activities of creating remuneration and benefits packages, tracking employee progress, bargaining

---

7.　Schuler, *op. cit.*
8.　Schuler, *op. cit.*; J. Pfeffer, 1998, *op. cit.*
9.　O. Lundy and A. Cowling, *Strategic Human Resource Management*, New York: Routledge, 1996.
10.　Lundy and Cowling, *op. cit.*
11.　Schuler, *op. cit.*
12.　Schuler, *op. cit.*; Lundy and Cowling, *op. cit.*
13.　Schuler, *op. cit.*

collectively with unions and evaluating employee performance remain under the aegis of the HR department.[14] Despite the traditional nature of these functions, however, they too have been updated as a result of the partnership which the HR department has with the organization as a whole in furtherance of the strategic goals of the organization. For example, remuneration and benefits packages include not only direct compensation, but performance-based pay and indirect benefits. While these topics may not seem to be radically different from those which were considered part of the remuneration packages a decade ago, they now must reflect the organization's position on flexible time, flexible place, job sharing, gainsharing, and other issues coming to the forefront as organizations increase their efforts to be more competitive.[15]

9. In addition and partially as a result of a familiarity with the legal and regulatory environment which stems from its environmental scanning, the HR department is the department within the firm that is typically responsible for highlighting the need for compliance with laws regarding employment-related areas such as discrimination, privacy rights and health, and safety issues. As a result it is charged with creating means of ensuring and measures that ensure that compliance. These necessary activities are also part of the process of facilitating the implementation of the strategic plan of the organization.

10. In summary, it appears that the HR department is responsible for activities such as the adaptation of the employee to the work of the company, the adaptation of the workforce to the goals of the company and the adaptation of the retention programs to the needs and interests of the employees so as to ensure the organization's ability to compete successfully and to achieve its strategic objectives. These activities increase the success of the corporation by generating productivity improvements, ameliorating the quality of work life, ensuring increased legal compliance, presenting the organization with a source of competitive advantage and insuring future work force flexibility.[16]

B. Staffing the HR Management Department

1. Specialists vs. Generalists

11. Human resource management today requires a breadth and a depth of knowledge that is greater than in earlier, more stable times. While both staff members and top leaders need to be functional experts regarding the activities performed and need to be capable administrators, when the HR department is viewed as a strategic partner, it must also be able to act as a business consultant and to solve problems taking into account the global environment. As a result, today's management of human resources differs greatly in scope of activity from yesterday's personnel management.

---

14. Lundy and Cowling, *op. cit.*
15. Pfeffer, 1998, *op. cit.*
16. Schuler, *op. cit.*

12. Specialists in the HR department focus on the specific human resource activities. These specialists typically come from backgrounds in which they have acquired technical information regarding human resource practices and policies, including law, industrial and organizational psychology, industrial labour relations, counseling, medical or health science, social service, organizational development, organizational change and design, total quality management, or, given the recent emphasis on technology.[17]

13. Line managers, as HR generalists, are also important to the human resource function. One step along the career path of many line managers is in the HR department.[18] During this phase of their careers, they spend two to three years receiving exposure to human resource practices and issues. At the end of this period of time, they have had exposure to the same areas as human resource specialists, although the managers will have had that exposure at a far more general level. The line managers then will be human resource generalists within the organization. After becoming an HR generalist, it is possible for a manager to lead the HR department or to be the general manager at one of the firm's installations.[19] In point of fact, spending part of one's career in the HR department will become more and more prevalent, as 65 per cent of managers have identified it as a critical step along a career path for a manager in the year 2000.[20]

2. Centralization vs. Decentralization

14. With increasing numbers of line managers spending some of their career learning human resource practices, the question of arena of responsibility for human resource practices becomes relevant. In an organization with centralized human resource practices, the headquarters location is where the policy creation and decision making take place.[21] In these centralized organizations human resource management is typically more likely to reflect a recognition of human resource management as a strategic partner in achieving the goals of the entire organization.

15. In a decentralized organization, human resource activities are generally performed at lower levels and decisions are made either at the divisional, regional or departmental level.[22] Thus, while decentralized human resource management allows the organization to have decisions made in the environment in which they are to be enforced, when the human resource function is decentralized, much of the ability to coordinate activities on a broad scale and to exchange information is limited. The practice of decentralized human resource management, then, enables several smaller HR departments within the same organization to be strategic partners, but makes

---

17. Schuler, *op. cit.*; K. Legge, *Human Resource Management*, London: Macmillan Press Ltd., 1995; J. Storey, *op. cit.*
18. Schuler, *op. cit.*
19. Schuler, *op. cit.*
20. Schuler, *op. cit.*; *Reinventing the CEO*, Korn/Ferry International and Columbia University, 1989.
21. Jackson and Schuler, *op. cit.*
22. Jackson and Schuler, *op. cit.*

coordination across them more difficult. The creation of a group of HR generalists rotating through these smaller HR departments would tend to facilitate the coordination of otherwise decentralized human resource practices.

C. Partnership in HR

16. Partnership in human resource management has arisen from a recognition of the value that the human resource function and the human resources of an organization can have in the implementation and achievement of the strategic goals of that organization. Although implementation is frequently discussed as important, strategic management literature regarding bow to carry out implementation is remarkably sparse.[23] Nevertheless, it has been recognized that the implementation of the strategy is an important element in the achievement of the goals.[24] Since implementation involves the workforce of the company, human resource management is seen as critical to implementation of organizational strategy and, as a result, to the accomplishment of organizational goals. The interaction between human resource management and an organization's strategy and goals goes beyond filling the organization's staffing requirements to include providing training, socialization, motivation and to meeting other needs which are equally important to the success of the strategy implementation process.

17. Thus the current issues in human resource management practice highlight the value of the strategic partnership between the HR department, the management, and all the employees in managing the human resources of an organization. Because of the vital role that human resource managers play in implementing the strategic plans made by the governing bodies within an organization, and because of the knowledge that they possess as a result of their environmental scanning, they are well suited to assist in preparing an organization for the changing context that it faces. A more detailed way in which each of these partners can contribute to managing the firm's human resources is shown in Exhibit 1.

18. In summary, there are a number of areas in which changes have arisen as a result of the recognition of human resources as a partner in managing the firm from a view of human resource management as being the functional area responsible for hiring and firing. In particular, the focus tends to shift away from being specialists toward being generalists; away from conflict and toward harmony with workers; away from individual-focused, narrowly developed human resource practices, and toward team-focused, broadly developed practices; away from operational issues and attraction/retention/motivation issues, and toward an organizational view based on benefiting strategy and the bottom line; and away from a domestic and internal focus and toward a global and external focus.[25]

---

23. A. Nutt. Thompson and A.J. Strickland, *Crafting and Implementing Strategy*, New York, McGraw Hill, 1998.
24. J.M. Bryson and P. Bromiley, 'Critical factors affecting the planning and implementation of major projects', *Strategic Management Journal*, Vol. 14, 1993, pp. 319–337.
25. Schuler, *op. cit.*

Exhibit 1. Elements of the Human Resource Management Partnership

Line Managers	Human Resource Professionals	Employees Unions
Include human resource professionals in the process of creating a business strategy and putting into place means of achieving the business strategy.	Assist line managers, employees and unions in developing and implementing elements of human resource function.	Implement FIR activities in conjunction with line managers and human resource professionals.
Work in tandem with human resource professionals, unions and employees to develop and implement elements of the human resource function.	Work in tandem with line managers to forge links between human resource activities and the business.	Become responsible for managing their own behaviour and their careers in organizations.
Share responsibility for managing the human resources of the company.	Assist employees in voicing their concerns to management.	Recognize the value of and need for flexibility and adaptability.
Set policy that supports ethical behaviour.	Create policies and practices to support ethical conduct and an environment which supports them.	Represent the needs of all workers.

Adapted from S.E. Jackson and R.S. Schuler, *Managing Human Resources: A Partnership Perspective* 7th ed., Cincinnati, Ohio: South-Western, 2000, p. 25.

19. In part this emphasis on partnership reflects a recognition that the HR department is more than a representative of the sum total of the human capital in the organization. In fact, the HR department has been recognized as not only a match-maker between the skills of the employee and the needs of the organization, but as a partner to the organization in formulating the strategy and planning the implementation of those strategies in pursuance of the organization's goals. Perhaps in recognition of this new partnership, human resource directors have been included in the long-range planning process to a greater degree than ever before. In addition, this partnership has resulted in a view of the HR department not as a cost center, but as a server of internal customers. The emphasis on the partnership between the organization and the HR department in creating and implementing strategic plans is apparent throughout the rest of this chapter, especially in reference to those organizations which are future-focused.

D. HR Management Reflects Changing Context

1. Globalization of Industry

20. As a result of the globalization of industry, many firms now must compete on a global basis rather than on the regional basis previously favored in order to survive.[26] Thus strategic human resource management in this international context requires focus not only on the functions, policies and practices of human resource management but also on the issues facing multinational enterprises (MNEs).[27] Differing national cultures have different human resource management implications.[28] One of the challenges which faces organizations as they globalize their operations is the adaptation of their HR practices to the new set of cultures in which the organization is operating and the creation of a manner of operation which is both comfortable to the organization, and appropriate for those cultures. [29]

21. Diversity plays an important role in organizations now more than ever. As an additional by-product of the globalization of industry, the relevant market sectors have broadened to include far-reaching areas of the globe. This market change is true for firms all over the globe. As organizations become more global and begin to do business in greater numbers of areas, the number and variety of cultures represented in their workforce also changes. As this number increases and as organizations attempt to treat each different culture with respect, practical issues can arise which may make doing business increasingly more difficult. For example, which religious and secular holidays need to be honored based on the cultures represented in the workforce? Similarly, questions may arise regarding what the official language of the workplace will be and whether the speaking of other languages to co-workers will be accepted.

2. Organizational Changes

a. Downsizing
22. Downsizing, or 'right-sizing' as it is euphemistically called in the United States, is a significant features of the competitive landscape. Major businesses have announced layoffs of tens of thousands of employees. The ways in which these layoffs are handled raises some interesting human resource issues. First, it is not unusual for these layoffs to be tied to re-organizations or re-structuring of the organization. Often as a part of the re-organization of the company, although some jobs have been eliminated, other jobs have been created and need to be filled. The employees to be laid off often are given the opportunity to interview for these jobs and sometimes are required to interview to retain their current jobs. Managing this process correctly will limit the adverse reactions to the interview process common in those with long tenures in their current position. One way in which some companies minimize the

---

26. C.A. Bartlett and S. Ghoshal, *Managing Across Borders: The Transnational Solution*, London: London Business School, 1991; Schuler, *op. cit.*

27. Schuler, *op. cit.*

28. G. Hofstede, *Culture's Consequences*, Beverly Hills, CA: Sage, 1980.

29. P. Dowling, D. Welch, and R.S. Schuler, *International Human Resource Management*, 3rd ed., Cincinnati, Ohio: South-Western, 1999; N.J Adler and F. Ghadar, 'Strategic Human Resource Management', in Pieper, R. (ed.), *Human Resource Management: An International Resource Comparison*, New York; de Gruyter, 1990; P.R. Sparrow, R.S. Schuler and S.E. Jackson, 'Convergence *or* divergence: Human resource practices and policies for competitive advantage worldwide', *The International Journal of Human Resource Management*, Vol. 5, 1994, pp. 267–299.

number of employees to be laid off is by giving skill upgrades and additional training in order to enable them to remain with the company in another capacity.

b. Mergers and acquisitions

23. Similar re-hiring situations arise in the case of mergers and acquisitions. At the time in which the merger takes place, the transition team identifies both the skills and abilities necessary to run the newly created entity, and the skills possessed by the employees currently with the organization. Efforts are then made to match current employees with the jobs available, with line and human resource managers often playing the hiring role, selecting from the available pool of talent. The HR department of the new organization, often one of the first areas created, is thus crucial to the success of the new venture, providing training and guidance in selection of employees for the new work teams, and acting as a strategic partner by assisting in determining the needs of the newly created organization.

c. Innovation in technology

24. An additional type of organizational change, which is often paired with the shift from an industrial to a service economy, is the change in the level of innovation that results from changes in technology. Innovation is often credited with increases in productivity. But, in order for that increased productivity to exist, the human element must be considered as part of the changes. Innovation typically requires upgrading the skills of employees generally through further training. The rationale behind the need for attention to the human element in the adoption of new technology is apparent if one recognizes that current employee skill sets may need to be changed in order to ensure its successful adoption. Attention to the human element results in creating an environment that is conducive to the use of the new technology. As technical innovations become more rapid in the workplace, the rate at which the workforce will be expected to adapt to the changes in technology will also increase. This need for adaptability will further necessitate the ability of the workforce to be flexible, and to learn quickly. These needs have the potential to change the demo graphics of the workforce.

d. Innovation of practices

25. Innovation is not limited to technology, however, work practices and procedures such as manufacturing processes, also can be fertile ground for innovation. Many organizations are currently or have recently gone through re-engineering processes.[30] Re-engineering examines organizational processes and identifies ways to re-organize their value creating processes in order to improve measures of performance. For these innovations to be successful, the human resources of the organization – i.e. the people – must be taken into account. For example, over the last several years, a practice innovation called total quality management has become more prevalent in US manufacturing facilities. Total quality management (TQM) has been defined as 'the generation of structures and a culture of quality to pervade all aspects

---

30. A. Hammer and J. Champy, *Reengineering the Corporation: A Manifesto for Business Revolution*, New York: Harper Business, 1993.

of the organization'.[31] From the human resource perspective, the cultural element of this definition requires the integration of quality into the training and socialization processes that take place within the organization. Training and socialization alone, however, are insufficient for successful innovation. Once these training and socialization endeavors have taken place, the HR department plays an integral role in supporting the company culture of total quality through ensuring the presence of the appropriate practices, policies and philosophies. This preservation of an atmosphere favoring innovation is viewed as being a necessary condition for innovation to take place.[32] In addition, TQM indicates that there is a link between the company and the customer, whether that customer is an internal one, such as a different division, or an external one, such as a major client.[33] At some level, this represents an acknowledgment of the influence of the stakeholders on the organizations, a factor which will be discussed later in this chapter. Customers may be viewed as strategic partners who can help in the improvement of the product or the service produced.[34]

e. Innovation in process

26. Just-in-time (JIT) manufacturing is an innovative manufacturing process which derives from the Japanese manufacturing system.[35] It depends on employee input in order to achieve its twin goals of constant improvement and elimination of waste.[36] In order to support JIT manufacturing, employees must be involved in the manufacturing process, and must be able to increase and update their skills to keep up with the technological changes. As a result HR departments must support the manufacturing process with ways to allow the employees to increase and update their skills.

f. Teams

27. Teams also dot the landscape of the current workforce. In part supporting TQM and JIT initiatives, teams are found in many manufacturing workplaces. For example, Kodak's black and white division, led by a 15-member team and nicknamed 'Team Zebra', has brought itself from being the worst place in the firm to work to being one of Kodak's leading business units.[37] Teams are part of the workplace from the boardroom on down. A great deal of research has been done on the effect of top management teams, and on communication within teams.[38] Human resource management impacts teams by helping to create an atmosphere conducive

---

31. Legge, *op. cit.*, p. 219.
32. R.M. Kanter, 'When a thousand flowers bloom: Structural, collective and social conditions for innovation in organization', *Research in Organizational Behavior*, Vol. 10, 1988, pp. 169–211.
33. Legge, *op. cit.*
34. Legge, *op. cit.*
35. Legge, *op. cit.*
36. Legge, *op. cit.*
37. Schuler and Jackson, *op. cit.*
38. *See* e.g. S.E. Jackson and M.N. Ruderman, *Diversity in Work Teams: Research Paradigms for a Changing Workplace*, Washington, D.C., American Psychological Association, 1995; R.A. Guzzo, E. Salas, and Associates, *Team Effectiveness and Decision Making in Organizations*, San Francisco; Jossey-Bass, 1995; D.C. Hambrick, 'Top management groups: a conceptual integration and reconsideration of the "team" label', *Research in Organizational Behavior*, Vol. 16, 1994, pp. 171–214.

to the functioning of teams, by empowering workers to work with other team members to craft solutions to problems facing the organization and by socializing and training workers to work within the team structures.

3. Outsourcing

28. Outsourcing has also become one of the strategies used by industry both in response to uneven demand patterns and as a means of reducing fixed wage costs. A typical service organization that outsources its employees will establish a core of employees who will work for the organization year round. In times when work is required beyond that baseline, additional employees will be hired temporarily to meet the needs of the organization. In a manufacturing organization, the make or buy decision is often the relevant decision, based on a criterion of the short-term cost or benefit of each option. Outsourcing operates similarly, with an organization deciding to outsource the work needed to create a particular component if it is less expensive to do so. From the human resource perspective, effective human resource managers must deal with the fluctuations in the size of the workforce that this practice brings and must be able to identify the key means of selection and training for these temporary employees.

4. Legal

29. The legal landscape for employment relations in the United States has changed over the past several decades. Issues such as workplace violence and sexual harassment have been brought to the forefront. Other issues such as privacy invasion and workplace security are also being grappled with. One major set of changes over the last several decades has been in and around the enactment of legislation prohibiting discrimination. With the enactment of the Civil Rights Acts of 1964, there has been an increasing amount of focus on the representation of minorities in the workforce. Interestingly, one of the original types of plans that organizations implemented in order to come into compliance with this act, affirmative action, has come under fire of late for being discriminatory. While that issue has not been determined definitively, the trend in some states tends to be to strike down affirmative action programs. Possible substitutes for these are programs that attempt to redress differences in economic opportunities. Additional pieces of legislation such as the Age Discrimination in Employment Act of 1967 and the Americans with Disabilities Act of 1990 have both increased the scope of protection and have included increasing numbers of American workers in protected classes.

30. The legal system in the United States is fragmented, with laws enacted on federal, state, and local levels. Thus organizations operating in a variety of different areas are likely to experience differing local laws regarding (e.g. laws regarding discrimination based on sexual preference vary greatly among cities and states in the US). Human resource practice in this environment requires frequent environmental scanning and attention to the changes to and to local differences in the rules under which business takes place.

Exhibit 2. Stakeholders and their Objectives in HRM

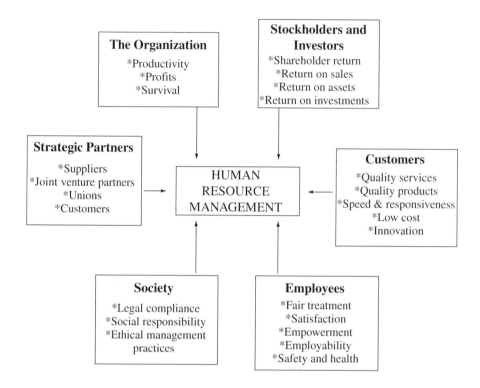

Adapted from S.E. Jackson and R.S. Schuler, *Managing Human Resource: A Partnership Perspective*, 7th ed., Cincinnati, Ohio: South-Western, 2000, p. 9.

E. Forces Impacting HR Management

1. Pressures for Social Responsibility

31. Organizations are also faced with increased social pressure to behave in a socially responsible manner. In part this pressure comes from society at large, in its role as one of several stakeholders of the organization. Other stakeholders and their objectives are shown in Exhibit 2.

As a stakeholder, society has shown interest in a variety of different topics. For example, the natural environment has been one subject of society's interest, with the genesis of a movement known in the US as the greening of America. Issues such as the location of factories and the choice between greenfield and brownfield sites, which previously were relegated to the strategy domain of the relevant organization, have taken on strong social and human resource components, both domestically and abroad, as organizations locate operations in countries where labour is less expensive.[39] As these organizations have learned as a result of these global moves, managing a workforce around the world is drastically different from managing a workforce only in the United States. This topic will be discussed further later in the chapter along with issues of strategic international human resource management. Now we expand on the stakeholder model.

2. Elements of the Stakeholder Model

a. The organization as stakeholder

32. The organization as a whole can be viewed as a stakeholder of human resource management as shown in Exhibit 2. The organization's objectives of improving prod-uctivity, improving profitability and surviving in general all impact human resource management. Each of these objectives necessitates a more effective utilization of the firm's human resources. As a result, the objectives of the organization give the organization as a whole a stake in the operation of the HR department.

b. Employees as stakeholders

33. The employees are one of the most important stakeholders in the organization, even in those organizations not owned by the employees. The emphasis placed on the role of the employees within the organization has increased, particularly in light of the adoption of strategies of total quality management and customer-focused management. Just as the value of the worker was recognized by the advances in human resource practice that took place in the manufacturing sector segments, such as the automotive industry and the high-technology factories, as the US workforce becomes more focused on the service sector, the employees who are providing those services of necessity must become more important. This increased importance results in increased training and development of these employees, and in a focus on creating positive long-term relationships with these employees. When the organization is owned by its employees as is the case for companies with Employee Stock Ownership Plans (ESOPs), the employees also carry out the role played by the investors as described below.

c. Customers as stakeholders

34. The emphasis on customer service and strategic partnering with customers has become more prominent, in part as a result of the JIT manufacturing initiatives and TQM. The consequences of the new partnership with customers are many. First, job descriptions have changed, which in turn results in needs for different skill sets for the jobs. Second, customers have been included in the performance evaluation process in many organizations. Since the customers are now part of the evaluation process, an emphasis on customer service is a logical result. Third, these customers often act as part of the design team when new products are being designed. For example, this pattern has been followed by some of the major automotive manufacturers.

---

39. *See* e.g. the special issue of the *Academy of Management Review* devoted to this topic, which was published in October, Vol. 20, 1995, No. 4.

Finally, customer satisfaction surveys are being undertaken by increasingly large numbers of organizations to determine how better to serve their customers.

d. Investors as stakeholders

35. Investors are viewed as one of the most important stakeholders because without their capital, the business could not continue. The time orientation of the investors is a driving force for the corporation as well. To the extent that investors are focused solely on the short-term profits of the corporation, the good of the corporation can be jeopardized.[40] In the case of corporations such as United Airlines and others that are owned by the employees, the long-term good of the organization may supplant an interest in immediate profit. In either case, the capital transfer from the investors is dependent on their willingness to continue to invest in a company with that particular strategic focus.

e. Strategic partners as stakeholders

36. The role of strategic business partner is a relatively new one for the HR department.[41] However, as the focus of the department has shifted to include both long- and short-term goals, and to act as an internal supplier of skills to the organization, the role of strategic business partner has emerged. As a strategic partner, the HR department has the opportunity not only to assist in the implementation of strategic plans, but also to help adapt the implementation, of the plan to the environment in which the plan is to be implemented.

f. Society as stakeholder

37. Society in general is viewed as being a stakeholder as well. Societal needs are made manifest in several different arenas: the legal framework under which the organization operates, the social mores of the areas in which the organization operates, and the constraints imposed by the natural environment. The legal framework is used by society as a means of enforcing the needs of society as a whole and of the environment. Although these two types of needs are often both interpreted by and protected through society at large, they do not represent the limitations of society's interest in the practices of the organizations. In particular, this recognition of needs may be a result of the pressure exerted by society both through legislation and through organized activity – both in support of and in opposition to corporate practices.

38. Global expansion also attracts attention to issues of workplace safety and practices of large organizations operating either in the US alone or worldwide. Thus human resource managers realize that decisions made on benefits and working conditions become issues for which the company must answer as a result of the ever-present nature of the media. As a result, including the HR department in both the strategic planning process and the implementation process is crucial to the preservation of a positive public impression of the company, which may in turn assist in preserving revenue generation for the company.

---

40. A.A. Buckho, 'The effects of employee ownership on employee attitudes: An integrated causal model and path analysis', *Journal of Management Studies*, Vol. 30, 1993, pp. 633–657.
41. Schuler, *op. cit.*

39. From the institutionalist perspective, practices have a life of their own once they have been standardized across an industry.[42] On a societal level, pressures exist that seek to preserve the status quo, at least in terms of practices, in all industries. Thus those who believe that legitimacy is of primary importance will seek to conform to the industry standard. On the other hand, other societal forces favour innovation, Thus innovative organizations may attempt to improve on the standard or change it entirely in an attempt to gain a competitive advantage. These differing perspectives point up the difference between those who believe that there is one best way for all situations and those who believe that an action is only appropriate for the particular environment in which it is undertaken. Further discussion of these perspectives is found at the conclusion of this chapter.

F. Strategic Human Resource Management

40. Strategic human resource management has been recognized as a source of value added for the firm. For example, Kanter[43] notes that strategic human resource management assists organizations in dealing with 'strategic surprises', which require the company to exhibit both flexibility and innovation.[44]

41. Given the characteristics the company must exhibit, it is no surprise that, strategic human resource management has two foci: integration and adaptation.[45] These two components are made up of a variety of elements, notably the practices and procedures, policies and processes, and programmes and philosophies undertaken by a given company. In line with the focus on strategic partnership, human resource management serves as a means of aligning the strategic plans of the organization with the implementation of these plans. This alignment takes place through the use of the human resources of the organization to further the strategic needs of the organization.

42. These strategic needs are derived from the long-range plans of the organization, but are implemented in the environment in which the company currently finds itself. As such, human resource managers are well positioned to assist in this activity, given the scans of the competitive environment which they perform and given their knowledge of the internal characteristics of the firm.

43. One indication that human resource practitioners are included in the strategic planning process seems to be the terminology used for the strategic plan of the organization. Generally when the strategic plans are known as strategic business objectives, there is an impact on the human resource philosophy. This philosophy indicates

---

42. P.J. DiMaggio, 'Constructing an organizational field as a professional project: US art museums, 1920–1940', in Powell, W.W. and DiMaggio, P.J. (eds), *The New Institutionalism of Organizational Analysis,* Chicago, University of Chicago Press, 1991, pp. 267–292.
43. Kanter, *op. cit.*
44. Lundy and Cowling, *op. cit.*
45. R.S. Schuler and S.E. Jackson, *Strategic Human Resource Management: A Reader,* London: Blackwell, 1999.

Exhibit 3. HRM Activities

Organizational strategy
Begins the process of identifying strategic needs and
provides specific qualities to them

Internal Characteristics → ↓ ← External Characteristics

Strategic Bussiness Needs
Expressed in mission statements or vision statements
and translated into strategic bussiness objectives

↓

STRATEGIC HUMAN RESOURCE MANAGEMENT

Human Resource Philosophy → EXPRESSION of how to treat and
Expressed in statements defining value people.
business values and cultures

Human Resource Policies → ESTABLISHMENT of guidelines for
Expressed as shared values action on people-related bussiness
(guideliness) issues and HR programs.

Human Resource Programs → COORDINATION of efforts to
Articulated as human resource facilitate change to address major
strategies people-related bussiness issues.

Human Resource Practices → MOTIVATION of needed behaviour.
For leadership, managerial and
operational costs

Human Resource Processes → DEFINITION of how these activities
For the formulation and are carried out.
implementation of other activities

Adapted from Schuler, R.S. 'Strategic Human Resource Management: Linking People with
the Strategic Needs of the Bussiness', *Organizational Dynamics*, 1992, p. 20.

the role which human resource are viewed to play in the organization. For example,
it provides guidelines for acting on business issues related to people, and for developing the human resource programmes and practices based on strategic needs.

44. As human resource management has come to be viewed as an integral part of
the organization, five principle activities have come to the forefront for strategic
human resource management: creating a philosophy, establishing policies, coordinating programmes, motivating practices and defining processes. Each of these activities
derives from the strategy of the organization and its business needs, and is shaped by
both internal and external characteristics. These activities are outlined in Exhibit 3.

45. The programmes and practices noted above are the coordinated efforts of the
HR department geared toward sustaining and supporting the organizational activities
and changes undertaken as a part of the strategic plan. HR programmes derive from
the firm's strategic aims and intentions, and involve human resource management

issues. The practices are geared around managing and leading employees and performing operational roles.[46] Managerial roles focus on the traditional elements of planning, organizing, delegating and coordinating, while leadership roles establish direction, motivate and inspire employees and align people in the creation of desired changes. Operational roles, on the other hand, are more facilitation oriented, describing daily activities. These roles are often reinforced by HR practices.

46. These reinforcing HR practices, in turn, derive from HR policies, which act as guidelines for creating actual programs and practices, without resorting to being the rules for behaviour in given situations. HR practices are the means by which all other HR activities are identified, planned and put into action. As such, HR practices represent a large portion of strategic HR management activity. Their success depends in large measure on the level of participation by employees in both the planning and implementation stages.[47] Consistency in participation and involvement of employees between these two stages is important to the success of the practices. Recognition of this need for consistency also brings an awareness of other aspects of strategic human resource management, and results in a greater need to act in a systematic manner. Thus the keys to strategic human resource management could be said to include both consistency and systematic operation.

G. Strategic International Human Resource Management

47. Human resource management has also become international in scope. As a result of the costs *of* research and development *of* new products and of marketing, many organizations view the marketplace as being global in nature. However, along with the view of the marketplace as being global comes concerns regarding the applicability of products and services across national boundaries. In particular, customs and tastes differ from region to region and country to country.[48] Thus many organizations become MNEs as a means of surviving. As a result, they need to manage globally in order to survive, and to manage locally, in order to take into account the different cultures in which they operate.[49] Thus there are several relevant issues for strategic international management of human resources practices.

48. One of the issues which arises when multinationals begin to face issues of cultural differences is how they link the human resource practices of their units in all sectors of the globe into a unified set of human resource policies and practices. Issues of interest to these organizations centre around both transfer of learning and innovation across units of the firm through human resource policies and practices and coordination on a global scale.[50]

---

46. Schuler, *op. cit.*
47. Schuler, *op. cit.*
48. Hofstede, *op. cit.*; Dowling et al., *op. cit.*
49. Bartlett and Ghoshal, *op. cit.*; Adler and Ghadar, *op. cit.*
50. Schuler, *op. cit.*; Taylor, *op. cit.*

49. Strategic international human resource management is the result of internationalizing the human resource management approach being used in organizations which have identified the value of human resources for the firm. Strategic international human resource management is defined as being 'human resource management issues, functions, policies and practices that result from the strategic activities of MNEs and that impact the international concerns and goals of those enterprises'.[51]

50. The practice of strategic international human resource management is dependent upon two strategic MNEs components: inter-unit linkages and internal operations.[52] Inter-unit linkages are concerned with the ways in which the units of a firm which are scattered throughout the globe are integrated, controlled, and coordinated.[53] Internal operations, on the other hand, encompass the remaining issues.[54] For example, internal operations would be concerned with the way a unit operates in concert with the laws, culture, society, politics, economy, and general environment of a particular location.

51. As noted previously, for US companies, managing an American workforce differs drastically from managing a foreign workforce. Nevertheless, many organizations that operate internationally have adopted the human resource practices of their parent Country.[55] As they take different views of operating internationally, their level of sensitivity to the cultural variance grows, and some organizations alter their policies accordingly.[56] Others adopt local practices, which makes standardization across national boundaries within one organization more difficult.[57]

III.   What are Some of the Theoretical Frameworks that are
       Applicable in Studying the Human Resource Management Field?

A.   *Resource Dependence Theory*

52. Resource dependence theory stems from the relationship between an organization and its constituencies. This theory emphasizes the need for resources as

51.   Schuler, *op. cit.*, p. 42; *citing* R.S. Schuler, P. Dowling, and H. DeCieri, 'An integrative framework of strategic international human resource management', *International Journal of Human Resource Management*, December, 1993.
52.   Schuler, *op. cit.*
53.   S. Ghoshal, 'Global strategy: an organizing framework', *Strategic Management Journal*, Vol. 8, 1987, pp. 425–440; J.R. Galbraith, *The Value Adding Corporation*, CEO Publication, University of Southern California, 1992; B.J. Punnett and D.A. Ricks, *International Business*, Boston: PWS-Kent, 1992; Schuler, *op. cit.*
54.   Schuler, *op. cit.*
55.   R.J. Ballon, *Foreign Competition in Japan*, New York; Routledge, 1992; S. Taylor, 'National origin and the development of organizational capabilities: The case of international human resource management in two Japanese MNCs', presented at the Western Academy of Management Annual Meeting, Banff, Canada, 1996.
56.   Adler and Ghadar, *op. cit.*
57.   Adler and Ghadar, *op. cit.*; Taylor, *op. cit.*

being primary in the determination of policies and procedures.[58] Organizations are viewed as being able to succeed by gaining and retaining control over scarce valuable resources.[59]

53. Within the organization, the HR department can be viewed as being a holder of scarce resources in the sense that it controls access to the skills necessary for the achievement of strategic goals, and that only through it can another department gain access to needed resources.[60] On a broader level, a firm may be able to lure and retain the top talent as a result of some competitive advantage linked to the improvements in the environment of the organization made by the HR department either alone or in concert with some attractive remunerative scheme.

B. Competitive Advantage Theory

54. Competitive advantage theory dictates that a competitive advantage exists if the resource is rare, inimitable, non-substitutable and valuable.[61] The application of this theory to human resource practice has been viewed as a study of what effective organizations do with people.[62] These competitive advantages are sustained through continued training, support of organizational culture, selection processes, and other traditional human resource practices. This assessment, however, begs the question of why performance of traditional HR practices can result in a competitive advantage. Competitive advantage can arise when HR management is viewed as a strategic player within the organization, and as such is included in the entire process of creation and implementation of strategies for the organizations, including the implementation of traditional HR practices.

C. Institutionalist Theory

55. Institutionalism suggests that organizations operate in a manner consistent with the rationalized myths which will garner them legitimacy in their external

---

58. S.E. Jackson and R.S. Schuler, 'Understanding human resource management in the context of organizations and their environments', *Annual Review of Psychology*, Vol. 46, 1995, pp. 237–264; J. Pfeffer and Y. Cohen, 'Determinants of internal labor markets in organizations', *Administrative Science Quarterly*, Vol. 29, 1984, pp. 550–572.
59. Jackson and Schuler, *op. cit.*
60. P.O. Osterman, 'Internal labor markets in a changing environment: Models and evidence', in Lewin, D., Mitchell, O.S., and Sherer, P.D. (eds), *Research Frontiers in Industrial Relations and Human Resources*, Madison, WI: Industrial Relations Research Association, 1992, pp. 273–308; Pfeffer and Cohen, *op. cit.*
61. J. Barney, 'Firm resources and sustained competitive advantage', *Journal of Management*, Vol. 17, 1991, pp. 99–120; J. Barney, 'Integrating organizational behavior and strategy formulation research: A resource based analysis', *Advances in Strategic Management*, Vol. 8, 1992, pp. 39–61; I. Dierickx and K. Cool, 'Asset stock accumulation and sustainability of competitive advantage', *Management Science*, Vol. 35, 1989, No. 12, pp. 1504–1511; A.A. Lado and M.C. Wilson, 'Human resource systems and sustained competitive advantage: A competency-based perspective', *Academy of Management Review*, Vol. 19, 1994, pp. 699–727.
62. R.S. Schuler and I.C. MacMillan, 'Gaining competitive advantage through human resource management practices', *Human Resource Management*, Vol. 23, 1984, pp. 241–255.

environment.[63] This external environment is made up of a broad variety of stakeholders. This adherence to rationalized myths in an attempt to retain legitimacy results in both survival and constraints on organizational actions.[64] In part one of the sources of this diffusion of operating myths is the professionalization of the industry.[65] Other sources include local social mores and the nation-state (in the sense that laws institutionalize certain practices as discussed previously).[66] Institutionalization is a source of both structure and practice in the workplace.[67]

56. In the human resource arena there are a number of forces arguing for institutionalization of practices and policies. Certainly among these forces, the primary one is the emphasis on environmental awareness, which aligns well with the emphasis HR departments must now place on environmental scanning. For example, as the trend toward an educated workforce continues, and as organizations create more HR generalists, it becomes increasingly more likely that expectations will exist regarding which policies and procedures are 'appropriate' for a given organization in a given location. These expectations are often coloured in some manner by the interaction of the policies and procedures with the legal system under which the organization operates, and the practices of other organizations in the industry. Institutionalism thus provides a means by which a firm can avoid the pitfalls associated with adopting an inappropriate set of policies and procedures.[68]

57. However, there are also several arguments against institutionalization. By definition institutionalization requires adoption of what amounts to standardized practices.[69] Because competitive advantage requires inimitability, this adoption cannot by definition provide a competitive advantage, but can only produce competitive parity. Thus in a changing environment, adoption of institutionalized practices can relegate an organization in the position of follower of the pack rather than its leader. Thus in formulating HR practices and policies, an organization must decide whether it is content in following or not, and, if not, how it can distinguish its practices in a way that will create a competitive advantage.

---

63. J.W. Meyer and B. Rowan, 'Institutionalized organizations: formal structure as myth and ceremony', *American Journal of Sociology*, Vol. 83, 1977, pp. 340–363; P.S. Tolbert and L.G. Zucker, 'Institutional sources of change in the formal structure of organizations; The diffusion of Civil Service reform, 1880–1935', *Administrative Science Quarterly*, Vol. 28, 1983, pp. 169–189.
64. Meyer and Rowan, *op. cit.*
65. DiMaggio, *op. cit.*
66. Meyer and Rowan, *op. cit.*; P.J. DiMaggio and W.W. Powell, 'The iron cage revisited: institutional isomorpbism and collective rationality in organizational fields', *American Sociological Review*, Vol. 35, 1983, pp. 147–160.
67. L.B. Edelman, 'Legal environments and organizational governance: The expansion of due process in the American workplace', *American Journal of Sociology*, Vol. 95, 1990, pp. 1401–1440; L.B. Edelman, 'Legal ambiguity and symbolic structures: Organizational mediation of Civil Rights law', *American Journal of Sociology*, Vol. 97, No. 6, pp. 1531–1576; J.N. Baron, F.R. Dobbin, and P.D. Jennings, 'War and Peace: The evolution of modem personnel administration in US industry', *American Journal of Sociology*, Vol. 92, No. 2, 1986, pp. 350–383.
68. Jackson and Schuler, *op. cit.*
69. Jackson and Schuler, *op. cit.*

D. Agency Theory

58. Agency theory is perhaps one of the most related theories to human resource practices. From the legal perspective, an agency relationship exists between an employer and an employee. Agency theory posits that this relationship may be subject to difficulties to the extent that the employer and the employee (in legalese, the principal and the agent, respectively) have differing goals, and when monitoring the employee's actions is difficult for the employer.[70] Agency theory has made recommendations regarding the ways in which the interests of the employers and employees can be aligned.[71] Agency theory has also been used in studies of occupation-based job-pricing differences as a predictor of differences in job pricing methods and pay variability.[72] HR management can use this theory as a lens through which to view the practices and policies that it promulgates.

E. General Systems Theory

59. General systems theory views systems as made up of complex, independent parts.[73] Inputs to this open system come from the environment, are transformed during processing through the system, and are returned to the environment. Using an open systems model, human resource management is studied as a subsystem within the larger system of the organization.[74] A competence management model of organizations has been described by Wright and Snell[75] who viewed human resource management through the lens of the open systems perspective. Here skills and abilities come from the human resources in the environment and are the input to the system as the organization hires new employees. These skills and abilities are then acted upon as the employees go about their jobs, resulting in outputs such as satisfaction for the employee and performance for the organization. Another example of general systems theory is the multilevel organizational systems approach that has been applied to the understanding of training implementation and transfer.[76] General systems theory is useful to FIR management as a means of understanding the role of HR in the larger context.

---

70. K.M. Eisenhardt, 'Agency theory: An assessment and review', *Academy of Management Review*, Vol. 14, 1989, pp. 57–74; Jackson and Schuler, *op. cit.*

71. *See* e.g. Eisenhardt, *op. cit.*; Jackson and Schuler, *op. cit.*

72. J.M. Newman and M.A. Huselid, 'The nature of behavioral controls in boundary occupations: Agency theory at the edge', *Advances in Global High-Technology Management*, Vol. 2, 1992, pp. 193–212.

73. L. von Bertalanffy, 'The theory of open systems in physics and biology', *Science*, Vol. I, 1950, No. 11, pp. 23–29.

74. D. Katz and R.L. Kahn, *The Social Psychology of Organizations*, New York: Wiley, 1978; Jackson and Schuler, *op. cit.*

75. P.M. Wright and S.A. Snell, 'Toward an integrative view of strategic human resource management', *Human Resource Management Review*, Vol. 1. 1991, pp. 203–225; Jackson and Schuler, *op. cit.*

76. S.W.J. Kozlowski and E. Salas, 'A multilevel organizational systems approach for the implementation and transfer of training', in Ford, J.K. and Associates, (eds.), *Improving Training effectiveness it? Woi* Organizational*, Hillsdale, NJ: Erlbaum, 1994.

F. Human Capital Theory

60. Human capital theory appears largely in the economics literature in reference to people's productive capacities.[77] The crux of this theory is that people are of value to the organization because they make it productive. In essence the organization has invested in people just as if they had invested in machinery, viewing them as an additional type of capital. As a result, all the costs related to training, retraining, motivating, and monitoring the organization are viewed as additional investments in the human capital of the firm, just as maintenance of machinery would constitute an investment in the capital of the firm.[78] Given the ways of attaining and maintaining human capital, HRM logically is a means of increasing the value and level of an organization's investment in human capital.[79] Human capital can be attained by either hiring from outside the organization or by training and developing human capital already within the organization.[80] The decision to 'buy or make' depends on a comparison between the projected value to the organization, which will be realized when the capital is deployed and the costs to the organi-zation of each option, given the current environmental context.[81]

G. Life Cycle Theory

61. Life cycle theory notes that there are several stages of the life of an organization. These stages have been described as start-up, growth, maturity, decline and revival.[82] As an organization moves through these stages, researchers have suggested that HRM practices which fit with the life-cycle stage of the organization will result in organizational effectiveness.[83]

H. Role Behaviour Theory

62. Role behaviour focuses on the interdependent role behaviours as building blocks for the organizational system. According to Katz and Kahn,[84] role behaviours are defined as 'the recurring actions of an individual, appropriately interrelated with the repetitive activities of others so as to yield a predictable outcome'. The primary

---

77. G.S. Becker, *Human Capital,* New York; National Bureau of Economic Research, 1964; Jackson and Schuler, *op. cit.*
78. E.G. Flarnholtz and J.M. Lacey, *Personnel Management, Human Capital Theory and Human Resource Accounting,* Los Angeles: Institute of Industrial Relations, University of California, 1981; Jackson and Schuler, *op. cit.*; W.F. Cascio, *Costing Human Resource: The Financial Impact of Behavior in Organizations.* Boston: PWS-Kent, 1991; Flamholtz and Lacey, *op. cit.*
79. Jackson and Schuler, *op. cit.*
80. Jackson and Schuler, *op. cit.*
81. Jackson and Schuler, *op. cit.*
82. L. Baird and L Meshoulam, 'Managing the two fits of strategic human resource management" *Academy of Management Review,* Vol. 13, 1988, pp. 116–128; Smith et al., *op. cit.*; Jackson and Schuler, *op. cit.*
83. Jackson dnd Schuler, *op. cit.*
84. Katz and Kahn, *op. cit.*

means by which the organization sends role information through the organization, supports desired behaviours, and evaluates role performances is human resource management. Schuler and Jackson[85] used this theory to link HR practice with the competitive strategy of the organization. Different strategies require different role behaviours of the employees and thus require different human resource practices. Therefore, human resource management is effective when the expectations which it communicates internally and the ways in which it evaluates performance are congruent with the system's behavioural requirements.[86]

I. Organizational Change Theory

63. Organizational change theory focuses on the 'difference in form, quality, or state over time in an organizational entity'.[87] Organizational change theory adds two pieces to the understanding of human resource management. First, in management of organizational change, organizations need to ensure congruence between the stated goals and stated changes and the enacted changes. In part this depends on clarity of communication. Second, organizations need to look at the way in which change is implemented. The success of implementation is dependent both on communication and on buy-in. Organizations experience difficulty in implementing changes to the organizational structure or practices when those changes are foisted upon employees.

J. Transactions Cost Theory

64. Transactions cost theory takes an economic viewpoint of the creation of governance structures which establish, monitor, evaluate, and enforce exchanges previously agreed upon.[88] Central to this theory are two assumptions: bounded rationality and opportunism. Opportunism assumes that if any potential for advantage exists, it will be taken. On the part of employees, the potential for opportunism exists when the employee is specially trained or possesses specialized knowledge or skills which have a market value to other organizations. The context in which the organization operates dictates the specific needs of the firm as well as whether those needs are likely to be satisfied internally or externally, and at what cost. Bounded rationality dictates that there are a limited number of options that can be assessed by any given organization prior to making a decision. In part, the context in which the organization operates also dictates the set of options that must be considered prior to making

---

85. R.S. Schuler and S.E. Jackson, 'Linking competitive strategy with human resource management practices', *Academy of Management Executive*, Vol. 3, 1987, pp. 207–219.
86. *See* e.g. N. Fredericksen, 'Toward a broader conception of human intelligence', *American Psychologist*, Vol. 41, 1986, pp. 445–452.
87. A.H. van de Ven and M.S. Poole, 'Explaining development and change in organizations', *Academy of Management Journal*, Vol. 20, 1995, pp. 510–540.
88. O.E. Williamson, 'Transaction-cost economics: The governance of contractual relations', *Journal of Law and Economics*, Vol. 22, 1979, No. 2, pp. 233–261; O.E. Williamson, 'The modem corporation: origins, evolution, attributes', *Journal of Economic Literature*, Vol. 19, 1991, pp. 1537–1568; Jackson and Schuler, *op. cit.*

a decision. Human resource activities seek to take advantage of bounded rationality while attempting to prevent the exercise of opportunism through the execution of contracts, the creation of monitoring and compliance assurance systems and through the revision of the contracts when necessary.

K. Strategic Contingency Theory

65. Strategic contingency theory recognizes that there are several strategic typologies. The choice made by an organization of which strategy to pursue requires systematic management of human resources in order to ensure appropriate and successful implementation. Strategic contingency theory posits that the choice between various typologies is dependent upon the environment within which the organization operates.[89] Two of the most well-known of these typologies are the defender-reactor-analyser-prospector theory proposed by Miles and Snow[90] and the five forces framework created by Porter.[91] Following this recognition of the value of circumstances in selecting a strategy, the choice of human resource practices and strategies is similarly viewed as being most effective when their selection is contingent on strategies pursued by the organization.[92] For example, prospectors may find it more important to look externally for people with a more current technological background so as to get the most cutting edge abilities within the company. In contrast, an organization pursuing a reactor strategy would value knowledge about the organization's own process over technological advances.

66. Porter also offers a typology which distinguishes organizations based on a focus on product differentiation, cost leadership or market breadth.[93] Schuler and Jackson[94] have adopted Porter's typology to describe the role of HRM in various of these strategies using the role behaviour perspective. Thus under either model noted, HR practices need to be consistent with the business strategy chosen by the organization in order for implementation of that strategy to be successful.

L. Organizational Learning Theory

According to organizational learning theory perspective offered by Kogut[95] prior learning facilities the learning and application on new, related knowledge.[96] This idea

---

89. Lundy and Cowling, op. cit.
90. R.E. Miles and C.C. Snow, 'Designing strategic human resource systems', Organization Dynamics, Vol. 16, 1984, pp. 36–52.
91. M.E. Porter, Competitive Strategy: Techniques for Analyzing Industries and Competitors, New York: Free Press, 1980.
92. Lundy and Cowling, op. cit.
93. Schuler and Jackson, 1987, op. cit.
94. Jackson and Schuler, op. cit.
95. Kogut, B. 'Joint Ventures: Theoretical and Empirical and Perspective,' Strategic Management Journal, Vol. 9, 1988, pp. 319–332.
96. W.M. Cohen and D.A. Levinthal, 'Absorptive Capacity: A New Perspective on Learning and Innovations,' Administrative Science Quarterly, Vol. 35, 1990, pp. 128–152.

can be extended to include the case in which the knowledge in question is itself a set of learning skills constituting a firm's absorptive capacity. This capacity increases as a function of the previous experience, its learning processes, and the need for information the firm considers lacking in order to attain its strategic objectives. In the foreign market entry, advocates of the internationalization process school have argued that firms expand slowly from their domestic bases into progressively distant areas. Learning from previous expansions is the driving force behind new investments.[97]

M. Information Processing Perspective

This perspective is based on the premise that organizations are created to facilitate the flow of information for effective individual and organizational decision making.[98] The focus is on the capacity and facilitation characteristics of organizational structure and practices such as human resource ones that support, encourage, and reward transfer of information within the organization, across its boundaries to IJV partners and the IJV itself, and that enables the organization to acquire knowledge to transform the data and information. Learning theory then enters to address how the organization can use this information in a creative way to better deal with and learn from the environment and its own experienes.[99]

IV. WHAT ARE SOME OF THE KEY ISSUES RELEVANT TO THE PRACTICE OF HUMAN RESOURCE MANAGEMENT THAT ARE LIKELY TO CARRY US INTO THE 21ST CENTURY?

A. Leadership

67. In contrast to companies which practice traditional management and focus on stability, today's leading companies are increasing the emphasis put on empowering their workers and on the qualities of change, motivation, and vision. As a result leadership has become increasingly necessary.[100] In addition, when companies expand globally, they are often competing for the same employees as the major organizations headquartered in that country. Thus, one of the challenges for human resource managers is to craft a hiring programme that not only identifies leadership potential of candidates but also provides development opportunities for them that help fulfil that potential once they are employed.

---

97. H.G. Berkema, O. Shenkar, F. Vermeulen, and J. Bell, "Working Abroad, Working With Others: How Firms Learn to Operate International Joint Ventures" *Academy of Management Journal*, 1997.

98. W.G. Egelhoff, 'Information-Processing Theory and the Multinational Enterprise,' *Journal of International Business Studies*, 22, Third Quarter, 1991, pp. 341–367.

99. R.L. Daft and K.E. Weick, 'Toward a Model of Organizations as Interpretation Systems,' *Academy of Management Review*, Vol. 9, 1984 pp. 284–295.

100. J.P. Kotter, A *Force for Change: How Leadership Differs from Management*, New York: The Free Press, 1990.

B. Pay for Performance

68. Pay for performance has also become an issue for many organizations. It is intended to serve as a linkage between the strategic goals of the organization and the activities of the individual, and to serve as a means of reinforcing organizational norms. Its success depends on an assumption that money motivates performance, and that differential performance can be recognized adequately in this manner. Notably organizations such as Lincoln Electric have been using this strategy for decades, with a great deal of success in many but not all countries. In recent years, other companies have recognized the potential for improved performance available through this practice and have attempted to copy it. When instituting a programme such as this when an organization operates overseas, special care must be taken to align the incentives and bonuses paid for exceptional performance with items that actually motivate the members of that culture and are legally feasible. For example, stock options, which are valuable to US workers, are typically not subject to the same tax benefits globally. Thus HR managers must adapt the HR programs, policies, practices and philosophies of the organization to reflect the different environments in which it is operating.

C. Effectiveness

69. Effectiveness in a human resource context can be viewed as matching the right person for the job with the right job for the person. In part, it results from a knowledge of both the tasks to be done and the pool of talent available to perform those tasks. As organizations are seeking to improve their bottom line through improvement of efficiency, product quality and decrease in costs, the value of human resource effectiveness is being documented in the academic literature[101] and is becoming more obvious to organizations. From the perspective of the human resource manager, effectiveness translates into a need to be aware of the environment in which business is being done, both on a local and on a global scale, and of the skills, abilities and competencies represented within the organization. This awareness, paired with knowledge of the strategic plan of the organization and the steps necessary to achieve those strategic goals, will allow a human resource manager to ensure that the person with the right behaviours, competencies and motivation is available when and where needed.

D. Technology

70. Technology is the process used to transform inputs into usable outputs.[102] It varies both by degree of continuity and level of knowledge required by the system. As technology has become more advanced, and as these changes have taken place at

---

101. M.A. Huselid. S.E. Jackson, and R.S. Schuler, 'Technical and strategic human resource management effectiveness as determinants of firm performance', *Academy of Management Journal*, Vol. 40, 1997, pp. 171–188.
102. Jackson and Schuler, *op. cit.*

increasing speed, organizations have been forced to keep up with these changes. This need to keep up has meant that organizations are put in the position of requiring increasing levels of technical skill from their employees and future employees. This requirement, in turn, changes the level and type of training sought by members of the organization as well as changing the minimum desirable set of skills for candidates being hired. Here the cooperation between HR management and union representatives can assist in providing training and encouraging employee flexibility.

E.   Flexible Work Arrangements

71.   One of the most valuable alternative work arrangements for employees is flexible work arrangements. These arrangements often fall into three main categories: re-designed job, flexible time and flexible place.

1. Job Re-design

72.   Re-designing jobs creates a means of restructuring the jobs to allow practices such as job sharing. Typically this re-design takes place through the use of job design and job analysis processes. From these processes are culled the essential skill set needed to perform a particular job. When employees share a job, each fulfils the requirements of the job, but only part time. While it does require some coordination on the part of the employees, it often creates employment opportunities for those who previously would not be able to perform the essential tasks on a full-time basis.

2. Flexible Time

73.   Flexible time allowances, or flextime, as it is commonly called in the US, allows employees to schedule their working hours in a way in which they are better able to perform their jobs while also being able to take care of their personal needs. When flextime programmes are instituted, flextime and coretime (the time during which an employee must be at the office) are typically identified, and employees are allowed to structure their remaining work hours when they choose to work.[103] Flextime has been credited with increasing employee productivity, and as a means of accommodating differences in religious obligations and family responsibilities, some of which are protected under the law. For example, many companies allow employees to work four 10-hour days, rather than working five 8-hour days.

3. Flexible Place: Telecommuting

74.   As a means of being flexible as to the place where the duties of the job are to be performed, some organizations allow telecommuting, the practice of telephoning in via computer modem from wherever an employee is to a central office computer

---

103.   Jackson and Schuler, 2000, *op. cit.*

and working on and through that computer. As well as being a benefit to employees, it also benefits employers who often are able to accommodate needs such as parents who need to be available to sick children, but can still spend the day doing productive work. An additional benefit realized by organizations in the northeastern part of the US during the blizzard of 1996 was that employees could telecommute, allowing firms to remain open although virtually no employees could actually get to the office.

F. HR for Learning and Innovation

75. In some of the best organizations, keeping the process of change flowing continuously has become a top priority. In recent years, such organizations have been referred to as *learning organizations*. When the environment is complex and dynamic, learning may require a lot of exploration and experimentation. When the environment is more stable, learning is more likely to occur through a systematic process of testing alternative approaches.[104] In either case, innovation occurs through a continuous process of learning and change.

76. For learning organizations, successful innovation is not an infrequent and special event with a clear-cut beginning and end; it is a never-ending process that becomes part of the daily routine. Learning organizations innovate by learning from their past experiences, learning across parts of the company, learning from customers and learning from other companies. They have both the drive and the capabilities to improve their performance continuously. At Yahoo!, a provider of Internet search engines and other services, all employees experiment constantly to satisfy customer demand. Yahoo! receives thousands of suggestions and comments from users who are eager for sites that suit their particular needs. Employees who read these submissions are fully empowered to make changes as they see fit. At Yahoo!, continuous learning and innovation create a sustainable competitive advantage.

77. In learning organizations, continuous innovation is supported by several organizational factors, including a fluid and flat organizational level, and a variety of human resource management practices. When appropriately aligned, these factors create a context of innovation.

G. One Best Way?

78. As is perhaps apparent from the discussions of the differing needs and interests of employees above, the one-best-way approach to the management of human resources appears outdated. For example, some firms have focused on the acquisition of technical expertise as a source of competitive advantage.[105] With organizations

---

104. S.E. Jackson and R.S. Schuler, 'Managing Human Resources for Innovation and Learning,' in R. Berndt (ed.) *Challenges of Management* Vol. 7: *Management of Innovations/Innovative Management*, Zurich: GSBA, 2000.
105. Jackson and Schuler, 2000, *op. cit.*

operating in diverse cultures and with a diverse set of employees in many of those cultures, there is no perfect prescription such as technical expertise for success. Instead, organizations must retain flexibility in addressing human resource planning and management issues.

79. One means of addressing these needs is through the use of systematic analysis. Systematic analysis provides a blueprint for a means through which organizations can approach this problem. In systematic analysis, the organization first identifies how the practices within the firm affect the employees and the behaviours of those employees. Second, the organization takes its unique characteristics into account. Third, the organization uses the results of the environmental scanning done by the HR department to assess the changes in the environment. Finally, the organization goes through a trial and error process, where decisions as to which actions to take are made, implemented and assessed in terms of their ability to generate the intended results without undue unintended consequences.

80. Human resource departments play a strong role in the systematic analysis process for several reasons. First, HR departments are able to assess the current internal situation in the organization. Second, as a result of their constant environmental scanning, the HR department knows a great deal about the environment in which the organization is operating. Third, knowing the current set of skills, abilities and competencies possessed by members of the organization and the means of motivating these employees, the HR department is uniquely positioned to assist the organization in both implementation and assessment of adapting current practices to the operational environment. Thus the HR department is a valuable strategic partner in identifying the best way for an organization to proceed in a specific environment.

V. SUMMARY

81. The nature of human resource management has changed dramatically in the US in recent years. Organizations that previously held themselves apart from the global market are now active participants. Competition is viewed as a global phenomenon in many industries. The geographic scope of the talent pool has also increased to a great degree. As a result, the role of the HR department has also changed. Increasingly, the HR department is being recognized as an asset to the strategic planning process, since it is both the locus of implementation of the strategic plans of the organization and a valuable source of knowledge about the internal and external environment in which the organization is operating. The changes in this environment take place at high speed. This chapter has attempted to: (a) describe the overall changes taking place; (b) explain the current context in which human resource managers operate and the consequences of that Context; (c) identify some of the theoretical frameworks that can be used to understand how context shapes HR activities; and (d) identify some of the issues in the forefront of current human resource management practice in the US. As globalization continues, human resource management must continue to address the issues noted and adapt to the speed and level of changes in order best to serve the interests of all its stakeholders: the employees, society, strategic partners, customers, investors, and the organization itself.

Each of these interests is likely to be served most effectively by a partnership among the line managers, HR professionals, employees and unions that determines the strategic direction of the organization.

Select Bibliography

B.E. Becker and M.A. Huselid, 'High Performance Work Systems and Firm Performance: A Synthesis of Research and Managerial Implications,' *Research in Personnel and Human Resources Management*, in G. Ferris (ed.), Greenwich, CT: JAI Press, 1998.

C. Brewster and A. Hegewisch (eds), *Policy and Practice in European Human Resource Management*, New York, 1994.

I. Brunstein, *Human Resource Management in Western Europe.* New York, 1995.

J.M. Bryson and P. Bromiley, 'Critical Factors Affecting the Planning and Implementation of Major Projects', *Strat. Mgt. J.*, 1993, pp. 319–337.

A.A. Buckho, 'The Effects of Employee Ownership on Employee Attitudes: An Integrated Causal Model and Path Analysis', *J. Mgt. Stud.*, 1993, pp. 633–657.

P. Cappelli and A. Crocker-Hefter, *Distinctive Human Resources are the Core Competencies of Firms*, Report no. R117Q00011-91 (Washington, D.C.: U.S. Department of Education, 1994); *High Performance Work Practices and Firm Performance*, U.S. Department of Labor: Washington, D.C., 1993.

L. Davidson, 'Measure What You Bring to the Bottom Line,' *Workforce*, September 1998, pp. 34–40.

T. Donaldson and L.E. Preston, 'The Stakeholder Theory of the Corporátion: Concepts, Evidence, and Implications,' *Academy of Management Review* 20, 1995, pp. 65–91.

E. Freeman and J. Liedtka, 'Stakeholder Capitalism and the Value Chain,' *European Mangement Journal*, Vol. 15(3) June 1997, 286–296.

L. Gratton, V. Hope Hailey, P. Stiles, and C. Truss, *Strategic Human Resource Management*, London: Oxford University Press, 1999.

C. Handy, 'A Better Capitalism,' *Across the Board*, April 1998, pp. 16–22.

M.A. Huselid, S.E. Jackson, and R.S. Schuler, "Technical and Strategic Human Resource Management Effectiveness as Determinants of Firm Performance," *Academy of Management Journal* 40, 1997, pp. 171–188.

S.E. Jackson and R.S. Schuler, 'Understanding Human Resource Management in the Context of Organizations and their Environments', *Ann. Rev. Psych.*, 1995, pp. 237–264.

S.E. Jackson and R.S. Schuler, *Managing Human Resources: A Partnership Perspective*, 7th ed., Cincinnati, Ohio: South-western, 2000.

J.P. Kotter, *A Force for Change*, New York, 1990.

E.E. Lawler III, *The Ultimite Advantage: Creating the High Involvement Organization*, San Francisco: Jossey-Bass, 1992.

E.E. Lawler III, S.A. Mohrman and G.E. Ledford, *Employee Involvement in America: An Assessment of Practices and Results*, San Francisco: Josey-Bass, 1992.

K. Legge, *Human Resource Management*, London, 1995.

O. Lundy and A. Cowling, *Strategic Human Resource Management*, New York, 1996.

J.P. MacDiffie and J. Drafcik, 'Integrating Technology and Human Resources for High-Performance Manufacturing,' *Transforming Organizations*, T. Kochan, M. Useems (eds), New York: Oxford University Press, 1992, pp. 210–226.

J. Pfeffer, *Competitive Advantage Through People*, Boston: Harvard Business School Press, 1995.

J. Pfeffer, *The Human Equation*, Boston: Harvard Business School Press, 1998.

M. Poole, *Human Resource Management, Vols. I, II, and III*, London: Routledge, 1999.

A.J. Rucci, S.P. Kirn, and R.T. Quinn, 'The Employee-Customer-Profit Chain at Sears,' *Harvard Business Review*, January–February, 1998, pp. 83–97.

R.S. Schuler, 'Human Resource Management: Domestic to Global', in M. Warner (ed.), *International Encyclopedia of Business and Management*, London: Blackwell, 1994.

R.S. Schuler and S.E. Jackson, 'Linking Competitive Strategies with Human Resource Management Practices', *Acad. Mgt. Exec.*, 1987, 207–219.

R.S. Schuler, S.E. Jackson, and J. Storey, 'HRM and Its Link with Strategic Management,' in J. Storey (ed.) *Human Resource Management: A Critical Text*, London: IT, 2000.

R.S. Schuler and I.C. MacMillan, 'Gaining Competitive Advantage through Human Resource Management Practices', *Hum. Res. Mgt.*, 1984, pp. 241–255.

R.S. Schuler and S.E. Jackson, *Strategic Human Resource Management: A Reader*, London: Blackwell, 1999.

P. Sparrow and J.-M. Hiltrop, *European Human Resource Management in Transition*, New York, 1994.

J. Storey, *Human Resource Management: A Critical Test,* 2nd ed., London: ITL, 2000.

A.A. Thompson and A.J. Strickland, *Crafting and Implementing Strategy*, 10th ed., New York: McGraw-Hill, 1998.

SOURCES OF REGULATION

Chapter 7.   International Labour Law

*L. Swepston**

I.   INTRODUCTION

A.   *Definition*

1.   International labour law covers both the substantive rules of law established at the international level, and the procedural rules relating to their adoption and implementation.

B.   *Historical Development*

2.   Moves towards international labour Conventions date back to the beginning of the nineteenth century. It was felt that labour legislation could not be solidly established in individual countries unless supported by parallel standards adopted internationally. The first two Conventions were adopted by a diplomatic Conference in Berne in 1906. The Treaty of Versailles in 1919 provided for the establishment of an International Labour Organisation having as its principal purpose the adoption of Conventions and Recommendations.

3.   Since then the International Labour Conference, the principal deliberative body of the ILO, has met regularly, normally once a year. It has adopted 183 Conventions and 191 Recommendations as of June 2000.

4.   In 1944 the Conference, meeting in Philadelphia, adopted a Declaration to redefine the aims and purposes of the Organization, which was incorporated in the ILO Constitution in 1946. The Declaration affirmed, in particular, that 'labour is not a commodity', that 'freedom of expression and of association are essential to sustained progress', that 'poverty anywhere constitutes a danger to prosperity everywhere' and that 'all human beings, irrespective of race, creed, or sex, have the right to pursue both their material well-being and their spiritual development in conditions of freedom and dignity, of economic security and equal opportunity'.

---

*   This chapter has been updated from earlier versions written by N. Valticos and K. Samson.

C. The Purposes of International Labour Law[1]

5.   The main argument originally advanced in favour of international labour law related to international competition. It was felt that international agreements on conditions of labour would prevent competition at the expense of the workers and favour fair competition. For some time, these arguments were given less emphasis, since it was felt that costs and the competitive value of products depended on many factors other than labour costs.[2] However, the question of the role and effect of labour standards in relation to trade has come to the fore again and has been the subject of intense debate with the globalization of the world's economy. It lies at the heart of discussions concerning the harmonization of the activities of the ILO and the World Trade Organization, and some propose requiring observance of minimum labour standards as a condition of trade liberalization.

6.   At the end of the First World War, a further argument was put forward, namely that action against social injustice serves the cause of peace. This led to the establishment of the ILO in the Treaty of Versailles, at the same time that the League of Nations was set up.

7.   Today, social justice remains an essential driving force behind international labour law. Even in developed countries, in spite of significant improvements in labour conditions during the 20th century, many social problems still subsist, while exploitation and hardship continue to affect workers in vast areas of the world. Notions of social justice constantly evolve, and now embrace the general welfare of mankind.

8.   In addition to these basic purposes, the function of international labour law is also to promote balanced economic and social progress, to regulate labour matters of an international character and to serve as a guide to governments, workers, and employers.

II.   THE SOURCES OF INTERNATIONAL LABOUR LAW

A.   ILO Sources

1. The Constitution of the ILO

9.   The Constitution of the ILO lays down a number of principles, such as freedom of association and non-discrimination, which are regarded as a direct source of

---

1.   For further details, *see* N. Valticos and G. von Potobsky, *International Labour Law*, 3rd ed., Deventer, 1996; Bartolomei, von Potobsky and Swepston, *The International Labor Organization: The International Standards System and Basic Human Rights*, Westview, 1995.
2.   For an early analysis of this question, *see* Herbert Feis: 'International labour legislation in the light of economic theory', 1927, reproduced in Werner Sengenberger and Duncan Campbell (eds): *International Labour Standards and Economic Interdependence*, International Institute for Labour Studies, Geneva, 1994, pp. 29–55.

law. This has been reinforced with the adoption of the Declaration of Fundamental Rights and Principles at Work in 1998 (see below).

2. Conventions and Recommendations

10. Conventions create international obligations for the States which ratify them, while Recommendations aim at providing guidance for policy, legislation, and practice. ILO Conventions have specific features because they are adopted in an institutional framework, the Conference which adopts them has a tripartite structure, and they are designed to be more effective than normal diplomatic treaties. The provisions of ILO Conventions and Recommendations are described as *international labour standards.*

11. Conventions and Recommendations are adopted in the framework of the ILO, which has 175 member States. Its deliberative organs are *tripartite*, being composed of representatives of governments, employers, and workers. This structure has been a source of strength for the ILO, though it has also given rise to a certain number of difficulties, for example, as regards the designation of workers' representatives by countries with several trade union movements and by those where there is no real freedom of association. The designation of employers' representatives by communist countries was also a cause for controversy before the end of the Cold War.

12. The ILO is comprised of three main bodies. The most representative is the *International Labour Conference* which normally meets once a year (though on occasion special sessions are convened to deal with maritime questions). It consists of delegations from member States which should comprise two government delegates, one employers' and one workers' delegate.[3] The latter two delegates must be nominated in agreement with the most representative organizations of employers or workers of their countries. Every delegate votes individually. The *Governing Body* consists of 56 members, 28 representing governments (including permanent seats for those of the ten countries of 'chief industrial importance') and 14 each representing employers and workers. Its members are elected every third year at the Conference by their respective groups.[4] The *International Labour Office* is the permanent secretariat of the Organization. Its Director-General is appointed by the Governing Body.[5]

13. Conventions and Recommendations are adopted by the International Labour Conference, normally after discussion at two successive sessions. The Office prepares preliminary reports reviewing law and practice in the different countries on the questions concerned. Each item is considered by a special technical committee of the

---

3. Most delegations include a larger number of people as advisers, in order to cover the wide range of subjects dealt with in the Conference.
4. Amendments to the ILO Constitution adopted in 1986 would double the size of the Governing Body and abolish the permanent government seats; the number of ratifications required for their entry into force has not yet been attained.
5. The current Director-General is Juan Somavia of Chile.

Conference. Conventions and Recommendations must be adopted by the Conference itself, by a majority of two-thirds of the delegates present.

14. The main problem encountered in framing international labour standards arises from the diversity of national economic, social, and political conditions. However, the view persists that ILO instruments should remain universal in character. In order to take account of the diversity of conditions in the world, recourse is had to various types of flexibility clauses inserted in Conventions.[6] As concerns the level of the standards, they should be relevant to the greatest number of countries, while also requiring a significant advance upon average existing practice in order to have a dynamic thrust. Standard-setting policy is giving rise to difficult discussions in the ILO that are likely to continue for some time. The employers' group and a certain number of governments favour more general, 'framework' Conventions as compared to highly detailed Conventions which may be ratified by fewer Members, and some are calling for a suspension of the adoption of new standards until older instruments have been revised and brought up to date.[7]

15. The question of choice between a Convention and a Recommendation is discussed regularly. Recommendations are used mainly to supplement Conventions, in order to indicate in greater detail the manner of giving effect to their provisions or to advocate the establishment of higher standards. Free-standing Recommendations are adopted to deal with subjects that are not yet ripe for a Convention or do not lend themselves to the adoption of Conventions which would give rise to international obligations.

16. Changes in conditions and conceptions may make it necessary to revise international labour standards. ILO Conventions adopted since 1929 contain clauses providing that a revising Convention does not entail the abrogation of the original instrument, but that, unless otherwise provided, the original instrument shall cease to be open to ratification as from the entry into force of the new Convention, and ratification by a State of the latter shall involve the denunciation of the original text. More than 50 Conventions have been revised by subsequent instruments, sometimes to make them more flexible, but frequently also to raise earlier standards.

3. Declaration of Fundamental Rights and Principles

17. In 1998, the ILO adopted a new kind of instrument. The Declaration of Fundamental Rights and Principles at Work codifies the ILO's long understanding of the fundamental human rights contained in its Constitution and standards, as comprising freedom of association and the right to bargain collectively; freedom from

---

6. *See* J.F. McMahon, 'The Legislative Technique of the ILO', *British Year Book of International Law*, 1965–66, pp. 31–68; Valticos and von Potobsky, *op cit.*, pp. 57–61; Bartolomei, von Potobsky and Swepston, *op cit.*, pp. 37–45; ILO document GB.244/SC3/3 (November 1989); and *Handbook of Procedures on International Labour Standards*, available through ILOLEX, on-line at the ILO website.
7. A policy document on standards policy in the ILO was submitted to the Governing Body of the ILO in November 2000. See doc.gB.279/4.

forced labour; freedom from child labour; and freedom from discrimination. It provides that all States, even if they have not been able to ratify the Conventions which embody these principles, have 'an obligation, arising from the very fact of membership in the Organization, to respect, to promote and to realize, in good faith and in accordance with the Constitution, the fundamental rights which are the subjects' of the eight ILO Conventions recognized as fundamental. The Declaration's follow-up procedures involve *annual reports* by all States that have not ratified all eight of the fundamental Conventions, and the examination of these reports by a panel of Expert Advisers and the Governing Body. *Global reports* are also provided for, each of which focusses on one of the four subjects covered, and examines its application around the world.[8] Global reports are then discussed by the International Labour Conference, giving rise to a discussion in the following November session of the Governing Body which should adopt a plan of action for technical assistance. All of this work is done in a promotional framework, and is aimed at providing assistance to member States to implement the fundamental rights and principles covered by the Declaration.

4. Other Less Formal Instruments

18. In other cases as well, standards are laid down in texts less formal than Conventions and Recommendations. These include, for example, the Tripartite Declaration of Principles concerning Multinational Enterprises and Social Policy, adopted by the Governing Body in 1976, and Conference resolutions on such questions as the independence of the trade union movement and the relation of trade union rights and civil liberties. The ILO has also adopted a number of codes of conduct and guidelines illustrating best practice in various respects.

5. Interpretation

19. The ILO Constitution provides that any question or dispute relating to the interpretation of the Constitution or a Convention shall be submitted to the International Court of Justice, but there has been only one such case, in 1932.[9] On the other hand, the International Labour Office is frequently consulted by governments as to the interpretation of Conventions: the opinions given are communicated to the Governing Body and published in the *Official Bulletin*.

6. Case Law

20. The ILO supervisory bodies (discussed below) have built up a body of so-called 'case law' as to the scope and meaning of various ILO Conventions. The

---

8. The Global Reports are to cover freedom of association (2000), forced labour (2001), child labour (2002) and discrimination (2003) before beginning the rotation again.
9. Article 37 of the Constitution would allow the establishment of a tribunal for purposes of interpretation, but it has never been thought worthwhile to establish it.

Committee of Experts on the Application of Conventions and Recommendations has pointed out that although its terms of reference do not allow it to give definitive interpretations of Conventions, it has to consider and express its views on the meaning of certain provisions of Conventions in order to carry out its function of evaluating the implementation of Conventions.[10] The Governing Body Committee on Freedom of Association (see below) has formulated an important body of principles in the course of examining cases submitted to it.

7. Instruments Adopted at Special Conferences

21. In some cases, special governmental Conferences have dealt with questions which concerned only a limited number of countries, such as the Agreements concerning Rhine Boatmen of 1950, the 1956 European Convention concerning Social Security for Workers Engaged in International Transport, and the 1980 European Agreement concerning the Provision of Medical Care to Persons during Temporary Residence. Instruments relating to performers and to teachers have been adopted by conferences convened by other organizations (UNESCO et al.) with the cooperation of the ILO.

22. On three occasions the ILO Governing Body has carried out a systematic review of ILO Conventions and Recommendations, leading to the adoption in 1979 and again in 1987[11] of a classification of existing standards (particularly to identify priority instruments and instruments to be revised and of possible subjects for new instruments). The latest review is due to be completed in 2001. In each of the last two reviews a number of Conventions and Recommendations have been listed as instruments to be promoted on a priority basis, those in need of revision are identified, as well as possible new subjects. In the course of the latest review the Governing Body has identified 69 of the ILO's 183 Conventions as fully up to date and representing the Organization's policy on the matters they cover, with others to be reconsidered and revised, abrogated, or withdrawn. A Constitutional amendment, now open to ratification, would permit abrogation of out of date Conventions. Pending its coming into force, the Governing Body has approved the discontinuance of detailed reporting on a number of Conventions considered obsolete, and in the June 2000 Conference session five Conventions which never entered into force were withdrawn.

B. *United Nations Instruments*

23. While the UN's mandate is not for labour matters as such, it has touched on them, mainly in instruments concerning human rights. The 1948 Universal Declaration of Human Rights and the two 1966 International Covenants on human

---

10. *See* e.g. Report III(4A), International Labour Conference, 73rd Session, 1987, para. 12; *ibid.*, 78th Session, 1991, paras 9–13.
11. *See* ILO: *Official Bulletin*, Vol. LXX, 1987, Series A, Special Issue.

rights contain various provisions relating to labour matters. Reference should also be made to the 1965 Convention on the Elimination of All Forms of Racial Discrimination, the 1979 Convention on the Elimination of All Forms of Discrimination against Women, and the 1989 Convention on the Rights of the Child, all of which contain provisions relevant to labour law. The 1990 Convention on the Protection of the Rights of All Migrant Workers and Members of their Families has not yet entered into force.

C. European Instruments

1. Council of Europe Instruments

24. The 1950 European Convention on Human Rights deals essentially with civil and political rights, including the prohibition of forced labour and the right to form trade unions. The most comprehensive instrument adopted by the Council of Europe on social questions is the 1961 European Social Charter. Its most original feature was the recognition of the right to strike, subject to certain restrictions. An additional protocol to the Charter containing four additional substantive articles was adopted in 1987. A further protocol to strengthen the procedures for supervising the implementation of the Charter was adopted in 1991, and in 1995 another additional protocol provided for a system of collective complaints. Finally, the Council of Ministers adopted a Revised Social Charter in April 1996, which entered into force on 1 July 1999.

25. The Council of Europe has also adopted a number of social security instruments. The 1964 European Code of Social Security was based on ILO Convention No. 102; a revised Code was adopted in 1990. The 1972 European Convention on Social Security deals with equality of treatment between nationals and foreigners and the maintenance of rights acquired abroad.

2. European Communities Standards

26. Provisions of a social character are to be found both in the basic treaties of the European Communities and in various acts adopted under the Communities' legal system. A Charter of Fundamental Social Rights for Workers – in the form of a non-mandatory declaration dependent on a programme of implementing measures – was adopted in 1989. A protocol on social policy adopted in 1991 in connection with the conclusion of the Maastricht Treaty on European Union has been adhered to by all Member States of the Union except the United Kingdom. The 1997 Treaty of Amsterdam reaffirms the commitment to a number of social rights, particularly those relating to discrimination, and allows greater access to recourse at the European level.

D. Instruments in the American Region

27. The Organization of American States adopted the American Convention on Human Rights in 1969. Like its European counterpart, it deals mainly with civil and political rights, but includes the prohibition of forced labour and the right of

association, *inter alia,* for economic, labour, and social purposes. In November 1988, a protocol to the Convention dealing with economic, social, and cultural rights (covering the right to work, conditions of work, trade union rights, and social security, among its workers' rights provisions) was adopted. The Organization of Central American States adopted a Social Security Convention in 1967, and the countries of the Andean group adopted instruments on social security and migration of workers in 1977. The North American Free Trade Agreement (Canada, Mexico, and the United States) also has labour provisions.

E. Instruments in the African Region

28. The Organization of African Unity adopted the African Charter of Human and Peoples' Rights in 1981: it deals both with civil and political rights, and with economic, social, and cultural rights. In 1998 it adopted the Ouagadougou Protocol to the Charter on the Establishment of an African Court of Human and Peoples' Rights, which must receive 15 ratifications to come into force. A General Social Security Convention was concluded by the African, Malagasy, and Mauritius Organization in 1971.

F. Instruments in the Arab Region

29. The League of Arab States adopted the Arab Labour Standards Convention in 1907. Since then, the Arab Labour Organisation has adopted a series of Conventions on labour matters.

G. Bilateral Treaties

30. Bilateral treaties in the labour field aim at regulating the admission to and conditions of employment of nationals of the contracting countries. Such treaties are based on the principle of equality of treatment of the nationals, of the States concerned. They are very numerous and their scope has broadened over the years. They include treaties on limited subjects or groups, labour treaties of more general scope, conventions on migration and social insurance agreements.

H. Relation between Sources

31. The plurality of sources of international labour law makes necessary measures of coordination and consultation aimed at preventing the adoption of conflicting standards. In case of conflict, regard should be had to the standard most favourable to workers.

III. THE CONTENT OF INTERNATIONAL LABOUR LAW

32. ILO standards can be categorized in several ways. There are fundamental human rights standards, and more technical instruments. Some Conventions can be called 'promotional' – i.e. the obligations they create on ratification are oriented more towards adopting and pursuing a policy than toward precise obligations to be carried out in specified ways. The first set of four subjects below cover the fundamental human rights standards of the ILO, and if they are applied it makes the achievement of all the others much more feasible.

A.   Freedom of Association and Protection of the Right to Organize

33. Freedom of association has special importance for workers, as an essential means to defend their interests, and is vital also to employers. The principle of freedom of association is embodied in the Constitution of the ILO. The basic instrument in this field is the Freedom of Association and Protection of the Right to Organize Convention, 1948 (No. 87), which has been ratified by 133 States.[12] It provides that workers and employers, without distinction whatsoever, shall have the right to establish and to join organizations of their own choosing without previous authorization. The Convention also provides that the organizations shall have the right to draw up their constitutions and rules, to elect their representatives in full freedom and to organize their activities, that they shall not be liable to be dissolved or suspended by administrative authority, that they shall have the right to establish federations and confederations, and that all such organizations shall have the right to affiliate with international organizations.

34. While Convention No. 87 does not deal expressly with the right to strike, the case law of the ILO supervisory bodies is that this right is inherent in the right to take action to defend workers' interests.[13]

35. The freedom of action of trade union organizations depends to a great extent on the civil liberties enjoyed in each country. This was stressed in a resolution adopted in 1970 by the International Labour Conference, and is frequently cited by ILO supervisory bodies.

36. The Right to Organize and Collective Bargaining Convention, 1949 (No. 98), ratified by 147 countries, provides for protection of workers and trade union leaders against acts of anti-union discrimination and against interference in trade union matters. It also provides for the promotion of voluntary negotiation between employers and workers with a view to the conclusion of collective agreements.

37. A Convention (No. 135) and Recommendation (No. 143) of 1971 provide for the protection and facilities to be afforded to workers' representatives in the undertaking. The Rural Workers' Organizations Convention (No. 141) and Recommendation

---

12.   All numbers of ratifications listed here are as of 31 December 2000.
13.   *See* 'Freedom of Association and Collective Bargaining', *General Survey by the Committee of Experts on the Application of Conventions and Recommendations*, Report III(4B), International Labour Conference, 81st Session, 1994, pp. 61–78; J. Hodges-Aeberhard and A. Odero de Dios: 'Principles of the Committee on Freedom of Association Concerning Strikes', *International Labour Review*, Vol. 126, 1987, p. 543; ILO Law on Freedom of Association: Standards and Procedures, ILO, 1995.

(No. 149) of 1975 state basic guarantees for such organizations and also provide for policies to encourage their growth. The Labour Relations (Public Service) Convention (No. 151) and Recommendation (No. 159) of 1978 are concerned with the right to organize of public employees and the determination of their conditions of employment. A Convention (No. 154) and a Recommendation (No. 163) of 1981 deal with the promotion of collective bargaining. A number of other instruments either deal with freedom of association issues directly, or presuppose its existence in providing for the involvement of workers' and employers' representatives in their functioning.

B. Forced Labour

38. There are two important Conventions in this area. The Forced Labour Convention, 1930 (No. 29) – the most widely ratified ILO Convention (by 155 States) – provides for the suppression of forced labour, subject to a limited number of exceptions (e.g. prison labour under defined conditions, compulsory military service, etc.). The Abolition of Forced Labour Convention, 1957 (No. 105), which has been ratified by 151 States, requires the immediate and complete abolition of any form of forced labour when imposed as a means of political coercion or education or as a punishment for holding or expressing views ideologically opposed to the established political, social, or economic system; as a method of mobilizing and using labour for purposes of economic development; as a means of labour discipline; as a punishment for having participated in strikes; or as a means of racial, social, national, or religious discrimination.

C. Discrimination in Employment and Occupation

39. While there are a number of ILO Conventions which include the concept of non-discrimination, the main instrument is the Discrimination (Employment and Occupation) Convention, 1958 (No. 111), which has been ratified by 145 States. The Convention defines discrimination as including any distinction, exclusion, or preference made on the basis of race, colour, sex, religion, political opinion, national extraction, or social origin, which has the effect of nullifying or impairing equality of opportunity or treatment in employment or occupation. Certain distinctions are not deemed to be discrimination, such as those based on the inherent requirements of a particular job, those affecting an individual who is justifiably suspected of or engaged in activities prejudicial to the security of the State (provided that s/he has a right to appeal) and certain special measures of protection or assistance. The Convention and its supplementary Recommendation indicate the methods to be used to eliminate discrimination.[14]

---

14. It is now of historical interest that in respect of apartheid in labour matters in South Africa, in 1964 the International Labour Conference adopted a Declaration, which was updated in 1981, 1988, and 1991. The Declaration condemned the policy of apartheid and called upon the Government of South Africa to renounce it. The Conference also established a detailed programme for the elimination of apartheid in labour matters. Following fundamental constitutional and political changes in South Africa and the country's return to membership of the ILO, the Declaration was rescinded by the International Labour Conference in 1994.

40. The Equal Remuneration Convention, 1951 (No. 100), lays down that each State should promote and in so far as consistent with the methods of wage determination in operation in its country, ensure the application of the principle of equal remuneration for men and women workers for work of equal value. It has received 149 ratifications. The question of employment of workers with family responsibilities is dealt with in a 1981 Convention (No. 156) and Recommendation (No. 165), applicable to both men and women.

D. Child Labour

41. Child labour was the subject of a Convention (No. 5) adopted at the first session of the International Labour Conference in 1919, to set a minimum age for work in industrial undertakings. It was followed by a number of others over the years, culminating in the Minimum Age Convention, 1973 (No. 138). This Convention covers all economic activities, both employment and other kinds of work, and requires States to set a minimum age for entry in the world of work at 15 or the end of compulsory schooling, whichever is higher; or 14 or the end of compulsory schooling for developing countries. It includes a number of flexibility clauses, and has now been ratified by 104 countries. This Convention, a very technical instrument, revises ten earlier minimum age Conventions.

42. The ILO had not earlier adopted a child labour Convention with a human rights orientation, so in 1999 the Conference adopted – unanimously – the Worst Forms of Child Labour Convention (No. 182). Some countries have stated that their low development level does not allow them to abolish child labour in the short term. Convention No. 182 provides that there are certain forms of child labour – such as slavery, involvement in the sex trade, engagement in illegal activities, and very dangerous employment – that cannot be accepted even in the short term, and ratifying States engage themselves to abolish them in the shortest possible time. The Convention has been ratified very rapidly by member States, picking up 28 ratifications in its first year and another 30 by the end of 2000.

43. The ILO's child labour Conventions are supplemented by the International Programme for the Elimination of Child Labour (IPEC). This is a technical assistance programme, well financed by outside donors, which works in a growing number of countries around the world to combat child labour with the eventual goal of its total elimination.

E. Employment

44. Many Conventions have been adopted in the field of employment. The most important is the Employment Policy Convention, 1964 (No. 122), under which ratifying States (91 up to now) have to declare and pursue, as a major goal, an active policy designed to promote full, productive and freely chosen employment. The Convention was supplemented by a more detailed Recommendation No. 122, and the standards have been further supplemented by Recommendation No. 169 adopted in 1984. These standards are supplemented by active ILO technical assistance for employment stimulation and creation, with a recent emphasis on the creation of small- and medium-sized enterprises.

45. Other ILO instruments deal with the maintenance of *employment services* (Convention No. 88 of 1948), the *abolition of fee-charging employment agencies* (Convention No. 96 of 1949) and *private employment agencies* (Convention No. 181 of 1997), *vocational guidance and training* (Convention No. 142 of 1975) and *vocational rehabilitation and employment of the disabled* (Convention No. 159 of 1983). In 1998 the ILO adopted a new Recommendation on job creation in small and medium enterprises (Recommendation No. 189).

F. Wages

46. While the level of wages cannot be regulated internationally, various Conventions and Recommendations concerning minimum wage fixing machinery were adopted in 1928 and 1951. The most recent instruments on this question – Convention No. 131 and Recommendation No. 135 of 1970 – provide for a system of minimum wages to cover all groups of wage earners whose terms of employment are such that coverage would be appropriate. Protection in the payment of wages and the question of labour clauses in public contracts have been covered by instruments adopted in 1949. A Convention (No. 173) and a Recommendation (No. 180) concerning the protection of workers' claims in the event of employers' insolvency were adopted in 1992.

G.   General Conditions of Work

47. The first Convention adopted by the ILO, in 1919, was the Hours of Work (Industry) Convention (No. 1), which provided that, subject to exceptions, working hours should not exceed eight in the day and 48 in the week. Although not ratified by the major industrial countries, this Convention exercised a considerable influence. In 1935 the ILO adopted the Forty-Hour Week Convention (No. 47), and then a number of sectoral Conventions based on the standard of the 40-hour week. In 1962 the Reduction of Hours of Work Recommendation (No. 116) set the principle of the progressive reduction of normal hours of work with a view to attaining the social standard of the 40-hour week. Hours of work and rest in road transport are the subject of a Convention and a Recommendation adopted in 1979. Weekly rest of not less than 24 hours per week was provided for by a 1921 Convention (No. 14) relating to industry and by a 1957 Convention (No. 106) relating to commerce and offices. A 1957 Recommendation (No. 103) advocates that the period of rest be at least 36 hours.

48. The first Convention on holidays with pay (No. 52) was adopted in 1936 and provided for an annual holiday of at least six days. In 1954 a Recommendation (No. 98) set the standard at two weeks and in 1970 a revised Convention (No. 132) raised it to at least three weeks. In 1974 a Convention (No. 140) and a Recommendation (No. 148) made provision for paid educational leave.

49. The questions of workers' spare time, welfare facilities for workers and workers' housing have been dealt with in Recommendations of 1924, 1956, and 1961.

50. A Convention (No. 171) and a Recommendation (No. 178) of 1990 lay down conditions to be observed in regard to night work, including limitation of duration of such work and rest periods. They replace a number of earlier Conventions which prohibited night work for women, now an outmoded concept – see below, para. 58.

H. Occupational Safety and Health

51. A large number of instruments deal with safety and health at work. Some concern the general framework for policy, legislation and implementation of measures designed to secure occupational safety and health (Convention No. 155 and Recommendation No. 164 of 1981), the establishment of occupational health services (Convention No. 161 and Recommendation No. 171 of 1985) and prevention of major industrial accidents (Convention No. 174 and Recommendation No. 181 of 1993). Others deal with protection against risks or processes, such as radiation, benzene, carcinogenic agents or substances, asbestos, chemicals, dangerous machinery, air pollution, noise and vibration, or establish health and safety standards for particular branches of activity, such as commerce and offices, the construction industry, dock work, and work at sea. The Safety and Health in Mines Convention (No. 176) was adopted in 1995, and a new instrument on safety and health in agriculture is likely to be adopted in 2001.

52. Standards have also been established to provide compensation for injury due to occupational accidents and diseases. The most recent texts on this question are Convention No. 121 and Recommendation No. 121 of 1964 (with an expanded list of occupational diseases adopted in 1980). The system of compensation for occupational diseases provided for is based on lists of diseases which are to be considered as of occupational origin when contracted by workers in specified forms of work.

I. Social Security

53. Between 1919 and 1936, a series of instruments based on the concept of social insurance was adopted to protect given categories of workers against particular contingencies. Since 1944, the wider concept of social security has been adopted, aimed at providing a basic income to all in need of such protection, as well as comprehensive medical care. Comprehensive standards based on that approach were laid down in the Social Security (Minimum Standards) Convention, 1952 (No. 102). It deals with nine branches of social security: medical care, sickness benefit, unemployment benefit, old-age, invalidity and survivors' benefits, employment injury benefit, family benefit, and maternity benefit. Since then, further instruments establishing more advanced standards have been adopted in respect of all these branches except family benefit (Conventions Nos 121, 128, 130, and 168 of 1952, 1964, 1967, and 1988). The Maternity Protection Convention, 2000 (No. 183) is the most recent of these instruments. A general discussion on this will take place in 2001.

54. Standards have also been adopted with a view to ensuring equality of treatment of nationals and non-nationals in social security (Convention No. 118 of 1962 in respect of workmen's compensation for industrial accidents) and the maintenance of acquired rights and rights in course of acquisition in the nine branches of social security covered by Convention No. 102 (Convention No. 157 of 1982 and Recommendation No. 167 of 1983).

J. Social Policy

55. Several instruments relating to social policy as a whole were adopted (in particular Convention No. 117 of 1962) to encourage governments to pursue systematic action in this field. In 1977 the ILO Governing Body adopted a Tripartite Declaration of Principles concerning Multinational Enterprises and Social Policy.

K. Industrial Relations

56. In addition to the adoption of the Conventions on freedom of association, described above, the ILO has dealt – mainly in Recommendations – with various aspects of industrial relations, such as voluntary conciliation and arbitration, cooperation at the level of the undertaking, consultation at the industrial and national levels, and communications and examination of grievances in the undertaking. Standards relating to termination of employment by employers, originally dealt with in a Recommendation (No. 119) of 1963, are now laid down in a Convention (No. 158) and a Recommendation (No. 166) of 1982.

L. Employment of Women

57. In the field of employment of women, international action has been guided by two main considerations. Originally, the desire to protect women against excessively arduous conditions of work was the ruling factor. Subsequently, this was supplemented and partly replaced by the concern to ensure equality of rights and of treatment between women and men (see above). The basic ILO approach now is that women should be provided special protection only in so far as conditions of work place them specifically at risk with relation to reproduction.

58. One form of prohibition in earlier years concerned *night work in industry.* In addition to a 1906 Convention adopted before the ILO was established, three ILO Conventions dealt with the subject (1919, 1934, and 1948), successive revisions rendering the standards more flexible. A protocol to the 1948 Convention, adopted in 1990, permits more extensive derogations from the prohibition of night work by women. This is accompanied by the adoption of standards to regulate the conditions of night work for workers generally. Protective standards for women are also contained in the Conventions on *maternity protection* (No. 3 of 1919, No. 103 of 1952 and No. 183 of 2000) and on underground work in mines (No. 45 of 1935), as well as in certain Conventions dealing with occupational safety and health (e.g. lead poisoning, benzene, maximum weight for the manual transport of loads).

M. Older Workers

59. Recommendation No. 162 of 1980 laid down standards on equality of opportunity and treatment for older workers, on their protection in employment and on preparation for and access to retirement.

N. Migrant Workers

60. The principal instruments are the Migration for Employment Convention (Revised), 1949 (No. 97), and the Migrant Workers (Supplementary Provisions) Convention, 1975 (No. 143). The former provides for assistance and information to migrants for employment, for regulation of recruitment, and for granting to lawful immigrants treatment not less favourable than that applied to nationals in respect of labour matters and social security. The latter provides for the suppression of trafficking in migrant workers and of illegal employment of such workers, and for measures to promote equality of opportunity and treatment of migrant workers lawfully within the national territory. Both Conventions are supplemented by Recommendations. Instruments relating to the protection of the rights of foreign workers in the field of social security have been referred to in section I above. In a General Survey of 1998, the Committee of Experts found that these instruments had such a great level of detail that many States could not ratify them, and those that had could not apply all their provisions. The ILO Experts found that many of the same concerns applied to the United Nations Convention on the same subject, which has not yet received sufficient ratifications to enter into force. The Experts proposed that consideration be given to revising them in the fairly near future.

O. Other Special Categories of Workers

61. In general, ILO Conventions apply to all workers falling within their scope, irrespective of nationality, and a number expressly state this. In other cases, however, Conventions or Recommendations have been adopted to deal with particular problems arising in various areas.

62. More than 50 Conventions and Recommendations deal with various aspects of employment and social security of *seafarers*. They are adopted through a special procedure aimed at ensuring participation of the representatives of seafarers and shipowners (as workers and employers in this sector are known in the ILO), and there are special conditions for their entry into force. One Convention adopted in 1976 (No. 147) deals with the general question of minimum labour standards for merchant ships. Special standards have also been adopted in respect of fishermen and dockworkers.

63. A number of instruments deal with *workers in agriculture, and* extend to these workers the rules applying to industry, e.g. as regards rights of association and workmen's compensation (Conventions Nos. 11 and 12 of 1921). Others take into account the special features of work in agriculture. Special standards have been adopted for plantation workers (Convention No. 110 and Recommendation No. 110 of 1958 and a 1982 protocol to the Convention), and for tenants and share croppers (Recommendation No. 132 of 1968). As indicated above, a draft instrument on safety and health in agriculture will be before the 2001 Session of the Conference.

64. *Indigenous and tribal peoples* are protected under the Indigenous and Tribal Peoples Convention, 1989 (No. 169), which replaced Convention No. 107 of 1957 on the same subject. These standards were adopted in collaboration with the UN and other interested specialized agencies, and deal comprehensively with the situation of these peoples. The earlier standards had an integrationist approach, which was eliminated when the Convention was revised. Convention No. 169 provides for action to protect the rights of these peoples and to guarantee respect for their integrity, based on the principles of consultation and participation. A series of earlier Conventions which sought to protect indigenous workers primarily in dependent territories in regard to recruiting, long-term contracts and penal sanctions for breaches of employment contracts and to lay down special standards for workers in non-metropolitan territories with respect to social policy, rights of association, and labour inspection have now lost their pertinence and are proposed for abrogation.

65. Reference may also be made to Convention No. 149 and Recommendation No. 157 of 1977 relating to *nursing personnel*, to Convention No. 151 and Recommendation No. 159 of 1978 on labour relations in the *public service*, to Convention No. 175 and Recommendation No. 182 of 1994 concerning *part-time workers*, and to a series of other instruments on particular categories of workers.

P. Labour Administration

66. General provisions on the organization and functions of labour administration are laid down in the Labour Administration Convention (No. 150) and Recommendation (No. 158) of 1978. Standards relating to *labour inspection* are contained in Convention No. 81 of 1947 (for industry and commerce, with a protocol of 1995 to permit extension to the non-commercial services sector) and Convention No. 129 of 1969 (for agriculture) and their supplementary Recommendations. *Labour statistics* are dealt with in instruments of 1985 (Convention No. 160 and Recommendation No. 170), which revised earlier Conventions on the same subject.

67. Arrangements for tripartite consultations at the national level with respect to ILO standards, and regarding ILO activities more generally, are provided for in Convention No. 144 and Recommendation No. 152 of 1976.

IV. THE IMPLEMENTATION OF INTERNATIONAL LABOUR STANDARDS

A. Obligations in Respect of Standards

68. The ILO Constitution requires Member States, in all cases, to submit ILO Conventions and Recommendations to their competent authorities (normally the

legislature) within a year to 18 months of adoption, for consideration of implementing action and, in the case of Conventions, of ratification. They must also supply reports not only on Conventions which they have ratified but also, when requested by the Governing Body, on unratified Conventions and on Recommendations, to indicate the position of their law and practice, the difficulties encountered and future prospects. The latter reports yield a 'General Survey' by the Committee of Experts.

B.   Ratification of Conventions

69.   By ratification, a State undertakes to give effect to a Convention. The ratification of ILO Conventions cannot be accompanied by reservations, an exception to general international practice, though as indicated above there are flexibility clauses in many ILO Conventions which allow choices to be made at, or shortly following, ratification. At 31 December 2000, there had been 6,856 ratifications of ILO Conventions. Generally, a Convention enters into force after receipt of two ratifications. International labour Conventions and Recommendations are minimum standards and do not affect any law, custom or agreement which is more favourable for workers.

70.   Conventions can be denounced by States which have ratified them, usually at intervals of 10 years. In addition, ratification of a revising Convention results in the automatic denunciation of an older instrument on the same subject.

C.   Reports on Ratified Conventions

71.   Each State is required by the ILO Constitution to supply reports on the measures taken to give effect to ratified Conventions. Originally, reports were due each year on every ratified Convention, but with the increase in the number of Conventions and of ratifications, the reporting periodicity has been extended several times. Reports are now requested every two years on a group of twelve key Conventions dealing with freedom of association, non-discrimination, forced labour, child labour, employment policy, labour inspection, and tripartite consultation. For other Conventions, reports are in principle called for once in five years, but they can be requested at shorter intervals where the supervisory bodies note serious problems of application or when employers' or workers' organizations submit observations on difficulties of implementation.

D.   The Incorporation of International Conventions in
National Law as a Result of Ratification

72.   In a number of countries, the ratification of a Convention makes it part of national law and directly enforceable at the national level. However, to be applied effectively in such cases, a Convention must be self-executing. Most ILO Conventions are not drafted in this way, and require supplementary measures or regulations for their application.[15]

---

15.   *See* Virginia Leary, *International Labour Conventions and National Law*, The Hague, 1982.

V. The Supervisory Machinery of The ILO[16]

73. The ILO has established a diversified system of supervision. The existing procedures fall into two main groups, relying respectively on the examination of reports and on consideration of complaints.[17]

A. Procedures Based on the Examination of Periodic Reports

74. Most supervision takes place on the basis of regular reporting and dialogue with the ILO's supervisory bodies. The reports supplied by governments on the application of Conventions and of Recommendations are examined in the first instance by the *Committee of Experts on the Application of Conventions and Recommendations,* which is composed of 20 independent persons. The Committee's comments take the form either of 'observations' contained in its printed report or of 'direct requests' addressed directly to the governments concerned.[18] The Committee also prepares general surveys each year on one or several related Conventions and Recommendations. The reports of the Committee of Experts are submitted to a tripartite *Committee on the Application of Conventions and Recommendations* at each session of the International Labour Conference. This body discusses with the representatives of the governments concerned selected cases of important discrepancies noted by the Committee of Experts. In 1968, a procedure of 'direct contacts' was introduced, under which representatives of the ILO visit countries with the agreement of the governments concerned to discuss difficulties in the implementation of ILO standards. This procedure has been applied to some hundreds cases since then. At times, it has also involved extensive fact-finding. Since the Committee began keeping records of this kind in 1964, it has recorded over 2,200 cases, concerning more than 150 countries or territories, in which governments have taken measures in direct response to comments by the supervisory bodies. Many more such instances are recorded of measures taken in order to allow ratification, or to improve application without the prompting of the ILO.

B. Procedures Based on the Examination of Complaints

75. The ILO Constitution makes provision for two kinds of contentious procedures. The procedure of *complaint* under article 26 of the ILO Constitution allows complaints to be filed by any member State against another member State on the application of a Convention which both have ratified. This procedure may also be initiated by the Governing Body on receipt of a complaint from a delegate to the Conference or on its own motion *(inter alia,* when seized of a representation by an employers' or workers' organization under the procedure described below). In nine

---

16. Complete details can be found in *Handbook of Procedures relating to International Labour Conventions and Recommendations,* Geneva, ILO, 1998, available also online under ILOLEX (see next note).
17. They are supplemented by the non-supervisory promotional procedures provided for under the 1998 Declaration.
18. All the Committee's observations, as well as the rest of the supervisory material mentioned here, are contained in the interactive data base *ILOLEX,* available on-line or on CD-ROM.

cases, the Governing Body has appointed a Commission of Inquiry to investigate the issues. Some of the more recent of these cases concerned the employment of Haitian workers on sugar plantations in the Dominican Republic (1983), trade union rights in Poland (1984), employers' organizing rights in Nicaragua (1990), political discrimination in public service employment in the Federal Republic of Germany (1987) and discrimination, particularly against minorities, in Romania (1991). A complaint filed in 1996, following the examination of earlier representations, alleged massive forced labour in Myanmar, and the Commission of Inquiry found that these allegations were amply justified. Commissions of Inquiry receive written submissions, hear witnesses and, when necessary, make on-the-spot visits. A number of other complaints have been referred to the Committee on Freedom of Association (see below) or were the subject of an agreed settlement reached with the assistance of the ILO.

76.   The Myanmar case referred to above led in June 2000 to the first instance of the ILO's use of article 33 of the Constitution, which provides that the Governing Body may propose to the Conference 'such measures as it may deem wise and expedient' to secure observance of the findings of a Commission of Inquiry.[19] The ILO continues to follow up this case.

77.   *Representations* may be made under article 24 of the Constitution by employers' or workers' organizations on the ground that a State does not secure the application of a ratified Convention. They are considered by a three-member committee of the Governing Body, and then by the Governing Body itself. Fewer than 100 representations have been submitted during the existence of the ILO, since 1919, but 23 were submitted in the years 1993–95. The pace has slowed down somewhat since then, but the striking increase in recourse to this procedure in recent times appears to reflect growing difficulties in numerous countries in securing observance of ratified Conventions.

C.   Special Machinery in the Field of Freedom of Association[20]

78.   In the field of freedom of association special machinery was set up by the ILO in 1950, in agreement with the Economic and Social Council of the United Nations, for examination of complaints by governments or by employers' or workers' organizations. Since the procedure draws its authority from the ILO Constitution, it may be invoked against States which have not ratified the freedom of association Conventions. The machinery comprises two bodies:

The *Committee On Freedom of Association*[21] is a tripartite body of nine members, appointed by the Governing Body from among its members and presided over by an

---

19. See Provisional Record 6–4, International Labour Conference, 88th Session, Geneva, 2000 – to be published in time in the *Proceedings of the International Labour Conference* for this Session.
20. *See* ILO, *Procedure for the Examination of Complaints Alleging Infringement of Trade Union Rights*, 1985; ILO, *Law on Freedom of Association: Standards and Procedures*, 1995.
21. *See* von Potobsky, 'Protection of Trade Union Rights – twenty Years' Work by the Committee on Freedom of Association', *International Labour Review*, April 1972, pp. 69–83; A.J. Pouyat, 'The ILO's Freedom of Association Standards and Machinery: A Summing Up', *op. cit.*, May–June 1982, pp. 287–302.

independent person. It has dealt with some 2,000 cases on a wide range of issues. While generally basing itself on written submissions, it may in appropriate cases hear representatives of the parties and also resort to the procedure of direct contacts, mentioned above. Such visits have taken place to a large number of countries, including Argentina, Canada, Chile, Colombia, Cuba, Ethiopia, Nicaragua, Paraguay, Poland, Surinam, Tunisia, Turkey, and others.

The *Fact-Finding and Conciliation Commission*,[22] composed of independent persons, may undertake more extensive investigations, similar to a commission of inquiry. A case may not be referred to the Commission without the consent of the government concerned, and in the early years, several governments refused to give their consent. Subsequently, a number have done so, but if the governments concerned have ratified the Conventions the tendency is to have resort to the article 26 procedure which does not require consent. The most important cases concerned Japan (1966), Chile (1975), and South Africa (1992). The Commission may consider cases concerning States that are not Members of the ILO but are Members of the UN, as happened with regard to South Africa and the United States (during a brief withdrawal).

D. Special Studies and Inquiries, Promotional Measures, Technical Cooperation

79. Apart from the established ILO supervisory procedures, various *ad hoc* studies and inquiries have been undertaken by the ILO in the field of labour standards. Many have concerned freedom of association, either as regards the situation in given countries or regions or as regards ILO member countries as a whole. Investigations and studies in the field of forced labour took place from 1951 to 1959. Missions of ILO officials have visited Israel and the occupied Arab territories every year since 1978 to consider and make recommendations concerning the situation of Arab workers of these territories. For 30 years, until 1994, there were regular reports on the situation of workers under apartheid. Implementation of ILO standards is also sought through technical cooperation, training, and seminars. Experts on international labour standards form part of ILO multidisciplinary teams that advise member States in the various regions.

VI. SUPERVISORY MACHINERY ESTABLISHED BY OTHER ORGANIZATIONS

80. Other international organizations, in particular the United Nations, UNESCO and regional organizations, have established a great variety of more or less elaborate supervisory procedures for the implementation of the instruments adopted by them. In many instances, these arrangements derive not from the constitutional instrument of the organization, but from the provisions of the respective Conventions – in particular, the 'treaty bodies' which supervise the implementation of six basic human rights conventions of the United Nations. Generally, supervision is based on the

---

22. *See* ILO, *Digest of Decisions of the Freedom of Association Committee of the Governing Body of the ILO*, Fourth Edition, 1996.

supply of reports by government and their examination by different expert bodies, but provision is also made for inter-State or individual complaints, particularly in the case of the European and American Conventions on Human Rights and the International Covenant on Civil and Political Rights. The arrangements under the European Social Charter for examination of periodic reports, are largely based on the ILO system.

SELECT BIBLIOGRAPHY

ILO, *International Labour Conventions and Recommendations 1991–1995* (instruments are also published in the ILO *Official Bulletin* and available as offprints).
– *International Labour Standards,* Report of the Director-General, Part 1. *International Labour Conference*, 70th Session, 1984.
– *The Impact of International Labour Conventions and Recommendations*, 1986.
– *ILO Law on Freedom of Association: Standards and Procedures*, 1995.
D. Harris, *The European Social Charter*, Charlottesville, 1984.
C.W. Jenks, *Human Rights and International Labour Standards*, New York, 1960.
E.A. Landy, *The effectiveness of International Supervision – Thirty Years of ILO Experience*, New York, 1966.
H. Bartolomei de la Cruz, G. von Potobsky, and L. Swepston, *The International Labour Organization – the International Standards System and Human Rights*, Boulder, Colorado, and Oxford, 1996.
W. Sengenberger and D. Campbell (ed.), *International Labour Standards and Economic Interdependence*, Geneva, 1994.
N. Valticos and G. von Potobsky, *International Labour Law*, Deventer, 2nd ed., 1994.
N. Valticos, *Droit international du travail*, Paris, 2nd ed., 1983.

Chapter 8.   The European Union and Employment Law*

R. Blanpain

I.   INTRODUCTORY REMARKS

1.   There is no doubt that the European Union (EU) has extremely high ambitions regarding employment and social policies. The successive European Treaties, including the Amsterdam Treaty, include ambitious goals, like:

- A high level of employment and social protection;
- Equal treatment;
- Improved living and working conditions;
- Proper social protection;
- Social dialogue;
- Upwards harmonization;
- Combating of social exclusion.

2.   Notwithstanding that the different national system of labour law are confronted with the same challenges within the large European common market, such as globalization of the economy, new technologies and the like, they remain widely divergent and will continue to do so. The diversity is greater than is usually realized.

3.   Indeed, some system are very formal (e.g. Germany), other rather informal (e.g. Italy). Great divergence can also be found in the degree of organization, trade union structure and trade union ideology. The same goes for the role and the structure of employers' associations. May be the most divergent factor lies in the difference in legal culture between various countries, especially regarding the role of legislation and collective bargaining. Continental European countries tend to be legal interventionist, the UK not, while the Scandinavian countries favour collective bargaining to regulate conditions of work.

4.   An equally striking difference concerns the legally binding effect of collective agreements. In the UK, collective agreements are in principle not legally binding, while they are binding in continental countries and even can be extended by a

---

*   *See* Blanpain R., *European Labour Law*, 7th and revised ed., Kluwer, The Hague, 2000, p. 548.

Governmental measure to all employees and employers of a given sector of activity or a country as a whole.

The role of Governments in employment relations, particularly in the area of income policies is another topical example. In certain countries income policies limit the freedom of collective bargaining, like in Belgium. In other countries, like Germany, income policies might be unconstitutional.

One can go on. Diversity is the general rule and this will stay so. In other words, there is no European system of employment law or industrial relations. The systems are mainly national and will remain so for a long time to come. This will even be more so when the EU will composed of some 28 odd Member States.

II. Competences Regarding Labour and Employment Matters

5.   The EU competences regarding labour law and employment matters are limited to the powers conferred by the Treaty upon the Community. These must be exercised by taking the principles of subsidiarity and proportionality into account. This means that the Community shall take action only if and insofar as the objectives of the proposed action cannot be sufficiently achieved by the Member States and can therefore, by reason of the scale or effects of the proposed action, be better achieved by the Community. Any action of the Community shall not go beyond what is necessary to achieve the objectives of this Treaty.

A.   Legislative Competence

6.   The Treaty allows the Community to formulate regulations, directives or recommendations with either unanimity of the votes in the Council of Ministers, or with qualified majority. Some matters are excluded from the competence of the Community regarding social matters.

1. Qualified Majority

7.   This concerns following matters:

– Health and safety;
– Working conditions;
– Information and consultation;
– Equal treatment between men and women with regard to labour market opportunities and work;
– Integration of excluded persons.

2. Unanimous Voting

8.   This concerns following matters:

– Social security and social protection of workers;
– Job security;

– Representation and collective defence of the interests of workers and employers, including co-determination;
– Third country nationals;
– Financial contributions for promoting employment.

To this has to be added to power of the Council take appropriate action to combat discrimination based on sex, racial or ethnic origin, religion or belief, disability, age or sexual orientation (art. 13 TEC) and that unanimity is also necessary when decisions are made relating to the rights, and interests of employed persons (art. 95 TEC).

3. Excluded Matters

9.   This concerns following matters:

– Pay;
– Right of association;
– Right to strike;
– Right to impose lockouts.

B.   *Guidelines and Peer Pressure: Employment Policies*

10.   In the area of employment the TEC cannot take measures, which would lead to the harmonisation of Community legislation. The Member States are in the first place competent as regards employment policy. The role of the EU is merely suppletive. A European coordinated employment strategy is provided for.
European strategy shall consist of:

– drawing up guidelines;
– writing annual reports;
– adopting incentive measures;
– exchanging information and best practices;
– promoting innovative practices and recourse to pilot projects; and
– making non-binding recommendations.

National policies consist of:

– implementing the European guidelines; and
– drafting of annual reports to the Council.

C.   *The European Social Fund*

11.   The European Social Fund aims to improve employment opportunities for workers in the internal market and to contribute thereby to raising the standard of living; and to render the employment of workers easier and to increase their geographical and occupational mobility within the Community, and to facilitate their adaptation to industrial changes and to changes in production systems, in particular through vocational training and retraining. The Fund spend some 47 billion ECU between the 15 Member States for the period 1994–1999, which amounts to almost 10 per cent of the EU-budget.

III. THE ROLE OF SOCIAL PARTNERS: CONSULTATION AND COLLECTIVE BARGAINING

12. The role of the social partners bas been dramatically enhanced at the occasion of the Treaties of Maastricht and Amsterdam: from consultation with the European Community regarding the implementation of Community directives to collective bargaining at European level. In consequence the social partners are titled to real involvement in the shaping of European labour law from the initial certain countries where this is legally possible, in the implementation of Council directives. At the same time a stronger legal basis has been id for European-wide collective bargaining and mechanisms were introduced, ensuring a binding effect of European collective agreements erga omnes.

The social partners can conclude collective agreements, which if they fall within the social competence of the Community can be legally binding by the Council by way of a Council Directive. This means that the social partners are part of the legislative framework within the EC.

13. It is the Commission, which has the task of promoting the consultation of the social partners at Community level, and will take any relevant measure to facilitate their *dialogue*. To this end before submitting proposals in the social policy field the Commission consults management and labour on the possible direction of Community action. If, after such consultation, the Commission considers Community action advisable, it consults the social partners on the content of the envisaged proposal. The partners forward to the Commission an opinion or, where appropriate, a recommendation. On the occasion of such consultation the social partners may inform the Commission of their wish conclude an agreement on the matters under discussion. The duration of the procedure shall not exceed nine months, unless the social partners and the Commission decide jointly to extend it. If an agreement is concluded it can be made, as indicated, early generally binding by way of a Community Directive.

14. At present three inter-industry-wide European agreements have been concluded, namely:

– on parental leave (14 December 1995);
– part-time work (6 June 1997); and
– fixed term contract (18 March 1999).

15. The social partners which are involved in the process of negotiation are: UNICE, CEEP for the employers and the ETUC for the workers. Needless to say that other 'social partners' are anxious to join the club. When this seemed impossible UEAPME introduced a request to the European Court. This way UEAPME wanted to obtain its recognition as a full-fledged European Social Partner. UEAPME is of the opinion that it has the right, as the representative of the SMEs in Europe, to participate in the negotiating and conclusion of European-wide collective agreements.

The Court (1998), however, refuted UEAPME's claim on the following grounds: according to the standing European law, no one of the social partners has a right to participate in the negotiations. Moreover, UNICE also has SMEs amongst its members. So, the Court concluded, these enterprises are adequately represented. It will surprise no one, after what we said above, that we deeply regret this judgment. First, from a democratic point of view. Indeed, one expects from the social partners that they replace in a sense the democratically elected EP in this legislative process. How then can the Court refuse UEAPME at the table of negotiations, since it organizes the larger part of the SMEs? Also from the point of view of employment, the Court's decision has to be rejected. Indeed, everyone recognizes that it are the SMEs, which are the job creators par excellence, and yet they are kept at length. It is, however, especially in the area of fundamental social rights that this judgment is totally inadequate. The right to collectively bargain is a fundamental right, belonging to the core of fundamental rights laid down by the ILO. The already mentioned Conventions 1987 and 1998 deal explicitly with freedom of association and collective bargaining. All EU Member States, as well as the national social partners, belong to the ILO. The ILO Conventions, moreover, are a part of the general principles of law, the Court has to respect and apply. In other words, when criteria for representativity are not clearly spelled out at European level, the Court had to look for inspiration in the ILO Conventions. The ILO has repeatedly id that the criteria of representativity need to be objectives precise and known forehand. The Court should have directed the Commission to establish these criteria and to respect them. Pending legal procedures introduced by UEAPME concerning the directives implementing framework agreements have however been put to an end according to an operation agreement concluded between UNICE and UEAPME, 12 November 1998.

IV. THE EMU: A SCENARIO FOR SOCIAL DUMPING AND A DUAL SOCIETY

A. *Macro-economic: Inflation and NAIRU*

16. The EMU intends to maintain a non-inflationary economy. Such an economy presupposes a certain degree of unemployment. So it is that a certain level of increasing unemployment is 'the instrument' to contain inflationary tendencies.

The EMU approach translates a certain economic vision, represented by the Chicago school, favouring supply-side economics, which has gradually conquered the world since the beginning of the 1970s, first the UK and the USA, then Western Europe and later Latin- America, Africa, Asia and since the beginning of the 1990s, Central and Eastern Europe.

Supply-side economics are not – in contrast to the economy policy inspired by Keynes – centred on demand and full employment, but directed at the control of inflation. This theory accepts a so-called national degree of unemployment, which is, so the argument goes, mainly the consequence of structural rigidities on the labour market. When inflation is threatening to accelerate, the (Independent) Central Bank will intervene and eventually raise the interest rate. This has a negative effect on employment.

The idea is that the economy will become overheated when unemployment is too low. The leading economic school is of the opinion that accelerating inflation is unavoidable unless a certain number of workers are unemployed. The minimum employment needed to check inflation, is called NAIRU, which stands for 'non-accelerating inflation rate of unemployment'. The minimum is not a standard, but differs from period to period and from country to country.

17. The use of unemployment as a weapon to contain inflation is a blunt instrument and leads to lasting- and great damage. Certain enterprises close down,]machines become idle, and investment decreases. Bankruptcies are on the increase. Long-term unemployed workers become unemployable and are no longer fit to work.

Moreover, the acceleration of inflation can have many different causes. Price rises can be a consequence of the increased retribution of public services, like transport, or of the increase of taxes on wine or on tobacco or of certain services, like medical services, which are also determined by the government, or have to do with the rising price of petroleum, which is imported.

In short, enterprises and workers are often the innocent victims of anti-inflationary policies, when in fact they are not responsible at all for the eventual acceleration of inflation, as the price of the goods/services they produce may have diminished and inflation goes up for reasons, which have nothing to do with their behaviour on the labour markets.

When financial credit becomes more expensive, 'cross-sectionally, small companies that do not have significant buffer-stock cash holdings are most likely to trim their investment ... around the periods of tight money.' Nevertheless, it is argued that employment will be especially created by SMEs.

B.   Flexibility

18. Micro-economic supply-side economics are intended to free enterprises from certain regulatory constraints by providing enterprises with more flexibility, so as to promote economic growth and consequently create more jobs. Protective labour measures, such as a minimum wage, working time restrictions, dismissals and others are looked upon as hindrances to growth and should be done away with.

Labour cost especially has to go down. The worker has to be paid according to, and in relation to, the economic value that he adds in the process.

It is up to the Member States and their national social partners to see that the necessary flexibility is introduced. In any case, they have no other choice, as the market forces will oblige them to do so anyway.

19. The fact that social policy in the EU remains mainly a national affair means that social dumping – the deliberate attraction of investment on the basis of lower wage costs and lower working conditions – is not only accepted, but globally, and on a European scale, intentionally organized as the way to enforce more flexibility. The market will play in full: the more expensive operators will have to give up, unless they succeed in becoming cheaper, which means reducing the cost of their operations.

In a global, market driven economy, services and goods have to become continuously better and cheaper. This means, that enterprises will invest in those countries where costs are the lowest. There are, certainly, other factors, which come into play when companies decide to invest, but labour costs may be an important one. Consequently, European nations competing with each other will also do their utmost to diminish labour costs because everyone else is doing it. So, the trend is downwards, and is the direction that the social harmonization in Europe will go in.

It is similar to a theatre. When spectators on the first row stand up in order to see the stage better, the others have to get up in order to see something and then the benefit the first standing spectators had, is done away with. So it is with the downward spiral of wages and labour conditions. Labour cost must be reduced; others do the same, and again the former countries are no longer competitive. So, they downsize their costs even more; this means more restructuring, relocations, and more machines to replace workers, more dismissals. It is clear that national social systems cannot stand on their own and must yield in the face of a fierce globalized market economy. They have to give way to the lowest social denominator.

C. An Evaluation

20. The European employment strategy can be summarized in three main points.

The first is the goal of achieving and maintaining a non-accelerating inflation role of employment (NAIRU).

The second is a generalized flexibility of wages and labour conditions, which introduces job insecurity in the lives of many workers as a strategic element to contain inflation.

And the third point is the organization of an ongoing competitive battle, which will be waged between the national social and fiscal systems of the Member States in and outside the EU. A country with high wage costs or which spends more on social policies than others will become less competitive. This means a kind of institutionalized social dumping between the EU Member States themselves and outside the EU.

Europe has no 'core' social competencies, which could bring about a real European social policy, including a proper employment strategy, which would involve wages, working conditions – e.g. job security – and social security, being based on fundamental social rights, European minimum standards.

Such a policy will only be possible when the EU has the competence to make decisions, including about 'core' matters and fiscal affairs, with a qualified majority.

What things are about now is a harmonization downwards and not 'while the improvement is being maintained' as Article 136, rather naively promises.

Obviously, inflation has to be kept under control, as well as public finances. But, is it conceivable that Europe is riot empowered to take appropriate social measures to combat unemployment and establish minimum standards? That a European collective agreement concerning pay would have no proper European legal status? That a European minimum wage will never be possible and that even the idea of a European social security system could always be countered by the veto of one Member State?

21. In short, the TEC beyond Amsterdam is much more than a choice or a preference for a free market economy, with which most will agree. It is a definite and final choice for a certain type of ultra-liberal (conservative) policy, which precludes almost forever, a proper European social policy, employment included. Once the Treaty of Amsterdam is ratified, this political choice will indeed become quasi-eternal.

V. THE 'ACQUIS COMMUNAUTAIRE'

A. In General

22. European labour law sets a framework, leaving a lot of room for national developments. The main point covered by European labour law relate to:

- free movement of workers (art. 39 TEC);
- individual employment contracts (1991);
- protection of young people at work (1994);
- equal treatment (art. 141 TEC and 5 directives);
- motherhood (1992);
- working time (1993);
- safety and health (art. 137 TEC and directives);
- collective redundancies (1975–1992–1998);
- transfer of undertakings (1997–1998);
- insolvency of the employer (1980);
- European works councils (1994);
- parental leave (1996);
- posting of workers (1996);
- part-time (1997);
- reversal of the proof in case of discrimination (1997); and
- fixed term contracts.

Let us consider some of the most important issues.

B. Free Movement of Workers

23. Freedom of movement constitutes a fundamental right of workers and their families. It is however not an autonomous, but a purposeful right within the framework of the economic objectives of the Community; this right is only conferred for reasons of the performing of an economic activity. It is a contribution to the economic needs of the Member States.

'Mobility of labour is looked upon as one of the means by which the worker is guaranteed the possibility of improving his living and working conditions and promoting his social advancement, while helping to satisfy the requirements of the economies of the Member States.'

It should be underlined that Article 39 TEC concerning the free movement of workers has a *direct effect* on the legal orders of the Member States and confers on individuals rights which national courts must protect.' Article 39, however, does not aim to restrict the power of the Member States to lay down restrictions within their own territory on the freedom of movement of all persons subject to their jurisdiction in the implementation of domestic criminal law.'

In order to be truly effective, the right of workers to be engaged and employed without discrimination necessarily entails as a corollary the employer's entitlement to engage them in accordance with the rules governing freedom of movement for workers. The rule of equal treatment can be relied upon as well by a worker as by an employer.'

Free movement of workers entails the right to work in another Member State under the same conditions as national workers; it includes the right to move freely within the territory of Member States for this purpose and the right to stay in a Member State. The number pf EU nationals resident in another Member State is only 5.5 million out of 370 million. There are also some 12.5 million third country nationals.

24. The Court has ruled consistently that the notion 'worker' in Article 39 of the TEC has a Community meaning in law. The term 'worker' and 'an activity as an employed person' may not be defined by reference to the national laws of the Member States. If that were the case, the Community rules on free 'movement for workers would be frustrated, as the meanings of those terms could be fixed and modified unilaterally, without any control by the Community institutions, by national laws which would thus be able to exclude at will certain categories of persons from the benefit of the Treaty.'

'It is appropriate therefore, in order to determine their meaning, to have recourse to the generally recognized principles of interpretation, beginning with the ordinary meaning to be attributed to those terms in their context and in light of the objectives of the Treaty.' In this respect, it must be stressed that the terms 'worker' and 'activity as an employed person' define the field of application of one of the fundamental freedoms guaranteed by the Treaty and, as such, may not be interpreted restrictively.

'Nevertheless, a person who has worked only as a self-employed person before becoming unemployed cannot be classified as a 'worker' within the meaning of Article 39 of the Treaty, not even when the person concerned previously worked as an employed person.'

25. The concept of 'worker' must, the Court rightly ruled, be defined in accordance with objective criteria, which distinguish the employment relationship, by reference to the rights and duties of the persons concerned. The essential feature of an employment relation, however, is the fact that for a certain period of time a person performs services for and under the direction of another person in return for which he receives remuneration.' The Court therefore retained three criteria: (1) performance of services (2) in subordination for (3) remuneration.

26. The job has to have an economic nature within the meaning of Article 2 of the TEC. Consequently, the Court ruled that the practice of sport is subject to Community law only insofar as it constitutes an economic activity in the meaning of Article 2.'

'This applies to the activities of professional or semi-professional football players, who are in the nature of gainful employment or remunerated service.'

It follows logically that:

'where such players are nationals of a Member State they benefit in all the other Member States from the provisions of Community law concerning freedom of movement of persons and of provision of services. However, those provisions do not prevent the adoption of rules or of a practice excluding foreign players from participation in certain matches for reasons which are not of an economic nature, which relate to the particular nature and context of such matches and are thus of sporting interest only, such as, for example, matches between national teams from different countries.'

Community law is also applicable to football trainers.' There is no need to underline that the free movement of professional soccer players is *defacto* not respected given the restrictions imposed upon players for reasons of nationality on one hand and the systems of blockade which operate in the case of a transfer of players from one club to another, at international as well as national level on the other hand. Fifa and Uefa, which have set up international cartels to monopolize professional soccer on a worldwide basis, are violating Community law relating to competition in general and to Articles 81 and 82 of the TEC in particular.

27.   This was more than confirmed in the *Bosman* Case (1995), where the Court of Justice did justice, which was more than overdue in sports, especially regarding the transfer system in which sportsmen, especially soccer players were – and still are outside the EU – treated like cattle which can be sold and bought. The Court reaffirmed that free movement of workers applies to professional sports and that it constitutes a fundamental right. Transfer systems designed to block players and nationality clauses limiting EU players to be lined up are contrary to Article 39. This landmark decision is a marvellous example of the contribution of European law to human rights and human dignity.

C.   Equal Treatment for Men and Women

28.   Here, The EC played an important role, first by adopting Article 141 in the EC Treaty, which contains the principle of equal pay for equal work, and consequently by adopting several directives:

– 1975: relating to the application of equal pay for men and women;'
– 1976: relating to the implementation of the principle of equal treatment for men and women as regards access to employment, vocational training and promotion, and working conditions;'
– 1978: concerning the progressive implementation of the principle of equal treatment for men and women in matters of social security;
– 1986: on the implementation of the principle of equal treatment for men and women in occupational social security schemes;'
– 1997: on the burden of proof in cases of discrimination based on sex.

One has also to mention the role of the Court of Justice, which has tremendously enhanced the principle of non-discrimination.

29.   Article 141 is part of the social objectives of the Community aimed at social progress, as laid down in the preamble preceding the Treaty. The Court has repeatedly stated that the respect for fundamental personal human rights is one of the general principles of Community law, the observance of which it has a duty to ensure. There can be no doubt that the elimination of discrimination based on sex forms part of those fundamental rights.' It is part of the foundation of the Community. In particular, since Article 141 appears in the context of the harmonization of working conditions while improvement is being maintained, the objection that the terms of this article may be observed in no other way than by raising the lowest salaries must be set aside.' It is clear that the 6 instruments, namely, Article 141 and the

5 directives, form one body of rules that are complementary to each other and fortify each other.

Article 141 and the directives have a general scope of application, which follows from the nature of the principle of equal treatment, and thus apply to the private sector as well as to the public sector,' and to the self-employed.

30. Community law prohibits direct and indirect discrimination: direct on grounds of sex, indirect when other criteria are used, which are *prima facie* objective and acceptable, but *defacto* lead to a discriminatory treatment of one sex.

31. Exceptions to the rule of equal treatment relate to:

– the nature of the activity;
– protection of women; and
– positive discrimination.

32. The possibilities for positive discrimination are enhanced in the new Article 141, 4 TEC, which reads as follows: 'with a view to ensuring full equality in practice between men and women in working life, the principle of equal treatment shall not prevent any Member State from maintaining or adopting measures providing for specific advantages in order to make it easier for the underrepresented sex to pursue a vocational activity or to prevent or compensate for disadvantages in professional careers.' A Declaration attached to the Treaty of Amsterdam clarifies that the Member States in adopting such measures have to aim in the first place at the improvement of the situation of women in employment and occupation.

33. Article 141 of the TEC concerns equal pay equal work or work of equal value. The notion, pay' in the meaning of Article 141 and the equal treatment directives belongs to advanced legal technology.

34. This was confirmed in *Douglas Harvey Barber v. Guardian Royal Exchange Group* (1990), which related to Barber's right to an early retirement pension on his being made compulsory redundant. Barber's conditions provided that, in the event of redundancy, members of the pension fund established by the Guardian were entitled to an immediate pension subject to having attained the age of 55 for men and 50 for women. Staff who did not fulfil those conditions received certain cash benefits calculated on the basis of their years of service and a deferred pension payable at the normal pensionable age, which was fixed at 62 for men and 57 for women. Barber was made redundant when he was aged 52. The Guardian paid him the cash benefits provided for in the severance terms, the statutory redundancy payment and the *ex-gratia* payment. He would have been entitled to a retirement pension as from the date of his 62nd birthday. It was undisputed that a woman in the same position as Mr. Barber would have received an immediate retirement pension as well as the statutory redundancy payment and that the total value of those benefits would have been greater than the amount paid to Mr. Barber. Therefore, Barber contended that he was discriminated against.

35. In deciding this case the Court took a number of important decisions on principle, while confirming some others:

1. The fact that certain benefits are paid after the termination of the employment relationship does not prevent them from being in the nature of pay, within the meaning of Article 141 of the EC Treaty;'
2. Compensation in connection with redundancy constitutes a form of pay to which the worker is entitled in respect of his employment and which is paid to him upon the termination of his employment relationship, whether it is paid under a contract of employment, by virtue of legislative provisions or on a voluntary basis;
3. Unlike the benefits awarded by national statutory social security schemes, a pension paid under a contracted-out scheme constitutes consideration paid by the employer to the worker in respect of his employment and therefore falls within the scope of Article 141;
4. It is contrary to Article 141 to impose an age condition which differs according to sex in respect of pensions paid under a contracted-out scheme, even if the difference between the pensionable age for men and that for women is based on the one provided for by the national statutory scheme;
5. The Court emphasized the fundamental importance of transparency and, in particular, of the possibility of a review by the national courts, in order to prevent and, if necessary, eliminate any discrimination based on sex;
6. If the national courts are under the obligation to make an assessment and a comparison of all the various types of consideration granted, according to the circumstances, to men and women, juridical review would be difficult and the effectiveness of Article 141 would be diminished as a result. It follows that genuine transparency permitting an effective review is assured only if the principle of equal pay applies to each of the elements of remuneration granted to men or women;
7. The Court held that, according to its established case-law, Article 141 applies directly to all forms of discrimination which can be identified solely with the aid of the criteria of equal work and equal pay referred to by the article in question, without national or Community measures being required to define them with greater precision in order to permit their application;
8. The direct effect of Article 141 may not be relied upon to claim entitlement to a pension, with effect from a date prior to that of his judgment, except in the case of workers or those claiming for them who have before that date initiated legal proceedings or raised an equivalent claim under the then applicable law.

36. Directive No. 76/207 of 9 February 1976 aims at the implementation of the principle of equal treatment as regards access to employment, vocational training and promotion, and working conditions. This includes selection criteria for access to all jobs or posts, whatever the sector or branch of activity, and to all levels of the occupational hierarchy, as well as to vocational guidance, vocational training, advanced vocational training, and retraining; these must be accessible on the basis of the same criteria and at the same levels without any discrimination on grounds of sex. It is interesting to note that offers of employment do not fall within the scope of the directive. Equal treatment relates also to dismissals.

37. Council Directive 97/80 of 15 December 1997 deals with the burden of proof in cases of discrimination based on sex.' The directive reverses the proof provided the plaintiff establishes the fact from which it may be presumed that there has been direct or indirect discrimination.

38. On 17 July 1996, the European Commission adopted a code of practice concerning the application of equal pay for women and men for work of equal value. The aim of this code is:

(i) to provide concrete advice to employers and partners in the collective bargaining carried out at the level of the enterprise (sectoral and intersectoral) to ensure application of the principle 'equal pay for equal work' in all its elements; and
(ii) eliminate discrimination based on sex when the remuneration structures are based on systems of classification and evaluation of employment.

Designed in close collaboration with social partners, this code reflects as much as possible the approach proposed by them, i.e. a short code intended to be applied:

(i) in a voluntary and effective fashion and able to be used during the different phases of the collective negotiation; and
(ii) at the work place in the public and private sector.

Employers are encouraged to follow the recommendations contained therein by adapting them to the dimension and structure of their companies.

D.   *Restructuring of Enterprises*

39. During the 1970s, called by some the golden years for European labour law, three directives were adopted which were intended to protect the workers against the functioning of the common market. I remember from the discussions we had in the group of experts on labour law from the different Member States that the reasoning underlying those directives was the following: there is a larger market with an increase in scale to which the undertakings will have to adapt themselves; this means: restructuring, mergers, takeovers, collective dismissals, and bankruptcies. Indeed, it was said, the worker should not have to pay the price for the establishment of a common, bigger market; rather the worker should be protected against the social consequences of this restructuring. On the basis of this reasoning, three directives were proposed and, also due to the then political composition of the Council, adopted. These directives relate respectively to collective redundancies (1975), the transfer of undertakings or parts thereof (1977) and the insolvency of the employer (1980). One will notice, when analysing these directives, that the managerial prerogative concerning economic decisions remains intact. In short, the directives only address the social consequences of restructuring.

1. Collective Redundancies

40. Information concerning the collective redundancies must be given beforehand. This means before the decision is taken. The text of Article 2, § 1 is clear on

169

this point: it concerns an employer who is *contemplating* collective redundancies. The directive explicitly mentions that the employer has to consult the workers' representatives in good *time*. The directive only applies when the employer projects collective redundancies.

The purpose of the information is to enable the workers' representatives to make constructive proposals. The employer shall at least notify them of the reasons of the projected redundancies, the number of categories of workers to be made redundant; the number or categories of workers normally employed; the period over which the projected redundancies are to be effected; the criteria proposed for the selection of the workers and the method for calculating any redundancy payment (other than those arising out of national legislation and/or practice).

The directive holds irrespective whether the decision regarding collective redundancies is being taken by the employer or by an undertaking controlling the employer (Articles 2, 4). In considering alleged breaches of the information and consultation duties account shall not be taken of any defence on the part of the employer that the necessary information has not been provided to him by the undertaking, which took the decision leading to collective redundancies. The employer is obliged to consult the worker's representatives with a view to reaching an agreement. This is a very strong form of consultation, which is very close to collective bargaining. The consultations must cover ways and means of avoiding collective redundancies or reducing the number of workers affected, and of mitigating the consequences.

2. Transfer of Undertakings and Acquired Rights

41.   Directive No. 77/187 relates to the safeguarding of employees' rights in the event of transfers of undertakings, businesses or parts of businesses.' The purpose of the directive is to ensure that the rights of employees are safeguarded in the event of a change of employer by enabling them to remain in employment with the new employer on the terms and conditions agreed at the transfer. The purpose of the directive is therefore to ensure that the restructuring of undertakings within the common market does not adversely affect the workers in the undertakings concerned.'

42.   There is a transfer within the meaning of the directive where there is a transfer of an economic entity which retains its identity, meaning an organized grouping of resources, which has the objective of pursuing an economic activity, whether or not that activity is central or ancillary.

This definition summarizes the abundant case-law of the European regarding the notion of transfer. This case-law reads as follows. The key element of the definition lies in the fact whether the employees are, as a consequence of the transfer of the undertaking, confronted with a new, legal employer; in other words, the selling of a number of shares with the consequence that there is a new economic owner is not relevant.

> 'The directive is applicable where, following a legal transfer or merger, there is a change in the legal or natural person who is responsible for carrying on the business and who, by virtue of that fact, incurs the obligations of an employer *vis-à-vis* the employees of the undertaking, regardless of whether or not ownership of the undertaking is transferred.'

170

43. The directive applies provided that the undertaking in question retains its identity, as it does if it is a going concern whose operation is actually continued or resumed by the new employer, with the same or similar activities. In order to determine whether those conditions are met, it is necessary to consider all the circumstances surrounding the transaction in question, including, in particular, whether or not the undertakings' tangible and intangible assets and the majority of its employees are taken over, the degree of similarity between the activities carried on before and after the transfer of the period, if any, for which those activities ceased in connection with the transfer.

It is therefore 'necessary to determine, having regard to all the circumstances of the facts surrounding the transaction in question, whether the functions performed are in fact carried out or resumed by the new legal person with the same activities or similar activities, it being understood that activities of a special nature which pursue independent aims may, if necessary, be treated as a business or part of a business within the meaning of the directive.'

The directive may thus apply in a situation in which an undertaking entrusts another undertaking by contract with the responsibility for running a service for employees, previously managed directed, for a fee and various benefits the terms of which are determined by agreement between them.

44. The rule of thumb is that the rights and obligations of the employee arising from his contract of employment in the case of a transfer are automatically transferred. In other words, the employees who are employed on the date of transfers are automatically transferred to the new employer with all their acquired rights, whether they or the new employer want it or not. Therefore, the terms of the contract work or of the working relationship may not be altered with regard to the salary, in particular its day of payment and composition, notwithstanding that the total amount is unchanged. The directive does not preclude, however, an alteration of the working relationship with the new head of the undertaking in so far as the national law allows such an alteration independently of a transfer of the undertaking.'

As the Court has repeatedly held, 'the Directive is intended to safeguard the rights of workers in the event of a change of employer by making it possible for them to continue to work for the new employer under the same conditions as those agreed with the transferor.

It is likewise settled case-law that the rules of the Directive, in particular those concerning the protection of workers against dismissal by reason of the transfer, must be considered to be mandatory, so that it is not possible to derogate from them in a manner unfavourable to employees.

It follows that in the event of the transfer of an undertaking the contract of employment or employment relationship between the staff employed by the undertaking transferred may not be maintained with the transferor and is automatically continued with the transferee.

45. Pursuant to the directive the transferee shall, following the transfer, continue to observe the terms and conditions agreed in any collective agreement on the same terms applicable to the transferor under that agreement, until the date of termination or expiry of the collective agreement or the entry into force or application of another collective agreement'. The directive does not oblige the transferee to continue to observe the terms and conditions agreed in any collective agreement in respect of workers who are not employed by the undertaking at the time of the transfer.

46. The provisions regarding acquired rights do not, unless Member States provide otherwise, cover employees' lights to old age, invalidity or survivor's benefits under supplementary company or intercompany pension schemes outside the statutory social security schemes in Member States. Member States have, however, to adopt the measures necessary to protect the interests of employees and of persons no longer employed in the transferor's business at the time of the transfer in respect of the lights conferring on them immediate or prospective entitlements to old-age benefits, including survivors' benefits, under the supplementary schemes (Article 3, § 4).

47. The directive protects the concerned employees in the case of a transfer against dismissal by the transferor or the transferee on the grounds of the transfer, except for economic, technical, or organizational reasons entailing changes in the work-force. In order to ascertain whether the employees were dismissed solely as a result of the transfer, it is necessary to take into consideration the objective circumstances in which the dismissal took place such as, in particular, the fact that it took effect on a date close to that of the transfer and that the employees in question were taken on again by the transferee.

48. If the contract of employment or the employment relationship is terminated because the transfer involves a substantial change in working conditions to the detriment of the employee, the employer shall be regarded as having been responsible for termination of the contract of employment or the employment relationship.

49. The directive provides that the transferor and the transferee shall be required to inform the representatives of their respective employees affected by the transfer with the following information:

– the date or proposed date of the transfer;
– the reasons for the transfer;
– the legal, economic, and social implications of the transfer for the employees; and
– the measures envisaged in relation to the employees.

The transferor must give such information in good time before the transfer is carried out. The transferee must give such information in good time, and in any event before the transfer as regards their conditions of work and employment directly affects his employees. If the transferor or the transferee contemplates measures in relation to his employees, he shall consult his workers' representatives in good time or on such measures with a view to seeking agreement.

VI. THE SOCIAL DIALOGUE

A. *In General*

50. The promotion of a social dialogue constitutes one of the key elements of European social policies. This follows clearly from Article 138, 1 TEC, which reads as follows 'The Commission shall have the task of promoting the consultation of management and labour at Community level and shall take any relevant measure to facilitate their dialogue by ensuring balanced support for the parties.' The notion of social dialogue self-evidently also includes collective bargaining, the conclusion of agreements between the social partners. Consequently, Article 139, 1 TEC says, should management and labour so desire, the dialogue between them at Community level may lead to contractual relations, including agreements.'

51. Collective bargaining, however, is a delicate flower. Indeed, quite a number of questions pop up over which opinions, especially between the social partners, diverse. First of all, what is the *division of tasks* between European and national levels? That the answer to that question leads to controversies, follows clearly from the rather heated discussions concerning the appropriateness of the conclusion of a European agreement on information and consultation rights of employees at national level. For the employers, this is an issue to be dealt with exclusively at national level and no business whatsoever for the Community, while the trade unions defend fiercely that this is a matter to be dealt with at European level and that European minimum requirements are necessary.

Secondly, there is the reality of the *power relationship* between the European social partners, or better the lack of power of European trade union in pushing the employers to the European bargaining table. Political pressures from the European Institutions, especially from the European Commission, however, efficiently compensate that lack of power. There is indeed a kind of situation, which one could call 'Damocles bargaining'. This goes as follows. The European Commission invites the European social partners to have a dialogue and negotiate an agreement on a given issue, let's say on information and consultation rights at national level. The parties and especially the employers know that the Commission, if no agreement is reached, will push for European legislation. So employers are put under pressure and have to consider to join or not to join and eventually to negotiate a given deal in order to prevent legislation, the outcome that would escape them almost completely anyway. So there is a sword, hanging above their heads.

52. There is, on top of that, the problem of *credibility*. The European social partners exist. They want to prove that they are more than mere lobbyists and are able and willing to play a constructive role. Concluding agreements is one way of indicating that they are doing more than merely talking to each other.

53. The Damocles tactic is now widely used at European level. This is not only so for inter-industry-wide agreements, like the ones we discussed concerning parental leave and part-time, but also for the level of the European enterprise. Let's take the example of the EWCs. Also here, enterprises are put under pressure of either negotiating an agreement, allowing for some flexibility or undergoing mandatory rules, which come into force when no agreement is reached.

54. A '*social dialogue*' between employers and trade unions at the European level has taken place for a number of years at Val Duchesse, near Brussels, and has led to informal agreements on such issues as motivation and vocational training, information and consultation with respect to the introduction of new technologies,

173

adaptability and flexibility on professional and geographic mobility, and the improvement of the functioning of the Common Market in Europe. However, the outcomes of these talks were labelled 'common orientations,' and did not even constitute informal guidelines. No real effort has been made to implement these 'common orientations' at national or sectoral levels. Undoubtedly, a number of sectoral talks do take place in various joint committees, but those talks mostly concern the sharing of information or consultation, not bargaining.

However, again, some positive change can be noted. As mentioned before, three important agreements have been concluded by UNICE, CEEP, and the ETUC, since and the social dialogue at sectoral level expands. But the developments in this area are more of a political than of an industrial nature. The agreements at European level constitute more another form of legislative machinery than genuine collective bargaining. The issue of who is a 'social partner' remains unsolved. At the same time, one has to note that at present more than 600 European Works Councils have already been established with information and some consultation rights.[1]

55. Up to now, their impact on European industrial relations remains uncertain. It remains an open question whether the EWCs will become bridgeheads for a full-fledged European industrial relations system, which might emerge in the 21st century. The chances are slim since the new economy is in a sense sapping the powers and the impact of the European social partners.

56. Moreover, more than another 1,000 councils still need to be established. All this is impressive and even fabulous. One is indeed talking about hundreds of meetings a year, where thousands of works council members meet. But fundamentally nothing has happened, since the power relations remained unchanged. The EWC does not affect the *managerial prerogative* and did e.g. not change the outcome of the shameless and brutal closure of the Renault plant in Vilvoorde (Belgium), where 3,000 workers lost their jobs.

B. The Sectoral Social Dialogue

57. Activities in all areas of the sectoral social dialogue gained momentum in 1996, with 30 joint opinions, memoranda, recommendations, and agreements being adopted. The majority of joint opinions were concerned with the preservation of the basic principles governing activities in the sectors concerned, or the safeguarding of employment in the industry. Agreements, opinions, and recommendations adopted in the sectoral social dialogue process included the following:

– agreements recommending the application of all or part of Council Directive 93/104/EC on *working time* were concluded in the *railways, sea transport, and civil aviation sectors*;
– the social partners in the *cleaning industry* adopted a memorandum on new services to private individuals and on agreements covering workers engaged in the new activities thus created;

---

1. Chapter 22 (Engels and Salas).

- the social partners in the *distributive trades and private security industries* issued opinions and recommendations aimed at improving their image and outlining ways of achieving greater professionalism;
- in the *agricultural sector* an agreement was formulated aimed at reducing working time and developing new areas of activity;
- the *fishing industry* considered the implications of environmental policy on its activities;
- health and safety issues were the focus of discussions in the *construction industry*; and
- the *textiles, clothing and footwear industries* commenced preparation of their own codes of practice in a context of widening international competition (regulation of child labour and respect for fundamental rights).

Another area where social dialogue is developing is at the cross-border level, via the interregional trade union committees set up by ETUC. These operate in close conjunction with the EURES network linking up Member States' national employment agencies in a number of regions.

Developments in cross-industry advisory committees and in the Standing Committee on Employment have also to be mentioned.

To these have to be added developments in the European Commerce Sector (agreement of fundamental social rights – 1999); a sectoral framework agreement in European agriculture (1997) and an agreement on child labour in the footwear sector (1998).

C. Divergent Views on the Future Role of the Social Dialogue

58. It is increasingly clear that employers and trade unions do have diverging agendas towards developing the agenda and role of the intersectoral EU-1evel social dialogue process, particularly in relation to the desirability of further framework agreements.

In March 1999, the ETUC made proposals for a social dialogue work programme involving the negotiation of framework agreements on the issues of temporary agency work, telework, access to life-long learning, and complementary social protection (portability of occupational pensions), together with possible recommendations on the revision of the 1993 working time Directive and anti-discrimination measures under Article 13 of the Treaty and sexual harassment.

UNICE, on the contrary, wants to give priority to the completion of an ongoing joint social partners' study of 'best practice' and 'factors for success' in the area of agreements balancing flexibility and security as promoted by the EU Employment Guidelines and also proposed joint work on health and safety issues. It reserved its position on the issues of sexual harassment and Article 13 measures.

The social partners' agreement on fixed-term work excluded workers supplied to a user enterprise by a temporary work agency, but stated that: 'It is the intention of die parties to consider the need for a similar agreement relating to temporary agency work.' In December 1999, the ETUC insists on negotiations over an agreement on the regulation of temporary agency work.

It is clear that the scope for, and desirability of, Community-level agreements continues to be controversial, both among the social partners and among EU institutions and governments. It is clear that the main motive for UNICE to engage in negotiations is the threat of the European legislator stepping in.

VII. CONCLUSIONS: EUROPE BEYOND 2000

59. At the start of the 21st century the face of 'social Europe' is dramatically changing. The impact of new technologies on the world of work cannot be overestimated. A new economy is emerging transforming the way enterprises are organized and products and services produced and delivered in a 24-hour economy. Knowledge and information are 'the' sources of added value. The economy is spurred by an ongoing amount of new applications and services, which are rendered by the net economy. Start-ups are in, and more important, attracting the best brains. The Internet has become an integral part of an e-commerce, which is only beginning. At this time, the new economy is simply an American one. 'The America on Line-Time Warner deal (2000) is the McDonalds of the mind'. The new economy is enhancing the dual society, between those, who participate in the new economy and those, who do not.

A 'new economy' is in. The job market has become even more dual than before: an increasing shortage of (skilled) labour and a remaining group of workers, who are not in a position to effectively take part in the growing economy, as they lack either the technical skills or the social skills, or both.

Both urgencies need to be constantly and urgently addressed.

60. The European Council held a special meeting on 23–24 March 2000 in Lisbon and set itself a *new strategic goal* for the next decade: *to become the most competitive and dynamic knowledge-based economy in the world capable of sustainable economic growth with more and better jobs and greater social cohesion.*

Businesses and citizens must have access to an inexpensive, world-class communications infrastructure and a wide range of services. Every citizen must be equipped with the skills needed to live and work in this new information society.

The rationale behind the launch of this new strategy is based on:

- the projection that by 2010, half of all jobs will be in industries that are either major producers or intensive users of information technology products and services;
- the fact that some 9 million people in the EU are teleworkers;
- the estimate that some 81 million of the 117 million people aged under 25 years in the EU are in educational institutions and should be groomed for employment in the 'knowledge economy'; and
- the belief that employment in the 'information society' is less stable than in the past and more dependent on high skills and adaptability.

61. The Commission's strategy is primarily aimed at reducing the skills gap between the EU and the USA with regard to internet access and the use of communications technology. The report highlights the risk that the next generation of workers could lack the necessary skills to meet the demands of the knowledge economy. It states that the demand for highly skilled workers in the information technology sector in Europe is already not being met and that by 2002 the number of unfilled job vacancies in this sector could reach 1.6 million. This in turn could then stunt the growth of software, services and telecommunications sectors.

The strategy calls on Member State governments and the social partners to act by:

- linking all schools to the internet by 2002;
- ensuring that all teachers are verifiably competent in information skills;
- providing all workers with the opportunity to learn information skills;
- establishing flexible frameworks to facilitate teleworking;
- adapting equipment to improve the employability of workers with disabilities;
- encouraging entrepreneurship through tax policies that reward risk-taking; and
- promoting the use of information tools to small- and medium-sized enterprises.

A. Marginal and Fundamental

62. The Treaty of Amsterdam (1997) has degraded European labour law to the rank of a second-class citizen, notwithstanding the Title on employment and a new chapter on social provisions. The hierarchy of objectives of the EU indicates clearly that social action in the Community is subordinate to non-inflationary monetary policies, which the EU is pursuing. Within the one, united European economic area, a battle of competition will be waged between enterprises with weapons like flexibility, lower wage costs, less standards, delocalizations, and downsizing, in other words social dumping. There will be a harmonization downwards.

On the other hand one has to recognize that quite a number of fundamental principles and labour laws have been affirmed and/or acted upon: thus equal treatment as well in the area of free movement of labour, with all it involves, as in the area of sexual equality where Community law and its implementation by the European Court has been of the highest importance. Important labour laws concern collective dismissals, acquired rights in case of transfer of enterprises, working time, and above all health and safety.

However, there is not yet a common social market and social policies, also in the area of equal treatment, are undermined by the crisis rather than enhanced. It is like taking an umbrella away when it is raining.

B. Hope: More Majority Voting and Fundamental Rights

63. Again, there is hope. The IGC (2000), which is engaged in preparing the enlargement of the EU, is addressing the issue of expanding the majority vote. Everyone realizes that maintaining unanimity when the Union expands to possibly 27 Member States means paralysing the decision making. Let us hope that more labour issues will fall within the reach of majority voting.

Moreover, when the European Council at Tampere Council (1999) met, ministers decided to initiate the drafting of a charter of fundamental rights in the EU. A joint body consisting of representatives of Member State governments, the Commission, the European Parliament and national parliaments, will draft the charter. Other EU bodies, social groups, and experts will be invited to give their views to the joint body. The idea is to present a draft document in advance of the European Council of December 2000. There is a good chance that fundamental rights will be included in the European Treaties. Remains to be seen whether the Council will go beyond a mere declaration but lay down directly enforceable rights for the European citizens, employers, and workers included. Legally enforceable fundamental standards would help to put 'social Europe' definitely on the map.

In the meantime, in November 1999, the European Commission issued an anti-discrimination package of proposals consisting of two draft Directives, a draft Decision establishing a Community action programme and a Communication to the European institutions. The legislative proposals are based on Article 13 of the European Treaty, which provides a new legal base for the Commission to issue proposals aimed at combating discrimination on grounds of sex, racial or ethnic origin, religion or belief, disability, age, and sexual orientation. This also looks promising. Both directives were eventually adopted: Council Directive 2000/43/EC of 29 June 2000 concerns the implementation of the principle of equal treatment between persons irrespective of racial or ethnic origin and Council Directive 2000/78/EC of 27 November 2000 establishes a general framework for equal treatment in employment and occupation.

C.   Power Relations

64. The debate should also be seen in *the* framework of the power relations between management and labour which have been dramatically affected, especially in a period in which the economic world becomes more and more international and almost totally escapes the grip of European actors, i.e. politicians, trade unions, and also employers and their organizations. It is quite clear that the social partners, the employers' associations as well as the trade unions lose influence and members, both at national as at European level, and even more so at world level. Trade unions are also losing power on the market place. Undertakings have become the main participants on the markets; they have their own specific strategies in which trade unions play less and less a role or no role at all. Decentralization, empowerment, individualization coupled with teamwork, driven by re-engineering and bench marking are the main characteristics shaping the industrial relations and human resources management policies of the enterprises today. In this 'brave new world,' collectively cooked up 'information and consultation schemes' seem to many of the protagonists more than outdated. No wonder, then, that many enterprises, and consequently their organizations, vehemently oppose not so much the idea of informing and consulting employees, but the thought of having trade unions back on their playing fields through the back door of EWCs. Many, especially US based undertakings, do not like that the power the trade unions lost in the market place is conquered back in political arenas.

65. These are some of the fundamental reasons why the European social partners failed in their attempt to conclude a European collective agreement on the issue of EWCs, although they tried very hard as their credibility as 'social partners' was and is at stake.

VIII.   A NEW ECONOMIC–SOCIAL BALANCE?

66. With the Treaty of Amsterdam (1997), the social map has been drawn up for some time to come. The socio-economic balance, which was pursued in Europe by

a whole generation since World War II, has been disrupted. The EU has chosen for iron-clad economic agreements, for supply side economics, a tough non-inflationary monetary policy on the one hand and a very soft social Europe, that is crushed by the storms of the extremely volatile international competition on the other hand.

The Treaty needs to be rewritten, especially as far as social policies are concerned. The EU should have the necessary competence to adequately monitor the market economy by way of socially inspired corrections. This is, however, not the case at present. Can one, under those circumstances still boast about a European social model?

Select Bibliography

B. Bercusson, *European Labour Law*, Butterworths, London, 1996.
R. Blanpain, *The Bosman case: The end of the Transfer System*, Peeters, Leuven, 1996.
R. Blanpain et al., *International Changes and European Social Policies after the Treaty of Amsterdam*, Kluwer, The Hague, 1998.
R. Blanpain, *European Labour Law*, 7th and revised ed., KLuwer, 2000.
R. Nielsen, *European Labour Law*, Djof Publishing, Copenhagen, 2000.

Addendum   European Labour Law after the European Top at Nice (December 2000)

A.   *Charter of Fundamental Rights of the European Union: Too Much and Too Little*

The European Council at Nice welcomed and adopted the Charter.
The Charter contains following social rights:

– Prohibition of slavery and forced labour
– Respect for private and family life
– Protection of personal data
– Freedom of thought, conscience, and religion
– Freedom of expression and information
– Freedom of assembly and of association
– Right to education
– Freedom to choose an occupation and right to engage in work
– Freedom to conduct a business
– Non-discrimination
– Equality between men and women
– Workers' right to information and consultation within the undertaking
– Right of collective bargaining and action
– Right of access to placement services
– Protection in the event of unjustified dismissal
– Fair and just working conditions
– Prohibition of child labour and protection of young people at work
– Family and professional life
– Social security and social assistance
– Freedom of movement and of residence.

Obviously, the Charter contains a lot of social rights. Some are fundamental; some are important but not fundamental. Here we can talk about an inflation of social rights as a far a Charter, to be included in the European treaties is concerned. We think for example about rights like the right of access to placement services, to protection in the event of unjustified dismissal and fair and to just working conditions. These are important points indeed, but not the 'core rights' one is thinking about when discussing a Charter of Fundamental Rights. The 1998 ILO Declaration, on the contrary, is concentrating on the real core social rights and the ILO solution seems to more appropriate.

As far as the binding effect of the Charter is concerned one is nowhere. The Presidency Conclusions of the Nice Top regarding the Charter read as follows: 'The European Council welcomes the joint proclamation, by the Council, the European Parliament and the Commission, of the Charter of Fundamental Rights, combining in a single text the civil, political, economic, social, and societal rights hitherto laid down in a variety of international, European, or national sources. The European Council would like to see the Charter disseminated as widely as possible amongst the Union's citizens. In accordance with the Cologne conclusions, the question of the Charter's force will be considered later.'

Later, means after enlargement and that some 30 Member States may have to unanimously agree to give binding effect to the Charter.

B. Unanimity and Qualified Majority

Here nothing changes. On the contrary, article 137 of the Treaty was re-written and looks now (draft) as follows

1. With a view to achieving the objectives of Article 136, the Community shall support and complement the activities of the Member States in the following fields:

(a) improvement in particular of the working environment to protect workers' health and safety;
(b) working conditions;
(c) social security and social protection of workers;
(d) protection of workers where their employment contract is terminated;
(e) the information and consultation of workers;
(f) representation and collective defence of the interests of workers and employers, including codetermination, subject to para. 5;
(g) conditions of employment for third-country nationals legally residing in Community territory;
(h) the integration of persons excluded from the labour market, without prejudice to Article 150;
(i) equality between men and women with regard to labour market opportunities and treatment at work;
(j) *the combating of social exclusion;* and
(k) *the modernization of social protection systems without prejudice to point (c).*

2. To this end, the Council:

(a) may adopt measures designed to encourage cooperation between Member States through initiatives aimed at improving knowledge, developing exchanges of information and best practices, promoting innovative approaches, and evaluating experiences, excluding any harmonisation of the laws and regulations of the Member States;

(b) may adopt, in the fields referred to in para. 1(a) to (i), by means of directives, minimum requirements for gradual implementation, having regard to the conditions and technical rules obtaining in each of the Member States. Such directives shall avoid imposing administrative, financial and legal constraints in a way which would hold back the creation and development of small and medium-sized undertakings.

The Council shall act in accordance with the procedure referred to in Article 251 after consulting the Economic and Social Committee and the Committee of the Regions, except in the fields referred to in para. 1(c), (d), (f) and (g), where the Council shall act unanimously on a proposal from the Commission, after consulting the European Parliament and the above mentioned Committees. The Council, acting unanimously on a proposal from the Commission, after consulting the European Parliament, may decide to render the procedure referred to in Article 251 applicable to para. 1(d), (f) and (g).

3. A Member State may entrust management and labour, at their joint request, with the implementation of directives adopted pursuant to para. 2.

In this case, it shall ensure that, no later than the date on which a directive must be transposed in accordance with Article 249, management and labour have introduced the necessary measures by agreement, the Member State concerned being required to take any necessary measure enabling it at anytime to be in a position to guarantee the results imposed by that directive.

4. The provisions adopted pursuant to this Article:

– *shall not affect the right of Member States to define the fundamental principles of their social security systems and must not significantly affect the financial equilibrium thereof;*
– shall not prevent any Member State from maintaining or introducing more stringent protective measures compatible with this Treaty.

5. The provisions of this Article shall not apply to pay, the right of association, the right to strike or the right to impose lock-outs.

C. The European Company Statute (SE)

An agreement was finally reached on the European Company Statute and Workers Participation. It will be a very weak instrument. First, it is voluntary; secondly,

Member States do not have to implement the provisions on workers participation and do not need to have such a system if the national legislation of the Member State, where the SE has its registered office does not foresee in equivalent provisions (e.g. Ireland, the UK).

The Council of Social Affairs of December 20, 2000 concluded as follows regarding the SE:

'The Council agreed unanimously on guidelines for political agreement on two acts concerning the European Company (SE):

- the Regulation on the Statute for a European Company;
- the Directive supplementing the Statute for a European Company with regard to the involvement of employees.

The rules relating to employee involvement in the SE are the subject of the Directive described below, on which agreement was also reached at the Council. The provisions contained in that Directive form an inseparable complement to the Regulation and must be applied in parallel.

This Directive supplements the Regulation as regards the involvement of employees in the affairs of European Companies, in order to ensure that the creation of an SE does not entail the disappearance or reduction of practices of employee involvement existing within the companies participating in the establishment of an SE.

Given the diversity of rules and practices in the Member States as regards the manner in which employees' representatives are involved in decision making within companies, a single European model is not intended. Nevertheless, procedures for the information and consultation of workers at transnational level will be ensured.

When rights to participate exist within one or more of the companies establishing an SE, those rights will be preserved through their transfer to the SE, once established, unless the parties involved decide otherwise.

When the management or administrative organs of the participating companies decide to set up an SE, negotiations will be started with the representatives of the companies' employees in order to reach agreement on ways to involve employees in the forthcoming SE. A special negotiating body (SNB) representing the employees of all the companies involved will then be established. In electing or appointing members of the SNB, it must be ensured that those members are elected or appointed in proportion to the number of employees employed in each Member State by the companies concerned.

In principle, such negotiations may continue for six months. The agreement negotiated will specify the scope of the agreement, the composition, number of members and allocation of seats on the employees' representative body, the functions and procedure for the information and consultation of workers, the frequency of meetings of the representative body, the financial and material resources to be available to that body, and if need be the arrangements for participation, as well as the date of entry into force of the agreement and its duration.

If no agreement is concluded, the arrangements for the information, consultation, and where appropriate participation of employees which are laid down by the legislation of the Member State in which the registered office of the SE is situated will apply. That legislation must comply with the reference provisions set out in the Annex to the Directive.'

D. Conclusion

The European Top of Nice (December) constituted a last and unique chance to give the EU the necessary competences to combat social exclusion and monitor the globalization of the economy from the social point of view in an integrated and comprehensive way. To do so successfully the Charter of Fundamental rights should have been integrated in the European Treaty and have binding effect; more majority voting regarding social affairs should have been provided for. This did not happen, on the contrary.

As said earlier, to change the Treaties unanimity between all the Member States is necessary. One Member State can veto any change. This happened in Nice: a.o. the Labour Government, for domestic reasons, undermined the European Social Model by vetoing more majority voting and amending article 137 of the Treaty

In short, the EU is socially handicapped. It will be so as long as Thatchers, Blair's and others veto European progress for purely national ill-conceived concerns. Indeed, social Europe is not so 'Nice'.

Chapter 9. Multinational Enterprises and Codes of Conduct

The OECD Guidelines for MNEs in Perspective

R. Blanpain

I. INTRODUCTION

1. The OECD Guidelines for Multinational Enterprises (MNEs) were first promulgated in 1976. They responded to the advent of MNEs on the world scene in the 1960s, and to their growing economic influence which gave rise to concerns, especially among some governments and the international trade union movement. At the time, wide-ranging debates of a social, economic and political nature about the role of multinational enterprises took place in the OECD as well as in other international organizations, like the UN and the ILO.

2. The Guidelines affirm that every country has the right to prescribe the conditions under which MNEs operate within its national jurisdiction, subject to international law and the international agreements to which it subscribes. They are not a substitute for national laws, to which MNEs are fully subject. They represent supplementary standards of behaviour of a non-legal character, particularly concerning the international operations of these enterprises.

3. Despite regular reviews of the OECD Guidelines, they have remained remarkably stable overall, as few amendments have been made to the original text.[1] This is also the case for the Employment and Industrial Relations chapter, where only one paragraph was amended slightly in 1979.[2] There are obvious reasons for adhering to the original 1976 text. The Guidelines were very carefully drafted with a major input by national delegations and after due consultation with the social

---

1. The major exception was the introduction of a chapter on Environmental Protection in 1991.
2. This concerned para. 8 referring to the threat to transfer the whole or part of an operating unit in the context of *bona fide* negotiations or the right to organize. An amendment was adopted in 1979 including a reference to the transfer of employees.

partners (BIAC and TUAC). In addition, the view has been taken that the effective application of the Guidelines depends to a large extent on their stability.

4. However, since 1976 the world has changed dramatically. Today's globalizing economy is driven by the massive introduction of information and communication technologies, which allow knowledge to be stored, manipulated and transmitted worldwide without significant costs. Since companies cannot organize all the increasingly available knowledge and expertise in their own house, they tend to increasingly externalize certain tasks and services. Enterprises are massively engaging in outsourcing and networking, entrusting tasks they used to do themselves to other enterprises which can provide them better and more cheaply. This trend is likely to increase further as bandwidth on the web becomes less of a constraint. Outsourcing, sub-contracting and use of the WWW are liable to change radically the way that companies conduct their business.

5. Human relations, inside as well as outside the enterprise, are becoming less hierarchical and more translateral: people work more as equals, and in more flexible ways. Henceforth, work may be increasingly performed in networks and teams, which may involve different formal enterprise structures. For example, workers may be employed by company A, but actually work in the laboratory of company B. Labour relations, previously more central, uniform, and controlled by way of collective bargaining, are now becoming more decentralized, even individualized. One example is the spread of teleworking, as a modern form of (mainly) home working.

6. At the same time, global Foreign Direct Investment (FDI) by MNEs has grown considerably. Today some 53,000 MNEs and their (estimated) 300,000 affiliates employ some 190 million people worldwide. They have an impact on every facet of industry, trade, services, and commerce. Moreover, FDI is now probably much more widely accepted as beneficial for economic development than it was in 1976. And it may, in the present political climate and the generalized acceptance of market economies, be subject to fewer government controls.

7. Consequently, there is no doubt that recommendations or guidelines, designed to encourage the positive contribution which multinational enterprises can make to economic and social progress and to help them resolve any difficulties to which their operations may give rise, are at least as relevant today as they were in the 1970s. This is shown, *inter alia*, by the present proliferation of company codes of conduct at the firm and industrial levels, as well as by the recent discussions in various international fora on the relationship between international trade, FDI, and labour standards.

8. The question therefore arose whether the OECD Guidelines, in particular their Employment and Industrial Relations chapter, still represented the state of the art and whether they are adequate in relation to the challenges of today's globalized economy. In this context, two questions are of particular importance:

– whether the content and language of the Guidelines needed to be adjusted, so that they remain credible relative to the problems of today and tomorrow; and

– whether they have been as effective as they could have been, and if not, what could be done to ensure their efficient implementation.

9. To that end another review was finalized in June 2000, after lengthy consultations between the OECD Governments amongst themselves and with BIAC, TUAC, and NGOs. The review related as well to the text of the Guidelines themselves as to the implementation procedure. Added were a.o. guidelines on child and forced labour, while other guidelines were made more precise, like paras 1d (discrimination) and 6 (notice in case of changes in operations) of the employment chapter.

10. These questions are especially relevant for the Employment and Industrial Relations chapter. Indeed, this chapter has been the object of numerous cases brought before the CIME since the adoption of the Guidelines, and the clarifications issued by the Committee render its content quite comprehensive.

11. At the same time, account should also be taken of developments relating to employment and industrial relations in other international organizations, like the ILO where new instruments have been adopted, such as the 1998 ILO Declaration on Fundamental Principles and Rights at Work. The Labor Side Agreement to NAFTA (1993), which contains principles relating to employment and industrial relations, is also relevant.

II. THE EMPLOYMENT AND INDUSTRIAL RELATIONS CHAPTER

A. *Content of the Chapter*

12. This chapter is one of 8 Guidelines chapters (the others referring to General Policies;[3] Disclosure of Information; Competition; Financing; Taxation; Environmental Protection; and Science and Technology). It consists of a chapeau and 8 paragraphs. The chapeau refers to 'applicable' law and regulations which is meant to acknowledge the fact that MNEs, while operating within the jurisdiction of particular countries, may be subject to national, sub-national, as well as supranational levels of regulation of employment and industrial relations matters.

---

3. The General Policies chapter provides a.o.

   – respect the human rights of those affected by their activities consistent with the host's government international obligations and commitments;
   – encourage human capital formation, in particular by creating employment opportunities and facilitating training opportunities for employees;
   – refrain from seeking or accepting exemptions not contemplated in the statutory or regulatory framework related to environmental, health, safety, labour, taxation, financial incentives, or other issues;
   – promote employee awareness of, and compliance with, company policies through appropriate dissemination of these policies, including through training programmes; and
   – refrain from discriminatory or disciplinary action against employees who make *bona fide* reports to management or, as appropriate, to the competent public authorities, on practices that crontavene the law, the Guidelines or the enterprise's policies.

13. Spread over 8 paragraphs, the chapter outlines the following rights and principles, expressed in each case as recommendations for the behaviour of individual enterprises. The text below presents largely verbatim extracts, regrouped under summary headings.

1. Freedom of Association (paras 1a and 7): *Enterprises should*

14. respect the rights of their employees to be represented by trade unions and other *bona fide* organizations of employees (para. 1a);
while employees are exercising a right to organize, not threaten to utilize a capacity to transfer the whole or part of an operating unit from the country concerned nor transfer employees from the enterprises' component entities in other countries in order to hinder the exercise of a right to organize (para. 7);

2. Child Labour (para. 1b): *Enterprises should*

15. contribute to the effective abolition of child labour and, in particular, not engage in the worst forms of child labour in their operations;

3. Forced Labour (para. 1c): *Enterprises should*

16. contribute to the elimination of all forms of forced or compulsory labour and, in particular, not engage in the use of such labour in their operations;

4. Discrimination (para. 1d): *Enterprises should*

17. not discriminate against their employees with respect to employment or occupation on such grounds as race, colour, sex, religion, political opinion, national extraction, or social origin – unless selectivity concerning employee characteristics furthers established governmental policies which specifically promote greater equality of employment opportunity or relate to the inherent requirements of a job.[4]

5. Collective Bargaining (paras 1, 2, 8): *Enterprises should*

18. respect the rights of their employees to engage in constructive negotiations with a view to reaching agreements on employment conditions (para. 1 a);
provide such facilities to representatives of the employees as may be necessary to assist in the development of effective collective agreements (para. 2a);
provide to representatives of employees information which is needed for meaningful negotiations on conditions of employment (para. 2b);

---

4. It is regretable that the OECD did not retain 'age' as a ground for non-discrimination.

enable authorized representatives of their employees to conduct negotiations on collective bargaining or labour/management relations issues with representatives of management who are authorized to take decisions on the matters under negotiation (para. 8)

in the context of *bona fide* negotiations with representatives of employees on conditions of employment, or while employees are exercising a right to organize, not threaten to transfer the whole or part of an operating unit from the country concerned nor transfer employees from the enterprises' component entities in other countries in order to influence unfairly those negotiations or to hinder the right to organize (para. 7).

6. Provision of Information–Consultation (paras 2c and 3): *Enterprises should*

19. to provide representatives of employees where this accords with local law and practice, information which enables them to obtain a true and fair view of the performance of the entity or, where appropriate, the enterprise as a whole (para. 3);

20. promote consultation and cooperation between employers and employees and their representatives on matters of mutual concern (para. 2c).

7. Health and Safety (para.4b): *Enterprises should*

21. take adequate steps to ensure occupational health and safety in their operations (para. 4b).

8. Observance of Employment Standards (para. 4): *Enterprises should*

22. observe standards of employment and industrial relations not less favourable than those observed by comparable employers in the host country.

9. Skills and Training (para. 5): *Enterprises should*

23. to the greatest extent possible, utilize, train and prepare for upgrading members of the local labour force in cooperation with representatives of their employees and, where appropriate, the relevant governmental authorities.

10. Reasonable Notice and Cooperation in Case of Major Changes
    (para. 6): *Enterprises should*

24. in considering major changes in business operations (in particular in the case of the closure of an entity involving collective dismissals), (i) provide reasonable notice of such changes to employee representatives and, where appropriate, to the relevant governmental authorities; and (ii) cooperate with the employee representatives and government authorities so as to mitigate to the maximum extent practicable adverse effects. In the light of the specific circumstances of each case, it would be appropriiate if management were able to give such notice prior to the final decision being taken.

11. Access to Decision Makers (para. 9): *Enterprises should*

25. enable authorized representatives of their employees to negotiate with representatives of management who are authorized to take decisions on the matters under negotiation.

B. The Clarification Process

26. Since the Guidelines are drafted in fairly general terms, it has been necessary, on occasion, to clarify their purpose and intent. A follow-up procedure has been established for this purpose within the CIME. Most of the requests for clarification to date have referred to the Employment and Industrial Relations chapter of the Guidelines. They have been raised either by national delegations or by TUAC and have usually referred to some disputed behaviour of a particular enterprise. The text below summarizes the most important issues raised and clarifications given, using, to a large extent, the original wording of the clarifications.

27. *The (non-)definition of a MNE*: The Guidelines do not define the term 'MNEs', a concept which embraces a diversity of situations found throughout the business world. Rather, they describe some general criteria covering a broad range of multinational activities and arrangements. These arrangements can include traditional direct investment based on equity participation, or other means which do not necessarily include an equity capital element. The sharing of knowledge and resources among companies or other entities does not in itself indicate that such companies or entities constitute a MNE.

28. Since the Guidelines reflect good practice for all enterprises, both multinational and domestic enterprises are subject to the same expectations wherever the Guidelines are relevant to both.

29. *Responsibilities of the various entities of a MNE:* All entities, including parent companies, local subsidiaries, as well as the intermediary level of the organization, are expected to cooperate and assist, as necessary, in observing the Guidelines. To the extent that parent companies actually exercise control over the activities of their subsidiaries, they have a responsibility for observance of the Guidelines by those subsidiaries. The concept of responsibilities of the various entities is relevant, *inter alia*, for those paragraphs of the Guidelines dealing with the provision of information to employee representatives (see, for example paras 2 and 3 of the Employment and Industrial Relations chapter).

30. The Guidelines do not make specific recommendations concerning the division of responsibilities between parent companies and their local entities, apart from the expectation that all entities will cooperate to ensure observance of the

Guidelines. It would be reasonable to expect that a 'prudent enterprise' would set up whatever internal procedures would be necessary to ensure that the Guidelines are known and applied by its various entities. The Guidelines do not, however, imply a model of corporate decision making, nor do they interfere with the way parent companies communicate with their affiliated entities. For example, they do not explicitly refer to the set-up of consultations between parent companies and local entities, although such consultation between the parent and local entities would undoubtedly assist in achieving the purposes of the Guidelines.

31. Freedom of association: The thrust of the Guidelines in this area is towards management adopting a positive approach towards the activities of trade unions and other *bona fide* organizations of employees and, in particular, an open attitude towards organizational activities of workers within the framework of national rules and practices. The Guidelines do not indicate what organizations in a specific sense should represent employees for collective bargaining purposes, or what criteria should be used for the selection of such organizations. They are not putting any obstacles in the way of recognition by management, in agreement with national laws and practices, of international trade union bodies (such as an International Trade Secretariat) as a '*bona fide* organisation of employees'. One clarification has noted that management should adopt a cooperative attitude towards the participation of employees in international meetings for consultation and exchanges of views among themselves, provided that the functioning of the enterprise's operations and the normal procedures governing relationships with employee representatives and their organizations are not prejudiced thereby.

32. Providing information for a true and fair view of the enterprise: Regulations and practices in Member countries, with respect to the provision of information by enterprises to employees, differ considerably. In some countries, statutory provisions are very extensive and detailed, whereas in others, management and labour representatives define, on the basis of need, the information which management is expected to provide on a 'good-faith basis'. Thus, there is no general approach to this question, as is illustrated by the many facets of information provision, which include the type of information to be provided, its degree of detail, whether provided to the individual entity or the group, the timing of provision, whether it covers the present situation, past developments, future outlook, etc.

33. Because of this diversity in Member country situations, the CIME has considered it neither feasible nor practical to give an authoritative and detailed list of items covered by the expression 'information enabling a true and fair view of the performance of the entity and, where appropriate, the enterprise as a whole.' However, it has noted that employees of MNEs may need and should have access to more specific information, beyond that available to the general public, and in a form suitable for their interests and purposes.

34. Enterprises should provide information on aspects of their performance, which will also enable users to assess, *inter alia*, likely future developments. In so doing, they should be guided by the information items enumerated in the Disclosure of Information chapter of the Guidelines. Where more specific information is necessary, management and labour should be prepared to discuss information requirements in a constructive manner, taking into account the specific situation of the enterprise and of local laws, regulations, and practices.

35. Certain activities of MNEs, for instance restructuring activities, can be put into perspective only if the information on the position of the enterprise as a whole is available. If restructuring, or similar decisions, results in negotiations where the position of the enterprise as a whole is a key element, then employee representatives should have access to the information which gives a true and fair view of the enterprise as a whole and which they need for meaningful negotiation on employment conditions. The term 'meaningful' must be applied in the circumstance of each case, but is considered to have operational value to persons experienced in labour relations. At the same time, considerations of business confidentiality may mean that information on certain points may not be provided, or may not be provided without safeguards.

36. Effective communication: Negotiations, consultations, cooperation, or the provision of information to employees imply effective communication between the parties concerned. As a general rule, management and labour representatives should communicate in a language effectively understood by employees or their representatives. Where this may be unreasonably difficult, such as when representatives from the parent company are involved, adequate interpretation and translation facilities should be provided.

37. Reasonable notice of change in operations: The text in para. 6 of the Employment and Industrial Relations chapter which deals with reasonable notice in case of major changes in business operations, must be read together with the General Policies chapter, which provides that enterprises take account of the established general policy objectives of those Member countries in which they operate. Paragraph 2 of that chapter provides particular guidance to MNEs as to how they should take account of the economic and social priorities of their host countries.

38. When a local subsidiary of a MNE is to be closed down, a company should seek all necessary information on the country's relevant aims and practices from the Government concerned. While this does not affect the right of the enterprise to reach decisions with respect to cutting back or terminating operations in a given plant, certain considerations should be carefully weighed in making such a decision. For example, when there is clear evidence of the profitability of a particular subsidiary, the company should give special consideration to this fact when contemplating the closing down of that subsidiary. This does not restrict the company's right to make such a decision, which may take account of other factors besides profitability.

39. Should reasonable notice, as stipulated in the Guidelines, be interpreted as notice given *before* a business decision affecting the livelihood of employees is actually taken or notice given after such a decision is taken but before it is implemented? Reasonable notice is linked to the recommendation that management cooperate with employee representatives and governmental authorities in order to mitigate the adverse effects of such changes. For such notice to be 'reasonable', it should be sufficiently timely for the purpose of mitigating action to be prepared and put into affect. Notice of changes should be given and the actual changes implemented in such a way that meaningful cooperation can take place. It would conform to the general intention of this paragraph, in the light of the specific circumstance of each case, if management were able to give such notice prior to the final decision being taken.

40. Should the management of an enterprise claiming to be an exceptional case because of 'sensitivity of business decisions and/or of particular jobs' be required to justify these claims? There may be circumstances in which the sensitivity of business decisions, in terms of possible serious damage to the enterprises concerned, is such that it would render it difficult for them, when considering changes in activities which would have major effects on the livelihood of their employees, to give employee representatives early notice of such changes. However, in the view of the CIME, such circumstances would be exceptional. In particular, there is no business sector or business activity where it could be considered that such circumstances would usually prevail. This would seem to imply that an enterprise would be expected to state the reasons why it considers that exceptional circumstances apply.

41. Finally, enterprises may on occasions be faced with a situation where their employees are not represented by trade unions and other *bona fide* employee organizations. In such cases, enterprises should take all practical steps towards meeting the objectives underlying the Guidelines text on reasonable notice, within the framework of national laws, regulations, and prevailing labour practices.

42. Transfer of a unit or of employees. Unfair influence during negotiations: An important issue with respect to para. 8 is the distinction between legitimate provision of information and threats to influence unfairly negotiations with employees (e.g. when threatening to transfer an operating unit from the country concerned or transfer employees from a foreign affiliate). It was recognized that 'unfair' was the key notion in this context. A distinction should be made between information given to employees on the likely consequences of certain employee demands for the future of the firm, and threats which would be an unfair use of management's negotiating power.

43. Conduct of negotiations. Access to decision makers: When negotiations or collective bargaining take place in the context of a parent-subsidiary relationship, the subsidiary may not be fully empowered to negotiate and conclude – an agreement. There may be special problems in the case of a subsidiary situated in a country different from that of the parent company. In these situations, the parent company is expected to take the necessary organizational steps to enable its subsidiaries to observe the Guidelines, *inter alia*, by providing adequate and timely information and ensuring that the enterprise's representatives carrying out such negotiations are duly authorized to take decisions on matters under negotiation.

44. Several clarifications have addressed the meanings of terms such as 'collective bargaining', 'labour–management relations' and 'negotiations'. In some countries, collective bargaining or labour–management relations are limited to conditions of employment in a more traditional sense (for example, wages, working hours, health, and safety standards). In other countries, there is a trend towards including information and consultations on the economic and financial management of the enterprise, extending to future production and investment plans to some extent. The CIME has noted that these terms, as they are used in the Guidelines, are sufficiently broad to permit a variety of interpretations in the light of different national situations. Their specific meaning is determined by reference to national regulations and prevailing labour relations and employment practices.

45. The Guidelines do not define what is meant by 'negotiations'. As a general rule, it implies an effort to reach agreement by the parties concerned. It may, however, be difficult in practice to distinguish between 'negotiations' and 'consultations', the latter term in some countries being used in situations where management retains the prerogative of a final decision in case of disagreement, after listening to the views of employee representatives. In some cases, 'consultations' may be understood to imply the effort to reach agreement, although management retains the final decision-making power. The Guidelines text does not institute a claim for opening consultations or negotiations in the absence of other relevant provisions. It supposes that such consultations or negotiations are conducted in the framework of national laws and practices of the host country.

46. Future production and investment matters: When dealing with the specific issue of consultation or negotiation in which future production and investment plans are involved, para. 9 avoids the need for defining the locus of the negotiations or the proper level of management to be involved in such negotiations. This depends on the decision-making structure of each MNE. Negotiations conducted in accordance with national practice should take place in a meaningful manner with management representatives in a position to directly influence decisions on investment matters and to engage in effective negotiations. Where negotiations are defined by national practice in a way that management, in case of disagreement, remains free to make the final decision, these negotiations should still provide employee representatives the opportunity to discuss with management representatives having real impact upon the final decision.

47. Central management has a range of possibilities from which to choose to enable meaningful negotiations with employee representatives, depending on various circumstances. Examples include:

– to provide the management of the subsidiary with adequate and timely information and to ensure that it has sufficient powers to conduct meaningful negotiations with employee representatives; and
– to nominate one or more representatives of the decision-making centre to the negotiating team of the subsidiary in order to ensure that management has sufficient power to conduct meaningful negotiations with employee representatives;

to engage directly in negotiations.

III. DEVELOPMENT IN OTHER INTERTNATIONAL ORGANIZATIONS

48. A number of important developments have taken place in other international and regional bodies, in particular the ILO and NAFTA.

A. International Labour Office

1. The ILO Tripartite Declaration of 1977

49. While the OECD Guidelines cover all major aspects of corporate behaviour, the ILO Tripartite Declaration of Principles concerning MNEs Social Policy, which was largely inspired by the OECD Code adopted a year earlier, sets out principles only in the field of employment, training, conditions of work, and industrial relations. Governments, employers, and workers, as well as MNEs themselves, are recommended to observe those principles.

50. Wherever these principles refer to the behaviour expected by MNEs, they parallel the OECD Guidelines and do not conflict with them. They can therefore be of use in understanding the Guidelines to the extent that they are more elaborate. However, the responsibilities for the follow-up procedures under the Tripartite Declaration and the Guidelines are institutionally separate. Requests for clarification by governments, trade unions, or other parties are often addressed to both international fora.

2. The ILO Declaration on Fundamental Principles and Rights at Work and its Follow-up (1998)

a. The ILO declaration

51. On 18 June 1998, the ILO adopted the Declaration on Fundamental Principles and Rights at Work and its Follow-up, thereby taking up the challenges of globalization, which have been the focus of considerable debate within the ILO since 1994. As its former Director-General has underlined,

> 'Although globalisation is a factor of economic growth, and economic progress is a prerequisite for social progress, the fact remains, that it is not in itself enough to guarantee that progress. It must be accompanied by a certain numbers of social ground rules founded on common values to enable all those involved to claim their fair share of the wealth they have helped to generate'.[5]

52. A first step in this direction was made at the World Summit for Social Development in Copenhagen in 1995, when the Heads of State and Government adopted specific commitments and a Programme of Action relating to 'basic workers' rights': the prohibition of forced labour and child labour, freedom of association, the right to organize and bargain collectively, equal remuneration for work of equal value, and the elimination of discrimination in employment. Parties to the corresponding ILO Conventions were requested to fully implement them and other governments to take into account the principles embodied in them. At the WTO

---

5. M. Hansenne, *ILO Declaration on Fundamental Principles and Rights at Work and its Follow-up*, Geneva, 1998, p. 1.

Ministerial Conference held in Singapore in 1996, governments renewed their commitment to observe internationally recognized core labour standards.

53. The 1998 ILO Declaration follows on from these commitments. It was adopted by all OECD Member governments, with the exception of one government which abstained. The full text of the Declaration is given below:

The ILO Conference

Recalls:

that in freely joining the ILO, the Members have endorsed the principles and rights set out in its Constitution and in the Declaration of Philadelphia, and have undertaken to work attaining the overall objectives of the Organisation to the best of their resources and fully in line with their specific circumstances;

that these principles and rights have been expressed and developed in the form of specific rights and obligations in Conventions recognised as fundamental both inside and outside the Organisation.

Declares that all Members, even if they have not ratified the Conventions in question, have an obligation, arising from the very fact of membership in the Organisation, to respect, to promote and to realise, in good faith and in accordance with the Constitution, the principles concerning the fundamental rights which are the subject of those Conventions, namely:

freedom of association and the effective recognition of the right to collective bargaining;

the elimination of all forms of forced or compulsory labour;

the effective abolition of child labour; and

the elimination of discrimination in respect of employment and occupation.

Recognises the obligation on the Organisation to assist its Members, in order to attain these objectives:

by offering technical co-operation and advisory services to promote the ratification and implementation of the fundamental Conventions;

by assisting those Members not yet in a position to ratify some or all of these Conventions in their efforts to respect, promote and to realise the principles concerning fundamental rights which are the subject of those Conventions; and by helping the Members by their efforts to create a climate for economic and social development.

Decides that, to give full effect to this Declaration, a promotional follow-up, which is meaningful and effective, shall be implemented in accordance with the measures specified in the annex hereto, which shall be considered an integral part of the Declaration.

Stresses that labour standards should not be used for protectionist traded purposes and that nothing in this Declaration and its follow-up shall be invoked or otherwise used for such purposes; in addition, the comparative advantage of any country should in no way be called in question by this Declaration and its follow-up.

b. The follow-up to the declaration

54. The objective of the follow-up is of a strictly promotional nature. It should allow the identification of areas in which the assistance of the Organization through its technical cooperation may prove useful to its Members to help them to implement these fundamental rights and principles. It is not a substitute for the established supervisory mechanisms of the ILO, which already provide the means of assuring the application of Conventions in the States that have ratified them.

55. For those that have not, the Declaration makes important new contributions. First, it recognizes that the Members of the ILO, even if they have not ratified the Conventions in question, have an obligation to respect and promote in good faith the principles and fundamental rights which are the object of these Conventions. It seeks to achieve this aim by asking each year those member states that have not ratified all core Conventions to submit reports on progress made in implementing the principles enshrined in them.

56. The second aspect of the follow-up is a 'global report' which will provide an overview of the progress made in the preceding four-year period both in countries which have ratified the core Conventions, and in those which have not. This report will serve as a basis for assessing the effectiveness of the action taken during the preceding period and as a starting point for action plans on future assistance. It will cover, each year, one of the four categories of fundamental principles and rights in turn.

57. The global report will be submitted to the annual ILO Labour Conference for tripartite discussion. It will then be for the Governing Body to draw conclusions from this discussion concerning the priorities for technical cooperation to be implemented for the following four-year period.

3. NAFTA: The Labor Side Agreement

58. Parties to the North American Free Trade Agreement (NAFTA) are Canada, Mexico and the United States. The NAFTA text is accompanied by a Labor Side Agreement (1993) that contains an Annex on labour principles which the Parties are committed to promote, subject to each Party's *domestic* law. They indicate broad areas of concern where the three countries have developed laws, regulations, and practices that protect the rights and interests of their workforces. These principles include: freedom of association and protection of the right to organize; the right to bargain collectively; the right to strike; prohibition of forced labour;[6] labour

---

6. 'The prohibition and suppression of all forms of forced or compulsory labor, except for types of compulsory work generally acceptable by the Parties, such as compulsory military service, certain civic obligations, prison labor not for private purposes and work extracted in case of emergency'.

protection for children; minimum employment standards;[7] elimination of employment discrimination;[8] equal pay for men and women; prevention and compensation of occupational injuries and illnesses; and protection of migrant workers.[9] The agreement recognizes the right of each Party to develop and promote its own national standards within the framework of these principles.

59. The NAFTA side agreement also encourages the development of enforcement institutions and provides for a regulatory mechanism to oversee the implementation of the agreement and discuss complaints and related issues.

IV. Corparate Codes of Conduct

60. Mention should also be made of private initiatives such as corporate codes of conduct and voluntary commitments by companies to observe labour standards. In November 1998, for example, Nike, Reebok and other clothing and shoe producers concluded an agreement with a number of American human rights organizations, in which they accepted that conditions of work in their subsidiaries in the third world would be reviewed. This agreement signifies an important break-through in the fight against exploitative forms of child labour.

61. Earlier in 1998, US apparel companies, trade unions and NGOs agreed to elements of a Code of Conduct and independent monitoring systems to ensure that member company products are made under decent and humane working conditions. The Code of Conduct would require member company contractors, *inter alia*, to prohibit child labour and worker discrimination; recognize the right to freedom of association and collective bargaining; and adopt a minimum or prevailing industry wage, and a cap on mandatory overtime. To cite another example, in October 1998, the ILO signed an agreement with Pakistan's carpet makers that aims to end child labour in the country's largest cottage industry. This deal followed a similar agreement concluded in 1997 with Pakistan's soccer ball industry to phase out some 7000 child workers in and around Punjab City, the centre of Pakistan's sporting goods industry.

62. These are only a few examples, which point to a proliferation of individual corporate codes of conduct in recent years and the increased interest of companies in 'good corporate citizenship'. Considerable activity in this area can be observed across the OECD region. In the United States, a majority of the larger companies are reported to have already adopted their own company codes.

---

7. 'The establishment of minimum employment standards, such as minimum wages and overtime pay for wage earners, including those not covered by collective agreements'.
8. 'Elimination of employment discrimination on such grounds as race, religion, age, or sex, subject to certain reasonable exceptions, such as established practices or rules governing retirement ages, and special measures of protection or assistance for particular groups designed to take into account the effects of discrimination'.
9. 'Providing migrant workers in a Party's territory with the same legal protection as the Party's nationals in respect of working conditions'.

63. A recent OECD survey of codes of corporate conduct established an inventory of 233 codes.[10] For this survey, codes of corporate conduct were defined broadly as '…commitments voluntary made by companies, associations, or other entities, which put forth standards and principles for the conduct of business activities in the market place.' The definition included self-obligations and negotiated instruments, but excluded codes of corporate governance.

64. The majority of the codes were issued by individual companies, although code activity extends beyond companies to associations and groups bringing together various stakeholders. Hundred and seven codes were issued by individual companies (mostly MNEs), 89 were issued by business associations, 33 by partnerships of stakeholders (such as those based on a management/labour agreement), and 4 by intergovernmental organizations (ILO, OECD, UNCTAD, UNCED).

65. Not less than 124 of the codes contained clauses relating to 'fair employment and labour rights', in particular non-discrimination (race, gender, age, sexual orientation, disability, religion) in employment; the right of association and the right to organize and bargain collectively; avoidance of child and forced labour; and maintenance of a healthy and safe environment.

66. A large majority of the company codes apply to the direct employees of the company or companies concerned. As a rule, they apply to the *global* operations of the company and do not differentiate between countries. Many company codes also entail some form of contractual obligation for contractors and sub-contractors; most of these seek to apply standards of fair employment and labour rights, especially with respect to banning child, forced and prison labour. The majority of such contractual engagements are found in light industry (e.g. apparel) and in services (retailers and distributors).

67. The survey found that one or more international standards are explicitly cited as a reference point in about 20 per cent of the codes surveyed. International standards cited most often relate to ILO Conventions and UN Declarations; six of them refer to OECD instruments (Bribery; Protection of Privacy; and MNE Guidelines). The most frequently cited ILO Conventions refer to Forced labour (C. 29 and 105); Freedom of association and the right to organize (C. 87); Right to organize and collective bargaining (C. 98); Equal remuneration (C. 100); Discrimination in employment and occupation (C. 111); Employment policy (C. 122); and Minimum age of employment (C. 138).

68. A code's effect and effectiveness depend on faithful implementation. Where codes that apply to contractors/sub-contractors involve the signing of an agreement, such an obligation by itself represents a certain guarantee that standards will be followed. There are also cases where a code makes adoption a prerequisite to

---

10. Working Party of the Trade Committee, 'Codes of Corporate Conduct – An Inventory', OECD General Distribution document (forthcoming).

membership in a business association or partnership or gives subscribers access to recognition marks, such as special logos or labels.

69. As far as monitoring is concerned, companies tend to prefer internal procedures. However, a quarter of the codes surveyed mention some form of corrective action to deal with non-compliance, including working with suppliers or other business partners to make improvements necessary to meet code standards. Other codes mention legal action, complaints to professional bodies, and expulsion or suspension from association membership. Eighteen per cent of the codes state that non-compliance could or will result in the termination of an existing contract or business relationship. Codes tend to target with such threats compliance problems with selected standards, notably those banning child labour and forced labour.

70. An important instrument in this context is the *Voluntary Statement of Business Practices*, which the US Government has developed, following consultations with business and labour communities. It establishes Model Business Principles (MBPs) which call on US companies operating overseas to provide a safe workplace, to recognize the rights of workers to organize, and not use either child or forced labour in the production of their products. The MBPs are to be used by corporations as reference points in framing their own codes of conduct and are based on a variety of similar sets of principles US companies have put into practice. They cover essentially the same guidelines for corporate behaviour regarding labour issues as those embodied in the OECD Guidelines, with the added provisions on child and forced labour.

71. Another example of an OECD government becoming active in promoting voluntary company codes is the Japanese Council on Industrial Structure (an advisory body for MITI), which recently proposed *10 Items for Better Corporate Citizenship*, in an effort to support enterprise guidelines on how to behave abroad.

V. IMPLEMENTATION PROCEDURES

A. *Procedural Guidance for National Contact Points (NCPs)*

72. NCPs have an important role in enhancing the profile and effectiveness of the *Guidelines. They are national fora where problems related to the guidelines can be dealt with.* While it is enterprises that are responsible for observing the *Guidelines* in their day-to-day behaviour, governments can contribute to improving the effectiveness of the implementation procedures. This of the greatest importance, given the voluntary nature of the Guidelines.

1. Core Criteria for Functional Equivalence in the Activities of NCPs

73. Visibility. In conformity with the Decision, adhering governments agree to nominate NCPs, and also to inform the business community, employee organizations and other interested parties, including NGOs, about the availability of facilities associated with NCPs in the implementation of the *Guidelines.* Governments are expected to publish information about their contact points and to take an active role in promoting the *Guidelines*, which could include hosting seminars and meetings on the instrument. These events could be arranged in cooperation with business, labour, NGOs, and other interested parties, though not *necessarily* with all groups on each occasion.

74. Accessibility. Easy access to NCPs is important to their effective functioning. This includes facilitating access by business, labour, NGOs, and other members of the public. Electronic communications can also assist in this regard. NCPs would respond to all legitimate requests for information, and also undertake to deal with specific issues raised by parties concerned in an efficient and timely manner.

75. Transparency. Transparency is an important criterion with respect to its contribution to the accountability of the NCP and in gaining the confidence of the general public. Thus most of the activities of the NCP will be transparent. Nonetheless when the NCP offers its 'good offices' in implementing the *Guidelines* in specific instances, it will be in the interests of their effectiveness to take appropriate steps to establish confidentiality of the proceedings. Outcomes will be transparent unless preserving confidentiality is in the best interests of effective implementation of the *Guidelines.*

76. Accountability. A more active role with respect to enhancing the profile of the *Guidelines* – and their potential to aid in the management of difficult issues between enterprises and the societies in which they operate – will also put the activities of NCPs in the public eye. Nationally, parliaments could have a role to play. On the international plane, increased accountability may be achieved through annual reports and annual meetings of NCPs. Such meetings will provide an opportunity to share experiences and encourage 'best practices' with respect to NCPs. NCPs will also be subject to review by the CIME, where experience would be exchanged and effectiveness of their activity could be assessed.

2. Institutional Arrangements

77. The composition of NCPs should be such that they provide an effective basis for dealing with the broad range of issues covered by the *Guidelines.* Different forms of organization (e.g. representatives from one Ministry, an interagency group, or one that contained representatives from civil society) are possible. It may be helpful for the NCP to be headed by a senior official. NCP leadership should be such that it retains the confidence of social partners and fosters the public profile of the *Guidelines.* NCPs, whatever their composition, are expected to develop and maintain relations with representatives of civil society, including the business community, labour unions, and other interested parties.

3. Information and Promotion

78. The NCP functions associated with information and promotion are fundamentally important to enhancing the profile of the *Guidelines.* These functions also help to put an accent on 'pro-active' responsibilities of NCPs.

79. NCPs are required to make the *Guidelines* better known and available by appropriate means, including in national languages. On-line information may be a cost-effective means of doing this, although it should be noted that universal access to this means of information delivery cannot be assured. English and French language versions will be available from the OECD, and web site links to the OECD *Guidelines* web site are encouraged. As appropriate, NCPs will also provide prospective investors, both inward and outward, with information about the *Guidelines*, particularly those seeking investment insurance, financial assistance, or other forms of government cooperation or assistance. A separate provision also stipulates that in their efforts to raise awareness of the *Guidelines*, NCPs will cooperate with a wide variety of organizations and individuals, including, as appropriate, the business community, employee organizations, other non-governmental organizations, and the interested public.

80. Another basic activity expected of NCPs is responding to enquiries. Three groups have been singled out for attention in this regard: (i) other NCP (reflecting a provision in the Decision); (ii) the business community, employee organizations, other non-governmental organizations, and the public; and (iii) governments of non-adhering countries.

4. Implementation in Specific Instances

81. When issues arise relating to implementation of the *Guidelines* in specific instances, the NCP is expected to help resolve them. Initially, issues will normally be dealt with by the NCP in whose country the issue has arisen. The NCP may also take other steps to further the effective implementation of the *Guidelines.*

82. In making an initial assessment of whether the issue raised merits further examination, the NCP will need to determine whether the issue is *bona fide* and relevant to the implementation of the *Guidelines.* In this context, the NCP will take into account:

– the identity of the party concerned and its interest in the matter;
– whether the issue is material and substantiated;
– the relevance of applicable law and procedures;
– the procedural status and relevant results with respect to the treatment of similar or identical issues in other proceedings at the domestic and international level; and
– whether the consideration of the specific issue would contribute to the purposes and effectiveness of the *Guidelines.*

Following its initial assessment, the NCP is expected to respond to the party or parties having raised the issue. If the NCP decides that the issue does not merit further consideration, it will give reasons for its decision.

83. Where the issues raised merit further consideration, the NCP would discuss the issue further with parties concerned and use its 'good offices' in an effort to contribute informally to the resolution of issues. This could include seeking the advice of relevant authorities, as well as representatives of the business community, labour organizations, other non-governmental organizations, and experts. Consultations with NCPs in other countries, or seeking guidance on issues related to the interpretation of the *Guidelines* may also help to resolve the issue.

84. As part of making available its good offices, and where relevant to the issues at hand, NCPs will offer, or facilitate access to, consensual and non-adversarial alternatives to assist in dealing with the issues at hand, such as conciliation or mediation. In common with accepted practices on conciliation and mediation procedures, these would be used only upon agreement of the parties concerned.

85. If the parties concerned fail to reach agreement on the issues raised, the NCP will express its views to the parties on how to implement the *Guidelines*, including recommendations as appropriate. This procedure makes it clear that an NCP will express its views, even when it feels that a specific recommendation is not called for.

5. Reporting

86. Reporting would be an important responsibility of NCPs that would also help to build up a knowledge base and core competencies in furthering the effectiveness of the *Guidelines*. In reporting on implementation activities in specific instances, NCPs will comply with transparency and confidentiality considerations as set out in para. C-4.

B.   *Procedural Guidance for the CIME*

87. The procedural annex to the Council Decision provides additional guidance to the Committee in carrying out its responsibilities, including:

– Discharging its responsibilities in an efficient and timely manner;
– Considering requests from NCPs for assistance;
– Reviewing the activities of NCPs;
– Providing for the possibility of seeking advice from experts.

88. The non-binding nature of the *Guidelines* precludes the Committee from acting as a judicial or quasi-judicial body. Nor should the findings and views expressed by the NCP (other than interpretations of the *Guidelines*) be questioned by a referral to LIME. The provision that CIME shall not reach conclusions on the conduct of individual enterprises has been maintained in the Decision itself.

89. CIME will consider requests from NCPs for assistance, including in the event of doubt about the interpretation of the *Guidelines* in specific circumstances. This paragraph reflects para. C-2c of the procedural annex pertaining to NCPs, where NCPs are invited to seek the guidance of the CIME if they have doubt about the interpretation of the *Guidelines* in these particular circumstances.

90. In reviewing NCP activities, it is not intended that CIME conduct annual reviews of each individual NCP, although the CIME will make recommendations, as necessary, to improve their functioning, including with respect to the effective implementation of the *Guidelines.*

91. A substantiated submission by a government or an advisory body that an NCP was not fulfilling its procedural responsibilities in the implementation of the *Guidelines* in specific instances will also be considered by the CIME. This complements provisions in the section of the annex pertaining to NCPs reporting on their activities.

92. Clarifications of the meaning of the *Guidelines* at the multilateral level would remain a key responsibility of the CIME to ensure that the meaning of the *Guidelines* would not vary from country to country. A substantiated submission by an adhering country or advisory body with respect to whether an NCP interpretation of the *Guidelines* is consistent with CIME interpretations will also be considered. This may not be needed very often, but would provide a vehicle to resolve a specific problem if it arises.

93. Finally, CIME may wish to call on experts in addressing specific issues or where specialized expertise is needed on broader issues (e.g. child labour, human rights). Experts could be called on to report to CIME on individual issues and/or on improving the effectiveness of procedures. For this purpose, CIME could call on OECD in-house expertise, international organizations, the advisory bodies, NGOs, academics, and others.

VI. CONCLUSIONS

94. The nature of the OECD Guidelines. Guidelines for enterprises, as an instrument to monitor corporate conduct, are growing in importance. There is a broad consensus that the OECD Guidelines should be *voluntary* or better *non-legally binding.* They do represent Member countries' firm expectations for MNE behaviour. As such, they are morally binding, as they translate the 'mores' of the international community. The same can be said of the Tripartite Declaration of the ILO (1977), of the ILO Declaration on Fundamental Principles and Rights at Work (1998) and the NAFTA Labor Side Agreement.

95. There is an equally broad consensus that the OECD Guidelines should be stable and consistent. This is especially the case for the Employment and Industrial Relations chapter, which continues to be a positive and progressive statement of good practice of industrial relations in OECD countries.

96. The OECD Guidelines and the ILO Tripartite Declaration. The ILO Declaration is addressed to governments, employers, and workers organizations, while the OECD Guidelines are recommendations to MNEs. The ILO Declaration sets out principles only in the field of employment, training, working conditions, and industrial relations. Wherever the principles of the ILO Declaration refer to the behaviour of enterprises, they parallel the OECD Guidelines and do not conflict with them. They can, therefore, be of use in understanding the OECD Guidelines to the extent that they are more elaborate, as in the case of the Employment and Industrial Relations Chapter. This consistency between the two codes of conduct needs to be maintained.

97. Scope of application of the OECD Guidelines. The Guidelines are recommendation addressed to enterprises operating in OECD countries. However, para. 2 of the introduction stipulates that, 'since the operations of MNEs extend throughout the world, international cooperation in this field should extend to all States'. Thus, MNEs are encouraged to extend good corporate practice throughout the universe of their operations.

98. One should consider whether it would be appropriate to extend the applicability of the Guidelines to activities of MNEs beyond OECD territory. The introduction to the Guidelines, as quoted above, seems to be pointing in that direction. Arguably, the Guidelines do represent universally accepted principles and fundamental rights. Indeed, it might be difficult for MNEs to distinguish in their overall corporate conduct between the countries in which subsidiaries or intermediary levels operate. Moreover, the OECD survey of corporate codes of conduct finds that when companies set standards for the direct employees, these usually apply to the global operations of the company. Problems of extraterritoriality do, in principle, not arise, since these are voluntary guidelines addressed to MNEs, not to Governments. Indeed, under the Guidelines, the recommendations are also addressed to parent companies situated outside OECD territory. There is, however, a problem of implementation, since there are no contacts points in non-OECD countries.

99. The (non-)definition of the MNE. The guidelines do not define the term MNE, but rather describe some general criteria covering a broad range of multinational activities and arrangements. These arrangements can include traditional international direct investment based on equity participation, or other means which do not necessarily include an equity capital element.

100. The clarification by the CIME that '*all entities, including parent companies, local subsidiaries, as well as intermediary levels of the organisation, are expected to co-operate and assist, as necessary, in observing the Guidelines. To the extent that the parent companies actually exercise control over the activities of their subsidiaries, they have a responsibility for observance of the Guidelines by those subsidiaries*' seems to be adequate in addressing possible issues at stake.

101. In this context, the question arises as to whether the definition includes also sub-contractors in case of out-sourcing. For example, would an MNE also have responsibility for the observance of labour standards by its sub-contractors? As outlined further above, many voluntary company codes already entail some form of contractual obligation for contractors or sub-contractors to live up to standards of fair employment and labour rights, in particular concerning a ban on child labour, forced and prison labour.

102. It nevertheless remains a fact that sub-contractors are, in relation to a MNE, a third party. Consequently, a sub-contractor is solely responsible for his own behaviour. From this point of view, the definition of the MNE would not cover sub-contractors. However, if the (contractual) relationship between an MNE and a sub-contractor was of such a nature that the MNE was in fact exercising a significant influence over the activities of the sub-contractor, it could be argued that this relationship might be covered by the definition. In such a case there might be, depending on the realities of the relationship, a responsibility for the MNE to ensure the observance of the Guidelines by a sub-contractor.

103. Child labour and bonded labour. There was strong support for amending the Guidelines by including two core labour rights contained in the ILO Declaration of 1998, namely, the elimination of all forms of forced or compulsory labour and the effective abolition of child labour. The credibility of the Guidelines required that Governments, at the occasion of the Review 2000, should recommend to the MNEs to make a positive contribution on those issues.

104. Information to employee representatives. One ought to take account of developments in other regional organizations, such as the 1994 European Works Council Directive. The issue of information has become of major importance in a globalizing economy. Consequently, a more precise guideline seems warranted, if the Guidelines want to remain credible.

105. Information rights should be strengthened and consequently Para. 3 could read as follows (additions in italics): [Employees should] '*regularly* provide to representatives of employees information which enables them to obtain a true and fair view of the performance of the entity *and* of the enterprise as a whole. *The information should, in particular, relate to the structure of the enterprise, the economic and financial situation, overall prospects and manpower planning, investments, substantial changes in operations, cut-backs or closures of undertakings, establishments or important parts thereof and collective redundancies, taking into account legitimate requirements of business confidentiality*'.

106. Non-discrimination. Non-discrimination is one of the core fundamental principles retained in the 1998 ILO Declaration. It is also retained in many private codes of corporate conduct issued by MNEs business associations. In these codes, non-discrimination is sought on the following grounds: race, gender, age, sexual orientation, disability, and religion. Similarly, the NAFTA Labor side agreement contains the following principles: 'elimination of employment discrimination (on such grounds as race, religion, age, sex, or other grounds)' and 'equal pay for men and women'. It is regretable that the OECD Guidelines omit 'age' as a ground for non-discrimination.

107. Implementation. The implementation procedure, especially the role of the NCP has been strengthened. The NCPs will determine to a great extent whether the OECD Guidelines develop into a credible instrument for the social monitoring of the activities of MNEs worldwide.

Chapter 10. Conflicts of Laws in Employment Contracts and Industrial Relations

F. Gamillscheg and M. Franzen

I. INTRODUCTION

1. Where an employment contract involves one or more foreign countries, it must be determined which of the different laws governs the contract before litigious questions can be resolved.

For example, if an American company hires an engineer in Brussels of American (Belgian/Swiss) nationality for work to be executed in Bolivia, a dispute may arise on which legal basis he may claim compensation for unfair dismissal.

The question is answered by Conflict of Law rules. Every country has its own set of such rules. They are also known as Private International Law, though these rules are not 'international', but national in character. Truly international sources governing conflicts of law in our field are not numerous, though of growing importance.

2. The conflict of law rule is dependent upon the essence of the subject matter, i.e. labour law norms. In substantive labour law we distinguish three categories of norms:

(1) As a rule the employment relationship, as established by the employment contract, forms part of the general law of contract. The norms governing the employment relationship are mandatory; they cannot be abrogated by contract. Yet it is left to the employee to claim his rights through the courts or grievance procedures. In continental European law this category of norms is classified as private law.
(2) A number of issues (safety at work, protection of children or pregnant mothers, or of handicapped persons, maximum hours, non-discrimination, etc.) are often considered to be of such fundamental importance that special authorities (factory inspectorates, social security officials, etc.) are organized to ensure compliance with the rules governing these issues, if necessary by means of compulsion. The enforcement of these norms may even take place against the will of the protected employee. In countries with a Roman law tradition these protective rules (or at least the associated regulations on penal sanctions and coercive measures, etc.) are classified as rules with the character of 'public law'. The distinction

between these two modes of enforcement as such is also known in Anglo-Saxon countries.

(3) Industrial relations are also governed to a growing extent by legal norms. They are often classified as 'collective' norms. The phenomenon of collective labour law does not fit very well into the distinction between private and public law. It resembles the latter (e.g. the duty of fair and equal treatment, the mandatory nature of industrial norms contained in collective agreements, etc.), yet without being subject to state control.

3. The distinction between labour law rules, as described in para. 2, is reflected in international labour law. The conflict of laws of the employment contract is regarded as forming a part of the conflict of laws of the contract in a search for the appropriate law, foreign or domestic, controlling the contract. The rule thus indicating the proper law of the contract belongs in the category of so-called multilateral conflict norms.

For example, suppose that the employment contract were governed by the law of the place where the work is done/or where the seat of enterprise is located/or by the law chosen by the parties concerned. In all these cases the applicable law may be foreign, if the place of work/seat of the enterprise/chosen law is foreign. If in our first example above the dismissal is governed by Bolivian law, then there is no difficulty for American or Belgian judges to apply that law.

In the field of public law as described above each authority only applies its own law, and the sole question is whether or not the respective norm is to be applied. If the answer is no, the authority refrains from action. As a rule – this is universally accepted – the application of these protective norms is contingent on the fact that the work is executed within national boundaries. The conflict of law norm is unilateral. For example, the German factory inspectorate (*Gewerbeaufsicht*) is only responsible and German safety regulations only apply if the work is done in Germany. Work done abroad (i.e. beyond the border) lies outside the jurisdiction of such authorities even if German citizens are working there (*infra* no. 19).

As concerns collective labour law, most of the answers are still uncertain; only a few sets of rules are generally accepted (*infra* no. 26).

II.   SOURCES

A.   *International Sources*

4.   Written norms in International Labour Law which relate to the employment relationship or to individual aspects thereof may be found in certain conventions of the ILO and in bilateral treaties.[1] In 1980 the EC proposed a Convention Regarding the Law Applicable to Contractual Obligations (hereinafter: EC-Convention) which also applies to the labour relationship.[2] It is based on the preparatory work of numerous

---

1.   *Cf.* M. Simon-Dépitre, *Acts of the 2nd International Congress of Labour Law*, 1957, Geneva, 1961, p. 332; Stefan Szászy, *International Labour Law*, p. 23.

2.   O.J. No. L 266 of 9 October 1980. The draft has been made a part of the new Law on Private International Law for the Federal Republic of Germany of 1986; *cf.* F. Gamillscheg, *Zeitschrift für Arbeitsrecht*, 1983, p. 307.

experts (*see* the report of Prof. Lagarde and Prof. Giuliano). After being ratified by the Member States of the EC, it has come into force in 1991.

The Council Directive of the EC concerning the posting of workers in the framework of the provision relates to some aspects of conflicts of laws in employment contracts. This directive was adopted by the Council of Ministers of the EC in autums 1996.[3] According to this directive the employee who is sent abroad to perform work temporarily on the territory of another Member State is entitled to claim the 'hard core' of the working conditions such as minimum weekly hours of work, minimum paid holidays or minimum rates of pay which apply for work in the receiving State regardless of the proper law of his employment contract. Laws providing such working conditions have to be considered as mandatory rules for the purposes of Article 7, para. 2 of the the EC-Convention (*infra* no. 20).[4] According to its Article 20 the EC-Convention does not affect the application of provisions of the EC which lay down choice of law rules relating to contractual obligations.[5]

B.   National Sources

5.   A number of states have written multilateral conflict norms, mostly contained in a general code of Private International Law. Thus, Article 6 of the European Convention (*infra* no. 17) has become part of the new German law on Private International Law (Article 30 of the Introductory Law to the Civil Code, EGBGB). In Switzerland, Article 121 of the Federal Law on International Private Law, 1987, refers to the ordinary place of work; the parties are free, however, to choose either the law at the employees domicile or the law at the seat, domicile or ordinary residence of the employer. Article 32 of the Polish Law on Private International Law, 1965, grants the parties the right to choose the applicable law. In Austria, the former Article 44 of the 1978 Austrian Act on Private International Law refers to the law at the place of work. Austria is now part to the EC-Convention and has therefore repealed Article 36–45 of the Austrian Act on Private International Law.[6] Written conflict norms are also contained in the respective codes of Hungary, Albania, and Kuwait.

Numerous norms determine the scope of application of this or that particular law. They cannot be listed here. They generally provide that the norm must be applied to all work executed within the territorial boundaries of that country, regardless of the

---

3.   O.J. No. L 18/1 of 21. January 1997; *cf.* W. Däubler, *Industrial Law Journal.* 1998, p. 264; P. Davies, *Common Market Law Review* 1997, p. 571; M. Franzen, *Zeitschrift für Europäisches Privatrecht.* 1997, p. 1055. First and second draft of this Directive *O.J.* 1993 no. C 187/5.

4.   A. Lyon-Caen, *Revue du Marché commun*, 1991, p. 108; E.Jayme/C.Kohler, *Revue critique de droit international privé*, 1995, pp. 1, 32.

5.   EC-Member States with a general high salary level like Austria, Belgium, France, Germany, and the Netherlands have in the meantime enacted own national rules providing the mandatory application of certain working conditions to employees working temporarily in the receiving state; cf. for example sec. 7, 7a–c Arbeitsvertragsrechts-Anpassungsgesetz (Austria), and Arbeitnehmer-Entsendegesetz (Germany). The existence of those laws shows that in general national rules governing the employment contract are not to be considered as 'norms with direct applicability' (*cf. infra* no. 15), they only apply if the law of the State they belong to is the proper law of the employment contract. In consequence they are not mandatory according to Article 7, para. 2 of the EC-Convention (*infra* no. 20).

6.   *Cf.* M. Schwimann, *Internationales Privatrecht*, 2nd ed., 1999, p. 76.

nationality of the parties. For example, this is the case with section 196 of the British Employment Rights Act, 1996.

6.   Norms such as the following are not genuine sources of Private International Law: for example section 92c of the German Commercial Code provides that the mandatory provisions for the protection of the Commercial agent are freely negotiable if his place of business is located outside the territory of the EC and the European Economic Area. Section 7(2)(g) of the British Sex Discrimination Act permits the non-engagement of a woman because of her sex when the position involves tasks which, according to the law or customs of the place of work, cannot be performed by a woman. Article L 122-14-8 of the French Code du Travail obliges the French employer to carry home and to re-employ a French employee sent abroad to work with an affiliated company in case he is dismissed there.[7] Such norms are not conflict rules. They apply when German or British or French law is the proper law. Whether this is the case, is a preliminary question and an issue in itself. But, of course, their very existence may be taken into consideration when the conflict rule itself is being elaborated by the judge.

7.   In many parts of the world, as in the United States or the Nordic countries, International Labour Law is still a product of case law; to what extent it has achieved the status of customary law must be determined in a country-by-country survey. The spectrum of opinions and solutions is accordingly broad. But this has the advantage that, in the course of the years, certain standard solutions have been developed for certain typical recurrent situations. It is especially fascinating for the scholar of comparative law to uncover how, on this basis, the same solutions have simultaneously gained acceptance in different countries totally independent of one another, which of course is an indication that the solution satisfies the interests of the parties involved.

If the European codification will achieve its goal of unifying the different legislations will have to be seen. The convention (and accordingly the new German Act) obliges the Member States to interpret the uniform rules in an international mind, Article 18 EC-Convention, 36 EGBGB.

III.   THE PROPER LAW OF THE EMPLOYMENT CONTRACT

8.   There are three main approaches to resolving the question of the applicable law:
(1)   the classical method;
(2)   the territorial connecting factor; and
(3)   the compromise as embodied in Article 6 of the EC-Convention.

A.   *Autonomy of the Parties*

9.   The prevailing opinion in many industrialized countries such as the USA, Sweden, formerly also Germany or Switzerland, still adheres (or adhered) to

---

7.   *Cf.* the case Cour de cassation (chambre sociale) 30 June 1993, *Revue de jurisprudence sociale*, 1994, p. 245.

general international contract law and thus the principle of party autonomy. This principle provides that the parties to the employment contract have the right to choose the law governing the contract. If they fail to do so, other substitute criteria apply (*infra* no. 14)

In the United Kingdom[8] general opinion also supported the precedence of the will of the parties in determining the proper law; on the other hand, a series of new protective laws (for example legislation against unfair dismissal or sex discrimination) each contain an independent norm limiting their application to work performed at home regardless of the proper law. That the proper law is not to be superseded by these special norms can be seen definitively in section 204 Employment Rights Act 1996, where it is written that the proper law of a labour contract 'apart from this Act' can be English or foreign law.[9]

10.   As a rule, an implied choice of law is as effective as an express one. Such a choice exists when the parties intended to submit their contract to a particular legal system but this intention can only be derived from other circumstances. For example, in a contract relating to country A and country B the six-week period of notice is referred to as the 'legal period' of notice. This would be evidence of the intention of the parties to submit the contract to the law of country A if the legal notice period in country B is only four weeks.[10] A reference to the rules of tax or of social insurance law may also be an indication of a tacit choice of law, but this is not necessarily so.

11 .   Article 3 of the EC-Convention is satisfied with 'sufficient certainty' of the choice of law; the former section 44 para. 3 of the Austrian Law on Private International Law required on the other hand, an express choice[11] (which may, however, be verbal).[12] Swiss law demands an unequivocal choice to be derived from the contract itself or the circumstances of the case.

12.   In general international contract law it is disputed whether the choice of law must be made from among those systems to which the contract entertains material

---

8.   The United Kingdom also ratified the Rome Convention. It may be permitted, as a last homage to the great jurist that was F.A. Mann, to cite his evaluation of the Convention in *International Comparative Law Quarterly*, 1983, p. 265: 'This is one of the most unnecessary, useless, and, indeed, unfortunate attempts at unification or harmonisation of the law that has ever been undertaken ... Nothing ... is apt to eliminate the conclusion that the Convention results from a misconceived initiative, would be likely to corrupt our present law and should be rejected – the sooner the better, if insecurity and imtation all over the world are to be avoided'.

9.   *Cf.* B. Hepple and P. O'Higgins, *Employment Law*, 4th ed., 1981, section 21; Dicey/Morris, *On the Conflict of Laws*, 13th ed., 2000, II, p. 1301; *Industrial Relations Legal, Information Bulletin* No. 454 (1992).

10.   *Cf.* Rechtbank Amsterdam, 7 May 1957, *Ned. Jur.*, 1957, No. – 646.

11.   *Cf.* Oberster Gerichtshof (OGH), 27 January 1987, *Zeitschrift für Arbeits- und Sozialrecht* 1988, p. 56 (the express choice of exclusive competence of a Swiss court is not sufficient to displace the Libyan place of work as connecting factor); Oberlandesgericht Linz, 14 January 1991, *Sammlung arbeitsrechtlicher Entscheidungen*, No. 10982; Schwimann, *Zeitschrift für Arbeits- und Sozialrecht.* 1992, p. 5.

12.   Sections 36–45 of the Austrian Law on Private International Law were repealed after Austria has acceded to the EC-Convention in 1998 (*see also supra* no. 5).

bonds. This does not have to be resolved here; no cases have, as yet, been found where the parties to the employment contract have chosen a totally unrelated legal system. In practice the choice lies exclusively between the law of the place of work and the law at the seat of the enterprise. One must be careful, however, not to misinterpret the required 'close' or 'legitimate' connection of the contract to the chosen law as a purely territorial connection. The work is carried out in a place where the legal system is of course of the greatest significance for its execution, but the issue still remains essentially one of the employment relationship. A legal relationship has its roots not in a place but in a legal system. The law does have a sphere of territorial validity, where it is the *lex fori*; however, this territorial factor is but one of several potentially relevant determining aspects. The place of work is an important point of consideration but far from being the only one.

13. Article 3, para. 1 of the EC-Convention, equally incorporated into Article 27 of the German Law, permits the parties to select the governing law 'applicable to the whole or a part only of the contract'. In the field of labour law, this is, however, not a good solution. It is a perversion of party autonomy to allow them to select portions of different legal systems and to construct for themselves out of these a mosaic to suit their own tastes. This may be tolerable for general International Contract Law where parties are of equal economic strength. In Labour Law, however, this would lead to all the dangers which the opponents of party autonomy always, unjustly, conjure up (*infra* no. 16). For example, it would be bad law to allow the parties to submit their contract to German law in general and to the law of X for all the questions concerning employee inventions or pension rights. Partial references which take into consideration certain peculiarities of the place of work, e.g. hours of work or holidays, which the employer for practical reasons cannot avoid, are of course not excluded.

The (express) choice of the governing law may also take place in course of the employment, even when the contract has come to its end.[13]

14. When the parties omit to choose the proper law a number of written norms state which law applies. In Italy, Article 25 d.p. (disposizioni preliminari al Codice Civile) refers to common nationality of the parties, and, in the absence of this, to the place of conclusion of the contract. Article 10, no. 6 of the Spanish Civil Code refers to the place of performance, as do Article 121 of the Swiss Act on Private International Law and Article 33 of the Polish Law, each with further details. Italy and Spain are now part to the EC-Convention.

To the extent that the law is silent, the determination of the proper law becomes the responsibility of the judiciary and the academic community. A number of different approaches have been worked out.

(1) The search for general connecting factors. In early days, Romanic and Anglo-Saxon countries regarded the *locus contractus* as the connecting factor for contracts. Savigny replaced the place of contract with the place of performance and found many supporters. Even today there are decisions based on these two rules.

---

13. *Cf.* Court of Appeal Paris, 27 November 1986, *Revue critique de droit international privé*, 1988, p. 314.

As standard criteria for all conceivable cases, however, they fail to satisfy the wide spectrum of interests involved.

(2) Eminent scholars have for a long time required that every type of contract should have the connecting factor that is most appropriate to it. This is said to be the place of the characteristic performance, a formula due to the late Professor Schnitzer, Geneva, formerly Berlin, and set forth in Article 117 of the Swiss Act or section 29 of the Hungarian law on Private International Law or in Article 4 para. 2 of the EC-Convention. For an employment contract the characteristic factor would be the place of work. To date, however, this proposition has not prevailed because there are too many cases in which the acknowledged interests of the parties require other solutions.

(3) In the practice of important industrial countries another method predominates. It endeavours to find the suitable connecting factor for every single contract as such. This theory aspires to a maximum of individual case justice, purchased, to be honest, with a high measure of uncertainty: for, in the final analysis, it is the judge who subsequently decides on the predominant connecting factor and with it on the proper law. This method has recourse to a stock of typical criteria. If one of them is especially germane, i.e. 'most significant', or, where many factors arise, if these all point to the same law, then this is taken to be the centre of gravity of the contract and thus leads to its proper law. It is an 'English' or 'French' contract, therefore English or French law applies. Examples of typically recurrent connecting factors in a legal system are the place of performance; the seat of the enterprise; common nationality; reliance on prior contracts; the place of contract; the place of origin of payment or of instructions; agreements as to currency used for payment; participation in pension plans of the parent enterprise; language of the contract; etc.

In another variation of this method it is not the cumulation of connecting factors but rather a decision on the alleged intent of the parties based on these connecting factors that is emphasized. This so-called 'subjective' theory arises from the assumption that the parties had a free choice of law; since they failed to exercise it, the judge makes the choice in their stead as he deems they reasonably and fairly would have done. Both methods lead, as a rule, to the same result. The objective approach is more generally accepted. The subjective has, on the other hand, certain advantages.[14]

On the basis of these methods a number of principles have been developed and applied by the courts, without their relinquishing the prerogative to decide otherwise. According to these principles the place of work emerges as the most relevant connecting factor. If the centre of gravity is the place where the work is usually done, the proper law of the contract does not change merely because the work is temporarily completed elsewhere. An example would be a travelling salesperson, working within country A who takes a trip to country B (*infra* no. 17).

For persons hired at the seat of the enterprise specifically for work abroad the seat of the enterprise prevails as the connecting factor. This line of thought is even more dominant when the employee is a citizen of the 'sending State' (common nationality being an additional element). The argument which supports this decision is that the

---

14. *Cf.* Gamillscheg, *International Encyclopaedia of Comparative Law*, l.c., No. 18.

legal system at the place of work may be unknown and unfamiliar, often for both parties, so that they, if only for this reason, would prefer their own law. Executive and management personnel, for whom transferrals are common, are usually subject to the law at the seat of the enterprise. This connecting factor best corresponds to their vital interest that the proper law does not change with every new place of work.[15]

For sailors the rule still prevails that the law of the flag is to be applied, but this is a very doubtful solution.[16] In determining the applicable law of a maritime employment contract under the EC-Convention this rule may be counteracted by all circumstances of the case according to the 'unless'clause (Article 6, para. 2, *infra* no. 17).[17] Such an analysis may, when the flag is the only connection to a flag of convenience state and other more significant links exist with one other state, especially the state of the former flag, require application of the law of the latter state. In many European countries (for example Denmark, France, Germany, Norway, or the United Kingdom) international shipping registers have been installed as an (probably not very effective) instrument against flagging out. Provided that a ship is registered in the German International Shipping Register it flies the German flag but the flag is not to be considered as a connecting factor when the sailor does not have his domicile or habitual residence in Germany (Section 21 para. 4 of the German Law of the Flag Act). If this is the case the maritime employment contract shall be governed by the law of the country the contract is more closely connected with; important connecting factors may be the domicile, habitual residence or the nationality of the sailor.[18]

B. Lex Loci Laboris

15. A strong trend among scholars and judicial bodies which has also found its way into a number of statutesn such as section 51 of the Hungarian Act, deny the parties the option of choosing the law applicable to the employment contract and demand instead a link independent of their intention. The employee – according to the basic idea behind this view – is economically too weak to resist the choice of law imposed by the employer. Thus, this choice would typically deprive the employee of the protection afforded by the law which would normally be applicable. 'Normally applicable' means the law of the place of work.

Many arguments have been assembled to support this view: the oldest explanation is that labour laws are so-called *lois d'ordre public*. This means that they are so

---

15. An example of this type of a middle-management employee is M. Gary Wuetig, who served International Harvester in Chicago, Greece, Great Britain, and France where he was dismissed, *see* Court of Appeal Paris, *supra* note 7. *Cf.* also the former section 44 I of the Austrian Act and Oberster Gerichtshof, 8 April 1992, *Zeitschrift für Arbeitsrecht und Sozialrecht*, 1992, p. 17.
16. *Cf.* Kahn-Freund, *Rabels Zeitschrift für ausländisches und internationales Privatrecht*, 1958, p. 200; Lagarde, *Revue critique de droit international privé*, 1991, p. 319; Gamillscheg, *Internationales Arbeitsrecht*, p. 137.
17. *Cf.* the Opinion of Advocate General Marco Darmon, in the Case 72/91, European Court of Justice, 17 March 1993, I-887, No. 81; German Bundesarbeitsgericht (BAG), 24 August 1989, in *Arbeitsrechtliche Praxis. Nr. 28 zu IPR-Arbeitsrecht*; Déprez, *Revue de jurisprudence sociale*, 1994, pp. 235, 244.
18. *See* German Bundesarbeitsgericht (BAG), 3 May 1995, in *Entscheidungssammlung zum Arbeitsrecht*, no. 3 Art. 30 EGBGB; Bundesverfassungsgericht 10 January 1995, in *Arbeitsrechtliche Praxis*, No. 76 Art. 9 Grundgesetz.

important and so closely related to the social order of the state of the forum that their application is mandatory and independent of the proper law of the contract. The effect is the same when labour laws are characterized as *lois de police et de sureté*, a notion derived from Article 3 para. 1 of the French Civil Code. Labour laws as *lois de police* are, above all, protective labour laws with public law reinforcement, but not exclusively. Frequently, all mandatory norms, especially those against dismissal, are included under this designation. Another premise is the notion of territoriality. Courts and authors often rely, without further discussion, on the explanation that labour laws are 'territorial'. Yet this notion is very unclear: 'Nobody knows exactly what this means'.[19] Finally, in the context of present judicial trends attention must be drawn to a modern theory, connected, above all, with the names of, *inter alia*, Francescakis, de Nova, Malintoppi, de Winter which categorizes norms such as labour law norms into a special class of 'norms with direct applicability'. This dogmatic construction has found its way into Article 7, para. 2 of the EC-Convention and consequently into the German Law as well.[20]

As already mentioned, the main idea is to protect the worker against an abuse of power by the employer. This fear of abuse with regard to the freedom of contract is enhanced with a growing distrust of large multinational enterprises (MNEs). So, English legislation, which prescribes the application of the new protective laws to work performed within its boundaries, independent of the proper law, was justified by the wish to extend the advantages of these laws to the employees of the American MNEs working in England.[21]

16.   Yet the criticism of party autonomy is unfounded. Freedom of contract under substantive law and the choice of the governing law under the conflict rules are not comparable. When in substantive law a protective norm is excluded (e.g.: severance pay for unfair dismissal), the employee does not receive this protection: instead of X, there is non-X. When, on the other hand, through a choice of law, X (e.g. the law at the place of performance) is excluded in favour of Y (the law at the seat of the enterprise), non-X is, to be sure, still valid, but Y applies with all its protective provisions. We must now, until there is evidence to the contrary, assume that X and Y offer equivalent protection. With this assumption, however, the employer's incentive to abuse his economic and intellectual advantage through the choice of law is lost. On the other hand, the mandatory application of the *lex loci* may be hazardous to an employee who is sent to a country with (a) insufficient social protection; or (b) which delegates the regulation to collective agreements which do not apply *in casu*. Here the protection, which, for fear of abuse, the denial of the freedom of choice is intended to assure, results in the reverse.

Furthermore, even when the legal system at a distant place of work is socially comparable, it is often an unknown factor for all involved. This uncertainty concerning the legal position may deter an employee, even more than is already the case, from seeking judicial vindication of his rights, and his union will only rarely be in a

---

19. See Blanpain/Dumortier, *Belgian National Report to the 11th International Congress of Comparative Law*, Caracas, 1982, p. 16.
20. Another example is French Cour de Cassation, 19 March 1986, *Revue critique d.i.p.*, 1987 p. 554.
21. *Cf.* B. Hepple, *Encyclopedia of Employment Law*, Vol. 1, No. 1, 1999, International Employment Contracts. No. 1-9004.

position to give proper advice and assistance. The judge, for his part, will be compelled to obtain costly expert opinions on the foreign law involved even when the dispute concerns a matter that is clear under domestic law and the ties to the overseas place of work have long been disrupted. Finally, it should be borne in mind that in all developed labour law systems judges are accustomed, in one form or another, to reviewing the fairness of the provisions contained in the employment contract, so that agreements through which the interests of the employee may be unfairly violated are treated as null and void. On the other hand, rigid application of the *lex loci laboris* will often give the employer the same possibilities for abuse. Many important employee issues, such as protection against dismissal, competition after termination of the employment relationship, rights to employee inventions, pensions, etc. could be manipulated by say, sending an employee – especially professional and managerial employees – to countries which offer less protection. When it is within the employer's power to direct such a transfer the employee will be obliged to comply. Evidence that the transfer was made *in fraudem legis* will not be adducible in all cases.

C. Article 6 of the EC-Convention

17. Still distrusting party autonomy as such for fear of abuse by the employer, yet mindful of the deficiencies of the place of work as the only connecting factor, the ECConvention steers a middle course which seeks to offer the employee a maximum of protection: Party autonomy is not excluded, but it works only in favour of the employee. The applicable law as such, in the absence of choice, is determined in the following way, Article 6, para. 2 EC:

> '… an employment contract shall, in the absence of choice in accordance with Article 3, be governed:
> (a) by the law of the country in which the employee habitually carries out his work in performance of the contract, even if he is temporarily employed in another country; or
> (b) if the employee does not habitually carry out his work in any one country, by the law of the country in which the place of business through which he was engaged is situated; unless it appears from the circumstances as a whole that the contract is more closely connected with another country, in which case the contract shall be governed by the law of that country.'

Thus the authors of the Convention pay all due tribute to the place of work but no longer insist upon it being the sole connecting factor. Another country may be more closely connected with the contract.

Note: The place of work is not only rejected where the other connecting factor is 'manifestly' more intrinsic to the contract. Of two connecting factors the more intrinsic one is adopted.[22] Yet there is no doubt that the place of work is the rule and the 'unless' clause the exception.

---

22. A similar escape from the mandatory application of the *lex loci* is permitted in Swiss law by Article 15. This norm empowers the judge to deviate from the ordinary conflict rule if another law has a 'much more close' connection with the case. *Cf.* Bucher, 'Les nouvelles regles de droit int. privé suisse dans le domaine du droit du travail'. in *Melanges A. Bérenstein*, 1989, p. 147.

The 'unless' clause will permit the actual practice to continue applying the law of the home State to the employment contracts of people who are sent abroad by their company (permanently[23] or with the intention of returning to continue work at home). The case is open when an employer of X engages a co-citizen of X in country Y where the employee resides, as when an American company engages in Brussels an American citizen living in Brussels for work in Belgium. Whether this employee's contract is more closely connected with the United States or with Belgium may depend on additional factors; thus the judge will be more inclined to apply American law with a high-ranking manager than with a blue-collar worker.

For example in Germany the 'unless' clause was applied by the Federal Labour Court when an American airline engaged pilots of American nationality with habitual German residence for work to be executed in Germany. Due to the specific circumstances of the case the German Federal Labour Court held that the pilots' employment contracts were more closely connected with the state of New York where the seat of the airline was situated.[24]

18. If the parties choose a law other than that which is described in Article 6, para. 2, the choice is valid, but '… shall not have the result of depriving the employee of the protection afforded to him by the mandatory rules of the law which would be applicable under para. 2 in the absence of choice' (Article 6, para. 1)

Thus the idea of the principle of the most favourable law, has achieved a breakthrough. Its purpose is to prevent abuse of the party autonomy as well as to allay misgivings about submitting the employment contract to an unfamiliar or underdeveloped local law. This theory involves the joint application of both legal systems. The employee is entitled to claim the norm more favourable to him.[25] In this way the well-known Labour Law principle of the most favourable law seems to be incorporated into Conflicts Law. This solution was also adopted in the former Section 44, para. 3 of the Austrian Law on Private International law before Austria acceded to the EC-Convention (*see supra* no. 5). The French courts and literature followed the same line already before the entering into force of the EC-Convention.

---

23. Contra to the German Bundesarbeitsgericht (BAG), 30 April 1987, in Arbeitsrechtliche Praxis. No. 15 zu § 12 Schwerbehindertengesetz. The court would have applied Saudi Arabian law, had the parties not expressly agried on the application of German law (the case was still governed by the law prior to the new Article 30 EGBGB). *Cf.* Cour de Cassation, Chambre sociale, in its decision of 29 May 1991, *Revue critique de droit international privé*, 1992, p. 471 and Déprez, *Revue de jurisprudence sociale*, 1994, pp. 235, 237.

24. *See* Bundesarbeitsgericht 29 October 1992, in *Arbeitsrechtliche Praxis*, No. 31 zu IPR-Arbeitsrecht. *Cf.* also the case Cour de cassation (Chambre sociale), 28 October 1997, in *Praxis des Internationalen Privat- und Verfahrensrechts*, 1999, p. 261: an employment contract between a French citizen and a French company concluded in France in French language was governed by french law though the contract was executed in Pakistan.

25. *Cf.* the example of the Luxembourg Cour d'appel, 3 December 1992, *Pasicrisie Luxembourgeoise*, 1993, 1, p. 30. The court compared the French and Luxembourg provisions concerning protection against dismissal and found out that the French laws provided a shorter period of notice whereas the Luxembourg provisions did not grant compensation for unfair dismissal like the French did. Therefore the court held that the French norms concerning protection against dismissal were on the whole more favourable and had to be applied to the case.

In Spanish Law Spanish workers employed by Spanish companies abroad can claim all advantages accorded by Spanish Law, Article 1.4 Estatuto de los Trabajadores.[26]

Yet reliance on the principle of the more favourable law is not a good solution. In substantive labour law it is used to decide when norms and formative factors in the labour relationship of different levels of authority require simultaneous application:

The statute (conferring e.g. a minimum of three weeks vacation) gives way to the more favourable rule agreed upon at a lower level (i.e. collective agreement or employment contract: four weeks). On the other hand, in German law, where these questions have been dealt with most thoroughly, it is undisputed that this principle is not valid when norms on an equal level (e.g. two collective agreements) conflict. This is particularly true of temporal succession: a new collective agreement replaces the former even if the former was more favourable to the employee. Where two concurring collective agreements are simultaneously in effect, there are also several ways of handling the problem; but the principle of the most favourable law is expressly excluded as a possible solution.

The same must apply in a clash between two legal systems existing side by side. They are, as explained above, considered to be in principle equal, even though different in detail. System A might extend less protection against dismissal, but on the other hand a higher standard wage intended to cover this risk. System B emphasizes job security with a lower salary level. No reason is to be seen why the few employees who enter into a legal relationship with contacts to A and B should enjoy the advantages of both legal systems, higher salaries and absolute job security.

Another example may be furnished by paid holidays. Suppose that in the state of common nationality ('the sending state') the national law of which has been agreed upon by the parties, some 12 Christian holidays are to be kept without loss of pay, whilst work is done in a Muslim State with 10 other paid holidays: Is our worker entitled to 22 such luxurious days? Or, to push the example to the absurd: is a construction worker working in an Arab country under a German employment contract entitled to weekly rest on Friday (like the rest of the people working on the site) and to the 50 per cent bonus for Sunday work according to the collective agreement that was settled in the home country? The answer is clearly no in both cases.

The objection to the cumulation of advantages could only be avoided by comparing the legal systems in question as a whole. Such a global comparison is, however, impossible. It would be arbitrary in the extreme to suggest that the English or the German or the law of New York or that of Saudi Arabia were best.[27]

With the principle of the most favourable law, the employer loses all interest in a choice of law, for that would only cost him money. What would remain would be the rule of the law of the place of work with all the disadvantages described above (combined according to Article 6 of the European Convention with all the uncertainties of the 'unless' clause) .

---

26. Cf. Galiana Moreno, 'Notas para el estudio del Articulo 1.4 del Estatuto de los Trabajadores', *Actualidad Laboral*, 1987, p. 2169. – In general *cf.* A. Marin Lopez, *Derecho internacional privado espanol*, II, 7th ed., 1993, p. 382.

27. This would be particularly true for an international court. For the European Court, for instance, it would be unthinkable to decide that law X in Europe was better than law y; at least the judges would be very reluctant to say so! *See also* the hesitations expressed by Rodière, *Revue critique de d.i.p*, 1988, p. 691.

IV. The Sphere of Application of the Protective Norms with Public Law Character

19. Most legal systems are familiar with the above (*supra* no. 2) described classification of protective labour law norms into (1) mandatory norms to be enforced by courts or through the ordinary grievance, procedure and (2) protective provisions of such social and political importance that their enforcement is entrusted to special authorities (factory inspectorates, governmental agencies, etc.), including penalties for non-observance and extending to closure of the plant. These categories remain in use even though the distinction between private and public law, as such, is not universally accepted. We should now attempt to bring the application of both these types of provisions into a coherent system.

(1) The jurisdiction of domestic authorities is limited territorially. Each authority enjoys the power of enforcement only within the boundaries of the state which has set it up: Any direct activity abroad, such as prevention of violations of domestic legislation at a place of work beyond the frontiers, would be a violation of the sovereignty of that state where the work is being carried out. For example, a factory inspector of state A may not cross the border into state B in order to close a site there because of its insalubrity, even if the majority of persons employed there are border-crossers (citizens of state A).

(2) The limitation sub (1) does not mean that the local authority or court is prevented from trying to obtain results abroad through pressure exercised at home. Employers may, indeed, be compelled to act in the desired manner by means of all appropriate measures. For example, a company the seat of which is in country A may be penalized in order to compel it to introduce the necessary hygienic standards at the site in B.

(3) This does not mean that the courts and authorities extend at will the scope of their own public labour law. It goes without saying that no one wants to establish a world law. Therefore, in practice the concept prevails that public protective labour law or its equivalent and administrative labour law may in principle only be applied if the work is performed within the state. The sphere of validity and sphere of application, the jurisdiction of the factory inspectorate and the execution of the norm all come together.

(4) At times, a protective public law norm only concerns the relationship between the employer and the state (e.g. the obligation to allow factory inspectors on the premises or to maintain a register). Most often, however, it includes prohibitions and obligations in favour of the employee, which could just as well be included in the employment contract (e.g. prohibition of employment for more than eight hours daily). This private law core of the public law norm may form a part of the employer's duty of care and therefore be a part of the appropriate law. This situation opens the way for the application of public law to work performed (mostly by nationals) abroad. Of course the extent to which protective domestic norms are to be included in the appropriate law depends on the conditions at the place of work and cannot be addressed by a general rule. In any case, in the absence of an analogous norm abroad (or when the norm in effect there does not apply *in casu*), nothing prevents its being enforced as part of the duty of care or even as an implied provision of the employment contract.

(5) Officials may neither exercise their authority nor perform administrative acts in a foreign state, nor will local authorities act on their behalf unless obliged to do so under an active treaty between the two states.

Whether local courts take into consideration the orders and prohibitions in effect at a foreign place of performance depends upon the nature of these norms.

Here, too, the protective social provisions will have what we have called a 'private core'. In so far as this core affects the relation between employer and employee, consideration may be given to it by the judge of the forum and an attempt must be made to harmonize this set of rules with the proper law of the contract.[28]

20. The EC-Convention, though it does not contain any precise rules on these questions, nevertheless opens the gate for consideration of all the propositions described above (1)–(5). As concerns the public (or otherwise cogent) norms of the forum, Article 7, para. 2 (Article 34 of the German Act) declares:

> 'Nothing in this Convention shall restrict the application of the rules of the law of the forum in a situation where they are mandatory irrespective of the law otherwise applicable to the contract.'

With regard to the application of the private core of the respective norms of the foreign place of work, Article 7, para. 1 reads:

> 'When applying under this Convention the law of a country, effect may be given to the mandatory rules of the law of another country with which the situation has a close connection, if and in so far as, under the law of the latter country, those rules must be applied whatever the law applicable to the contract. In considering whether to give effect to these mandatoy rules, regard shall be had to their nature and purpose and to the consequences of their application or non-application.'

The words 'effect may be given, emphasize that all is left to the discretion of the judge, so that there is no obstacle to the development of sensible rules in this unexplored field of conflict of laws.[29]

V. THE SCOPE OF THE PROPER LAW

21. Questions of qualification, e.g. the correct classification of the relevant legal issue or norm into the categories of private international law, are not infrequent in international labour law. For example, unjust dismissal may be viewed under one system as a breach of the employment contract, in another as a tort, in a third as a question of industrial relations and in still another as a breach of a collective agreement. It is generally accepted that such questions of classification are decided

---

28. For more details *see* F. Gamillscheg, *Internationales Arbeitsrecht*, l.c. para. 11, *Revue critique de droit international privé*, 1961, pp. 265, 477, 677.

29. Article 7 has been the most controversial problem of the EC-Convention. Plans for reform of this provision are under discussion, *cf.* A. Junker, *Praxis des Internationalen Privat- und Verfahrensrechts*, 2000, p. 65ff.

according to the *lex fori*. This means that the ideas of the law of the forum govern. Of course this is, like every aspect of private international law, highly controversial.

22. In many systems, the legal capacity to conclude contracts is determined separately. Thus, e.g. the continental European systems rely on the nationality of the subject; in other countries, like the United States, legal capacity is determined by the proper law.

International labour law is in keeping with this rule. The question is not unimportant since employment contracts are often entered into by minors and the legal systems concerned facilitate the conclusion of such contracts by various means, e.g. by reducing the age limit or presuming the existence of parental consent.

Local rules on legal capacity are often held to be applicable in order to protect local commerce, *cf.* Article 11 of the EC-Convention. In the field of employment law, the solution is, however, open to doubts: it does not sufficiently take into consideration that the protection of commerce must be weighed against the protection of the under-aged employee.

23. According to general opinion the form of the employment contract or other agreements and declarations (e.g. agreement on competion, notice, etc.), is based on the principle *locus regit actum* together with any supplementary provisions, *cf.* Article 9 para. 1 of the EC-Convention. In so asserting, it is overlooked that this rule owes its origin to the desire to facilitate the conclusion of contracts (*favor negotii*), while in labour law the purpose of form stems primarily from the desire to protect the worker. The result is that any relaxation of the formal requirements in the conclusion of transactions runs directly counter to the purposes of the law.

24. The following key-words are meant to give the reader an idea of the subject matter covered by the proper law of the employment contract: conclusion, nullity, rescission, and interpretation of the contract; payments for work completed in the event of void contracts, the employee's obligations of performance, and loyalty; limitations on liability for defective work; agreements in restraint of competition; the employer's duty of care; salary; equal treatment (in a number of cases, such as the differentiation between white-collar and blue-collar employees; for other forms of discrimination *see infra* no. 25); the obligation to pay salaries in the event of non-performance of work (in cases which are covered by social security different solutions may impose themselves); liability of the employer; employee inventions; periods of notice; justification of dismissal,[30] compensation, re-instatement with or without backpay; impact of business transfers on employment contracts;[31] company pensions, and others.

---

30. German Bundesarbeitsgericht, 24 August 1989, in *Arbeitsrechtliche Praxis* No. 30 zu IPR-Arbeitsrecht; this solution is not generally accepted, *cf.* S. Krebber, *Internationales Privatrecht des Kündigungsschutzes bei Arbeitsverhältnissen*, 1997, p. 212ff.
31. German Bundesarbeitsgericht, 29 October 1992, in *Arbeitsrechtliche Praxis* No. 31 zu IPR-Arbeitsrecht; but this solution is not generally accepted, *cf.* A. Junker, *Internationales Arbeitsrecht im Konzern*, p. 240; H. Kronke, Netherlands International Law Review 1989, p. 1; F. Gamillscheg, *Recueil des Cours 181*, (1983), p. 328.

25. In most countries the application of a foreign law is not left to the discretion of the judge or the parties, though the judge may refer to the parties in order to ascertain the content of the foreign law. Yet foreign law is not to be applied in every case: if it would lead to a result which *in casu* (even taking into consideration that the case is closely connected with the foreign country where a system of different cultural values may exist) would violate elementary principles of justice, it will not be applied: objection of public policy, *ordre public*, the so-called reservation clause. *Cf.* Article 16 of the EC-Convention: 'The application of a rule of any country ... may be refused only if such application is manifestly incompatible with the public policy ("*ordre public*") of the forum.'

The ordre public device functions as an emergency valve alleviating the uncertainty of the content of the foreign law which is to be applied according to the conflict rules. Whether the result is manifestly incompatible with our standards is a question to be answered above all in the light of the fundamental rights and liberties of the employee and the basic principles of a good social order.

Examples would be discrimination based on race, sex, or religion[32] etc.; failure to compensate for deprivation of vested rights; life-long employment contracts: usury wages; excessive periods of notice or agreements not to compete; insufficient protection against dismissal; excessive penalties; right of the husband to interfere with the wife's employment contract, and so forth. The reservation clause does not apply when the foreign proper law is merely somewhat less favourable than the *lex fori*; it must be a 'manifest' disadvantage. For instance, it has been decided that the Belgian *ordre public* was not violated when a commercial agent under German law received no severance pay or again, when a period of notice under Nigerian law was reduced to one day. German courts have often applied American law in regard to notice, even though the German law would have granted somewhat broader claims. Differences between the political systems in East and West were not considered as being a sufficient reason to fall back on the public policy device.[33]

Renvoi, i.e. the reference back to the *lex fori* by the proper law, is not admitted, Article 15 of the EC-Convention, Article 35 EGBGB.[34]

VI. COLLECTIVE LABOUR LAW (INDUSTRIAL RELATIONS)

26. Up until now the international aspects of collective labour law have been widely neglected. Few attempts to elucidate the subject have been made. It would be premature, therefore, to present a set of rules; however, a number of suggestions may be proffered.[35]

---

32. In the United States the scope of the Civil Rights Act has now been extended to work abroad, Civil Rights Act,1991; *Social Labour Bulletin*, 1992, p. 219; Zimmerman, *International Labour Review*, 131, 1992, p. 217ff.

33. *See* textbooks on private international law; Gamillscheg, *Internationales Arbeitsrecht*, *l.c.*, para. 7; Dumortier, *l.c.*, passim.

34. To the contrary, but erroneously, the Austrian OGH in an obiter dictum in its decision of 3 July 1986, in *Zeitschrift für Rechtsvergleichung*, 1987, p. 289.

35. *Cf. also* G. Lyon-Caen and A. Lyon-Caen, *Droit Social International et Européen*, 8th ed., 1993; Pierre Rodière, *La convention collective de travail en droit international privé*, 1987; Curt W. Hergenröder, *Der Arbeitskampf mit Auslandsberührung*, 1987.

27. Not infrequently collective agreements on the regulation of work done abroad are concluded in a specific country between unions and employers organizations or companies. Thus, the collective agreement receives an extra-territorial quality. No 'territoriality' or similar concept should be a hindrance to this. A separate question is how far a general agreement concluded to regulate work within the country extends to employees working for the company (temporarily or habitually) abroad.

The question of really international collective agreements, i.e. concluded by a pool of unions of different countries with a MNE will not fail to be an important topic of the near future.

28. Strikes and lock-outs are so closely related to the public order of the place of the dispute that no other legal system could possibly apply. Hence, the law relating to industrial disputes is territorial. This law also determines the private law consequences of participation in the dispute. Nevertheless, a more favourable regulation included in the proper law should prevail.

29. The sphere of application of the legislation on works councils is usually unilaterally determined according to the principle of territoriality in a statutory system, as in Germany or France. Thus the German Works Constitution Act governs enterprises in Germany, the French provisions enterprises in France,[36] and so forth. No universal rule envisaging the application, or even consideration, of some kind of foreign plant representation law has yet, so far as we know, been developed.

In consequence, the Federal Labour Court has declared void the dismissal in Germany of a foreigner employed under foreign law on the grounds that the works council was not consulted, as required under German law. The authority of the works council also covers employees transferred abroad temporarily, but does not cover those employees who are permanently working abroad. The mere fact that their employment relationship is subject to German law makes no difference.

Under section 106 of the Works Constitution Act, the information due to the works council in economic matters is delegated to the so-called economic committee (*Wirtschaftsausschuß*). If the seat of the company is situated abroad, an economic committee cannot be formed there or meet there; but if the enterprise has one or more domestic factories with a work force totalling more than 100, the smallest number under section 106, then the economic committee must be established for the benefits of the domestic staff, the information being limited to matters affecting and concerning them. If an enterprise with its seat of business abroad has several plants in France, a central work's council (*Comite central d'enterprise*) must be set up for them.[37]

The private international law aspects of co-determination of the employees in the Supervisory Board of the company are questions of international company law. The composition of such a board is, in principle, a question to be decided by the law at the seat of the enterprise. Another option would be to apply the law under which the company was incorporated.

---

36. *Cf.* Cassation, Assemblée Plenière, 10 July 1992, *Droit social*, 1993, p. 72.
37. *See* decision of the French Cour de Cassation of 29 June 1973, *Droit social* 1974, p. 48, and the comments of Francescakis, 'L'arret Compagnie Internationale des Wagons-Lits', *Revue critique de droit international privé*, 1974, p. 273, and Dumortier, *l.c.*, p. 346.

Thus, the sphere of application of the German legislation on co-determination is limited: an enterprise with its seat abroad is not subject to a German '*Mitbestimmung*', even where its domestic plants are concerned. On the other hand, enterprises with their seat in Germany are, of course, subject to the Act. Nevertheless, there are two important limitations: it is prevailing opinion, with regard to the 1976 Co-determination Act, that persons employed in the foreign plants of a specific enterprise are not to be included in computing the minimum number of employees required under section 1 (2,000 employees) and that any such employees have no voting rights in the Supervisory Board elections.

Select Bibliography

J. Dumortier, *Arbeidsverhoudingen in het Internationaal Privaatrecht*, Antwerpen, 1981, 409 pp.

P. Fieschi-Vivet, *La règle de conflit applicable au contrat de travail international*, 1987 Dalloz, chronique p. 255.

F. Gamillscheg, *Internationales Arbeitsrecht* (Arbeitsverweisungsrecht), Tübingen, 1959, 454 pp.

– *International Encyclopaedia of Comparative Law*, Private International Law, ch. 28 Labour Contracts, Tübingen/Paris, Vol. III, 28 pp.

– 'Rules of public order in private international labour law', Academie de Droit International', La Haye, *Recueil des Cours*, Vol. 181, pp. 289–347.

A. Junker, *Internationales Arbeitsrecht im Konzern*, Tubingen, 1992, 597 pp.

O. Kahn-Freund, 'Notes on the conflict of laws in relation to employment in English and Scottish law', *Selected Writings*, London, 1978, pp. 259–272.

G. and A. Lyon-Caen, *Droit social international et europeén*, 8th ed., Paris, 1993, 323 pp.

F. Morgenstern, *International Conflicts of Labour Law*, Geneva, 1984, 129 pp.

C. Reithmann/D. Martiny, *Internationales Vertragsrecht*, 5th ed., 1996.

P. Rodière, 'Conflits de lois en droit du travail', in *Juris-Claeur de droit international*, Fasc. 573–1, Paris, 1966.

INTERNATIONAL DEVELOPMENTS
AND COMPARATIVE STUDIES

Chapter 11. Freedom of Association

*B. Creighton**

I. THE CONCEPT OF FREEDOM OF ASSOCIATION

1.   Most international instruments that are directed to the protection of fundamental human rights make reference to the notion of freedom of association.
Sometimes they do this in recognition of a general right to associate for social, political, religious, commercial or industrial purposes. In other instances they do so with
specific reference to freedom of association for trade union purposes. Whether the
latter should be regarded as simply a manifestation of the former, or as a fundamental human right *sui generis*, is a matter of some debate.[1] For present purposes it will
be used as a 'shorthand expression for a bundle of rights and freedoms' relating to
membership of associations of employers and workers.[2] In particular, it will be used
to refer to the rights and freedoms that are guaranteed by the ILO Freedom of
Association and Protection of the Right to Organize Convention, 1948 (No. 87) and
the Right to Organize and Collective Bargaining Convention, 1949 (No. 98).

2.   This is not to suggest that Conventions Nos 87 and 98 are exhaustive of the
concept of freedom of association for trade union purposes. They clearly are not.
They do not, for example, make any express reference to the right to strike or to take
other forms of industrial action (although, as will appear presently, this omission is
more apparent than real). They are entirely silent on issues such as the right *not* to
associate, integrity of union premises, confidentiality of union communications, and
union officials' rights of access to their members. They accord only very limited
recognition to the right to be represented by a trade union for purposes of collective
bargaining and to the duty to bargain in good faith. In addition, some observers
would argue that they are outmoded in certain respects, and/or that they embody a
'Eurocentric' conception of freedom of association, for example in relation to trade
union pluralism.[3]

---

*   The author wishes to acknowledge the research assistance of Michelle Kossenas and Deborah
     Siemensma in the preparation of this chapter.
1.   *See* C. Wilfred Jenks, *The International Protection of Trade Union Freedom*, London, 1957, p. 63.
2.   F. von Prondzynski, *Freedom of Association and Industrial Relations*, Lonon, 1987, p. 13. For further
     consideration of the concept of freedom of association *see* S. Leader, *Freedom of Association: A
     Study in Labor Law and Political Theory*, New Haven, 1992.
3.   *See* further paras 42–48.

3.   The fact remains, however, that Conventions Nos 87 and 98, and the associated supervisory procedures, have acquired a degree of acceptance amongst the international community that not only renders them uniquely authoritative in relation to freedom of association, but which also sets them apart from almost all other international standard-setting instruments in the field of human rights. This is reflected in the fact that Convention No. 87 has been ratified by all OECD countries apart from New Zealand, Korea, and the United States, whilst Convention No. 98 has been ratified by all members apart from Canada, Korea, Mexico, New Zealand, and the United States. It is appropriate, therefore, that these Conventions and the associated jurisprudence should constitute the principal focus of this examination of the international protection of freedom of association. It must be emphasized, however, that they are by no means the only international standard-setting instruments to accord formal recognition to freedom of association for trade union purposes.

II.   INTERNATIONAL RECOGNITION OF FREEDOM OF ASSOCIATION

A.   *The Universal Declaration of Human Rights, 1948*

4.   Article 20(1) of the Universal Declaration of Human Rights, which was adopted by the United Nations General Assembly in 1948, states that 'everyone has the right to freedom of peaceful assembly and association', subject to the proviso that 'no one may be compelled to belong to an association' (Article 20(2)). Article 23(4), meanwhile, provides that 'everyone has the right to form and to join trade unions for the protection of his interests'.

There is no express reference to a right not to join in Article 23. It is unclear, therefore, whether the guarantee provided by Article 23 must be read subject to the qualification set out in Article 20(2), or whether the right to form and to join trade unions should be regarded as a fundamental human right standing apart from the more general notion of freedom of association which is embodied in Article 20(1), and as such not subject to any correlative right not to join. It is interesting to note in this context that of the other international instruments which deal with freedom of association for trade union purposes, only the African Charter on Human and Peoples' Rights (1981) and the Additional Protocol to the American Convention on Human Rights (1988) make specific reference to a 'right not to join'.

5.   The declaration is not a binding instrument in international law. Nevertheless, it does set out a series of internationally recognized norms in the field of human rights, and as such it serves to flesh out the general references to human rights in the United Nations' Charter. In some respects, the significance of the Declaration has been diminished by the adoption in 1966 of the International Covenant on Economic, Social and Cultural Rights (ICESCR) and the International Covenant on Civil and Political Rights (ICCPR), both of which *are* binding upon ratifying States.

B.   *The 1966 Covenants*

6.   Both the ICESR and the ICCPR were adopted by the United Nations General Assembly in December 1966. They became operative in January 1976, when they had received the requisite number (35) of ratifications. In July 2000, the ICESCR had been ratified by 142 Member States of the United Nations and 5 non-Member States, whilst the ICCPR had also been ratified by 142 Member States, and by 3 non-Member States.

7.   Article 8(1) of the ICESCR deals with a number of fundamental aspects of freedom of association for trade union purposes:

'The States Parties to the present Covenant undertake to ensure:

(a) The right of everyone to form trade unions and join the trade union of his choice, subject only to the rules of the organization concerned, for the promotion and protection of his economic and social interests. No restrictions may be placed on the exercise of his right other than those prescribed by law and which are necessary in a democratic society in the interests of national security or public order or for the protection of the rights and freedoms of others;

(b) The right of trade unions to establish national federations or confederations and the right of the latter to form or join international trade union organizations;

(c) The right of trade unions to function freely subject to no limitations other than those prescribed by law and which are necessary in a democratic society in the interests of national security or public order or for the protection of the rights and freedoms of others;

(d) The right to strike, provided that it is exercised in conformity with the laws of a particular country.'

These guarantees are subject to two significant qualifications:

'2. This article shall not prevent the imposition of lawful restrictions on the exercise of these rights by members of the armed forces or of the police or of the administration of the State.

3. Nothing in this article shall authorize States Parties to the International Labour Organization Convention of 1948 concerning Freedom of Association and Protection of the Right to Organize Convention to take legislative measures which would prejudice, or apply the law in such manner as would prejudice, the guarantees provided for in that Convention.'

8.   Article 22(1) of the ICCPR refers to the right 'to form and join trade unions for the protection of his interests' as a specific manifestation of 'the right to freedom of association with others', whilst Article 22(2) states that:

'No restrictions may be placed on the exercise of this right other than those which are prescribed by law and which are necessary in a democratic society in the interests of national security or public safety, public order (*ordre public*), the protection of public health or morals or the protection of the rights and freedoms of others. This Article shall not prevent the imposition of lawful restrictions on members of the armed forces and of the police in their exercise of this right.'

Article 22(3) preserves the integrity of Convention No. 87 in the same manner as Article 8(3) of the ICESCR.

9. The supervision of the effect given to these Covenants is dealt with in Articles 16 to 20 of the ICESCR, and Articles 19 and 21 of the ICCPR.[4]

C. Regional Standards Relating to Freedom of Association

10. There is now an extensive range of regional instruments relating to fundamental human rights. Many of these standards make specific reference to the concept of freedom of association, often with heavy reliance upon the principles embodied in Conventions Nos 87 and 98. This influence is particularly marked in Articles 5 and 6 of the European Social Charter, 1961 (which was drafted with ILO assistance):

> '5.   With a view to ensuring or promoting the freedom of workers and employers to form local, national or international organizations for the protection of their economic and social interests and to join those organizations, the Contracting Parties undertake that national law shall not be such as to impair, nor shall it be so applied as to impair, this freedom. The extent to which the guarantees provided for in this Article shall apply to the police shall be determined by national laws or regulations. The principle governing the application to the members of the armed forces of these guarantees and the extent to which they shall apply to persons in this category shall equally be determined by national laws or regulations.
>
> 6.   With a view to ensuring the effective exercise of the right to bargain collectively, the Contracting Parties undertake:
>   (1) to promote joint consultation between workers and employers;
>   (2) to promote, where necessary and appropriate, machinery for voluntary negotiations between employers or employers' organizations and workers' organizations, with a view to the regulation of terms and conditions of employment by means of collective agreements;
>   (3) to promote the establishment and use of appropriate machinery for conciliation and voluntary arbitration for the settlement of labour disputes; and recognize:
>   (4) the right of workers and employers to collective action in cases of conflicts of interest, including the right to strike, subject to obligations that might arise out of collective agreements previously entered into.'

11. Other important regional instruments which include specific provision relating to freedom of association include the American Declaration of the Rights and Duties of Men, 1948 (Article 22); the Charter of the Organization of American States, 1948 (Article 43(2)); the European Convention for the Protection of Human

---

4. *See* further N. Valticos and G von Potobsky, *International Labour Law*, 2nd ed., Deventer, 1995, pp. 258–259.

Rights and Fundamental Freedoms, 1950 (Article 11); the Labour Standards Convention adopted by the League of Arab States, 1966 (Articles 76–84); the American Convention on Human Rights, 1969 (Article 16); the African Charter on Human and Peoples' Rights, 1981 (Article 10) and the Protocol to the American Convention on Human Rights, 1988 (Article 8). Both the Charter of the Organization of American States and the Protocol to the American Convention on Human Rights make express reference to the right to strike. As indicated, Article 10(2) of the African Charter and Article 8(3) of the Protocol to the American Convention stipulate that no one may be compelled to join an association/union.

D.   Freedom of Association and the ILO

12.   Article 41 of the original Constitution of the ILO[5] set out a number of 'methods and principles' which were considered to be of 'special and urgent importance' for the attainment of the objectives of the fledging organization. They included 'the right of association for all lawful purposes by the employed as well as by the employers.'

13.   These imperatives also found recognition in the Declaration of Philadelphia of 1944, Article I(b) of which affirmed that 'freedom of expression and of association are essential to sustained progress', whilst Article III spelled out the 'solemn obligation' of the ILO 'to further among the nations of the world programmes which will achieve':

> 'the effective recognition of the right of collective bargaining, the co-operation of management and labour in the continuous improvement of productive efficiency, and the collaboration of workers and employers in the preparation and application of social and economic measures.'

The Declaration was annexed to the Constitution in 1946, at which time a new Preamble was adopted which also endorsed 'recognition of the principle of freedom of association' as one of the main methods by which social justice, and therefore 'universal and lasting peace', could be attained.

14.   As is apparent from Article III of the Declaration of Philadelphia, one of the most distinctive features of the ILO is the tripartite structure of its key decision-making organs: The International Labour Conference and the Governing Body. The principle of tripartism is also reflected in the Committees of the Conference and of the Governing Body, and permeates everything the organization does. The *sine qua non* of meaningful tripartism is the existence of free and effective organizations of employers and of workers. That in turn is dependent upon respect, at both national and international level, for the principles of freedom of association. This does much to explain the high priority that is accorded to this issue in the Constitution of the ILO, in the standard-setting activities of the Conference, in the work of the supervisory bodies, and in the promotional and technical activities of the Office.

---

5.   Article 427 of the Treaty of Versailles.

15. The Conference endeavoured to recognize this logic by adopting a general Convention on freedom of association in the mid-twenties. However, these endeavours foundered in the face of employer (and government) insistence that the right to form and join trade unions must carry with it a correlative right not to join. This proposition was not acceptable to the workers' group, 'and in these circumstances it was thought preferable not to proceed with the matter'.[6]

16. The Conference returned to this issue in the period immediately after the Second World War, and in 1948 and 1949 adopted the pivotal Conventions Nos 87 and 98.[7] These were not, however, the first ILO instruments to make reference to the principles of freedom of association. That distinction belongs to the Right of Association (Agriculture) Convention, 1921 (No. 11), Article 1 of which states that:

> 'Each Member of the International Labour Organisation which ratifies this Convention undertakes to secure to all those engaged in agriculture the same rights of association and combination as to industrial workers, and to repeal any statutory or other provisions restricting such rights in the case of those engaged in agriculture.'

This was an important affirmation of principle. It is clearly appropriate that agricultural workers should have the same rights of association as other workers. But the efficacy of the Convention was severely circumscribed by the fact that there was no adequate international protection for the rights of association of the industrial workers with whom it was meant to ensure parity. Put simply, if municipal law denied full freedom of association to industrial workers, it would be entirely consistent with the Convention also to deny such freedom to agricultural workers so long as they were not placed in any worse position than their colleagues in industry. Workers in agriculture are now entitled to the protections set out in Conventions Nos 87 and 98 in the same way as any other workers. To that extent, Convention No. 11 may be said to be of little practical relevance. Nevertheless, effective recognition of the principle of freedom of association for agricultural workers does raise special problems. This was reflected in the adoption in 1975 of the Rural Workers Organisations Convention (No. 141).

17. Article 2 of the Right of Association (Non-Metropolitan Territories) Convention, 1947 (No. 84) stipulates that 'the rights of employers and employed alike to associate for all lawful purposes shall be guaranteed by appropriate measures', whilst Article 3 seeks to protect the right of representative trade unions to conclude collective agreements with employers or employer organizations. The Convention endeavours to encourage the fair and expeditious settlement of both individual and collective disputes: preferably through conciliation machinery involving representatives of employers and workers, but also with the involvement of public

---

6. *See* C. Jenks: 'The International protection of Trade Union Rights', in E. Luard (ed.), *The International Protection of Human Rights*, London, 1967, pp. 213–214.
7. For a helpful summary of the background to the adoption of Conventions Nos 87 and 98, *see* H. Bartolomei de la Cruz, G von Potobsky and L Swepston. *The International Labor Organisation: The International Standards System and Basic Human Rights*, Boulder Colorado, 1996, pp. 167–171.

officers if necessary (Articles 5, 6, and 7). There is also formal endorsement of consultation with representatives of employers and workers 'in the establishment and working of arrangements for the protection of workers and the application of labour legislation' (Article 4), and in the establishment and operation of dispute-resolution mechanisms (Articles 6(2) and 7(2)).

18. Convention No. 84 was the first of three Conventions on freedom of association which were adopted in the period 1947–49. It was followed by the Freedom of Association and Protection of the Right to Organise Convention 1948 (No. 87) and the Right to Organise and Collective Bargaining Convention 1949 (No. 98). Taken together these two Conventions have played, and continue to play, a central role in the international protection of freedom of association for trade union purposes. They have, however, been complemented by a number of later instruments which deal with more specific applications of the principles of freedom of association.

19. The Workers' Representatives Convention 1971 (No. 135) (and accompanying Recommendation No. 143) is principally concerned with the protection of workers' representatives against prejudicial treatment based on their status or activities as representatives or as union members (Article 1), and with the facilities with which they should be provided at the level of the enterprise to enable them to carry out their functions promptly and efficiently (Article 2).

20. The Rural Workers Organisations Convention 1975 (No. 141) (and accompanying Recommendation No. 149) restates the basic principles of freedom of association with specific reference to the position of rural workers (Article 3); requires steps to be taken to facilitate the establishment and growth of voluntary, strong and independent organizations of rural workers (Article 4), and obliges ratifying States to (Article 5(1)):

> '... adopt and carry out a policy of active encouragement to these organizations, particularly with a view to eliminating obstacles to their establishment, their growth and the pursuit of their lawful activities, as well as such legislative and administrative discrimination against rural workers' organisations and their members as may exist.'

'Rural worker' for these purposes means 'any person engaged in agriculture, handicrafts or a related occupation in a rural area, whether as a wage earner or ... as a self-employed person such as a tenant, share-cropper or small owner-occupier' (Article 2(1)).[8]

---

8. Article 2(2) makes clear that 'tenants, share-croppers or small owner-occupiers' in this context includes only those who 'derive their main income from agriculture, who work the land themselves, with the help only of their family or with the help of occasional outside labour', and that it does not include those who permanently employ workers, employ a substantial number of seasonal workers or have any land cultivated by share-croppers or tenants.

21. The Labour Relations (Public Service) Convention 1978 (No. 151) (and accompanying Recommendation No. 159) was adopted in response to what was perceived to be a gap in the guarantees provided by Convention No. 98 by virtue of the fact that that instrument 'does not deal with the position of public servants engaged in the administration of the State' (Article 6). Convention No. 151 applies to all persons employed by public authorities 'to the extent that more favourable provisions in other international labour Conventions are not applicable to them' (Article 1(1)), but permits some discretion in relation to its application to 'high-level employees whose functions are normally considered as policy making or managerial, or to employees whose duties are of a highly confidential nature' (Article 1(2)). It stipulates that there should be adequate protection against anti-union discrimination (Article 4); that public service organizations should be fully independent of the authorities (Article 5); that representatives of such organizations should have access to appropriate facilities (Article 6); that measures appropriate to national conditions should be adopted for the negotiation by employee organizations and the public authorities of terms and conditions of employment of public employees (Article 7); that there should be suitable machinery for the settlement of disputes (Article 8); and that (Article 9):

> 'Public employees shall have, as other workers, the civil and political rights which are essential for the normal exercise of freedom of association, subject only to the obligations arising from their status and the nature of their functions.'

In other words, it applies to public servants essentially the same guarantees as are provided to other employees by Convention No. 98 – albeit subject to the recognition of the special character of the public service which is inherent in Articles 1(2) and 9.

22. The Collective Bargaining Convention, 1981 (No. 154) (and accompanying Recommendation No. 163) sets out a number of measures which should be adopted to promote collective bargaining so as more effectively to achieve the objectives set out in the Declaration of Philadelphia, in Article 4 of Convention No. 98 and in para. 1 of the Collective Agreements Recommendation, 1951 (No. 92).

23. Taken together, these eight Conventions constitute a comprehensive, even if not exhaustive, code for the protection and promotion of freedom of association. A number of other international labour standards make specific reference to the principles of freedom of association (for example Article 2 and the Appendix to the Merchant Shipping (Minimum Standards) Convention 1976 (No. 147)), whilst others may be said to complement them (for example the Tripartite Consultation (International Labour Standards) Convention 1976 (No. 144)). Table 1 summarizes the state of ratification of the eight 'freedom of association' Conventions as of 3 July 2000.

---

9. By its nature, Convention No. 84 was relevant only to countries which had responsibility for non-metropolitan territori es. This explains why it has been ratified only by Belgium, France, New Zealand, and the United Kingdom, and why it is now of little practical relevance.

Table 1. Ratification of Freedom of Association Conventions (3 July 2000)

	Convention	Ratifications*
No. 11	Right of Association (Agriculture) 1921	119 [24]
No. 84	Right of Association (Non-Metropolitan Territories) 1947[9]	4 [4]
No. 87	Freedom of Association and Protection of the Right to Organize 1948	130 [26]
No. 98	Right to Organize and Collective Bargaining 1949	146 [24]
No. 135	Workers' Representatives 1971	66 [19]
No. 141	Rural Workers' Organizations 1974	37 [16]
No. 151	Labour Relations (Public Service) 1978	36 [15]
No. 154	Collective Bargaining 1981	30 [9]

* Figures in square brackets indicate the number of ratifications by members of the OECD.

24. Formal standard setting is by no means the only way in which the ILO seeks to protect and to promote the principles of freedom of association. Jenks,[10] for example, considered that the mere fact of the existence of the ILO, has played a major role in helping to promote and to protect the principles:

'The main contribution of the International Labour Organisation to the promotion of freedom of association transcends the particular procedures for the protection of freedom of association ... It has been to give employers' and workers' organizations a new international status which has given a powerful impetus to their development and influence throughout the world, particularly in countries of recent industrialization and underdeveloped areas generally. It has given such organizations a recognised official position; has ensured them the international contacts, outlook and experience necessary for their growth to maturity at a reasonably rapid rate; and has in many cases furnished, through the decisions of the International Labour Conference, the essentials of their programmes of action.'

25. In more concrete terms, the Conference has adopted a number of resolutions which complement the formal freedom of association standards in certain areas. The most important of these were the resolutions concerning the Independence of the Trade Union Movement of 1952[11] and Trade Union Rights and Their Relation to Civil Liberties of 1970.[12]

---

10. *See* Jenks, footnote 1, p. 67.
11. *See* ILC, 35th Session, 1953, *Record of Proceedings*, p. 451.
12. *See* ILC, 54th Session, 1971, *Record of Proceedings*, pp. 733–736. *See also Trade Union Rights and Their Relation to Civil Liberties*, Geneva, 1969, which was submitted to the 54th Session and which helped pave the way for the adoption of the 1970 resolution.

26. The 1952 resolution was largely concerned with the need for the trade union movement to maintain a proper measure of political independence 'so as to be in a position to carry forward its economic and social mission irrespective of political changes in each country.' This was not to suggest that trade unions should not establish relations with political parties, or engage in constitutional political activity, but rather that such relations or activity 'should not be of such a nature as to compromise the continuance of the trade union movement or its social and economic functions' in the event of political change within the country. This latter was a particular source of difficulty during the Cold War period, where legislation in Eastern Bloc countries generally established a formal connection between the trade union movement and the governing party. This issue is clearly of reduced significance since the break-up of the Soviet Union and the advent of pluralist political systems in Eastern Europe.[13]

27. The 1970 resolution embodied a clear affirmation of the need for proper respect for civil liberties as an essential pre-condition of respect for the principles of freedom of association. In particular, it emphasized the importance of (para. 2):

> '(a) the right to freedom and security of person and freedom from arbitrary arrest and detention;
> (b) freedom of opinion and expression and in particular freedom to hold opinions without interference and to seek, receive and impart information and ideas through any media and regardless of frontiers;
> (c) freedom of assembly;
> (d) the right to a fair trial by an independent and impartial tribunal;
> (e) the right to protection of the property of trade union organizations.'

The resolution also called on the Governing Body to adopt a number of measures intended to strengthen the contribution of the ILO to the protection and promotion of the principles of freedom of association and related civil liberties.[14]

28. In June 1998 the Conference adopted, by an overwhelming majority, a Declaration on Fundamental Principles and Rights at Work. This commits all Member States to respect, promote and realize in good faith the principles set out in seven core human rights instruments. Those instruments include Conventions Nos 87 and 98, together with the Forced Labour Convention 1930 (No. 29), Abolition of Forced Labour Convention 1957 (No. 105), Equal Remuneration Convention 1951 (No. 100), Discrimination (Employment and Occupation) Convention 1958 (No. 111), and Minimum Age Convention 1973 (No. 138). The Declaration is not open to ratification, and does not have any binding effect in international law. Nevertheless, it does incorporate a 'follow-up' procedure which in effect imposes reporting obligations upon all Member States irrespective of whether they have ratified the Conventions concerned.[15]

---

13. *See* further Bartolomei et al., footnote 7, pp. 195–196.
14. One of the more tangible results of this resolution was the publication of a *Digest of decisions and principles of the Freedom of Association Committee of the Governing Body of the ILO*, Geneva, 1972 [henceforth '*Digest*']. The fourth edition of the *Digest* appeared in 1996.
15. *See Your Voice at Work*, ILC, 88th Session, 2000.

As such, it constitutes an important re-affirmation of the foundational principles of the ILO.[16]

29. The Office has also endeavoured to promote respect for, and the implementation of, the principles of freedom of association through a wide range of educational activities; publications; audio-visual materials, and the provision of technical cooperation. This latter can include assistance in the preparation of labour legislation, training of labour inspectors etc. In principle, all such activities should themselves be consistent with the principles, and should be structured and implemented in such a way as to promote respect for the principles in the future. Other technical cooperation activities – such as the administration of public works projects on behalf of other international agencies, or individual donor countries – might also be expected to provide a vehicle for the promotion of the principles of freedom of association, and of international labour standards in general. Indeed this is an important part of the rationale for ILO involvement in such activities in the first place. Attractive as this logic may appear in the abstract, it has proved far from easy to put it into effect in practice.[17]

E.   Conventions Nos 87 and 98

30. The substance of Convention No. 87 can be summarized by reference to eight basic propositions:

(i) All workers and employers, without distinction whatsoever, have the right to establish, and subject only to the rules of the organization concerned, join organizations of their own choosing without prior authorization (Article 2). 'Organization' for these purposes means any organization of workers or employers for furthering and defending the interests of workers or of employers (Article 10).

(ii) Workers' and employers' organizations have the right to draw up their constitutions and rules, to elect their representatives in full freedom, to organize their administration and activities, and to formulate their programmes (Article 3(1)). The public authorities must refrain from any interference which would restrict these rights, or impede their exercise (Article 3(2)).

(iii) Workers' and employers' organizations must not be dissolved or suspended by administrative authority (Article 4).

(iv) Workers' and employers' organizations have the right to form and to join federations and confederations (Article 5). Such federations and confederations in turn have the right to affiliate to international organizations of workers and employers (Article 5), and also to enjoy the guarantees provided by Articles 2, 3 and 4 (Article 6).

(v) The acquisition of legal personality by organizations, federations and confederations must not be made subject to conditions of such a character as to restrict the application of Articles 2, 3 and 4 (Article 7).

---

16. For an analysis of the Declaration in the context of 'the ILO's identity crisis', *see* B Langille, 'The ILO and the New Economy: Recent Developments' *The International Journal of Comparative Labour Law and Industrial Relations*, Vol. 15, 1999, p. 229.

17. *See* further *Your Voice At Work*, footnote 15, Part III.

(vi) In exercising their rights workers, employers and their organizations are to respect the law of the land (Article 8(1)), which in turn must not be such as to impair, or be applied so as to impair, the guarantees provided by the Convention (Article 8(2)).

(vii) According to Article 9 the extent to which the guarantees provided by the Convention are to apply to the armed forces and the police is to be determined by national laws or regulations. These are the only permissible derogations from the generality of the Convention.

(viii) Ratifying States must take 'all necessary and appropriate measures' to ensure that employers and workers may freely exercise the right to organize (Article 11).

31. The substance of Convention No. 98 can be summarized by reference to six basic propositions:

(i) Workers are to enjoy adequate protection against acts of anti-union discrimination at the time of hiring, during employment, and in relation to termination (Article 1).

(ii) Worker and employer organizations are to enjoy adequate protection against interference by other organizations and by employers in their establishment, functioning, or administration (Article 2).

(iii) Machinery appropriate to national conditions is to be established, where necessary, to ensure respect for the rights guaranteed by Articles 1 and 2 (Article 3).

(iv) Article 4 directs that where necessary, measures appropriate to national conditions must be taken to encourage and to promote the full development and utilization of machinery for voluntary negotiation between employers or employers' organizations and workers' organizations 'with a view to the regulation of terms and conditions of employment by means of collective agreements.'

(v) Article 5 confers upon ratifying States a discretion similar to that in Article 9 of Convention No. 87 in relation to the armed forces and the police.

(vi) According to Article 6, the Convention 'does not deal with the position of public servants engaged in the administration of the State'. It also provides that the Convention is not to be construed as prejudicing the position of such workers in any way.

32. Neither Convention makes any express reference to the right to strike.[18] However the supervisory bodies have consistently taken the view[19] that it is an integral part of the free exercise of the trade union rights which are guaranteed by Conventions Nos 87 and 98,[20] and by the Constitution of the ILO. This view has come under increasingly critical scrutiny in recent years in the Conference

---

18. *See* however Abolition of Forced Labour Convention 1957 (No. 105), Art. 1(d) and Voluntary Conciliation and Arbitration Recommendation 1951, paras 4, 6, and 7.

19. *See* for example *Digest*, paras 473–475 and the *General Survey by the Committee of Experts on the Application of Conventions and Recommendations on Freedom of Association and Collective Bargaining* [henceforth '*General Survey*'], Geneva, 1994, paras 145–151.

20. Particularly, by Articles 3, 8, and 10 of Convention No. 87.

Committee on the Application of Conventions and Recommendations – largely at the initiative of the employer members of that Committee.[21]

III. APPLICATION OF THE PRINCIPLES OF FREEDOM OF ASSOCIATION

A. *The Supervisory Bodies*

33. The supervisory procedures of the ILO relating to freedom of association are described elsewhere in this volume.[22]

34. The examination of periodic reports on Conventions Nos 87 and 98 constitutes an important part of the work of the Committee of Experts on the Application of Conventions and Recommendations.[23] For example, in 1999, the Committee addressed 'observations' to 88 of the 128 States that had ratified Convention No. 87 at that time, plus 'direct requests' to 49 States (including 35 to countries which had also received an observation). It also addressed 'observations' to 36 of the 145 States that had ratified Convention No. 98, together with 16 'direct requests' (including 4 to countries which had also received an observation).[24]

In 2000, the Committee addressed 'observations' to 40 of the 130 States which have ratified Convention No. 87, plus direct requests to 16 States (including 10 which had also received an observation). It also addressed 'observations' to 62 of the 146 States which have ratified Convention No. 98, together with 38 'direct requests' (including 10 to countries which had also received an observation).[25]

In total these observations occupied 126 pages of the Committee's 1999 Report to the Conference, and 81 pages of the Committee's 2000 Report to the Conference.[26] Table 2 outlines observations directed to members of the OECD in relation to the freedom of association Conventions in calendar years 1999 and 2000.

35. The Committee of Experts has also conducted a number of 'general surveys' on freedom of association and collective bargaining under Article 19 of the Constitution.[27] The most recent of these was in 1994,[28] and the Committee's report

---

21. *See* for example ILC, 80th Session, 1993, *Record of Proceedings*, pp. 25/10–12 and 25/58–64; ILC, 81st Session, 1994 *Record of Proceedings*, pp. 25/179–180.
22. *See* also Valticos and von Potobsky, footnote 4 pp. 295–299.
23. Governments which have ratified 'core' human rights Conventions such as Nos 87 and 98 are normally required to provide a report on law and practice in relation to those Conventions once every two years.
24. Direct requests were also addressed to the Netherlands in relation to non-metropolitan territories in respect of Convention No. 87.
25. Direct requests were also addressed to a number of countries in relation to non-Metropolitan territories in respect of both Conventions No. 87 (one case) and No. 98 (two cases). The Committee also made one observation in relation to a non-metropolitan territory under Convention No. 87.
26. Report of the Committee of Experts on the Application of Conventions and Recommendations, ILC, 87th Session, 1999, Report III (Part 1A), pp. 199–294 and 322–351; Report of the Committee of Experts on the Application of Convention and Recommendations ILC, 88th Session, 2000, Report III (Part 1A), pp. 165–202 and 221–263.
27. Article 19(5)(e) empowers the Governing Body to request governments to provide reports on unratified Conventions 'at appropriate intervals'. One Convention or a group of related Conventions is normally dealt with under this procedure each year.
28. *See* footnote 19. Conventions Nos 87 and 98 were dealt with separately in 1956 and 1957. They were dealt with jointly in 1959, 1973, 1983, and 1994.

Table 2. *Observations of Committee of Experts to OECD Members on Freedom of Association Conventions 1999–2000**

Country	Convention	Observations of committee	Reference
Australia	No. 87	Adoption of new legislation; limitation on strike action; continued concern in relation to secondary boycott provisions in legislation; request that the Government also take measures to amend State legislation.	1999, pp. 204–206
	No. 98	Concern re: exclusion of certain categories of employees from protection against unlawful and unfair dismissal; primacy given to individual over collective relations through Australian Workplace Agreement procedures; deductions of pay in all strike cases; pre-selection of bargaining agent at greenfields site before workers are employed.	2000, pp. 222–225
Austria	No. 87	Eligibility of foreign workers for office in works councils.	1999, p. 207
Belgium	No. 87	Point to the need to ensure by law that objective, pre-established and detailed criteria are adopted in establishing rules for the access of professional and workers' organizations to the National Labour Council.	1999, p. 216
Canada	No. 87	Definition of 'essential employees' in Newfoundland; unacceptable restrictions on the right to strike for health workers in Alberta; exclusion of certain workers in some Provinces from the right to organize.	1999, pp. 222–223
Denmark	No. 87	Representation of foreign seafarers in collective bargaining by organizations of their own choosing.	1999, p. 230
	No. 98	Extended coverage of collective agreements to foreign seafarers; potential for an overall draft settlement to cover collective agreements involving an entire sector when organization representing most of the workers in that sector reject the draft settlement.	2000, pp. 230–231

Table 2. (Continued)

Country	Convention	Observations of committee	Reference
Finland	No. 98	Application of legislation to senior white-collar employees for the purpose of negotiating collective agreements; consequences of 'savings agreements' (i.e. local collective agreements for civil servants and other State employees deviating from nationwide collective agreements and whose explicit purpose is the saving of costs).	2000, p. 234
Germany	No. 87	Prohibition on right to strike in public service.	1999, pp. 239–240
	No. 98	Collective bargaining rights of teachers.	2000, p. 235
Greece	No. 87	Infringement of the right to strike; freedom of association of seafarers; limitation on the right of workers employed in public or utility undertakings to take strike action.	1999, p. 241
	No. 98	Adoption of legislation under which workers in the public service may enjoy the right to bargain collectively.	2000, p. 236
	No. 154	Adoption of legislation pursuant to which employees in the public service can benefit from bargaining collectively.	2000, p. 434
Japan	No. 87	Prohibition on the right to organize of fire-fighting personnel and prohibition on the right to strike of public servants.	1999, pp. 248–250
	No. 98	Promotion of negotiation rights of public employees who are not engaged in the administration of the State; exclusion of certain matters from negotiation in national medical institutions and State enterprises.	2000, pp. 240–241
Mexico	No. 87	Imposition by law of trade union monopoly. Prohibition on foreigners from being members of trade union executive bodies.	1999, p. 254–255
	No. 87	Continued concern re: trade union monopoly imposed by legislation and the Constitution on State employees; prohibition of foreigners from being members of trade union executive bodies; restriction on the right to strike of employees in banking institutions belonging to the public sector; restriction on the right to strike of State employees.	2000, pp. 184–186

Table 2. (Continued)

Country	Convention	Observations of committee	Reference
The Netherlands	No. 98	Jobseekers Opportunity Act – The Committee noted with interest that, in relation to one of the programmes, there had been an extension of pay range and relaxation of restrictions on duration of working week. It requested to be kept informed in relation to a programme that provided a total income of 8/9ths of the legal minimum wage.	2000, pp. 246–247
New Zealand	No. 11	Decline in union membership and the negotiation of collective employment contracts without a union.	2000, p. 62
Norway	No. 87	Proposed legislative intervention in relation to the right to strike in particular sectors and compulsory arbitration.	1999, pp. 263–264
	No. 98	Compulsory arbitration as a means of resolving labour disputes.	2000, p. 247
Poland	No. 87	Restrictions on the right to organize for senior public servants; restitution of trade union assets; representativeness of trade union organizations.	1999, p. 275
Portugal	No. 87	The need expressly to repeal legislative provisions that are contrary to Constitution and ratified international instruments. No practical obstacles to the establishment of workers' and employers' organizations.	1999, p. 275
	No. 98	Compulsory arbitration – inconsistent with the promotion of collective bargaining.	2000, p. 251
Spain	No. 87	The Committee noted the approval of regulations governing trade union elections and consultation with employees. It requested that the Government keep it informed in relation to proposed legislation concerning the minimum level of services to be maintained in the event of a strike.	1999, p. 280
Switzerland	No. 87	The need to amend legislation in relation to the right of public servants (other than those exercising authority in the name of the State) to take strike action.	1999, pp. 281–282
Turkey	No. 87	Legislative amendments restrict the right of workers' and employers' organizations to elect their officers in full freedom; draft Bill in relation to the right to organize of public servants; continued concern in	1999, pp. 287–288

Table 2. (Continued)

Country	Convention	Observations of committee	Reference
		relation to restrictions on industrial action re: collective bargaining and the imposition of compulsory arbitration.	
	No. 98	The Committee noted judicial decisions in which compensation was granted in cases of anti-union discrimination; concerns re: limitations on collective bargaining; imposition of compulsory arbitration.	2000, pp. 257–258
United Kingdom	No. 87	The Committee noted with satisfaction the restoration of trade union rights for employees of Government Communications Head Quarters; proposed simplification of law and Code of Practice on industrial action and ballots; concern that law prohibits unions from disciplining members who refuse to participate in industrial action; concerns re-absence of immunity in respect of civil liability for sympathetic industrial action; need for protection against termination of employment in relation to industrial action.	1999, pp. 289–291
	No. 98	Amendments to legislation do not sufficiently address the potential for anti-union discrimination.	2000, pp. 260–261

* There were no observations directed to the Governments of Czech Republic, France, Hungary, Iceland, Ireland, Italy, Luxembourg, and Sweden in the period under review. It should be noted however that New Zealand has ratified only Conventions Nos. 11 and 84, whilst Korea and the United States have not ratified any of the freedom of association Conventions.

provides an invaluable source of information as to the application of the two Conventions.

36. The Governing Body's Committee on Freedom of Association (CFA) was established in 1951, essentially to act as a filter mechanism for the Fact-Finding and Conciliation Commission on Freedom of Association (FFCC). After a relatively slow beginning, the number of cases submitted to the CFA has increased steadily over the years. For example, between 1951 and 1960 a total of 230 complaints were lodged with the Office. For 1961 to 1970 the figure was 400, whilst between 1971 and 1980 it fell back slightly to 350. Between 1981 and 1990 the figure rose to a new peak of 570. Between 1991 and 1999 the figures fell again to 502. Overall, the Committee has examined more than 2000 alleged breaches of the principles of freedom of association. In doing so, it has almost entirely usurped the role of the

FFCC.[29] It has also established an elaborate jurisprudence, the key features of which are set out in the *Digest*.[30]

37. In terms of geographical distribution, around half of all cases come from Latin America, followed by Africa and Europe. In the past, cases concerning Africa, Asia and eastern Europe made a relatively modest contribution to the workload of the Committee. However, there has been a significant increase in the number of complaints against governments from all three regions in recent years. Only a very small number of cases relate to Middle Eastern countries.

38. In terms of subject matter, most complaints raise a number of different issues. Historically, about half of all complaints related to human rights violations, including deaths, torture, ill-treatment, detention, intimidation, harassment, etc. of trade union leaders, activists and members. This is still a major focus of complaints, even though the proportion of such complaints has declined somewhat in recent years. The other major sources of complaint are: (i) unfair labour practices, for example dismissals, transfer or demotion of union activists, employer or government support for one union rather than another, etc.; (ii) interference by the public authorities in the right to organize, for example denial of the right to organize to certain groups of workers (notably, public servants), refusal to register trade unions, deregistration, seizure of union assets, etc.; (iii) interference with the collective bargaining process, for example by subordinating bargaining outcomes to government policy; and (iv) the imposition of legal or practical constraints upon the right to strike.

39. In terms of outcomes, the great majority of complaints are upheld in whole or in part. This is of considerable significance in light of the fact that the CFA consists of three representatives of each of governments, employers and workers (plus an independent chair), and that it invariably arrives at its decisions by consensus.[31] It means that decisions often represent a 'lowest common denominator' in the sense that they represent that which was acceptable to the members of the Committee in that particular instance. On the other hand, the fact that the decisions of the Committee are consensual does make them uniquely authoritative – especially in relation to contentious issues such as the right to strike.

40. Tables 3 and 4 provide a detailed breakdown of the work of the CFA in calendar year 1999.[32] Table 5 lists all complaints against members of the OECD over the period 1995–99.

---

29. The FFCC has dealt with only six cases since its inception. For practical purposes it is now of relevance only as a means of dealing with complaints against Governments which are members of the United Nations but not of the ILO and which have accepted the jurisdiction of the Commission. The most recent such case was complaint against the Government of South Africa which was submitted by the Congress of South African Trade Unions in 1988, and which was finally examined by the Commission in 1992 – *see* the report of the FFCC concerning the Republic of South Africa presented to the Governing Body at its 253rd Session (Geneva), May–June 1992. South Africa subsequently re-joined the ILO in 1994.
30. *See* footnote 14.
31. A dissent has been recorded only once in the history of the Committee.
32. The cases dealt with in 1999 are to be found in the 274th to 276th Reports of the Committee on Freedom of Association.

Table 3. Committee on Freedom of Association 1999 – Complainant and Subject Matter of Complaint

Region	No. of cases	Complainant					
		National trade union(s)	International trade union organization(s)	National/ international trade union organizations	National employer organization(s)	International employer organization(s)	International/ National employer organizations
Africa	11	5	4	2	—	—	—
Northern Europe	1	1	—	—	—	—	—
Western Europe	2	2	—	—	—	—	—
Eastern Europe	7	7	—	—	—	—	—
Latin America	38	16	13	9	—	—	—
Middle East	1	—	—	1	—	—	—
Asia	7	3	2	2	—	—	—
North America	5	5	—	—	—	—	—
Total	72	39	19	14	—	—	—

Table 3. (Continued)

Region	Complainant	Subject matter of complaint				
	International employer / trade union organizations	Human Rights	Unfair labour practices	Interference right to organize	Interference collective bargaining	Interference right to strike
Africa	—	5	2	9	6	6
Northern Europe	—	—	—	—	1	1
Western Europe	—	—	—	1	2	1
Eastern Europe	—	2	1	5	4	2
Latin America	—	16	23	23	18	9
Middle East	—	—	—	1	—	—
Asia	—	3	1	7	5	4
North America	—	—	—	3	4	4
Total	—	26	27	49	40	27

Table 4. Committee on Freedom of Association 1999 – Decision and Outcome

Region	No. of cases	Decision				Outcome					
		Not call for further examination	Definitive conclusions	Request to be kept informed	Interim conclusions	Substantially sustained	Partially sustained	Not sustained	Issues substantially resolved	Insufficient information	Referred to experts
Africa	11	—	1	6	4	8	2	—	—	—	2
Northern Europe	1	—	1	—	—	1	—	—	—	—	1
Western Europe	2	1	1	1	1	1	1	—	—	—	—
Eastern Europe	7	1	—	4	2	4	2	—	1	1	3
Latin America	38	5	7	21	17	14	9	—	4	16	4
Middle East	1	—	—	1	—	1	—	—	—	—	—
Asia	7	—	—	6	2	6	1	—	—	1	1
Canada	5	—	—	4	2	4	1	—	—	—	1
Total	72	7	10	43	28	39	16	—	5	18	12

Table 5. Complaints to Committee on Freedom of Association Against OECD Members 1995–99*

Country	Case	Year	Issue and Report	Outcome
Canada	1758	1995	Restrictions on collective bargaining – public service sector, 297th Report, paras 190–230	Upheld
	1779–1802	1995	Elimination of collective bargaining, pay reductions to government employees, interruption of contracts, 297th Report, paras 190–271	Upheld.
	1800	1995	Restrictions on collective bargaining, public sector wage fixing, federal public sector, 299th Report, paras 155–186	Upheld
	1733,1747, 1748,1749, and 1750	1995	Restrictions on the right to strike and the right to organize – public, parapublic and municipal sectors, 299th Report, paras 187–247	Upheld
	1802	1995	Restrictions on collective bargaining – public sector, 299th Report, paras 248–284	Upheld
	1806	1995	Compliance with collective agreements – restrictions on collective bargaining arbitration – teachers, 300th Report, paras 101–129	Upheld
	1737	1996	Biased conduct, interference, policing in private sector labour dispute, 305th Report, paras 102–116	No further examination
	1859	1997	Restrictions on collective bargaining – public sector, 306th Report, paras 177–247	Upheld
	1900	1997	Legislative repeal of statutory access to collective bargaining, termination of existing right to organize and nullification of collective agreements, 308th Report, paras 139–193	Upheld
	1928	1998	Denial of right to bargain collectively, interference with independence of arbitration, 310th Report, paras 134–184	Upheld
	1943	1998	Interference in arbitration and labour tribunals, 310th Report, paras 185–242	Upheld
	1943	1998	Governmental interference in arbitration and labour tribunals, 311th Report, paras 151–169	Upheld

Table 5. (Continued)

Country	Case	Year	Issue and Report	Outcome
	1951	1998	Interference with collective bargaining, denial of rights to organize, bargain collectively and strike, lack of protection against anti-union discrimination and employer interference, 311th Report, paras 170–234	Upheld
	1951	1999	Interference with right to bargain collectively and right to organize – Education sector, 316th Report, paras 214–228	Upheld
	1975	1999	Right to organize, bargain collectively and strike – workers employed in subsidized jobs, 316th Report, paras 229–274	Upheld
	1985	1999	Interference in collective bargaining right to strike – postal workers, 316th Report, paras 275–325	Upheld
	1943	1999	Independence of arbitration – tribunal appointment and revocation procedures – public sector, 318th Report, paras 103–118	Part upheld
	1999	1999	Interference with the right to bargain collectively, 318th Report, paras 119–171	Upheld
Czech Republic	1762	1995	Interference with the right to strike and organize – Collective bargaining – public sector, 297th Report, paras 272–284	Part upheld.
Denmark	1861	1996	Violations of trade union rights, interference, harassment, right to freedom of association, 305th Report, paras 229–253.	Part upheld
	1882	1997	Interruption of lawful industrial action – hospital sector, legislative extension of collective agreements, 306th Report, paras 369–438	Part upheld
	1933	1998	Insufficient protection against anti-union discrimination, dismissal of a workers' representative, 309th Report, paras 186–223	Not upheld
	1958	1998	Interference in collective agreements, and collective bargaining – public sector, 312th Report, paras 1–77	No further examination
	1950	1998	Restrictions on the right to strike and interference in free collective bargaining, 312th Report, paras 430–461	Upheld

Table 5. (Continued)

Country	Case	Year	Issue and Report	Outcome
	1971	1999	Interference with collective bargaining and the right to strike, 317th Report, paras 1–61	Upheld
France/ French Polynesia	1858	1996	Violent clashes, maltreatment arrests and repression of trade unionists, 305th Report, paras 289–314	Not upheld
France (Guiana)	1929	1998	Arrest and deportation of trade union leaders and activists, 310th Report, paras 393–431	Upheld
Germany	1820	1996	Right to bargain collectively, restrictions on the right to strike – teachers, 302nd Report, paras 80–110	Part upheld
Iceland	1768	1995	Interference with the right to strike/ lockout on ferry, right to bargain collectively, 299th Report, paras 71–112	Upheld
Japan	1991	1999	Unfair and discriminating labour practices – anti-union discrimination, 318th Report, paras 232–271	Upheld
Korea	1865	1996	Right to organize, arrest and detention of trade union official, registration of organizations, 304th Report, paras 221–254	Upheld
	1865	1997	Right to organize, arrest and detention of trade union leader, registration of organizations, 306th Report, paras 295–346	Upheld
	1865	1998	Arrest and detention of a trade union leader, government refusal to register newly established organizations, government adoption of labour law amendments contrary to freedom of association, 309th Report, paras 120–160	Upheld
Mexico	1844	1995	Annulment of registration of organisation, interference with right to organize, 300th Report, paras 61–66	Upheld
	1927	1999	Acts of anti-union discrimination within the framework of collective bargaining with a minority trade union, 313th Report, paras 118–131	Not upheld
	1974	1999	Anti-union discrimination – dismissal of workers threats of arrest, 318th Report, paras 298–307	Part upheld

* There were no complaints against the Governments of Australia, Austria, Belgium, Finland, Greece, Hungary, Ireland, Italy, Luxembourg, The Netherlands, New Zealand, Norway, Sweden, Switzerland, and the United States in the period under review.

B. *The Principles as Developed*

41. It is beyond the scope of the present work to describe the jurisprudence of the Committee of Experts and the CFA relating to freedom of association in any detail. It is, however, proposed briefly to examine four issues which are of special practical significance and/or which have generated particular controversy over the years: (i) the right of workers to join the trade union of their choice; (ii) the 'right' of trade unions to represent their members for purposes of collective bargaining; (iii) the subordination of bargaining outcomes to government policy; and (iv) the imposition of legislative and other restrictions upon the right to strike. The *Digest* and the *General Survey* provide a more detailed picture of the jurisprudence of the supervisory bodies. In certain respects this jurisprudence reflects concerns and debates that are now of diminished significance – notably the circumstances of the Cold War era. Nevertheless the supervisory bodies have not resiled from any of the fundamental principles which have been developed over the last half century, even though there have been significant shifts of emphasis in some areas in response to an ever-changing social, political and economic environment. Whether those changes have been sufficient – or excessive – is itself an important subject for debate. Further analysis of specific aspects of the principles, and of these debates, can be found in the texts and articles listed in the Select Bibliography at the end of this chapter.

C. *Choice of Union*

42. Article 2 of Convention No. 87 provides that

> 'Workers and employers, without distinction whatsoever, shall have the right to establish and, subject only to the rules of the organisation concerned, to join organisations of their own choosing without previous authorisation.'

According to the Committee of Experts this is 'one of the fundamental aspects of freedom of association'.[33] It has, however, generated a number of problems in practice – notably in relation to trade union pluralism, membership size as a criterion for registration, the concept of 'most representative union' and restrictions on the number of unions in a given enterprise, occupation or branch of activity.

43. Both the Committee of Experts and the CFA have consistently taken the view that Article 2 does not make trade union pluralism mandatory. But they have also insisted that conformity with the Convention requires that diversity must be possible if workers so choose.[34] This has caused considerable difficulty in relation to countries where labour legislation provides, directly or indirectly, that only one trade union may be established for a given category of workers and/or that all unions must belong to a single hierarchical structure. Such provision is seen not only to be contrary to Article 2, but also to facilitate acts of interference in the internal affairs of unions on the part of employers or government.

---

33. *General Survey*, para. 107.
34. *General Survey*, paras 91 and 107, *Digest*, paras 287–291.

44. The Committees have recognized that workers, employers, and governments may feel that multiplicity of trade unions is not conducive to the development of the strong and independent unions which are an essential pre-condition of adequate respect for the principles of freedom of association. They consider, however, that freedom of choice is of paramount importance, and that fragmentation can best be avoided if unions are encouraged voluntarily to form strong and united organizations, rather than having such unity imposed on them by legislative dictat.[35] The fact remains, however, that governments in many developing countries consider that some form of union monopoly is in the best interests of both workers and of the State. Such governments frequently claim that the Committees' insistence on the possibility, if not the reality, of pluralism is symptomatic of the 'Euro-centric' character of the Conventions and of the associated jurisprudence.

45. One of the ways in which governments sometimes seek to discourage an excessive proliferation of trade unions is by stipulating that to be recognized as a trade union in law, organizations must have a certain minimum number of members. Such requirements are said to prevent the proliferation of small, non-viable unions which might be susceptible to employer domination, and which might lack the resources adequately to service their members. The Committees have taken the view that such requirements 'should be fixed in a reasonable manner so that the establishment of organizations is not hindered'.[36] Inevitably, there can be no hard and fast rules as to what constitutes a 'reasonable figure' for these purposes. The CFA has for example determined that a 20-member limit 'does not seem excessive', whereas limits of 50 members, or a high proportion (for example 50 per cent) of workers in an industry or undertaking, have been considered to be unacceptable.[37]

46. There are some countries where there is no requirement that unions be of a specified size in order to exist as a union, but where *registered* unions are accorded certain legal and industrial privileges.[38] Where size is a pre-condition for such registration, the supervisory bodies will look at the surrounding circumstances, including the capacity of unregistered bodies adequately to represent the interests of their members, in deciding whether a given limit is acceptable. In 1989, for example, the CFA determined that a 1,000 member requirement (in an optional registration system) was excessive because it 'might be liable to deprive workers in small bargaining units or who are dispersed over wide geographical areas of the right to form organizations capable of fully exercising trade union activities'.[39] As against this, it might also be

---

35. *See General Survey*, paras 91–96 and *Digest*, paras 292–299.
36. *See General Survey*, para. 81.
37. *See Digest*, paras 254–258. *See also General Survey*, para. 94.
38. On registration in general, *see General Survey*, paras 71–75.
39. Case No. 1385 (New Zealand), 265th Report paras 260–282. *See also* case No. 1559 (Australia) 284th Report paras 200–263 where the Committee determined that the 10,000 member limit embodied in Federal industrial legislation was unacceptable, notwithstanding that the majority of trade unions in that country operated outside the Federal system. In New Zealand the Employment Contracts Act 1991 removed all legal recognition of trade unions. In Australia the relevant legislation was amended in response to the decision of the CFA – *see* B. Creighton, 'The ILO and the Protection of Fundamental Human Rights in Australia' (1988) 22 *Melbourne University Law Review* 239, pp. 269–270, 276–278.

said that the need to be capable of effectively exercising trade union rights is precisely the kind of factor which would justify a relatively high membership requirement. It is also necessary to recognize that it be appropriate to apply different principles in situations where the trade union movement is 'immature' as compared to those where the movement is well-established and 'mature'.

47. The Committees have accepted that legislation which distinguishes between 'most representative' trade unions and other unions is not necessarily incompatible with Article 2 so long as: (i) 'representivity' is determined according to objective, pre-established and precise criteria; (ii) non-representative unions are still able to exist and to represent their members, at least in relation to individual grievances; (iii) that the distinction between 'most representative' and other unions is limited to matters such as collective bargaining, consultation by the authorities and nominating delegates to international organisations (most obviously, the ILO); and (iv) that a most representative organization that has exclusive bargaining rights must be obliged 'to represent fairly and equally all workers in the bargaining unit, whether or not they are members of the trade union'.[40]

48. Requirements that members of a trade union must all belong to the same or similar branch of economic activity, occupation, etc. are not necessarily incompatible with Article 2. However, there must still be a possibility of pluralism in relation to each branch of activity, etc., and first-level organizations must retain the freedom to form or join federations or confederations of their own choosing.[41]

D. *The 'Right' to Union Representation*

49. Self-evidently, respect for the principles of freedom of association requires that individual workers should have the right to form and to join trade unions, and that they should have adequate protection against victimization on account of having done so. These imperatives find clear recognition in Article 2 of Convention No. 87 and in Article 1 of Convention No. 98. Since the fundamental purpose of trade union organization is to enable workers to deal on more equal terms with employers through the power of the collectivity, it seems reasonable to suppose that respect for the principles of freedom of association would also require that workers should have the right to insist that their union be permitted to represent their interests in negotiations with their employer. This is not, however, the position which has been adopted by the supervisory bodies.

50. Both the CFA and the Committee of Experts have consistently emphasized the desirability of union recognition for purposes of collective bargaining, and of bargaining in good faith.[42] They have not, however, been prepared to carry this logic through by requiring that conformity with the principles of freedom of association in general, and Article 4 of Convention No. 98 in particular, requires that employers must be obliged to recognize and bargain in good faith with the union(s) to which

---

40. *General Survey,* paras 97–99 and *Digest,* paras 309–315.
41. *General Survey,* para. 84 and *Digest,* para 292.
42. *See* for example *General Survey,* paras 240 and 243 and *Digest,* paras 821–823.

their employees belong (subject to any permissible qualifications in terms of representivity). They have based this refusal on the premise that:

> 'Nothing in Article 4 of the Convention [i.e. No. 98] places a duty on the government to enforce collective bargaining by compulsory means with a given organisation; such an intervention would clearly alter the nature of bargaining.'[43]

In other words, the CFA seems to consider that if employers were compelled to recognize the union(s) to which their workers belong this would deprive any resultant bargaining of its 'voluntary' character. This view can be sustained on the basis of the wording of Article 4, but it is not *impelled* by it. For example, it could equally be argued that in order to 'encourage and promote the development and utilization of machinery for voluntary negotiation' as required by Article 4, it is necessary that there be some means whereby recalcitrant employers can be forced to come to the bargaining table. This approach certainly seems to be more consonant with the intent of Article 4 than a line of reasoning which holds that it is contrary to the Convention expressly to deny certain groups of workers the *right* to engage in collective bargaining, for example because of the sector of the economy in which they are engaged,[44] but that it is permissible for an employer to achieve the same result by declining to negotiate with the union to which those workers belong.

51. It is important to appreciate that the supervisory bodies have not suggested that it is inconsistent with the principles of freedom of association for the law to oblige employers to negotiate with trade unions which satisfy certain criteria (for example, as to representativity).[45] The point is that they have not been prepared to recognize that the absence of such mechanisms severely compromises the notion of the *right* to engage in collective bargaining which is ostensibly protected by Article 4 of Convention No. 98. The limitations of the jurisprudence regarding the 'voluntary' character of collective bargaining have become increasingly evident in light of the recent trend, especially in developed economies, towards the individualization of employment relationships with the attendant practice of preferencing industrial agreements over the end-products of processes of collective bargaining.[46]

---

43. *Digest*, para. 846. *See also Digest*, paras 844–845. The Committee of Experts is equally insistent upon the 'voluntary' character of collective bargaining – *General Survey*, paras 248 and 265.
44. *See Digest*, paras 729–805.
45. For the principles governing this issue are *General Survey* paras 238–243 and *Digest*, paras 824–843.
46. *See General Survey*, para. 236 and *Digest*, para. 911. *See also* the decision of the CFA in Case No. 1698 (New Zealand), 292nd Report, paras 675–741 and 295th Report, paras 132–262, and the observation of the Committee of Experts in relation to Australia in 1998 and 2000 – ILC, 86th Session, 1998, Report III (Part 4A), pp. 223–224 and ILC, 88th Session 2000, Report III (Part 4A), pp. 223–225.

E. Interference with Bargaining Outcomes

52. Despite their rather ambiguous attitude to compulsory recognition for purposes of collective bargaining, the supervisory bodies have been most zealous in their insistence upon the autonomy of the bargaining process:

'The principle of voluntary negotiation of collective agreements, and thus the autonomy of the bargaining partners, is the second essential element of Article 4 of the Convention No. 98.[47] The existing machinery and procedures should be designed to facilitate bargaining between the two sides of industry, leaving them free to reach their own settlement. However, several difficulties arise in this respect, and an increasing number of countries restrict this freedom to various extents. The problems most frequently encountered concern unilateral decision as to the level of bargaining; the exclusion of certain matters from the scope of bargaining; making collective agreements subject to prior approval by the administrative or budgetary authorities; observance of criteria pre-established by the law, in particular as regards wages; and the unilateral imposition of working conditions.'[48]

53. Whilst the subordination of bargaining outcomes to government policy etc., is, *prima facie*, incompatible with the principles on freedom of association, the Committees have recognized that in some circumstances governments may legitimately seek to influence the outcomes of the bargaining process.

54. One means of doing this which may be acceptable is for legislation to require that agreements are to become operative only a reasonable length of time after they have been filed with the relevant public authority. If this authority considers that the terms of the agreement were manifestly incompatible with economic policy objectives which are recognized to be in the general interest, the agreement could be referred to an appropriate consultative body, upon which both employers and workers should be represented. This body could then have the power to draw the attention of the parties to any considerations of general interest to which they might care to refer. In the final analysis, however, the decision as to whether or not the agreement becomes operative must rest with the parties.[49]

55. In extreme cases, compelling reasons of national economic interest may justify more far reaching interference with the autonomy of the participants in the bargaining process. However, any such interference: (i) should be imposed only as an exceptional measure; (ii) should be limited to the extent necessary to deal with the situation in hand; (iii) should operate only for a reasonable period; and (iv) should be accompanied by adequate safeguards to protect workers' living standards.[50]

---

47. The first is the requirement that the public authorities take appropriate measures to *promote* collective bargaining – *General Survey*, paras 235–247.
48. *General Survey*, para. 248.
49. *General Survey*, para. 253 and *Digest*, paras 872–874.
50. *General Survey*, para. 260 and *Digest*, para. 899.

56. Despite the importance attached by the supervisory bodies to the autonomy of the bargaining process, governments seem increasingly prepared to disregard international norms in this respect. This is clearly borne out by the high proportion of the complaints which are summarized in Table 5 which relate to attenuation of the right to engage in collective bargaining and inference with the outcomes of the bargaining process – especially in the public sector.

F. Interference with the Right to Strike

57. It was noted earlier that neither Convention No. 87 nor No. 98 make any express reference to the right to strike. However, the supervisory bodies have repeatedly insisted that:

> ' … the right to strike is one of the essential means available to workers and their organisations for the promotion and protection of their economic and social interests. These interests not only have to do with obtaining better working conditions and pursuing collective demands of an occupational nature, but also with seeking solutions to economic and social policy questions and to labour problems of any kind which are of direct concern to the workers.'[51]

Denial of this right is considered to constitute a restriction on the means available to trade unions to further and to defend the interests of their members, and 'to organise their administration and activities and to formulate their programmes'. As such, it is incompatible with Articles 3, 8 and 10 of Convention No. 87. It is also considered to be inconsistent with the obligation to accord proper respect to the principles of freedom of association which is a necessary incident of adherence to the Constitution of the Organisation.[52]

58. It is clear that the right to strike is not limited to the protection and promotion of purely occupational interests: rather it extends to 'the seeking of solutions to economic and social policy questions and problems facing the undertaking which are of direct concern to the workers.'[53] On the other hand, it is also clear that strikes of a purely political nature do not fall within the scope of the principles.[54]

59. The concept of the 'right to strike' includes not just the collective withdrawal of labour in the conventional sense, but also extends to other forms of industrial action, including the go-slow, work-to-rule, sit-down strikes and picketing, so long as they remain peaceful.[55] It may also include sympathy action so long as the action

---

51. *General Survey*, 1983, para. 200. *See also General Survey*, paras 146–151 and *Digest*, paras 473–476.
52. Denial of the right to strike might also be said to be 'inconsistent' with the guarantees provided by Article 4 of Convention No. 98 since recourse to strikes and other forms of industrial action can be seen to be an instant of 'voluntary' collective bargaining. In fact the supervisory bodies never seem to have adopted this approach, although as a matter of logic it has much to commend it.
53. *Digest*, para. 479.
54. *General Survey*, para. 165 and *Digest*, para. 481.
55. *General Survey*, paras 173–174 and *Digest*, paras 496–497.

in support of which it is taken is itself consistent with the principles of freedom of association.[56]

60. The supervisory bodies have accepted that governments may legitimately impose certain pre-conditions of the taking of strike action. These may include the giving of notice of strike; the imposition of cooling-off periods; the holding of ballots; the attainment of a stated quorum in a ballot; and recourse to compulsory conciliation and arbitration. However, all such pre-conditions must be 'reasonable', and must not be such 'as to place a substantial limitation on the means of action open to trade union organisations'.[57]

61. Legislative or common law provisions which expose workers and/or their unions to actions for damages and/or injunctions in respect of the legitimate exercise of the right to strike may deprive workers of the right to take strike action in order to protect and to promote their economic and social interests.[58] Similarly, the Committees have taken the view that penal sanctions should be imposed only where there have been violations of strike prohibitions which are themselves in conformity with the principles of freedom of association. Even where penalties are in order, the sanctions imposed should be proportionate to the offences committed, and sentences of imprisonment should never be imposed for organizing or participating in peaceful strikes.[59] Dismissal of trade union leaders or members for exercising the right to strike is considered to be contrary to the principles of freedom of association.[60]

62. Probably the most vexed issues which arise in the context of international protection of the right to strike relate to the imposition of restrictions on the right to strike in the public sector, in essential services and in times of national emergency.

63. Both the Committee of Experts and the CFA have recognized that the right to strike may be prohibited or curtailed in the public sector and in relation to essential services. However, they have also made clear that this may be done only in limited circumstances, and subject to appropriate procedural and substantive safeguards.

64. As concerns public servants, the Committee of Experts has stressed that prohibition of the right to strike 'should be limited to public servants exercising authority in the name of the State'. It has also recognized that it will often be difficult in practice to draw and maintain a distinction between public servants in this narrow sense and public sector employees more generally. This has led the Committee to suggest that 'one solution might be not to impose a total prohibition on strikes, but rather to provide for the maintaining by a defined and limited category of staff of a

---

56. *General Survey*, para. 168 and *Digest*, para. 486.
57. Digest, para. 498. *See also Digest*, paras 499–514 and *General Survey*, paras 170–172.
58. *See Digest*, para. 594 and the Report of the FFCC concerning the Republic of South Africa, presented to the Governing Body at its 253rd Session (Geneva, May–June 1992), para. 666.
59. *See General Survey*, paras 174–178 and *Digest*, paras 598–604.
60. See *General Survey*, paras 139 and 179 and *Digest*, paras 570–571 and 590–593.

negotiated minimum service when a *total and prolonged* stoppage might result in *serious* consequences for the public'.[61]

65.   The definition of what constitutes an 'essential service' in this context has been a constant source of difficulty for the supervisory bodies. However the core concept is clear enough: 'essential services are only those the interruption of which would endanger the life, personal safety or health of the whole or part of the population'.[62] The problem is, of course, to determine which services will meet those criteria. Attempts to do so have generated an extensive, if not entirely consistent, jurisprudence.[63] The Committees have, however, evinced an increasing preparedness to recognize that a service which is not 'essential' in the strict sense of the term may become 'essential' by reason of its duration or extent, or the particular circumstances of the country concerned.[64]

66.   The Committees have also exhibited an increasing preference for arrangements for the provision of appropriate levels of minimum service as an alternative to outright prohibition of strikes and other forms of industrial action. To be acceptable, such arrangements 'must genuinely and exclusively be a *minimum* service, that is one which is limited to the operations which are strictly necessary to meet the basic needs of the population or the minimum requirements of the service, while maintaining the effectiveness of the pressure brought to bear'. Furthermore, the workers concerned must have the right to participate in the process of determining what constitutes a minimum level of service for these purposes.[65] Where the minimum service option is not sustainable, then workers who are to be deprived of the right to strike must be provided with appropriate 'compensatory guarantees'. These might include:

> 'conciliation and mediation procedures leading, in the event of deadlock, to arbitration machinery seen to be reliable by the parties concerned. It is essential that the latter be able to participate in determining and implementing the procedure, which should furthermore provide sufficient guarantees of impartiality and rapidity; arbitration awards should be binding on both parties and once issued should be implemented rapidly and completely.'[66]

67.   Curtailment of the right to strike may also be justified in times of acute national crisis, but only for a limited period. Requisitioning of labour may be permissible in such circumstances if it is used purely for the purpose of 'maintaining essential services in circumstances of the utmost gravity', and subject to appropriate procedural and substantive safeguards.[67]

---

61.   *General Survey*, para. 158. *See also Digest*, paras 531–539.
62.   *General Survey*, para. 159. *See also Digest*, para. 540.
63.   *See* especially *Digest*, paras 544–545.
64.   *General Survey*, para. 160 and *Digest*, para. 541.
65.   *General Survey*, para. 161.
66.   *General Survey*, para. 164. *See also Digest*, paras 546–553.
67.   *Digest*, para. 573.

IV. EVALUATION AND FUTURE DIRECTIONS

68. It is, of course, impossible accurately to measure the practical impact of the ILO standards on freedom of association. Nevertheless, there is a substantial body of evidence which suggests that over the years, this impact has been very considerable.

69. It is clear that many countries need to, and do, amend their law and practice in order to enable them to ratify Conventions Nos 87 and 98. Even governments which have not ratified the Conventions frequently take account of their requirements in framing their labour legislation. Indeed the normative effects of the principles of freedom of association are such that some commentators have suggested they have acquired a status akin to the rules of customary international law.[68]

70. Once a State has ratified either or both of the Conventions, it is obliged to maintain its law and practice in conformity with their requirements for the future. It is the function of the Committee of Experts and the Conference Committee on the Application of Conventions and Recommendations to try to ensure that this happens. Some impression of the degree of success attained by the supervisory bodies in this respect can be derived from the fact that between 1964 and 2000 the Committee of Experts has noted 2,230 'cases of progress' – that is cases in which law and practice have been amended in order to bring them into conformity with the requirements of a ratified Convention. A very substantial proportion of these have related to Convention No 87 or 98. For example, in its 2000 Report the Committee noted 27 such cases, of which 7 related to one or other of Conventions Nos 87 and 98.[69]

71. It is also clear that over the years the work of the CFA has produced significant results both in relation to industrial law and practice, and in terms of securing the release of imprisoned trade unionists, preventing executions, ensuring that dismissed workers are reinstated, etc.[70] In many instances, even totalitarian regimes with poor human rights records have proved to be surprisingly responsive to the pressure of international public opinion as represented by the supervisory bodies. Even where a government has appeared to be wholly unresponsive in the short term, previous ILO activity has often provided basis for legislative reform after a radical change of regime – as occurred in many of the countries of eastern Europe following the collapse of the Communist regimes in those countries.

---

68. *See* G. von Potobsky, 'Protection of Trade Union Rights: Twenty Years' Work by the Committee on Freedom of Association' (1972) 105 *International Labour Review* 69 at p. 83, and Jenks, footnote 1, p. 6. For a decisive repudiation of this proposition at national level, *see* the observations of the High Court of Australia in *Victoria v Commonwealth* (1996) 187 Commonwealth Law Reports 416, pp. 543–544.
69. ILC, 88th Session, 2000, Report III (Part 1A), at paras 99–100. In 1999, 17 out of 39 cases related to these the Conventions. *See also* ILC, 87th Session, 1999, Report III (Part 1A), at paras 203–205.
70. *See* for example the reprieve and release of a Sudanese trade union leader who had been under sentence of death in the aftermath of a military coup in that country in 1989, Case No. 1508 (Sudan), 270th Report, paras 369–412 and 272nd Report, para. 11.

72. It would be quite erroneous to suggest that the principles of freedom of association are accorded a proper level of respect in all of those countries which have ratified Conventions Nos 87 and 98, let alone in those which have not done so. This is patently not the case. This is borne out by the number, and gravity, of complaints presented to the CFA. It is also borne out by the number and complexity of the issues dealt with in the observations of the Committee of Experts. These trends appear certain to continue as organized labour struggles to maintain and to enhance its position in an increasingly difficult economic and political environment. In this regard, it is impossible to be other than concerned at the cavalier attitude to the principles and to the pronouncements of the supervisory bodies by governments in a number of developed countries in recent years.[71] This bodes ill for the future, not only of the principles and the associated supervisory procedures, but ultimately of the tripartite structures of which they are the cornerstone.

73. This is not to suggest that the principles and procedures are, or should be, immutable. It may well be that the jurisprudence of the Committee of Experts and of the CFA need to be reconsidered in certain respects – for example in relation to union pluralism, recognition for purposes of collective bargaining and the concept of 'essential services': indeed the 1994 *General Survey* suggests that there has been at least a partial re-evaluation of this latter concept. It may also be necessary dispassionately to evaluate the efficacy of the supervisory procedures, to try more precisely to define the proper relationship between the Committee of Experts and the CFA, and to try constructively to build upon the momentum generated by the adoption of the Declaration on Fundamental Principles and Rights at Work and the associated 'follow-up' procedure. It is certainly necessary to establish and maintain a more coherent relationship between respect for ILO standards on human rights and the provision of technical assistance to Member States than has been the case hitherto. But it is also of the utmost importance that those countries, especially in the developed world, which have traditionally prided themselves upon their commitment to respect for fundamental human rights should adopt a more positive approach to respect for the principles of freedom of association and the associated supervisory procedures than has been evident in the recent past. Failure to do so must inevitably undermine respect to these fundamental values not only in those countries themselves, but also in those countries which are in the process of industrialization and/or which are emerging from long periods of totalitarian rule.

SELECT BIBLIOGRAPHY

H. Bartolomei de la Cruz, G. von Potobsky, and L. Swepston, *The International Labor Organization: The International Standards System and Basic Human Rights*, Boulder Colorado, 1996.
H. Bartolomei de la Cruz, *Protection Against Anti-Union Discrimination*, Geneva, 1976.

---

71. *See* for example B. Creighton, 'The ILO and the Protection of Freedom of Association in the United Kingdom', in K.D. Ewing, G. Gearty, and B.A. Hepple (eds), *Human Rights and Labour Law*, London, 1994.

R. Ben-Israel, *International Labour Standards: The Case of Freedom to Strike*, Deventer, 1988.

L. Betten, *International Labour Law: Selected Issues*, Deventer, 1993.

B. Creighton, 'The ILO and Protection of Freedom of Association in the United Kingdom', in K.D. Ewing, C. Gearty, and B.A. Hepple (eds), *Human Rights and Labour Law*, London, 1994.

B. Creighton, 'The ILO and the Protection of Fundamental Human Rights in Australia', *Melbourne University Law Review*, Vol. 22, 1998, p. 239.

B. Gernigon, A. Odero, and H. Guido, 'ILO Principles Concerning the Right to Strike', *International Labour Review*, Vol. 137, 1998, p. 441.

J. de Givry, *Droits de l'homme travail et syndicats*, Paris, 1989.

E.B. Haas, *Human Rights and International Action – The Case of Freedom of Association*, Stanford, 1970.

J. Hodges-Aeberhard and A. Odero de Dios, 'Principles of the Committee on Freedom of Association Concerning Strikes', *International Labour Review*, Vol. 126, 1987, p. 543.

ILO, *General Survey by the Committee of Experts in the Application of Conventions and Recommendations on Freedom of Association and Collective Bargaining*, Geneva, 1994.

ILO, *Digest of decisions and principles of the Freedom of Association Committee of the Governing Body of the ILO*, 4th ed., Geneva, 1996.

C.W. Jenks, *The International Protection of Trade Union Freedom*, London, 1957.

C.W. Jenks, 'The International Protection of Trade Union Rights', in E. Luard (ed.), *The International Protection of Human Rights*, London, 1966.

E.A. Landy, *The Effectiveness of International Supervision*, London, 1966.

B. Langille, 'The ILO and the New Economy: Recent Developments' *The International Journal of Comparative Labour Law and Industrial Relations*, Vol. 15, 1999, p. 229.

S. Leader, *Freedom of Association: A Study in Labor Law and Political Theory*, New Haven, 1992.

A. Pankert, 'Settlement of Labour Disputes in Essential Services', *International Labour Review*, Vol. 119, 1980, p. 723.

N. Valticos, 'Les méthodes de la protection internationale de la liberté syndicale', in *Recueil des cours*, Vol. 1-1975, 79.44.

N. Valticos and G von Potobsky, *International Labour Law*, 2nd ed., Deventer, 1995.

Chapter 12. The Changing World of Work

R. Blanpain

I. The Network-Society

1. We live in a new society.[i] We have been catapulted out of an industrial society into an information and network society. The worldwide competition for investments and jobs and the new communication technologies are challenging the old paradigms of social protection, stable jobs and industrial relations systems. Supply side economics tend to push labour law, collective agreements, minimum wages and social security to the sidelines. The search for a new balance between economics and social policy has to be launched again.

2. This is especially the case as we are increasingly confronted with contradictory developments. Yesterday, the problem no. 1 in Europe was unemployment. Today there is a growing shortage of labour. There is battle for the brains. 'British industry is short of plumbers, joiners, and electricians, but even more hard pressed to find skilled foremen to oversee their work ... It was revealed that managerment had been forced to employ two million to were not fully proficient for the job they were doing.[1] There are other contradictions. Today, there is more added value and wealth created than ever before in history and yet their is a growing number of poor. There is an increasing gap between haves an haves not. Worldwide two billion people have to live on less than one US $ today. 'The richest country in the history of the universe, the USA, tolerates a poverty rate of about 20 per cent among its children, and about 35 per cent among its black children'.[2] In the European Union there are 55 million poor and five million people without a roof over their heads.

A. Information Technologies

3. Today the economy becomes more and more globalized. Information and communication technologies are by far the most important factor fostering this globalization.

---

1. J. Kelly, 'Skills shortages highlighted', *Financial Times*, 27 June 2000.
2. Weinstein M.? 'Upward Mobility Isn't the Rule', *International Herald Tribune*, 21 Febraury 2000.

This follows an historical pattern. The development of our societies has always been technologically driven, at the pace of the agricultural society and horses until the 18th century, since then on the basis of machines, of electric and steam power in the industrialized societies, and today and tomorrow in the orbit of the information revolution. This technological development is all pervasive, dominating, and dramatically affecting our societies in general and the labour markets in particular.

One of the reasons why most government job schemes fail is that many decision makers fail to realize that we have been catapulted, forcefully and brutally, out of the industrial society into what may be termed an information society: many politicians still want to restore and go back to the earlier model, to the industrial society of yesterday.

4.   Indeed, only yesterday Fordism was still riding high. It lasted triumphantly for some thirty years (1950–1980) and was characterized by the following features:

– almost everyone who could work had a job, neatly 'tailored';
– almost everyone earned a 'reasonable' salary; and was
– a brave 'consumer'.

There was enough money to finance transfers for the benefit of the sick and the handicapped, to pay for pensions, to support (some) unemployed and the like.

Employers and trade unions regularly programmed – with success – social progress. Everyone had a place on the labour market, often colourless and boring, but could see himself and especially his children grow in the system. The children would study, do better and climb the social ladder. There was a 'social arrangement' in which employers and employees could find common ground: economic growth on the one hand and social progress on the other were monitored collectively by employers and trade unions, including through collective bargaining, often with the consent of or in concertation with the welfare state.

Consumption then was geared to, we would now call rather, primary needs. Everybody wanted a TV, a refrigerator, a car, a roof over his head. Our society was one of consumers, targeting useful things: 'a society of the useful'. Steady consumption made the economic machine run smoothly.

5.   Those glorious thirty years are definitively behind us. 'We are in a New World. Freer, but less secure.'

This move into the information society is as drastic, brutal and fundamental as the transition from the agricultural society to the industrial society in the 19th century, when our (great)-grandparents were driven from the barn and the field into the sweatshops and the cities.

More than that, in those earlier (industrial) days, we were merely moving from one sector to another: from the primary sector to the secondary, from agriculture to manufacturing. An analysis at first sight may lead us to conclude that today we are massively stepping into the third sector: the services. This is evidenced by less than 10 per cent of the economically active population left in agriculture, less than 30 per cent in manufacturing and 50 per cent or more in the service sector.

6.   However, things are not that simple. There is much more to it: at present, sectors are merging into each other. What we are really experiencing is a tertiarization of agriculture and manufacturing on the one hand and a (partial) industrialization of services on the other. All this is obviously the result of the massive and creative introduction of new technologies, especially of information–communication technology, where in the form of bits – not atoms – knowledge is stored, manipulated, and transmitted worldwide without significant costs.

As a consequence, the source of economic value is shifting from the material to the non-material. Where previously wealth had to do with the yield of land (agriculture) and underground deposits (mining) and yesterday opulence was the result of produced goods, today and tomorrow, wealth means knowledge, inventions, and intellectual property. What are involved are 'things' which the customs officer does not see pass through national borders; the newer wealth has to do with 'invisible', which pass underground, above the ground, through satellites and are sent around the world on the information highways.

New technologies are likewise replacing traditional raw materials, such as copper as a medium for transporting bits with fibres, which are cheaper and lighter to install and, equally important, perform better.

7. A couple of examples may serve to illustrate our reasoning more clearly. Take the cost structure of a pound of butter or a car. Only 20 per cent or less of the cost of making butter relates to the agricultural work; 80 per cent or more goes to research and development, including genetic engineering, storing, marketing, distribution, and the like. The cost of a car is less and less related to the financing of the chassis or to paying the assembly-line workers involved, of whom there are fewer every day, but results from expenditure/investments for conception, design, R&D, intellectual property, marketing, distribution, licences, financing, insurance ... all services, many of which can be operated over information–communication highways.

Products and goods, agriculture and manufacturing, are thus in the grip of 'services'. Even more, it is clear that goods and services go hand in hand. Industry remains the motor of the economic machine, but is *de facto* 'service-driven'.

Now, it is plain that these services have become so varied, so specialized, so rapidly evolving and so demanding, that a single enterprise cannot simply house all the services it may need and maintain them at top-level quality. Moreover, they are not needed constantly, but only at specific points in time. On top of that, these services can be very expensive, since top quality commands top rewards. And lastly, they can be provided via the information highways from anywhere, even from the other side of the globe, at possibly only 10 per cent or even less of the cost at home.

8. New products and services pop up every day. To give one example: privately built satellites make satellite pictures available useful for crop monitoring, scouting for oil and gas resources, better management of urban sprawl, environmental concerns, and the like.[ii]

'IT Skills in the 21st Century', a study of 500 companies based in London found that the ratio of users to professional specialists has moved dramatically since 1994. Then, the ratio was 13:1. By 1997 it had risen to 28.1 and is forecast to reach 40:1 by 2000. In 1994, 25 per cent of the workforce interacted with IT systems regularly. By 1997, this had risen to 75 per cent and is expected to hit 90 per cent in 2000. IT will become one of the key management skills of the next century. IT demands a new generation of senior managers. E-commerce is coming to us like a tidal wave and senior management must be able to ride the wave'.[iii]

At the same time 'a record number of industrial robots were introduced (1997) around the world and rapid growth is forecast into the next century. Worldwide new robots are predicted to climb from 84,900 in 1997 to 119,800 in 2001, an increase of 41 per cent. In 2001 there will be some 873,000 robots. Most robots are used in the motor industry, but they are also widely employed in electronic assembly. As the price of robots fall they may become more widely used in many other areas including services, like cleaning, surgery, robots for the disabled, and so on. In 1997, *Japan* used 277 robots for every 10,000 workers in manufacturing, followed by *Germany* with 90, and *Sweden* and *Italy* with just over 60'.[iv]

Everyday, we fall from one amazement to the other. Yesterday, it was the Encyclopaedia Britannica going on line: 44 million words; then it was the Oxford English Dictionnary: 60 million words and 20 volumes. Today it is the electronic book. 'At last count, about 98 per cent of the words in Webster's English Dictionnary were registered as domain names'.[3]

B. *Externalization and Outsourcing*

9. This major movement, driven by the tertiarization of industry and agriculture, goes logically hand in hand with the 'big bang' of the (bigger) companies. These may literally explode. Enterprises are engaging in outsourcing, entrusting tasks they used to do themselves to other enterprises which can provide them better and more cheaply. A vast sub-contracting exercise is carried on. Gone are the days of enterprises that controlled raw materials, having their own coal and ore mines, their own railway system and so on up to the final product, including its distribution. Outsourcing is in.

10. *India*'s software export industry, worth more than $1 billion a year, has become one of the most dynamic sectors of the Indian economy, fuelled by demands of offshore clients for low-cost, high quality products and services. There are now more than 700 software companies in *India*. In 1995, 104 companies out of the Fortune 500 outsourced their software development to *India*. Indian software sales to *Europe* were just 5 per cent of total exports in 1994. The proportion, driven by euro-related business hit 23 per cent for the first half of 1998, part of an overall 65.6 per cent rise in software sales. '*India* is offering low-cost labour intensive software services. About a fifth of the 40,000 Indian software engineers servicing foreign clients are employed on year 2000 solutions'.[v]

More *USA* software companies look overseas to take advantage of cheaper labour. For every US programmer, a company could employ 1.3 British programmers, 1.6 Canadians, 5 Mexicans or 6.7 Indians.[vi]

11. A report by the Belgian Foundation for the Enterprise (1998) reveals that an increasing number of enterprises concentrate themselves on their core business. Cleaning is the highest on the list of outsourcing (65 per cent of enterprises); high are also software (62 per cent), legal counselling (60 per cent) and the

---

3. Wessel R., 'Dot-compound Words Apply German Dynamic. English Terms Unite as Short Domains Run out', *Wall street Journal*, 20 April 2000.

administration of payment and social security (58 per cent). The reasons are self evident: the developments in the area of software go too fast; outsourcing of legal counselling and wage administration has to do with the growing complexity of the legal and social regulations. Activities, which have a strategic or a confidential character, are the least outsourced.

Other activities which are outsourced are: transport (48 per cent); maintenance (45 per cent); hardware (40 per cent); advertising (39 per cent); security (38 per cent); selection (37 per cent); catering (29 per cent); R&D (24 per cent); accountancy (10 per cent); financial services (9 per cent); others (9 per cent); administration of stocks (6 per cent).

Of the larger Belgian enterprises, employing more than 1,000 employees, 99 per cent were outsourcing one or more activities; of companies with 100–199 employees, 96 per cent outsourced; of companies with 50–99 employees 72 per cent outsourced and of SMEs (1-50 employees) 68 per cent outsourced.[vii]

Ford Motor company, Belgium, in a plan to shed 2,400 workers (1998) plans to transfer parts of its business to smaller external enterprises, where wages are lower, e.g. the textile sector.[viii]

'The case for outsourcing everything is likely to get dramatically stronger as bandwidth on the web becomes less of constraint. Outsourcing and handling everything over the web could change the way that companies conduct their business'.[ix]

Even the job and investment costs of production can be outsourced to more specialized companies. Virtual manufacturing means that small companies can concentrate on the design and marketing of sometimes products, which are manufactured by others.[x]

12. Electronic commerce is on the move. B2B and B2C are in. 'The Internet bas opened up the possibility of doing business with the best possible supplier, no matter where they are located. The time needed to conclude a deal has been reduced, often to several minutes, thanks to safer online transmission of documents. The need for costly business trips, long telephone discussions and face-to-face negotiations behind closed doors bas been greatly reduced and may soon be a thing of the past. The result is that the carefully nurtured long-term business relations between companies that were for so long key to the success of Japan and Germany, a relationship whose cohesiveness was fastened by cross stock holding, are now falling apart. Electronic commerce has thrown the procurement market open to suppliers of all sizes, addresses, and backgrounds, rendering the more fraternalistic business model obsolete'.[4]

13. Also the push for 'shareholder's value is up. The European social model is under heavy pressure. Wealthy pension funds look at short-term return on investment. They push companies to restructure and get costs down. Employees are stakeholders of the second zone. CEOs, compensated by stock options gladly oblige and downsize as an easy way to get shares up. Wall street rewards shares of companies that restructure and get the 'headcount' down. This means that that the trust between employee

---

4. Nezu R., 'E_commerce: A Revolution with Power', www.oecd.org.

and the enterprise is a thing of the past, also for those employee that stay. Enterprises become money machines.

'In addition to leading a big increase in hostile bids, Europe accounted in 1999 for an astonishing $1.6 trillion of the global total of $3.8 trillion of mergers and acquisitions. ... Much of this activity is been guided by American investment banks and driven by Anglo-Saxon shareholders, the classic case being the $183 billion hostile takeover last year of Germany's Mannesman AG by Vodafone AirTouch PLC of Britain. ... In the past a German company would have been expected to thwart such a hostile bid by political string-pulling, deft use of cross-share-holdings and other anti-raid devices. Instead, Mannesman opted to get the best deal for its shareholders confirming the view ... that, in Europe too, maintaining shareholder value has become the only viable management strategy ... There can be no doubt that the Old World's traditional economic and social assumptions are being swept aside'.

C. Chains of SMEs

14. Enterprises are evolving, to a larger extent than before, into coordination centres of outsourced services and activities. A car is the (international) result of the input of perhaps hundreds of companies, possibly spread around the globe. Enterprises are becoming part of one or preferably more networks, are federations of 'bits and pieces of activities' in which especially smaller SMEs, legally independent but economically linked up on the basis of 'tooth and nail' agreements, deliver services and/or (sub-) products to one or more of the coordinating centres. Most of the time, the outsourcer retains the economic power if need be, for reasons of price, quality or just-in-time delivery, the outsourcer can change sub-contractors and choose them, eventually, from a global panoply of bidders. Performance is no longer for the benefit of another department within the company, but for a client: we get chains of SMEs, looking for and performing for clients, always on the move. A client, working for other clients.

These SMEs in turn will also sub-contract, will have certain tasks performed by other enterprises and grow, while networking.

II. CONSEQUENCES FOR THE LABOUR MARKETS

15. The consequences of these developments are manifold and have far-reaching repercussions on the nature of enterprises, on the kind and number of jobs, on labour law and industrial relations systems, on HRM and, plainly on society at large. Let us try to evaluate their impact.

A. Networking

16. The hierarchical enterprise, the pyramid with the managing director and the board atop the descending ranks of the managers, the middle managers, the foremen and the white- and blue-collar workers at the bottom of the pile, organized like an army or a governmental organization, belongs to the glorious years of Fordism, i.e. to the past. Labour relations in those enterprises were subordinate, tended to be more uniform, collective, controllable, and controlled, including by way of collective bargaining.

Now, networking is the key word. People-relations, inside as well as outside the enterprise, are becoming less hierarchical and more lateral: working more as equals, on the basis of capability, according to the value one can add and in teams. Work will thus be performed in networks, in teams, which may extend over different formal enterprise structures; employed by company A but partly performing in the laboratory of company B. People will be able to work if they can bring added – non-material – value and will be paid accordingly.

The worker of today and tomorrow will thus perform in one or more networks, on his own, but mostly as part of a team, in the framework of shorter or longer projects, for which he will be contracted. The worker will have to assemble and monitor his own portfolio of work, most often as an independent worker and in a sense becoming his own employer. Labour relations will at the same time be less collective, less uniform, freer, less controllable, and controlled. Collective arrangements will be mere frameworks or simply fade away.

17. The old, hierarchical enterprise, where someone could start his career as a lift attendant and eventually end up as the managing director at the top of the pyramid is definitely becoming an oddity in the landscape of work. Enterprises will be composed of a small core of permanent staff; the rest will probably be more peripheral workers, who will deliver specific services as part of teams, evolving in their own networks, possibly across boundaries and regions.

Permanent jobs, full-time and lifelong until retirement, will be the great exception, other than perhaps for those engaged in a (slimmed-down) public sector and possibly in other protected workplaces.

New technologies are also affecting the retail industry, where we are moving from a distribution economy to a search economy. Consumers will want to shop over the Internet and have goods delivered, even if that means paying a premium. 'These changes will force companies to build new competencies. One example might be an ability to deal with consumer queries on line', says Prof. Gary Hamel.[xi]

The new company, called '*the individualised corporation*', in order to be successful, needs to develop three core capabilities:

– the ability to inspire individual creativity and initiative in all its people, built on fundamental faith in individuals;
– the ability to link entrepreneurial activity and individual expertise by building an integrated process of organizational leaning; and
– to continuously renew itself.[xii]

B.   Job Shift

18. The factors thus far enumerated constitute the main reasons for the ongoing dramatic job shift, which is only just beginning. Job loss is also caused by other factors such as robotization and automation, through which repetitive work in particular is shed on a massive scale. Rifkin judges that 'more than 75 per cent of the labour force in most industrial nations engage in work that is little more than simply repetitive tasks'.[xiii]

Philips announced (November 1998), as indicated earlier, that it will close 1/3 of its enterprises worldwide for reason of overcapacity for the year 2002. This means of the existing 244 sites, only 160–170 will remain.[xiv]

Siemens, the largest German engineering and electronics group, plans to sell business worth 10. 3 billion $, including all its loss-making semiconductor activities, in one of the biggest restructuring operations in recent German corporate history. The businesses being shed employ 60,000 people. The group wants to improve return on capital to 8.5 per cent.[xv] This corporate transformation of Siemens may be only a first step.[xvi] Siemens is under pressure from investors to deliver big improvements in earnings and as many as 20,000 redundancies are mooted, mostly in Germany.[xvii]

A fifth of manufacturing jobs in the *UK* pharmaceutical industry have been lost over the past six years as companies shifted production to countries with lower taxes and fewer regulations (1998). This has led companies to set up plants in countries such as *Puerto Rico, Singapore, India* and *Ireland*, which have more favourable tax regimes and lower labour costs.[xviii]

Let us also mention that Merril Lynch axed (October 1998) 3,400 jobs, or 5 per cent of its worldwide workforce amid the volatility of financial markets during that period,[xix] while the British Engineering Employer's Federation (October 1998) warned that Britain's slowing economy will cut engineering output by 1 per cent next year and destroy 100,000 jobs.[xx]

19. In Asia, the crisis killed 24 million jobs. 86 per cent of the dismissed in the Korean Banking and financial institutions were women.[xxi] Eight out of every 10 Japanese worry about losing their jobs or about pay cuts, the Asahi Shimbun newspaper reported.[xxii]

October 9, 1998 *Le Figaro*, a leading French newspaper reported following American downsizings:
*Raytheon:14,000 (1998); *Levi's: 2,500 (1998); *Toys'R'Us 1,200 (1998); *Boeing: 18,000 to 28,000 (1998); *Motorola: 15,000 (1998); *Intel 3,000 (1998); *Compact-Digital: 17,000 (1998); *General Motors: 16,000 to 24,000 in Europe (1998); *Kodak: 16,600; (1997);[xxiii] *Shell-Texaco: 4,000 (1998).[xxiv]

In the US in 1998 some 677,795 jobs were lost, which constitutes a record for the last 10 years. 'Workers likely to be laid off in 1999 are midlevel managers with manufacturing firms or other export-dependent companies, workers who provide less bang for the buck'.[xxv]

To this can be added:
Alcatel: 12,000 (1999);[xxvi] *Heinz: 4,000 (1999);[xxvii] *NEC 15,000 (1999);[xxviii] *Renault: 9,300 (1999);[xxix] Boeing: 6,700 (1999);[xxx] *Japan Banks: 21,000 (1999);[xxxi] *Sony: 17,000 (1999);[xxxii] *Ericsson 11,000 (1999).[xxxiii]

20. On the other side, digital media, the industry responsible for designing and creating content for the Internet and other digital formats, such as CD Roms[xxxiv] could create 80,000 jobs in Britain over the next eight years. At the same time call centres have become a phenomenon of the 1990s, as selling an ever growing list of commodities – from life assurance to plastic windows – is done over the telephone.

In the *UK*, there were 162,000 agents at 4,000 call centres handling 25 million domestic and international calls a week in 1996. Employment may rise to almost half a million by the year 2000. For *Europe* one expects the figure to reach 1, 2 million.[xxxv]

C. Kinds of Jobs

21. This line of thought brings us to the three types of work, which Robert Reich identified, in '*The Work of Nations*' (1992), namely: routine production and services, in-person services and creative inputs.[xxxvi]

Routine production and services: this category covers manual work, but also activities performed by middle or senior management responsible for routine tasks of supervision and the application of specified rules, and certain computer activities such as the processing of financial transactions (cheques, credit card payments), hospital invoices, social operations (administration of wages, health insurance), etc.

Similarly, *in-person services* mostly comprise routine activities, but in this case performed by people who come into direct contact with the customers, patients, and all recipients of the services concerned. The category covers sales assistants, waiters and waitresses, hotel workers, hairdressers, hospital staff, taxi drivers, cleaners, etc.

22. Creative inputs are the work done by certain engineers, public relations experts, lawyers, managers, designers and planners, financiers, authors, artists, journalists, and the like. This category covers people who perform non-routine activities, who are capable of distancing themselves from the everyday reality by virtue of their capacity for abstract thought and who, by manipulating ideas, images, sounds, or materials, make a creative contribution that enables certain problems to be solved more effectively. These contributions may range from energy conservation to space exploration, encompassing in their span activities such as financial speculations, a work of art, a musical composition, a new software development, or a television production. Such creative contributions are generally effected via increasingly internationalized networks, on the basis of non-hierarchized team-based work, in meetings, through formal and informal channels, by way of telecommunications, and in supersonic aircraft. Here, time and energy are predominantly spent on identifying solutions and implementing the scheme and strategy to be followed, activities, which generally contribute a high added value.

It is a matter of making creative use of know-how and experience. Such work is interesting and pays well. The more a person performs creative work, the more creative they become. According to Reich, some 15–20 per cent of workers in the *USA* fall specifically within this category, although this is not to say that others do not also apply creativity in their work, a point to which we will come back later.

The 'training of creative contributors' signifies a learning process in which young people and adults receive an education and training, which equips them to grasp problems and work out solutions. Four types of ability need to be developed: abstraction, systematic thinking, experimentation, and communication with others (through languages, technology, etc.).

It is obvious that routine or repetitive jobs are on the decline.[xxxvii] In-person services are faring little better. Creative workers are really the only ones, who are flourishing. They are able to offer their creative services on the world market.

The worker who performs routine production or service activities is under threat on the one hand from automation and on the other from cut-throat competition from low-wage countries, with production being provided at much lower wages and under far less favourable working conditions in *India*, *China*, etc.

A continuous decline in routine jobs can therefore be predicted, with middle and routine management jobs also coming under threat. Draconian reductions in wage costs would be needed in order to halt this trend; moderate reductions would at best merely slow down the rate of decline.

In-person services are faring little better. Here too, automation is playing a large part (the telephone, computerized telesales of goods, theatre seats and airline tickets, Tele-banking services, automatic check-in in hotels, etc.). Growing competition, both from workers who have lost their routine jobs and from immigrant workers, is forcing wages downwards. In addition, in the case of many services the recipients are people for whom money is in short supply (the disabled, the sick, the elderly). Some jobs are only part-time or too ill paid to provide a real living (casual labour). Health care budgets, etc. are being cut. In the non-market sector, there is scope for creating jobs *ad infinitum* but the funds are yet not sufficiently available.

23. Creative workers are really the only ones, who are flourishing. They are able to offer their creative services on the world market.

The only people, who are really contributing a high added value, and being well rewarded for it, are creative workers.

This leads to a *battle for the brains*. One fitting example is the information technology. *Western Europe* faces a potential shortage of 1.6 million workers in information technology within the coming four years resulting in excessively high wages, low productivity and delayed investment in the sector. The skills shortage amounts to some 12 per cent of the demand for IT workers by 2002.[xxxviii] One does not expect any decrease in demand after 2000.[xxxix] In *Belgium* (1998) there was a shortage of at least 10,000 engineers and IT specialists.

The battle for the brains takes many forms. One is attracting foreign students to its universities and research centres. The *USA* is leading that dance with not less than 560,000 foreign students. In *Massachusetts*, the budget of the universities exceeds the one of the entire industrial sector in that State. Moreover, brilliant students, returning home become Prime ministers, leading industrialist, academics. They are a product of continued American influence. The French now, with only 130,000 foreign students out of a total of two million university students, want increase their share of the part of the world-elite. They claim that there is a world market of 200 billion dollars to be conquered. *France* has created 'Edufrance' in order to win 'la bataille de la matière grise au XXIe siècle'.[xl]

Another form is the attraction of skilled workers. This is why the *USA* Congress is expected to approve controversial legislation to expand the number of visas for highly skilled foreign workers by more than 300,000 over the next three years.[xli]

A second form is the attraction of skilled workers. In the very tight market for talented high skilled workers, companies engage in battles not to loose skilled workers to foreign competition. This is why the *USA* Congress is expected to approve controversial legislation to expand the number of visas for highly skilled foreign workers by more than 300,000 over the next three years.[xlii] 40,000 French work in Silicon Valley. Germany wants to import 30,000 IT specialists from Poland, Tjechia, Slovenia, and India.

According to management guru Peter Drucker, 'knowledge workers own the means of production. They can walk out the door. It follows that companies have much to learn in attracting and holding knowledge workers.[xliii] Creative workers are in the 'driver's seat'.[5] They are a nightmare for the employers. Traditional HRM is put on its head. The knowledge workers are footloose, have less commitment to the company, but more to the team and the project they work on. Their employment contracts are open-ended.[xliv]

24. There is what Robert Reich calls the 'secession of the succesful'. 'The cosmocrats comtitute a world within a world, linked to each other by mynad global networks but increasingly cut off from their "neighbours"'.[6] The working elite turns on itselfs, linked by e-mail, internet and waps.

D. Decentralized and Atomised Labour Relations

25. It is this combination of factors, which lies behind the rising rate of unemployment in our advanced countries of workers, who miss the necessary know how and social skills. The trade unions, which are consequently losing a good number of their members in the process, are finding their position becoming all the weaker. They have to bear the full brunt of the technological revolution and its impact on the labour market. Members in traditional sectors are fading away, and with them traditional trade union strength. Trade unions are on the defensive and trying to hang on, still fighting for the stable jobs which are no longer there. The newer activities, the new workers especially, are difficult to organize. Their organizations at international level have no 'clout'.

In its most recent World Labour Report 1997–1998, devoted to 'Industrial Relations, Democracy and Social Stability', the ILO observes that in the majority of countries around the globe trade union representation has declined in the past decade. The unionization rate has dropped by over 20 per cent in over half the 66 countries for which comparable data could be collected. Moreover, in 48 countries in the developing world the unionization rate has fallen, or remained, under 20 per cent of the formal, organizable (wage earning) labour force. Britain At Work reports 'that two thirds of work places in the Britain have no employee representatives and nearly half of them do not have joint consultative committees to represent the views of the workforce'.[xlv]

26. In the USA, efforts to revitalize the USA labour movement are running into serious troubles, threatening any significant comeback after more than 20 years of trade union decline. After the 1995 election of John Sweeny as AFL-CIO president,

---

5. Maitland A., 'Balance of power shifts to employees in e-commerce world', *Financial Times*, 28 June 2000.
6. Mickcklethwait J.and Wollridge A., 'Piloted by a new ruling class?'. *Financial Times*, 27–28 May 2000. Globalisation is throwing up a new elite whose power lies in their ideas, connections and sheer hutzpah'.

the *USA* unions launched a highly publicized campaign to restore lost power and influence through membership drives. But figures show private sector unionization continues to decline from 10.8 per cent in 1994 to only 9.7 per cent in 1997.[xlvi]

27. The same goes for employers' associations. Their role in the conclusion of collective agreements, at sectoral–regional level is losing much of economic rationale. Companies feel that they are on their own in the economic wars, which are waged internationally, and want to act accordingly, taking their own specific challenges, strengths and weaknesses into account.

The he-days of the social partners are over.

28. Externalization and outsourcing mean that labour relations, previously global/ uniform and controllable by way of collective bargaining, are now becoming more decentralized, even atomized, individualised and more independent. Telework, as a modern form of (mainly) home working, is growing more and more fashionable, with the added element of redundant employees, especially managers, starting to work as independent consultants from their home base or elsewhere.

No wonder that strike activity has become increasingly rare in Western industrialized societies. *UK* working day losses per year have fallen considerably during the 1990s. In 1997, only 10 working days were lost per 1,000 employees. Figures for *Denmark* were 41 working days, for the *USA* 38 working days, for *New Zealand* 18 working days, and *Ireland* 69 working days. For the years 1997–1998, the *UK* lost 62 working days per 1,000 employees. Losses in other countries were: *Sweden* 80 working days, *Italy* 201, followed by *Spain* with 469 working days, and *Greece* 327 days. This contrasts with *Japan* with 3 working days, *Austria* with 4 days and *Switzerland* with one working day lost.[xlvii]

Nonetheless, one has to take into account that in (rare) economies with lower unemployment, like the *USA*, workers may take up demands again. 'Their fights, wage on all industry fronts, have been surprisingly successful', one report indicates. 'The number of work stoppages in 1998, for instance, rose to 34 from 29, reflecting the growing number of employees going on strike'.[xlviii]

29. The days of confrontation and the previously hostile and adversarial atmosphere between management and labour in the *UK*, however, seem to belong to the past. For the *UK*, Prime Minister Blair endorses 'the clear message of the TUC that *Britain* works best when union and employers work together'. The TUC has established six principles for partnership in the workplace, between a company and a trade union, representing employees, namely:

– a shared commitment to the success of the enterprise;
– a recognition of legitimate interests, accepting that there might be differences of priorities, so that the partnership arrangements can embody a degree of trust and respect;
– a commitment to employment security and one of accepting job flexibility;[xlix]
– a focus on the quality of working life;
– partnership has to be transparent with genuine consultation and with the commitment from companies to listen to employees and their unions; and
– partnership requires adding value to the workplace.

'The TUC believes employers will have to allow unions to exercise greater influence over strategic decisions. It will require managers to relinquish some control, changing workplace culture from a command structure to one of problem solving. The TUC favours a range of partnership institutions, ranging from works councils to a national forum'.[1]

E. Flexibility

30. Micro-economic supply-side economies, the OECD insists, are intended to free enterprises from certain regulatory constraints by providing enterprises with more flexibility, so as to promote economic growth and consequently create more jobs. Protective labour measures, such as a minimum wage, working time restrictions, dismissals and others, are looked upon as hindrances to growth and should be done away with. Labour cost especially has to go down. The worker has to be paid according to, and in relation to, the economic value that he adds in the process.

It is up to the Governments and their national social partners to see that the necessary flexibility is introduced. In any case, they have no other choice, as the market forces will oblige them to do so anyway.

Flexibility (= adaptability = deregulation), or more freedom for management to manage its business, relates to many issues and can take many forms.

Flexibility can be unilateral, individual, legislated, or negotiated, the latter meaning that flexible arrangements are possible only if they are agreed upon with the representatives of the employees, at enterprise or even sectoral level.

Flexibility is a major and probably lasting trend in our employment system. But workers have paid a price in higher job instability and more inconvenient working hours, including night work, weekend work, and long shifts, 'with unwelcome consequences for the personal lives of many employees'. In a major forthcoming study, the ILO, underlines that there are in practice four major types of flexibility,[li] namely regarding: * employment contracts; * pay; * working time, and * work organization.

31. Working time is undoubtedly the 'king' of flexible arrangements. There has been a trade off between less man-hours in favour of longer machine hours and flexibility. Almost everything has become possible and is discussed in the framework of a wholesale reorganization of work: weekend work, shift-work, overtime, part-time, annualization of working time. The 35 hour week is definitely been instituted in *France* and discussed in being discussed in *Italy* and *Spain*, and is on many trade unions agendas.

No doubt we will have to work longer in the future, not only due a shortage of qualified people in certain sectors but in order to keep our pension system going, as the demographic evolution is pointing in that direction.[lii]

The 24 hour economy and the consumer start to dominate the debate. Night work is on the increase. In the *USA*, which is in many ways leading the way into the 24 hour world, 20 million people regularly work at night; in the *UK* the figure is a little over 1.5 million people, that work at some time over the night. As the consumer is more and more dictating his will in our market economies, millions more will have to work non-conventional hours to satisfy the demand for goods and services imposed by the consumers' wants.[liii]

Finally, we have to add that the EMU pushes for more flexibility. As well the European Central Bank as the OECD are constantly claiming for less rigidities in the labour markets.[liv]

F. The Dual Society. The Informal Economy

32. There is no doubt that these developments lead to dual societies, to a world of more poor and rich and between them the guns of private police. The European Union, to give one example, has more than 54 million poor, over 3 million or more without a roof over their heads, and their numbers are increasing. In Wallonia, the French-speaking region of *Belgium*, almost one person in two lives from social security aid in one form or another. Poverty doubled in the last 10 years. In Brussels 9 per cent lives below the poverty line; 30 per cent just above.[lv] The biggest risk groups are youngsters and single mothers. According to Commissioner P. Flynn of the European Commission, only 7 per cent of the unemployed in the EU have the chance to learn new skills, as against 93 per cent who are 'left on tender-hooks in a dead-end of no learning', 50 per cent of workers over age 55 are no longer in the labour market and 20 per cent of young people reaching the labour market have no recognised skills.

33. The EU the employment rate has declined to 60.5 per cent in 1997[lvi] from 65.5 per cent in 1973. This means a rate of jobless of 39.5 per cent. Even if the maximum potential of the EU labour supply is taken as 80 per cent of working age population, close to 20 per cent of that population is currently unemployed.[lvii] 53.3 per cent of *USA* jobholders are employed in the services vs. 39.7 per cent in the EU. '*Western European* Governments are not doing enough to create employment, the European Commission said in a critical report (October 1998) on job creation across the EU. In the *USA* there is an employment rate of 74 per cent. The report singled *Germany* out for very poor job creation over the last years.'[lviii]

In Great-Britain 2 million children work of which 500,000 are less than 15 years of age.[lix] There are 12 million poor in the *UK* of which 4 million are children, a number that has tripled the last 20 years.[lx]

This also the case for the *USA*. 'The rich are getting richer and the poorer are finding themselves even further adrift', says Jef Gates. '*USA* census Bureau statistics for 1996 showed that the top fifth of American households were receiving 48.2 per cent of the nation's income compared with a bottom fifth surviving on 3.6 per cent. Supply-side economic measures from Reagan and Tatcher eras have created not so much a trickle-down but trickle-up effect'.[lxi] The same message can be read in a study by the Economic Policy Institute:[lxii] ' ... most workers' real wages are still not back to the levels of 10 years ago. Nor have the living standards of most working families fully recovered from the early 1990s recession ... American families are working harder to stay in the same place and are seeing little gains in the overall economy. Amidst positive overall growth significant economic disparities persist as trends in wages, income and inequality in the 1990s continue to follow patterns set in the 1980s.' The report adds '*USA* jobs have grown less secure and less likely to offer health and pension benefits. Middle class wealth (the value of tangible assets such as houses and cars, plus financial assets, minus debts) has also fallen. ... The main reason for common income trends is a continuing wage deterioration among middle- and low-wage earners and white-collar and some college educated workers ... The share of wealth held by the top 1 per cent of *USA* households went up from 37.4 per cent of the national total in 1989 to 39.1 per cent in 1997 while the share held by the families in the middle fifth of the population dropped from 4.8 to 4.4 per cent'.[lxiii]

34. In its World Employment Report 1998–1999, the ILO reports that up to one-third of the world's three billion workers will be either without a job or under-employed in 1999 with the growing global recession. It estimates that the number of jobless will reach 150 million by the end of 1998, with a further 25 to 30 per cent of workers under-employed (between 750 and 900 million people) either working substantially less than full time. The Asian financial crisis has added 10 million new unemployed to the total since it began in mid-1997. In *Thailand, Malaysia, Indonesia* and the *Philippines* 40 million people lived on less than 1$ a day (1997). By 2000, the number could be 100 million. 'The social consequences have been alarming. Households are coping by rationing food, pulling children out of school, and in some cases resorting to illegal activities. Violence, street children and prostitution are all on the increase and the social fabric is under increasing strain.[lxiv]

The ILO indicated also that 66 million young people between 15 and 24 years of age are looking for work but not finding any. These figures do not take into account the considerable numbers of those who have given up to find work or involuntary part-time workers.

The report also refers to the rapid rising unemployment in *central* and *eastern European* countries and *Russia. Latin American* countries have had substantial growth but this has not led to significant expansion of job opportunities.

The ILO concludes that the *Asian* financial crisis 'has shown the cost of neglecting social concerns'. The pace of globalization has been primarily driven by market forces and national, and to some extent, international rules, institutions and practices needed to render its consequences socially acceptable have been insufficiently developed'. The report finally confirms its belief in the benefits of a global economy, but insists that depressed world commodity prices, the introduction of the EMU, asset price 'bubbles' and further liberalization of trade with increased competition will affect future employment trends'.[lxv]

There is thus no need to stress that prostitution, crime, drug use, violence, and racism are on the rise, inevitably accompanied by more alarm systems, more private police, and the like. Unemployment is society's gangrene.

35. 'At the same time, the ILO observes a growing 'informalisation' of the labour force and employment relations, a phenomenon which appears to go together with falling income levels, lower standards, and diminished access to collective representation. Of the 15.7 million new jobs in Latin America between 1990 and 1994, 84 per cent were in the informal sector.

In Asia the informal sector accounts for 40–50 per cent of the urban labour force – varying, from 10 to 20 per cent in the newly industrial countries of southeast Asia (before the recent financial crisis) to 65 per cent or more in *Bangladesh* and *India*. In Africa, as stated earlier, the informal sector covers 60 per cent of the urban labour force and 90 per cent of the additional jobs in the 1990s. Work in the informal sector is often highly unstable, precarious, unsafe, or even inhuman.

36.   'Informalisation' appears to be linked to a stagnation or decline of the formal sector and reflects according to the ILO three factors:

(1) the rapid growth of the urban population and labour force;
(2) the impact of the economic stabilization and restructuring programmes introduced in the 1980s in many African and Latin American countries which caused a contraction of public sector employment, retrenchment for many industrial workers and a fall in real wages; and
(3) the quest for increased flexibility and deregulation required on account of the growing competitiveness in global markets, which has resulted in enhanced capital intensity and reduced labour costs. Many retrenched workers or members of their families are drawn into the informal sector for lack of other employment opportunities and income.

The distinction between formal and informal employment is increasingly blurred and more global corporations operate in both. In other words, informal labour is not necessarily a characteristic of economic backwardness or a consequence of lack of access to capital, but can be part of a global strategy in which modern firms depend for their expansion or survival upon forms of labour that conform to the standards of the informal sector such as no minimum wages, no welfare benefits, no unions, no legal protection, and no job security.

37.   This phenomenon is not limited to the developing world. 'One may estimate that roughly 10–15 per cent of all wage earners in *western Europe*, probably less in *northern Europe*, and twenty per cent of all wage earners in *southern Europe* are employed in the informal sector, in small firms and under highly flexible or poor employment conditions, with signs of a rising trend in recent years. This does not include the unemployed – currently averaging 11 per cent in the European Union – and on the rise in most other parts of the world. None of these figures takes into account the unknown number of people involved in illegal activities and begging'.[lxvi]

In *Italy*, one fifth of the work force escapes at every form of control. This concerns more than five million people. Italian flexibility means that a company, which has 15 employees, will not hire more people officially for the reason of the extra costs this brings about. Instead they will hire 15 others on the black market.[lxvii]

38.   In *eastern Europe*, thousands of companies have, due to the recent crisis in *Russia*, been forced to bankruptcy. They range from furniture workshops in eastern *Poland*, to Hungarian food traders and Ukrainian sugar merchants. Many of them operate in the 'grey market' beyond the reach of official statistics. To survive, companies have to re-learn the tricks of the past, such as barter and payment in advance for all shipments.[lxviii] According to a report of the European Bank for Reconstruction and Development, the outlook is gloomy for the former east bloc. In the *Commonwealth of Independent States* Gross Domestic Product stood at 55 per cent of 1989. In *central and eastern Europe*, *Slovakia* and *Slovenia* last year saw their return to 1989 levels, joining *Poland*, which passed this milestone a few years ago.

30 million Russians face extreme poverty.[lxix] The worst-affected Russians will be families with children. In *eastern Europe*, and the countries of the former Soviet Unions, millions have seen their living standards deteriorate in the transition from planned to market economies. 'Around 147 million people (approximately one in three) live on less than US $4 a day, a tenfold increase since 1989'.[lxx]

39. The spread of HIV/Aids has wiped out hard-won increases in life expectancy, with 29 per cent of Zimbabwe's population between 15 and 49 infected. Another ten countries have infection rates above 10 per cent.

All developing regions have seen setbacks in poverty reduction. The World Banks forecast for 1998–2001 suggest that only south Asia and China will have enough economic growth to meet the international standards of halving poverty by 2015'.[lxxi]

In its latest report, the World Bank underlined that 'weak world trade growth, falling commodity prices and a lack of external finance will condemn developing countries to their slowest growth since 1982'.[lxxii]

At the other side, in the formal sector, there are those who have an employment. Having a job seems to contribute to workers satisfaction. According to an international survey of 50,000 employees in 18 countries most workers are satisfied with their working lives, with less than one in 10 expressing any discontent. Only three per cent of workers in industrialized countries say they are 'very dissatisfied' with their job or workplace. There seems to be a similar pattern of age and work satisfaction in 17 of the countries studied. 'Employees in their 20s have a fairly high positive view of work but this falls to a low point around the mid-30s and thereafter rises into a person's 60s'. Having a trade union in the work place seems to make workers satisfaction lower. 'Jobs satisfaction is higher in public sector employment while better educated workers are slightly less satisfied than those who are less well educated'. 'The Irish are the most satisfied workers followed by the Danes, the Dutch, the Belgian, the Austrians, and the Swedes. Workers who are the most satisfied come from southern European countries such as Greece, Portugal, Italy, and Spain, although the French are more dissatisfied than any except the Greeks. British and German workers are halfway in the satisfaction league table. The USA is the only country where job satisfaction levels have been recorded for more than 25 years. At the start of the 1970s 56 per cent of American workers said they were very satisfied at work: now the figure has fallen to 47 per cent'.[lxxiii]

III.   CONCLUDING REMARKS

A.   A New World of Work

40. Our world of work is undergoing a revolution. We have been catapulted into a new information society, where the realities and the truths of yesterday are becoming increasingly irrelevant. Globalization and new technologies are causing enterprises to explode into networks of teams where work will be done on a project basis, fundamentally altering the employment relationship, the role of the social partners and the like. There is a need for a mental revolution, especially in the area of vocational training, in order to grasp the challenge before us and what has to be done in order to respond creatively and appropriately to the call of new opportunities which the information society offers. There is no shortage of work.

We are looking forward to a new social era. There should be a *social roof* on top of the societal building, containing *social rights* and a *floor, containing minimum standards* of protection at the bottom of the house, so that in between both *the free market can play in full,* including a degree of flexibility, necessary to conduct a business in the XXI century.

Various means should be explored to introduce and to follow-up on these measures. We should not only consider the role of the law, especially of *legislation* in its broadest sense and *collective bargaining,* which have been traditional measures of protection. Measures have to be taken, as well at international, regional as national level.

B.   Fundamental Rights

41.   The ILO Declaration of 1998 on Fundamental Principles and Rights at Work is a hope giving start, but the road is long and narrow.

'The Declaration states that all Member States of the ILO, whether or not they have ratified the Conventions in question, have an obligation to respect, promote and realise the principles concerning:

(a) freedom of association and the effective recognition of the right to collective bargaining;
(b) the elimination of all forms of forced or compulsory labour;
(c) the effective abolition of child labour; and
(d) the elimination of discrimination in respect of employment and occupation'.

The Declaration recalls that these principles have been developed 'in the form of specific rights and obligations in Conventions recognised as fundamental both inside and outside the Organisation'.

42.   The EU should include a list of fundamental social rights in the Treaty of the European Community.

One should also address newer avenues, like *corporate codes of conduct.*

Also the *consumer power* has to be brought into the picture. Consumers' attitudes can have a wide impact. Here *social labelling* comes into play.

In the search for a new social era we should not only look at the fundamental and other social rights to be implemented, but also at the *kind of institutions, notions and categories, which suit the information society.*

This last point means that we have to radically reorganise the labour market and tackle categories like employees and self-employed, which have been sacro saint over the last decades.

The question is then how to organize the labour market in order to suit the needs of the information society, and, at the same time, to see to it that enough added value and wealth is created to be able to establish and guarantee an adequate system of social protection, which should shield the worker of the XXI century as far as his needs for income, health, and safety, also regarding social security (unemployment, sickness insurance, pension ...) are concerned in a globalized volatile economy.

C. Avenues and Propositions

43. It seems to me that following avenues and propositions need to be explored, namely the need for:

a. basically one labour market;
b. one basic category of workers;
c. payment according to added value;
d. the end of age limits;
e. vocational training vs. job security; and
f. a free labour market.

Finally, in the search for employment for all, we need to address issues like *employment policies and training.*

'Globalisation has only one true meaning and significance. More than ever, we are all in the same boat. But it does not mean that we are powerless in charting of its course'.[7]

'Capitalism as an economic system has brought undeniable benefits, but it also divides rich from poor ... '. We would like to conclude by Charles Handy who argues in his recent book: *The Hungry Spirit*',[8] for a future with values that are more sustaining than the values of the free market'. Or to put it otherwise: 'on a quest for purpose in the modern world'.

NOTES AND BIBLIOGRAPHY

i *See* Blanpain R., 'Social Dialogue – Economic Interdependence and Labour Law', *Reports to the 6th European Congress for Labour Law and Social Security*, Warsaw, 13–17 September 1999, 39–125; Hirst P. and Thompson G., *Globalisation in question*, Polity Press, 1999; Freeman R.B. and Rogers J., *What workers want*, New York, 1999, 226 p.; Hansenne M., *Un garde-fou pour la mondialisation. Le BIT dans l'après-guerre froide*, Genève, 1999, p. 147.
ii David L., 'Information is heaven-sent. Data gleaned from satellites is available on a pay-per-view basis', *F.T.*
iii Manchester Ph., 'Scarcity of IT people with business minds', *F.T.*, 5 November 1998.
iv Williams F. 'More and more robots populate world's factories', *F.T.*,14 October 1998. United Nations Economic Commission for Europe and the International federation of Robotics, *World Robotics 1988*, Geneva, 1998.
v Nicholson M., '2000 reasons why India's software industry is feeling joyful', *F.T.*, 12 November 1999, p. 7; Guha Krishna, 'Indian software exports exceed 50 per cent growth rate', *F.T.*, 28 January 1999.
vi Taylor R., 'US Groups take advantage of cheaper labour costs abroad', *F.T.*, 8 April 1999.

---

7. Moisi D., 'The dark side of triumph. The fall of the Berlin wall opened a bright future. But almost 10 years on, the hopes of a new world order have failed to materialise', *F.T.*,14 September 1998.
8. London, 1997, 272 p.

   vii *De Standaard*, 19 October 1998.

  viii Tegenbosch G., 'Ford-directie verlaagt zelf arbeidskosten', *De Standaard*, 2 September 1998.

    ix Jackson T., 'Internet breathes new life into software rental', *F.T.*, 5 October 1998.

     x Marsh P., 'Cutting out the core. How two manufacturers outsource the job itself', *F.T.*, 26 November 1998.

    xi Houlder V., 'Interview Gary Hamel. Many retailers make the costly mistake of not preparing for the impact the Internet will have on consumer habits', *F.T.*, 22 October 1998.

   xii Goshal S. and Bartlett C.A., *The Individualised Corporation. A fundamentally new Approach to Management. Great Companies ate defined by pourpise, process, and people*, Heinemann: London, 1998, p. 14.

  xiii *Op. cit., The Annals of the American Academy*, 1996, p. 19.

  xiv 'Een Philips-fabriek op drie moet dicht', *De Standaard*, 3 November 1998.

   xv Bowley G., 'Siemens plans to shed businesses in $10bn shake-up. Lossmaking chip operations to be sold in restructuring', *F.T.*, 5 November 1998.

  xvi Bowley G., 'Siemens restructures. Germany's biggest corporate transformation in years may be only a first step', *F.T.*, 5 November 1998.

 xvii Bowley G., 'It's payback time for Siemens' industrious unit chief', *F.T.*, 13 October 1998.

xviii Pilling D., 'Drugs industry "being driven from UK" ', *F.T.*, 17 October 1998.

  xix Corrigan T. and Harris C., 'Axe falls on Wall Street. The worldwide jobs cuts in investment banking announced by Merril Lynch this week will not be the industry's last', *F.T.*, 15 October 1998.

   xx Brown K., 'Engineering group predict 1per cent output fall', *F.T.*, 23 October 1998.

  xxi L.M., 'Asie. La crise a déjà supprimé 24 millions d'emploi. Les ravages causés par la crise asiatique n'en finissent de s'amplifier. Le BIT, qui estime nécessaire un nouveau contrat social, souligne la relance du travail des enfants', *Le Figaro Économique*, 19 March, 1999.

  xxii *F.T.*, 26 April 1999.

 xxiii Le G.Y., 'Raytheon supprime 14.000 emplois', *Le Figaro Économique*, 9 October 1998.

 xxiv Dendooven P., 'Shell en Texaco zetten mes in organisatie. Ingreep gevolg van lage prijzen', *De Standaard*, 13 November 1998.

  xxv Simons J., 'Global discord sparks layoffs. Mergers also have displaced workers', *The Wall Street Journal*, 19 Novemer, 1998; 'Suppression d'emplois massive aux Etats-Unis', *Le Figaro Économique*, 8 January, 1999.

 xxvi Daudet A., 'Alcatel supprime 12000 emplois', Le Figaro Économique, 12 March 1999.

 xxvii Lewis W., 'Heinz to cut 4,000 jobs in global restructuring', *F.T.*, 18 February 1999.

xxviii Nusbaun A. and Price C., 'NEC to shed 15,000 after biggest loss', *F.T.*, 20/21 February 1999.

 xxix AFP., 'Renault verjongt personeel', De Standaard, 13/14 March 1999. Renault wanted to shed 9,300 older workers by 2003 and hire 3,300 youngsters.

  xxx P.K., 'Boeing: nouvelle réduction d'effectifs', *Le Figaro Économique*, 16 March 1999.

xxxi Tett G. and Nakamae N., 'Japan Banks to cut 21,000 jobs in exchange for $60bn', *F.T.*, 9 March 1999.

xxxii Nakomoto M., 'Sony restructuring plan lifts shares 9 per cent', *F.T.*, 10 March 1999.

xxxiii Burt T., 'Ericsson shake-up sees job losses of 11,000', *F.T.*, 26 January, 1999.

xxxiv Rawsthorn A., 'Digital media "could create 80,000 jobs"', *F.T.*, 3 November 1998.

xxxv ' A clear line to new business', *F.T.*, 10 September 1998.

xxxvi P. 174.

xxxvii Thus Nissans' restructuring plan involving a cut of 14 per cent of the workforce (21,000 workers), 'Japan Inc'., *F.T.*, 19 October 1999; CH.G.,' Renault inflige un traitement de choc à Nissan. Le constructeur français supprime 21,000 emplois et ferme cinq usines', *Le Figaro Économique*, 19 October 1999; Mitsubishi sheds 9.900 jobs over 5 years, 27 October 1999.

xxxviii Peel Q., 'IT Workers. Skill shortage hits W. Europe', *F.T.*, 23 September 1998.

xxxix Black G., 'Specialist skills. Shortfall at all levels. Demand for Emu-related skills is expected to be greater than for the year 2000 computer date problem', *F.T.*, 5 November 1998.

xl Bollaert B., 'Pour combattre le déclin du français et faire pièce au pouvoir d'attractions des Anglosaxons. La France veut sa part du marché des élites mondiales', *Le Figaro*, 7–8 November 1998.

xli Wolffe R., 'US visa plan for high-tech workers', *F.T.*, 25 September 1998; *See also* Marsh P., 'US group moves north to find skilled engineers', *F.T.*, 20 September 1999.

xlii Wolffe R., 'US visa plan for high-tech workers', *F.T.*, 25 September 1998.

xliii Jackson T., 'Reflections of a knowledge worker', *F.T.*, 27 April 1999.

xliv Capelli P., *The New Deal at Work. Managing the market-driven workforce*, Boston, 1999, p. 307.

xlv Taylor R., 'Employees lack a voice in half of the workplaces. Trade unions survey shows results of membership decline', *F.T.*, 24 September 1999.

xlvi Taylor R., 'Union revival is "hitting snags"', *F.T.*, 22 October 1998.

xlvii According to the UK's Office for National Statistics, reported in 'UK sheds image of militant industrial disputes', *F.T.*, 15 April 1998.

xlviii Liu B., 'US workers going on strike again – because they can', *F.T.*, 27 April 1999.

xlix This means limiting compulsory redundancies and making joint agreements on staffing.

l Taylor R., 'Blair signals sea change for trade unions', *F.T.*, 22 April 1999.

li *Negotiating flexibility. The Role of Collective Bargaining in Labour Market Flexibility,* Geneva, (manuscript 1997). *See further* Standing G., *Global Labour Flexibility. Seeking Distributive Justice*, London, 1999, 441 p. Sarfati H., *Flexibilité et céation d'emplois. Un défi pour le dialogue social en Europe*, Paris, 1999, p. 227.

lii Taupin B., 'Pourquoi il faudra travailler plus longtemps', *Le Figaro Économique*, 25 March 1999.

liii Kreitzman L., 'Something of the night about too many of us', *F.T.*, 13/14 March 1999.

liv Calle M.C., 'Duisenberg: la croissance par la flexibilité du travail', *Le Figaro Économique*, 16 December 1998; Nicaud G., 'Zone Euro: L'OCDE prône la flexibilité du travail. L'Ocede explique que la mobilité des travailleurs peut permettre d'absorber les chocs économiques régionaux', *Le Figaro Économique*, 25 March 1999; Balls A., 'Jobless rate is top priority' (the single curency means that the need for flexibility in eurozone labour markets is even greater', *F.T.*, 24 September 1999.

lv 'Armoede is verdubbeld in Wallonië', *De Standaard*, 29 September 1998.

lvi Employment rates by broad sector, 1997, in percent were as follows: Europe: agriculture 3.0 per cent; industry 17.8 per cent, services 39.7; jobless 39.5 per cent; USA: agriculture 2.0 per cent; industry 17.7 per cent; services 54.3 per cent; jobless 26 per cent.

lvii European Commission, *The Future European Labour Supply*, Brussels, 1999, p. 7.

lviii Mitchener B., 'Report Assails EU Job-Creation Efforts. Growth Urged for Region's Employment Rate', *The Wall Street Journal*, 15 October 1998.

lix Validire J.L., 'Social: les cacaphonies de l'Union Européenne. Rapporteur du Parlement Européen sur les "liens entre le système commercial et les normes de travail" André Sainjon plaide pour une plus grande cohérence des pays de L'UE'., *Le Figaro Économique*, 30 Septembre 1998.'

lx J.D., 'L' écart entre riches et pauvres s'accroît outre-Manche. Le Royaume-Uni adopte le salaire minimum', *Le Figaro Économique*, 1 April 1998.

lxi Donkin R., 'Working on a new ethic', *F.T.*, 28 August 1998.

lxii *The State of Working America 1998–1999*, Washington, 1998.

lxiii Taylor R., 'Wages of US workers start to bounce back', *F.T.*, 7 September 1998.

lxiv Chote R., 'Poverty coming back to E Asia', *F.T.*, 28 september 1998.

lxv Taylor R., 'World Unemployment. Third of all workers affected, says ILO Report. Asia crisis will add to jobless total', *F.T.*, 24 September 1998.

lxvi Visser J., 'Globalisation and informalization of labour: is there an organised response?', in: *IIRA, 11th World Congress. Developing competitiveness and social justice: the interplay between institutions and social partners*, 22–26 September 1998, Bologna, Italy, Vol. 3, pp. 35–39.

lxvii R.H., 'Italie: le travail noir indispensable à la croissance. La capitale c'est Rome', *Le Figaro Économique*, 9 February 1999.

lxviii Bobinsky C., and others, 'Eastern Europe's companies are forced to re-learn old trading tricks', *F.T.*, 24 September 1998.

lxix According to the World Bank. 'Extreme poverty is defined as those living on less than half the official subsistence minimum income which stood at $35 a month in February 1998' (Jack A., é30m Russians face extreme poverty, World Bank to warn. Economy forecast to decline 8.3 per cent, hitting families worst', *F.T.*, 19 April 1999.

lxx Chote R., 'Efforts to reduce poverty falters', according to the World Bank, *F.T.*, 27 April 1999.

lxxi *Idem*.

lxxii 'Chote R., 'Developing nations face slow growth', *F.T.*, 8 April 1999.

lxxiii Study by David Blanchflower at the US National Union of Economic Research and Prof; Andrew Oswald, Economics Department of the University of Warwick (Taylor R., 'Irish Workers "most satisfied"', *F.T.*, 26 April 1999).

Chapter 13. Job Creation and Labour Law: From Protection towards Pro-action

*M. Biagi**

I. FROM EMPLOYMENT PROTECTION TOWARDS PRO-ACTION: IS THERE ANY ROLE LEFT FOR LABOUR LAW IN JOB CREATION POLICIES?

1. The title chosen for this study implies a comparison between the regulatory and functional role of labour law. A number of questions should be answered in this respect. First of all, is there, on the one hand, an interplay between the job creation function and employment strategy, and employment policy and labour law on the other? Secondly, is labour law called upon to perform a new function (promoting employment) and, in so doing, is it moving away from its original mission of protecting people at work? Thirdly, how is labour law reacting to this pressure in the various national/regional contexts? Is it re-directing its focus or simply resisting those pressures and, as a result, impeding job creation policies to produce the expected results? Overall, in most of countries, is it true that labour law and industrial relations have shifted from a protective approach to one which has as its main object the promotion of business competitiveness and employment growth? Undoubtedly, a radical change in the goals of labour law is under way. From the traditional role of static protection of the individual employee, it is now moving towards a dynamic perspective of employment promotion. The aim of this work is to investigate to what extent, and how, labour law and industrial relations might contribute to a job creation/employment promotion policy.

2. One should recognize that a possible misunderstanding seems to have deeply conditioned the scientific debate, at least in Europe, over the last twenty years, i.e. the tendency of equalizing *sic et simpliciter* the *policies of labour* with *policies for employment.* Yet they are two profoundly different concepts. Employment policies, on the one hand, are aimed at increasing the overall level of employment in a determined, socio-economic system. These policies are made up of measures operating in different areas other than in the labour market. For example fiscal policy, industrial policy, public spending policy, or also policies supporting job creation at the local

---

* I would like to thank Michele Tiraboschi for his great help in the drafting of this study.

level, policies aimed at guaranteeing an efficient use of EU structural funds, policies laid down to fight the evasion of tax and compulsory social contributions, policies for the emergence of undeclared labour, etc. Labour policies, mainly active labour policies, are instead something quite different. The latter are made by measures set up to promote the opportunity of employment of a specific target of the population (long-term unemployed, unqualified unemployed, young people, women, disabled, immigrants, etc.). These measures operate at different levels of intervention, such as education, training, vocational guidance, etc. Consequently, they do not have an impact – if not marginally and indirectly – on the overall unemployment level. At most, they can influence the duration and, above all, the distribution of unemployment between the different groups of individuals, contributing to but not penalize further the so-called outsiders versus the insiders.

3.   This chapter takes into account the fact that there is little evidence that employment protection really has an effect on employment. It is not by chance that the OECD came to the conclusion in the Employment Outlook of 1999 that such a relationship was not supported by empirical evidence. This view was not a surprise to those who study job creation. Consequently, it seems more advisable to discuss here to what extent and how labour law could create some pre-conditions necessary to ensure better employment performance.

4.   In comparing diverse cultural and juridical experiences of job creation, special attention will be paid to some specific strategies emerging at supra-national level and then implemented domestically. In this respect, particularly relevant are:

(a) the *guidelines* drawn up since 1994 by the OECD (so-called *Job Strategies*), which represent ten recommendations addressed to national governments to fight unemployment);
(b) the *EU employment guidelines* (so-called *European Employment Strategy* as provided by the employment chapter of the Amsterdam Treaty).

5.   It is important to underline that these types of strategies for job creation are mainly developed in countries and geographical areas in which there is a high level of unemployment. In contrast, other countries or geographical areas such as the US and Canada, follow a more laissez-faire approach to job creation, allowing the level of unemployment to be 'governed', by market forces. In the US and Canada, we may find some policies at the local level, which contribute, directly or indirectly, to create employment.

6.   In the United States, in particular, no single document sets out a national employment strategy in as comprehensive a manner as in European countries, for instance. The American conception is that of a cause and effect relationship between economic performance and employment growth.

7.   Japan represents a quite different case, for until recently, the low level of unemployment did not necessitate the adoption of any government-run job creation strategy. However, a number of fundamental features of the Japanese system (such as the life-time/long-term employment system, seniority-based wage policy, etc. ...)

are now being challenged by the rapid change in the economy with a significant increase in the level of unemployment and a rapidly ageing society. The Japanese case remains a very difficult one to categorize. On the one side, Japan is experimenting with some policies that may fall into an overall job creation strategy, but in many areas of labour law, Japan seems tempted to resort to a mere de-regulatory approach.

8.   The following areas of job creation strategy will be discussed:

(a) improving employability, which is a preventive approach to unemployment, which includes modernizing public employment services, encouraging life-long learning, tackling youth unemployment and preventing long-term unemployment. This analysis will include a discussion of public and private employment services, temporary work agencies, the transition from passive to active measures and the role of social parties in the development and implementation of this strategy;
(b) adaptability in enterprises and evaluating the need for incentives to job creation at the enterprise level;
(c) encouraging entrepreneurship through increasing incentives and removing obstacles to starting new business, self-employment and encouraging the inclusion of young people and women in the labour force;
(d) creating new jobs by developing new markets and regulating black market work;
(e) the involvement of social parties and local level support in the formation of job creation strategies; and
(f) investing in jobs through public aids.

II.   CREATING NEW JOBS: THE OECD AND EUROPEAN EMPLOYMENT STRATEGIES

A.   *Introduction*

9.   There are divergent views on what should be the role of the State in the context of a job creation policy. The OECD strongly supports a market-oriented strategy to create new jobs and fight unemployment. This strategy could be defined in terms of State abstention, and in some ways reflects the US neo-liberal attitude toward the regulation of the labour market. Contrary to this idea, the EU approach to unemployment is more articulated and still based on the pivotal role of the State in the implementation of an employment strategy. Since the publication in 1993 of the White Paper on *Growth, Competitiveness and Employment*, the EU Commission has indicated a number of features in the national employment systems that have resulted in lower employment creation for a given level of output, such as a slow adaptation to the new international division of labour and of the gap between qualifications of the labour force and the needs of the market, insufficient flexibility of labour markets with respect to work organization and statutory or conventional conditions that discourage business from taking on employees, wage increases not leaving enough scope for employment creation, taxes and other statutory contributions heavily burdening labour and affecting especially the lower qualified, and employment policies excessively based on passive assistance.

10. Over the past few years the European Union has adopted a strategy that in many aspects resembles that of the OECD. In fact, the idea of maintaining high levels of protection and guaranteeing equal employment opportunities is strongly balanced by a more market-oriented approach toward the mechanism of governing labour market. Though the OECD is stressing a de-regulatory approach, while the EU has concentrated much more on the issue of a labour market open to all. Maximizing employment opportunities through 'employability', 'adaptability' and 'entrepreneurship' are now common goals both for the OCED and the EU.

B.   The OECD Jobs Strategy

11.   Since 1992 the OECD has undertaken a major *Job Study* to examine the fundamental aspects of the employment and unemployment in the OECD Member countries. This study analyses the effects in numerous countries of a range of economic and labour factors on unemployment. Macro-economic management, competition from low-wage countries, faster technological change, and slow adjustment to new jobs, and skills are just some of the factors examined. The OECD Jobs Study finds that much unemployment is the unfortunate result of society's failure to adapt to a world of rapid change and intensified global competition. Rules and regulations, practices and policies, and institutions designed for an earlier era have resulted in labour markets that are too inflexible for today's world. Based on this finding, the OECD set out a broad programme of action designed to deal with job creation policies. The OECD strategy is based on ten recommendations representing a balanced mix of macro-economic and structural policies. The recommendations have been developed against the background of the tight budgetary constraints faced by virtually all governments. The focus throughout is on the design of policies that facilitate and encourage participation in work, thereby keeping to a minimum the numbers of those who have to live wholly on income support. It is important to underline that these recommendations do not apply to governments alone. In many cases responsibility for action to improve employment performance lies most directly with employers, trade unions and individual workers.

12.   The OECD strategy for job creation contains a range of macro-economic and structural policies aimed at reinforcing innovative and adaptive capacity and improve conditions for job creation:

i.   Sustainable growth can occur only when stable prices and public finances are the foundation of macro-economic policy, along with strong structural policies;

ii.   Employment, living standards and growth in productivity is largely based on technological development. Economies must therefore create the most favourable conditions possible to encourage and assist technological research and development and the creative use of new technology in ways of increasing high productivity and well-paid jobs;

iii.   Legislation, those directly governing work time and regarding enterprise and investment taxes and social security payments, should facilitate the use of flexible work contracts and create incentives to part-time work for employers and employees;

iv. The State should work to create a climate that spawns entrepreneurship, rationalizing and simplifying regulations to invigorate enterprise creation of new enterprises, while removing bureaucratic policies that hinder the creation or growth of new entities. The climate must also be fair to small as well as large enterprises, and these measures should be supported by public awareness campaigns to educate investors, entrepreneurs and other regarding the progressive entrepreneurial policies and to remove negative connotations towards business failure;

v. To help prevent rising unemployment, wage and labour costs should be more flexible reflecting the local conditions and individualized skill level;

vi. To reform employment security provisions for the private sector to avoid inhibiting new hirings. Overly zealous security provisions make employers fearful of hiring new workers;

vii. To strengthen the emphasis on active labour market policies and reinforce their effectiveness. Public spending on labour market programmes in almost all countries is still dominated by passive measures. Active programmes must correspond to the needs of either individual client groups or specific labour market problems. Active measures should be coordinated with unemployment and related benefit systems;

viii. Education policies, from early childhood education to training for low-skilled workers must be implemented to improving skills for the labour force. In addition, policies to ease the transition from school to work should be implemented;

ix. Remove disincentives to joining the labour force and improve the availability of active assistance programs geared to prepare people for the workforce, while at the same time preserving equality and social cohesion; streamline unemployment and related benefits so that protection is achieved with fewer burdens on the market; and

x. Increase competition in the market.

C. The European Employment Strategy

13. The European Employment Strategy (EES) is based on *guidelines* (GLs) laid down yearly by the Council as provided by the Employment Chapter of the Treaty. They constitute an example of 'soft laws', as an alternative to the traditional legislative approach based on directives and regulations. GLs are actual rules in that Member States are bound by the principles which are stated, regardless of the contingent political domestic situation. Nevertheless, since harmonization in this field of Community action is openly rejected, examples of 'hard laws' in employment matters would have been inappropriate. 'Soft laws' are certainly normative in character, while at the same time, representing a method of Community guidance. Employment guidelines belong to this category of 'norms', since they recognize the principle of subordination while, at the same time, create an expectation that the performance of the Member States will be in conformity with them.

14. By including employment in the Community policies and thus making the promotion of employment a matter of common concern, and so requiring Member

States to coordinate their policies in order to achieve a high level of employment in the context of balanced and sustainable economic progress, the new Title ensures the development of employment initiatives and the creation of a consistent policy at the European level. The extraordinary European Council meeting on Employment in Luxembourg in November 1997 gave life to these new provisions by developing an agreed-upon coordinated process for implementation. The culmination of these efforts was the adoption of the 'Luxembourg Process on Employment Guidelines and National Action Plans,' which endorses a coordinated strategy aimed at the development of active job creation policies.

15. The Employment Guidelines are based on four core themes or pillars aimed at promoting: (1) employability, (2) entrepreneurship, (3) adaptability, and (4) equal opportunities. They set out the Community priorities for each of the objectives (the common ends that all Member States and social partners must pursue to promote employment growth in a given year) and establish the main steps of the process of implementation for that year. The essence of the Luxembourg process is to identify common ends without imposing common means.

16. Pillar 1 ('improving employability') focuses on the skills gap between job seekers and available jobs. While skill development and life-long learning remain a key objective for the whole work-force, here there is particular emphasis on ensuring that young people and the unemployed (particularly the long-term unemployed) are equipped to profit from new and ever-changing employment opportunities in the current labour market. Two key elements of this pillar are early intervention, before individuals become long-term unemployed, and customized and targeted assistance to meet individual needs. This pillar also marks the first time the EU has provided clear, quantified targets for Member States in giving a new start to young and long-term unemployed people, and in increasing access to training for the unemployed. While respecting the diversity of national industrial relations and labour market systems, Member States are now under the obligation to act within the constraints of parameters jointly agreed upon each year. Guidelines 1, 2 and 3 (of 1998, 1999 and 2000) clearly prescribe actions which can be quantified. For instance, every unemployed young person must be offered a new start before reaching six months of unemployment (in the form of training, re-training, work practice, a job or other employability measures). This opportunity must be offered to every unemployed adult before reaching twelve months of unemployment. Furthermore, active measures to promote employability should affect at least 20 per cent of those who are unemployed. On top of that, for 2000 guideline 6 requires each Member State to 'define lifelong learning in order to set a target according to national circumstances for participants benefiting from such measures'. Member States are now in part bound by quantified targets in employment matters.

17. Pillar 2 ('encouraging entrepreneurship'), is based on the belief that the creation of more and better jobs requires a dynamic and enterprising climate for businesses to expand and hire workers and for new businesses to come into being. The definition of entrepreneurship as utilized for this pillar is broad, covering the start-up and running of new enterprises, development of existing enterprises, encouragement of initiative within large firms, generation of new sources of employment (including different forms of self-employment), and creation of networks among enterprises, and between enterprises, and local authorities.

18. Pillar 3 ('improving adaptability'), aims at developing the ability of both enterprises and workers to evolve along with technology and markets. This idea includes industrial restructuring and the development of new products and services, adaptability in terms of the organization of work, working patterns' and contracts, as well as adaptability in terms of regulatory and training systems. This pillar is an explicit recognition of the need for 'flexurity'; the balance between the need of businesses for flexibility, and the needs of employees for security and employability. This pillar directly affects labour law regulations. In fact, in order to promote the modernization of work organization and forms of work 'the social partners are invited to negotiate, at the appropriate levels, in particular at sectoral and enterprise levels, agreements to modernize the organization of work, including flexible working arrangements, with the aim of making undertakings productive and competitive and achieving the required balance between flexibility and security'. These agreements may cover such areas as the expression of working time as an annual figure, reduction of working hours, reduction of overtime, development of part-time working and life-long training and career breaks. Each Member State is to examine the possibility of legislating the inclusion of more adaptable types of contracts, taking into account the fact that forms of employment are increasingly diverse. At the same time, those working under new forms of work contracts should continue to enjoy adequate security and higher occupational status, compatible with the needs of business. To renew skill levels within enterprises, Member States are to re-examine the obstacles, in particular tax obstacles, to investment in human resources. To remove such obstacles, member states may take such actions as to provide tax or other incentives for the development of in-house training. Further, they will examine any new regulations to ensure their contribution to reducing barriers to employment and helping the labour market adapt to structural changes in the economy.

19. The EU does not advocate improving job creation by simple de-regulation of the labour market. In fact, a significant emphasis is placed on the need to ensure equal opportunity for everyone and a labour market open to all. Pillar 4 prioritizes equal opportunities, with the twin social and economic objective of modernizing societies so that women and men can work on equal terms with equal responsibilities to develop the full growth capacities of European economies. It recognizes both the social need to counter discrimination and inequalities between women and men, and the economic loss resulting from not making full and effective use of the productive capacities of all sections of the population. In addition to this focus on closing the gender gap in Europe's economic and social life, this pillar emphasizes the integration of people with disabilities into working life. In this area labour law regulation plays the traditional function of balancing the driving forces of the market with attention to social integration.

20. Following the adoption of the EU Council, all Member States must each develop a National employment Action Plan (NAP) setting out the means which they propose to take to implement the Guidelines. The NAPs, which must be submitted to the Council and Commission for purposes of recommendations, are expected to reflect the priorities of the Union as defined under the four core themes. While these duties are not accompanied by resulting sanctions in the event of non-performance and do not advocate measures to harmonize national provisions, the expectation is that such a process will have an indirect impact on Member States' policies and thereby lead to greater cooperation and convergence.

D.   OECD and EU: A Common Goal but Different Strategies?

21.   Despite the different philosophies of job creation strategies, the practical solutions proposed by both OECD and EU for their member countries significantly converge, especially in how each organization approaches the concepts of employability, adaptability and entrepreneurship.

22.   A key reason for the partial implementation of the OECD Jobs Strategy is the perception that undertaking reform involves a conflict with policy objectives concerning equity and social cohesion. In particular, concern has been expressed that the Jobs Strategy recommendations to enhance wage flexibility and to reform social transfer systems would be at odds with the policy objectives of ensuring some degree of equity across members of the labour force or the population at large. Nevertheless, it is true that the few countries have followed the OECD Jobs Strategy have had improved labour market outcomes – the United Kingdom, the Netherlands, New Zealand, and, to some extent, Ireland. It is also undeniable that we can find deteriorating conditions in some of those that have not done much to implement these new ideas. These results may be an indication that the Strategy works. Studies have demonstrated the importance of a strategic approach to reform. Pursuing a comprehensive approach to reform is likely to bring greater benefits than concentrating efforts in a few area, even though comprehensive reforms cannot be easily implemented in the short run.

23.   Also the European Union authorities have now understood the importance of implementing job creation strategies in a comprehensive policy. However, unlike the OECD, they believe that comprehensive reforms cannot be achieved without the cooperation of social parties.

III.   COMPARATIVE OVERVIEW: IMPROVING EMPLOYABILITY

A.   Introduction

24.   The OECD Jobs Study and the EU Employment Guidelines are both based on the assumption that active labour market policies (ALMPs), if properly managed, will raise the employability of the unemployed, in particular the long-term employed who for the most part are unskilled workers. Instead of simply providing the unemployed with some income support such as subsidies and unemployment insurance, which may be acceptable when countries have lower levels of unemployment, these forms of assistance are more burdensome in countries with high levels of unemployment. When high unemployment exists, it may be preferable to adopt preventive measures in addition to income support, which will help the unemployed to develop competitive. 'Improving employability' implies a preventive approach to unemployment: modernizing public employment services, encouraging life-long learning, tackling youth unemployment and preventing long-term unemployment, and easing the transition from school to work.

25. Although there is a wide consensus regarding the necessity to move from passive to active labour market policies, there is a stark contrast with how different countries are approaching this movement. In Europe, the approach is to gain a wide consensus with social parties at the national, regional and local level to implement such policies. In Germany for instance, efforts are made at both the regional and national level to create a tripartite 'job alliance for jobs, training and competitiveness' aimed among other things to deal with vocational and continued training. Tripartite agreements performing a job creation function have also been signed in Spain and in Italy. This practice is labelled as 'social concertation'.

26. In other countries, for example the UK, active labour policies and measures are implemented unilaterally by the government without the significant cooperation of the social partners. Likewise, in the United States, the government has implemented the welfare-to-work policy aimed at removing disincentives from entering the labour market. In the US, active employment policies are rare and generally only at the local level and/or at the level of single enterprises. Only in exceptional cases management and labour enter collective bargaining on this matter.

B. The Role of Public Employment Services

27. With respect to improving employability, one idea common to both European countries and Japan is that of re-regulating the area of public employment services (PES). Following the indication laid out in the ILO conventions 34/1933 and 96/1949, the majority of countries have experimented a model of either public monopoly in the area of job placement or a strictly regulated private job placement system. In fact, on the basis of the constitutional principle that labour is not a commodity, the ILO provided a system of free public employment agency under the control of a central authority and a drastic limitation of private employment agencies even in the case of non-profit agencies. The historical experience of this monopoly demonstrates a very low level of efficiency and effectiveness in matching unemployed people with available jobs. For example, in Europe, only four out of every 100 job vacancies were filled through the use of the public monopolistic agency. For this reason, it became a conventional, although not necessarily accurate idea that perhaps high unemployment levels were caused by the bureaucratic public employment agencies. Until the 1990's it was only the UK in continental Europe which allowed private placement agencies. Now, the privatization and de-regulation trend has affected the whole of Europe. The European Court of Justice has clearly indicated that any form of monopoly in the placement area is in direct conflict with the general rule on competition, at least in cases where the public services alone are not able to provide effective assistance to unemployed people. The same conclusion has been

reached by ILO, which adopted in 1997 a new convention on private employment agencies (convention No. 181/1997).

28. Although international bodies and individual countries agree that the PES should be re-regulated, the approach to such re-regulation is diverse. For example, the OECD proposes that new regulations should create competition for the services that have traditionally been provided by the PES. In addition, the OECD advocates that PES should be mainly geared towards monitoring and supporting the motivation and job-search efforts of the unemployed who claim income support, and, if required, refer them to ALMPs, thereby contracting out much of the placement services and other ALMPs to private agencies. On the other hand, the European employment strategy advocates modernizing the PES to enlarge its role in providing ALMPs, to become more comprehensive, more de-centralized (e.g. more locations close to where people live) and more efficient.

29. The UK, for example, has always had a public–private approach. Specifically, it has experimented with the contracting out of the training function of the PES. In the UK, Training and Enterprise Councils (TECS) are private enterprises under contract with the Department of Education and Employment. The TEC then contracts out with service providers. The first contract is to a 'Training Agent' who assesses the needs of the jobseeker and then contracts with a Training Manager to develop a training program and either provide that training or contract with another to provide such training. In the Netherlands, training is also contracted out in a hybrid manner, with the PES providing a large percentage of its own training and contracting out only some of the training to private institutes.

30. Sweden, Denmark, Italy, and Spain, recognizing the benefits of competition, have all to some degree reformed the role of the PES and instituted competition in the form of private agencies.

31. The European Employment Strategy sets the following targets for PES: '(1) obtain substantial access to vacancies; (2) develop arrangements for the systematic case management of all registered unemployed jobseekers; (3) contribute to the coordinated delivery of all public services to jobseekers, focused on their re-integration; and (4) develop strong partnerships with other relevant actors in the market.' Further, the strategy states that there is a need for a more active approach to the promotion of occupational as well as geographic mobility in Europe as a means of increasing job opportunities and improving job matching.

32. Historically, PES was simply a bureaucratic contact for unemployed people to locate available jobs. Although the specific role of the PES can differ depending on the national structure, with current reforms, PES now offer free services, including the provision of information to jobseekers and employers as well as active job matching. In addition, public service tasks, such as checking the availability of the unemployed and producing quantitative and qualitative labour market information, promote the re-integration of the unemployed into employment through active labour market policies (e.g. training courses). In some countries, the PES administers unemployment benefits. In others, such benefits are administered by a separate agency. The advantage of separating the administration of benefits from the PES is obvious. The PES is therefore left freer to provide more active services. However, the disadvantage resulting from the separation of these two functions is that it creates two agencies dealing with partially overlapping activities and creates difficulties in keeping the unemployed person in contact with available vacancies.

33. PES operates in a number of ways to fill vacancies. The four methods are: self-selection, conditional self-selection, administrative matching and selective matching. In the first two, the PES is passive. For example, self-selection is often based on an open-file system containing all relevant information to which employers and jobseekers have direct and independent access without involvement from the PES. The conditional self-selection model consists of online or card registers with vacancy information. When a jobseeker finds a position in which he is interested, he approaches a PES staff member and is interviewed for an initial screening. These two approaches are termed semi-open self-service systems. Administrative matching, on the other hand, means that notified vacancies are communicated to potentially suitable jobseekers who register with the PES. Selective matching is even more resource intensive than administrative matching in that this method of mediation requires PES personnel to screen candidates for available vacancies. Normally, mediation services offered by the PES is obligatory for unemployed benefit recipients and generally voluntary for other jobseekers.

34. A process for evaluating the mediation of referring jobseekers to vacancies is essential in ensuring efficiency and effectiveness of PES. The evaluation can be both of the performance of the PES and also of its impact. PES can surely have an impact at the micro-level by matching vacancies and jobseekers. However, it remains questionable whether a PES can have a positive impact at the macro-level, specifically, whether its activities can lead to an increase in employment, to a reduction of unemployment and to an avoidance of high rates of unemployment. Importantly, it should be noted that PES can only impact job creation if the following is true: (1) the PES fills jobs that would otherwise been left vacant; or (2) the PES fills job vacancies that would not have been filled as quickly otherwise. The PES can only impact a reduction of unemployment if: (1) unemployed jobseekers placed by PES would have not been placed in this or another comparable job otherwise; or (2) unemployed jobseekers would not have found this or another comparable job as quickly through other methods.

35. EU countries are working in a number of ways to modernize PES. For instance, Spain, in collaboration with social partners and autonomous regions, has developed and implemented a number of projects to improve PES from many perspectives. Spain is also working to increase the use of new technologies in PES, for example, there is a goal to establish in the year 2000 a service to enable companies to connect with the computer system of the PES to select and arrange interviews with suitable candidates and submit job offers. In addition PES will provide a computer 'bulletin board,' which can be accessed by both employers and jobseekers from remote computers (e.g. home pc). The PES will also develop the SPE-Social Media Partnership in employment programmes, with the aim of gaining a higher profile in mass media so that job vacancies and the employment policy objectives are advertised more broadly. In step with the trend to de-centralize, a large part of the responsibilities of INEM (National Employment Institute) have been transferred to regional bodies to better serve the specific needs of geographical areas.

36. Similarly, Japan has worked in concert with a tripartite body established by the Labour Minister to drastically reform the PES. Importantly, previously the PES had a monopoly on all placement services except those identified by law. However, the tripartite body has now established a short list of occupations that will be served by the PES, leaving the rest to private agencies. Further, the tripartite body was reacting to the fact that only 20 per cent of new recruits had been placed through PES. Like Japan over the last ten years, most European countries have also abolished the state monopoly of PES (e.g. Portugal, Austria, Germany, Italy, Sweden, Iceland).

37. In the Netherlands, social partners as well as the local and regional authorities are integral to the development of modernizing PES. The PES provides information and advice, placement services and vacancy filling for all jobseekers. In addition, the Netherlands has given the work of implementing measure to make local markets more effective and to re-integrate those left out of the job market through mainly private actors. The Netherlands aims to follow Denmark and Sweden by emphasizing life-long learning as the approach to improving employability.

38. In the Asian context, Korea is late in modernizing the PES, although at least some private employment services exist. The PES is administered by both the Labour Ministry and under local government control. Unlike the situation in Europe, where the private employment agencies have mainly concentrated on finding skilled labour jobs, private employment agencies in Korea have a good record in finding jobs for unskilled persons.

C.   The Role of Private Employment Services

39. The OECD and the EU both advocate the development of private employment services (PRES) to foster competition and thus improve the efficiency and effectiveness of placement services.

40. PERS have taken on a number of different forms depending on the country. For example, there are now private-for-profit employment agencies; private sector firms which compete directly with PES, government funded private firms; and finally, there are partnership arrangements with private firms and community organizations for placement.

41. The increase in PRES, although seen as a move to de-centralize, modernize and improve employment services, may also be cause for concern. Studies on the role of PRES demonstrate that the focus of these agencies is highly-skilled or specially-skilled jobs and focused principally on experienced jobseekers who are already employed. PRES mainly operate in large metropolitan areas with large enterprises as clients. These characteristics may have negative implications for efficiency. Specifically, PES are intended to offer free information and create market transparency to facilitate job matching. If the PRES replaces the PES, the access to information will be restricted, thereby restricting efficiency.

42. Another important argument in favour of continuing the use of the PES is social justice. As discussed above, PRES serve the most promising jobseekers. Therefore, the elimination of the PES would result in hardship for smaller and medium-sized companies and organizations and those in less prosperous areas. Furthermore, hard-to-place jobseekers (e.g. the long-termed unemployed and the low or no-skilled workers) would not be served, resulting in the marginalization of this population and a rise in hard-core unemployment. PES, as a public intervention against market failures, may serve another purpose. For example, PES can supply unemployed jobseekers with hope that they will find employment, and it can provide much needed job training for those without skills. The PERS is not designed to assist the large numbers of long-term unemployed or low-skilled unemployed people. With respect to these populations, the public intervention of the PES seems to be an efficient and effective service, which can combine job placement with other active labour market policies.

43. In Japan PERS have gained access to a wide range of employment within the white collar area. Similarly, as mentioned above, most European countries have now liberalized the restriction on PERS.

D.   Transition from Passive to Active Measures

44. The EU employment guidelines for 2000 recommends the transition from passive to active employment policies in order to implement new active labour market policies (ALMPs) to improve employability. The guidelines specifically state that Member States should 'provide incentives for unemployed or inactive people to seek and take up work or measures to enhance their employability and for employers to create new jobs ... develop a policy for active ageing, encompassing appropriate measures such as maintaining working capacity, life-long learning and other flexible working arrangements, so that older workers are also able to remain and participate actively in working life.'

45. Generally, EU countries implement their labour market policy through centralized organizations and/or institutions, as in Spain, France, Germany, Portugal or through de-centralized organization/institutions, as in Denmark, The Netherlands, UK, and Belgium. This situation is becoming less clear as all European countries are moving towards implementing their ALMPs in a de-centralized manner with an emphasis on geographical needs.

46. The UK, and likewise the United States, has implemented federal welfare to work strategies aimed at removing disincentives to work and at the same time providing unemployed with job training, and counselling during the period of unemployment. For example, these programmes provide the unemployed with financial support yet at some point require their participation in work training with personal advisers and job counsellors. The approach to these programs is to provide individually tailored assistance to the unemployed. The UK also have individual programmes for those who are of certain ages or have been unemployed for a certain amount of time. For instance, those individuals remaining unemployed after three months participate in an in-depth review of their job-search activity and are eligible for progressively more intensive help. Furthermore, those hard-to-place individuals (e.g. ex-offenders, people with disabilities, people with literacy or numeracy problems, those who speak English as a second language, etc ...) are eligible for more intensive job-search assistance at an earlier stage. The UK also has various programmes that intensify according to the jobseekers age and time of unemployment (e.g. three months of employment; 25 years of age or older and unemployed for six months, 50 years of age and 12 months of unemployment; those with 18 months of unemployment and those of 25 years of age or older and two years of unemployment). The U.S., however, has no national initiative to train and place either those long-term unemployed or specially disadvantaged groups.

47. Along these lines, Portugal is working to remove disincentives to work by implementing the 'new unemployment protection scheme', which allows partial or full unemployment payments with part-time work and allows some payments to continue for 30 days when a beneficiary attends professional training for at least six months. National legislation is aimed at improving employability through implementing active employment measure is implemented based on geographical needs in accordance with Territorial Pacts and Regional Employment Networks. The percentage of money budgeted for ALMPs now have grown to 50 per cent of the employment policy cost. Emphasis is placed on providing access to ALMPs for the unemployed to improve this group's employability and assist their integration into the labour market. The government's target in Sweden is that all young people under the age of 25 will be offered regular work, suitable training, practical work experience or a job-creating measure not later than 100 days after the start of unemployment.

48. In Australia, vocational training has become an integral part of the government's economic restructuring and involvement in ALMPs. Australia started the New Apprenticeship System in the mid-to-late 1990s to increase flexibility in traineeships and apprenticeships. Further, to protect apprentices and trainees, the Workplace Relations Act 1996 protects the integrity of their special rates of pay.

49. In Latin America, preparing young people for today's market is the largest challenge to achieve improved employability. The public education system is geared towards preparing youth for traditional jobs, which are becoming ever more scarce. The restructuring of federal education programmes and developing active training programmes are essential to improve the skill of the workforce, the quality of products, improve technologies and the quality of jobs. To this end, the social parties' role is essential, yet the strength of these parties has not yet been fully explored.

E. *The Role of Social Parties*

50. In continental European countries in particular, the process described in the previous sections has created a lot of conflict and social resistance. Consequently, national governments were not able to unilaterally implement measures expected to improve employability, for instance, the privatization of employment services, the abolition of the public monopoly on placement services and the easing of the transition from school to work or aiding those long-term unemployed. Therefore, the liberalization process for these countries has taken place with the collaboration with the social partners at the national, regional, and local levels.

51. EU Employment Guidelines pay much attention to this profile. Recognizing that 'the actions of the member states alone will not suffice to achieve the desired results in promoting employability', the EU solicits the social parties at the supranational, national, and local level 'to conclude as soon as possible agreements with the view to increasing the possibilities for training, work experience, traineeships or other measures likely to promote employability of the young and adult unemployed and to promote entry into the labour market.' Moreover, the EU 'in order to reinforce the development of a skilled and adaptable workforce,' asks both Member States and social partners 'to develop possibilities for life-long learning, particularly in the fields of information and communication technologies.' In this respect, each Member State is asked to 'set a target according to national circumstances for participants benefiting from such measures.' Over the last few years, continental Europe has become a laboratory for bilateral and tripartite agreements at the local, regional, and national level aimed at improving employability.

52. In Germany the social partners are currently involved in a process called 'Alliance for Work, Training and Competitiveness', which is a forum providing a permanent framework for dialogue between all groups of society to discuss employment issues and potential solutions. The Alliance, for example, declared that all parties were in favour of an employment-oriented and longer-term collective bargaining policy. Further, the Alliance came out in favour of further reform of regional industry-wide collective agreements, a reform aimed at encouraging necessary branch-related differentiations. The social partners are also contributing with Governments to modernize educational systems and to make them more relevant to the new economy.

53. Sweden has a strong tradition of collaboration between the Government and the social partners on issues of working life. Other countries who have given a strong role to the social partners at the national, regional, and local level include Denmark and The Netherlands.

F. Promoting a Labour Market Open to All

54. The move towards active measures with the involvement of private enterprise and market forces in the area of improving employability may risk increasing the marginalisation of weaker parties, for example the aged, women, disabled, ethnic minorities, low-skilled workers and the long-term unemployed. In response to this risk, the EU employment guidelines state that each member state will 'give special attention to the needs of the disabled, ethnic minorities and other groups and individuals who may be disadvantaged, and develop appropriate forms of preventive and active policies to promote their integration into the labour market.'

55. In the UK, for example, the Government promotes equal opportunity and fights discrimination through various commissions, Equal Opportunities Commission, the Commission of Racial Equality (CRE) and the Disability Rights Commission. Each Commission works independently and takes its own actions towards equality. Further, the UK has developed a pilot project to educate employers as to equal opportunity laws. This service provides employers with information regarding equal opportunities from a single source. The UK still has a disproportionately high unemployment rate among ethnic minorities.

56. Portugal is working to implement a number of measures to integrate the disabled, ethnic minorities, immigrant communities, and other disadvantaged members of society (e.g. drug addicts) into the workforce. The actions implemented to achieve these goals include: increasing the employability of the disabled through professional rehabilitation as well as public interventions to facilitate integration into the job market, promoting socio-professional integration of particular targeted groups (e.g. the long-term unemployed, low-skilled workers), developing activities which serve to provide professional training skills and also contribute to the employability of socially disadvantaged groups. In Spain, 1999 marked a year when a number of legislative measures and adjustments to active employment policies were introduced to facilitate the effective incorporation of the disabled into the labour market as well as those marginalized members of society.

57. In contrast, the US has strong legislation to protect weaker parties (minorities, women, aged, disabled) from being denied employment for which they are qualified. However, the policies are passive in that they do not promote integration for weaker parties into the job market unless those parties are already employable.

IV. COMPARATIVE OVERVIEW: ADAPTABILITY

A. *Introduction*

58. There is overwhelming agreement on the need to revise the legal/contractual framework on which labour law is presently based. Rules which could fit for the manufacturing production process cannot be entirely kept after having already entered into the era of the knowledge-based society.

59. Labour law and the entire social model have to be modernized, at least in the European Union countries. A complete rethink of the organization of work in the context of the information society is an absolute priority. This does not mean simply de-regulation. Instead, this approach implies a new balance between security (progressively more in terms of employment rather than of jobs) and flexibility – also technically conceived of as a way of allowing management and labour to negotiate in order to deviate from legislative provisions, taking into account more closely specific situations of single enterprises and/or local labour markets.

60. Modernizing labour law obviously means different things in various contexts. In Europe, labour law could cooperate to launch a strategy of employment creation making permanent/open-ended employment contracts more attractive to

employers. In some national contexts hyper-protective, anti-dismissal legislation has induced remarkably precarious hiring arrangements. Human resources should be regarded as the main capital of the European economy. The real protection lies in training, possibly an obligation of management to provide employees with continuous education for the duration of their working life.

B.   Modernizing Work Organization

61.   According to the European Commission's Green Paper 'Partnership for a new organization of work', successful modernization of work should be based on the full involvement of the social partners. Modernizing work organization should take place mainly at the workplace between management and workers (and their representatives) so that the diverse nature of each situation in each individual sector can be uniquely tailored to the sector and the size of the company. Social partners can foster modernization by identifying points of common interest and sharing ideas to meet the necessary balance between flexibility and security.

62.   Modernizing work organization includes such phenomena as creating flexible working times, increasing training, shortening working hours, developing new forms of work individually adapted to special sectors or particular regions and Government interventions such as incentives for innovation, training and increased investment in new technology. Finally, all parties, management, social partners and Government must invest time, energy, and resources to improving training opportunities so that the demand for skilled workers does not go unmet.

C.   Working Time, Reduction of Hours and Part-time Work

63.   The reduction of working time has been a continuous trend in Europe since 1983. Since 1983, the number of hours worked per person has fallen to 38. The reduction in hours is partly due to new flexibility in working relationships, the growth in part-time work and in the service industry. Further, this phenomenon may be also the result of more women in the marketplace. Working time reductions associated with an increase in employment are also usually associated with an increase in current wages. Reduction in working time usually favours employment, but, because of the resultant productivity gains, there is not a one-for-one relationship between the increase in employment and the reduction in working time.

64.   Corporations, because of the resulting increase in the hourly wage, usually is not inclined to reduce working time. In addition, employees usually prefer an increase in purchasing power over a reduction in working time. However, when a reduction in working time either prevents a reduction in employment or leads to an increase in employment, both parties can support it as a common goal. Therefore, reductions occur when it is initiated through a Government incentive or through collective action of the employer and employees.

65.   France has one of the most advanced policies in Europe to reduce working time. It is the only country where the Government provides large subsidies to support part-time work schemes. For example, the Robien Act of 30 May 1996 provides employers with a 40 per cent rebate in social security contributions for a year and 30 per cent for the next six years when they reduce working time by 10 per cent to save or create an additional 10 per cent in the number of jobs. Employers therefore gain a rebate over seven years. The commitment to maintain the additional employees, however, only lasts for two years. In France, 37 per cent of companies involved in the Robien plan have reduced the working week whilst others have linked the reduction and flexibilization of working schedules.

66. In 1998, the Aubry I Act was passed in order to encourage labour and management to negotiate the transition to a 35-hour work week. The Government itself also made a commitment to reduce the working week to 35 hours. The commitment includes aid to companies that apply this reduction. The actual implementation of the reduction of hours, however, is a subject of collective bargaining, which may be characterized as either a reduction in the working week or in the annual working hours. Therefore, flexibility of working hours in France is a subject of both legislative action and collective bargaining.

67. In the logic of fighting unemployment, part-time work plays a central role. This type of contract could facilitate reconciliation between family duties and work responsibilities and guarantee more opportunities for jobs in a flexible manner – which is acceptable for both employers and employees. In Europe only the Netherlands seem to have taken full advantage of this kind of work arrangement. Roughly, 40 per cent of the Dutch work with this type of contract. Government legislation has guaranteed the worker the right to ask employers to reduce or make flexible the working hours and schedule of work. Part-time work is widespread in northern European countries. Instead, the use of this contract is much less utilized in the Mediterranean countries, France and Germany. In the latter cases, the use of part-time work is sustained by financial subsidies from the government. However, the success of part-time work in these countries as a measure for job creation is not very clear.

D. *Facilitating the Diversification of Working Relationships as well as New Forms of Work*

68. One way to adapt work organization to the needs of the new economy, where employment is increasingly individualized and diverse, is to encourage the flexibility of the employment contract. Especially in countries where the level of protection against dismissal is very high, we see a trend towards flexibilization in the legally admissible types of work contracts. However, this strategy does not seem to produce satisfactory results in the long run for at least two reasons: (1) empirical research demonstrates that this type of contract aimed to increase flexibility in the labour market can produce some results in economies with low unemployment and a highly developed market; (2) people employed under this kind of contract usually have low skills, because the enterprise does not invest in these employees.

69. A good example of this phenomenon can be seen in Spain. The amount of temporary work in Spain had grown dramatically in the 1990s; however, unemployment

did not fall. Simply, the temporary work through agencies changed the nature of available jobs from permanent employment to those of non-permanent nature without benefits or guarantees.

E. Supporting Adaptability in Enterprise: Some Examples

70. In Sweden, a law passed on 26 May 1999 gives employer's associations the right to participate in drawing up labour legislation, the legislation regulating part-time work and also one re-examining the legal framework of temporary work. Further, Sweden created the 'Rotation-Employment' measure to enable companies to improve their workers' qualification through recruitment of temporary workers to substitute permanent workers during training. Further, measures were introduced to revitalize and modernize business. In 2000, measures are to be implemented to assist with on-going training in the scope of re-qualification and modernization of the national productive system. These measures will include training for professional re-conversion to permanently adapt workers' skills to the needs of the changing market place and other ideas to achieve 'life-long training' and training for senior staff and managers of SMEs. Priorities for Sweden include updating the legislative framework to adjust it to new forms of employment, to ensure appropriate legal protection of workers involved in atypical forms of work, and to continue the fight against illegal employment.

71. In Portugal, the priorities for adaptability include strengthening training and technical support for SMEs, increasing training of the employed population, re-structuring companies to make them stronger and more competitive in coordination with the regional development objectives and to assist those workers who are in danger of losing their job as a result of re-structuring. Training and technical support is particularly lacking in Portugal. For example, over the last years, only an estimated 10 per cent of SMEs took advantage of the training subsidies available. This situation is particularly urgent because a significant number of poorly qualified workers are concentrated in SMEs. Portugal has set a five-year goal to get 10 per cent of the total working population into training, with an appropriate distribution between men and women, and to include information and communication technology areas in 50 per cent of ongoing training activities. New instruments are being implemented to assist displaced workers during re-structuring.

72. Spain's adaptability policy is a result of concerted action with the social partners. For example, adaptability is to be largely achieved through changes in collective bargaining by providing more clauses allowing flexibility: e.g. related to the ordering and structure of wages, types of contracts offered, ordering of working hours, and the functional mobility of professional training. In addition, the Interconfederal Agreement on Collective Negotiation also offers new possibilities for modernizing and rationalizing the structure of collective negotiations and increasing their scope. The bodies collaborating to achieve goals in adaptability are the social parties, the Ministries of Labour, Education and Culture, the autonomous regions, the National Institute of Public Administration FRCEM and the Spanish Federation of Municipalities and Provinces.

73. The UK, unlike other European countries, is implementing programmes largely without the significant involvement of the social partners. To achieve the goal of adaptability the UK, has concentrated efforts on the tax incentive structures for business so that there can be a larger investment in human capital. For example, training costs are fully tax deductible and can be set off against profits. In addition, the government has initiated programmes such as Career Development Loans and Small Firms Training Loans to provide incentives for continued training.

V.   Comparative Overview: Encouraging Entrepreneurship

A.   *Entrepreneurship and Job Creation Opportunities*

74. In a strict sense, entrepreneurship aims to reduce the burden on business, including lowering taxes, and simplifying administrative procedures to start-up and maintain businesses. Teaching entrepreneurship skills has become a priority in a number of Member States with a number of novel programmes being started. Encouraging entrepreneurship is especially important for women and other groups who are at a disadvantage in the subordinate labour market. Self-employment is both a way to employ disadvantaged groups, but also a way to provide them with special advantages. In addition, the growth of SMEs is essential for job creation and for the expansion of training opportunities.

B.   *The EU Experience*

75. The Netherlands have implemented a number of programmes to make it easier to start up and run a business. The government has set a target to reduce administrative costs by 15 per cent compared with 1998. To do so, attention is being placed on limiting administrative costs created by legislation. An external body will examine all new regulations to assess their impact on administrative costs. The government is also implementing actions geared to create a more centralized source of information for entrepreneurs: setting up one central point where entrepreneurs can obtain all the forms they need, promoting the multiple use of data and encouraging the practice of transferring data from business to government agencies using modern data communication techniques. In addition, a uniform virtual registration system for businesses and a basic business register is being developed to be ready by the end of 2000.

76. Germany has implemented a number of policies aimed to reduce the administrative burden for start-up companies, to promote the development of self-employment, create jobs at the local level, and to fully exploit the employment potential of the service sector, and revise the tax system so that it is 'employment friendly'. A project group was established to follow up on all substantive indications of more efficient processes and regulations and convert them into action, if feasible. A mailbox was even established so that enterprises have an opportunity to directly report bureaucratic obstacles to the ministry. The bureaucratic cost oversight agencies were established to streamline agencies and the simplification and acceleration of planning and approval process. The SME-Dialogue (*Mittelstandsdialog*), which is part of the 'Alliances for Jobs' already contains concrete proposals for the reduction of bureaucratic obstacles with the goal to reduce administrative costs and the amount of time spent dealing with agencies for start-ups and smaller enterprises. Long administrative processes are being shortened by establishing 'virtual City Halls' or 'virtual market places,' which places the information exchange, communications and interactive processes onto the net. The federal Government will create a catalogue of measures for the reduction of bureaucratic obstacles for start-ups and small- and medium-size enterprises to be implemented by 2001. The administrative process for start-ups and small- and medium-sized enterprises is to be simplified. This will include easier access to federally funded loans. To promote self-employment and strengthen the economic productivity of small- and medium-size companies the young enterprises will be assisted financially through federal Government loans and the EU. Start-ups by women will be favoured. Take-overs, as a special form of start-up are supported through a special programme. Funding for various programmes is supplemented by support from the private risk capital market. A comprehensive counselling and education program is available to start-ups and is supported by individual Chambers of Commerce, the Federal Government and other partners in the economy.

77.   The Swedish government has proposed a Bill to achieve a clearer and more effective central authority structure to promote business development and growth. The new authority would focus on the needs of entrepreneurs and companies. Tasks currently handled by the National Board for Industrial and Technical Development and ALMI Företagspatner AB will be transferred to the new authority. The Government Offices' special group for the simplification of rules and regulations, the Simplex Commission, will intensify its work in 2000, including the training and further support of ministries and authorities in particular problem and consequence analyses, in the common effort to achieve fewer, fairer, and more intelligible rules.

78.   In Portugal, 60 per cent of jobs are in small- and medium-sized companies. The greatest potential for employment growth is also seen in these companies, rather than in large companies. Thus, Portugal recognizes the importance of supporting these industries, encouraging entrepreneurship, initiative and innovation as well as stronger training for businessmen, and decision makers – including women and young people in the business world. The range of initiatives to encourage entrepreneurship include: measures facilitating red tape and tax procedures, educational initiatives to value scientific curiosity, group work, communication capacity, and self-esteem.

C.   *The United States Experience*

79.   While Europe has been slow to fully embrace the concept of entrepreneurship, in countries like the US, entrepreneurship is a commonly accepted value. The curricula of universities and even lower levels of education involve training for entrepreneurship or 'business training'. The high-tech explosion has only magnified the US' emphasis on entrepreneurship. For example, Harvard College expressed concern recently over the number of start-up businesses that were being run out of

its undergraduate dormitory. The Massachusetts Institute of Technology (MIT) runs a famous contest every year 'the Business Plan Competition', which provides $50,000 US for the winner with the best business plan. The competition is one example of the general emphasis on learning about teamwork and the dynamics of starting a new business, which are important experiences for future entrepreneurs. In addition, such programmes like that of MIT, which are common in the US, require students to develop full business plans, create new products or services, and develop methods of obtaining financing.

VI. CREATING NEW MARKETS AND NEW JOBS

A. Introduction

80. The labour market is rapidly and continually evolving; however, the legal framework does not always accurately reflect the dynamism of socio-economic phenomena. A legal framework reflecting the reality of an industrial society does not seem to be adequate to govern the new phenomena. Norms written to accomplish the needs of a Fordistic system of production are not able to represent and satisfy the new organizational forms of work both in the so-called information and knowledge society as well as in the so-called third system (health and social system activities, household and non-commercial activities). The result is a legal crisis: widespread evasion of legislated norms. In other words existing laws lose their meaning and effectiveness. The potential of the new economy in terms of job creation opportunity is restricted by an outdated legal framework.

81. There are two important consequences of the outdated framework and the new economy. The first is the inability to exploit undeveloped employment potential in the new Information Society, and the second is the inability to capitalize on employment potential currently existing. The result is a high instance of unemployment, yet a shortage of labour able to perform tasks for a new economy, and simultaneously, we see growth in the informal economy. Job creation strategies should take on the task of developing new sources of jobs, for example in information technology (IT). Second, strategies should be aimed at increasing the number of jobs in existing markets, for instance regulating and encouraging markets that are currently growing in the informal sector (black market work). Both these initiatives require the creation of incentives to encourage new investment, subsidies, or the removal of existing barriers.

82. One of the greatest potentials for job creation lies in the field of IT. The information and knowledge society is in need of people who can work with new technology with adequate skills. The unemployed are mainly workers without appropriate skills to enter into the new economy.

83. In addition to creating new jobs in the field of technology, other employment sectors are growing as the result of sociological changes. The ageing of population in many countries and the movement away from extended families, as the result of migration, divorce, and other modern phenomena has created the need for a whole sector of household services (e.g., assistance for the elderly, house maintenance and cleaning, child care, home aid for people who are ill).

84. Lastly, there is a growing sector of black market work, which functions partly as the result of outdated regulations, which restricts the flexibility of the labour market. Black market work can take on many forms, usually in industries that are labour intensive and offer low profits, such as construction, agriculture, retail, catering and domestic services. The existence of black market work has negative consequences for both the suppliers of services and for the economies in which this work occurs. Further, black market work causes distortions of competition in the internal market and a loss of revenue to the State, reducing the ability of the State to provide services. Bringing this economy under regulation would offer greater protection to those black market workers, while enhancing competition in the market.

B.   Society of Knowledge and Communication

85. The EU Employment Strategy addresses the challenges posed by the new society in the information age. The new economy has the potential to indirectly assist in the accomplishment of other job creation goals. For example, the technology sector offers an opportunity to open the labour market to all. Technological advancements have the potential to include workers who may have been traditionally at a disadvantage in the industrial labour market. For example, with the ability to work remotely and with adaptable equipment, people located in rural or less prosperous regions and disabled people do not have to miss out on job opportunities.

86. The US is currently leading the pack in taking hold of the new economy. Although the US has no comprehensive job creation strategy, this sector of the economy has nonetheless begun to create job opportunities for highly skilled labour. The question remains, however, for whom is the US creating jobs and whether is this benefiting US citizens. As in Europe, and other countries of the world, there is a gap in the supply and demand of highly skilled labour. Every year, tens of thousands of skilled workers from a wide range of countries (e.g., India, Pakistan, China, Myanmar) enter the US to work in the IT field. The current debate is whether older American IT workers, who are more costly in terms of salary and training, are being excluded from the market. Surely, this debate is relevant in European countries, and employment strategies will have to pay attention to the impact of the new economy on older workers. The European Commission has raised this very question. As the European Commission has warned, these types of issues are challenges where the contribution of the social partners is essential.

87. Another area of concern is the 'brain-drain' on those countries who are supplying the world with IT workers. For example, India is in great need of highly skilled workers. Yet qualified workers, who have the opportunity to live in Europe, Canada, Australia or the US and earn a very good salary, are likely to leave. Ireland, South Africa, and Pakistan are also suffering a 'brain drain'. The new economy poses two risks for individual countries: (1) if it does not modernize, it may lose its most talented, highly skilled labour and continue to fall further behind; (2) alternatively, if countries modernize and ignore the input from social parties, there are huge risks of marginalizing diverse sectors of the population (e.g., older workers).

88. The overall objective of the EU employment strategy is that creating new jobs can only take place if jobseekers develop adequate skills to join the ranks of the information economy. It is estimated that in less than 10 years, half of all jobs will be in industries that are either major producers or intensive users of information technology products and services. The transformation of traditional skills is essential. Computer hardware, software, services and telecommunications is the fastest growing sector and provides new jobs at a rapid rate. Moreover, technological changes are also occurring in fields having nothing to do with technology. For example, one of the fastest growing information technology areas is business to business communication (ordering materials, arranging for delivery of raw materials, etc ...). The result is that the entire economy is affected by the new economy and a large sector of the working population will need adequate skills.

89. The European Commission has stated that reaping the possible benefits of the information economy requires developments in education, from providing access to computers, and the internet in all schools, to providing opportunities for advanced training after school, wide public access to the internet, flexible and clear regulation so that even small- and medium-sized business can take advantage of available technology.

90. According to the European Commission, the real challenge in closing the skill gap is re-training those workers who are already in the labour force. Many workers have low numeracy and literacy skills. Further, many have none or little training in 'informacy' (e.g. using a personal computer for word processing, etc ...). Further, much of existing training is organized for the young, not for those who have been working for 10, 20, or even 30 years and have lost their jobs.

91. Ireland has developed a programme to try to close the gap for older workers. It has launched an industry-driven programme called 'Fast Track to Information Technology' for approximately 3,500 long-term unemployed people who will receive technical and personal skills training and will be offered full-time employment in the IT-industry. Likewise, other European countries have launched initiatives for training for the benefit of older workers. Finland is raising the number of training places which will provide adult education, with special attention to female participation. Austria is developing IT training for the unemployed at the PES. Other European countries are developing training, but mostly geared at students and young people. For example, Germany has introduced seven new IT-professions, while Austria has launched new apprenticeship schemes.

C. *The Third System and the Household Services Sector*

92. Another idea to combat high unemployment, which has been promoted by the EU Employment Strategy, is that of developing a normalized 'Third System'. This term refers to a wide range of organizations, encompassing cooperative, mutuals,

associations, foundations, charities, voluntary, and not-for-profit organizations that are: (1) responsive to unmet needs not provided by the public or private sectors; (2) community oriented and based; (3) not for profit; (4) draw upon the 'gift economy' (e.g. volunteer work). Third System organizations can be defined as private, not-for-profit organizations working for a local community or for groups of people living in the community and to some extent controlled by the community itself. The Third System Organizations (TSOs) may in fact perform several roles: advocacy, wealth re-allocation (grant-making foundations) and the production of social services. Since the 1980s, TSOs throughout Europe have shifted their role to that of entrepreneurial producers of services of collective interest, with a certain degree of autonomy.

93. A good example of the potential for the Third System is the household services area (e.g. assistance to the elderly, child care, domestic cleaning, home maintenance). The legal framework created for the needs of the industrial society does not provide relevant norms for this sector. As a result, the household services sector remains basically without adequate regulation. This sector, which has great potential to contribute to new employment creation and local development in various ways, remains paralysed as a result of the lack of applicable regulations, which could both stimulate supply and demand. Estimates produced in different countries of the potential impact on job creation of regulating the household services industry are impressively high, for example it is estimated that in Germany, up to 166,000 jobs could be created in the provision of home help for the elderly. The estimate for the UK is 71,000 jobs. Thus, the Third System could play a pivotal role in meeting needs for those who receive services and meeting needs of jobseekers, while spurring local development.

94. Of all European countries, perhaps France has the most advanced system for developing the household services sector within the Third System. France has introduced the 'cheque domicile' for the purchase of home care services for children, handicapped and the elderly. This innovative approach assigns purchasing power to private citizens, making them clients and not users.

95. In the US, the household services sector has become very developed over the last 15 years. From 1986 to 1996 employment grew by 50 per cent in this sector, while employment generally grew at 19 per cent. The strong development in these services is partly the result of the fact that in the US, 61 per cent of mothers with children under six years of age work outside the home. This sector is largely characterized by non-profit organizations on a regional or national basis, including church and public facilities. Government programmes in the area of child care have sustained growth in this sector by providing subsidies to families for the costs of child care outside the home. For example, the Federal Child Care Tax Credit provides families with children an income tax credit. Further, the Head Start Programme supports child care facilities that serve low-income children as a priority, and Aid for Families with Dependent Children provides single parents with training and subsidies for the children to attend care centres outside the home. Government policy has therefore, created incentives for the growth of this industry, while allowing private non-profit organizations to thrive independent of government control. In this way, families who need services yet cannot afford them, with assistance from the government, can utilize private services outside the home.

D. Normalizing Black Market Work

96. The undeclared work across the EU involves four main groups: 'moonlighters' and multiple job holders, the inactive population (students, people taking early retirement, housewives, etc.); unemployed people; and third-country nationals illegally resident in the EU. The age and gender of undeclared workers depends largely on the sectors affected. In the Scandinavian countries, the Netherlands, Belgium and the UK, such activity seems to be the preserve of young, skilled males, whereas illegal immigrants were perceived to be a big problem in France, Germany, and Austria. In Southern Europe, undeclared workers seem to be young people, women working from home and illegal immigrants.

97. The growth of undeclared work is fostered by a number of factors: high levels of taxes and social security contributions; the inability of existing legislation to provide useful norms in the new economy and for new types of work; time-consuming bureaucratic procedures for registering certain jobs or gaining access to certain professions; the industrial structure (with a large number of SMEs in the industrial sector and the pattern of unionization of labour).

98. Although the extent of the underground economy as a percentage of gross domestic product (GDP) cannot be accurately assessed, there is evidence that the Scandinavian countries, Ireland, Austria, and The Netherlands have relatively low levels of such activity, around five per cent, while other countries, such as Italy and Greece were estimated to have an underground economy that accounted for around 20 per cent of the gross domestic product.

99. Normalizing undeclared work will require reducing the advantages of being in the undeclared economy, such as adapting inappropriate legislation to new forms of work, reducing obstacles and burdens to starting business and perhaps enforcing stronger sanctions for participation in undeclared work. Belgium for example is now making a stronger effort to enforce its laws against undeclared work with the hope that this enforcement will reduce this market.

VII. JOB CREATION POLICY AT THE LOCAL LEVEL AND
      THE ROLE OF SOCIAL PARTIES

A. Introduction

100. While job creation strategies at local level have traditionally been implemented in the United States, in Europe the awareness of the opportunities that exist at local level for developing employment is quite recent. Only in recent decades have most EU Member States developed an institutional and administrative de-centralization process in their employment policies, reflecting the importance which is now being placed on the job strategies rooted at local level. Based on the experience of a number of Member States, the EU Commission has indicated 17 fields with potential for employment in a local perspective: home help services, child care, new information and communication technologies, assistance to young people facing difficulties, better housing, security, local public transport services, the revitalization of urban public areas, local shops, tourism, audio-visual services, the cultural heritage, local cultural development, waste management, water services, protection and conservation of natural areas, and the control of pollution (Communication from the Commission on a European strategy for encouraging local development and employment initiatives, COM(95)273; see also the Communication from the Commission to the Council, the European Parliament, the Economic and Social Committee and the Committee of the Regions, *Acting Locally for Employment. A local dimension for the European Employment Strategy,* (COM(2000) 196 final).

B. In Search of Best Practices: The EU Experience

101. Much of the debate about the role of labour market institutions on the levels of unemployment has focused on trade unions and especially on the possible distortive effects of collective bargaining on matching on supply and demand of labour. These neo-liberal approaches, based on the idea that unions are one of the principal causes of labour market rigidities to restore full employment, have been progressively increasing at least in Europe. In these countries, characterized by a strong legislation aimed to protect the workers, the actions of governments alone do not seem sufficient to pursue an effective job creation strategy. In these countries the goal to create a new framework more friendly toward the will of enterprise to hire new people can be pursued only through the involvement of a social partner. In fact, social partners can play a decisive role across the whole of the labour market. Through joint negotiation, formal and informal practices, institutional and other forms of partnership, they can exercise a significant influence on the way the labour market is managed. Best practices can be found in every EU Country (see: for instance Territorial Employment Pacts: <http//www.inforegio.cec.eu.int/pacts/EN/ LIST/>).

102. Asturias (Spain) is undergoing a process of industrial re-conversion particularly in the coal mining and steel-making sectors. It has the highest regional unemployment level in Spain (17.92 per cent). The mining areas have been hardest hit. The job creation schemes that the regional and local authorities chose to adopt in 1998 seem to be working. One of the schemes is to set up an institutional cooperation through the development of associations 'Casas del Consorico' and an observatory. These will provide information, documentation, and analyses of the action themes in the Pact. The signatories of the Pact plan to finance through the creation of a fund designed to supplement aid to projects involving investments of less than 40 million pesetas. The social partners hope to set up a committee, the 'Mesas para el Pacto', which will coordinate the fight against unemployment. They plan on providing support for networks of business partnerships and creating regional mobile advisory teams, which help and supervise businesses. The local government hopes to develop industry through the integration of new technologies into industrial areas and undertaking regional industrial development.

103. Youth unemployment seems to be the target of the job creation schemes adopted in Molsheim-Shirmeck region of France. The signatories agree that by informing SMEs of employment aid for young people, developing sandwich courses in businesses with more than 50 employees and promoting apprenticeships in the crafts sector, the number of job vacancies in the area especially for young people will be increased. Job finding will be made easier for young people once new employment services and opportunities have been created. It is estimated that 250 new jobs will be created each year through the use of sandwich course contracts. The regional authorities hope to create jobs in the area by increasing access to these contracts and by creating an insertion solution for every long-term unemployed person. The job creation schemes that were adopted during the months of January and September 1998 are numerous. They are adjusting the supply of labour to the demand, improving employment guidance for young people, making teachers aware of the realities of business life (visits to businesses and three-day courses under the local Economics Education Committee) and making summer jobs available in the community's engineering departments. Others include simplifying administrative procedures and creating a resource centre intended to structure supply and demand for services. Funds will be provided in order to finance these programmes and to open a youth centre. A job-initiatives-counter will be set up at Schirmeck.

104. The Halle Vilvoorde region in Belgium has a job shortage. Very few jobs can be found in the primary and secondary sectors. The region suffered much when the Renault car plant closed down. The closure resulted in the loss of 3,100 jobs. The unemployment rate stands at 6.05 per cent. Most of the people unemployed in Halle Vilvoorde are long-term unemployed and over 40 years old. Almost a third of the unemployed in the area do not speak Flemish (the language of the region). The region is highly dependent on Brussels for employment. The Halle Vilvoorde local pact encourages training, counselling, and supervising unemployed people. Priority will be given to the higher risk groups of the unemployed. Job opportunities will be created for the unemployed by providing training for those workers who feel threatened by unemployment. They feel they might lose their job due to changing circumstances in their companies. Re-establishing former Renault employees into the labour market is one of the aims of the local government. Several job creation schemes have been adopted targeting such employees. These include offering job seekers the chance to expand their skills through temporary employment in companies (through internships, individual vocational training projects or subsidized labour jobseekers will be given the opportunity to find work), improving the match between training and company needs and organizing in-company training. In-company training will focus on adapting workers to changes in industry and organizing an awareness-raising campaign, which will publicize employment measures being implemented by various governments. Other job creation schemes include developing additional business sites in the area (one of the region's weaknesses), promoting child care facilities and the establishment of neighborhood services. Promoting child care and environmental projects has created jobs. Projects that allow the long-term unemployed to look after the children of employees while their parent's work. Protection of the environment as well as job creation is stressed when municipal greenery projects are promoted. These projects encourage employment by employing jobseekers to maintain public parks and shrubbery in the municipality.

105. Residents of Sonderjylland (Denmark) know all about hard times. With a high female unemployment rate, an unskilled workforce (employees with little to no qualifications), and ageing labour force' the region is extremely fragile. As a result, the area is sensitive to economic fluctuations. The local government is hopeful that the job creation schemes they chose to adopt in July of 1998 will correct the problems of the past. They feel that creating new jobs will eliminate some of the problems that they have had. The job creation schemes of the Sonderjylland target women who have had difficulties entering the labour market, young people with little to no experience and older workers who wish to remain in the labour market but on a part-time or more flexible basis. One of the schemes is to establish a secretariat that will act as a go-between between actors at the community level and those at the regional level. The secretariat will consist of two people who undergo specialized training. From this training they will become familiarized with the range of subsidies and measures which may be employed in the implementation of the pact. By coordinating the measures needed to fight unemployment and sponsoring cross-border projects (measures which respond to business needs), people who feel they are at risk of being marginalized and SMEs receive assistance. To create jobs in the area' regional authorities have taken a regional approach to employment.

106. In 1997, 19,528 people under the age of 24 were unemployed in Dublin (Ireland). These people account for 24.5 per cent of the total unemployed in the region. Unemployment in the area currently stands at 12.8 per cent compared to the national average of 11.8 per cent. Long-term unemployment as well as youth unemployment remains a problem. For instance, 52 per cent of the unemployed are classified as long-term unemployed. To Dublin residents it is not only important to reduce long-term unemployment in disadvantaged and excluded groups (disabled people and travellers) it is a necessity. Creating jobs means identifying a skills base needed to meet the demands of local businesses, providing training in information and communication technologies and implementing the programs designed to help tackle the issue of long-term unemployment. These programs are the Whole Time Jobs Initiative Program, the Core Skills Program and Organized Labour Streams. The local authorities hope to fight youth unemployment by implementing the Luxembourg guarantee to young people within six months of leaving full-time education and the development of linkages between schools and the business sector, local authorities and community organizations. The guarantee is to provide a training place for young people. The Train and Build Project is a project that aims to establish a company-community business offering between young people and businesses. This offers educational support to young people from disadvantaged communities and builds skills to the third level initiative. The social partners hope that by implementing the Social Economy Development programme which aims to research, facilitate and develop social economy projects the social economy will be helped. Some of the job creation schemes included in this pact are establishing networks and linkages both at the local and regional level, implementing the Economic Profile Project and setting up the Core Pact group. The Economic Profile Project will review and evaluate issues such as sustainable employment, job creation and raizing the skills base. The Core Pact group along with focus groups is designed to tackle long-term unemployment and youth unemployment with in-depth expertise.

107. The region Noord-Brabant located in the Netherlands is struggling. It is difficult to fill vacancies in the area due to long-term unemployment and lack of an adequately trained workforce. Lack of flexibility threatens business competitiveness.
High levels of inactivity exist, especially among older workers. The social partners of
Noord-Brabant agreed to the following job creation schemes when they adopted their
local job pact in February 1998. Exchanging information between the various governments on what works, setting up a series of sectoral employment projects which will
help fix staffing problems in companies and the qualitative mismatch between supply
and demand and implementing projects like RegioMet. RegioMet is a partnership of
metalworking companies, which targets long-term unemployed people in disadvantaged neighbourhoods. The La Poubelle project inserts the long-term unemployed.
Suitable candidates among the long-term unemployed are selected for a job. The candidates undergo a training course and once they are deemed to be qualified for a regular job the 'soon to be' employee will be given a subsidized position in the company.

108. Employees in Vienna (Austria) feel threatened by corporate downsizing.
Fighting long-term unemployment requires restructuring the local economy, raizing
qualification levels through active labour market policies and improving equal
opportunity between men and women. Some of the job creation schemes that have
been adopted are re-integrating the unemployed into the labour market, improving
the attractiveness of Vienna as an economic and business centre and implementing
projects like the Training Account Programme. This program will give grants to
finance individual training courses. The WiedereingteigerInnen Programme supports
re-orientation, training, job searches' and new business start-ups for women and men
returning to the labour market after time-off. The Flexwork project specializes in
finding contractual work in companies for older and long-term unemployed people.
The Home Service project provides employment for long-term unemployed women.
The women receive an hourly wage plus social security benefits in exchange
for domestic services carried out in private homes. The WAFF (Weiner
ArbeitnehmerInnen Fyrderingsfords) acts as a promoter of active labour market
policies and human resources. The Mayor of Vienna acts as president of WAFF,
whereas representatives from the district, the political parties and the social partners
sit on the advisory committee. The WAFF budget is derived from City Council and
private sector funds. Every WAFF project receives co-financing from the European
Social Fund.

109. People are leaving Ita Lappi (Finland) in search of work. The region is losing their best-trained young people. In order to get people to stay, action plans and
job creation schemes promoting tourism and economic growth have been adopted.
Preventing migration, developing telework, providing support for sub-contracting
and setting up seasonal jobs in the field of forestry are just some of the job creation
schemes that have been implemented. Others include developing ecotourism and
modernizing the areas' image in order to attract tourists and investors.

110. The economy in Stromstad (Sweden) is declining. The unemployment rate
stands at 13.9 per cent. Entrepreneurs in the area realize that in order for jobs to be
created there is a need for economic cooperation. The success that the local government has been having with their job creation schemes relates to the fact that their

schemes pertain to all sectors of the economy (fishing, agriculture, and commerce) and they focus on improving local skills. Appointing a project manager is one of the job creation schemes. The project manager will be responsible for project management, the distribution of data, and evaluation of individual projects and the quantification of NTERREG funds for interregional cooperation. Other job creation schemes include developing and enlarging the fishing sector, establishing computer communication centers in rural areas, promoting tourist activity in the region, and increasing access to the Norwegian market.

111. Job creation schemes adopted in the UK include those in Haringey, North London (England), and those at Easterhouse and Coatbridge. One of the schemes is to set up a steering group, which makes decisions regarding policy development and financial control. The Local Employment Observatory develops innovative research methods in order to improve understanding of the local labour market. The local government hopes to create jobs by improving the employability of people. Employability means an employee who is flexible and mobile. Employers want employees who are willing to take on new tasks.

112. In an attempt to fight unemployment and social exclusion the regional and local authorities of Florina and Kozani (Greece) have come up with job creation schemes and start-up plans. To the residents in these regions job creation means keeping the population of the area active, providing women access to the labour market and enhancing the efficiency of existing development projects and programs for the creation of sustainable employment. In Florina, women especially are affected by increasing unemployment rates. In Kozani, unemployment stands at 17 per cent, which is the highest in Greece. The economic crisis that hit industry in the area had a direct effect on the mass lay-off of personnel. The local government hopes to developing the primary sector by enhancing agricultural development through the processing of farm products, giving aid to private and cooperative units which process farm products in the area and promoting local farm products. One of the job creation schemes that the regional authorities of Florina have come up with is to establish an employment observatory. The aim of the observatory will be to speed up the adjustment process of the workforce and entrepreneurs to industrial changes and to create networks at the national and transnational level. This will improve communication channels through the transfer of experience, know-how and information, develop an electronic advertizement service and make the management of human resources within the local labour market possible.

113. Creating a Concertation Commission which approves and monitors projects is just one of the many job creation schemes that the Milan Municipal administration and the social parties (except for the CGIL) agreed to and adopted in February 2000. The Concertation Commission will be a tripartite body made up of representatives from the Milan Municipality, the Province and signatory associations. The President of the Commission will be the Milan Municipality and the signatories will nominate the two Vice-Presidents, one from the employer's side and the other from the trade union side. The Commission will meet at least six times a year. When the Commission is in session it will meet with representatives from the city associations that deal with the social economy, physical-mental handicaps, and immigration. The Milano Lavoro One-stop shop is a job creation scheme aimed at helping the match between supply and demand of labour. It will be set up on the basis of a convention between the Municipality and the Province of Milan. The One-stop shop is aimed at helping businesses hire workers. It gives the authorization needed for dependent work and self-employment. The terms for hiring under a fixed-term contract can be found in the Milano Lavoro One-stop shop. A business can hire under a fixed-term contract when hiring the first employee. This type of hiring is allowed when employers have up to five employees and the parties agree on the importance of placing special attention on the use of contracts or quasi-subordinated work for people over 40 who have been excluded from the labour market. A person with whom a previously stipulated contract had been stipulated is another requirement for hiring under contracts of dependent work. According to the procedures established by the Concertation Committee, public or private enterprises will be able to apply for self-financing, co-financing or financing on behalf of a third party. One-stop shop funds originate from Municipal, Provincial, Regional, and EU sources. The financial measures taken by these sources are hand outs in the form of financial aid or normative aid. The government in situations they deem necessary hands out financial aid. Normative aid is more complex in that there are certain rules governing state aid. Once the Concertation Committee has chosen which enterprise would be most beneficial to finance they will coordinate-training courses. These courses should reflect the needs expressed by the demand of labour. The training of Milano Lavoro will consist of a small staff. Through the use of training and guidance courses and work programs, the Milano Lavoro will be able to carry out activities. The aim is to provide the cooperation needed to create employment insertion methods. The training programs that the Concertation Committee chooses to institute will operate in partnership with public and private institutions in training suppliers and in finding suitable training offers.

114. Different from western Europe and other areas of the world, such as Central and Eastern Europe, the US has a tradition of leaving the task of improving the employment situation to private enterprise. However, since the 1970s, local governments have developed local business incentives such as tax forgiveness, tax increment finance authorities, industrial development bonds, and other incentives. Although this may be locally driven action, it is not usually in concertation with social parties. The growth of public-private partnerships has also grown somewhat in recent years to create local educational and training opportunities. This movement however, has largely been based on employers' needs for highly skilled labour, and the federal Government has no specific widespread policy to pursue these local efforts.

VIII. INVESTING IN JOBS – THE LOGIC OF STATE AID

115. Most governments have, over the course of time, developed a wide range of financial incentives to support employment and job creation strategies at national and/or local level in addition to the reorganization of the labour market, the active labour market policies and the different incentives of a normative nature aimed at the flexibilization/modernization of the employment contract. Tax and financial measures play an increasing role in encouraging/discouraging employers to hire new workers or some groups of workers. The same type of measures may also give an incentive to the enterprizes to invest in vocational training, to locate an undertaking in a depressed or underdeveloped area of the country, to start new business in deprived urban areas, etc.

116. Seemingly, their use has affected the distribution of existing job vacancies between the different groups of workers (young people, old people, women, disabled people, immigrants, long-term unemployed, etc.), rather than actually creating additional jobs with respect to those spontaneously produced by the economic system itself. Further, it has been rightly pointed out by different scholars that, in the drive towards a policy supporting employment, a misguided shortcut would be to widen the incentives indefinitely. In such a case, the incentive is no longer capable of altering the system of entrepreneurial convenience: the incentive for all is tantamount to an incentive for no one. In effect, most of the employment incentives represents one of the most evident examples of how the economic incentives of employment are frequently indirect assistance for the entrepreneurial system, offering no significant correspondence with the increase in employment levels.

117. The case of incentives favouring work/training contracts in Italy is meaningful in this regard. Introduced by Act no. 863/1984, work/training contracts allow companies to take on young people up to the age of 32 under a fixed-term contract for a maximum duration of 24 months. This contractual arrangement, the subject of multiple interventions of reform on the part of the legislator, is supported through reductions in wage levels set by industry-wide agreements and fiscal and social contributions incentives. The European Commission has recently intervened on the matter of the compatibility of this incentive mechanism for employment with the Community regulation on competition matters. With the decision of 11 May 1999, the Commission confirmed the presence of social benefits in the work/training contracts which are determined and adjusted according to both the geographical area in which it is used, and the type of company involved, whereby a constant jurisprudence of EU Court of Justice denies the legitimacy of incentive measures which are not generalized. Inasmuch as such benefits (recognized by the Italian legislator to such a contractual arrangement) have been found to be incompatible with the discipline on State aids to companies, the Commission, on behalf of the beneficiaries, ordered the Italian Government to recover the corresponding assistance without creating additional employment. In accordance with the discipline on employment aids, the application of social benefits has, in fact, been held admissible on the condition that they are directed: (a) to the net creation of relatively stable employment for unemployed workers or those who have lost a previous job; (b) to the hiring of young people under the age of 25 or 29 if they have a University degree; (c) to create additional jobs in the case of benefits granted following the transformation of work/training contracts of an indefinite duration.

118. The Commission's decision, apart from confirming how frequently State aids for employment do not represent a measure supporting employment levels but rather an occult support for companies, indicates how in this matter, too, the room for manoeuvring left to the national legislator is somewhat limited. The EU Treaty, in giving rise to a regime understood to ensure that the competition in the common market is not distorted by the behaviour of companies and public actors, has actually eroded significant powers of the Member States in pursuing policies aimed at supporting the productive and employment systems. In this perspective, further limits which have affected, in no small way, the Italian Government's employment policies are also those relating to monetary policy and market regulation.

119. The principle of transparency of social costs hampers, for instance, public support for unproductive companies with the sole aim of maintaining employment levels, which has been the dominant model of employment policies, above all in the South and in the depressed area of the Europe. Of equal hindrance (or at least greatly limiting) is the adoption of policies concerning the emersion of undeclared work, such as the so-called contracts of emersion of black work experimented in Italy in that they bring with them advantages for the company and territory putting undeclared workers on a equal footing with new hirings. The Community regime of State aids, therefore, subordinates employment policies to a restricted choice of incentives tools, which must not lead to a differential advantage in favour of certain categories of companies. The EU Treaty, in fact, considers that, without rigorous control and strict limits, employment aid can have negative macro-economic effects which cancel out its immediate effect on unemployment levels and job creation strategies. If the financial measures supporting employment are used to protect firms exposed to intra-community competition, they could have the effect to delaying adjustments needed to ensure the competitiveness of the enterprises in the global competition. Besides, this kind of aid, if granted in an uncontrolled way, will shift unemployment from rich regions to poor ones without helping to resolve the employment problems distorting the competition to an extent contrary to the common interest. This is the reason why Article 92(1) of EU Treaty (Article 87 of the consolidated draft) stipulates that' any aid granted by a Member State or through State resources in any form whatsoever which distorts or threatens to distort competition by favouring certain undertakings or the production of certain good shall, in so far affects trade between Member States, be incompatible with the common market.

120. A number of job creation measures are out the scope of Article 87 of EU Treaty. This is the case of aid to individuals that does not favour certain undertaking or the production of certain goods. For instance: aid to improve the personal situation of the worker in the labour market or to help him/her to find a job; aid to supplement the income of certain workers; aid to foster the mobility of the workers; aid creation of self-employment activities etc. This is also the case of aid that does not have an effect on the trade between Member States like neighbourhood care services and other local employment initiatives. The Commission considers that *de minimis* aid, which encompasses most forms of aid promoting self-employment and local employment initiative does not effect on trade between Member States.

121. With regard to the financial measures within the scope of Article 92(1), these can be considered compatible with EU Treaty only in relation to the creation of employment for workers who never have had a job or who have lost their previous job. The Commission will be favourably disposed towards aid to promote job sharing and work sharing, which allows that the overall amount of work available to be distributed among a larger number of jobs with shorter working hours, aid to create job in SMEs and in region eligible for regional aid and aid to encourage firms to recruit certain disadvantaged groups of workers experiencing particular difficulties entering or re-entering in the labour market. In this latter case, there is no need for net job creation, provided that the job falls vacant following voluntary departure and not redundancy. In the other cases the EU Commission requires that financial aid will ensure that the job created is a stable one. In any case, the aid should be temporary. The amount of aid per worker should be justified and it should not be higher than required to create or maintain jobs. Finally, it should not represent too high a proportion of the firm's total production cost.

IX. CONCLUSIONS

122. In many countries there is a shift in importance from measures on the demand-side to those on the side of supply. One might add, in this regard, that the initiative of regulation (either de- or re-regulation) seems to be more and more on the supply side. Unquestionably, an important role is played in this context by the employment services, be they public or private. Increasingly, Governments no longer invest financial resources in public-spending projects, but try instead to make public employment services more pro-active and efficient. 'Employability' seems to be really a dominant perspective, although interpreted in various ways, in all domestic systems.

123. The second notion which has been investigated here is 'adaptability'. This word has been also translated into the term 'flexurity', meaning the need to reconcile flexibility and security. Labour law has not (not yet, at least) abandoned its original function of protecting people at work. The emphasis on training policies, and particularly on life-long learning, cannot simply be considered as a way of progressively empowering employees at the expense of job security. In this context regularization of undeclared work is an additional theme of action which implies a re-thinking of the role of labour law.

124. 'Promoting a labour market open to all', to put it in EU employment strategy terms, is an equally vital aspect. It involves the well-known theme of equal opportunities, paying special attention to the issue of the gender gap in employment. Not surprisingly in North America and in Japan, a right to equal (or, at least, comparable) treatment between typical and atypical employees cannot be affirmed – or certainly not to the extent which is accepted within the European Union. This is, in actual fact, an area where the combination of the 'protective' and 'promotional' function of labour law should be explored further. The key-issue seems to be the position of those we might term 'non-competitive jobseekers', meaning those who would not be employed unless their cost of labour were significantly reduced in comparison with other applicants who enjoy a stronger position in the labour market. Labour law should not continue to protect everybody in the same way. This, at the end of the day, would only penalize those in need of more protection. The real issue is what is the price to be paid for this inevitable project of modernization.

125. The question is not so much *whether* but *how* the modernization (in terms of re-regulation) of labour law could be better achieved. None should claim in this regard that a 'coordinated corporatist strategy' might well be considered an appropriate way of accelerating Government-sponsored (or even Government-run strategies) in employment promotion. Evidently, not only in Europe (and, more specifically, in the European Union) have the social parties contributed to speeding up and facilitating the necessary reforms of employment legislation. Collective bargaining should increasingly perform a job creation function.

126. Some conclusions can be tentatively drawn on the basis of this study. There is substantial agreement on the need to revise the legal/contractual framework, on which labour law is presently based, in all the countries, mainly with reference to Continental Europe. Rules which could fit for the manufacturing production process cannot be entirely kept after having already entered into the era of the knowledge-based society.

127. Labour law and the entire social model have to be modernized, at least in European Union countries. A complete rethink of the organization of work in the context of the information society is an absolute priority. This does not mean simply de-regulating, which would only serve to undercut terms and conditions of employment to the detriment of employees. Instead, this approach implies a new balance between security (progressively more in terms of employment rather that of jobs) and flexibility – also technically conceived of as a way of allowing management and labour to negotiate in order to deviate from legislative provisions, taking into account more closely specific situations of single enterprises and/or local labour markets.

128. Modernizing labour law obviously means different things in various contexts. In Europe labour law could cooperate to launch a strategy of employment creation making permanent/open-ended employment contracts more attractive to employers. In some national contexts, hyper-protective, anti-dismissal legislation has induced remarkably precarious hiring arrangements. Human resources should be regarded as the main capital of the European economy. The real protection lies in training, possibly an obligation of management to provide employees with continuous education for the duration of their working life.

129. There is a tendency not simply towards de-unionization, but also towards pressures leading to the 'de-laborization' of employment relations. Commercial-style contractual arrangements are on the rise and in the service sector (a sort of laboratory to predict the future of the e-economy), 'economically dependent workers' (i.e. quasi-subordinate, semi-self-employed people) frequently exceed the number of those who are employed in the traditional sense. The social partners should then define appropriate rules for this new workforce to combine fairness of treatment with business efficiency. The law-maker should not be in any hurry to intervene in this subject matter.

130. 'Protection' and 'promotion' are not terms to be conceived of alternatively or in opposition. Much depends on what we mean by 'protection'. If (and when) labour law focuses not simply on employment relationship but also (and mainly) on career development, the modernization effort will be greatly facilitated. Is guaranteeing every employee a minimum of ten days or so of training on a yearly basis, a way of protecting him/her? Without doubt, but at the same time it is also a way of promoting his/her position in the labour market.

131. In the future, labour law should not so much contribute to creating new jobs, but rather to creating an institutional environment which is more favourable to employees in the era of the new economy. Work organization is changing profoundly and at a speed unknown in the past. Labour law has a unique opportunity to regulate the new economic context. Its survival depends on how quickly it will be able to take on new challenges – it is really a question of adapting or dying.

SELECT BIBLIOGRAPHY

Addison J.T., 'The US Employment Miracle in Comparative Perspective', in *Comparative Labor Law & Policy Journal*, Vol. 19, 1998, No. 2, 283 seq.

Biagi M. (ed.), *Job Creation and Labour Law. From Protection towards Pro-action*, Kluwer, 2000.

Biagi M., 'The Impact of European Employment Strategy on the Role of Labour Law and Industrial Relations', in *The International Journal of Comparative Labour Law and Industrial Relations*, 2000, 155 et seq.

Biagi M., 'The Implementation of the Amsterdam Treaty with Regard to Employment: Coordination or Convergence?', in *The International Journal of Comparative Labour Law and Industrial Relations,* 1998, 325 et seq.

Blanpain R. (ed.), *Deregulation and Labour Law. In Search of a Labour Concept for the 21st Century*, in *Bulletin of Comparative Labour Relations*, Kluwer, 2000, No. 37.

Blanpain R., 'The World of Work and Industrial Relations in Developed Market Economies of the XXIst Century. The Age of the Creative Portfolio Worker', in Blanpain R. and Biagi M., *Non-Standard Work and Industrial Relations*, in *Bulletin of Comparative Labour Relations*, 1999, No. 35.

Campbell M., *The Third System Employment and Local Development*, Policy Research Institute Leeds Metropolitan University Bronte Hall, UK, August 1999.

Choater R., 'The Job Creation Barrier', in *Comparative Labor Law & Policy Journal*, Vol. 19, 1998, No. 2, 280 et seq.

Craver C.B., 'Promotion and Regulation of Job Opportunities in the United States', in *Promotion and Regulation of Job Creation Opportunities*, XIV World Congress of Labour Law and Social Security, Seoul, Korea, September 1994.

Communication from the Commission to the Council, the European Parliament, The Economic and Social Committee and the Committee of the Regions, *Acting Locally for Employment: A Local Dimension for the European Employment Strategy*, COM(2000) 196 final.

Crouch C., 'Labor Market Regulations, Social Policy and Job Creation', in Gual J. (ed.), *Job Creation: the Role of Labor Market Institutions*, Elgar, Cheltenham, 130 et seq.

European Commission, *Green Paper Living and Working in the Information Society: People First*, COM(96) 389.

Foden D., 'The Role of the Social Partners in the European Employment Strategy', in *Transfer* 1999, No. 4, 5 et seq.

Foden D. and Magnusson L. (ed.), *Entrepreneurship in the European employment strategy*, Brussels, ETUI, 1999.

Lefresne F., 'Employability at the Heart of the European Employment Strategy', in *Transfer* 1999, No. 4, 460 et seq.

Marsden D., *Management Practices and Unemployment*, The OECD Jobs Study Working Paper, No. 2, OECD, Paris, 1995.

Marsden D., *The Impact of Industrial Relations Practices on Employment and Unemployment*, The OECD Jobs Study Working Paper, No. 3, OECD, Paris, 1995.

Mazumdar D., *Constraints to Achieving Full Employment in Asia*, ILO, Employment and Training Papers, No. 51/1999.

Meulders D. and Plasman R., 'The Third Pillar: Adaptability', in *Transfer* 1999, No. 4, 481 et seq.

Mosley, Hugh, *The Role of the Social Partners in the Design and Implementation of Active Measures*, ILO, Employment and Training Papers, No. 27/1998.

OECD, *Implementing the OECD Job Strategy: assessing Performance and Policy*, OECD, Paris, 1999.

OECD, *Implementing the OECD Jobs Strategy: Lessons from Member Countries*, OECD, Paris, 1997.

Renshaw G., *Achieving Full Employment in Transition Economies*, ILO, Employment Paper, No. 7/2000.

Tronti L., 'Benchmarking Employment Performance and Labour Market Policies: The Result of the Research Project', in *Transfer* 1999, No. 4, 542 et seq.

Chapter 14. Subordinate Employees or Self-employed Workers?

C. Engels

I. INTRODUCTION

1. The distinction between self-employed and subordinate workers has raised difficult questions for many decades both in civil law and common law jurisdictions. Neither legal system has developed a test to answer the question as to which worker is independent and which one is a subordinate employee. It is a remarkable phenomenon that one of the cornerstones of labour law has remained largely undefined,[1] leaving judges a wide latitude in deciding individual cases.

2. From the point of view of terminology it has to be stressed that the concept of worker is used in this chapter to refer to any person performing services for another person or entity. Whether these services are performed in a relationship of subordination or not is irrelevant for the 'worker' concept. Those workers who are performing their services is a subordinate relationship, will be further referred to as employees, while the others will be referred to as self-employed workers.

3. This chapter looks into the different ways legal systems try to make the distinction between the various kinds of performers of services and at the consequences of falling on one side of the dividing line, or the other. The question will equally be raised whether this *summa divisio* still makes sense in the present day and whether the addition of a third category of workers, next to the subordinate employees and the self-employed workers would be an acceptable and useful way of coping with the increasing difficulties of distinguishing between both kinds of workers.

II. THE IMPORTANCE OF THE DISTINCTION

4. It is clear that over the years the scope of labor law and particularly social security law has widened beyond its original scope. Quite often the social security laws are applied not only to subordinate employees, but to a host of work relationships in

---

1. *See* B. Brooks and C. Engels, 'General Overview', in Employed or Self-employed', B. Brooks and C. Engels (guest eds), *Bull. Comp. Lab. Rel.*, Vol. 24, 1992, p. 2, hereinafter referred to as 'Employed or Self-Employed'.

which no contract of employment exists, but where those who deliver the services are in a very similar relationship to a contract of employment. Thus, the concept of a subordinate employee is still very central to the whole debate on the applicability of labor and employment laws and social security laws.

5. In most legal systems, the status of subordinate employee, and thus the existence of a contract of employment brings into play, the protective provisions of *labor law*. Those who work on an independent contractor basis, usually are not covered by protective labor law provisions. The prototype of the self-employed worker (e.g. the baker or butcher operating their own store, with or without help of others) is not protected by any legislation similar to the many and often quite detailed provisions of labor law. In some legal systems, rules have been developed by which self-employed workers are to a certain extent protected against either themselves or other contract parties. One can think here of regulations concerning the obligation of shop owners to close their shops on Sundays or any other day of the week and rules establishing maximum opening hours. While such rules may have originated at least partly from concerns in respect of fair competition, they have as a side effect that they curtail the maximum number of working hours of the self-employed workers concerned.

6. Labor law foresees, at least in most legal systems, some forms of security of employment, either directly through legislative action, or indirectly through collective bargaining. While the substance of the protection that is granted may differ greatly, protection against untimely termination of contracts of employment or unjustified termination is part of most, if not all legal systems. Even in those systems in which the rule of at will employment still reigns, the termination of employment contracts is subject to some form of scrutiny, be it from the legal provisions dealing with prohibitions on discrimination on certain grounds, such as race, religion, nationality, sex, age, and disability.[2]

7. Labour law does not only establish rules dealing with individual terminations, it equally regulates collective dismissals, plant closures and transfers of businesses. In this respect reference has to be made to provisions dealing with information and consultation of employees and/or their representatives in case the company for which the employees are working goes through some form of restructuring that has or potentially could have an important impact on the employees and their livelihood. In Europe this area of the law has been heavily inspired by European directives and their implementation into national law. A number of EU directives immediately come to mind:

1. the collective dismissals directive;[3]
2. the transfer of businesses directive;[4]

---

2. *See* C. Summers, 'Similarities and differences between labour contracts and civil and commercial contracts, General report', in General Reports of the XVI World Congress of Labour Law & Social Security (Jerusalem, Israel, 3–7 September 2000, 58, hereinafter referred to as 'Similarities and differences').
3. Council Directive 98/59/EC, 20 July 1998, on the approximation of the laws of the Member States relating to collective redundancies, OJ 12 July 1998, no. L 225, 16.
4. Council Directive 77/187/EEC, 14 February 1977, on the approximation of the laws of the member States relating to the safeguarding of employees' rights in the event of transfers of undertakings,

3.   the European works council directive;[5] and
4.   the insolvency directive.[6]

All these directives foresee some employee protection through information and consultation of the employees or their representatives, or some financial security in respect of major company restructuring. Similar rules do not exist with respect to self-employed independent contractors.

8.   Labor law provisions quite often reduce the employees' liability for mistakes and errors committed in the execution of their contract of employment. While an independent contractor may be liable towards its contract party for any mistake made, however slight, employees are normally not held liable for minor mistakes. Belgian law for example determines that the employee will only be liable in case of fraud, gross mistakes, or repetitive minor mistakes. While this may not be important for all professions, this could be a major issue for a medical doctor working in a hospital. If he/she is an employee, the liability of the doctor is more restricted than when working as a self-employed. However, if he/she is an employee, the hospital will be co-liable as the employer, towards the patients of the doctor.

9.   Major differences often exist in the applicable *social security systems*, both with respect to the coverage granted to the self-employed and with respect to the contributions to be paid by both parties to the employment relationship. The self-employed worker is not covered against the risk of unemployment, the pensions obtained through government systems are normally much lower, etc. The self-employed is supposed to look after him/herself. Not surprisingly, at the contribution side, the social security systems for employees are much more costly than those for the self-employed. A prime example here is the Belgian system of social security for subordinate workers. The contributions are extremely high and consist of a combination of employer and employee contributions. For higher level incomes, the costs become prohibitive, especially if one start comparing the level of these contributions to the level of contributions paid by a similarly situated self-employed worker.

10.   It is not only for the worker that the change in status (from subordinate employee to self-employed service provider) will influence the social security contributions to be paid. Also for the employer some fundamental changes in the applicable contribution rates will take effect. It is well known that Belgian social security

---

(*Contd.*)

businesses or parts of businesses, OJ 5 March 1977, no. L 61, 26, as amended by Directive 98//50/EC, 29 June 1998, OJ 17 July 1998, no. L 201, 88.
5.   Council Directive 94/45/EC, 22 September 1994, on the establishment of a European Works Council or a procedure in Community-scale undertakings and Community-scale groups of undertakings for the purposes of informing and consulting employees, OJ 30 September 1994, no. L 254, 64 and Council Directive 97/74/EC, 15 December 1997 extending, to the United Kingdom of Great Britain and Northern Ireland, Directive 94/45/EC on the establishment of a European Works Council or a procedure in Community-scale undertakings and Community-scale groups of undertakings for the purposes of informing and consulting employees, OJ 16 January 1998, no. L 10, 22.
6.   Council Directive 80/987/EEC, 20 October 1980, on the approximation of the laws of the Member States relating to the protection of employees in the event of insolvency of their employer, OJ 28 October 1980, no. L 283, as amended by Directive 87/164, 2 March 1987, OJ 11 March 1987, no. L 66, 11.

contributions to be paid on subordinate employment run extremely high. The employer social security contribution rate is around 35 per cent of the employee's gross wages and could run up to 50 per cent of the gross wages for blue-collar workers.[7] The employee him/herself contributes at the rate of 13.07 per cent of the employee's gross salary, prior to performing any tax deductions. This percentage applies regardless of the level of salary of the employee concerned, this is applicable to the simple low level white-collar worker and the highest level manager. This means that there is no distinction made on the basis of the income level, as far as the percentage of the contributions concerned. The same percentages apply across the board, without any ceiling being foreseen above which no contributions would be due.

11. With regard to the self-employed workers it should be stressed that the contract party (ex-employer) does not pay any contributions whatsoever. Furthermore, the social security system for the self-employed foresees an income ceiling above which no contributions are due on the income surpassing the ceiling. The latter is certainly the most noticeable distinction as far as the level of contributions is concerned. Also the applicable rates are different for self-employed and subordinate workers. Up to around US$8,979[8] the contributions to be paid by the self-employed run at 16.70 per cent; a second tier of income between US$8,979 and US$63,708 requires a contribution of 12.27 per cent. On the income that surpasses the ceiling of US$63,708 no contributions are due at all.

The rates of contributions to be paid by the self-employed are certainly not advantageous to the self-employed who is earning a low income. For the lowest income tier the contribution rates for the self-employed are significantly higher, namely 16.70 per cent as compared to the 13.07 per cent the employee would pay. For the middle tier of income the self-employed pays less than what he/she would have paid as an employee with the same level of income. However, the global contributions the self-employed pays for an income that does not surpass the second level ceiling is still less advantageous. The system for the self-employed has, however, a built in ceiling above which no contributions have to be paid. For the income above US$63,708 the self-employed does not pay any contributions at all. The higher the income of the self-employed the more advantageous the applicable social security system is compared to that of the subordinate employees. It should thus not come as a surprise that workers with high income levels may seek an independent status rather than the protective environment of subordinate employees.

12. Also from a *tax law* point of view most often different systems apply to self-employed and subordinate workers. The distinction that is made in labour law between those performing on a self-employed basis and subordinate workers thus has repercussions far beyond the mere application or inapplicability of labour law provisions.

13. Subordinate workers performing in furtherance of a contract of employment are subject to provisions that are mandatory to a much larger extent than would be

---

7. Some slight variations apply depending on the number of employees employed by the company.
8. Rate applied: 1 US$ = 44 Belgian Francs (BEF).

the case in commercial law. This means that the protective provisions cannot be set aside by the parties (employer and employees), but have to be respected even in case both parties would like to deviate from them. As Professor Clyde Summers wrote :

'In broad terms, the most significant difference between individual employment contracts and civil or commercial contracts is the scope of the freedom of contract. General contract law, at least in market economies, starts from the principle premise of freedom of contract; the parties should be free to agree to any terms which they find mutually acceptable. ... Freedom of contract is of course not an absolute freedom; it may be limited by general principles of public policy, good faith, unconscionability and various statutory limitations. This is true for all contracts, but the limitation of freedom of contract in employment contracts is of quite a different order.'[9]

14. First of all there are limitations on whom the employer can contract with. One can think here of rules with respect to minors, prohibitions on discrimination, requirements to hire certain numbers of handicapped, etc. Furthermore, content wise there are many issues that are regulated in a mandatory fashion, as far as employment contracts are concerned. Deviations are quite often only allowed when they are to the benefit of the employee, not to his or her detriment. How and when the contract can be terminated is largely regulated by laws and regulations dealing with security of employment. And most of all, as Professor Summers points out, there is the fact that employment contracts are subject to rules not set by government, legislators, or courts, but to rules that are part of collective bargaining agreements that are bargained between private parties.[10]

III. THE TESTS DEVELOPED TO MAKE THE DISTINCTION BETWEEN EMPLOYEES AND SELF-EMPLOYED

A. *The Absence of a Full Definition*

15. No single legal system seems to have been able to clearly define the concept of employee, beyond a very broad definition. An employee is generally described as a worker who performs services in exchange for remuneration and in a relationship of subordination towards his/her contract party. Such a worker is then performing services in furtherance of an employment contract or an employment relationship with an employer.

16. In the absence of a sufficiently clear legislative definition of the employee concept, case-law was forced to develop tests in order to be able to distinguish between the self-employed worker and the employee. It is remarkable to notice that very similar developments took place in common law and civil law jurisdictions. While in its extreme form a civil law legal systems relies on its legislature to make

---

9. *See* C. Summers, Similarities and differences, 50 et seq.
10. *See* C. Summers, Similarities and differences, 51.

the law and on the courts to apply it, in this area of the law there is not much of a distinction between the civil and common law jurisdictions. Writes Professor Paul L. Davies:

> '...despite generalised differences between common law and civil law systems about the roles assigned to it, respectively, judges and legislation as sources of the law, the importance of judicial case-by-case determination of employee/self-employed distinction is emphasised in many civil law countries.'[11]

17. Given the absence (or impossibility) of a full definition of the employee concept and the difficulty certain workers faced in proving their subordinate status under the law, legislators quite often introduced legal presumptions. For example, commercial sales representative are presumed to be working in a subordinate relationship to their principal (the employer) in Belgian law. The Belgian presumption is rebuttable. This means that when confronted with a claim of the sales representative, based upon his/her subordinate status, the counterpart can always prove that the sales representative is not a subordinate employee but an independently operating sales agent. Given the often exiting difficulty in proving the subordinate status for employees often performing away from the company premises, the legislator considered it appropriate to shift the burden of proof. Self-evidently the legislator can also establish irebuttable presumptions.

B. The Freedom of Choice

18. Unless a specific legal act determines in a mandatory fashion that a given job or task needs to be performed either as an employee or as a self-employed worker, the parties can decide this issue. It is up to the parties to the contract to decide whether they want the job to be done by a subordinate employee or by a self-employed independent worker. This being said, it does not mean that the parties are granted the ability to decide whether a given work relationship is an employment contract or not. The parties can never pass the ultimate judgement on the nature of the contract that they concluded. The label that the parties have stuck on the contract is thus not determinative. This does not mean that the parties cannot structure their collaboration in a given way, as long as they take all the consequences attached to their choice. This means that once the parties have opted for a collaboration on an independent basis, they should leave each other the required degree of freedom and independence, both from a legal and from a practical perspective, that corresponds with the chosen independent structure. Such a choice, when followed up with a practical implementation that fully corresponds with the choice, is respected by the law unless the law would irebuttably determine the nature of a given work relationship.

19. Given the mandatory nature of many laws and regulations governing the employment relationships, it does not come as a surprise that the labelling effort

---

11. *See* P.L. Davies, 'Wage employment and self-employment – a common law view', in Reports to the 6th European Congress for Labour Law and Social Security, Warsaw, Poland, 13–17 September 1999, 166. *See also* B. Brooks and C. Engels, in Employed or Self-Employed, p. 1.

undertaken by the parties, either directly (such as calling the contract a contract for the independent delivery of services) or indirectly by using references to the tax status of a self-employed worker, or the voluntary submission to the social security status of self-employed workers, will as such not bind a court of law.

20. In theory, any kind of job can be performed either as an employee or as a self-employed worker. In order to make a difference, two out of three of the constituent elements of an employment relationship will equally be present in a contract for services (i.e. performance and remuneration), contract with a self-employed worker. The main difference lays in the fact that the employee performs his/her services in a relationship of subordination towards the employer.

21. For most kind of jobs, the law will not specify whether they have to be performed either as an employee or as a self-employed. Exceptions do exist, however. In *Belgian* law for example, those performing as company directors are by law presumed to be doing this as self-employed, independently operating workers. The law establishes an irrebuttable presumption that they are self-employed. This means, self-employed as a company director. This does not restrict a company director from holding a job within the same company, as an employee, subject to the authority of the board of directors.[12] A combination of jobs is then required: one as a director, performed as a self-employed, and one as an employee, separate from the director job and performed in subordination to the employer. For *Italy* it is stated that the accumulation of the position as a director and as an employee in the same company is legally acceptable.[13] Also under *Scottish* law, '*it is clear that directors qua directors are not employees. It is equally clear that if a director works for the company in some role quite distinct from the management role as director he is an employee*'.[14] The same also seems to be true for *Argentina.*[15]

22. Whether or not certain tasks could be performed in furtherance of an employment contract, and thus in a relationship of subordination, was a question that was raised particularly with respect to the liberal professions, such as doctors and lawyers. While it seems to be generally accepted now that the nature of the tasks performed by a doctor, the kind of training and education required and the necessary diagnostic freedom the doctor requires in order to properly perform his/her job, do not prevent the existence of an employment contract with a hospital in which the doctor is performing the services, the same has not always been true. However, the move away from the idea that liberal professions were always performed in complete independence[16] happened gradually.

---

12. *See* Engels, C., Het ondergeschikt verband naar Belgisch Arbeidsrecht [Subordination According to Belgian Labor Law], Brugge, Die Keure, 1989, 644, pp. 329–457. C. Engels, 'Belgium, in Employed or Self-employed, pp. 44–49.
13. *See* S. Liebman, 'Italy', in Employed or Self-employed, p. 97.
14. *See* F. Davidson, 'Scotland', in Employed or Self-employed, p. 169.
15. *See* B. Nazar-Anchorena, in Employed or Self-employed, p. 14.
16. *See* A. Supiot, 'Wage employment and self-employment', in Reports to the 6th European Congress for Labour Law and Social Security, Warsaw, Poland, 13–17 September 1999, p. 130.

23. The discussion on the nature of the work relationships of medical doctors and hospitals is not closed. It often has to be determined on a case by case basis whether such relationship is a contract of employment (employment relationship) or a relationship with an independent contractor of services. However the discussion is closed with respect to the legal possibility of having a medical doctor perform in a subordinate employment relationship.[17] This now seems to be totally accepted in most legal systems. A similar discussion is circulating with respect to the status of lawyers working in big law firms. The debate is very similar to the one that went on a couple of decades ago with respect to medical doctors in the *Belgian* legal world. The argument is that the independence needed by a lawyer to defend the client's interest can conflict with an employment relationship with the law firm. The same old arguments are used to defend the position that the lawyer in the law firm is necessarily self-employed. This position is totally untenable and outdated, and has been abandoned in most jurisdictions. Whether or not such lawyers are independent performers of services or subordinate employees to the law firms should depend on the way they are actually required or could contractually be required to perform. A case by case investigation into the different work environments of these lawyers would undoubtedly point out that some of them are working as employees and some as independent contractors, just as for any other profession. Most jurisdictions have already taken this step. There is no legal text that would prevent the same move in Belgian law.[18]

C. Performance by a Physical Person, Not a Legal Entity

24. None of the legal systems reviewed accepted the possibility for a legal entity to be an employee. Most of the time it is stated that the employee is a physical person, who is required to personally perform the services for which the parties contracted. Self-evidently certain exceptions to this rule exist.[19]

The question arises as to what effect the incorporation of an individual worker will have, where the corporate objective of the new legal entity is to perform the same or similar services as the individual previously performed him/herself. The legal entity cannot of course personally perform the services, but has to do so through the workers that work on its behalf. These performances could be delivered by a worker, operating either as an independent contractor with the company, or as an employee of the same company. The issue then is to know how the relationship with the original company for whom the work is performed has to be qualified. Does the

---

17. With respect to the Belgian situation, *see* Engels, C., 'De juridische duiding van de overeenkomst tussen ziekenhuis en ziekenhuisgeneesheer, Arbeidsovereenkomst of overeenkomst tot zelfstandige samenwerking' [The legal determination of the agreement between hospital medical doctors and the hospital], in Arbeidsrecht, Confrontatie Tussen Theorie EN Praktijk [Labor Law: A Confrontation between Law and Practice], Antwerp-Apeldoorn, Maklu uitgevers, 1993, pp. 31–109.

18. *See* Engels, C., Het Ondergeschikt Verband Naar Belgisch Arbeidsrecht [Subordination According to Belgian Labor Law], Brugge, Die Keure, 1989, 644, pp. 56–59.

19. For *Germany* it is reported that an employee home worker may still be an employee if the home worker does not have more than two employees assisting him or working for him. *See* M. Weiss, cited in P.L. Davies, 'Wage employment and self-employment – a common law view', in Reports to the 6th European Congress for Labour Law and Social Security, Warsaw, Poland, 13–17 September 1999, p. 174.

interposition of a legal entity (e.g. a one man company) rule out the qualification of the relationship as an employment relationship?

25.   One-man companies are allowed in all of the member states of the European Union.[20] If the creation of such a one-man company would in itself allow avoidance of employee status for the person performing the services, the establishment of such companies would permit the avoidance of the application of protective and inflexible labor law provisions. Even though courts may not be inclined to easily lift the corporate veil,[21] it should be stressed that the mere establishment of a legal entity in a work relationship should not be seen as fundamentally altering the relationship between the provider and the recipient of services.[22]

26.   The issue made headlines in the Belgian legal community with respect to two highly publicized cases (first degree and appeals level) dealing with the social security status of a manager of a first division soccer club. Instead of performing directly for the club, the soccer coach was performing as a managing director of his own company. The latter company had concluded an agreement with the company of the coach. In furtherance of this agreement, the coach's company had to put 'a coach' at the disposal of the club. The agreement had an annex naming the coach personally as the coach chosen by his company to be put at the disposal of the club. The club itself declared in the annex that it agreed that the named coach would perform the services. The courts hearing the case disregarded the corporate entity that had been created and judged the relationship between the coach personally and the club. The courts rightfully held that there was still an employment relationship, regardless of the valid or invalid existence of a corporate entity. Rightfully so, the courts were not convinced that the mere creation of a corporate entity ruled out the possibility of the existence of an employment contract.

D.   The Different Tests that were Developed

27.   Various tests have been developed in order to determine ways to make the distinction between those operating as subordinate workers or employees, and those who are not. It is interesting to note that the tests that were developed over time in civil and common law jurisdictions, do not differ much.[23] The tests that are applied all seem to

---

20.   Twelfth Council Company Law Directive 89/667/EEC, 21 December 1989, on single-member private limited liability companies, OJ 30 December 1989, no. L 395, 40.
21.   *See* P.L. Davies, 'Wage employment and self-employment – a common law view', in Reports to the 6th European Congress for Labour Law and Social Security, Warsaw, Poland, 13–17 September 1999, p. 188.
22.   *See* C. Engels, 'Subordinate employees or self-employed workers?, an analysis of the employment situation of managers of management companies as an illustration' Comp. Lab. L. J., forthcoming. *See also* C. Engels, 'Het sociaal statuut van de manager in de managementvennootschap' [The social law status of the manger of a management company], Soc. Kron. 1992, pp. 353–362; C. Engels, 'De managementvennootschap en het sociaal recht. Update naar aanleiding van het geval Leekens' [The management company and labor and employment law. An update at the occasion of the Leekens case] Orientatie, 1995, pp. 192–210.
23.   *See* B. Brooks and C. Engels, Employed or Self-employed, p. 1.

refer to a host of factual circumstances on the basis of which decisions are being taken to label a given work contract either as an employment contract or as a contract for the independent delivery of services. None of the characteristics or facts seem to be determinative themselves. It is the overall situation that is taken into account and the basis on which decisions are made. There is of course a difference in the criteria which are taken into account in the different countries[24] and thus a difference in how the tests may actually be applied.

28. The various tests that have been developed and used in order to distinguish wage employment from self-employment, all reflect the system of industrial relations in which they were developed and its stage of development.

29. One of the early tests was the *actual control test*. The employer, under this test, is the entity (legal or natural person) actually controlling the work performed by the workers. Such control can be exercised either personally or through the intervention of supervisors. What is required under this test is the *actual exercise of control.* A mere possibility of such a control being exercised would not suffice. While this test may have been useful to deal with the employment status of large numbers of blue-collar workers working in large industries under the direct supervision of a superior, it is no longer a viable test. For a very large number of workers this test would not allow them to qualify as workers. The actual control test included the idea that the employer could actually control the performance and give guidelines with respect to the work to be performed. '*Central to the notion of subordination is the idea of control of one party over the way in which the other party performs the task. In this sense the control test is an echo of the past.*'[25]

30. The traditional control test became inadequate to protect persons whose technical skills and expertise *prima facie* make them independent of the business enterprise. Rapid technological change has created workers whose technical independence 'prevents' them from being considered subordinate to anyone, at least as far as the technical side of the performance is concerned. Courts therefore tended to move away from a test that included actual control, to a test emphasizing the employer's *ability to exercise* control, without there being a requirement to actually use the right of intervention, through control and direction.[26]

31. Both versions of the control test were difficult to apply to new work arrangements under which people work according to the organizational needs of the enterprise, such as home workers, casual workers or contingent workers, and temporary workers, etc. The emergence of these types of arrangements meant that courts had to re-shape the traditional tests. One way of looking at the issues is to ask the question whether the individual is part and parcel of the organization for which the work is being performed and are they therefore subordinate to it. Self-evidently the

---

24. *See* A. Supiot, 'Wage employment and self-employment', in Reports to the 6th European Congress for Labour Law and Social Security, Warsaw, Poland, 13–17 September 1999, p. 136
25. *See* B. Brooks and C. Engels, Employed or Self-employed, p. 4.
26. *See* B. Brooks and C. Engels, Employed or Self-employed, p. 4.

application of the *organizational test* brings along difficulties in its application to cases of casual workers not fully integrated in the organization of the enterprise.

32. A test most often not seen as an entirely independent test is the *economic dependency test.* This test goes back to the fundamental reason why labour law came into existence in the first place, namely to offset the power of the employer in the absence of any sufficient counter balance, and the fact that workers are dependent on the income from their labor to survive. While judges will often be influenced by the existence of a relationship of economic dependence of one party to the other, this criterion is often not seen as absolutely necessary, nor as a sufficient reason to hold a worker to be a subordinate employee or a self-employed worker.[27]

33. Most of the time courts will not make a choice between one test or the other when confronted with the question as to the employment status of a worker, but instead a *hybrid test* of all the above tests will be applied. Judges will look at the economic dependence of the worker concerned. They will try to determine whether actual control is being exercised. If this is the case, quite often they can already come to the conclusion that an employment contract exists. If not, the follow-up questions as to the right to exercize authority need to be asked. The integration of the worker in the company will equally be seen as an indication in the direction of a subordinate employee status.

E. European Labour Law

34. The question of who is protected under a given labour law instrument is not only a question raised under national law. The same issue arises in regional systems, such as the well developed system of the European Union (EU). Within the EU various kinds of legal measures exist (Treaties, regulations, directives, decisions, etc.), in which the notion of worker appears. When used at European level, the notion of worker does not refer to the general notion as used in this paper. The 'worker concept' stands against the concept of the self-employed performer of services. Worker therefore means subordinate worker.

35. At the European level an additional question needs to be raised: Is the worker concept, if and when used in the European measures necessarily a concept defined at European level, or is the actual content of the concept filled in and defined at national level? When the transfer directive grants protection to workers in the case of transfer of the business to which they belong, it is then up to the different Member States to give a definition of who is protected by the national implementing measure of the directive, or is the concept necessarily defined at European level? Can the different Member States determine who is granted the freedom of movement of workers through defining the latter concept unilaterally and at a national level?

---

27. *See* B. Brooks and C. Engels, Employed or Self-employed, p. 5.

36. A uniform answer cannot be given to this question. Some European measures require the worker concept to be defined at European level, while others leave the definitions up to the individual Member States. With respect to the Treaty article dealing with the freedom of movement of workers, the European Court of Justice stated that the said concept was a European concept. The Treaty itself did not give a definition of the concept. The European Court of Justice did so through its abundant jurisprudence. The Court came to a definition which broadly refers to the basic elements relied on in most legal systems. The Court considered that the essential feature of an employment relationship is *'that for a certain period of time a person performs services for and under the direction of another person in return for which he receives remuneration.'*[28] The Court was faced with the same question with respect to the employee concept used in the transfer directive. While the Commission had argued that a European definition was indispensable, the European Court of Justice did not follow the reasoning, since the directive was not intended to provide uniform protection throughout the Community.[29] The amended version of the Transfer directive now explicitly foresees that the employee concept is a national concept, further to be defined at national level.[30]

IV. CONTRACT LABOUR

37. The term contract labour surfaced in discussions at the International Labour Organisation (ILO). It is defined in a recent draft ILO Convention and Recommendation as *'work performed for a natural person or legal person (referred to as the "user enterprise") by a person (referred to as the "contract worker") where the work is performed by the contract worker personally under actual conditions of dependency on or subordination to the user enterprise and these conditions are similar to those that characterize an employment relationship under national law and practice and where either:*

(i) the work is performed pursuant to a direct contractual arrangement other than a contract of employment between the contract worker and the user enterprise; or
(ii) the contract worker is provided for the user enterprise by a subcontractor or an intermediary.'[31]

---

28. *See* ECJ, *Deborah Lawrie-Blum v. Land Baden-Württemberg,* 3 July 1986, Case no. 66/85, ECR 1986, 2121, Nos 16–17.
29. *See* C. Engels and L. Salas, 'Cause and Consequence, what's the Difference in respect of the EC Transfer Directive?', in Labour Law and Industrial Relations at the Turn of the Century, Liber Amicorum in Honour of Prof. Dr. Roger Blanpain, C. Engels and M. Weiss (eds), Kluwer Law International, The Hague London Boston, 1998, 274 es. *See also* ECJ, *Foreningen af Arbejdsledere I Danmark v. A/S/ Danmols Inventar, in liquidation,* 11 July 1985, Case no. 105/84, ECR 1985, 22; (recent case) ECJ, *C.P.M. Mueussen v. Hoofdirectie van de Informatie Beheer Groep,* 8 June 1999, ECR 1999, 3289.
30. Council Directive 77/187/EEC, 14 February 1977, on the approximation of the laws of the member States relating to the safeguarding of employees' rights in the event of transfers of undertakings, businesses or parts of businesses, OJ 5 March 1977, no. L 61, 26, as amended by Directive 98//50/EC, 29 June 1998, OJ 17 July 1998, no. L 201, 88.
31. Article 1(a) Proposed Convention on Contract Labour.

The draft Convention itself states that it shall not apply to workers who, in accordance with national law and practice have a recognized contract of employment.[32]

38. There was some discussion within the ILO as to whether a third category of workers was being created, in between the two existing categories of subordinate labour on the one hand and self-employment on the other hand. While some representatives tried to state this was not the case, one cannot but logically accept that the category of 'dependent independents' or 'independent dependents', does in reality constitute some intermediary category.

39. The draft Recommendation that accompanies the draft Convention further explains what the dependency is about. The draft Recommendation retains a number of characteristics that would be taken into account in order to determine whether the self-employed is actually to some extent dependent on its contract party so that he/she would fall within the category of contract labour and therefore is entitled to the protection the draft Convention and Recommendation intend to put forward. The draft Recommendation highlights some of the features of dependency that would be taken into account :

> 'in determining whether the conditions of dependency or subordination referred to in paragraph (1) above are met, a Member could consider one or more criteria, including but not limited to, the following:
>
> (a) the extent to which the user enterprise determines when and how work should be performed, including working time and other conditions of work of the contract worker;
> (b) whether the user enterprise pays amounts due to the contract worker periodically and according to pre-established criteria;
> (c) the extent of supervisory authority and control of the user enterprise over the contract worker in respect to the work performed, including disciplinary authority;
> (d) the extent to which the user enterprise makes investments and provides tools, materials and machinery, among other things, to perform the work concerned;
> (e) whether the contract worker can make profits or run the risk of losses in performing the work;
> (f) whether the work is performed on a regular and continuous basis;
> (g) whether the contract worker works only for a single user enterprise;
> (h) the extent to which the work performed is integrated into the normal activities of the user enterprise;
> (i) whether the user enterprise provides substantial job-specific training to the contract worker.'[33]

---

32. Article 2.1 Proposed Convention on Contract Labour.
33. Article 5.4 Proposed Recommendation on Contract Labour.

40. While the ILO Convention and Recommendation foresee some protection that needs to be granted to the contract workers (more than to the true self-employed, but less than to the normal subordinate workers), it still considers them to be outside the category of employees.

The concept of contract labour as a kind of intermediary category between self-employed workers and employees remains far from accepted. Within the ILO context the debate continues. In some countries, the discussion has progressed further.

Examples of the extension of the scope of some labour law provisions, so as to include 'dependent contractors' could be found for example in the *United States* and *Sweden*. In the latter country the legislation dealing with collective bargaining was extended to commercial travellers, tenants of filling stations, and timber haulers using their own horse or tractor.[34]

A more recent example is *Germany,* in which the scope of some protective provisions is extended to include 'employee-like persons' ('arbeitsnehmerähnliche Personen'). *'In German law the conditions to be treated as employee-like are the obligation personally to provide the work and the fact of doing the majority of the work or receiving more than half of one's income from a single "employer"'*.[35]

V. CONCLUSION

41. The discussion on the concept of 'contract labor' within the ILO and the introduction of similar concepts such as 'employee-like workers' in different national legal systems highlights a more fundamental issue. Is it still acceptable or even desirable to continue the fundamental distinction between subordinate employees on the one hand and self-employed workers on the other hand? Given the difficulties, both from a theoretical and from a practical point of view in clearly drawing the demarcation line between self-employed workers and employees (and more so, the demarcation lines between self-employed, employee-like, and employee), the more fundamental question surfaces as to the abolition of the distinction.

42. Does it really make sense, for example, to continue the effort to try to distinguish between self-employed commercial agents on the one hand and subordinate sales representatives on the other hand?[36] Looking at the definition of what the relevant European directive states[37] it is clear that only the element of subordination is making the difference between this commercial intermediary and the sales

---

34. *See* P.L. Davies, 'Wage employment and self-employment – a common law view', in Reports to the 6th European Congress for Labour Law and Social Security, Warsaw, Poland, 13–17 September 1999, p. 184.
35. *See* P.L. Davies, 'Wage employment and self-employment – a common law view', in Reports to the 6th European Congress for Labour Law and Social Security, Warsaw, Poland, 13–17 September 1999, p. 186.
36. *See* C. Engels, 'Contract Labour, de afhankelijke zelfstandige of de zelfstandige afhankelijke' [Contract Labour, the dependent independent or the independent dependent], in Liber Amicorum Prof. Dr. Roger Blanpain, Brugge, Die Keure, 1998, pp. 274–275.
37. Council Directive 86/653/EEC, 18 December 1986 on the coordination of the laws of the member States relating to self-employed commercial agents, OJ 31 December 1986, no. L 382, 17.

representative who is acting as a subordinate employee.[38] The commercial agent, according to the directive, has to conclude transactions he/she is *instructed* to take care of, has to communicate to the principal all available *information* and must comply with all reasonable *instructions*.[39] In exchange for these obligations the agent is granted some employee like protection among other things, with respect to commissions, the termination of the contract and with respect to the potential loss of clientele resulting from such termination. Making the distinction between the subordinate and self-employed commercial intermediary has become extremely difficult, if not impossible in many cases if it is taken for granted that also the independent agent has to obey instructions. The qualifier 'reasonable' that goes with the definition of the instructions the agent has to obey, cannot make the difference here. One cannot sensibly argue that the subordinate sales representative not only has to obey the reasonable, but also the unreasonable instructions of the his/her contract party. Does the case of the commercial intermediaries not underline the fact that the traditional labour and employment distinction self-employed vs. subordinate worker is outdated?

---

38. Article 1.2, Council Directive 86/653/EEC, 18 December 1986 on the coordination of the laws of the member States relating to self-employed commercial agents, OJ 31 December 1986, no. L 382, 17:

    'For the purpose of this Directive, "commercial agent" shall mean a self-employed intermediary who has continuing authority to negotiate the sale or the purchase of goods on behalf of another person, hereinafter called the "principal", or to negotiate and conclude such transactions on behalf of and in the name of that principal.'

39. Article 3, Council Directive 86/653/EEC, 18 December 1986 on the coordination of the laws of the member States relating to self-employed commercial agents, OJ 31 December 1986, no. L 382, 17.

Chapter 15.   Working Conditions and Globalization*

J.-M. Servais

1.   In public debate today on the future of labour, it is taken for granted that social policies and their implementing legislation will have to adapt to more open and competitive markets, and to a way of organizing production that is at one and the same time more complex, segmented and dependent on new techniques. This hypothesis would seem to be confirmed by recent socio-economic developments; it also reflects the view of labour market management held in a country such as the United States, the driving force behind globalization. We know how reluctant the American government is to take action on labour issues; American legislation, for example, focuses more on fundamental rights at work, and most labour regulations stem from collective agreements concluded at the enterprise level or at that of its subsidiaries.

2.   Bringing social policies up to date re-ignites the debate on the optimal synthesis between the guarantees given to workers, job creation, and competitiveness, or in other words, between development and the values and rights that a given national community holds dear. We might at this point usefully recall how these factors were balanced in the past and briefly review the foundations of the measures protecting wage-earners.[1]

3.   Social regulations constituted a response to the concerns arising from the 'social question', i.e. the miserable condition of workers at the beginning of the industrial age. It has perhaps not been pointed out often enough that the first to be stirred by the workers' plight included humanist employers such as Charles Hindley in Great Britain and Daniel Le Grand in France, doctors such as Louis-René Villermé, economists such as Jérome-Adolphe Blanqui, and civil servants (the history books mention the Belgian Inspector General of Prisons and Social Welfare Institutes, Edouard Ducpétiaux), in addition to thinkers, politicians, and union leaders of the emerging social and socialist movements.

---

*   The opinions expressed in this article are those of the author and in no way reflect those of the institution to which he belongs.
1.   *See also* P. Verge and G. Vallée, *Un droit du travail? Essai sur la specificité du droit du travail*, Cowansville (Quebec), Yvon Blais, 1997, in particular pp. 171 et seq.

4. They were prompted to act – and were later joined by their national governments – for several reasons, which were undoubtedly primarily social. Often, however, those reasons were tinged with disquiet at the economic and even military consequences of sapping the physical strength of a large proportion of the population and with concern to preserve social and political stability. Improvements in a company's conditions of employment could, of course, increase costs, at least in the short term. Those employers who viewed progress favourably therefore sought to neutralize its effects with regard to their competitors, at first nationally, then abroad, by means of labour regulations that were applicable to all. This contributed to the development of national and international labour law, and was clearly one of the factors at the origin of the International Labour Organisation (ILO).[2]

5. Concern for social or simply human justice, employers' fears that their social spending would rise more rapidly than that of their competitors, and the desire for social and political stability were therefore associated, even though it is difficult to assess the exact role each played in the development of labour regulations.

6. Examining those factors in terms of the situation today should enable us to shed a more accurate light on the current state of policies protecting work. There are indeed many fracture lines in social life and at the workplace. They constitute so many 'prints'[3] of the social question as it arises in the new century or millennium. This contribution identifies those prints (I) before reflecting on the solutions found in practice (II) and on the adjustments that will have to be made in labour policies and their legal instruments to overcome the problems thus defined (III).

I.   PERSISTENT SOCIAL MALAISE

A.   *Countless Social Fracture Lines*

7. Each national community, to maintain unity and prevent 'criminal' groups from taking control, is based on a series of basic norms that set the framework for relations between its members. The norms may be moral or religious in origin, but the State seeks to impose rules and penalties corresponding to the situation in a society at a given time. If the socio-economic context changes, those rules will also have to change, sometimes radically. This is what happened when the modern States emerged.[4] We may be undergoing another period of great upheaval, what with technological changes, the opening of borders and the growing internationalization of markets. In any event, social ties are breaking down all over, at school, in marriages and families, in the community. In cities and towns, insecurity and delinquent behaviour are so widespread that they

---

2.   *See* J.-M. Servais, 'The International Labour Organisation', in R. Blanpain (ed.), *International Encyclopedia of Law*, The Hague, Kluwer, 1996, pp. 1 et seq.

3.   D. Behar, 'Question urbaine et question sociale: quel lien pour quelle politique publique?', *Problèmes économiques*, No. 2574, 24 June 1998, pp. 1–5.

4.   *See* for example, M. Stolleis, *Histoire du droit public en Allemagne. Droit public impérial et sciences de la police 1600–1800*, Paris, PUF, 1998, in particular pp. 603–604.

have taken on a political dimension;[5] up to a point, social conflict has been displaced from the factory to the poorest parts of the cities and their public transport systems.

8. Certain outpourings of public feeling serve as warning signs: the reaction to the death of Diana, Princess of Wales, or, a few years ago in Belgium, the so-called 'white' march of protest against the established Belgian authorities, reflect sentiments that are difficult to define in rational terms. They are probably the expression, via the media, of the anxiety and frustrations projected on public figures whose charisma cannot be explained in any convincing way.

9. This having been said, growing job insecurity, under-employment and the absence of employment are probably the main reasons social relations are crumbling. In Japan, an unemployment rate of over four per cent has given rise to fears that the current depression will have a serious impact on the kind of society that country has built since the Second World War. That rate cannot be compared to those in Europe or, even worse, in developing countries, where unemployment entails processes of exclusion and marginalization on which there has been no shortage of comment.[6]

10. Even in places like the United States, where the unemployment rate remains low, acts of aggression and violence in the workplace are on the rise, and a widespread feeling of job insecurity reigns.[7] This is expressed in opinion polls and lies, along with the growing income inequality – some people do not earn enough to support themselves and their families – at the heart of the social debate in the country. This sense of insecurity was no doubt engendered by the mass lay-offs attending the restructuring of major American enterprises, and mobility, which has always been characteristic of the United States, has apparently usually led to a lower-paid job. The fact that job security is based essentially on collective enterprise agreements and not on a labour code or its equivalent reinforces that instability. Combined with growing wage disparities affecting low-skilled workers, it results in a polarization of the workforce and undermines social integration. What is more, analysts have revealed the existence of a self-perpetuating form of social exclusion that leaves the members of certain ethnic minorities out-of-work generation after generation; they may lose all reference to work in their lives.

11. In what is a new phenomenon, in eastern and central Europe impoverishment now affects large sectors of the population, including those with a job, while the problem remains endemic in very many developing countries. Here again, the gap between the haves and the have-nots is growing.

---

5. *See also* J. Donzelot, 'La nouvelle question urbain', Esprit, November 1999, pp. 87–114.
6. G. Rodgers, Ch. Gore, J.B. Figueiredo (eds), *Social Exclusion: Rhetoric, Reality, Responses*, Geneva, International Institute for Labour Studies, 1995; J.B. Figueiredo and A. de Haan, *Social exclusion: an ILO perspective*, Geneva, International Institute for Labour Studies, 1998; *See also* R. Castel, *Les métamorphoses de la question sociale, une chronique du salariat*, Paris, Fayard, 1995, and 'Centralité du travail et cohésion sociale', in J. Kergoat, J. Boutet, H. Jacot and D. Linhart, *Le monde du travail*, Paris, La Découverte, 1998.
7. ILO, *World Labour Report 1997–98: Industrial relations, democracy and social stability*, Geneva, 1997, p. 116.

12. Historically, governments adopted at least three kinds of policy to maintain or restore social stability among their citizens: enlightened despotism, laissez-faire and the Welfare State. In the 18th century, Prussia and Austria applied a virtuous authoritarianism, the classic example of the first kind of policy. The government had its own view of the problems encountered and imposed the remedies it deemed appropriate, in a way that brings to mind certain modern politicians who are brilliant technocrats and consider themselves to be in a privileged position to understand the difficulties of their people and how to solve them.

13. The laissez-faire strategy adopted elsewhere could not be more different: the governments concerned let the 'invisible hand' of the market make the adjustments required, including in the field of labour.

14. The third policy satisfied the citizens' desire, in particular in western Europe, to see the State establish rules, institutions and practices safeguarding them from social risks. It is based on a recognized duty of solidarity and, more often than not, on the explicit or tacit agreement of the large employers' and workers' federations. This is often referred to as the Welfare State or, in Germany, the Social State.

15. And yet, none of the three policies in their modern forms – and in their implementation through standards and legal institutions – has managed to mend the social fractures mentioned above in any significant way. On the contrary, those fractures seem even more pronounced now than in the recent past. The modern forms of enlightened despotism have often been mere alibis for personal gain; they do not always – and quite understandably – correspond to the needs and desires of the population; the risks of making a poor policy choice are obvious. The laissez-faire policy has never been able to guarantee a living wage for the most underprivileged, particularly during a slump; in practice, some form or other of social security system (the 'safety net') often corrected the more heartless facets thereof. And criticism has been heaped on the Welfare State on the grounds that it is too cumbersome to cope with the globalization of the markets for capital, products, and labour; for it to survive unchanged in a world in which trade in capital and goods has been liberalized presupposes an inter-State solidarity that does not really exist. In short, if the State wants to continue playing a role in the conception and implementation of social policies, it will have to adapt.

B. The Labour Scene Diversifies

16. The lack of success in policies has been compounded by the significant loss in power of the traditional social players. The internationalization of the market economy and its regionalization in Europe in particular have inevitably limited – although not to the extent some would claim – the scope for action of the public authorities, in particular with regard to labour affairs. A Keynesian national policy pre-supposed complete control by the State of economic instruments. It cannot function in the same way if the States lose some of that control. And yet governments are called on to be active more than ever before, in particular on the problems of employment and social protection.

17. They frequently turn to employers' and trade union organizations for help, but the latter are also faced with serious difficulties, in the same context. The predicament facing the unions is well known, with membership rates falling in many countries. Employers' organizations are also going through a period of upheaval. Diversification, the segmentation of interests both for trade unions (the concerns of stable wage-earners differ considerably from those of the unemployed and workers in contingent employment) and employers' federations (the interests of small- and medium-sized businesses may be very much at odds with those of multinationals) affect them both to the point that their respective monopoly on representation is open to challenge. Many companies, especially the bigger ones, seek to preserve their freedom of action when it comes to personnel management. They have nevertheless been known to create relatively informal networks among themselves. Staff policies crop up on the agenda at meetings of CEOs of America's biggest firms or of business councils set up elsewhere. The leaders of Japan's main enterprises hold sectorial, intersectorial or industrial group coordination meetings, notably in response to the ritual spring labour offensive (the *shunto*). For the trade unions, the segmentation of interests has put the tradition of fellowship among workers to the test. Moreover, the group that was in the past most favourably disposed towards union action, the regular wage-earners, is shrinking, while a large number of all kinds of organizations claim to represent what are often very specific interest groups (consumers, environmentalists, women, ethnic minorities, local communities, the unemployed, etc.) that overlap with those the unions seek to represent.

18. In short, for employers' associations and for workers' federations, the byword is competition rather than unified action.

19. Another phenomenon is the rising strength of the new world players, first and foremost the multinationals. Some of them (albeit as yet only a few) no longer even have privileged ties with a specific country; their headquarters are located wherever their principal leaders are to be found at any given moment. The regional groups, such as the European Union, Mercosur or NAFTA, constitute other new world players. Non-governmental organizations (NGOs) have for their part used the new communication technologies to create transnational networks which can carry great weight.[8] All of these players have adapted more quickly to the opening of borders and trade liberalization than the more rigidly-structured public authorities themselves.[9] Certain groups have an acknowledged ability to make themselves heard in the media.

20. The diminished role of the State reflects not only the growing importance of international actors. Local and municipal activities are also multiplying. Here, too, NGO initiatives have changed the local landscape. Increasingly, the public authorities entrust NGOs with tasks that they cannot or no longer wish to carry out, starting

---

8. *See also* J.T. Matthews, 'Power shift', *Foreign Affairs*, January–February 1997, pp. 50–66.
9. This is also the explanation for some of the difficulties currently facing international organizations, whose structures and modes of action continue to depend on inter-State relations. The efforts of those organizations to bring representatives of the global civil society into the fold reflect their desire to adapt to this new reality.

a process of privatization that does not involve the business sector but nevertheless relieves the authorities of certain responsibilities. Other public institutions below the level of the State have also been observed to be increasingly active. Most American states have an official observer at the World Trade Organisation. The German *Länder*, the Belgian language communities and the British local authorities send representatives to the European Union. France's Rhône-Alpes region has established direct relations with Geneva and Turin, with a view to dealing with cross-border issues such as seasonal workers. Many large companies are endeavouring, again more frequently than in the recent past, to develop social activities locally.

21. Borders are therefore becoming more permeable and less dissuasive. The situation in some respects approximates, on a global level, that prevailing in western Europe mainly in the 17th but also in the 18th century, when each nation's identity was not as well defined as it later was. Reports from well-off travellers show that they could move without any special administrative hindrance as far as the borders of the Ottoman Empire. Relations of that kind imply a certain sharing of views and interests. The fall of the communist regimes in Russia and its neighbours led in particular to a greater convergence in individual concepts of the organization of production and work. This is just one more facet of the ongoing process of globalization.

C.   The New Social Question

22. The above comments notwithstanding, social fractures, observed in particular around the labour market, and the loss of strength of the traditional social actors, give rise to fears that solidarity will be undermined and that society will split into two categories, the haves and the have-nots, which will take the place of the classes that emerged from the Ancien Régime in Europe.

23. It is significant that the word 'social' in 'social question' now has another connotation. Historically it referred to the division of society into classes and especially to the proletariat and its relations with a dominant, property-owning middle class.[10] Solidarity, as it developed in the 19th and 20th centuries, was occupational and class-related, uniting those whose station in life and risks were similar. In the new century, the social classes have largely disintegrated in Europe, or at least the effects of the class system are no longer as strongly felt on the labour market. The situation has become similar, from that point of view, to conditions in the United States and Japan. The social question facing industrial societies and developing countries today concerns the impoverishment, not of the working class but of all those, wage-earners and the self-employed, swept up, usually because of their forced inactivity but also because of their inadequate salary or precarious employment, in a current that is carrying or keeping them away from established structures.

---

10.   *See* for example A. Lalande, *Vocabulaire technique et critique de la philosophie*, Paris, PUF, 1962, p. 998.

II. Questions about the New Policies

24. It may be difficult to reverse the causes of growing work precarity, for wage-earners and the self-employed, but the most detrimental effects thereof should be corrected.[11] This brings us back to the foundations of work protection: since protection is essentially placed within an economic framework, its regulation must not become hostage to competition between enterprises; since work is still a fundamental part of life in society, some form of stability must be maintained; since the object of protection is the worker himself, certain human values must be upheld.

25. The first step is to examine to what extent those values can be ranked and to draw conclusions in terms of action to be taken. The second is to query the real possibilities for costing labour standards. The third is to focus on the principal modes of social regulation, to ask whether some are better than others or whether there are alternatives to legal regulation.

A. *Three Categories of Standards*

26. A careful analysis of the labour standards adopted by the ILO shows that they, and consequently the values they embody, may be classified into three categories.[12] The first concerns the fundamental rights of men and women to work; the second covers standards of a programmatic nature; the third relates to the more technical provisions of labour and social security legislation. The distinction may provide a useful reference framework for a broader discussion of the future not only of international but also national and regional labour regulations. In particular, more frequent recourse to programmatic standards should lead the way out of certain impasses.

27. In most countries, the standards in the first category are derived from basic constitutional principles concerning public freedoms or social rights. They relate to freedom of association and the right to collective bargaining, the abolition of child labour and forced labour, and equal pay and equal opportunities in terms of employment. Their fundamental nature is recognized by almost all, and international treaties have given them clear pre-eminence.

28. The United Nations Covenants on Civil and Political Rights and, in particular, on Economic, Social, and Cultural Rights are one example. Another is the ILO Constitution and several ILO conventions, and the Declaration on Fundamental Principles and Rights at Work and its Follow-up, adopted in June 1998 by the

---

11. *See* in particular ILO, *Decent work*, Report of the Director-General to the 87th Session (June 1999) of the International Labour Conference, Geneva, ILO, 1999; *see also* for example J.F. Beffa, R. Boyer, and J. Ph. Touffut, 'Le droit du travail face à l'hétérogénéité des relations salariales', *Droit social*, No. 12, December 1999, pp. 1039–1051.

12. *See* J.M. Servais, 'Le droit international en mouvement: déploiement et approches nouvelles', *Droit social*, May 1991, No. 5, pp. 449 et seq, comp.; W. Jenks, *Law, Freedom and Welfare*, London, Oceana Publications, 1963, p. 103.

International Labour Conference. These texts, which are succinctly worded, enshrine general principles that can be applied in many ways. This is why they sometimes give rise to the same difficulties of interpretation (a balance must be struck between excess laxity and extreme radicalism) as national constitutional rules.

29. It must be emphasized that the Declaration adopted by the ILO in 1998 has a greater potential to extend beyond the purely inter-State framework than the other international instruments mentioned above, even if it is intended mainly for the Member States. It focuses on all the previously mentioned fundamental social rights, which it lists without detailing the specific means for their implementation. Its binding force is limited, and the follow-up procedures considerably less demanding than the ILO's traditional control mechanisms. Although it is therefore aimed first and foremost at the Member States, which are invited to adopt implementation measures, it can easily, because of the general nature of its wording, be referred to directly by the new global players. It can be used to define the shared rules to be followed by the ILO and the major international financial institutions in the action they take at country level. It can be taken up in the social charters adopted by regional bodies (in particular the European Union, the Council of Europe, NAFTA, Mercosur); more often than not, the latter are already largely based on ILO standards. What is more, the Declaration can be invoked by NGOs calling for the establishment of a list of basic principles to be respected with regard to social policy. It can serve as a source of inspiration for multinational companies when they draw up their social codes of conduct or define the criteria to be observed in their so-called social reports or their social audits. In that case, private initiatives supplement national legislation on these different points and often ensure improved compliance.

30. The basic labour standards enshrine the essential principles of law and order giving the workers themselves the possibility 'to claim freely and on the basis of equality of opportunity their fair share of the wealth which they have helped to generate, and to achieve fully their human potential'.[13] They are therefore based on the notions of liberty and democracy. Incorporating those standards into constitutional texts establishes their pre-eminence; when incorporated into legislation they can be accompanied by sanctions in the event that they are violated. Without underestimating the usefulness of other, non-legal measures in promoting the application of the standards in specific socio-economic circumstances, the importance of legal measures is not and indeed cannot be open to doubt.

31. The second category of standards covers provisions of a more programmatic rather than directly obligatory nature. They essentially prompt action: they set the goals to be reached through promotional work by the public authorities and their implementation requires the adoption of a variety of measures (training, information, public-awareness campaigns, etc.) which are not all legal in nature. These standards are worded in general and flexible terms, and they place no immediate obligation on the employer or on any other person, but rather contain an obligation of means for

---

13. *See* the ILO Declaration on Fundamental Principles and Rights at Work and its Follow-up, adopted by the International Labour Conference on 18 June 1998.

the States concerned to adopt measures: carrying out certain activities, drawing up or implementing certain projects, working towards certain goals, etc.

32. These standards are to be found in particular in areas such as employment, occupational training and the abolition of discrimination. Thus, Articles 1 and 2 of the ILO Convention (No. 122) on Employment Policy, 1964, stipulate as follows:

"*Article 1*

1. With a view to stimulating economic growth and development, raising levels of living, meeting manpower requirements, and overcoming unemployment and under-employment, each Member shall declare and pursue, as a major goal, an active policy designed to promote full, productive and freely chosen employment.

2. The said policy shall aim at ensuring that

(a) there is work for all who are available for and seeking work;
(b) such work is as productive as possible; and
(c) there is freedom of choice of employment and the fullest possible opportunity for each worker to qualify for, and to use his skills and endowments in, a job for which he is well suited, irrespective of race, colour, sex, religion, political opinion, national extraction, or social origin.

3. The said policy shall take due account of the stage and level of economic development and the mutual relationships between employment objectives and other economic and social objectives, and shall be pursued by methods that are appropriate to national conditions and practices.

Article 2

Each Member shall, by such methods and to such extent as may be appropriate under national conditions

(a) decide on and keep under review, within the framework of a coordinated economic and social policy, the measures to be adopted for attaining the objectives specified in Article 1; and
(b) take such steps as may be needed, including when appropriate the establishment of programmes, for the application of these measures."

By the same token, Articles 2 and 3 of the ILO Convention (No. 111) concerning Discrimination (Employment and Occupation), 1958, provide that:

"*Article 2*

Each Member for which this Convention is in force undertakes to declare and pursue a national policy designed to promote, by methods appropriate to national conditions and practice, equality of opportunity and treatment in respect of employment and occupation, with a view to eliminating any discrimination in respect thereof.

Article 3

Each Member for which this Convention is in force undertakes, by methods appropriate to national conditions and practice

(a) to seek the cooperation of employers' and workers' organizations and other appropriate bodies in promoting the acceptance and observance of this policy;
(b) to enact such legislation and to promote such educational programmes as may be calculated to secure the acceptance and observance of the policy;
(c) to repeal any statutory provisions and modify any administrative instructions or practices which are inconsistent with the policy;
(d) to pursue the policy in respect of employment under the direct control of a national authority;
(e) to ensure observance of the policy in the activities of vocational guidance, vocational training and placement services under the direction of a national authority; and
(f) to indicate in its annual reports on the application of the Convention the action taken in pursuance of the policy and the results secured by such action."

33. These standards seek to make the public authorities' action in those areas more coherent and systematic; they define objectives, create mechanisms and structures adapted to the programmes chosen; they provide, as the case may be, for concrete measures concerning the labour market and the means of evaluating their effectiveness. In terms of employment, for example, some of these measures are apparently geared towards the immediate future (exemption from social security contributions to encourage the employment of young people at a given time), while others tend to lay the groundwork for a strategy to fight unemployment (such as the makeover of the occupational training system or, more simply, encouraging geographical or professional mobility).

34. It should be added that one legislative act can encompass both directly binding provisions and programmatic standards. Equal opportunity and equal pay legislation provide ample illustration thereof: promotional measures are accompanied by rules annulling acts of discrimination in the area considered.

35. In European and international law, programmatic standards are used as a matter of course to influence State action. Examples thereof can nevertheless also be found in domestic legislation. Japanese law imposes an obligation 'to endeavour' to take a measure as opposed to an 'obligation to do so', leaving it up to the administrative authorities – usually the Ministry of Labour – often with the trade unions and employers' associations, to convince enterprises to do all they can to translate the spirit of the law into action. In 1986, for example, an amendment to the Japanese Old Persons' Employment Stability Act required employers 'to endeavour' to postpone the mandatory retirement age, which until then had been well under 60, to 60 or beyond. A further amendment was introduced in 1990, making it mandatory for employers to 'endeavour' to re-employ retired workers, if they requested, until they reached the age of 65. Under this new rule, the Ministry of Labour ordered the drawing up of action programmes for that purpose. The government nevertheless subsequently found it necessary to increase the impact of the measures taken and in 1994 introduced a compulsory retirement age of 60 years. The law also strengthened the Ministry of Labour's administrative powers to encourage employers to keep their staff until age 65.[14] While the policy to extend the active working age can change because of momentary economic difficulties, the technique used seems deeply rooted in the country's legal tradition.

36. Programmatic standards reflect a determination to regulate by setting objectives. They are broadly based on other techniques for implementing social policies and sometimes refer to them explicitly: definition of political projects, adoption of economic measures, information and training campaigns, the use of non-legal technical norms, etc. This category contains standards to facilitate communication between social groups and other institutions, with a view to enabling them to solve the problems identified.[15] As has been said, they 'surround a process'. The European directives are a good example of such standards, as they are based, at least in part, on human resources management methods. Monitoring their application consequently gives rise to specific problems in that it involves the means used rather than the end results obtained.

37. Enacting legislation of this kind does not amount to 'deregulation' or to adopting a strictly voluntarist attitude, leaving the social partners entirely free to set the terms of their industrial relations.[16] Quite the contrary, the contacts between parties take place within a framework and objectives governed by legal rules, i.e. accompanied by the threat of sanction in the event of any breach.

38. Programmatic standards give rise to little debate. They are generally well-accepted, except when they increase the administrative burden on enterprises. Furthermore, insufficient use has been made of the means they afford for overcoming differences of opinion and for drawing up more adequate social policies on certain important matters, such as working time arrangements.

39. Most labour standards belong to a third group, with a more specifically technical content. They deal with working conditions, industrial justice, labour administration and social security. Most of the debate on the future of the legal protection of labour focuses on them. National – and international – lawmakers are faced with sometimes contradictory objectives, with tension between the different concerns of employers and wage-earners, or other groups, and the need to bring them in line with the public interest. Choices have to be made. Those choices are sometimes the fruit of semi-official negotiations and reciprocal concessions; at others they are the result of delicate arbitration. In democratic societies, the legislative branch often seeks a minimum consensus to guarantee that the standard will be effective.

---

14. *See* ILO, *World Labour Report*, Geneva, 1995, p. 82.
15. See on this point B. Hepple (ed.), *The making of labour law in Europe. A comparative study of 9 countries up to 1945*, London, Mansell, 1986, p. 10.
16. Comp. Wedderburn, 'The social charter in Britain. Labour law and labour courts', *The Modern Law Review*, Vol. 54(1), January 1991, pp. 3–4.

40. Agreement is more easily reached on topics like occupational health and safety than others. In those areas, employers and workers share the same broad concerns, related in good part to technical developments, even if their views differ on the practical methods of application or the pace of the planned reform. Hardly surprising, for example, that many European standards deal with occupational health and safety. A common approach is much more difficult to find on topics over which the proponents of a rigid system on the one hand and those of flexibility on the other tend to face off. Working time is a striking example. There has been heated debate on how to adapt the old rules on working hours to the new technical constraints and social aspirations. Any deadlocks usually do not stem from bureaucratic wrangling or the national system's lack of elasticity: they arise from the difficulty of reconciling varied and differing points of view on basic issues. For many years, for example, the waiver of the prohibition of night work for women employed in industry divided the world of labour. Solutions are today to be found in most European labour laws. It is also true that the European authorities worked hard towards that goal.

41. This type of agreement on the basic principles for a set of regulations is usually lacking today, hence entire sections of labour law have been laid open to question. A compromise seems all the more unlikely in that the workers' and even the employers' federations find it harder than in the past to speak on behalf of all those they represent. Technical standards focus most discussions on the best possible synthesis between economic objectives and labour protection. It is therefore above all in terms of those standards that the cost of labour law and social security must be examined.

B. *The Cost of Labour Standards*

42. There is obvious confusion in the discussions about the economic advantages and disadvantages of certain rules or types of labour regulations. The fact that the controversy concerns specialists from different fields – sociologists, political scientists, philosophers and many others in addition to lawyers and economists – only adds to the confusion.

43. To clarify the issue, the first thing required is the capacity to evaluate the economic impact of those standards relatively accurately. A quantitative or qualitative method can be chosen, but most of those who have tried their hand at the evaluation have opted for the second.[17] Many claim that satisfactory employment and labour protection gives enterprises – and economies – a very real competitive edge. It stimulates staff motivation and increases productivity. This so-called 'high road' argument seems in many respects convincing, but it has not put an end to the debate. Many employers still believe that paying low salaries and limiting expenditure on working environment arrangements will help them cut costs. What is more, in

---

17. There is a wealth of literature on the subject, but it is well worth rereading, for example, R. Freeman and J.L. Medoff, 'What do unions do?', New York, *Basic books*, 1984, or W. Sengenberger and D. Campbell (eds), *Creating economic opportunities. The role of labour standards in industrial restructuring*, Geneva, International Institute for Labour Studies, 1994.

Europe and Japan, where the phenomenon was until recently limited, a sharp increase has been observed in the recruitment of contingent workers, so as not to incur the financial risks of contracts without limit of time.

44. Exact figures seem to be expected in an area where it is apparently impossible to be certain of anything. How, then, to define accurately the economic effect of provisions on job security? And yet, for want of facts and figures, the vague and often in many respects irrational fear subsists that a limited period of notice for terminating an employment contract can jeopardise company competitiveness.

45. Reliable indicators are needed to evaluate the economic impact of implementing the values embodied in certain rules. Sometimes the law presumes what that impact is to limit the payment of certain benefits. Belgian legislation on the promotion of employment and the 'preventive' safeguard of productivity limited the salary increases obtained by collective bargaining under a complex system that nevertheless takes into account developments in the salary costs in Germany, France, and the Netherlands, neighbouring States considered to be Belgium's principal competitors. And while the purely economic and the socio-economic effects should not be overlooked, a distinction must be made between them. We cannot place enough emphasis on the importance of defining and selecting the factors to be used in constructing the indicators. How to explain, to take the example of legislation on redundancies, that recent analyses on the economic effects of dismissals did not include Japan, where growth was particularly spectacular in the 1980s and where it is especially difficult to lay off a worker? Also, clear distinctions must be made for the size of the enterprise and between the micro- and macroeconomic levels. Legislation on the prevention and compensation of occupational accidents, to give another example, obliges enterprises to cover certain costs, but it can also allow them to save more. The effects thereof on the national accounting would nevertheless appear on the whole to be even more positive.[18]

46. These indicators can be used as a basis on which to consider the application of certain values in different socio-economic contexts, separating that which is absolute (the protection of workers' lives) from that which is relative (worker comfort) in terms of values and their means of implementation.

C.   Autonomous Standards, Heteronomous Standards, and Alternatives to Social Regulation

47. More satisfactory replies to these questions should help strike an optimum balance between the legal option – which implies the use of coercive measures – and other techniques for implementing certain social objectives that rely principally on persuasion and rationality. The latter option includes obtaining political commitments, adopting economic measures, launching training initiatives and information campaigns and establishing 'technical' (as opposed to 'legal') standards and practical

---

18.   D. Andreoni, *Le coût des accidents du travail et des maladies professionnelles*, Geneva, ILO, 1985.

guidelines. These different means can be implemented in the absence of a true legal framework, and are quite improperly referred to as 'soft law', a comment that in no way diminishes their usefulness as evidenced, for example, by the countries of the European Union in their coordinated efforts to promote employment.[19]

48. The concept of 'rights', in particular with regard to social rights, is nevertheless ambiguous and calls for clarification. It refers first and foremost to a means of implementing a policy (by hypothesis social); it is used to demand a certain kind of conduct under threat of punishment. Both the policy and the conduct can of course at times seem perfectly detestable (imagine they had been imposed by a brutal dictator), but that does not necessarily affect the binding nature of the legal rules in which they are expressed.

49. To this positivistic concept of rights – and of law – is added another that gives the rights themselves – rather than the power that enforces them – a specific goal, the pursuit of certain values (such as social justice) based on moral or religious precepts, or on a vision of society and the relations between its members.

50. Invoking principles and setting social objectives when drawing up and implementing policy seems an eminently reasonable and often very desirable thing to do. However, the affirmation in this context of moral 'rights' that everyone should enjoy does not automatically make them those rights in nature. To proclaim, for example, the right to work without an accompanying threat of sanction for failure to respect that right is tantamount to expressing a wish or a political message that is certainly important but carries no legal weight.

51. Again, these remarks are in no way intended to detract from the usefulness of such proclamations or their capacity to convince. In many cases, moreover, the socio-economic situation prevents the adjunction of a legal dimension that would ensure permanence and coercion. When, however, the force of law is added – and only then – the lawmaker's intent can be discerned in the specific rule adopted and the legal standard interpreted in terms of that intent.

52. If the legal option is chosen, then a decision must be made on the most appropriate form of regulation. Regulation can be left to voluntary and private initiative (self-regulation), be imposed by the State (which gives the regulations permanence and makes them foreseeable and binding), or originate (in an agreement) in a dialogue to be defined between the social actors. A satisfactory mix of all three depends on the circumstances in each country, in particular in a democratic society, on the degree of social consensus that can be attained.

---

19. *See* H. Borstlap, 'Modernized Industrial Relations. A condition for European employment growth. A Dutch view', *The International Journal of Comparative Labour Law and Industrial Relations*, Winter 1999, Vol. 15(4), pp. 365–382. In the same issue, *see* J.H. Pedersen, 'Mainlines in Danish labour market policy as presented in the Danish National Action Plan', pp. 383–401 and J. Chozas Pedrero, 'The Luxembourg process and the Spanish experience', pp. 403–418.

53. More specifically, in terms of legislation the first step is to decide which regulatory functions concerning employment and work are to remain in the hands of the State and its administrations and which are to be left to the private sector. The question arises *inter alia* with regard to the following functions: employment services/agencies; social protection (social security, social benefits, social aid); settlement of labour conflicts (individual or collective; conflicts of law or of interests); even inspection of working conditions.

54. Another option is to distinguish, in those areas left to the private sector, between the functions falling only to the commercial sector (for example, the multinationals) and those falling to players that are not directly profit-seeking (employers' associations, unions, and so on). The latter cover in particular regulations reached by collective agreement at different levels above the enterprise. Another choice consists in whether or not to include new actors in the bargaining process: global, regional, or local institutions; other associations representative of civil society, etc.

55. While the calls for a new social pact are indeed multiplying, the parties thereto remain to be defined. One natural path to follow in the search for a consensus would appear to be a return to the principles of liberty and democracy on which modern societies were built. Freedom of association, expression, and assembly most assuredly give all those facing the same problems the possibility to set up institutions that act as intermediaries between the citizens and the State; in France there was talk of a 'boom' in the number of associations in the social sector.[20] Three kinds of groups have taken on a significant role in the establishment or application of social policies:[21] employers' and workers' organizations, social associations that do not fit into the previous category, and other NGOs whose purpose is social.

56. The ILO is very familiar with the term 'employers' and workers' organizations', which is used to refer to professional organizations that aim to promote and defend the interests of employers and workers.[22] The concept is broad in scope. With regard to the workers, it covers trade unions and, no matter what the words used, associations with similar goals for wage-earners or the self-employed, even the poorest and weakest among them. The participation in traditional trade union action by associations coming from the most underprivileged sectors of the population, in particular the informal rural or urban sector in developing countries, seems to have gained widespread acceptance.[23]

---

20. G. Malaurie, 'Le boom des associations', *Problèmes économiques*, No. 2605, 24 February 1999, pp. 22 et seq.
21. ILO, *World Labour Report 1997–98: Industrial relations, democracy and social stability, op.cit.,* pp. 47 et seq.
22. In particular in the Conventions (No. 87) on Freedom of Association and Protection of the Right to Organize, 1948, (No. 98) on the Right to Organize and Collective Bargaining, 1949, and (No. 141) on Rural Workers' Organisations, 1975.
23. *See* ICFTU, *The Global Market – Trade Unionism's Greatest Challenge*, 16th World Congress of the International Confederation of Free Trade Unions (Brussels, 25–29 June 1996), Brussels, 1996, pp. 67–69.

57. The second group of associations consists of those whose aim is social but that were created for different, often more limited purposes: the promotion and defence of women, consumers, the environment, small businesses, civil liberties, local or neighbourhood interests, students, parents of pupils, community or ethnic minority concerns, etc.; some take the form of cooperatives. Like workers' and employers' associations, these groups act as an intermediary between their members and the public authorities or intergovernmental institutions. They have several characteristics in common with professional organizations. For example, they are democratically created (by association) and make decisions by democratic process; this usually ensures that their structures are transparent and facilitates verification of their representativity and their objectives. Relations of greater trust can therefore be developed among these groups, and between them and the workers' federations. In fact, there are countless examples of alliances reached for industrial campaigns or for broader purposes.

58. The non-governmental organizations with social goals that make up the third group are not fundamentally based on associative principles. They run the gamut from churches, charitable organizations and aid networks (in particular for the unemployed) to projects for technical cooperation, assistance or development and the protection of occupational health and safety. They include men and women with practical experience who work for their own sake to train, insert and rehabilitate people headed for social exclusion (the chronically unemployed, the homeless, welfare recipients or those on a minimum guaranteed income, heavily indebted households, clandestine immigrants, drug addicts or simply the destitute). These institutions often work together with the local authorities, their development agents and their social workers. The absence of the same transparency in terms of representativity and resources can make it more difficult to carry out joint projects with this category of group. At times, however, they have proven to be useful partners.

59. The last two categories of groups, in particular those with a supra-national, regional or global structure, have recently had a visible impact on social, national and international policies. Yet the action they take is often erratic or unexpected, as it depends on the media coverage it gets and on financial sponsorship. Professional organizations, on the other hand, because they are permanent and truly representative – even when union members account for only 5–10 per cent of the active population, the unions usually have a membership rate that is markedly higher than that of the other groups – are a permanent part of the labour scene.

60. More generally, what possibilities do these 'civilian' groups really have to take action? To what extent can they contribute to social policies and under what conditions? These questions have given rise to a wealth of literature.[24] One must also ask:

(a) Can a better tie-in be found between legal measures and the action of these groups? In cases where their activities are carried out principally in the field, some of them have taken part in real negotiations (in South Africa, Ireland, Italy,

---

24. *See* for example the March–April 1999 issue of *Esprit,* on the topic 'A quoi sert le travail social'.

Latin America), the outcome of which may be purely political or also legal, i.e. accompanied by sanctions.

(b) Might more programmatic but directly threatening labour rules not promote recognition of the social actors and give them a freer hand, while channelling their efforts towards objectives defined in advance by the public authorities?

61. We shall consider those questions below.

62. With regard to State regulations, it must be decided what institution is to issue the rules: parliament, government, the judicial authorities, the administration (centralized or not), the local authorities, etc. Thought will also have to be given to the extent to which (criteria; means chosen; institutions required) the public authorities will, by producing binding rules or by encouraging or assisting the citizens and their associations, find the most adequate solutions of and among themselves. In that case, legislation essentially provides a framework for private initiative.

63. Two further questions arise. The first concerns coordination of these different sources of regulations; the second, which is essential to the credibility of any system, concerns the way in which the regulations are applied and controlled, the place of the judges and the role ('policemen', conciliators, mediators?) of labour inspectors. In the specific case of unilateral initiatives by the employer (the example of many codes of conduct), specific information must be provided on the legal validity and duration of the undertaking and on the means of verifying effective implementation – no easy task.

64. All these options depend on the kind of policy chosen. The responses vary from State abstention to the concentration in State hands of decision-making power; we have already mentioned how unlikely it is that these radical positions will provide solutions to the social problems of job and income precarity. Between the two extremes, however, there lies an entire range of modes of participation in the establishment and application of social policies. Dialogue can take an almost infinite variety of forms, including, for example, consultation before legislation is enacted. All that remains to be said is to underscore the need to broaden the bases of social consensus to encompass all actors in social life, including associations representing the most underprivileged.

III. A Need for Innovative Formula for Social Relationships

65. Reformulating labour policies in a way that deals with all the problems mentioned requires a series of measures. They relate to the levels of dialogue, the role of the State and the content of the discussions.

A. *Broadening the Levels of Dialogue*

66. First point: there must be more levels of dialogue. Discussions usually take place at the national, sector or company level, with the focus on one or the other, depending on the country and the period.

67. With the opening of borders to capital and products and the regionalization and subsequent globalization of the economy, an obvious need has arisen for labour-management relations at those levels, too. It is in fact above all on those levels that the new actors on the labour scene operate and that any alliances will therefore be most easily concluded. There are examples of negotiations at those levels, but not many. The pioneering role of the European Union in this respect is well known, with in particular the establishment of European works councils and the conclusion of true collective agreements at the level of a multinational (such as Danone), a sector of activity (the footwear industry) or at intersectorial level (with collective agreements on parental leave, part-time work and fixed-term contracts). Other initiatives are also worthy of note. The Japanese have established an essentially tripartite liaison conference that meets twice a year to discuss multinational labour issues. As a result, the Association of Japanese Overseas Companies has published a non-binding code of conduct for national investors abroad. Companies such as Honda and Matsushita have established transnational ties of cooperation with trade unions as part of their strategy to develop human resources. The trade unions, working with other groups, have launched worldwide campaigns that have been picked up in the media (for example, the 1999 Seattle meeting) and in some cases resulted in discussions. Programmatic standards have sometimes been adopted – for example by the European Union – to facilitate relations at those levels.

68. The levels of negotiation should also be diversified locally. Here, too, a significant number of experiences and arrangements have met with success. Take, for example, Italy, where hours – in the workplace, for public transport and public and private services – were re-organized in several major cities. Associations of women, users, shop owners, neighbourhoods, etc., coupled their efforts with those of the unions and the public authorities (at times also employers' associations) to improve the links between the requirements of city-dwellers in their private and working lives.[25] The Garment Industry Corporation, a tripartite body set up by New York's apparel industry to protect the industry and its jobs by upgrading qualifications and marketing methods and by using new production and management techniques, furnishes another example,[26] as do local employment initiatives in Belgium and Ireland which were also proven successes.[27]

---

25. S. Bontiglioli and M. Mareggi (eds), 'Il tempo e la città fre natura e storia. Atlante di progetti sui tempo della città', *Urbanistica Quaderni*, May 1997, No. 12; M.C. Belloni and F. Bambi (eds), *Microfisica della cittadinanza. Città, genere, politiche dei tempi*, Milan, Franco Agneli, 1997.

26. B.G. Herman, *See what? The New York apparel industry in the global economy: Inevitable decline or possibilities for industrial upgrade?* Working paper (International workshop on global production and local jobs: New perspectives on enterprize networks, employment and local development policy, Geneva, 9–10 March 1998), International Institute for Labour Studies, Geneva, 1998.

27. OECD (Labour Management Programme), *The role of trade unions in local development*, Paris, 1997; M. Geddes, *Local partnership: a successful strategy for social cohesion?* Dublin, European Foundation for the improvement of living and working conditions, 1998; comp. J. Bauer and D. Bell (eds), *The East Asian Challenge for Human Rights*, Cambridge, Cambridge University Press, 1999, p. 23.

B.   A Renewed Role for the State

69.   In every case, the State – or more specifically the public authorities at national, regional and local level – has an important role to play: to recognize these actors, to promote their development and improve their access to information (by removing obstacles such as anti-union practices), to recognize the institutions they create (for example, by taking part in their creation) and to facilitate relations between them. The State can do this by means of the programmatic rules we referred to earlier. That is the second point. In short, the State is not so much a tutor as it is a source of inspiration and a mediator creating an environment that is conducive to dialogue. It sets up communications structures to facilitate dialogue;[28] it opens the bodies implementing labour policies for vocational training, credit, social security, etc., to those representative players; it extends the scope of their autonomous negotiations or has them systematically participate in the drafting of labour policies and of the laws that translate them into lasting and to varying degrees binding measures. The same applies to inter-State authorities.

70.   This mission has a special dimension when it comes to specific kinds of activity, such as those of the informal sector or small- and medium-sized businesses, where social dialogue is more difficult to put into practice. Yet successful attempts have been made to set up a favourable framework. The achievements of the districts of Emilia Romagna in Italy are an oft-cited example.[29] Even in the informal sector, success stories are not unheard of.[30]

71.   The strengthening of the capacities of social negotiators should lead, if it is well done, to a consolidation of the State's own position in the globalized context. The State, as we have pointed out, should not promote only these renewed forms of participation, it must also ensure good coordination between the different levels.

C.   Standards with What Content?

72.   The broadening of the bases for social dialogue, the third point, is intended to facilitate the search for the best possible answer, in a given community at a specific point in its history, to the recurring question of the relationship between quality of work and quantity of employment.

---

28.   *See also* A. Supiot (ed.), *Au-delà de l'emploi. Transformations du travail et devenir du droit de travail en Europe.* Report to the European Commission, Paris, Flammarion, 1999, in particular pp. 270, 271; *see also* F. Durán López, 'Globalización y relaciones de trabajo', *Civitas*, No. 32, Nov.–Dec. 1998, pp. 869, 888. For a more general vision of the new role of the State, *see* P. Evans, 'The Eclipse of the State? Reflections on Stateness in an Era of Globalization', *World Politics*, Vol. 50 (I), October 1997, pp. 62–87.

29.   F. Pyke, G. Becattini, and W. Sengenberger (eds), *Industrial districts and inter-firm cooperation in Italy*, Geneva, International Institute for Labour Studies, 1990; F. Cossentino, F. Pyke, and W. Sengenberger, *Local and regional response to global pressure: the case of Italy and its industrial districts*, Geneva, International Institute for Labour Studies, 1996.

30.   ILO, *op.cit.*, pp. 175 et seq.

73. Research in this field has been carried out mainly within the model, or paradigm, of the labour market, an appropriate framework for explaining the trade-off between employment and remuneration in a labour relationship, especially when the relationship was long-lasting. The framework is less suitable when the model incorporates the more unstable forms of employment that have recently proliferated, and self-employment. It is inappropriate for the analysis of other activities such as volunteer (or very low paid) work done individually (babysitting, care of the elderly, the handicapped, etc.) or within an institution or association, training and re-training, and leave for family reasons (maternity leave, parental leave, etc.) or for civic duties (military service). Although many of these activities are socially useful, they do not really fit into the paradigm of exchange for profit.

74. Efforts have been made to take fuller account of these developments in socio-economic analysis. Researchers[31] focusing on labour market arrangements have pointed out that the new institutional arrangements increasingly comprise ongoing training, that the heterogeneity of individual needs requires greater flexibility in the organization of work, and that atypical forms of employment call for renewed consideration of the relationship between work and other useful activities. They have put forward the concept of the transitional labour market to define the principal conditions for implementation of these new arrangements (in terms of organization, income policies, labour policies, and their fiscal repercussions).

75. The future of the labour market is viewed in some quarters with great pessimism, and the rapid spread of the informal sector in both industrialized and developing countries is underlined to justify *inter alia* the payment of a guaranteed citizenship income.[32]

76. Other, notably French, researchers[33] have more clearly distanced themselves from the framework of the labour market. They emphasize that a working life can take many forms in the course of a career: employment, self-employment or entrepreneurship; volunteer and paid work; work in the public or private sector; training courses, internships or re-training; activities of a private (housekeeping) or public nature (military service, political activities). They underscore the ambiguity of the legal criterion of subordination, a decisive element in the employment relationship.

77. From this perspective, formulas have been proposed that outline possible scenarios for working lives that are made up of modules to be coordinated, with work alternating with re-training and leave (maternity or parental leave, military service, etc.).[34] Improved qualifications and greater independence – one goes hand-in-hand

---

31. *See New institutional arrangements in the labour market. Transitional labour markets as a new full employment concept*, Berlin, European Academy of the Urban Environment, 1998.
32. *See* G. Standing, *Global labour flexibility. Seeking distributive justice*, London, MacMillan, 1999.
33. *See* in particular A. Supiot (ed.), *Le travail en perspective*, Paris, LGDJ, 1998.
34. *See* the report by the Commission (*Commissariat général au Plan*) chaired by Jean Boissonnat, 'Le travail dans vingt ans', Paris, O. Jacob, *La documentation française*, 1995; *see also* A. Valli (ed.),

with the other – would ensure more satisfactory coordination between different individual activities – professional work, training and re-training, leave for specific reasons, volunteer or poorly paid but socially valuable work (childcare or care of the
elderly, assistance for the victims of all kinds of abuse, etc.) – and allow those kinds
of activity to be planned over an entire lifespan. They would help resolve the problem
of conflicting interests, first for the worker himself, then in his employment relationship, for example, the quest for a satisfactory balance between private life (family)
and professional activities.

78. These proposals cast a fresh light on the segmentation of working lives
observed in industrialized countries. They also enhance our understanding of the
various forms of professional activity carried out in developing countries, *inter alia*
in the informal sector. They can be used to justify payment of a minimum income,
or even the granting of limited credit for certain purposes (training, care of people in
need of care, social work within an association, etc.).

79. Their implementation nevertheless encounters major obstacles. First, we
must not be too hasty in declaring traditional employment a thing of the past, as is
borne out by the statistics. Salaried positions remain the best known guarantee of
income security.[35] Second, it is difficult to separate work and income and to reach a
consensus on how, in the absence of pay, a subsistence allowance is to be financed
(via income tax or turnover tax? via VAT?). But above and beyond those considerations, can a career really be laid out in this way? There is a difference, of course,
between insecurity and uncertainty: while social protection undoubtedly tends to
make those who work or want to work feel more secure in that it covers threats to
their lives, their health, their survival and that of their families, it is most emphatically not aimed – how could it be? – at preventing all mishaps, at completely organizing entire lives, in short at eliminating uncertainty. For the most enterprising
among us, uncertainty provides an incentive to create, to innovate and to undertake,
and is therefore a factor of progress.

80. Perhaps it would be better to proceed with more tangible situations, to have
recourse whenever possible to those programmatic standards we would like to see
more of and to encourage the social negotiators, who are closer to day-to-day reality, to assume a greater responsibility, where they have not already done so, in the
implementation of labour policies. Take the example of the Netherlands' system of
medical benefits; employers are responsible for managing the benefits but their
amount is fixed by the law.[36] By the same token, the diversification of situations has

---

Tempo di lavoro e occupazione. Il caso italiano, Rome, La Nueva Italia Scientifica, 1988, pp. 13–38
and 177–197; K.L. Ladear, 'Social risks, welfare rights and the paradigms of proceduralisation. The
combining of the liberal constitutional State and the social State', in J. de Munck, J. Lenoble and
M. Molitsz (eds), *L'avenir de la concertation sociale en Europe*, Louvain, Centre for the philosophy of law, Louvain Catholic University, 1995, p. 143.

35. R. Castel, 'Droit du travail: redéploiement ou refondation', in *Droit social*, No. 5, 1999,
pp. 438–442.
36. P. Auer, *Employment revival in Europe. Labour market success in Austria, Denmark, Ireland and
the Netherlands*, Geneva, ILO, p. 63.

obliged lawmakers in countries such as Belgium, France[37] and Italy to authorize derogations to labour rules (in particular concerning working hour arrangements) in collective agreements. The law does no more than set the framework for this greater flexibility, i.e. the conditions (and possible compensation) and scope of the exceptions allowed. In a similar vein, the law can define the circumstances – and the limits – in which the public authorities allow recourse to conciliation, mediation, and private arbitration of social conflicts.

81. Two avenues of reflection are open to the social negotiators and to the public authorities. The first consists in giving official recognition to those socially useful activities we mentioned earlier and to their protagonists. After all, the arts and the sciences already often do so. Social status must be accompanied by a corresponding decent wage provided by the beneficiaries or by State institutions. This would also result in a renewal of the analysis grids traditionally adopted for the informal sector and, again, in the incorporation of the activities of private associations.

82. Socially useful activities are understood to include but also to go beyond assistance for the most needy. Obviously, the aim is not simply to delegate a public service to private associations,[38] which might result simply in the establishment of a new market open to commercial groups or in bureaucratic red tape. Socially useful activities comprise the organization of systems such as the 'time banks' in Italy, France, and elsewhere, i.e. those exchange networks between private individuals where a service received is paid for by making time available to someone else (for example, babysitting in exchange for some minor household repairs). Obviously, many of these activities consolidate local community stability and help prevent the kind of social upheaval mentioned above, no matter where. The history of social security shows that, in the past, private institutions – relayed later on and only to a certain extent by public organisms – sprang up in many Western countries to meet the new and urgent needs arising from the industrial revolution and its social implications. By the same token it can be said that today, in many cases, these private groups fill a social void, meet an unsatisfied collective need.

83. The second path is to identify new forms of security that are compatible with a less stable employment sector. Institutions serving as points of anchorage in a context of increased mobility (from one company, one working relationship or one activity to another) must be invented or revived. The two examples below show that the idea is not pure speculation or out of this world.

84. The first concerns what in the Netherlands is called 'flexicurity', which seeks to combine employment flexibility with income security for the worker. On the basis of a broad consultation of the parties concerned, a law dated 1 January 1999 established a new regime for temporary workers: after having worked for the employment

---

37. For France, *see* G. Lyon-Caen, *Le droit du travail. Une technique réversible*, Paris, Dalloz, 1995, pp. 41 et seq.; Th. Revet, 'L'ordre public dans les relations de travail', in Th. Revet (ed.), *L'ordre public à la fin du XXIe siècle*, Paris, Dalloz, 1996, pp. 61 et seq.
38. *See* the issue of *Esprit* previously cited, pp. 108 et seq.

agency for a certain period of time (in principle 26 weeks, but that period can be and indeed has been extended by collective agreement), workers are considered to be under the benefit of an employment contract with the agency.[39] This gives them a home base that allows them to benefit more fully from the protection of labour and social security laws, while maintaining employment mobility.

85. In the second example, in the United States social benefits are obtained chiefly through the company and are in principle lost if workers leave their jobs (hence the question of transfer of acquired rights). In Silicon Valley, the Mecca of the new economy, Amy Dean, regional AFL-CIO head, has proposed her organization to offer workers who have become 'roving' – and thus especially mobile – the permanent link dropped by the companies and to provide them with health insurance, unemployment insurance and permanent training.[40] In several northern European countries – Belgium, Denmark, Finland, Ireland, and Sweden – the trade unions continue to handle – alone or otherwise – the payment of unemployment benefits.[41] The reason is to be found in their history, in the fact that they were the first to help the jobless, before the State took over responsibility for that task.

86. The ultimate aim of any labour policy and its implementation remains unchanged: to enable men and women to cope with the ups and downs that markets generate. Fear makes men weak of mind, Spinoza wrote. The democratic States have established mechanisms for the representation of their citizens in the decision-making process, including parliamentary systems and the workings of social dialogue in the broad sense. The opening of borders and the accelerated internationalization of economic exchanges have lowered each nation's capacity, and that of its participatory bodies, to control economic and social policies. The great difficulty, and at the same time the pressing need in the new century, is to make up for the democratic deficit,[42] to reinvent new institutions offering all those concerned the chance to take part, no matter at what level, in defining and implementing policies and programmes that provide them with decent work, meaning a job performed in conditions of respect for human dignity and with social protection covering the risks it entails.

SELECT BIBLIOGRAPHY

D. Andreoni, *Le coût des accidents du travail et des maladies professionnelles*, Geneva, ILO, 1985.

P. Auer, *Employment revival in Europe. Labour market success in Austria, Denmark, Ireland and the Netherlands*, Geneva, ILO.

---

39. *See* for example G. Heerma van Voss, 'The 'tulip model' and the new legislation on temporary work in the Netherlands', *The International Journal of Comparative Labour Law and Industrial Relations,* 1999 (winter), Vol. 15(4), pp. 419–430.
40. *See Le Monde*, 25 January 2000, p. 15.
41. Those countries are among those with the highest trade union membership rates: *see* ILO, *World Labour Report 1997–98: Industrial relations, democracy and social stability*, Geneva, 1997, p. 24.
42. Comp. J. Mazur, 'Labor's New Internationalism', *Foreign Affairs*, Vol. 79(1), February 2000, pp. 79–93.

Comp. J. Bauer and D. Bell (eds), T*he East Asian Challenge for Human Rights*, Cambridge, Cambridge University Press, 1999.

J.F. Beffa, R. Boyer and J.Ph. Touffut, 'Le droit du travail face à l'hétérogénéité des relations salariales', *Droit social*, No. 12, December 1999, pp. 1039–1051.

D. Behar, 'Question urbaine et question sociale: quel lien pour quelle politique publique?', *Problèmes économiques*, No. 2574, 24 June 1998, pp. 1–5.

M.C. Belloni and F. Bambi (eds), *Microfisica della cittadinanza. Città, genere, politiche dei tempi*, Milan, Franco Agneli, 1997.

R. Blanpain, *Institutional Changes and European Social Policies after the Treaty of Amsterdam*, The Hague, Kluwer, 1998.

–, 'Social dialogue. Economic interdependence and labour law', Report to the 6th European Congress for Labour Law and Social Security, Warsaw, 13–17 September 1999, Warsaw, Scholar, 1999.

– (ed.), 'Multinational enterprises and the social challenges of the XXIst century', in *Bulletin of Comparative Labour Relations*, No. 37, The Hague, Kluwer, p. 2000.

S. Bontiglioli and M. Mareggi (eds), 'Il tempo e la città fre natura e storia. Atlante di progetti sui tempo della città', *Urbanistica Quaderni*, May 1997, No. 12.

H. Borstlap, 'Modernised Industrial Relations. A condition for European employment growth. A Dutch view', *The International Journal of Comparative Labour Law and Industrial Relations*, Vol. 15(4), Winter 1999, pp. 365–382.

R. Castel, *Les métamorphoses de la question sociale, une chronique du salariat*, Paris, Fayard, 1995, and 'Centralité du travail et cohésion sociale', in J. Kergoat, J. Boutet, H. Jacot, and D. Linhart, *Le monde du travail*, Paris, La Découverte, 1998.

–, 'Droit du travail: redéploiement ou refondation', in *Droit social*, No. 5, 1999, pp. 438–442.

J. Chozas Pedrero, 'The Luxembourg process and the Spanish experience', *The International Journal of Comparative Labour Law and Industrial Relations*, Vol. 15(4), Winter 1999, pp. 403–418.

Commissariat général au Plan chaired by Jean Boissonnat, 'Le travail dans vingt ans', Paris, O. Jacob, *La documentation française*, 1995.

F. Cossentino, F. Pyke, and W. Sengenberger, *Local and regional response to global pressure: The case of Italy and its industrial districts*, Geneva, International Institute for Labour Studies, 1996.

J. Donzelot, 'La nouvelle question urbain', *Esprit*, November 1999, pp. 87–114.

F. Durán López, 'Globalización y relaciones de trabajo', *Civitas*, No. 32, Nov.–Dec. 1998, pp. 869–888.

European Academy of the Urban Environment, *New institutional arrangements in the labour market. Transitional labour markets as a new full employment concept*, Berlin, 1998.

P. Evans, 'The Eclipse of the State? Reflections on Stateness in an Era of Globalization', *World Politics,* Vol. 50(I), October 1997, pp. 62–87.

J.B. Figueiredo and A. de Haan, *Social exclusion: An ILO perspective*, Geneva, International Institute for Labour Studies, 1998.

R. Freeman and J.L. Medoff, 'What do unions do?', New York, *Basic books*, 1984.

M. Geddes, *Local partnership: a successful strategy for social cohesion?* Dublin, European Foundation for the Improvement of Living and Working Conditions, 1998.

G. Heerma van Voss, 'The 'tulip model' and the new legislation on temporary work in the Netherlands', *The International Journal of Comparative Labour Law and Industrial Relations,* Vol. 15(4), (winter) 1999, pp. 419–430.

B. Hepple (ed.), *The making of labour law in Europe. A comparative study of 9 countries up to 1945,* London, Mansell, 1986.

B.G. Herman, *See what? The New York apparel industry in the global economy: Inevitable decline or possibilities for industrial upgrade?* Working paper (International workshop on global production and local jobs: New perspectives on enterprise networks, employment and local development policy, Geneva, 9–10 March 1998), International Institute for Labour Studies, Geneva, 1998.

ICFTU, *The Global Market – Trade Unionism's Greatest Challenge,* 16th World Congress of the International Confederation of Free Trade Unions (Brussels, 25–29 June 1996), Brussels, 1996.

ILO, *World Labour Report,* Geneva, 1995.

–, *World Labour Report 1997–98: Industrial relations, democracy and social stability,* Geneva, 1997.

–, Declaration on Fundamental Principles and Rights at Work and its Follow-up, adopted by the International Labour Conference on 18 June 1998.

–, *Decent work,* Report of the Director-General to the 87th Session (June 1999) of the International Labour Conference, Geneva, ILO, 1999.

W. Jenks, *Law, Freedom and Welfare,* London, Oceana Publications, 1963.

K.L. Ladear, 'Social risks, welfare rights and the paradigms of proceduralisation. The combining of the liberal constitutional State and the social State', in J. de Munck, J. Lenoble and M. Molitsz (eds), *L'avenir de la concertation sociale en Europe,* Louvain, Centre for the philosophy of law, Louvain Catholic University, 1995.

A. Lalande, *Vocabulaire technique et critique de la philosophie,* Paris, PUF, 1962.

G. Lyon-Caen, *Le droit du travail. Une technique réversible,* Paris, Dalloz, 1995.

G. Malaurie, 'Le boom des associations', *Problèmes économiques,* No. 2605, 24 February 1999, pp. 22 et seq.

J.T. Matthews, 'Power shift', *Foreign Affairs,* Jan.–Feb. 1997, pp. 50–66.

comp J. Mazur, 'Labor's New Internationalism', *Foreign Affairs,* Vol. 79(1), February 2000, pp. 79–93.

OECD (Labour Management Programme), *The role of trade unions in local development,* Paris, 1997.

J.H. Pedersen, 'Mainlines in Danish labour market policy as presented in the Danish National Action Plan', *The International Journal of Comparative Labour Law and Industrial Relations,* Vol. 15(4), Winter 1999, pp. 383–401.

F. Pyke, G. Becattini, and W. Sengenberger (eds), *Industrial districts and inter-firm cooperation in Italy,* Geneva, International Institute for Labour Studies, 1990.

Th. Revet, 'L'ordre public dans les relations de travail', in Th. Revet (ed.), *L'ordre public à la fin du XXIe siècle,* Paris, Dalloz, 1996.

G. Rodgers, Ch. Gore, and J.B. Figueiredo (eds), *Social Exclusion: Rhetoric, Reality, Responses,* Geneva, International Institute for Labour Studies, 1995.

W. Sengenberger and D. Campbell (eds), *Creating economic opportunities. The role of labour standards in industrial restructuring,* Geneva, International Institute for Labour Studies, 1994.

J.-M. Servais, 'Le droit international en mouvement: déploiement et approches nouvelles', *Droit social,* May 1991, No. 5, pp. 449 et seq., comp.

J.-M. Servais, 'The International Labour Organisation', in R. Blanpain (ed.), *International Encyclopedia of Law*, The Hague, Kluwer, 1996, pp. 1 et seq.

G. Standing, *Global labour flexibility. Seeking distributive justice*, London, MacMillan, 1999.

M. Stolleis, *Histoire du droit public en Allemagne. Droit public impérial et sciences de la police 1600–1800*, Paris, PUF, 1998.

A. Supiot (ed.), *Le travail en perspective*, Paris, LGDJ, 1998.

– (ed.), *Au-delà de l'emploi. Transformations du travail et devenir du droit de travail en Europe*. Report to the European Commission, Paris, Flammarion, 1999.

A. Valli (ed.), *Tempo di lavoro e occupazione. Il caso italiano*, Rome, La Nueva Italia Scientifica, 1988.

P. Verge and G. Vallée, *Un droit du travail? Essai sur la specificité du droit du travail*, Cowansville (Quebec), Yvon Blais, 1997.

Comp. Wedderburn, 'The social charter in Britain. Labour law and labour courts', *The Modern Law Review*, Vol. 54(1), January 1991, pp. 3–4.

Chapter 16. Equality and Prohibition of Discrimination in Employment

R. Ben-Israel

I. THE NOTION

1. The principle of equality and prohibition of discrimination in employment (hereinafter: EPD) is based upon the legal and moral proposition that workers who are alike should be treated alike.[1] This proposition requires one both to analyse the circumstances under which two workers are considered to be alike and, as a consequence entitled to equal treatment, and to clarify what is meant by equality of treatment. The answer to these questions is determinative to the substance and scope of EPD. In principle, it is possible to answer these questions in different ways. For example, 'workers who are alike' could mean workers who are alike in every respect. The difficulty with this interpretation is that no two workers are alike in every respect. Alternatively, 'workers who are alike' might mean workers who, although not alike in every respect, are alike in some respects. The problem here is that while the first definition will likely exclude virtually all workers from its ambit, the alternative definition may well include within its scope every worker, because all workers are probably alike in some particular respect. As a result, neither of these definitions is capable of specifying what is meant by the proposition that workers who are alike should be treated alike. The same is true when the notion of equality of treatment is analysed. Thus, as, for example, equality of treatment can be expressed either in 'arithmetical' terms, which means providing the same thing to everyone; or in 'geometric' terms, which means giving to everyone in proportion, and if so, what will the criteria be?[2]

2. Consequently, for the proposition to have operative meaning, it must incorporate some external set of values. Without such imported values, the notion of EPD

---

1. Concerning the following approach to the notion of equality *see* P. Westen, 'The Empty Idea of Equality', Vol. 95, *Harvard Law Review*, 1982, p. 537.
2. *See* E. Vogel-Polsky, *Positive Action and the Constitutional and Legislative Hindrances to its Implemen-tation in the Member States of the Council of Europe*, Strasbourg, 1989 (hereinafter: Vogel-Polsky).

would remain meaningless, because it would be a mere linguistic formula without any bench mark on how it should be applied. EPD has no substantive moral content of its own. Consequently, the scope of EPD is determined in accordance with the moral values and social policy adopted either by the legislator or by the judiciary when called upon to adjudicate cases in which the matter of EPD is involved. Furthermore, because the substance of EPD is determined by reference to an external set of values, they can always be replaced by a new set. In particular, the scope of EPD may well be changed whenever it conflicts with other values which are preferred by the legislator or the judiciary at a particular time and place.

II. Sources of the International Labour Standard of EPD[3]

3. The doctrine of EPD is given expression in a large number of international instruments,[4] and is recognized as a positive right in numerous national constitutions and legislative enactments.[5] The general principle of equality is promoted by the United Nations, most fundamentally by the Declaration of Human Rights of 1948, which provides in Article 2 that 'everyone is entitled to all the rights and freedoms set forth in the Declaration, without distinction of any kind, such as race, colour, sex, language, religion, political or other opinion, national or social origin, property, birth, or other status'. This principle is reaffirmed by Article 2 para. 1 of the International Civil and Political Rights Covenant. In addition, the International Covenant on Economic, Social and Cultural Rights provides for an analogous right to equality, formulated in terms of an undertaking of the State Parties. Moreover, the fact that both the Declaration (Article 23) and the Covenant (Article 2, para. 3; Article 3, para. 7(a) and (c)) specifically deal with rights in the field of employment indicates that the general principle of non-discrimination applies to such rights.

4. On the ILO plane, the principle of EPD was referred to in its founding Constitution in 1919. But, it was in the Declaration of Philadelphia in 1944 that the ILO explicitly proclaimed as a fundamental principle, that 'all human beings, irrespective of race, creed or sex, have the right to pursue both their material well-being and their spiritual development in conditions of freedom and dignity, of economic security and equal opportunity'. This principle was consequently incorporated into the ILO Constitution and put into effect through a number of Conventions and Recommendations, the most comprehensive of which is the Discrimination (Employment and Occupation) Convention (No. 111) (hereinafter: Convention No. 111),

---

3. Hereinafter: ILSEPD.
4. On the international standard of EPD *see* N. Valticos, International Labour Law, in *International Encyclopaedia for Labour Law and Industrial Relations* (ed. in chief), Blanpain, Deventer, 1984. For a comparative study of the notion of EPD *see* Blanpain, Equality of Treatment in Employment, *International Encyclopedia of Comparative Law*, Chapter 10A, Tubingen, 1990 (hereinafter: Blanpain 1990).
5. For the extent to which equality in employment is guaranteed in constitutions *see* D. Ziskind, 'Labor Law in Latin American Constitutions', *Com. L.L.*, Vol. 6, 1984, p. 1; D. Ziskind, 'Labor provisions in Asian Constitutions', *Com. L.L.*, Vol. 6, 1984, p. 117; D. Ziskind, 'Labor Provisions in the Constitutions of Europe', *Com. L.L.*, Vol. 6, 1984 (hereinafter: Ziskind-charts).

adopted in 1958.[6] Furthermore, two ILO Conventions which deal with equality issues (Convention No. 111, and the Equal Pay Convention (No. 100), adopted in 1951) were included among the eight ILO Conventions which have been identified as being fundamental to the rights of human beings at work, irrespective of the level of development of individual States.

5.   Furthermore, in addition to the general guarantee of equality, there exist instruments which contain provisions expressly prohibiting, or seeking to eliminate, discriminatory measures in particular fields, or in relation to specific matters, or which prohibit discrimination on specific grounds only. For example, with respect to racial discrimination, one should note the United Nations' 1965 International Convention on the Elimination of All Forms of Racial Discrimination, Article 5, which provides that States Parties undertake to prohibit and eliminate racial discrimination in all its forms and to guarantee the right of everyone to equality before the law in the enjoyment of a specified number of rights without distinction as to race, colour, or national or ethnic origin, including economic, social and cultural rights, and in particular the right to work, to equal pay, etc.

In regard to gender discrimination, one ought to mention the 1981 International Convention on the Elimination of All Forms of Discrimination Against Women, which guarantees equality on the basis of gender. As far as the ILO is concerned, this attitude can be illustrated by the Equal Pay Convention (No. 100), adopted in 1951, which regulates the issue of EPD in connection with remuneration, the ILO Convention concerning Equal Opportunities and Equal Treatment for Men and Women Workers: Workers with Family Responsibilities (No. 156), which regulates discrimination in terms of family responsibilities; or the 1994 Part-time Work Convention (No. 175) which relates mainly to female work. As far as other grounds are concerned, one could mention for example the Migrant Workers Convention (No. 143), which deals with the equal treatment for migrant workers; or the 1989 Convention concerning Indigenous and Tribal Peoples, which regulates the employment of minorities.

6.   At the European level, various instruments have been adopted for the promotion and application of the principle of EPD. The European Social Charter of 1961, Article 1, para. 2, provides, *inter alia*, for the elimination of all forms of discrimination in employment, and Article 4, para. 3, recognises the rights of men and women workers to equal pay. The European Convention for the Protection of Human Rights and Fundamental Freedoms of 1950 provides more specifically in Article 14 that the enjoyment of the rights and freedoms set forth in the Convention – including the prohibition of forced labour, the right to form trade unions, and the right to equal pay – shall be guaranteed irrespective of sex, race, colour, language, religion, political or other opinion, national or social origin, association with a national minority, property, birth or other status.

In the framework of supra-national action against discrimination one should mention some of the recent developments: The proposal presented in November 1999 by

---

6. The examination of the International Labour Standard of EPD will rely mainly upon Equality in Employment and Occupation, *General Survey of the Committee of Experts on the Application of Conventions and Recommendations of the ILO*, 1996 (hereinafter: GS).

the European Commission under Article 13 EC which broadens the grounds of for-bidden discrimination to include sex, racial or ethnic origin, religion or belief, dis-ability, age, or sexual orientaion. The new Directive on the Burden of Proof which will come into force on 1 January 2001 that extends these new rules to situations covered by Article 119 EC Treaty (Article 141 EC) and by Directives 75/117/EEC, 76/207/EEC, 92/85/EEC and 93/34/EC. The fact that with the entry into force of the Treaty of Amsterdam in May 1999, positive discrimination is now recognized in the fourth paragraph of Article 141 EC. And as far as the definition of indirect discrim-ination is concerned, one should mention Article 2(2) of Directive 97/80/EC which will come into force on January 2001.

III. The Dynamic Definition of Equality

7.   As already mentioned, the notion of equality is an empty vessel, that acquires meaning by incorporating external values, without which it would remain a mere lin-guistic formula. Two varying schools of thought prevail in this respect. The varying approaches result from a conceptual evolution concerning the notion of equality in labour law and reflect an historical philosophic pendulum in this respect. At differ-ent stages, the notion of EPD was understood differently, starting with a narrow interpretation and later developing into a wider concept with a dual dimension. EPD in any specific legal system is formulated in light of one of these two schools. The variance between these schools is also reflected in relation to the question of whether the right to equality contains a negative as well as a positive feature. These approaches are as follows:

A.   Equal Treatment

8.   The first phase of the evolution of the notion of EPD, relates to the most eas-ily understood type of discrimination. According to this interpretation EPD means that like employees will be treated alike, basing equality in labour law on equal treat-ment. The focus of this approach is on ensuring fairness to the individual, by root-ing out direct discrimination on the basis of race, gender, or any other proscribed ground. Under this approach, the aspiration is for a 'colour-blind' society, whereby members of any status group should be treated 'equally' by the employer in the sense that their belonging to such a group should not be a factor in an employment deci-sion. As the focus of this concept of EPD is upon discrimination against the indi-vidual worker, this concept of equality is very often also related to as individual equality. The emphasis of this approach is upon the employers treatment, with no importance being attached to the outcome of his behaviour. Therefore, this concept of equality is referred to as formal or procedural equality. The equal treatment con-cept is premised on a neo-liberal, individualist free-market ideology, according to which the individual is perceived as the ultimate source of value and as an autonomous person whose choices about his own life should enjoy the utmost respect. The emphasis is on the option of personal choice provided thereby, while rejecting any outside interference even if it is meant to promote the social goal of equality.

9. Formal EPD is three dimensional: Equality before the law comprises its first dimension, the meaning of which is expressed in the equal treatment obligation imposed upon the legislature. In this sense, the principle of equality is designed to neutralize the State's power so that no arbitrary restriction can be imposed upon the autonomy of any individual. In light of the second dimension, formal EPD is expressed in the sense of prohibition of discrimination. In this sense formal EPD results from the universal recognition of employment equality as one of the socio-economic human rights, in which it is prescribed that society must prohibit employment discrimination. In light of the third dimension of formal EPD, it is expressed in the sense of guaranteeing individual equal opportunities. According to this significance of formal EPD, rooting out discrimination means only the removal of any non-relevant personal criteria which obstructs individual equal opportunities. Therefore, the extent of success of any worker has to reflect only his personal abilities and efforts. Consequently, formal EPD rejects the idea of equality having a positive dimension. The main reasons for such rejection, *inter alia*, are as follows:

10. First, the application of the equal treatment doctrine signifies only the relief from any obstacle preventing the individual from realization of his personality. Hence, taking positive measures other than removing existing personal restrictions is unacceptable according to this doctrine.[7] Moreover, it is argued that the outcome of imposing positive measures in favour of workers is also reflected in imposing restrictions upon the employer. Positive measures in this respect mean imposing restrictions upon the freedom of choice of the employer, by preventing him from hiring or firing employees at will, or by mandating him to provide special rights to employees of certain status groups, or to pay equal remuneration to his workers, and the like. Imposing restrictions upon the freedom of contract or freedom of choice of the employer, as is required if positive action is introduced, contradicts libertarian philosophy, which underlines the equal treatment doctrine.

11. However, as noted above, the application of the equal treatment doctrine recognizes the need to remove some obstacles, particularly those which prevent the individual from realization of his personality. The full significance of the equal treatment doctrine and the extent of its acceptance of some positive steps is traditionally

---

7. For affirmative action *see* Morris B. Abram, 'Affirmative Action: Fair Shakers and Social Engineers', *Harv. L. Rev.*, Vol. 99, 1986, p. 1312; Randall Kennedy, 'Persuasion and Distrust: A Comment on the Affirmative Action Debate', *Harv. L. Rev.*, Vol. 99, 1986, p. 1327; Robert Belton, 'Discrimination and Affirmative Action: an Analysis of Competing Theories of Equality and Weber', *N.C.L. Rev.*, Vol. 59, 1993, p. 531; Buchan T.A. Love, 'Justifying Affirmative Action', *Auckland U.L. Rev. Annual*, Vol. 7, 1993, p. 491; Christine M. Koggel, 'A Feminist View of Equality and Its Implications for Affirmative Action', *Com. J.L. Jur.*, Vol. 7, 1994, p. 43; Susan D. Clayton and Fay J. Crosby, *Justice, Gender, and Affirmative Action* (University of Michigan Press 1992); Joel Wm. Friedman, 'Redefining Equality, Discrimination, and Affirmative Action Under Title VII: The Access Principle', (23 *Tex. L. Rev.*, p.41); Cass R. Sunstein, 'Three Civil Rights Fallacies', (79 *Cal. L. Rev.*, p.751 (1991)); Stephen Keyes, 'Affirmative Action for Working Mothers: Does Guerra's Preferential Treatment Rational Extend to Childrearing Leave Benefits?', (60 *Ford. L. Rev.*, p.309 (1991) ; James E. Jones, Jr. 'The Genesis and Present Status of Affirmative Action in Employment: Economic, Legal, and Political Realities', (70 *Iowa L. Rev.*, p. 309 (1991)) James E. Jones, Jr., "Reverse discrimination" in employment, judicial treatment of affirmative action programmes in the United States', 120 *Int'l. L. Rev.*, p.453 (1981).

illustrated by two job seekers, one of them a minority group member, and both trying to get a certain job; and comparing them with two marathon runners, one of whom has chains on his legs.[8] In light of the equal treatment doctrine in this case, only the removal of the chains can be legitimately considered. On the employment plane, formal equality justifies only the removal of non-relevant considerations which concern the workers status group. Therefore, in light of this reasoning, unequal economic, social and political power is the unavoidable result of formal EPD, because according to this approach, unequal distribution of goods is not a relevant factor which has to be considered.

12. Second, in light of the equal treatment doctrine, it is argued that there is no justification in taking away a certain advantage from one person and giving it to another. This argument is also illustrated by the marathon race. Any action more than the mere removal of chains will create a situation in which the advantage of one runner will be taken away in order to give it to another, which is unacceptable under the formal EPD doctrine. Therefore, granting certain privileges to members of one group and taking them away from members of another contravenes the basis of formal EPD.

13. Third, a 'colour-blind' attitude comprises the heart of the equal treatment doctrine. In light of this theory, the colour of the worker is not relevant and cannot be considered in the process of admittance, promotion or dismissal of an employee. Therefore, positive action which is based upon consideration of the worker's colour goes counter to the most basic element of the equal treatment theory.

14. Fourth, recognition of the positive dimension of equality under such circumstances prescribes a collective and group advantage at the expense and denial of an individual advantage. Such attitude is in fact discriminating against the individual and is, therefore unacceptable according to the equal treatment approach.

15. Despite the above-mentioned arguments, even under the formal EPD principle some positive measures can be contemplated. Coming back to the marathon runners illustration, it could be said that the first runner has already gained a certain advantage by running while the other was still chained. Under such circumstances, providing equal opportunities to both runners means either to start the marathon anew, or to provide the chained one some advantage which will neutralize the disadvantage created by his being chained. By analogy, the chains can be compared to perpetuated and institutionalized group discrimination. Removal of the 'chains' is not enough to provide equal opportunities to workers who were victims of chronic group discrimination. Hence, even among supporters of the equal treatment concept there are those who are ready to accept certain positive actions, relating to more than the removal of existing barriers. Such supporters are ready to prescribe positive action in the case of personal and direct discrimination. But, adoption of group-positive steps bring about a situation whereby all members of the target group are compensated, and not only those who were victims of direct discrimination. Imposition

---

8. In this respect *see* Buchan T.A. Love, 'Justifying Affirmative Action', *Auckland U.L. Rev. Annual*, Vol. 7 1993, p. 491.

of collective compensatory measures is based upon models of collective responsibility or collective guilt, which contradict the liberal tenets centered, like the equal treatment principle, upon the autonomy and the self-realization of the individual personality. However, some of the formal EPD adherents, are ready to justify positive action related to status groups even without requiring proof of individual direct discrimination. Two arguments support this approach: The first argument is based upon the denial phenomenon. Accordingly, not only those who admit openly that they have been victims of direct discrimination suffered from such discrimination. People tend very often to deny the fact that they have been such victims, or they might not even be aware of their having been such direct victims. The second argument supports positive action even in cases of indirect discrimination. According to this argument, discrimination spreads in such a way that any group member has suffered in one way or another from direct or at least indirect discrimination.

B. Equality in Outcome

16. In a matter of time it was realized that members of minority groups do not get real equal opportunities. Even if two workers are endowed with the same qualifications, they might not have equal opportunities since membership in a certain status group plays a systematic role. Institutionalized and perpetuated discrimination prevents minority group employees from enjoying equal opportunities despite their entitlement to equal treatment. It was realized that guaranteeing formal EPD does not affect the unequal political, social, and economic distribution of power in society. Therefore, the next phase in the development of the notion of equality, required completion of the inadequate formal EPD principle by an additional concept. In light of this development, equality is understood as a dual concept which also embracess, in addition to the equal treatment/concept, the equal outcome/material equality/or group or collective equality concept. The new concept of equality provides material equality. Equality of outcome becomes the criterion of whether EPD in labour law is attained. Equality of outcome calls mainly for the following remarks:

17. In light of the first remark, it is noted that the need to provide equality in outcome shifted the emphasis from the individual to the status group. Equality in outcome is examined in relation to the status of the group and not in relation to the status of each of its individual members. It signifies that the specific group characterization or the fact of the perpetuated discrimination of such a target group must be considered to some extent. From the vantage point of material EPD, it is argued, that employment equality can be guaranteed only if and when all employees have the means for self-realization.

18. In the framework of the second remark, it is indicated that the guarantee of equality in employment in the sense of equality of outcome signifies that the degree of achievement of this goal must be determined independently from the individuals, personal efforts. Adoption of any policy which is based upon the victims fight against discrimination is unfair. It is unjust to impose upon the victim the fate of all his group co-members, and make him responsible for the social and economic status of his fellow members.

371

19. As far as the third remark is concerned, it is argued that any policy which reacts only against discrimination and does not adopt positive action to prevent discrimination will fail in its aim to achieve equality of outcome. The issue is no more a simple question of prohibiting discrimination, but becomes a problem whose solution requires some positive action. But, as already mentioned, it is not the individual victimized employee who must take such action. It is the State that is required to adopt the positive measures intended to correct the *de facto* unequal situation which violates the collective opportunities of members of target groups. Introduction of some positive measures might bridge the gap which stems from the differing personal characteristics and might abolish the economic and societal barriers. In this sense the positive action is meant to provide solutions to psychological and societal obstacles which are in fact the outcome of treating members of target groups as second class citizens. Positive action measures are supported also in light of the distributive justice doctrine which strives to achieve equality of outcome that will be reached by the redistribution of goods and power. Justice is interpreted under this doctrine as the claim to an equal distribution of social, economic and political power among the various status groups which comprise society. From this view-point, justice will be achieved by social engineering, by the adoption of positive action measures. In the framework of such social engineering, the collective factor can be considered, and it is legitimate for this purpose to apply even a non-colour-blind policy. In light of formal EPD, social justice was grasped as a *fair shake* principle. This principle is reflected in the labour law field in the individual equal opportunity principle. But, according to the distributive justice theory, or in light of the equality of outcome approach, the *fair shake* principle is being replaced by the *fair share* principle.[9]

C. Implementation

20. EPD in labour law is nowadays guaranteed in one way or another in most of the industrialized world. However, the scope, extent as well as substance of equality, vary from country to country and from time to time. On the international plane the concept of equality is defined by Article 1(a) of Convention No. 111 which provides that discrimination includes any distinction, exclusion or preference made on the basis of race, colour, sex, ... which has the effect of nullifying or impairing *equality of opportunity or treatment* in employment or occupation. As Blanpain explains, this definition is interpreted as relating to the dual dimension of equality which encompasses the equal treatment as well as equality in outcome.[10] On the comparative plane, equality in labour law is not always guaranteed in its dual concept. For example, Hepple affirms that the procedural EPD approach is still the primary concern of equality in labour law in the United Kingdom.[11]

---

9. In this respect *see* Morris B. Abram, 'Affirmative Action: Fair Shakers and Social Engineers', *Harv. L. Rev.*, Vol. 99, 1986, p. 1312.
10. Blanpain 1990, at § 27.
11. Hepple, 'Great Britain', in Blanpain (ed.), 'Equality and Prohibition of Discrimination in Employment', *Bull. Com. Lab. Rel.*, Vol. 14, p. 117, at p. 121.

21. Moreover, even when EPD in labour law is prescribed by applying both the equal treatment and the equal outcome approaches, it does not automatically follow that it also recognizes affirmative action. It is only in recent years that affirmative measures have begun to be legitimized. On the international plane the guarantee of the positive nature of equality in employment is still problematic. Although applied on an irregular basis, the principle of affirmative action is already recognized on the international plane also, e.g., by Article 1 para. 4 of the United Nations Covenant of 1965 concerning the Abolition of All Forms of Racial Discrimination, or by Article 4 of the United Nations 1979 Covenant concerning the Abolition of Sex Discrimination. On the comparative plane, the momentum generated by affirmative action in recent years is the outcome of the civil rights movement of the 50s in the USA, where institutionalized race and gender discrimination forced the conclusion that some positive measures had to be taken in order to out root such discrimination by leaning on the Equal Protection Clause included in the 14th amendment of the American Constitution. Recognition of affirmative action measures was approved in many of the Western countries, e.g. during the 90s affirmative action was provided by legislation in Northern Ireland where fair religious participation in the labour market was guaranteed by the Fair Employment Act (North Ireland) of 1989; in Germany, where fair gender representation in the federal service was guaranteed by the Frauenforderungsgestz of 1994; in Italy, where Act No. 125 of 1991 provided fair gender participation; or in Israel, where fair gender participation in the civil service was secured by the Civil Service Act (Amendment No. 7) of 1995.

IV. THE DISCRIMINATORY MODEL OF EQUALITY

22. Furthermore, EPD in labour law is challenged by a phenomenon, which can be best defined by using Simone De Beauvoir's epithet (in a wider sense), as the phenomenon of being the *Other*.[12] Equality is based upon comparison. The standard for comparison mirrors existing societal norms.[13] Thus, equality in labour law for most of the status groups, has come to mean equality with men (usually white, young, and healthy) (hereinafter: the male standard).[14] Hence, any status group which differs from the male standard is related to as the *Other*. Labelling a particular group of workers as such affects their social status, their self-perception and their opportunity to participate actively in the labour market. The very existence of the *Otherness* phenomenon involves a legal issue: It is questioned whether the model, according to which EPD in labour law is structured, really prohibits discrimination against all societal status groups (including those related to as the *Other*). Hence, EPD in labour law can not be defined unless some prior ex-legal policy decisions, concerning the structure of these models and the status of minority groups therein, are first

---

12. Simon De Beauvoir, *The Second Sex* (Penguin Books), Introduction, p. 16 ff.
13. Katharine T. Bartlett and Rosanne Kennedy, 'Introduction', in *Feminist Legal Theory, Reading in Law and Gender* (eds) Katharine T. Bartlett and Rosanne Kennedy, Westview press, Boulder, 1991, p. 5.
14. Catharine A. MacKinnon, Difference and Dominance: On Sex Discrimination, in *Feminist Legal Theory, Reading in Law and Gender* (eds) Katharine T. Bartlett and Rosanne Kennedy, Westview press, Boulder, 1991, p. 81.

provided. Policy decisions, that establish the criteria whereon the equality model is built, are affected by the social and economic framework in which labour relations function; by the definition of roles and tasks in the labour market; by the remuneration and promotion systems; by the particular work patterns characterizing the various status groups of which the workforce is comprised; as well as by the political system and the economic and social philosophy which it reflects. The model of EPD, in light of those ex-legal policy decisions can take various forms, some of which may even have discriminatory ramifications.

23. The question of whether A enjoys occupational equality can be phrased as follows: Are A and B treated alike? (assuming that A and B are alike). Hence, the traditional concept of equality entails the provision of a certain normative yardstick with which the treatment or opportunity accorded to A can be compared. The need of such a normative measurement is also relevant in the case of group discrimination. Under such circumstances, it is expressed in the following equation: Are members of group A and B treated alike? In this case, a work pattern, typical to members of group A serves as the yardstick to examine the occupational equality of employees who are members of other status groups. Analysis of equality in international and comparative labour law confirms two prepositions in this respect:

24. First, different work patterns characterize the work performed by the various status groups. This variety of work patterns results from biological differences concerning e.g., gender or the workers advanced age; it results as well as from cultural differences such as varying career patterns, which might themselves result from biological differences, existing between the various status groups comprising the labour market; and it sometimes results from existing prejudice, as in the case of statistical discrimination against women, workers with family responsibilities, elderly workers or the disabled ones and the like. Despite such variety, the male standard serves as the normative yardstick according to which equality of all status groups is measured. Generally speaking, this standard is based upon full-time employment and more often than not is also a time-demanding one, which causes the employee to stay away from home for long hours. Such a work pattern neither leaves the worker any leisure time, nor does it allow him to spend time with his family. In fact, the male work pattern is even counter to the international labour standard concerning hours of work and rest.

25. Secondly, examination of EPD in labour law on the international and comparative levels clearly indicates that although the male standard is generally used as a normative yardstick for comparison, in reality such use is performed by way of one of the following two distinctive models, which under the Feminist theory are related to as the Assimilation and the Accommodation Models.[15] Modern American Feminism was the first to examine equality from this viewpoint and to emphasize the importance the model has upon EPD in labour law. Although, those models were

---

15. In this respect *see* Christine A. Littleton, 'Reconstructing Sexual Equality' in *Feminist Legal Theory, Reading in Law and Gender* (eds) Katharine T. Bartlett and Rosanne Kennedy, Westview press, Boulder, 1991, p. 35.

developed in order to deal with gender discrimination, in the present framework they are applied in a broader sense, relating to employment discrimination which concerns most of the status groups.

A. The Assimilation Model

26. The Assimilation Model uses the male standard as the yardstick for comparison. This model is based upon the notion that status groups of employees, given the chance, are or could be just like men. Therefore, EPD in labour law should require social institutions to treat members of whatever status group is concerned as they already treat men. The Assimilation Model does not examine the neutrality of social institutions, but simply imposes upon them equal treatment of all employees without paying attention to any differences which may exist between them. Under this model, differences of any kind between the various status groups are ignored. Hence, in its broader sense discussed here, the Assimilation approach purported by Williams in relation to gender, denies the entitlement of any of the various status groups enjoyment of special rights.[16] Under the Assimilation model it is claimed that legislative distinction drawn on the basis of any differences, whether they are biological, cultural or societal, is inherently dangerous even when they purport to confer advantages. Equality, according to the Assimilation Model, means that only workers able to cope with the male standard are entitled to be treated alike. Implementation of this approach entails women entering the labour market to sacrifice their family life, or their particular relationship with their offspring, as male workers often do. The same can be said in relation to elderly workers. They will have to meet the standard set forth by young workers. Hence, according to the Assimilation Model, such workers will be integrated into the labour market as long as they are able to perform a full-time job and even work overtime when needed. Under this model elderly workers will have only two options, either to continue working full time or to retire, since according to this model the option of a graduated or flexible retirement is denied. Various arguments, generally economic ones, are provided under the Assimilation Model in order to support this approach and in particular to justify the denial of granting special rights provided therein. The following reasoning provides an illustration of the argumentation being voiced in this respect.

27. For example, the provision of special rights is denied because it is claimed that provision of such rights might only widen the gap between young, healthy, and white male workers which represent the norm, and other employees, who because of these rights being accorded to them might become the exception.[17] It is claimed that guarantee of special rights allows the firm to target and to discriminate against

---

16. In this respect *see* Wendy W. Williams, 'The Equality Crisis: Some Reflections on Culture, Courts, and Feminism', in *Feminist Legal Theory, Reading in Law and Gender* (eds) Katharine T. Bartlett and Rosanne Kennedy, Westview press, Boulder, 1991, p. 15.
17. For arguments against recognition of special rights *see* Eileen Trzcinski, 'Separate versus Equal treatment Approaches to Parental Leave: Theoretical issues and Empirical Evidence', *Law and Policy*, Vol. 13, 1991, p. 1.

protected status groups workers in wages, hiring procedures and promotions. It is therefore feared that workers of childbearing age, or of child-rearing age or of retirement age, regardless of whether they intend to have children, to raise children or to use retirement flexibility – may thus bear the repercussions of any adjustments made by the firms in response to mandated special rights. Moreover, the provision of special rights is denied because, it is argued, mandated special rights add a cost to the wage bill. The increase in labour cost which results from such mandated rights might make the employment of such employees less attractive. Prescription of such rights might therefore, result in creating two labour markets, in the framework of which only the secondary one will be open to participation of employees who are entitled to these rights. Furthermore, the provision of special rights might, as already mentioned, bring about a wage reduction of minorities salaries.

B.   The Accommodation Model

28.   The Accommodation Model as the former one, is also based upon the male standard.[18] By contrast to the Assimilation Model, this is rather an asymmetrical model, since it recognizes the differences which characterize the various status groups. Consequently, these differences are taken into account in the formation process of the EPD model. Accordingly, it is acknowledged that the very existence of differences between the various status groups, whether biological or cultural, prevent their members from coping with the male standard. Hence, in the interest of justice it is recognized that under this model the EPD of these employees can not be reached unless special rights are accorded to them. The guarantee of such special rights is meant to enable these employees to be integrated into the labour market. There are two facets to the Accommodation Model (narrow and broad, or sometimes the broad model is referred to as the Special Rights Model), each of which vary in the type and extent of recognized differences and entitlement to special rights.

1. Narrow Interpretation

29.   Under the narrow interpretation, it is agreed that differential treatment of biological differences such as pregnancy and perhaps breast feeding is necessary and justifies the provision of special rights in this respect.[19] But, at the same time it is argued that cultural or hard to classify differences such as career interests and skills do not justify the guarantee of special rights and therefore should be treated according to the Assimilation Model. According to this interpretation, cultural differences which result from the employee's family responsibilities do not call for accommodation. Moreover, differences in career types of male and female workers, which result from women's desire to choose a career that will enable them to perform their double role

---

18.   *See* Christine A. Littleton, 'Reconstructing Sexual Equality' in *Feminist Legal Theory, Reading in Law and Gender* (eds) by Katharine T. Bartlett and Rosanne Kennedy, Westview press, Boulder, 1991, p. 35.
19.   *Ibid.*

at home and at work are not accommodated. The same is true when the differing careers of elderly workers in comparison to those of young workers are concerned. Such differences are not relevant under this version of the Accommodation Model and should therefore be treated according to the Assimilation Model.

2. Broad Interpretation

30. The broad interpretation of the Accommodation Model affirms that the various status groups are different, and asserts that such differences relate to biological as well as to cultural factors.[20] According to this interpretation, the negative stereotype of members of various status groups such as women, elderly persons or of those encumbered with family responsibilities stems from cultural differences which evolved from biological ones. Therefore, in light of this model, society must take account of these differences and ensure that members of the various status groups are not punished for them. Hence, according to this type of the Accommodation Model, the guarantee of special rights must relate to all kinds of differences, and enable employees who are characterized by such differences to be integrated into the labour market as well as to perform their employer and employee duties. It is accepted that only in this manner will such employees be able to enjoy their right to occupational equality.

3. Justification

31. Both versions of the Accommodation Model are justified by various reasons, which can be discerned from the following arguments: The provision of special rights acknowledged under the Accommodation Model is justified on the ground that such rights comprise a certain type of affirmative action without which the discrimination against the relevant status groups will be perpetuated. Without special rights, vulnerable employees such as females, workers with family responsibility, elderly workers and the like will find it difficult to survive in the labour market, or will be unable to find alternative jobs once they become unemployed. Hence, it is argued that in order to provide workers, members of the various status groups, with equality in outcome in the long run, some protected measures must be prescribed in the short term.

32. Another reason very often raised in order to justify the guarantee of special rights focuses upon the possibility of its being a means for breaking the cycle that channeled women, elderly workers, or workers with family responsibilities, and the like, into low paying jobs that restricted the length of time they participated in the labour force.[21] According to this argument, it was claimed that mandated special rights imposed upon all employers might at a certain point neutralize the present

---

20. *Ibid.*
21. Eileen Trzcinski, 'Separate versus Equal treatment Approaches to Parental Leave: Theoretical issues and Empirical Evidence', *Law and Policy*, Vol. 13, 1991, p. 1.

negative approach to employment of members of target groups. For example, the availability of parental leave can shift the choices of women away from female dominated occupations. Women may thus choose occupations that they would have rejected before because these occupations provided neither leave nor easy exit and re-entry. Women's employment position would then improve, as it would enable them to enter the higher paid previously male-dominated occupations, which were previously rejected by women despite their higher wages. The same is true where flexible and graduated retirement is concerned. The provision of such rights might enable elderly workers to lengthen their stay in the labour market.

33. The prescription of special rights is also justified as a means of overcoming the employers lack of incentive to employment of target group employees, if and upon condition that the mandated special rights be phrased in the broadest possible sense.[22] The more general the special rights the broader the class of workers eligible and at risk of enjoying these special rights. The larger the group that can use the special rights, the smaller is the pool of alternative available employees. Under such circumstances the employer will have difficulties in finding alternative employees to whom the special rights are not applicable. Therefore, there will be an increase in the cost that the employer will have to pay if he relies upon statistical discrimination, the use of which is meant to prevent the employer from employing workers which have the potential of enjoying the prescribed special rights. At a certain point, the employer will come to the conclusion that it is economically preferable to provide the special rights rather than pay the cost of looking for employees who are not included in the risk group.

C. Implementation

34. Examination of labour law from a comparative and international view-point indicates clearly that nowadays the Accommodation Model in its wide interpetation plays a leading role, while the Assimilation Model has been relegated to a residuary role. The starting point was different. In the past, the Assimilation Model was the leading model and this model was applicable even in cases of pregnancy, as can be learned from the American case of Guerra.[23] The leading role of the Accommodation Model on the international plane can be discerned from Article 6 of Convention No. 111, where it is provided that special measures of protection or assistance provided for in other Conventions or Recommendations adopted by the ILO shall not be deemed to be discrimination. Moreover, it is also provided therein that any member State may, after consultation with representative employers and employees organizations, determine that other special measures designed to meet the particular requirements of persons who, for reasons of sex, age, disablement, family responsibilities or special social or cultural status, are generally recognized to require special

---

22. *Ibid.*
23. *California Fed. Sav. & Loan Ass'n v. Guerra.* 33 Empl. Prac. Dec. (CCH) § 34,227 (1984), *rev'd* 758 F.2d 390 (9th Cir. 1985), *aff'd*, 107 S.Ct. 683 (1987).

protection or assistance, shall not be deemed to be discrimination. A number of ILO Conventions adopted in this respect illustrate the fact that labour equality on the international plane is structured according to the Accommodation Model.

35. As far as the comparative plane is concerned, it could be said that the growing process of prescribing special rights in relation to pregnancy, childbirth, family responsibilities, flexible and gradual retirement, or disablement and the like, which we are witnessing today, is the best evidence of the increasing importance the Accommodation Model has recently acquired on this plane also. But it should be emphasized that EPD in labour law on the comparative plane is still structured according to the Assimilation Model, which is leading as long as protected legislation is not provided even if only in respect to issues which are not subject to such specific legislation. Hence, under legal systems where the range of protected rights is still very limited, employees who are members of vulnerable status groups will continue to work only if they can cope with the male standard.

36. However, the Assimilation Model as well as the Accommodation Model are both based upon the male standard, and consequently discriminate against members of the various status groups. The Assimilation Model is discriminatory in nature because target group workers in its framework are asked to work according to a pattern which does not fit their own characteristic work patterns. The Accommodation Model is discriminatory in nature because target group employees are treated in the framework of this model as an exception, as the *Other*. In fact, both models (the Assimilation and Accommodation Models) are inadequate, and call for a reform in this respect.

V. GROUNDS OF PROHIBITED DISCRIMINATION

A. *In General*

37. Generally speaking, the concept of EPD would imply the prohibition of all distinctions, exclusions or preferences in employment irrespective of the ground of such discrimination. But, in fact, EPD does not cut such a broad swath. Any definition of the concept of EPD must specify which grounds are protected under it. For example, as far as the ILSEPD is concerned, Article 1, para. 1(a) of Convention No. 111, refers to a list of seven grounds of prohibited discrimination: race, colour, sex, religion, political opinion, national extraction, and social origin.[24] Still, this list is not exhaustive since, under para. (b) of Article 1 other grounds can be added after consultation with the employers and workers organizations. It appears that certain grounds of prohibited discrimination, especially gender and race, have been given particular attention. Still, prohibited discrimination mainly in industrialized market economies and in international instruments extends beyond race and gender and in certain instances even beyond the seven accepted grounds prescribed by the ILSEPD

---

24. For detailed information related to the grounds of prohibited discrimination concerning the ILSEPD *see GS* §§ 28–64, 161–202.

to include such grounds as age, disablement, family responsibility, trade union membership, private life, educational level, place of birth, legitimacy of birth, sexual orientation, physical or mental state of health, medical history, and physical appearance.[25] Many of these additional grounds are in fact merely a development of already accepted ones, a sort of sub-classification of well-established grounds. For example, from a certain point of view maternity as well as marital status, family responsibility or even sexual harassment, can all be seen as further developments of the general prohibition of gender discrimination. The terms used in legislation in relation to these additionally protected grounds are not always defined; the fact that these various grounds are sub-classifications of established ones does not necessarily add to their clarification. Often, there is even a certain overlap between the various protected grounds.

38. Unfortunately, the enormous development of EPD in labour law took place mainly in industrialized market economies. By contrast, the pace of employment equality in the developing world is rather slower. As the Committee of Experts noted: 'Where there is no active employment policy that secures full and freely chosen employment, equality of opportunity and treament is a hollow expression'.[26] The low economic development of the developing countries, as well as the implementation of structural adjustment programs, do not contribute to the evolution of any employment equality law. Such programs very often impose devaluation measures entailing the falling of incomes, the removal of subsidies and the implementation of cuts in public expenditure. Such programs tend to abandon or drastically reduce those programs intended to remedy inequalities in order to decrease public expenditure in the name of economic efficiency. Furthermore, a different situation exists where former planned economy countries are concerned, mainly in Central and Eastern Europe. The problem these countries face, is the need to restructure their labour relations systems, as part of their transition to more market-oriented economies. Yet such a transformation might come at the expense of employment equality, or at least postpone its implementation.

B. Race (Colour, National Extraction, Social Origin)

39. The first family grouping of prohibited grounds is built upon the notion of race.[27] In this respect, one can also mention the additional grounds of colour, national extraction and social origin, which comprise three out of the seven basic grounds enumerated by the ILSEPD, and such further grounds as ethnic or national origin, language, social status, cast or tribe etc.[28] Under the umbrella of race, it

---

25. In this respect *see* Ziskind-charts.
26. *See* Equality in Employment and Occupation, General Survey of the Committee of Experts on the Application of Conventions and Recommendations of the ILO, 1988, § 251.
27. For detailed information in connection with such additional grounds of prohibited discrimination *see GS* §§ 30–34, 161–168.
28. It appears that certain grounds of prohibited discrimination, especially race, have been given particular attention. *See* in this respect Ziskind-charts.

seems logical also to consider various related grounds, such as colour, in as much as differences of colour constitute only one ethnic characteristic, albeit the most apparent one. Moreover, the term 'race' is frequently used in a different way, perhaps even erroneously, to refer to minority groups whose identity is based on cultural or religious characteristics, or to population groups which could more accurately be described as linguistic communities. Various legal systems combine nationality and ethnic or national origin together with race.[29] It can be said that, generally speaking, discrimination against ethnic minorities is considered as racial discrimination.[30] Still, distinctions can be drawn between the situation of ethnic minorities, and in particular, indigenous and tribal groups, and that of other minorities disadvantaged on racial grounds.

40. The concept of national extraction, which is included within the family grouping of race, covers distinctions between citizens of the country concerned made on the basis of a person's place of birth, ancestry or foreign origin. In some countries, racial minorities are comprised largely of immigrant workers, or the descendants of immigrants, who entered originally the country in order to perform low-paid labour.[31] In any event, they comprise persons whose ancestors or even themselves departed from their country of origin and entered a new society, frequently at a comparative disadvantage *vis à vis* the citizens of their new country. In some cases, the members of these ethnic minorities are citizens of the country where they now reside, and discrimination affecting them could be classified as being on the ground of national extraction. In some countries, regulations governing access to employment in the public sector still provide for a minimum length of time that a person must have been a national to qualify,[32] while in other countires, the prohibition against foreigners who have been naturalized or who have applied for citizenship from taking jobs in public employment has been abolished by law.[33] The problem of discrimination on the ground of social origin arises when an individual's membership in a class, or a caste determines his occupational future, either by denying him access to certain jobs or, by assigning him to certain jobs only. Still, such situations are today rarely encountered in so pronounced a form. For example, in India, implications arising out of untouchability were abolished by Article 17 of the Constitution, and in Japan, the problem of a minority living in a specific area (Buraku) and who were subject to discrimination concerning their social position, has been dealt with by statute.[34]

---

29. In this respect *see* e.g. *New Zealand,* Race Relations Act 1971, LS 1971-NZ 1, s. 5 and Labour Relations Act 1987, s. 211, LS 1987-NZ 1.
30. *See* e.g. Article 1 of the International Convention on the Elimination of All Forms of Racial Discrimination.
31. *See* in this respect: The Indigenous and Tribal Peoples Convention, 1989.
32. *See* e.g. *Algeria,* s. 31 of Decree No. 85-59 of the 23 March 1985 issuing model regulations governing employees of public institutions and administrations.
33. *See* e.g. *United States,* Immigration Reform and Control Act of 1986, s. 274(B), LS 1986-USA 1. Cf. decision of Commission of the European Communities against the Republic of France, 307/84.
34. In this respect *See* the *Japanese* Government's statement in E/CN.4/Sub.2/1983/39.

C. Sex (Civil or Marital Status, Family Responsibilities, Pregnancy and Confinement, Sexual Harassment, Sexual Orientation)

41. Discrimination on the basis of sex is one of the forbidden grounds set forth by the ILSEPD, and it is perhaps the most frequently applied ground on the national level. However, the inclusion of this ground is frequently not accompanied by a definition of how it should be understood. Therefore, the question has been whether the prohibition of discrimination on the ground of sex also covers cases of discrimination based on civil or marital status, familiy situations and responsibility, pregnancy and confinement, sexual harassment or sexual orientation. This question is relevant in all the cases where the employer in fact is not discriminating solely on the basis of sex, but on the basis of sex plus some other facially neutral qualification or characteristic. It should be noted that in such cases the employer does not discriminate against the class of men or women as a whole, but rather disparately treats a subclass of men or women by restricting their employment opportunities. This kind of discrimination is usually referred to as sex-plus discrimination. A typical example of sex-plus discrimination is the employer who refuses to employ married or pregnant woman, women over a certain age, or women with children of pre-school-age, while these criteria are not applied to married men, men over a certain age or men with pre-school children. Under such circumstances, neither males nor single females suffer by the standard. It is only the subclass of married women, or women over a certain age or women with pre-school-children that are treated unfavourably. It is well-accepted that EPD should prohibit discrimination in such situations, although it is debated whether such protection is provided under the prohibition of gender discrimination, or whether it requires a specific statutory prohibition of discrimination in respect of each of the above-mentioned situations. This question has been addressed in the United States, where the courts have held that, sex-plus discrimination is violative of the concept of EPD on the basis of sex.[35] For example, the sex-plus theory has been used to strike down no-marriage rules applied only to female employees;[36] similarly, the courts have invalidated policies that discriminate against unwed mothers,[37] or lesbians.[38] Moreover, in the Dekker Case,[39] the European court was prepared to extend the protection of the Equal Treatment Directive to a pregnant woman who refused employment on grounds of pregnancy despite being the most suitable applicant.

42. While the proposition that the prohibition of discrimination based on sex may cover acts of discrimination based on marital or family status, pregnancy and confinement as well as sexual harassment or sexual orientaion is judicially supported, still, in order to eliminate the uncertainty of the scope of the protection, statutory efforts should be made to ensure explicit protection for employees against discrimination in each of the sex-plus instances. For example, this was done at the

---

35. For example, the U.S. Supreme Court held in 1971 that disparate treatment of a subclass of a protected group violates the doctrine of EPD. *See Phillips* v. *Martin Marietta Co.*, 400 U.S. 542 (1971).
36. *See* United States Supreme Court of Appeals, Fifth Circuit, 1975, *Willingham* v. *Macon Telegrapgh Publishing Co.*, 507 F.2d 1084 (5th Cir., 1975).
37. *See Dolter* v. *Wahlter High School*, 483 F.Supp. 266 (N.D.Iowa 1980).
38. *See Valdes* v. *Lumbermen's Mutual Casualty Co.*, 507 F.Supp. 10 (S.D.Fla, 1980).
39. Case C-177/88 [1990] ECR 3841.

international level by the Workers With Familiy Responsibility Convention No. 156, which prohibits discrimination of workers with family responsibilities.

D. Ideological Freedoms and Beliefs (Political Opinion, Religion, Trade Union Membership)

43. A third group of prohibited grounds of discrimination focuses on various ideological freedoms and beliefs, such as political opinion and religion, which are explicitly included within the seven protected grounds provided by the ILSEPD, and trade union membership, which has been added in other international instruments.[40] The ground of political opinion provides protection for an employee's participation in political activities in which political opinions are expressed or demonstrated. As the Committee of Experts of the ILO stated, such a protection is not limited only to differences of opinion within the framework of established principles. Accordingly, even if certain doctrines seek fundamental changes in the institutions of the State, this does not justify excluding them from the protection of the ILSEPD, in the absence of the use or advocacy of violence to bring about such a result. On the national level, many systems provides that political opinion or beliefs, or political affiliation, are unlawful grounds of discrimination. Nevertheless, certain countries still prohibit the employment of persons not only in the public but even in the private sector,[41] or exclude persons from the protection afforded by the laws enshrining the principle of equality,[42] on the ground of their membership in certain political parties.[43]

44. In addition, the ILSEPD also aims to provide protection against discrimination affecting employment on the basis of religion, which is the consequence of a lack of religious freedom, of intolerance, and in some cases, of the existence of a State religion.[44] The free exercise of religious practice is hindered in particular in cases where a religion prohibits work on a day different from the day of rest established by law. This issue affects both the right to exercise one's own faith and also the right to act in accordance with it. For example, in the Netherlands, the Sunday Observance Act, while ensuring the observance of Sunday and certain Christian holidays, does not contain any regulation respecting non-Christian days of rest and holidays. The Supreme Court of the Netherlands ruled that while non-Christian religious holidays could not be regarded as enjoying equal status to those on the Christian calender, it would be unreasonable for an employer to demand the presence of a non-Christian employee at work on non-Christian holidays or days of rest, unless the work of the enterprise would be seriously disrupted.[45]

---

40. A large number of national Constitutions retain provisions that deal with ideological freedoms. *See* in this respect Ziskind-charts. For the third group of prohibited grounds of discrimination *see* GS §§ 186–202.
41. *See* GS § 46.
42. *See* e.g. *Chile*, Article 8 of the Constitution.
43. *See* e.g. *United States*: s. 703(f) of the Civil Rights Act of 1964; *see also* the Fair Employment Practices Act of *Nebraska* (s. 48-1109) and of *Nevada* (s. 613.360).
44. *See* GS § 41.
45. *See* Commission on Human Rights documentation E/CN.4/1986/37/Add. 5 §16.

45. The family grouping of prohibited grounds of discrimination concerning ideological beliefs is relevant also to the issue of trade union membership. Generally speaking, discrimination on such ground is prohibited. Such protection is not enshrined in Convention No. 111, but is provided by the Freedom of Association and Protection of the Right to Organise Convention, 1948 (No. 87).

E. Other Grounds (Family Responsibilities, Disablement, Health, Private Life, Age)

46. As already mentioned, at the international level, in accordance with Article 1 para. 1(b) of Convention No. 111, other grounds of prohibited discrimination may be determined after consultation with the representative employers and workers organisations. In this respect, the prohibition of discrimination on such additional grounds as family responsibilities, disablement, state of health, private life and age are of particular concern. Indeed, at the international level, some of these additional grounds have been secured by specific Conventions adopted for this purpose.

47. The Workers With Family Responsibility Convention No. 156 (hereinafter: Convention No. 156), aims at eliminating discrimination of workers with family responsibilities and prescribes an international labour standard.[46] Accordingly, the rights of WFR – who are engaged, or wish to be engaged in employment, must be guaranteed without being subject to direct or indirect discrimination. Moreover, the ILSWFR prescribes that specific protected rights must be guaranteed so as to enable WFR, as much as possible, to become and remain integrated in the labour force, and to re-enter the labour force after an absence due to family responsibilities, without being forced to chose between one's employment and family responsibilities. The ILSWFR (Article 1, para. 3 of Convention No. 156) applies the term 'family responsibilities' in a broad sense which includes a worker's dependant as well as other members of his immediate family who need this care or support.

48. The Vocational Rehabilitation and Employment (Disabled Persons) Convention No. 159, is aimed at eliminating discrimination of disabled persons. The term 'disabled persons' relates in this respect to individuals whose prospects of securing, retaining and advancing in suitable employment are substantially reduced as a result of a recognized physical or mental impairment. One ought to mention in this respect Article 4 of the above-mention Convention No. 159, which provides that special measures aimed at securing equality of opportunity and treatment for disabled workers shall not be regarded as discrimination against other workers. A number of countries have adopted provisions intended to make possible for disabled persons, and particularly veterans of war, to obtain or maintain a job by means of quota systems and the like.

49. A related question is the problem of including an employee's state of health or private life among the protected grounds. The protection of an employee's state

---

46. Hereinafter: ILSWFR.

of health concerns, e.g., whether it is legitimate to consider the past and present state of health of an employee where such information is not directly related to the specific job. It seems that the proposition that one's aptitude for a job must be assessed on the basis of the applicable current state of health, and not in terms of past or possible future health problems – is gaining today a foothold. Thus, the time is now ripe to adopt a defined standard which will not only include state of health among the protected grounds covered by the concept of EPD, but will define and clarify its scope. The problem raised by the spread of the Acquired Immune Deficiency Syndrome (AIDS) virus is largely responsible for the current impetus in this respect. The protection of a worker's private life relates not only to matters such as the worker's state of health, but to additional aspects such as sexual orientation. The latter can perhaps be protected either by including the employee's private life among the grounds of prohibited discrimination, or under the ground of sex, as a sex-plus situation. Whatever the basis, it seems that the issue of the employee's private life should be given particular attention in the future.

50.   While prohibition of discrimination on the basis of age is not ensured explicitly by the ILSEPD, it nevertheless is referred to within the framework of Convention No. 111, inasmuch as it is included among the subjects which require that special measures of protection be taken in accordance with Article 5, para. 2 of the Convention. Hence, in a number of countries the prohibition of discrimination on the ground of age has been prescribed,[47] in a number of countries, still, the guarantee of EPD on the ground of age is not inconsistent with the fixing of a retirement age. An example of prohibiting age discrimination at the national level can be learned from the case of the United States, where the adoption of the Age Discrimination in Employment Act of 1967 was aimed at resolving some of the senior citizens problems, such as higher rates of unemployment and arbitrary age limits in employment.[48]

VI.   EXCEPTIONS

51.   The guarantee of EPD, whether at the international or the national level, permits certain exceptions whereby differential treatment may be justified. Three specific exceptions are supported by Convention No. 111 in various Articles thereof, but they must be applied *stricto jure* in order to avoid undue restrictions on the application of the doctrine of EPD.

A.   *Inherent Requirements of a Particular Job*

52.   Any distinction, exclusion or preference in respect of a particular job based on the inherent requirements thereof is not deemed to be discriminatory but rather

---

47.   *See* e.g. *Canada*, s. 3(1) of the Canadian Human Rights Act; Colombia, s. 143 of the Substantive Labour Code; Spain, s. 4(2)(c) of the Act of 10 March 1980, to promulgate a Worker's Charter, LS 1980-Sp. 1.
48.   *See* LS 1967-USA 1.

constitutes a *bona fide occupational qualification* (BFOQ). This exception is not only self-evident, but is also prescribed by Article 1, para. 2, of Convention No. 111.[49] This exception is related to requirements that make it necessary that only persons of a given sex or age bracket be hired, or that persons possessing certain physical capabilities are required to ensure that the nature of the work in question be properly performed, or that the tasks involved be carried out safely, or that certain tasks deemed essential to the primary objectives of the enterprise be performed. It is not enough that the employer believes, no matter how sincerely, that the candidate must meet certain specific conditions to be eligible for the job.

53. Legislation seeking to eliminate racial or sexual discrimination often contains explicit exemptions to the principle of non-discrimination, in the form of either general provisions or lists or types of jobs for which a criterion such as sex may be prescribed as a necessary requirement; or they may combine both approaches, in which case a number of jobs are listed by way of illustration. Certain national legislation defines the scope of the concept of *bona fide* occupational requirement or qualification:[50] For example, the Canadian Human Rights Commission has published guidelines concerning the interepretation of the term *bona fide* occupational requirements, which are based on three main concepts:[51] (1) The enterprise may base job requirements only on the job's essential tasks; (2) The competence of each person who applies for a job must be assessed fairly, and the employer is not permitted to refuse to examine the application of persons merely by virtue of their belonging to a certain category; (3) The enterprise must be prepared, at least to some extent, to make the necessary accomodations in order to enable disabled persons and the adherents of certain religions to modify their work schedules, even if such accomodations entail a financial cost or business inconvenience to the enterprise.[52] One of the difficulties which is encountered in such cases relates to the burden of proof. Because, we are dealing with an exception to the rule against discrimination, it is generally up to the employer to prove that the special or unequal treatment is justified by objective reasons unrelated to a discriminatory criterion, or that this criterion constitutes an essential requirement for the work involved.

B. Security of the State

54. The second tradional exception is the security of the State exception. For example, in accordance with Article 4 of Convention No. 111, any measures affecting an individual who is justifiably suspected of, or who is engaged in, activities harmful to the security of the State is not deemed to be discriminatory.[53] In order to

---

49. *See GS* §§ 118–122.
50. *See* e.g. *Ireland*, s. 17(1) of the Employment Equality Act, L.S. 1977-Ire. 1.
51. *See* Guidelines of the *Canadian Human Rights Commission* concerning the limitations and modalities for the application of subsection 14(a) of the Canadian Human Rights Act to employment (Guide lines on Bona Fide Occupational Requirements) S1/82-3, filed on 13 January 1982.
52. Concerning the concept of reasonable accommodation, *see* e.g. *United States, Arizona*, s. 41-1461(8) of the Civil Rights Act.
53. *See GS* §§ 123–129.

constitute a sufficient ground for the application of the exception justified by activities harmful to the security of the State, the mere expression of opinion or of religious, philosophical or political belief is not sufficient.[54] Special care must be taken so that the measures provided to safeguard the security of the State will be clearly defined and do not themselves discriminate on the basis of political opinion or religion.[55] The security of the State exception provided in Article 4 of Convention No. 111 includes a procedural guarantee whereby there must be an appeals body which is separate from any administrative or governmental authority, thereby guaranteeing its objectivity and independence. This body must be competent to take testimony on reasons for the measures taken against the person in question, and to afford the claimant the opportunity to present his or her case in full.[56]

C. Special Measure of Protection

55. The third exception addresses the issue of protective legislation.[57] Under Article 5 of Convention No. 111, any distinction or preference is not deemed to be discriminatory, if such distinction or preference results from the application of special measures which are either provided for in other Conventions and Recommendations, such as maternity, or are designed to meet the particular requirements of persons who are recognized to require special protection or assistance by reason of sex, age, disablement, family responsibilities, or social, or cultural status. Still, it should be also remembered that, preferential treatment of minority groups, by virtue of protective legislation might make them less attractive on the labour market. Consequently, protective legislation might still fall under the rubric of indirect discrimination. Hence, in certain countries, preferential treatment even of minorities is considered as discriminatory in nature. This argument is often raised in connection with special rights accorded only to female workers with family responsibilites, and was the reason for regulating anew the issue of night work of female employees in 1990 by the ILO Convention concerning Night Work (No. 171).

VII. FIELD OF APPLICATION

56. Any definition of the concept of EPD must also address the scope of its application. For example, the protection against discrimination provided by Convention No. 111 (Article 1, para. 3) is applicable to all the stages of employment including: (1) The pre-hiring or pre-employment stage in connection with access to vocational

---

54. For examples of such decisions *see GS* § 125.
55. It could be compared to the principles of interpretation applicable to the notion of 'national security' in the International Covenant on Civil and Political Rights, in the *United Nations, Commission on Human Rights*, 41st Session, E/CN.4/1985/4, Annex, p. 5.
56. *See GS* §§ 128–129.
57. Article 5 provides two kinds of special measures of protection. The first kind relates to measures of protection that are provided for in international labour Conventions and Recommendations; the second kind relates to measures taken after consultation with workers' and employers' organizations. *See GS* §130.

training and employment, and placement procedures; (2) The general terms and conditions of employment; and (3) Specific issues such as equal remuneration or sexual harassment. While the scope of the ILSEPD is indeed comprehensive, its application at the national level varies significantly, and frequently its scope is narrower, relating only to a particular stage or to a specific issue. In addition, examination of various national experiences indicates that even where the general issue of EPD is not regulated by statute, certain specific matters such as admission policies, or equal remuneration are nevertheless frequently covered by legislation.

A. The Pre-employment Stage

57. Training and vocational guidance help determine a person's likelihood of gaining access to employment; As such, they play a major role in the application of the principle of EPD. Discriminatory practices in respect of access to training are usually caused by practices which are based on stereotypes. Hence, equality in vocational guidance can contribute to eliminate long-held misconceptions that certain trades or occupations are reserved for persons of particular features only. Therefore, EPD is not only extended, at least at the international level, to the likelihood of gaining access to employment but it also covers access to training, vocational guidance, and placement services.

58. The existence of a public employment service, by prohibiting discrimination in the placement process can contribute to the promotion of the concept of EPD.[58] The existence of a public employment service not only implies the observance of the principle of equality of treatment in the operation of the employment service,[59] but, it frequently imposes a ban on the application of discriminatory criteria during the course of the placement procedure.[60] For example, in Mexico or Morocco, the employment service is prohibited by law from receiving or filling offers for employment that contain discriminatory features. Very often, legislation concerning public employment services also imposes a prohibition on the employer as well, whereby he is prohibited from refusing to hire a person who is referred to him by the employment service if such refusal is based on discriminatory grounds.[61] Further, given the increasing use of private employment agencies, many countries have made applicable by statute the concept of EPD with respect to the provision of placement services by them as well. Consequently, these private agencies are required to adhere the

---

58. The Employment Service Convention (No. 88) and the Recommendation (No. 83), 1948 on the same subject contains provisions concerning placement services operated by the responsible authority. Paragraph 12(c) of the Recommendation provides that the employment service 'should not, in referring workers to employment, itself discriminate against applicants on the grounds of race, colour, sex or belief'.

59. *See* e.g. *Suriname*, s. 3(2) of the Labour Exchange Act.

60. *See* e.g. *FRG*, Regulation No. 167/81 of 15 September 1981 applicable to the Federal Employment Agency; in this respect *see also Denmark, Iraq, Mali, Yugoslavia*.

61. *See Israel*, s. 42A of the Employment Service Act, amended in 1988.

government's mandate in respect of equality of opportunity and treament in a manner similar to that which is imposed upon a public employment service.[62]

59. The applicabilition of EPD to access to employment means that every person has the right to seek employment on a non-discriminatory basis.[63] Thus, various national laws provide that recruitment for a job be based on objectively measured competence or merit, and no requirement that is unconnected with the performance of the task in question can be imposed.[64] Moreover, the employer is frequently forbidden by law from requiring into the political, religious or trade union views of persons seeking access to employment.[65]

60. The issue of offers of employment in advertisement and other media have created a new challenge to the application of EPD. In various countries, statutory action has been taken in this respect. The publication in the press of a discriminatory offer of employment, or the announcement of such an offer by the employer, is prohibited. In such cases, the law typically provides that it is unlawful to use or distribute forms of application for employment, or to publish an advertisement that contains or implies restrictions, conditions or preferences based on discriminatory grounds.[66] The same prohibition is often also imposed in connection with carrying out interviews or making written inquiries. No doubt the contribution that these measures have made to the implementaion of EPD is also expressed in the fact that they may help to revise the description of trades or occupations that carries a 'male' or 'female' connotation. The legal requirement that offers of employment be drafted in the most neutral terms contributes to this end, as well as to the prevention of indirect discrimination.

B. *General Terms and Conditions of Employment*

61. The principle of EPD applies to such issues as promotion, dismissal, retaliation and other general terms and conditions of employment. In this respect the principle is applied first to terms and conditions of employment in the area of job advancement, whereby promotions must be granted on the basis of the worker's individual suitability for the position. Hence, any discrimination based on unlawful

---

62. *See* e.g. *Denmark*, Notification Concerning Private Employment Agencies, dated 11 August 1986, issued in pursuant to the Act of 8 June 1978.
63. *See* Court of Justice of the European Communities, judgment of 10 April 1984, Case No. 79/83, *Harz* v. *Deutche Tradex GmbH*, in which the court did not accept the argument that the Directive concerning equal treatment created a right for a person to have a job. By implication, the Court expressed its preference for the employer's freedom of contract, subject however to the candidate's right to have his or her application for the post considered fairly.
64. *See* e.g. *Portugal*, Legislative Decree No. 392/79, s. 7(2).
65. *See* e.g. *Italy*, Act No. 300 of 20 May 1970 respecting the protection of workers' freedom and dignity, LS 1970-It. 2, s. 8.
66. *See* e.g. *Australia*, Victoria, ss. 18(1) and 27B of the Equal Opportunity Act 1977 as amended by the Equal Opportunity (Discrimination against Disabled Person) Act 1982 (discrimination on the basis of sex, marital status, existing or past physical or mental impairment), LS 1977-Aust. 1 and LS 1982 August. 1; *Canada*, s. 8 of the Canadian Human Rights Act; USA, s. 704(b) of the Civil Rights Act 1964.

grounds in the operation of the promotion system is forbidden.[67] Such a guarantee is of a particular importance in eliminating vertical segregation in occupations.[68]

62.   A second area which falls under the rubric of terms and conditions of employment relates to the issue of job security. This aspect of EPD is a counterpart of equal access of employment, by providing that dismissal from employment will not take place on discriminatory grounds. The guarantee of non-discrimination in job security confers the right to terminate an employment only when justified by reasons connected with the worker's conduct, ability or fitness to perform the work.[69] The fixing of a different age for mandatory retirement of men and women, is a controversial issue, and it has been treated differently in various countries. In some, such a provision is considered discriminatory, while in others it is regarded as a protective measure which, as such does not violate the concept of EPD and is lawful according to the ILSEPD.[70]

63.   The phenomenon of employers retaliation has grown in recent years, bring in in its wake the need to protect workers who either lodge a complaint, institute proceedings to enforce EPD, or who are a party to such proceedings in various capacities, e.g. as a witness. Hence, the application of EPD implies protection against employer retaliation. Protection against employer retaliation generally takes the form of a legal prohibition against using retaliatory measures if they are aimed at preventing workers from excercising their rights.[71] Explicit provisions protecting workers from dismissal by reason of having lodged a complaint, or instituted legal proceedings with respect to discrimination in the workplace appear in the legislation of some countries.

64.   Third, the application of the concept of EPD also relates to such terms and conditions of employement as hours of work, rest periods, annual holidays with pay, occupational safety and occupational health measures, as well as social security measures and welfare facilities and benefits provided in connection with employment.

VIII.   Remedies

65.   As already mentioned, in the Western countries, the development of EPD has recently entered a positive dynamic phase. This evolution is a development of the political muscle which members of certain status groups acquired (mainly women),

---

67.   *See* e.g. *Spain*, s. 8(2) of Act No. 8 of 10 March 1980 to promulgate the Workers' Charter, LS 1980-Sp. 1; *Portugal*, s. 10 of Legislative Decree No. 392/79 of 20 September 1979, LS 1979-Por. 3.
68.   Vertical segregation affects in particular women and minorities that are easily distinguished by race, colour, national or social origin.
69.   The issue of nondiscrimination in respect of termination of employment is dealt with specifically on the international level by the Termination of Employment Convention (No. 158).
70.   *See* the Judgments of the Court of Justice of the European Communities, dated 26 February 1986, *Marshall,* 152/84, *Beets-Proper*, 262/84.
71.   *See* e.g. *Guatemala*, s. 10 of the Labour Code, LS 1961-Gua. 1; *Honduras*, s. 10 of the Labour Code, LS 1959-Hond. 1; *Japan*, s. 104 of the Labour Standard Law, LS 1947-Jap. 3.

as well as of the growing awareness of human rights required to guarantee the principle of equality. It seems, however, that this dynamic development exposed and confronted the principle of EPD to, and with, a new challenge. In the post-industrial era, labour relations are confronted by a global competitive free market which results from the globalization process of the economy and the firm. The extent of competitiveness of the firm and its concomitant profits is very often based upon exploitation of cheap labour provided by a secondary labour force comprised of various status groups, such as, women, elder employees, immigrants, etc. Exploitation of this secondary labour force is institutionalized in various ways, e.g. atypical labour relations, second generation collective bargaining, precarious and part time work, etc. Basing labour relations upon the principle of equality has its cost. Equality has not only a political and social price, but also an economic dimension. The cost of equality under such circumstances rises from the special remedies which are applicable in the case of equality disputes and include the following remedial alternatives:[72] (a) Severance; (b) Extension (Reading in, or Reconstruction); (c) Positive Action. Hence, an economic conflict is created between the employers interest to reduce labour cost, and the workers interest to eliminate discrimination. In times of economic crisis, and of structural unemployment, this economic conflict is even magnified. This conflict challenges policy makers with a new dilemma with which they have to cope. They have to decide on methods of reconciliation between the conflicting interests.

A.   Severance

66.   The labour contract might prescribe two different arrangements, each relating to a different status group of employees. One of these arrangements might entitle certain employees with rights inferior to those provided to the other group. Such a contract is discriminatory and might bring about a nullity declaration of the contract as a whole. But more often than not it is enough under such circumstances to strike out only the discriminatory conditions. Applying the remedy of severance denotes the nullification of one of the two arrangements provided by the contract. Such nullification will result in both status groups enjoying the same rights. However, the need to nullify one of the arrangements only, requires a decision as to which of the two arrangements will be nullified. Theoretically we have two options: According to the first option, the more advantageous arrangement from the workers' viewpoint will be nullified. The result of such an option is that both status groups (the discriminated against and the one preferred) will derive no benefit from the better contract arrangement. The significance of this option is that the preferred workers will be deprived of their acquired contractual rights. According to the second option, it is suggested to nullify the worse arrangement of the two, according to which the workers are entitled to poorer conditions. The outcome of this option is that both status groups will benefit from the better arrangement provided by the

---

72.   For the relevant remedies *see* Justice Barak in Israeli H.Ct. *El-Al v. Daniloviz*, Vol. 48(5) P.D. 745 (1994).

contract. Under such circumstances, members of the preferred status group are not deprived of their acquired contractual rights. The idea of depriving workers of their acquired rights as prescribed by the first option is considered unreasonable considering the concept of equality in labour law, and until now has been rejected. The second option, according to which the employer is mandated to provide the discriminated group of workers with the better rights is accepted as a reasonable outcome. But, acceptance of the second option denotes an increase in the labour cost.

B. Extension

67. The extension remedy is relevant in a situation where the discriminatory feature of the contract is not reflected in two varying arrangements provided therein. The discriminatory nature is inferred from the fact that special contractual rights are accorded to one status group only, thus depriving members of other status groups from the enjoyment of such rights. Under such circumstances the severance remedy is not applicable since this is not a case which requires separation between the sick and healthy parts of the contract. Under the present situation, a new technique is used to provide employment equality. In this respect the extension/reading in/or reconstraction remedy/is affected to annul the discrimination of one status group in comparison to the other. *Prima facie* two options can also serve in this case. According to the first option, the discriminatory contractual provision of rights which are accorded to one status group only is annulled. That means that members of the preferred group are being deprived of their acquired contractual rights. The result of this option is expressed in the fact that all employees (the preferred ones as well as the discriminated ones) are treated equally since neither group is entitled to the rights prescribed by the contract of employment. According to the second option, the remedy accorded under its circumstances does not lie in nullification of the discriminatory arrangement provided by the contract, but rather by providing a judicial order meant to offset the discrimination by extending the contractual rights to the discriminated group of employees also. As already explained, the first option, because it violates protected employees rights, is considered to be unreasonable and therefore unacceptable under the principle of equality in labour law. Therefore, the extension prescribed by the second option is the proper solution under this principle. The right to impose such positive action is derived from the principle of equality which means that as long as the contractual discriminatory arrangement is not amended by the contract signatory parties, the prohibition of discrimination will be attained by providing the contractual special rights to the discriminated employees too. The application of such a remedy increases labour costs.

C. Positive Action

68. Examination of the specific remedies related to EPD disputes, requires reference to those traditional remedies which stem from the positive concept of equality. Several remedies can be mentioned in this framework, the most popular being the fair representation remedy. But from the viewpoint of labour cost, one should point out some additional positive remedies as follows:

1. Equal Pay for Work of Equal Value

69. It is quite often that a comparison of the wages paid to various status groups discloses a large gap which can be bridged, in part by the positive action principle of equal pay for equal work. However, this principle is inadequate to bridge the unequal and lower remuneration paid to the various deprived status groups, most of which are employed in the secondary labour market, and are paid a wage lower than the value of their work. Therefore, it is necessary to impose positive measures that entitles them to equal pay for work of equal value. Under such circumstances, equality can be attained by way of two possible options: Either by paying all workers the lower wage or by paying all workers the higher wage. But, since the first option is found unreasonable, under both principles, the discriminated against employees become entitled to higher wages. Adoption of the principles of equal remuneration for equal work or for work of equal value increases labour cost.

2. Special Rights

70. Treating equality in labour law as a positive right is also reflected in the special rights accorded to specific status groups. For example, this approach is reflected in the special rights accorded to workers with family responsibilities. Such special rights are meant to enable them to fulfil the double role in the family and in the plant. According rights such as maternity leave, parental or family vacation, etc. helps them perform their dual role. The prescription of such rights results in increasing labour cost.

D. *Implementation*

71. The practice of severance or extension can be illustrated by the case of equal remuneration provided on the international plane by the Equal Remuneration Convention, No. 100 of 1951, and on the comparative plane by legislation or jurisprudence which implements the international labour standard. The legislation of some countries explicitly provides that the lower rate of pay prescribed in the contract or agreement shall automatically be replaced by the higher rate. This is e.g. the case in Argentina, France, Luxembourg, Portugal, and in Equatorial Guinea. Moreover, in many countries, provisions in individual or collective agreements contrary to the principle of equal pay are deemed null and void according to legislation or jurisprudence. This can be ascertained from legislation in Argentina, Belgium, France, Germany, Ireland, Italy, Spain, and many other countries as well.[73] By contrast, the remedy of extension is provided rather by case-law as can be ascertained from jurisprudence dealing with equality disputes in general, e.g. in the United States in the case of *Welsh* v. *United States*,[74] or in Canada, from the case of *Schachter* v. *Canada*.[75]

---

73. *See* Equal Remuneration, General Survey of the Committee of Experts on the Application of Convention and Recommendations of the ILO, 1986 § 175.
74. 339 U.S. 333 (1969).
75. 93 D.L.R. (4th) 12 (1992).

IX. FUTURE OUTLOOK

72. As far as EPD in labour law is concerned there is no doubt that further legal, social, economic and educational steps must be taken on the comparative plane. These measures are required, for example: to enlarge the prohibited grounds of discrimination; to increase the scope of its application; to improve the legal procedures in order to better enforce employment equality rights; to increase the resources allocated to the promotion of employment equality, etc. However, it seems that these changes are already in motion. Nevertheless, the future of employment equality is somewhat clouded. It seems that any attempt to predict the future is to some extent not only presumptuous, but even self-deceptive, particularly in regard to the wide spectrum and extreme diversity of the various legal systems and their provisions of EPD in labour law. Despite everything, some guidelines as to the forecast of equality in the future can be formulated along the following lines:

A. *The Dynamics of Equality*

73. It should be re-emphasized that uprooting institutionalized discrimination is conditioned by: (a) The EPD in labour law being secured in its duality concept concerning equal outcome in addition to equal treatment; and (b) Its being recognized as a positive right permiting the introducion of affirmative action measures. Hence, the extent that institutionalized and perpetuated group discrimination decreases or increases depends upon the application of equality in the framework of the aforementioned two parameters. Institutionalized group discrimination will decrease if both parameters are implemented, and it might increase if it is applied only partially. The question of whether equality will continue to be applied in the aforementioned two parameters depends upon the movement of the political pendulum. Such movement is affected by the growing awareness of the principle of equality. From this viewpoint there are solid chances of future developments which will deepen the principle of EPD in labour law. However, this perspective might not be realized if a conservative backlash and adoption of a neo-liberal philosophy take place.

74. Notwithstanding, it seems that even the traditional EPD dual concept will have to be further developed in the coming years. It seems that the solutions provided by the traditional dual concept of EPD might not be adequate in view of the new types of discrimination facing a large part of the labour market. This forecast results from changes the labour market has undergone during the second half of the 20th century, caused by the intensified economic competition which globalization engendered, as well as, by the threatening phenomenon of the scarcity of work.[76] Consequently, the labour market was divided into three segments: The first one concerns the primary labour market which relates to full time and tenured workers, usually enjoying a large spectrum of rights acquired during their long period of

---

76. See J. Rifkin, *The End of Work, The Decline of the Global Labor Force and the Dawn of the Post-Market Era* (A Jeremy P. Tacher/Putnam Book 1995), p. 3.

employment. The second segment concerns the secondary market which relates to pricarious, atypical and peripheral workers, characterized by short-term and part-time employment usually accompanied by a very thin net of rights. The third segment concerns the structurally unemployed workers who are excluded from the labour market, and consequently, from society as well.

75. In light of such segmentation, it is most probable that the traditional dual concept of EPD will continue to be relevant where discrimination of primary labour market workers is concerned. But, unfortunately, the traditional dual concept of EPD will be inadequate regarding workers belonging to the secondary and third labour market segments. The inadequacy of the traditional dual concept of EPD, where secondary and third labour market segments are concerned, can be illustrated by many arguments, four of which will be presented bellow.

First, the traditional model of EPD is conditioned upon both employees (the discriminated against and the compared to) being employed by the same employer. But, the adaptation of atypical employment patterns such as, for example, in the case of outsourcing, made it impossible for the discriminated against secondary labour market employee to claim equality in comparison to the primary labour market employee. Thus, since under such circumstances, both employees are no longer employed by the same employer.

Second, it goes without saying that a tenured employee and a precarious one, even if employed by the same employer, are not treated equally. The discrimination, under such circumstances, is inherent in the varying patterns of their employment which were adopted by the employer. Under such circumstances, it will be impossible for the discriminated against precarious employee to claim equality. The precariousness and mobility, typical to secondary labour market employees, turns the enforcement of equality under such circumstances into an impossible situation technically, psychologically, and financially. Thus, the precarious employee will have to claim equality afresh every time he is obliged to confront a new employer.

Third, there is a large gap between the status and rights enjoyed by workers related to the primary labour market in comparison to the status and rights enjoyed by workers belonging to the secondary labour market. Hence, one could say that secondary labour market workers comprise a deprived group. The reason for their inferior and discriminatory situation lies in their belonging to the secondary labour market. In any event, however, they would not be able to claim equality under the traditional dual concept of EPD as the reason of belonging to the secondary labour market is not recognized as a prohibited ground of discrimination.

Fourth, the traditional model of EPD relates to discrimination of workers. This model is not relevant where the third labour market segment is concerned. The discrimination of those excluded from the labour market relates to a preliminary stage which is not covered by the traditional model of EPD. For this segment of the labour market, equality signifies first of all inclusion in society and in the labour market. But the traditional dual concept of EPD cannot provide it for them.[77]

---

77. *See* A. Giddens, *The Third Way, The renewal of Social Democracy*, at p. 102, who speaks of equality as inclusion and inequality as exclusion.

76. Hence, in the near future, in order to guarantee EPD, an additional distributive concept of equality will have to be added to the traditional one. In the framework of the new EPD concept, equality will serve as a distributive means, which will be used to overcome the discriminatory structure of the labour market which caused discrimination in the provision of work. While the traditional concept of EPD dealt with equality at work, the new distributive concept of EPD will be used in order to attain equal distribution of work itself.

B.   Final Remarks

77. Occupational equality in labour relations is undergoing a process of juridification. The juridification of employment equality turned the Law into an essential tool of reform. Under such circumstances, law becomes the key that can be used to limit political and social reforms as well as enable their implementation. Under such circumstances, the introduction of new legislation, without which the *status quo* reflected by existing norms and precedents will prevail, becomes vital. The above-mentioned *status quo* is more favourable to the male standard than to the interests of any other status group. As indicated before, however, law is not an instrument handled by the legislature but rather by society's policy-makers, a society which is comprised of groups, and where a person's status is determined according to the group to which he belongs. In such a society, powerful groups can influence the Law and use it to promote their interests. Sometimes, in order to evaluate the political power of the various status groups a parallel is drawn between them and the proletariat. While such a parallel is valid to some extent, there is a big difference between the situation of the proletariat and that of the various status groups referred to as the *Other*. The difference is expressed in the lack of concrete means of all status groups for organizing themselves into one unit which can stand face to face with the correlative unit, lacking in their case the required solidarity which characterized, *inter alia,* the situation of the proletariat. The various status groups are not even banded together, thus lacking even any community feeling which traditionally exists among workers of a plant. Therefore, the chances that all discriminated status groups will unite and gather enough political power to introduce reforms are not particularly good, although, some women's groups, as Schneider explains, might succeed in forming certain coalitions and asserting a certain collective identity.[78] Moreover, the case of the blacks in the United States, or Catholics in Northern Ireland, indicate that some status groups might acquire enough political influence to introduce some piecemeal reforms in their favour. It is claimed however, that such a strategy might perhaps reinforce rather than weaken the discriminatory structures of labour relations.[79]

---

78. Elizabeth M. Schneider, 'The Dialectic of Rights and Politics: Perspectives from the Women's Movement, in *Feminist Legal Theory, Reading in Law and Gender* (eds), Katharine T. Bartlett and Rosanne Kennedy, Westview press, Boulder, 1991, p. 318.
79. Katharine T. Bartlett and Rosanne Kennedy, 'Introduction', in *Feminist Legal Theory, Reading in Law and Gender* (eds), Katharine T. Bartlett and Rosanne Kennedy, Westview press, Boulder, 1991, p. 1, at p. 3.

78. The EPD system of any country is a subsystem in that country, along with other subsystems such as the industrial relations subsystem, or the political, economic, or human relations subsystems. As Reinolds explains, a subsystem that is not in harmony with other subsystems will either change those other systems so that harmony is established, or fail.[80] Therefore, if the political and social subsystems are already formulated or being reorganized in an antisocial mould which correspond to the criteria expressed by the key words of neo-liberalism: individualism, free market and competition, as well as a non-activist state – then it might become inevitable that occupational equality will also be expressed along such lines in the future.

SELECT BIBLIOGRAPHY

Aaron and Farwell (ed.), *Position of Women in Labour Law and Social Security Law, 10th International Congress, International Society for Labour Law and Social Security*, Vol. III, Washington, 1984.

Abram, 'Affirmative Action: Fair Shakers and Social Engineers', *Harv. L. Rev.*, Vol. 99, 1986, p. 1312 .

Bartlett and Kennedy (eds), *Feminist Legal Theory, Reading in Law and Gender*, Westview press, Boulder, 1991.

Belton, 'Discrimination and Affirmative Action: An Analysis of Competing Theories of Equality and Weber', *North Carolina Law Review*, Vol. 59, 1981, p. 531.

Blanpain, Equality of Treatment in Employment, *International Encyclopedia of Comparative Law*, Chapter 10A, Tubingen, 1990.

Blanpain (ed.), 'Women and Labour: A Comparative Study', *Bull. Comp. Lab. Rel.*, Vol. 9, 1978.

Blanpain (ed.), 'Equality and Prohibition of Discrimination in Employment', *Bull. Comp. Lab. Rel.*, Vol. 14, 1985.

Brown, Baumann, and Melnick, 'Equal Pay for Jobs ofiComparable Worth: An Analysis of the Rhetoric', *Harvard Civil Rights – Civil Leberties Law Review*, Vol. 21, 1986, p. 127.

Carnoy, 'The family, flexible work and social cohesion at risk', *Int'l L. Rev.*, Vol. 138, 1999, p. 411.

Clayton and Crosby, *Justice, Gender, and Affirmative Action*, University of Michigan Press, 1992.

Equality in Employment and Occupation, *General Survey of the Committee of Experts on the Application of Conventions and Recommendations of the ILO*, 1988.

Equal Remuneration, *General Survey of the Committee of Experts on the Application of Conventions and Recommendations of the ILO*, 1986.

Gilligan, *In a Different Voice*, 1982.

Heide, 'Supranational action against sex discrimination: Equal pay and equal treatment in the European Union' *Int'l L. Rev.*, Vol. 138, 1999, p. 381.

---

80. Reinhold Fahlbeck, 'The Demise of Collective Bargaining in the U.S.A.', in *The Changing Face of Labour Law and Industrial Relations, Liber Amicorum for Clyde W. Summers*, Blanpain and Weiss, (eds), Nomos Velagsgesellchaft, Baden-Baden 1993, p. 47.

Hodges-Aeberhard, 'Affirmative action in employment: Recent court approaches to a difficult concept', *Int'l L. Rev.*, Vol. 138, 1999, p. 247.

Jones, ' "Reverse Discrimination" in Employment: Judicial Treatment of Affirmative Action Programmes in the United States', *International Labour Review*, Vol. 120, 1981, p. 453.

Kennedy, 'Persuasion and Distrust: A Comment on the Affirmative Action Debate', *Harv. L. Rev.*, Vol. 99, 1986, p. 1327.

Koggel, 'A Feminist View of Equality and Its Implications for Affirmative Action', *Can. J.L. Jur.*, Vol. 7, 1994, p. 43.

Littleton, 'Reconstructing Sexual Equality' in *Feminist Legal Theory, Reading in Law and Gender* (eds), Bartlett and Kennedy, Westview press, Boulder, 1991, p. 35.

Love, 'Justifying Affirmative Action', *Auckland U.L.Rev. Annual*, Vol. 7, 1993, p. 491.

Landau, *The Rights of Working Women in the European Community*, Brussels, 1985.

MacKinnon, Difference and Dominance: On Sex Discrimination, in *Feminist Legal Theory, Reading in Law and Gender* (eds), Bartlett and Kennedy, Westview press, Boulder, 1991, p. 81.

Nussbaum, 'The capabilities approach', *Int'l. L. Rev.*, Vol. 138, 1993, p. 227.

Rubinstein, 'The Law of Sexual Harassment at Work', *Ind. L. J.*, Vol. 12, 1983, p. 1.

Schmidt (ed.), *Discrimination in Employment*, Stockholm, 1978.

Valticos, International Labour Law, in *International Encyclopaedia for Labour Law and Industrial Relations*, ed. in chief, Blanpain, Deventer, 1984.

Vogel-Polsky, *Positive Action and the Constitutional and Legislative Hindrances to its Implementation*, Strasbourg, 1989.

Weiller, 'The Wages of Sex: The Uses and Limits of Comparable Worth', *Harvard Law Review*, Vol. 99, 1986, p. 1728.

Westen, 'The Empty Idea of Equality', *Harvard Law Review*, Vol. 95, 1982, p. 537.

Chapter 17. Employee Privacy

F. Hendrickx

I. INTRODUCTION

1.   Privacy has had a place as an issue in several employment law books for quite some time. In the first place, this may be explained by the fact that privacy has gained more and more importance in the daily practice of labour relations. Employee privacy covers a broad range of issues, from personal data protection, medical screening, psychological testing, surveillance and monitoring of workers – internet monitoring being one of the new hot issues – to personal life style and personality matters. Another explanation however, relates to the true nature of the right to privacy. Indeed, the right to privacy is a fundamental human right. This right does not disappear when concluding an employment contract.

2.   Privacy is often an elusive legal concept, the precise content of which may be historically and culturally laden. Nevertheless, despite the nuances of legal derivation – from constitutional law, from the civil code or common law, from statute or administrative regulation – the general category cuts across a common concern and speaks to certain shared values. Collin Bennett adverted to these in his comparative treatment of the law of informational privacy. The fundamental issue addressed by the law, he opined, is

> 'the loss of human dignity, autonomy, or respect that results from a loss of control over personal information. Furthermore, the conviction that information privacy is an essential component of humanity is found in the literature and rhetoric of every country that has addressed this issue. In English we use the word 'privacy'. The Germans apply the related notion of *Die Privatsphäre* – literally a private sphere, a boundary between individual autonomy and social life. The French frame the problem as *la protection de la vie privée* with very direct references to the connection between *l'informatique* (information technology) and *les libertés* (human freedoms). The Swedes use the word *integritet*, which embodies the connotation that individuals have the right to be judged according to a complete profile of their personalities.'[1]

---

1.   C. Bennett, *Regulating Privacy: Data Protection and Public Policy in Europe and the United States*, 26–27, Ithaca, 1992.

3. As Bennett and others have pointed out, an axial principle around which the right to privacy turns is individual autonomy, a freedom from control or domination by others.[2] It plays out in *informational self-determination* – control of what is disclosed about oneself and to whom; in *freedom from control in the workplace* – by surveillance, computer monitoring and electronic supervision, even in control of one's dress and grooming; and *freedom from control in one's life off the job* – in sexual activity, recreation, association, and expression.

4. It should be at once obvious that the claim to individual autonomy is in sharp conflict with the demands of the modern employment relationship. Apropos of the right to disclose of oneself only as much as one freely wills, Roger Blanpain has observed that the modern employer

> 'wants to know almost everything about the candidate before hiring him or her. Hiring someone, after all, may be a significant investment. The employer will also want to monitor its employees during their employment – whether they are still fit to do the job, whether they need further training, and whether they can be promoted. As a result, the need for enterprises to know everything about the physical and mental health, motivation, relationships, beliefs, outlook, experience, competence, skills, ideas, religion, political opinions, offspring, and ethnic background, is, in a sense, exponentially growing.'[3]

5. Some techniques of human resource management seek to tie the employee to ever tighter bonds of loyalty to the employer and so to heighten employer controls of employee behaviour and attitude on the job and off. Some controls of off the job behaviour are connected to employer concern for liability – for sexual harassment if supervisor–subordinate or co-worker relationships turn bitter, for increased medical or workers' compensation costs from engaging in risky behaviour such as smoking, drinking, or sky-diving. Some is driven by employer concern for its image in the community, by regulating unpopular behaviour or speech. And some arises out of the felt need to display the exercise of power.

6. The following is unconcerned with the various legal theories of privacy. What follows, is a survey of privacy in labour relations from two angles. Firstly, an overview will be given of some general principles governing privacy. In international human rights thinking, important discussions are ongoing in relation to the application of a fundamental right, such as privacy, in private relationship, such as the employment relationship. This first part also tries to give an insight into the international perspective of privacy protection in the sphere of employment. A second part will concentrate on some substantial 'issues' related to employee privacy.

---

2. *See generally*, A. Westin, *Privacy and Freedom*, New York, 1968.
3. R. Blanpain, 'Employee Privacy Issues: Belgian Report', 17 *Comp. Labour Law J.*, Vol. 38, pp. 38–39, 1995.

II. GENERAL PRINCIPLES OF EMPLOYEE PRIVACY

A. The Right to Privacy as a Human Right

7.   The right to privacy is a fundamental human right. It is protected as such in most constitutions of industrialized – or post-industrial – countries. This 'fundamental rights' – nature of the right to privacy is important. Indeed, it gives employee privacy a meaningful respect.

8.   The real meaning of the right to privacy as a fundamental right could be illustrated by wondering what could happen if it were not 'fundamental' and thus not constitutionally protected. Let us discuss and compare English law with the law of continental European countries and the protection of the right to privacy under the European Convention of Human Rights, concluded in the framework of the Council of Europe.

9.   It has been argued already that, in England, privacy protection is 'piecemeal, incomplete and indirect'.[4] Therefore, legal scholars have often regarded the state of the English law as unsatisfactory.[5] While not completely ignored in English law, privacy protection is often indirect and incomplete.[6] It is a fragmentary protection through some kinds of torts, with particular fields of application, like for example trespass or nuisance. All this implies that employee privacy still needs to be protected all the way through contractual concepts. This may have different consequences than a 'fundamental' privacy approach. This may be illustrated with the case of reasonableness in unfair dismissal law in the UK. It is generally accepted that, under this law, a dismissal should be reasonable and that an overly broad justification thereof is undesirable. However, in UK unfair dismissal law the introduction of a justification amounts to a 'band of reasonable responses' test. It may happen that, within such concept, privacy becomes neglected. This is illustrated   in *Saunders v. Scottish National Camps Association*,[7] where a person was dismissed because of being homosexual and where the employer's response to the employee's privacy was in fact based on a test of 'the reasonable employer', i.e. reduced to that of the 'average' employer, without taking into account the possibility that a considerable proportion of employers might be wrong.[8]

10.   It may be argued that, the right to privacy being a fundamental right, justifications of privacy interferences should be dealt with along the lines of human rights protection mechanisms. For European employee privacy protection, this may mean that the case-law of the European Court of Human Rights at Strasbourg is education for privacy cases in the employer–employee relationships.[9]

---

4.   Bailey, S.H., Harris, D.J., and Jones, B.L., *Civil Liberties: Cases and Materials*, London, Butterworths, 1985, p. 352.
5.   Martin, A., 'Privacy in English law', in Robertson, A.H. (ed.), *Privacy and Human Rights*, Manchester, Manchester University Press, 1973, p. 96.
6.   Yang, T.L., 1966, p. 175.
7.   [1980] I.R.L.R. p. 175.
8.   *See* Wedderburn, *The Worker and the Law*, London, Sweet & Maxwell, 1986, p. 452.
9.   F. Hendrickx, *Privacy en arbeidsrecht*, Brugge, die Keure, 1999, 17 e.v.

11. Article 8 of the European Convention on Human Rights reads as follows:

1. Everyone has the right to respect for his private and family life, his home and his correspondence.
2. There shall be no interference by a public authority with the exercise of this right except such as is in accordance with the law and is necessary in a democratic society in the interests of national security, public safety, or the economic well-being of the country, for the prevention of disorder or crime, for the protection of health or morals, or for the protection of the rights and freedoms of others.

12. This article suggests that privacy should be protected along the lines of its second paragraph. A privacy case could then be dealt with as follows:

1. *legitimate purposes*: the right to privacy is a fundamental right and may only be interfered with for the protection of other legitimate interests or for legitimate purposes. The interests named in Article 8 are national security, public safety, economic well-being of the country, disorder, crime, health, morals, rights, and freedoms of others. Not necessarily all, but some of these rights or interests opposing the right to privacy might be relevant within employment relationships. Certainly, 'rights and freedoms of others' are recognized, meaning that if the employer has a very good reason to interfere with the employee's privacy, this has to be approved.
2. *described by law*: the Convention provides that 'there shall be no interference by a public authority with the exercise of this right except such as is in accordance with the law'. The meaning of this wording for employee–employer relationship is that any interference with the employee's right to privacy, should be in accordance with a clear and accessible norm.
3. *necessary and proportionate*: the words 'necessary in a democratic society' are the emanation of the proportionality principle or the 'least-means' principle.[10] 'Necessary' means 'proportionate to the legitimate aim pursued'.[11] It is believed that it is not a requirement of 'indispensable' but stronger than mere 'acceptable' or 'reasonable'.[12] Further, the expression 'in a democratic society' used in the wording implies that the necessity has to be interpreted against the background of democracy, implying a climate of broad mindedness and tolerance.[13]

13. One has to bear in mind that privacy cannot be defended at all costs. If an employer has a legitimate reason to interfere with the employee's privacy and complies with the human rights principles, he must be allowed to do so. Indeed, it must

---

10. Eissen, M.-A., 'The Principle of Proportionality in the Case-Law of the European Court of Human Rights', in *The European system for the protection of human rights*, MACDONALD, R.St.J., MATSCHER, F. and PETZOLD, H. (eds), Dordrecht, Nijhoff, 1993, 125–146.
11. *Handyside v. UK*, Judgment of the European Court of Human Rights, 7 December 1976, *Series A*, No. 24; *Dudgeon v. UK*, Judgment of the European Court of Human Rights, 23 September 1981, *Series A*, No. 45.
12. Delmas-Marty, M. and Chodkiewicz, C. (eds), *The European Convention for the Protection of Human Rights: International Protection Versus National Restrictions*, Dordrecht, Nijhoff, 1992, p. 326.
13. Rimanque, K., 'Noodzakelijkheid in een democratische samenleving – een begrenzing van beperkingen aan grondrechten' ('Necessity in a democratic society – a limit to limitations of fundamental rights'), in *Liber Amicorum Fréderick Dumon*, II, Antwerpen, Kluwer, 1983, p. 1224.

be recognized that the right to privacy is not absolute, and that privacy expectations are reduced in employment relationships. Under the European Convention on Human Rights it has been recognized that 'the claim to respect for private life is automatically reduced to the extent that the individual himself brings his private life into contact with public life or into close connection with other protected interests'.[14]

B. The Employment Environment

14. When studying employee privacy, specific attention must be drawn to the employment environment. Indeed, an employment relationship implies, as a general rule, a subordinate relationship. This means that the employer is contractually allowed to exercise authority over the employee. Being an employee implies that one's freedom is partly left behind in the sense that the employer can control personal behaviour. The employee's privacy is therefore qualified by the employment relationship. However, the individual is only subject to the authority of the employer in so far as this is embodied in the specific employment relationship. From this reality the concept of relevancy or non-relevancy is derived. Indeed, the employee's privacy can only be limited by the employer's authority in so far as this is relevant for the employment relationship.[15]

15. The relevancy-test implies that the employer must be able to justify interferences with the employee's privacy on the basis of the employment contract. However, the test may be applied in different ways. It may be interpreted as merely demanding a link with the employment relationship, or it could be interpreted as a necessity requirement of privacy interferences.

16. An employment relationship implies the co-existence of different rights and interests which limit the rights of the individual employee. Apart from the managerial prerogatives, there are also the rights of other employees (colleagues) and third parties (customers, society at large). It is obvious that one another limits the privacy claims of individual employees.

III. INFORMATIONAL SELF-DETERMINATION

A. Testing

1. Medical Testing: General Screening

17. All the industrial world shares a concern for health and safety in the workplace; all States impose an obligation on the employer to assure safe and healthful conditions toward which end employers commonly seek to screen applicants and test

---

14. *Brüggeman and Scheuten v. Germany*, Application No. 6959/75, Decision of the European Commission of Human Rights, 12 July 1977, *D.R.*, Vol. 10, p. 100.
15. G. Giugni, 'Political, religious and private-life discrimination', in F. Schmidt (ed.), Discrimination in employment, Stockholm, Almqvist&Wiksell International, 1978, pp. 191–193.

employees for their fitness to work. Consequently, all the States surveyed deal with medical testing. They take one or a combination of approaches: (a) to limit testing substantively, e.g. to allow employees to test only for those conditions having a close connection to job performance; (b) to limit testing procedurally, e.g. by regulation of who is authorized to conduct the examination or by requiring consultation with workers via a works council on what is to be tested for; or (c) to limit what an employer may do upon receipt of the test results even if medical testing is not otherwise regulated. The following outlines these approaches on a State-by-State basis from the more to the less rigorous in terms of the stringency of legal regulation.

18. Belgium's General Regulation for the Protection of Labour authorizes medical testing but only for certain jobs to be determined by employer-worker committees. The industrial physician is given control over the authorization of certain tests – alcohol, drug, or HIV/AIDS, depending upon the job at issue, i.e. respectively involving safety-sensitive work or exposure to surgical procedures. Thus, only such testing may be required as is essential for the fulfilment of the employee's obligations and the employer's obligation to afford a safe and healthful workplace.

19. France's Labour Code provides that all employees must undergo a medical examination, at least by the end of the probationary period, to insure that the employee is medically fit and free of infectious disease; annual medical examinations are required thereafter. However, the industrial physician is permitted only to transmit an opinion of medical fitness or unfitness to work, totally or partially. A duty to accommodate is imposed on the employer in the latter case; and appeal may be had to the labour inspector by the employer, the employee, or by an applicant.

20. Germany's Occupational Health Act authorizes the giving of medical examinations for health and safety reasons; and for some occupations such examinations are mandated by law. The scope of medical inquiry in limited to those purposes; i.e. to ascertain the ability of the candidate to do the work or to prevent accidents. The industrial physician, even if in the company's employ, is restricted to indicating the employee's capacity to perform; details of the employee's medical condition are (theoretically) not to be disclosed to the employer.

21. The Netherlands' Working Environment Act provides for a working environment service (WES) which is authorized to 'carry out medical examinations when workers are recruited' and allows the conditioning of certain types of work upon a finding of medical fitness, i.e. involving 'special danger for the lives or health of the workers concerned or [of] other persons', for example in coal mining, shipping, transportation, and the like. Questions of testing in the interests of health, safety, and welfare are also subject to consultation with statutorily mandated works councils. A bill proposed in 1992 would further restrict medical testing by requiring informed consent of the employee, giving the employee all results before they are communicated to the employer, and allowing the employer to review only a general conclusion of fitness or unfitness.

22. Austria's Workers Protection Act authorizes the medical service to institute a medical examination even where the employer has not itself established a test of physical fitness. Employees may be tested for exposure to harmful substances. But the means of carrying out such testing is subject to negotiation with the works council.

23.   Under Spain's General Occupational Safety and Health Ordinance employers are given the duty to arrange for pre-employment and periodical medical examinations subject to consultation with mandated workplace occupational safety and health committee established by the workers. Test results are subject to doctor–patient confidentiality. Action upon test results e.g. for HIV/AIDS or genetic tests, may implicate anti-discrimination law.

24.   Sweden requires that employers observe 'good labour market practice' as a basic principle of labour law. There is virtually no restriction on pre-employment medical screening as an aspect of the employer's freedom to 'hire at will'. Post-hire testing is legally required arising out of employer health and safety obligations under the Work Environment Act, and may be adopted toward that end even where not mandated. However, non-mandated post-hire testing may be subject to co-determination with the workers' representatives.

25.   In Canada (apart from legislation in certain safety-sensitive jobs) the common law restricts medical screening to a close relationship to safety and efficiency in the workplace, that is, the requirement must meet a standard of reasonableness.

26.   Australia, the United Kingdom, and the United States do not restrict medical screening as such, but various of these State's anti-discrimination laws may limit the employer's ability to act negatively upon the test results. In the United Kingdom, physician–patient confidentiality limits what a physician may report of an employee's test results, absent express consent. In the United States, the Americans With Disabilities Act forbids the giving of a medical examination until after a job has been conditionally offered, and requires that the medical information secured must be placed in separate medical files and be 'treated as confidential' – the latter is subject to allowance for disclosure to supervisors and managers who need to be informed of restrictions on an applicant's duties or other reasonable accommodations to the individual's statutory disability.

27.   In Japan, the Industrial Health and Safety Act requires employers to have medical examinations of employees conducted, but the precise medical defects discovered may not be disclosed.

2. Drug and Alcohol Testing

28.   A number of States require the testing of employees in certain especially safety-sensitive positions or in cases of accidents in such occupations, especially in transportation: Denmark, Finland, France, Italy, Japan, the Netherlands, Sweden, the United Kingdom, and the United States.

29.   In many States, drug use either in the general population or in the labour force is not considered a serious enough problem to warrant any special treatment: In

Belgium, occupational physicians have resisted systematic drug testing as an unwarranted intrusion into privacy. It is disfavoured by employers in Denmark, rare in Finland, is subject to an enterprise agreement with works councils in Germany (and, as to alcohol testing, requires reasonable cause on the basis of observable behaviour to require the individual employee to submit).

30. The Canadian common law approach requiring a reasonable relationship of a medical test to one's fitness or ability to perform the job would apply as well to drug or alcohol testing.

31. France draws a sharp distinction between drug and alcohol testing. The former is not considered a problem and no special legislation addresses it. On the latter, the courts have limited the employer's ability to conduct systematic screening to special safety-sensitive positions.

32. The legal framework in the United Kingdom is especially complicated and the employer's ability unilaterally to implement testing rules is open to question; thus, it has been argued that suspicionless testing of incumbent employees would be actionable as a breach of the contract of employment.

33. The Swedish labour court has sustained a construction company's drug testing to assure safety. The decision, which has become widely accepted, sets out the conditions sustaining the requirement including, among other things, objective need for the test in the context of the work performed.

34. In the United States, a few State courts have limited drug testing to safety-sensitive jobs; and drug and alcohol testing for incumbent workers is subject to negotiation with a union if one has been selected. Otherwise, employees are free to test as a screening device for applicants, before a return to work, or on a 'reasonable suspicion' or even a random basis for incumbent employees. At least fourteen States have legislated to regulate employment drug testing, e.g. to assure accuracy in testing and, in some cases, to require access to employee assistance plans in lieu of discharge; but none of these limit the nature of the employment for which testing can be required.

35. In Spain employers commonly test applicants and incumbents for drug or alcohol use, usually as part of general medical screening in the former case and frequently as part of a rehabilitative effort in the latter.

3. HIV/AIDS Testing

36. The propriety of testing applicants or employees for HIV/AIDS because of the special characteristic of the work, notably health personnel involved in invasive procedures, seems universally to be recognized. Alternatively, reliance on positive test results to disqualify applicants or employees for jobs not involving the serious threat of transmission could fall afoul or be subject to challenge on anti-discrimination grounds in Australia, Belgium, Canada, Finland, France, Italy, the United Kingdom, and the United States, but the basis of the challenge varies considerably. In the UK, use of the test result might be challenged on grounds of race or sex discrimination; in Australia and the US, on grounds of 'impairment' and 'disability' respectively; and in Italy, discrimination on grounds of HIV-infection is discriminatory in itself.

37. Systematic HIV/AIDS testing is forbidden (where seropositive persons do not constitute a threat) in Austria and France.

38. German law is complicated by separate legislation at the State level; there is no federal legislation. But because the general right of informational self-determination limits employer inquiries to those that are job related, that logic would extend to medical interrogations and could prohibit the employer's ability to require an HIV test where not job related.

39. There are no specially cognizable restrictions on HIV/AIDS testing in The Netherlands, Spain, or Sweden; but in each the actual situation appears to be more subtle. In The Netherlands, testing has been resisted by the government as unrelated to job content. In Spain, a Ministry of Labour Report recommended a distinction between 'risk companies' involving the threat of exposure and are expected to test, and 'normal companies' in which employees can refuse to be tested. And in Sweden, the obligation to abide by 'good labour market practice' could be read to limit HIV/AIDS status as job unrelated.

40. Japan's AIDS Prevention Act is a comprehensive regulation of physicians with respect to testing, surveillance, and reporting of HIV/AIDS; it reaches employment only indirectly, but it does not restrict the employer's ability to require such a test.

4. Genetic Screening and Monitoring

41. It may be necessary to distinguish genetic *monitoring* from genetic *screening*. Genetic *monitoring* tests are administered to see if members of the workforce are affected by potential mutenogenic substances in the workplace to which they may be exposed. Testing of that kind may be governmentally mandated, as an aspect of oversight of occupational health, or conducted pursuant to labour–management agreement. Genetic *screening* may be conducted to comb out applicants or employees who might be especially sensitive to such exposure or, more broadly, to eliminate from employment those who may be at heightened medical risk irrespective of workplace idiosyncracies and so pose a greater potential burden on the employer for lost time, accident or health insurance costs.

42. In Austria, the use of a genetic test would be subject to negotiation with the works council.

43. In France, the industrial physician is to decide to give a genetic test or not, either in screening or monitoring; but the physician's report can only deal with the applicant or employee's fitness for the job. So too, in Belgium, the industrial physician is most likely prohibited from communicating the results of a genetic test without the express consent of the employee.

44. In Canada, the use of a genetic test would likely be subject to a standard of reasonableness related to health or safety in the workplace. Monitoring and even screening would be permissible, however, subject to challenge on non-discrimination grounds, e.g. race, national origin, or disability.

45. Finland's Labour Protection Act (and its application) requires genetic monitoring; no provision deals with genetic screening.

46. Germany makes no separate provision regulating genetic testing. Two parliamentary reports were published outlining the major concerns, but no legislation has resulted. So, too, in Denmark, a bill was proposed in 1992 to restrict genetic testing, but it failed of passage. Neither is separate legislative provision made in Australia, Italy, the Netherlands, Spain, Sweden, or the United Kingdom though, again, in several of these States reliance on test results may be subject to challenge on anti-discrimination grounds depending upon the class adversely affected.

47. No federal law in the United States speaks directly to genetic screening though, again, reliance on test results is subject to challenge on anti-discrimination grounds. Eight States forbid or stringently regulate genetic screening.

5. Psychological and Honesty Testing

48. Employers may use a variety of devices to screen or test applicants or incumbents on psychological grounds: personality profiles can be developed from elaborate questionnaires, especially personality inventories; projective tests require interaction with and examination by a trained psychologist or psychiatrist; paper and pencil 'honesty' tests can be used to predict a propensity for theft; polygraphs ('lie detectors') or voice stress analysers can be used to assist in determining truthfulness either in screening applicants or in investigations of alleged misconduct. The States surveyed below are roughly in descending order of the extent of legal regulation.

49. The French Labour Code applies to psychological testing: it restricts testing to the 'particular characteristics of the job', for information that has a 'direct and necessary link' to those characteristics, is directly relevant to the ends sought, and does not discriminate against a list of protected classes. A 1993 circular of the Ministry of Labour elaborated on these requirements including that the techniques and methods must be reliable and accurate. These rights extend to both applicants and incumbents. If the requirement of reliability and accuracy come close to requiring professionally accepted test validation, then the scope for psychological testing would be considerably reduced.

50. Article 8 of the Italian Workers' Statute restricts the gathering of personal data, and it has been argued that to the extent psychological tests probe an employee's ideas, opinions, and convictions they are strictly forbidden.

51. No German law speaks specifically to psychological screening in the private sector; but the general principles of the law of personality (*Persönlichkeitsrecht*) have been widely understood to apply. By this reasoning, these devices would be viewed as inherently violative and their use could be justified only if employer's interest in giving them outweighs the strong privacy interest implicated, e.g. to fill a specific position where exposure to stress is intrinsic to the job.

52. The Netherlands would appear to take a similar approach, i.e. limiting such testing to those characteristics relevant to the particular position, subject to the further limits of anti-discrimination law.

53. In Canada, the use of the polygraph is prohibited in Ontario and New Brunswick. Psychological tests are not otherwise specifically regulated, although actions based on them are subject to challenge under anti-discrimination law.

54. Though the Australian Law Reform Commission cautioned in 1983 about the privacy concerns presented by psychological testing in all its forms, no special provisions has been made in Australian law (apart from the potential application of anti-discrimination law). Legislation in New South Wales bans the use of polygraphs and voice stress analysers in employment.

55. In Belgium, such psychological examinations as qualify as medical examinations would be treated as such; there is otherwise no separate treatment for psychological tests.

56. No special provision regarding psychological testing in any of its forms has been made: in Austria, though the introduction but not the use of psychological evaluation may be subject to negotiation with the works council; in Denmark, subject to the same reservation as well as to separate challenge on the collection and storage of personal data; in Finland subject to the application of data collection and storage law; in Sweden, subject to the same reservation; in the United Kingdom, subject to the same reservation; and in Spain.

57. In the United States, the use of the polygraph is strictly regulated by federal law and even more strictly by statute in twenty-seven States. A personality test, *if* it is a statutory 'medical examination' under federal disability discrimination law, could not be given until after a conditional job offer had been made and reliance upon the result might be subject to challenge on anti-discrimination grounds. An intermediate appellate court in California enjoined the use of a personality inventory (for the position of security guard) on the ground of the intrusiveness of the questions into religious belief and bodily functions. There have been no other challenges in the private sector, nor does any statute require professional validation for such tests. By the same token there are virtually no prohibitions upon the use of paper-and-pencil 'honesty' tests, though one state's prohibition on the use of lie detectors includes 'written examinations' and so would seem to reach such devices.

B.   *Questionnaires and Questions*

58. A similar diversity is reflected in the national approaches to questionnaires (or application form questions) and personal interview questions: from States that limit all questions to job relatedness and may require co-determination over the terms of the forms used, to those that only forbid questions bearing upon membership in a statutorily protected class or activity such as union membership. These will be outlined in order of descending rigour.

59. In France, the gathering and use of information about an applicant or employee was regulated extensively by the Act on Computer Science and Freedom of 1978, and even more stringently by the Act of 31 December 1992 under which any information gathered must have a 'direct and necessary link with the position offered or with the evaluation of the professional capacities'. Consultation with the works council is required over recruitment and evaluation of employees. Moreover, an elected employee personnel delegate has oversight under the law: if the delegate learns that an impermissibly intrusive question has been asked, the delegate may petition a court of competent jurisdiction to enjoin its use (though this provision is complicated and apparently rarely used). Moreover, a candidate's duty of candour does not apply to an impermissible question, e.g. into his or her private life; thus the candidate may lie in response to such a question.

60. In Germany, the individual right to informational self-determination limits employer questions only to those directly related to the job. A question, for example, of what an applicant is being paid in her current employment would be impermissible unless it had been made relevant to the hiring process, e.g. by the applicant's insistence that she would accept no less than her current rate of pay. The works council is given co-determination rights over the content of written questionnaires, but not of oral questions. As in France, a candidate may lie to an impermissible question.

61. Article 11 of Collective Bargaining Agreement no. 38 of 1983 stipulates that the recruiting employer may only ask such information relating to an applicant's private life insofar as this information is relevant for the job.

62. In Austria the consent of the works council is required for the introduction of personal questionnaires; questions of a personal or sensitive nature would be forbidden or subject to works council consent. It has been argued that the works council could not consent to questions that transcend what is necessary for evaluation for the job.

63. The principles of Finnish law applicable to testing apply as well to other information secured in the application process: the employer's authority to question is limited by discrimination law (and so a truthful applicant denied employment by virtue of answering an impermissible question could pursue an action against the employer); but the Personal Data File Act prohibits the recording of sensitive data including that bearing upon social, political, or religious beliefs as well as other very personal information.

64. Spain's Data Protection Act limits the collection and storage of data to that necessary for the legitimate objectives of the private enterprise: the storage of 'sensitive information' bearing upon ideology, religion, race, sex life, and the like is precluded. Thus, it can be argued that to the extent this information would not be recorded and stored it could not be inquired into.

65. In Australia it has been argued that questions that intrude into one's privacy are impermissible and so it would not breach the employee's duty of candour to refuse to answer; but it has also been acknowledged that industrial tribunals have not always proved receptive to the claim. In any event, questions that intrude into legislatively protected areas, e.g. sex discrimination, would be forbidden, the extent of these protections depending upon the law in the various States.

66. In Sweden, the United Kingdom, and the United States, employers are given almost unfettered ability to inquire save insofar as certain questions (or acting upon the results of truthful answers) would be violative of anti-discrimination law or, in the United States, are so intrusive (and so without business justification) as to amount to the tort of 'invasion of privacy' or 'infliction of emotional distress' under State law.

IV. EMPLOYEE DATA PROTECTION

A. International Law

67. On the international level, various legal instruments came into existence with regard to employee data protection. The most important instruments dealing with data protection are those drafted within the Council of Europe, the International Labour Organisation (ILO) and the European Union (EU).

1. Council of Europe Conventions and Recommendations

68. The Council of Europe adopted a specific convention with regard to personal data protection on 28 January 1981. It was the concern of the Member States of the Council of Europe to bring more unity in the national legal systems to protect the human rights on a higher level throughout Europe. To date, it still remains the world's only binding international legal instrument in this field, open to signature by any country, including countries which are not members of the Council of Europe.

69. The convention defines a number of principles for the fair and lawful collection and use of data. Notably, data can only be collected for a specific purpose and should not be used for any other reason. Data must be accurate, adequate for this purpose and stored only for as long as is necessary. The convention also establishes the right of access to and rectification of data for the person concerned (data subject), and requires special protection for data of a sensitive nature, for example on religion, political beliefs, genetics, or medical information.[16]

70. The desirability of adapting these data protection principles to the particular requirements of the employment sector, has lead to the adoption of Recommendation no. R(89)2 on the Protection of Personal Data Used For Employment Purposes. This

---

16. http://www.coe.fr/dataprotection/eintro.htm

recommendation was adopted by the Committee of Ministers on 18 January 1989 at the 423rd meeting of the Ministers Deputies.[17]

71. The Recommendation R(89)2 provides, among other things, that:

- Employers should, in advance, fully inform or consult their employees or the representatives of the latter about the introduction or adaptation of automated systems for the collection and use of personal data of employees. This principle also applies to the introduction or adaptation of technical devices designed to monitor the movements or productivity of employees;
- Personal data collected by employers for employment purposes should be relevant and not excessive, bearing in mind the type of employment as well as the evolving information needs of the employer. In the course of a recruitment procedure, the data collected should be limited to that which is necessary to evaluate the suitability of prospective candidates and their career potential. In the course of such a procedure, personal data should be obtained solely from the individual concerned. Subject to provisions of domestic law, sources other than the individual may only be consulted with his consent or if he has been informed in advance of this possibility;
- Recourse to tests, analyses and similar procedures designed to assess the character or personality of the individual should not take place without his consent or unless domestic law provides other appropriate safeguards. If he so wishes, he should be informed of the results of these tests;
- Personal data collected for employment purposes should only be used by employers for such purposes;
- In accordance with domestic law and practice or the terms of collective agreements, personal data may be communicated to employees' representatives in sofar as such data are necessary to allow them to represent the interests of the employees;
- Information concerning personal data held by the employer should be made available either to the employee concerned directly or through the intermediary of his representatives, or brought to his notice through other appropriate means;
- Each employee should, on request, be enabled to have access to all personal data held by his employer which concern him and, as the case may be, to have such data rectified or erased where they are held contrary to the principles set out in this Recommendation. In the case of judgmental data, each employee should have the right, in accordance with domestic law, to contest the judgment.

2. European Directive 95/46/EC

72. The international developments have also lead to the adoption of a specific instrument within the framework of the European Union, namely the European Directive 95/46/EC of 24 October 1995 regarding[18] data protection.

---

17. http://www.coe.fr/dataprotection/rec/r(89)2e.htm
18. O.J. 23 November 1995, L281/31.

73. It must be noted that the Directive has not been written only for labour relations or HR data. The directive applies to any operation or set of operations which is performed upon personal data (i.e. 'processing' of data). Such operations include collection, storage, disclosure etc. The directive applies to data that are processed by automated means (e.g. a computer database of customers) and to data that are part of or intended to be part of non automated 'filing system' in which they are accessible according to specific criteria (that is to say the traditional paper files, such as a card file with details of clients ordered according to the alphabetic order of the names). Clearly, the European Directive will apply to HR data processing activities and therefore also protects workers' privacy.

74. Data controllers (companies, employers) are required to observe several principles. These principles not only aim at protecting the data subjects but are a statement of good business practices which contribute to reliable and efficient data processing. Some examples of obligations imposed by the Directive:[19]

– Data processing is only allowed for limited purposes;
– Data should be processed fairly and lawfully and should be collected for specified purposes and used accordingly. The purpose of the processing should be explicit and should be legitimate;
– Data should be adequate, relevant and not excessive in relation to the purpose for which they are processed;
– Data should be accurate and where necessary kept up to date;
– Data controllers are required to take any reasonable step to ensure the rectification or erasure of inaccurate data;
– Data should be kept in a form which permits identification of individuals for no longer than it is necessary.

3. International Labour Organisation

75. While various national laws have established binding procedures for the processing of personal data, the ILO found that there was a need to develop data protection provisions which specifically address the use of worker's personal data. The ILO code of practice concerning the protection of workers' personal data was drafted to this end and adopted by a Meeting of Experts on Workers' Privacy of the ILO in 1996.[20] The Preamble of the code points out that the purpose thereof is to provide guidance on the protection of worker's personal data. It does not have binding force and it is not designed to replace national laws, regulations or international labour standards or other accepted standards. It should be used in the development of legislation, regulations, collective bargaining agreements, work regulations, policies, and other practical measures.

---

19. http://www.europa.eu.int/comm/internal_market/en/media/dataprot/backinfo/info.htm#int
20. ILO, *Protection of workers' personal data, An ILO code of practice*, ILO Geneva, 1997, p. 47.

413

76. Some general principles outlined in the code of practice are similar to those which can be found in other instruments as outlined above. Still, particular specifications are made with regard to the employment relationship. For example, it is stated that the mere fact that an employment contract is considered or has already been concluded does not entitle an employer to gather any information that he or she is interested in. The collection of personal data must be seen as an exception which needs to be justified.[21] The code also accepts a modification of the initial processing purposes within certain explicitly addressed limits. According to the code, it may be compatible with the original collection purposes to use personal data concerning the qualification or performance of workers in decisions to grant newly introduced fringe benefits.[22]

B.   National Laws

77. Various countries have comprehensive laws that deal specifically with the collection, storage and other processing of employee data held by private employers. Within the European Union, legislation must of course be in conformity with the standards of the European Directive 95/46/EC.

78. Therefore, the European regime has influenced the national legal systems in Europe, who adopted new legislation in order to bring national legislation in conformity with EU law.

79. In Spain, the Implementation Law (Ley Orgánica 15/99) of 13 December 1999 came into force on January 14, 2000. In the UK, the Data Protection Act 1998 received Royal Assent on 16 July 1998. Secondary legislation has been adopted and the Act entered into force on 1 March 2000. In Belgium, the implementation law was passed by the Parliament on 12 November 1998 and published in the Official Journal of 3 February 1999. Its entry into force is subject to secondary legislation that was published in December 1999. A new law was enacted by the Finnish Parliament on 10 February 1999 and entered into force on June 1, 1999. The Directive has been implemented in Austria by the Data Protection Act 2000 to enter into force January 1, 2000.

80. In the United States, federal law requires employee access to medical records which an employer is required to maintain (for the duration of the employment plus 30 years); an elaborate body of state law also regulates maintenance and access of medical records. In addition, at least sixteen states require employee access to personnel files, of which seven states allow an employee to enter an objection on the file to any matter claimed to be incorrect and to have that objection placed in the record. In contrast to the law, in many of the European States, no provision is made for external oversight of accuracy and completeness; but a very few States forbid the recording of employee association, political activity or non-employment activities by employers. Disclosure of the contents of employee files is regulated by the States in application of the tort defamation concerning injurious falsehoods, and, in most

---

21. Explanation 5.1.
22. Explanation 5.3.

States (but not all) by the tort of 'invasion of privacy' which forbids an unprivileged disclosure of an especially injurious fact that results in substantial injury to the employee.

81. In Japan, only Kanagawa Prefecture has an ordinance regulating electronically processed and manual files of private employers. It requires registration with the Governor of the Prefecture, limits the data that can be collected to those relevant to the employment relationship and requires a right of rectification.

V. SURVEILLANCE, MONITORING, AND OTHER CONTROLS IN THE WORKPLACE

A. *Surveillance and Monitoring*

1. General Protections

82. Some States treat employee surveillance and monitoring activities as particularized instances of more general protections, substantive and procedural.

83. France has a complex of laws (including criminal law) that combine to afford broad protection. The Labour Code prohibits unjustified intrusions into privacy interests, subject to a rule of proportionality under which the legitimacy of the employer's interest is weighed against the employee interest. Advance notice and consultation with the works council is required for the introduction of technology that would be used to monitor workers. In 1993, the Ministry of Labour issued a circular expanding upon the applicable principles and procedures. In the interplay of these provisions:

(a) listening to or recording speech in a private place without the consent of the person concerned is a crime, as is recording or transmitting a picture in those circumstances. These provisions have been held to apply to employer video-camera surveillance, telephone-call monitoring, and electronic eavesdropping. Under an Act of 21 January 1995, the Prefect of Police may authorize an employer's video surveillance of private places open to the public (e.g. in a department store to prevent shop-lifting), but such cannot be used to control employee behaviour, unless there has been prior consultation with the works council;

(b) under the Act of 31 December 1992, no information concerning an employee can be attained by means not made known to the employee beforehand. The courts have excluded evidence secured by these means (including a private detective's report) because these methods were not brought to the employee's attention prior to their use;

(c) the Directorate for Labour Relations of the Ministry of Labour, Employment and Vocational Training has permitted employers to require that identification badges be worn, but only for all employees who circulate throughout the enterprise. So, too, the CNIL, exercising its authority under the data protection act, has promulgated a set of guidelines governing the use of electronic badges for entrance, exit, and security purposes, distinguishing various levels of authorization depending upon the employer's justification, e.g. a record of entrance and exit of particular employees can be stored only for zones of particular risk and kept for a limited period, nor should workers' representatives free movement be affected;

(d) employers cannot open private mail addressed to workers; and

(e) case law has limited the extent to which the work rules can provide for searches of employees, their belongings or lockers. The protection of the employee's private life extends a prohibition upon an employer's reading of an employee's private papers (a diary) left in his desk even if written on the employer's time.

84. Germany recognizes the individual's right to conscience and belief, to freedom of association, and to the free development of personality. These have been held applicable to the employment relationship through various sections of the Civil Code, subject always to a balancing of countervailing employer interests. Nevertheless, the privacy (or 'personality') interest weighs most heavily and the burden is on the employer to show an overriding business need. Moreover, the works council is charged to protect these interests in framing work rules and works agreements. It has, for example, a co-determinative authority over the introduction of systems for the monitoring of the behaviour of employees by technical means. A complex body of law has grown up over the content of these substantive individual rights as well as over what matters are (and are not) subject to co-determination. A glimpse of how these have played out is indicated by:

(a) surreptitious telephone monitoring is a violation of privacy, but an announced interception is not; date, time, and duration of employee telephone usage may be recorded, but not the identity of those being called;

(b) interception or recording employee conversations by hidden microphones is a violation of the Penal Code;

(c) surveillance of an employee in a public area by a hidden video camera is a violation of the right of personality unless justified by a supervening business interest; a generalized interest in theft prevention will not suffice;

(d) searches at company gates may be authorized by collective or works agreements or introduced by the employer in response to a theft or a danger to safety;

(e) the introduction of computer systems that monitor the work performed by employees – their speed, accuracy, time away from the machine, etc. – and can store and compare that data with others and over time is subject to co-determination with the works council; and

(f) absent a collective or works agreement on point, an employee's enjoyment of life, e.g. playing the radio at work (when there is no customer or client contact and co-workers do not object) or even taking a drink (on a work break and in a non-safety sensitive job) is insulated from employer sanction.

85. In The Netherlands, the interplay of the constitutional guaranty of fundamental rights which, analogous to German law, is read to have 'third party' applicability, the Civil Code, the Data Protection Act, and the Works Council Act combines to afford broad protection of employee private interests:

(a) installation of video monitoring of workers at work has been enjoined (despite works council agreement) under the Civil Code. A situation of 'evident necessity' might justify such an installation, but in the case on point, it exposed employees to continuous and possibly protracted direct observation over which they could exercise no influence;

(b) computerized monitoring by the telephone exchange of operator response to calls for telephone information that allowed only for groups assessment was permissible (with the agreement of the works council), but not where individual work performance could be determined;

(c) owners of telephone lines are allowed to monitor their use if such interception is 'legitimate' and the power is not abused. The government has indicated that employer monitoring of telephones would be permissible to monitor technical quality, to prevent telephone misuse (e.g. by employees), or to permit executives to witness business transacted, but it also recommended that employees be informed of business practice in that regard.

2. Specific Protections

86. Other States treat the issues presented in a more piecemeal fashion, to afford greater or lesser protections. These are treated on a topic-by-topic basis below. (The omission of an entry for some of the States reviewed indicates either that the information is not readily available or, that no specific law or decision addresses the issue.)

a. Video surveillance

87. In Australia there is no direct regulation of optical surveillance devices, nor of electronic tracking devices (e.g. locational bracelets or badges, key cards, vehicular tracking devices, or the like) absent an actionable trespass.

88. In Belgium, a collective bargaining agreement regulates the protection of the employee's privacy in relation to the use of cameras at the workplace. The use of a camera is allowed in specific cases, such as health and safety, protection of property, control of production processes and employee monitoring. For the latter purpose, a strict procedure of information and consultation has been provided.

89. Finland prohibits the video surveillance of employees.

90. Spain would appear to prohibit the use of video cameras only in non-work areas, e.g. lavatories.

91. Sweden's Monitoring Cameras (Various Devices) Act sets out an elaborate set of regulation bearing upon video surveillance: hidden surveillance of employees is prohibited; surveillance in places open to the public requires a permit; surveillance in areas closed to the public is subject to union negotiations. Standards governing the issuance of permits are specified. (And as of 1987, over 2,500 such permits were issued.)

92. The United Kingdom's Employment Act of 1982 requires companies of more than 250 employees to inform their employees 'on matters of concern to them as employees', and this would arguably include the introduction and use of monitoring and surveillance devices.

417

93. There is no express prohibition upon video surveillance in Canada (but the Canadian Charter of Rights and Freedoms has been argued to limit an employer's ability to conduct such surveillance), Denmark, or the United States (but the common law tort of 'invasion of privacy' in most states would limit an employer's ability to survey places with a high expectation of privacy such as a lavatory).

94. There is no prohibition on video surveillance in Japan, and it is reported that the use of cameras in factories and shops has been increasing.

b. Telephone interception
95. Australia's Telecommunications (Interception) Act draws rather fine distinctions governing the equipment and circumstances of telephone interception; but, the use of equipment that is part of the telecommunications service to listen and record 'in the ordinary course of the operation of that' system is permissible.

96. In Belgium, as a principle, telephone interception and other controls of telecommunication are still prohibited by criminal laws. However, employee consent is one of the exceptions to said prohibition.

97. Canada prohibits the interception of telecommunications under circumstances where there is a reasonable expectation that the communication will be private; thus, if an employer warns employees beforehand that telephone conversations may be monitored the prohibition might not apply. Ontario has a stronger prohibition.

98. Finland extends the employee's right of privacy to telephone calls engaged in during work hours at the workplace. Under the Telecommunications Act, however, a register may indicate the numbers dialed from a given telephone, with the last four digits excised.

99. On the basis of a decision of Spain's Constitutional Court, construing the Spanish Constitution's guaranty of the secrecy of communications – especially of postal and telephone communications – it is believed that all forms of eavesdropping by an employer even into an employee's non-private communications would be prohibited.

100. Sweden flatly prohibits any interception of telephones without the employee's express consent, which extends to the tapping of internal telephone messages from one company extension to another.

101. The United Kingdom's Interception of Communications Act prohibits an unconsented-to interception of a telephonic communication.

102. In the United States, the federal Electronic Communications Privacy Act generally prohibits an interception of telephone communications, but it exempts the use of equipment furnished by the provider of communications service and used by the subscriber 'in the ordinary course of its business' or where one party gives prior consent to the interception. This 'extension phone' exemption permits employers to monitor telephone calls of customer service agents; but interception has been held actionable if it transcends that purpose or if personal calls are listed to. However, the states are not pre-empted in this area of regulation and some States, notably California, require the consent of both parties to the conversation to allow an interception.

c. Electronic eavesdropping

103. In Australia, five states have legislated to regulate the use of listening devices; generally, these are prohibited unless one party to the conversation has consented.

105. Finland prohibits the observation or recording of a person by use of a 'technical device'.

106. The law in Spain is treated in para. 93, *supra*.

107. In the United States, the federal Electronic Communications Privacy Act also applies to acquisition of the contents of an 'oral communication' by use of an electronic or mechanical device. Such is prohibited except under circumstances that would not justify an expectation of privacy in the oral communication. Thus, the recording of a worker by hidden microphone in a work area would be prohibited unless the circumstances deprived the employee of a legitimate expectation that his or her conversation would not be intercepted. Again, State law may be more protective than federal law, either by statute or by the common law.

108. Although, Japan generally allows employers to monitor employees and to evaluate their performance, in one case the use of a hidden tape recorder to monitor the employee's performance (as a diving instructor) was held to infringe upon the right of the employee and the customer; the use of such a device, if necessary, should have to be the product of prior consultation.

d. Telephonic message registration

109. Under Australia's Telecommunications (Interception) Act, the Telecommunications Commission has allowed the use of Telephone Information Management Systems so long as the user is informed that telephone calls are being logged by digit dialed, time, duration, and cost.

110. Danish law also limits employer telephone monitoring of the numbers called, but is inapplicable to the registration of incoming calls and to the manual monitoring of both outgoing and incoming calls. The Data Surveillance Authority may grant exemption in cases of overriding private or public interests.

111. Sweden's prohibition on telephonic interception has not been understood to extend to systems that record the number and cost of messages from a particular phone. If a link can be made between a particular person and the phone, the data could be subject to the Data Protection Act.

112. The United Kingdom's Interception of Communications Act includes dialing information (sender, receiver, duration of call) within its definition of a 'communication' subject to the Act.

113. In the United States, the use of 'caller ID' devices and the like is not prohibited by federal law; but State law may be more stringent.

e. Computer monitoring

114. Under an Order of the Danish Ministry of Labour, employees must be informed of the employer's use of any system of qualitative or quantitative control, e.g. in connection with video display terminals or other computerized systems.

115. It is arguable that the United Kingdom's employee informational rights under the Employment Act would have an effect similar to the Danish Order just discussed.

f. Search

116. No State would permit a private employer to conduct an unconsented-to search of an employee's person. Such conduct would be subject to both potential civil and criminal liability.

117. In Australia, unconsented to access to an employee's bag, personal effects, or company-supplied locker would constitute a trespass. Authority to do so, however, can derive from the awards or recommendations of industrial tribunals as, for example, in the retail industry in New South Wales.

118. In Belgium, the rules regulating employee searches are subject to regulation by collective bargaining and works agreements. There is case law that searches cannot be carried out in a humiliating or discriminatory manner; but also that employees can be dismissed for systematically refusing to be searched where circumstances would justify it.

119. Spain's Workers' Charter permits the search of a worker's person, locker, or personal effects during work hours at the workplace only if necessary to protect the property of the employer or of other workers. Such searches must respect the worker's dignity. The worker has the right to the presence of a legal representative or co-worker, but refusal to submit can be a cause to discharge.

120. In Sweden, a search of an employee's possessions and effects (backpacks, bags, baby carriages) would appear to be permissible if there is a legitimate need, that is, is consistent with 'good labour market practice' or where consent is given, an employee's refusal may constitute breach of the employment contract.

121. In Japan, the Supreme Court has held that a search of an employee's possessions is permissible if four conditions have been met: (1) the search is based on reasonable necessity; (2) it is implemented by methods considered generally acceptable; (3) it is made uniformly and systematically of all workers; and, (4) it is provided for in the rules of employment. There is a body of case-law applying these conditions; it has been held, for example, that an employee's private car is his absolute domain and may not be subject to search.

122. In the United States, the employer's privilege to search desks, lockers, brief-cases, handbags, and the like is subject to potential liability under State tort law for 'invasion of privacy', i.e. an unwarranted and substantial intrusion that a court would find highly offensive. Given this standard, routine inspections and searches 'for cause' have been sustained absent a high expectation of privacy by the employee, e.g. in the opening of mail marked 'personal'. But the standard of offensiveness is often quite high; in one case a State court held that a brief search of an employee's car parked on the company parking lot was permissible.

B. *Other Controls in the Workplace*

1. Dress and Grooming

123. In Australia, the common law had recognized the employee's right to dress as he likes so long as he does not offend public decency. That principle was tested in a 1982 case in which an employee insisted on wearing a caftan to work against his employer's wishes; but the court referred the case to a disciplinary board. The general proposition nevertheless continues to be relied upon.

124. In Finland, the right of an employer to impose dress and grooming standards depends on the nature of the job, the conditions and customs in the industry. Bus drivers can be expected to wear a uniform; waitresses a badge. But an absolute prohibition on long hair or beards (for men) would have to be justified; and religious objection may require an employer to accommodate the employee if possible.

125. Similarly, in France and Germany a rule of proportionality obtains; thus an employer may require the display of identifying badges or standard uniforms for customer contract positions, but not where such a specific business justification would be wanting, e.g. solely for the purpose of maintaining a corporate image.

126. Italy seems to take a similar approach, i.e. that one's attire is a personal matter, but there are circumstances where, for example, the employer can require the wearing of a uniform.

127. Much the same is the law in Spain where, for example, the Madrid High Court required an airline to show a legitimate business interest in forbidding male flight attendants from wearing beards.

128. Swedish employers do not generally regulate personal appearance or, if they do so, it is not by stringent regulation and such regulation as exists has tended to be dealt with by collective agreement. But religious belief, e.g. the wearing of a turban by a Sikh, has been held to require employer accommodation.

129. In the United Kingdom, the employer's ability unilaterally to adopt and to apply rules as part of the contract of employment has been held to be limited by an implied obligation of reasonableness, such that a unilaterally promulgated policy restricting a male employee's liberty to wear long hair has been held to that standard.

130. In the United States, apart from the application of anti-discrimination law, especially on grounds of religion, there are virtually no limits on the employer's ability to regulate dress and grooming. However, the District of Columbia forbids discrimination on grounds of 'appearance', and California legislation allows women to wear pants at work.

2. Expression in the Workplace

131. The Australia High Court has recognized a right of free expression in the workplace the content of which, however, remains to be seen. Direct or symbolic expression of a political nature would seem to be covered.

132. In Germany, one's right of free expression in the workplace is balanced against an obligation not to disturb the peace of the establishment; but restriction of freedom of opinion have been allowed only very rarely: for ideologicallyoriented employments and only to those employees whose job function is to shape the employer's position or institutional image.

133. In France, the Court of Appeals of Aix-en-Provence in 1993 opined in passing that shop rules could not proscribe all private conventions at work apparently as a rhetorical rebuttal to the employer's position concerning its reading of an employee's diary written on work time.

134. In the United States, the employees' right to engage in concerted activity for mutual aid or protection under the National Labour Relations Act would prevent an employer from disallowing dissident speech in non-work areas and in non-work time; nor could it forbid the wearing of union insignia or other displays of workplace protest in non-customer contact areas. But apart from regulation by anti-discrimination law, nothing prohibits an employer from forbidding other forms of speech, including political speech, or, contrary to the French hypothetical above, from prohibiting completely all non-work related speech.

VI. CONTROL OF EMPLOYEES OFF-THE-JOB

135. In most continental European countries, an employer has no control over an employee's private life unless there is a very close connection to the performance of the job. This includes sexual relationships between employees, recreational activity (cultural or sports activities), use of alcohol or tobacco, political expression and association. This has been stated as a flat expression of the law in Finland, France, Germany, Italy, and Sweden, and as a prediction of the law of Spain; but the widespread employment by 'affinity enterprises' (to use the French term), e.g. a church-related school, may be taken to allow restrictions not permitted for non-confessional employments.

136. Dismissal in the United Kingdom is subject to determination under a standard of a range of reasonable managerial response to the employee conduct presented, in application of which it has been argued that dismissal for off-duty behaviour that management (or the courts) finds offensive, such as engaging in an adulterous relationship, has been allowed.[23]

137. Australia would allow an employer to regulate private relationships if the conduct had an impact upon the employee's ability to perform his job duties. Thus an employee's having an affair with his employer's wife (in a small community) was held to justify dismissal.

138. Discrimination on the ground of political belief, conviction or opinion is prohibited in six Canadian provinces.

139. In Japan, activity undertaken in the employer's private life is sanctionable by the employer if it injures the company's honour or reputation; these activities must cause a loss of society's esteem for the company. Thus a steel company was held wrongfully to have discharged an employee for engaging in a demonstration against an American military base where he was only one of 30,000 of the company's employees.

140. In the United States, unless limited by State or federal legislation, e.g. church affiliation under anti-discrimination law, an employer is legally free to regulate employee off-duty behaviour: sexual non-fraternization with co-workers, political speech, charitable activity, drinking, smoking, hazardous recreation, and the like. But:

(a) twenty-five States have legislated to prohibit an employer from discriminating against applicants or incumbent employees on the ground of their off-the-job use of alcohol, tobacco, or 'lawful products' generally;
(b) seven States protect employee engagement in political activity, and a very few states have extended common law protection to political speech;
(c) two States forbid employers from regulating employee 'recreational' or 'leisure time' activity.

VII. CONCLUSION

141. One must be cautious about reliance on the law 'of the books', so to speak, as fully reflective of workplace realities. As some of the International Labour Organization studies relied upon here are candid in pointing out, the absence of law on point may only mean that employers do not interfere to any significant extent, and *per contra* there may be ways for employers to avoid (or evade) the law's reach. In Germany, for example, employers may require prospective executives to be evaluated by an independent 'assessment centre' which uses psychological testing and professional psychological evaluation that would be subject to challenge under the labour law, were the employer to administer them directly.

---

23. H. Collins, *Justice in Dismissal: The Law of Termination of Employment* (Oxford 1992), pp. 201–202.

With that *caveat*, it can nevertheless be said with only some oversimplification that the continental European countries tend to be more systematically protective of employee privacy than the English speaking ones, with both Japan and the United States as, in a sense, outliers – in this as in other areas.[24] The contemporary continental thinking reflected here – notably in France, Germany, and Italy – conceives of employment as a social relationship in which the employee's possession of a degree of personal autonomy in the relationship is an important value, either intrinsically or, as in Germany, as additionally connected to the political and social consequences of total institutional control.

From what appears, although Japanese law reflects analogous concerns for human dignity, the communitarianism of Japanese society, sometimes carefully engineered (which, among other things, strongly discourages litigation in defence of individual rights)[25] effectively commands a high degree of conformity and social control. So, for example, whether or not Japanese law countenances employer-imposed dress and grooming rules, it is virtually unthinkable that an applicant or employee would present herself with hair dyed in what to Westerners would be an inoffensive tea brown.

Again in contrast to the Continent, in the United States, the employment relationship is thought of far more as an economic than a social one. In the United Kingdom, Canada, and Australia, the common law concept of 'master and servant' still implies a residue of limits, of reasonableness in employer rules and orders, however attenuated at points. But the United States remains strongly committed to anti-statist, market-oriented, individualistic values. In this scheme, individual liberty in the employment relationship 'is more strongly identified as the employer's freedom from government constraint than it is with the employee's freedom from employer constraint'.[26] In other words, protection for the core of the claim to privacy – the employee's autonomy in the employment relationship – lies less in law than in the employee's freedom to quit and find an employer with less intrusive policies.

SELECT BIBLIOGRAPHY

Comparative Labour Law Journal, Vol. 17, No. 1 (1995), Symposium on Worker Privacy with country studies relied upon here on *Australia* (Ronald McCallum and Greg McCarry), *Belgium* (Roger Blanpain), *Finland* (Antii Suviranta), *France* (Jean-Emmanuel Rey and Jacques Rojot), *Germany* (Manfred Weiss and Barbera Geck), *Italy* (Roberto Romei and Selvana Sciara), *Spain* (Salvador del Rey Guanter), and *Sweden* (Reinhold Fahlbeck).

B. Creighton and A. Stewart, *Labour Law*, 2nd ed., Annandale, NSW, 1994 [Australia].

M. Finkin, *Privacy in Employment Law*, Washington, DC 1995 [US].

F. Hendrickx, *Privacy en arbeidsrecht*, Brugge, die Keure, 1999, 358 p.

---

24. *See generally*, S. Martin Lipset, *American Exceptionalism* (New York 1996) and especially Chapter 7.
25. J. Haley, *Authority Without Power: Law and the Japanese Paradox* (New York, 1991), Chapter 5.
26. M. Finkin, 'The Protection of Employee 'Personality' in the United States', 94 *Z Vgl R Wiss* 94, 118 (1995).

G. Halbach et al., *Labour Law: An Overview* (Angelika Haarkamp et al. trans.), Bonn, 1992.

ILO, *Conditions of Work Digest*, Vol. 10, No. 2, Geneva, 1991, on 'Workers' Privacy Part I: Protection of Personal Data'.

ILO, *Conditions of Work Digest*, Vol. 12, No. 1, Geneva, 1993, on 'Workers' Privacy Part II: Monitoring and Surveillance in the Workplace'.

ILO, *Conditions of Work Digest*, Vol. 12, No. 2, Geneva, 1993, on 'Workers' Privacy Part III: Testing in the Workplace'.

Proceedings of the 48th Annual Meeting, National Academy of Arbitrators (J. Najita, ed.), Washington, DC 1996, Ch. 7 in *'Privacy in the Workplace: International Perspectives'*.

K. Sugeno, *Japanese Labor Law* (Leo Kanowitz, trans.), Seattle, 1992.

Chapter 18. Security of Employment and Employability

J. Rojot

I. Introduction

1. Security of employment is a relatively new notion. Being employed, a little more than two centuries ago, was nothing to be proud of. Actually, a French nobleman in the XVIII century who engaged in gainful employment or worked for an undertaking for commercial or industrial purposes, except by Royal privilege aiming at developing certain trades, would lose his rank, privileges and condition.

It is only in recent times, following profound changes in society and widespread industrialization, that the status of the employee has become an enviable one. Even before World War Two, the percentage of wage earners in the population was quite low. However, by the 1960's it had reached more than 80% of the labour force in most European countries. Employment, the relationship between the employer and employee, is thus the dominant form, by far, for the performance of work. The contract of employment has displaced all other forms of legal frameworks of similar purpose, such as the contract of mandate, for instance.

II. The Notion of Employment Security

2. Within that framework, from a pure neo-classical economics point of view, labour is a commodity like any other. Employees sell their competence and their labour and employers purchase the amount that they deem necessary. Any hindrance to the smooth workings of the labour market can only be considered as an obstacle to the general good. Devices for securing employment against the will of any of the parties are therefore to be eliminated, as detrimental to all.

The 'employment at will' doctrine exemplifies that state of things. The US case in common law outside of the unionized sector, before the introduction of very small limitations, by European standards, exemplified such a case. In another context, this state of affairs is perfectly exemplified by a quotation of an Australian judge in 1964, who then wrote 'The law regarding Master and Servant is not in doubt. There cannot be specific performance of a contract of services, and the master can terminate the contract with the servant at any time and for any reason or for none ...'

3. However, it quickly appeared in practice that labour indeed is not a commodity like any other. All industrialized countries, even the ones with the doctrine closest to the neo-classical point of view, do mitigate, with damages in some cases, for example, the extreme point of view. This concept is in fact closely linked to the emergence of the idea of industrial relations as a legitimate practice and scientific discipline. If labour were an ordinary commodity, antitrust law would be enough to replace all of it. It was precisely and essentially illustrated with the decision of the US Supreme Court in the famous Danbury hatters case of 1908 in applying the Sherman Act to a union sponsored boycott. This point of view remained a powerful source of obstacles to union activities in the USA until the 1932 Norris-La Guardia Act was passed by Congress, even though the 1914 Clayton Act had provided by section 6 'That the labour of a human being is not a commodity or article of commerce'.

4. Legal issues aside, there are two major differences between labour and other goods. On the one hand, it has a specific nature, which differs from all other commodities able to be exchanged on the open market: it has no independent material existence, separate from the person of the worker and thus cannot be sold as they would be. On the other hand, the relationship between employer and employee has a different object for both of them. The employer is concerned with the product of labour and the employee is concerned with his availability and his effort. Two successive equilibriums at two different points in time must be established: between the wage which is fixed *ex ante* and the work which is expected but performed *ex post* and between the actual performance of work and the condition of the product of this work.

5. Nowadays, the whole of industrial relations and labour law in a country are testimony of the specific nature of work and the labour market. Actually, employment has now gained the status of a 'right' guaranteed by numerous Statutes and Constitutions, such as the Constitution of Japan and the preamble of the Constitution of France, not to mention the Article 1 of the European Social Charter: the right to work. Bob Hepple reminds us, however, that this right can be understood in different ways. In the above examples, it is an abstract right of the individual to benefit equally with others of every opportunity to enter freely into any occupation available and thus earn his living and, as well, to enjoy equally with others the benefits of the State manpower policies. A right of access to his job sometimes augments it, if he has one and so wishes, free of hindrance by any others. This right is often invoked by employers and/or non-strikers to gain injunctions against violent picket lines, as may be the case in France, for instance. But the right to work has existed in another philosophy, in the former democratic socialist European countries. It was enshrined also in the Constitution of the USSR for instance, it gave birth to a very concrete position, which could be seen as a guarantee of employment, if not a right to a particular given job. However, conversely it carried also as a twin consequence of the right, a legal duty to work and the strict observance of labour discipline. 'Evasion of socially useful work is incompatible with the principles of socialist society', and thus could be punished.

6. This latter concept has now disappeared in developed countries.

Besides, it must also be noted that Japanese Labour Law and industrial relations specialists, in its use of English language terminology, distinguish employment security from job security. 'Employment security' falls within the meaning of the Employment Security Act of 1947 which regulates recruitment, placement, employment exchange services, and vocational guidance. 'Job security' signifies the protection of employees against termination of their employment at the initiative of their employer. We shall restrict the analysis to the second of these definitions, taken however in a very broad sense.

III. THE TENSIONS ON EMPLOYMENT SECURITY

7.   Security of employment, understood now as the protection of the employee against dismissal, within only the abstract notion of a right to work without an absolute right in practice for job assignment, must be understood as the product of the tension between two opposite propositions: the need for employers to adapt to economic fluctuations on the stock market with the consequent necessity to adapt the workforce to business volume and the need for the employee for a continuous gainful income from his work.

8.   The expression of this need on the employee side has been masterfully described by Frederic Meyers in his classic comparative study of Mexico, France, Britain, and USA. He has developed the concept of property in his job by an employee in the sense that he could develop an individual right to retain, independently of the will and prerogatives of his employer, his position at work with its conditions attached.

> '(property) ... is of course used loosely, as an analogy to more traditional rights of property rather than as a category of them. Nevertheless it implies a change in the system of rights and obligations surrounding employment and the relationship of employer to employee ....
> ... To the layman at least, one of the essential characteristics of property is the right to retain undisturbed possession ... If employment is property, or analogous thereto, undisturbed possession means the right to continue in employment at the will of the employee. Protection against involuntary dismissal is a crucial characteristic to be sought if a system may be said to have property-like rights in employment'

He concluded that:

> 'The evidence of these four countries tends to support the conclusion that the classic liberal contractual approach to the employment relation in a complex industrial society is simply not a viable one. Workers do in fact tend to regard themselves as having some kind of right of possession in a job, and to devise institutions which invest control over incumbency from the hands of the employer and which express objectively a vesting of property-like rights in the workers. The devices by which this trend is expressed and the rates of change vary, of course, from country to country. In the United States, it is expressed primarily through the device of the collective agreement, and it may be farthest advanced in those jobs in the United States in which collective bargaining determines the basic character of the relationship of workers and employers to jobs. On the other hand, it is undoubtedly least far advanced in the unorganized segments of American industry, in which little has changed, so far as job control is concerned, since 1870.'

9.   On the other hand, powerful pressures have come to bear on businesses. The first and overriding pressure is the impact of technology. It is pointless to discuss

endlessly if the present technological changes constitute really a 'new' technology fundamentally different from the earlier waves of technical changes, such as the automation in the 1950's, or if they only are a demonstration of a continuous movement of incorporation of new technology in all equipment replacements in the workplace. It is enough to note that technological changes are indeed taking place. It is also just as pointless to argue whether it creates or destroys jobs. The evidence is that it does both, in different areas, but that the balance is in doubt.

10. However, some of the impacts of technology are beyond discussion and well established: It has allowed the growth of business organizations by permitting improved communications and the processing of information. It has brought an increased differentiation of functions within organizations, for instance in research, computer operations, marketing, etc .... In that way it has further broken the traditional working class by creating small categories of highly skilled technicians with specific interests, divergent beyond the tenuous link on their common status as wage earners. It has changed the contents of jobs, eliminating many average skills by automating them.

11. In a major way, and together with another factor already reviewed, it is bound to have a deep effect on the practices and styles of human resources management and the security of employment within firms. This used to exist in manufacturing in what was called the 'iron law of production'. Productivity was inversely correlated to versatility. One operation could be totally versatile, that is manufacture with almost every possible variation, as is also the case with a prototype or tool shop within a plant, with highly skilled employees and a variety of machines. But it could manufacture only one unit at a time, at the lowest degree of productivity. Another operation could have an extremely high productivity rate, of some several thousands of units per unit of time, as with a continuous process chemical plant, but it had no versatility and could produce units of only one product. Any move towards productivity, through assembly lines, transfer lines, batch production and the like involved a correlated loss of productivity. New technology, through flexible shops, computer aided manufacturing, computer aided design and finally computer integrated manufacturing has bent 'the iron law'. It is now possible to combine versatility with high productivity. For instance very different models of cars can be assembled together on the same line.

12. However, this progress has brought with it significant consequences for job design. The traditional way for job design was to establish a job description and to apply to it a system of pay and sanctions to ensure satisfactory performance. It worked rather well for simple tasks and simple technology. But the new jobs issued from the computer aided new technology, not for all of them but for a large part, are not amenable to that method. They included too many tasks of a different nature, which are not repetitive and for some of which the occurrence is unforeseeable. They are too complex to be described in advance. What is needed is no longer simply satisfactory compliance with predetermined standards but the need for a capability to make quick decisions and autonomous action in response to signals, the need for initiative. Therefore, the old way of job design can no longer work. What is now needed is the wilful cooperation on the part of employees, their goodwill, and that their capacity for innovation can be put to the service of the firm. Compliance with such needs cannot be demanded or bought as it could be in the old system.

13. Besides, it is significant to note the move of the economy of industrialized countries towards the services sector. Service industries, i.e. hotels, car rentals, banks, etc ... sell what can be considered as undifferentiated products. The product of one firm is just as good, because of market constraints, as the one produced by the next one. If the difference delivered to the customer cannot come from the nature of the service or from its cost it will have to come from the attitude of the employees of the firm with whom he will be in contact. Such an attitude of positive orientation towards the customer also cannot be imposed by an enforceable job description. As is the case with the technical jobs issued from the new technology, what is needed is a matter of attitude, initiative, individual responsiveness, and voluntary cooperation. Also here, it cannot be successfully ordered or bought.

These two changes, therefore, mean that the practices and policies of human resources management and security of employment for employees by the firms will have to change significantly.

14. On the other hand the impact of new technologies has strengthened this 'tertiarisation' of the economy. But it is a more complex issue that appears at first glance, for the sectors actually merge into each other. The tertiarization of agriculture and industry on the one hand is matched by the industrialization of services on the other hand.

To these deep movements must be added powerful economic changes including the following ones: the globalization of the world economies with increases in international competition and the entry of the newly industrialized countries on world markets; the shortening of product life cycles; the increased importance of quality as a competitive advantage; an accelerated pace of innovation; a greater differentiation in product markets.

These changes in the environment have a deep impact on management. Managerial responses can be grouped into three broad categories: cost containment; the introduction of various forms of flexibility, the adoption of styles of participative management, the latter one is not within our scope, but the other two are relevant here.

15. On the one hand, costs containment strategies took several forms: restructuring and streamlining of operations in order to avoid duplication of efforts; the introduction of wage freezes or pay caps, which occurred through either de-indexation, i.e. the decoupling of wage increases from increases into the cost of living, or concession bargaining, where typically wage concessions were gained in exchange for maintaining current levels of employment; and workforce reductions, where jobs were suppressed by whole categories as well as in numbers in any given category (i.e. positions in middle management or support activities). Thus job security was directly threatened.

16. On the other hand, the introduction of various degrees of flexibility also took several forms. Firstly wage flexibility was pursued independently of the wage limitation aspect implicit in costs containment strategies, it mostly aimed to link wages to profitability without regard to limiting the wage bill 'per se'. It had several aspects: The individualization of the wage; various forms of performance-linked wage; productivity agreements and the like. Secondly, non-wage flexibility was still more diverse. It can be categorized under four main categories according to an OECD study carried out in 1988:

– External quantitative flexibility. This includes temporary work, short-term contracts, part-time work, call contracts, 0 hours contracts, long trial periods before

definitely hiring, job-sharing, massive use of government sponsored schemes for the integration of the youth in the labor force, etc...
– Externalization. This includes sub-contracting, putting out work, use of self-employed, buying instead of making components, on-site use of independent contractors or of employees 'on loan' from other firms.
– Internal numerical flexibility. This includes the introduction of variable and flexible hours, new shift work patterns, including the increased use of night-work and overtime, week-end shifts, modulation, annualized duration of work to better adapt to the business cycle and modulation of the volume of manpower used according to demand while keeping constant labour costs.
– Functional flexibility. includes multi skilling, pay for knowledge, abolition of craft barriers, on-the-job and formal training, manpower forecasting and provisional human resources management, improvement of the adaptability of employees to change and the performance of multiple tasks.

17. Thus, flexibility is a multi-faceted concept, and it is present in different countries under different guises. In some, like Greece, Luxembourg and Portugal it mostly takes the form of 'legislated flexibility', where Government and/or Parliament have decided that providing additional flexibility in the working of the labour market is sound public policy. In others such as Belgium, Denmark, Italy, Spain, it takes the shape of an increase in 'negotiated and controlled flexibility', with an emphasis on collective bargaining rather than on statute law. In other countries, the trend is more towards 'individualized flexibility', whether it takes place against an active culture of bargaining with the unions as in Germany, or in the absence of much significant bargaining, like in France, where it sometimes reaches the level of 'informal' patterns of flexibility.

18. Flexibility in working arrangements is not only applied by law, but the trend goes much deeper. It extends beyond facilitating the use of the various tools available to ease its technical introduction. A marked trend towards the individualization of flexibility is noticeable in several cases for instance, side by side, or even sometimes within the framework of an active movement of negotiations with the trade unions. In several countries, (e.g. France, Greece, Spain), this marked trend is noticeable. Also in Great Britain, there is an increased diversity in working-time arrangements for full-time regular workers at local level, with a continuing trend towards greater functional flexibility. Some of these arrangements have been introduced by agreements with the union at company level. Some other agreements provide for a shorter working week or increased annual leave. In most other cases changes in working-time arrangements are introduced unilaterally by the employer, or after possible employee consultation as has been noted to be the case for the introduction of new technologies and other forms of work organization. In the Netherlands, agreements on working time with Works Councils have been given a status equal to collective agreements with unions, reflecting their similar importance.

19. This move towards, at the same time, decentralization and the informality of agreements that individualization represents is not surprising. It has been noticed elsewhere. However, it is to be noted that if functional flexibility increases the employee's security of employment, by making him adaptable to change within the enterprise by being able to fulfill a variety of positions, all other types of flexibility threaten it, not directly by work force reductions, but indirectly, by attacking the concept of the full time permanent job holder. Two of these schemes are prevalent in many industrialized countries and need to be described more in detail, however, in relation to part-time work and temporary work.

20. In most countries there is no legal and clear-cut definition of part-time work, other than an occasional, relatively vague, reference to work which is less than full-time. This is the case for instance, in Belgium, Denmark, Great Britain, Greece, Ireland, Italy, the Netherlands, Portugal, and Sweden. Usually, therefore, part-time work is referred to in relation to normal working hours and any period of time shorter than full-time, according to law and collective agreements, is thus considered to be part-time. In some other countries a more precise definition has tentatively been elaborated. Such is the case in France, where the Labour Code defines part-time work as any duration of work minus one-fifth of the legal duration (the 39-hour week as set by legislation or a lower standard established by collective agreement) and work by employees whose monthly duration of work is lower by at least 1/5 to the application over the (monthly) period of the legal (weekly) working time. It also now defines as part-time those employees employed over a year according to alternate working and non-working periods for which the duration of work over the yearly period is lower by at least 1/5 than the application of the legal (weekly) working-time to the same (yearly) period, minus holidays and vacations, established by statutes or collective agreements. In Great Britain, where there is no general definition whatsoever of the concept, part-timers are, for statistical purposes, usually defined as those working not more than 30 hours a week.

21. Surprisingly, the various European countries show a much wider diversity on the issue of temporary work than on the preceding one. However, an initial source of confusion is that various national studies refer to very different concepts under the heading of temporary work. There are at least four acceptable definitions of what is considered temporary work and it should be noted that some countries ignore some of them.

Additionally, the countries being considered seem to fall into two groups: the one where the normal employment relationship is defined as the (full-time) contract of employment for an indefinite duration, and all other forms which exist only by exception, as exemplified by France, and the ones where the employment relationship is undefined and shaped by the parties more or less as they see fit, barring rare and statutorily regulated exceptions.

22. At its simplest, temporary work is in practice the fact of an employer hiring an employee under a short-term contract. The work is indeed temporary because at the time of hiring the employee and employer know exactly when it will cease without further obligation of employment, either at the occurrence of a foreseeable event, e.g. the termination of a given task, the return of a sick or pregnant employee, or after that a given period of time has elapsed, e.g. a season, a month, etc. It is regulated in many countries (e.g. France), but not all (e.g. Great Britain, where it is unregulated, the Netherlands, where it is ignored by the law), or in order to avoid such regulation, by repetitive short-term contracts, an employer could deprive an employee of rights and protection accruing to him under a contract of employment for an indefinite duration, when such rights exist.

At its most complex, temporary work is conceived as interim work, or 'travail intérimaire'. In that case, temporary work is sometimes very strictly defined and it is categorized by the creation of a triangular relationship between, (a) the employer who is the enterprise (commonly referred to as the 'agency') of temporary work, which cannot lawfully carry any other activity than the provision of temporary employees for enterprises which are its customers, (b) the employee of this employer sent on an 'assignment' to a customer, (c) the enterprise which is the customer of the enterprise of temporary work, called the 'user'. This tripartite relationship comes about through the conclusion of two contracts: (a) a contract which places employees at a disposition, that is a commercial contract, passed between the Enterprise of Temporary Work (ETW) and the Enterprise User, which provides for the conditions, discussed below, under which the temporary employee(s) are put at the disposal of the user, (b) a contract of assignment, which is a contract of employment, passed between the Enterprise of Temporary Work and the temporary employee, which includes the conditions of the contract of putting at disposition plus additional ones. Specific obligations fall to each party, particularly the user and the agency. This system is totally ignored by law in Greece, was also previously ignored but is now regulated in Luxembourg, Austria, and the Netherlands, was previously expressly forbidden in Spain and Italy, where it has been recently recognized and regulated. It does not exist in the form described in Great Britain.

One may also distinguish between other categories of temporary work.

23. An important one is labour only sub-contracting, where a labour contractor puts his employees at the disposal of another employer on the latter's premises for the operation of the latter's machines and equipment. This should be distinguished from the independent sub-contracting of services, performed on his own by an independent enterprise or self-employed individual and also from subcontracting on the premises of another employer for a given and specific task by a specialized enterprise (e.g. security, cafeteria, etc.)

The distinction is important for in some countries one or two of the three might be unlawful whilst the other ones might be permissible. In France, for instance the first mode is strictly prohibited and to this day evokes memories of the XIXth Century system of 'marchandage' or 'putting out', dreaded by organized labour.

Another very particular aspect of temporary work is that of an employer hiring employees in his own employment, but from a private employment agency. The employees are hired by him, either for a determinate or indeterminate duration, but they are provided by this agency, by way of exception to the monopoly given to manpower or unemployment state organizations in many countries for the placement of workers (e.g. France, Italy).

24. The last category is 'casual labour' whereby unskilled laborers can be hired by the day, or even part of the day, without entering into a formal contract of employment, sometimes without even a record of their employment being kept and their wages paid in cash. It exists lawfully only in Great Britain and Ireland.

Finally, one might also consider work 'on call', whereby the employee remains at the disposal of the employer, but is only expected to work when the employer needs him might be seen as more of a category of temporary work than part-time work. The employee may have to work seldom and after long intervals for the same employer. 'Work on call' for instance, is regulated in Germany.

25. Very clearly, the number of employees in such schemes is rising. A 1996 survey of 6,000 workplaces by the European Foundation pointed to an increase over the last three years of 23% in part-time work, 27% in temporary work and 13% in subcontracting. These figures have been confirmed by other studies. Evidence shows, for instance that the growth in the number of temporary works bureaus, representing what we described above as the most complex form of temporary work, is dramatic. Between 1969 and 1994, their numbers grew, for instance, from 126 to 10,250 in Japan, 13 to 102 in Norway, 50 to 600 in Switzerland, 1,200 to 9,000 in the UK, 2,300 to 15,000 in the USA, and 450 to 5,011 in France. However, both the European Foundation survey and other sources tend to indicate that the impact of these forms of flexibility tends to impact very differently on different categories of employees, according to their different skills, age group, industry sectors, sex, etc.

26. It is clear, indeed, that most of the managerial manpower policies deeply threaten the traditional 'job ownership' concerns with employment security developed by the employees. To meet the requirements of employer' needs and employee' needs, a series of steps have been taken at different levels in different countries, however under very different shapes, guises and degrees of compulsion. As Hepple wrote:

> 'The measures adopted are deeply rooted in the political, social and economic traditions of each country. This, together with the enormous diversity of job security measures, makes it impossible to present any kind of comprehensive summary. Even where common minimum standards have been adopted – for example, among the Member States of the EC – it is striking how divergent are the methods used to implement these common obligations. The mixture between law and collective bargaining is different; the methods of legal enforcement are extremely varied; and the standards are reflected in many baffling forms.'

We shall then follow his lead and limit ourselves to a general presentation of the main issues, illustrated with some examples.

IV. DISMISSAL FOR CAUSE AND DISMISSAL FOR ECONOMIC REASONS

27. The first types of steps to be considered concern the protection of the individual employee from dismissal by the employer, and here, one should look first at the cause of the dismissal of an employee. It can occur for several reasons and theoretically can found its justification in different legal doctrines, for instance the law of master and servant or the disciplinary and managerial powers of the employer, or the non performance of a contractual obligation falling upon the employee.

28. In some countries a major difference is made between 'collective dismissals' and 'individual dismissals'. However, in some other countries, while dismissal is tightly regulated, no difference is made between individual and collective dismissals. The 'summa divisio' does not run between the individual and the collective, but between dismissals for economic reasons and dismissals for cause, the latter being understood as meaning for cause other than economic (including, therefore, but not limited to, an offence on the part of the employee dismissed). It is true that dismissals for economic reasons tend to be collective more often than not and that the opposite is the case for dismissals for cause. However, a single employee may well be dismissed for economic reasons and a group of employees might be conceivably dismissed for cause, after a fight, or an unlawful strike, for instance.

29. In France, for instance, for a long time, there was no difference between dismissals according to the reason for which they were decided by the employer. An Act of January 3, 1975, for the first time, created the notion of dismissal for economic reasons. The Act required an employer to secure the authorization of the relevant administrative authorities before proceeding lawfully to a dismissal, individual or collective if it was caused by 'an economic reason whether structural or conjunctural'. However, the Act failed to give a definition of what constituted an 'economic reason', and it fell initially to the courts to provide it. Since then, the regulation of dismissals for economic reasons was deeply overhauled, notably by an Act of December 30 1986 which suppressed the requirement of the administrative authorization, and an Act of August 2, 1989 which finally provided a legislative definition of what constituted an 'economic reason'.

As 'non inherent to the person of the employee, resulting from a suppression or a transformation of a job, or a substantial change in (the conditions of) the individual contract of employment (between employer and employee), consecutively, notably (but not only), to economic difficulties or technological changes'.

30. In Britain, the more restricted legal concept of 'redundancy' means a dismissal by reason of which either the employer ceases to carry on business at the place where the employee worked, or a reduction in the requirements of the employer for employees to do work of a kind which the employee was engaged to do.' In the USA and Canada the concept of 'layoff' is used in collective agreements to define a suspension of the employment relationship with a right, acquired for a certain duration of time, to be recalled with seniority in priority if work again becomes available at the same firm. In some Scandinavian countries and India, 'layoff' is a concept restricted to temporary workforce reductions, while dismissal is the usual method of making a permanent reduction, with different rules applying to each of these techniques'.

V. COMPANY LEVEL PROVISIONS IN ORDER TO REDUCE
  THE LEVEL OF DISMISSALS

31. Even though, the formerly very high levels of unemployment appear, at least at the present time, to have abated in the EU and North America, the impact of unemployment was such that whatever the legal constraints emanating from national statutes, that many companies had implemented elaborate procedures to deal with lay-off and massive economic dismissals. Because of the changes in technology discussed above, faster market fluctuations, increased national and international competition and a lower rate of growth since the late 1970's, many companies were driven towards a relocation of production, total or partial plant closure and large redundancies. They came to the view that some of the costs associated with these operations were unavoidable, such as discharge and severance pay, but also that other important costs, such as a loss of goodwill, legal suits, bitter strikes, loss of morale by personnel and bad media coverage and company image could be avoided if these operations were conducted in a planned and more open manner.

Thus the management of massive dismissals came to include a series of steps elaborated by enterprises on their own, independently of legal constraints. Some of the schemes elaborated by large companies can be briefly summarized.

32. First, some general principles of 'good behaviour' by management in conducting dismissals are outlined. The importance of giving early warning and as much notice as possible, once a decision was reached to effect a collective dismissal is considered essential, as well as the need to communicate these decisions as soon as they are reached. Besides, individuals who are to be dismissed should be informed first, before anybody else, individually by their immediate supervisor and by way of a private meeting. Then, the remaining employees should be informed immediately afterwards. In order to reduce resentment as far as possible, local management should lead the operations and not the head office. Good communications should be consistently maintained to avoid the danger of rumours and suspicion. Consultation with employees' representatives is essential, of course within the law, but also above and beyond the mere satisfaction of legal requirements. The union(s) should be notified and the union's propositions should be seriously studied and integrated as far as possible in the social plan. Room to negotiate with the union should be foreseen and left for the total number of dismissals and the occupations in-plant across which may occur, the selection procedure of the dismissed employees, the procedures and a period of actual dismissals. They can take place in the case of a complete closure of a plant, with the majority in one go with only a maintenance crew left or in a phased 'run down' over a period of time.

33. Second, the implementation of the dismissals includes the establishment of an orientation and relocation cell on the spot. It includes roughly 1 person for each 100 employees to be relocated, who should be a member of management. The cell should be located on company premises, near to the entrance and should be allocated enough resources to carry out its work (phone, secretariat, etc.). It should comprise in every case of at least two members specializing in inside and outside the plant related issues. It sits on a permanent basis for 6 to 12 months, on a full time basis, is easily accessible with its members present at most times and works autonomously within an allocated budget. Its members are knowledgeable on statutes, law, regulations, etc. The cell should be established as soon as possible after the dismissals have been announced, information about it should be widespread. Its work is to inform dismissed employees of the conditions of their dismissal and of their rights and prerogatives. It is also to establish contacts with all the businesses which surround the closing plant and/or survey their needs, with municipal authorities, employment agencies and the like and facilitate the finding of a new job by the dismissed employees. It may continue its operations for some time after the actual closure.

34. The role of the cell is important, for there is evidence that massive dismissals have a serious impact on all employees. A general attitude of uncertainty and possibly anger of those under the potential threat of whole scale dismissal until that the stage of nominative terminations has been announced. Then there is a possible state of confusion and demotivation for those who remain on the company's rolls, together with relief. Finally, a deeper feeling of confusion and uselessness linked to the loss of job for those who are actually dismissed. This is the more acute if they had held office for a long period, and all concerned fear having to live in a world no longer structured by stable habits. They are under heavy psychological stress, are likely to show impatience, irritability and improvizibility. All kinds of individual action are possible, possibly coalescing into collective action. Of course they have concerns about the future, a fear caused by uncertainty about their financial situation and insecurity about finding a new job. Usually, their behaviour goes through four phases: first a temporary denial of reality, a belief that 'it is not true' and that a miracle solution will appear. Then, when reality is undeniable it leaves room for diffuse aggression and anger. After that, as the situation develops depression and apathy replace them. Finally resignation and the acceptance of reality settles in.

35.   The attitude of the unions ranges from an extreme position, that the dismissals are unacceptable under any circumstances with a refusal to negotiate and an outright refusal to consider any of the management's proposals, to a reluctant acceptance to bargain. It also takes place through series of steps. At first usually, for either tactical or emotive reasons, they adopt a stance of refusal to accept the need for the redundancy itself and require that all jobs be kept. After more or less time depending on the reasons, there is room to search for the best possible agreement given the circumstances, initially negotiating a maximum compensation package while trying to keep the numbers of employees concerned down to as few as possible. After that the union will try to negotiate measures for reducing that number, then discuss the mode of selection of redundant employees and the criteria to be used, and finally try to improve the treatment of the employees to be dismissed in terms for instance of added severance pay, recall provisions and assistance in finding alternative employment.

36.   A social plan is considered a must, whether it is required or not by statute law, as is the case in Germany and France (even though the two similar words recover very different realities).

The plan should be both elaborate and credible. It includes the criteria of selection of employees to be dismissed and the implementation of those criteria resulting in a list of those whose employment is to be terminated. A search for individual solutions besides termination or in the case of termination, which may rely on a qualitative data base on personal job profiles available in the industry or the region. It also provides for the information for the concerned parties, the use of an outside resource such as Government representatives or industry regional local officials, meetings with unions and/or workers representatives, required or not by law, provision for help in looking for jobs for the dismissed employees, and, possibly, the spreading of the redundancies over time to avoid disruption to the local labour market and to ease the finding of jobs.

Tools used in a social plan include public employment services and occupational retraining schemes, grants to workers who move (relocating grants), regional development subsidies – institutional training or on the job subsided training, work experience programmes for young people, and the like, depending on national and local availability.

37.   Every possible means is used to avoid dismissals and to maintain employment for the largest number and/or to ease voluntary retirement. Even though, depending on the national legal framework, some of these means may or may not be

available in different countries, a list of a general nature would include the following, in order of severity:

The first provision to be taken when dismissals are foreseen is probably to stop hiring and wait for voluntary severance and retirements to reduce manpower to the required size. Such a measure is, however, almost always insufficient in itself and also endangers the age balance of the staff, with consequent problems in the demography of the enterprise's labour force. Next are cuts in overtime, although this is not always easy given the balance of skills requirements for production. Then, reduced hours below the usual norm or a shorter work schedule may be applied. Sometimes, this can take the shape of compulsory vacations during slow business periods or unpaid additional vacation days. Some countries, like Italy or France have introduced a system of partial unemployment (chomage partiel), whereby State help is available to compensate employees on shorter work schedules. A further step is to put a stop to the use of temporary staff and short-term contracts or withdrawing work contracted out in order to bring back work for the benefit of the permanent staff. This is of course, subject to in-plant work abilities and available skills. In some other countries, like in the USA, employees can be put on temporary lay off with possible recall within a given time frame, after which they will be definitively redundant. More and more often, also, postponement of pay increase or even salary cuts have been negotiated in exchange of the maintenance of the present level of staffing. Work sharing is often talked about but little practiced, principally for reasons of costs, notably in terms of benefits to be paid to all even if the wage is reduced by individual, adaptation in changes in working practice/and/or adjustment of shift work. Other provisions include the re-classification of employees which may be accompanied by demotion, the downgrading of job responsibilities with or without red circling and the elimination of levels of supervision. There are also the possibilities of internal mobility transfers of employees across the company's facilities, with or without training, interplant or intraplant. Other types of measures include early retirement, which at first saves money specially for managers, for younger employees generally get lower wages, but this involves a loss of the company's institutional memoir works which can offset the apparent gains and can be used only once, gliding retirement at full pay or not. External relocation, may also be seen, with employees being placed in other enterprises with or without a trial period and a compensation package for expenses such as moving and possibly a wage guarantee allowances and a return guarantee. Then another set of provisions include definite separations, with or without outplacement, sometimes with help to migrant workers to return home, voluntary resignations in exchange for higher severance pay, 'window' plans whereby employees are given an opportunity to quit while keeping benefits and reduced pay for sometime, re-training, sabbaticals, extended notice of termination with severance pay, help to volunteers to set up their own businesses with company money or loans, with equipment from the closed plant, with technical advice and counsel, and with help to other businesses which hire former employees.

38. Of course, these enterprise plans take place in the broad national framework of employment security, legal and contractual obligations. Here also, only examples of provisions included in such frameworks can be given as illustrations of the extremely wide diversity of situations.

VI. LEGAL AND CONTRACTUAL LIMITS TO ECONOMIC DISMISSALS

39. In the broad sense defined above, economic dismissals are the object of various regulations in different national frameworks, ranging from narrow restrictions to almost complete freedom. Authorization by public authorities of economic dismissals and subsequent hirings, when dismissals have been authorized, is now almost a thing of the past. It did exist in France and Portugal, for example but it was abolished in both countries in the 1980's. The traditional example is that of the Netherlands, where neither an employer nor an employee can terminate a contract of employment without the authorisation of the Director of the District Labour Office. As in the case of France mentioned above, this authorization is refused in only a very small number of cases.

However, in France also, for instance, the administrative authorization to effect a dismissal is still necessary in special individual cases for ' protected employees', i.e. employees representatives, whether for economic dismissals or dismissals for cause.

In other countries, such as Belgium and Germany, the power of public authorities is limited to the postponement of the dates of dismissals.

40. Weaker obligations apply in certain countries, for instance, in the USA a 1988 Federal Law obliges employers in some circumstances to provide advance notice of plant closures and thus of consequent employment terminations.

41. In many cases, the administrative authorities do not intervene directly in dismissals for economic reasons, but the law provides for a role for employee representatives. These rights include at a minimum, and in their weakest form, simple information. In the USA for instance, plant closures must be announced in advance. However, in most European countries, this right of information goes way beyond a simple notice and includes consultation via a complex and lengthy procedure, which has as its objective, at each of its steps, to allow the employee representatives to challenge the number of dismissals and the conditions under which they will occur. 'Social Plans', even though the same term covers very different content, for instance spell out in detail all provisions taken to minimize the numbers and consequences of the dismissals as well as the fate of the redundant employees. Information and consultation of employee representatives, for instance, must occur in Belgium, France, the Netherlands, Spain, etc. In the UK, for instance, information rights are exercised by the union, and not by members of elected works councils, reflecting the diversity of the European Industrial relations systems.

Generally, the extent of the obligations varies with the size of the undertaking.

42. Finally, in some exceptional cases, notably in Germany, employee representatives' powers extend even further. There, the right of co-determination covers recruitment, transfers and dismissals, as spelled out by the law. Thus, in those cases, the provisions for dismissals cannot be implemented without the consent of the works council. Dismissal for economic reasons follows the rules for individual dismissals for cause, with additional provisions, notably the duty of information of the works council, the duty to reach a compromise of interests with it, and a social plan. In cases of persistent disagreement between management and the works council, a labour court will adjudicate.

VII. Legal and Contractual Limits to Dismissal for Cause

43. In the United States and Canada, a dual system exists. Some rules are applicable to all employees. Some additional limits, reached through collective bargaining apply only in the union sector.

44. In the USA, for instance, outside of the union sector, which now is relevant to only a minority of employees, probably less than 15%, the doctrine of 'employment at will' prevails. It, however, is contained within certain limits set down in Federal statutes, State laws and the common law developed by the judiciary. The National Labor Relations Act protects employees, who attempt to form unions and to bargain collectively, against discriminatory actions by employers, including threats to employment security. Federal Laws on the minimum wage and occupational health and safety prohibits employers from the same type of actions against employees exercising their rights under these laws. Finally, the Civil Rights Act of 1964 prohibits such types of actions for reasons of an employee's race, colour, religion, sex, or national origin. Other Federal Laws were added similarly protecting the handicapped, Vietnam veterans and disabled workers.

State laws were added to the Federal framework, adding other cases of protection of employment security. For instance, Wheeler notes that starting in 1911 state statutes on worker's compensation contained provisions stating that an employee could not be terminated for filing a claim under the statute, and that now one State, Montana, has adopted legislation requiring cause for dismissal.

45. However, for a long time, this was the only limit to 'employment at will'. However, Wheeler further notes that:

> 'Perhaps the liveliest area of employment law in the United States at this writing is the increasing case by case restriction of the "employment at will" doctrine by the courts under the common law. Courts in some jurisdictions have held that the employee can sue the employer for damages if they are terminated (1) in violation of public policy (as in "whistleblower cases"; (2) in violation of the employer's own policies that are found to be a part of the contract of employment...; (3) in violation of obligations of and fair dealing that are implied in law to be part of the contract; (4) in a manner which is abusive'

46. In the union sector, the situation is very different. Most collective agreements contain a provision holding that termination can occur only for just cause and include another provision that provides for a grievance procedure culminating in arbitration in cases of disagreement upon the existence or not of that just cause.

In theory and in practice, there is thus still a large distinction between the two situations. In Canada, roughly starting from a similar legal distinction between the union and non-union sector, the evolution has been different. First, the union sector covers a much larger share of the labor force. Second Adams and Adell note that:

> 'the differences between the rights of the two classes of employees are gradually shrinking. For one thing, all employees are now protected by various substantive statutory regimes, ..., For another, the common law courts have narrowly being narrowing the concept of cause for dismissal, thereby bringing it more in line with the concept of just cause applied in the organized sector'

47. At the opposite point of the spectrum is the case of Germany where in part the same provisions apply to dismissals for cause as to individual dismissals, the former being considered as several individual dismissals together, and the economic reason being one of the three reasons allowed for 'ordinary' dismissals, together with the personality and the behaviour of the employee. 'Extraordinary dismissals' concern cases where it becomes intolerable to maintain the employment relationship any longer. Except for delays, they obey the same principle as ordinary dismissals: the works council is informed under penalty of voiding the dismissal. For extraordinary dismissals, the works council may express reservations, which will help the case of the employee in court, but the employer can proceed. In cases of ordinary dismissal, the works council may object to the dismissal and the employee if he objects cannot have his employment terminated other than by court proceedings.

Midway between these two extremes are some countries which follow the written Roman Law tradition, where statutory rules apply as a matter of public policy to all employees, but where dismissal is possible at the employers initiative but can be contested if it is abusive or without a real cause.

48. In France, for instance, the central concept is, unlike in the USA, one of an individual contract of employment. Therefore, all kind of dismissals, redundancies, terminations are to be understood under the legal category of the breakdown of the contract of employment. Employment security is, therefore, best analysed as the regulation or mitigation of the right, on the part of the employer, to break an employee's individual contract of employment.

49. This concept has historical roots. After the fall of the monarchy and of the ancient order of laws, the civil code, promulgated in 1804, provided in section 1780, in order to prevent the return of slavery, that one could sell one's services only for a definite period or a definite task. Therefore, it was unlawful to sell one's services for life. Besides, out of the 2281 sections of the code, only two, including this same section 1780, dealt specifically with the contract of employment, assumed therefore, as far as its legal status was concerned, to fall for its regulation under the title of the code devoted to the general law of contracts. Thus, as any other contract, the contract of employment was implying the complete reciprocity between the parties. Employer and employee where legally equal and the Courts, in the absence of a specific statute, and after initial wavering, quickly decided that the right of unilateral termination of a contract of employment, implicit into section 1780, applied to both parties.

Apart for the cases of dismissals for economic reasons, a slow evolution regarding dismissals for cause culminated with the Act of 1973 which submitted to them severe limitations from the part of the employer, who must follow a specific procedure which provides the employee with procedural guarantees and can lawfully dismiss only if it is for cause, and the cause must be real and serious with the burden of the proof falls equally on both parties and not only on the employee as a plaintiff. The notion of real and serious cause itself has been the subject of legal and judicial developments much beyond the frame of this paper.

50. In many countries other provisions limit the curtailment of employment security, such as a delay of notice before that the dismissal becomes effective, severance pay, often computed in regard of the duration of services, free time available during the period of notice to look for a job, 'procedural justice' provisions regarding dismissal, such as the right of the employee concerned to be heard before the decision, to be assisted by a fellow employee and the like.

Provisions have also sometimes been enacted against 'constructive dismissal' i.e. pressure by the employer until the employee quits on his own, which is then considered as an abusive dismissal.

VIII. GOVERNMENT ACTIVE MANPOWER POLICIES

51. The field here is so varied and diverse according to the country and industry that only very general indications can be provided.

First, supply oriented procedures include income protection, which is made essentially of the unemployment compensation system which may itself includes two parts, one based on insurance, the other on public help and funds and is mentioned here only for the record but will not be discussed. It should simply be noted that for most systems, benefits are decreasing with time and that increasing concern has been paid to 'poverty traps' i.e. the risk that receiving the allowance be dissuasive for the unemployed to undertake a lower level of paid activity which could be conducive to later new employment.

The second level of supply oriented provisions include measures promoting the relocation of the employees. The whole continuing education and training system could be seen as falling under this heading. It is, however, way outside the scope of this paper.

52. Second, demand oriented policies have multiplied and in many countries, several types of governmental help are available to those who hire employees, create a business or help the unemployed to be re-hired. There is notably help towards the employment of the youth or of the long-term unemployed. 'Work experience' contracts exist in the UK. Contracts called employment-solidarity are present to that end, even though they are of a very different nature, in Italy and in France. Other incentives to hiring include for instance the decreasing of wage-based social security contributions for small employers hiring of the first employee or certain types of employees.

IX. CONCLUSION

53. A question often raised nowadays around a new buzzword asks if job security is not a thing of the past. In the new flexible world, what counts is employability. That is, the capacity of the employee to fit the available types of employment. However, this raises many questions. It appears indeed that the old model where quasi life-time employment with an acceptable wage in exchange for unquestioned loyalty and obedience is quickly disappearing. What will replace it? In the worst of the worlds, employability has shifted the burden of employment security back on the employee alone. It is his task to create and maintain his employability. We have gone full circle from 'employment at will' and back there. Those who succeed will adapt and prosper, the others will join the ranks of the outcasts from the information society. In the best of worlds, employability rests on the availability of training and efficient mechanisms of equilibrium in the labour market, without undue bureaucratic pressure on enterprises, and employability is a shared responsibility between a string of enterprises and the individual. The technical and legal means of ensuring this equilibrium are still to be developed.

Chapter 19. National Trade Union Movements

G.P. Cella and T. Treu

I. INTRODUCTION

1. National trade union movements are fundamental elements of any developed industrial relations and labour law system. Yet, as Clegg[1] points out, 'there exists no systematic theory of trade unionism and even less of national labour movements'. This section will focus on national trade unions. Reference will be made to broader aspects of the labour movement when they are indispensable for an understanding of unionism.

For analytical purposes the models will be presented and interpreted as follows:

(1) union membership (or density), structure and internal organization;
(2) union presence or influence at the workshop level;
(3) forms of union action;
(4) political action and relations with political parties;
(5) trade unions and state intervention in industrial relations.

Each aspect will be considered in terms of the situation of the last decades along with basic historical references as needed. Finally, an attempt will be made to give an overall appraisal and interpretation of the models and trends.

II. TRADE UNION STRUCTURE

2. A first series of elements for the identification of the various models of unionism concerns structural characteristics such as the quality and quantity of trade union membership, patterns of union organization and their internal government (i.e. internal structure, regulations). These elements are all related in part to the characteristics of the labour force, on the one hand, and to the methods used by organized labour to achieve its aims on the other.

---

1. H. Clegg, *Trade Unionism under Collective Bargaining*, Oxford, 1976, p. 1.

A. Craft-Occupational Unions

3. The first type traditionally identified is the *craft union*, composed of workers in the same trade able to control the labour supply and hence unilaterally to impose their conditions and terms of work on the employers. The craft union flourished in numerous industries of the nineteenth century which relied on a rather small number of highly skilled workers and formed the backbone of the oldest trade union movements, led by Britain and the United States, where it later survived the development of mass production industry, the consequent standardization of labour and the decline of traditional skills. On the contrary, in continental Europe craft unionism, in the true sense of the term, has hardly gone beyond the early stages of union history or very limited areas of the labour force. In most late developing countries the timing and conditions of industrialization – plus the absence of a significant guild tradition – tended to exclude the basic pre-requisites for such a model.

4. However, over the past few decades craft (or, more generally, *occupational*) unions have undergone a profound change in order to survive. Besides adopting collective bargaining as the major method of action (like their competitors, the industrial unions), they expanded, or attempted to expand, into weakly organized industries and occupations with little regard for original boundaries (in much the same way as general unions, *see* below). This accounts in part for the highly complex organization of these trade union movements.

B. White-Collar Unions

5. An equally important development is the rapid and widespread growth of another type of occupational union: the organization of white-collar employees. It developed in all countries much later than blue-collar unionism and is still much less widespread in the private sector. Attempts to organize manual and white-collar employees into the same union have rarely been totally successful, not even in those countries dedicated to industrial unionism, for example Germany and Sweden. This is particularly true for employees with medium standards of professional qualifications, who continue to grow increasingly disenchanted with the general objectives and attitudes of national labour movements. They were the first to create separate organizations or confederations (the French CGC is among the best known), but in most countries are not organized at all in the private sector. Managerial personnel are in a similar situation (often the law forbids their unionization in the same organization as other employees).

6. The types of white-collar organizations are as variable as those of blue-collar. Some white-collar unions cover the relevant occupation within a single sector or industry: e.g. most national or local government employees in the public service. Others are more strictly occupational, since they group one or several occupations separately from the others within the same sector (e.g. airline pilots, assistants and air controllers in many countries). Some of the largest unions organize white-collar occupations across industrial boundaries, even beyond the industrial sector, e.g. the two largest unions affiliated to the Swedish TCO.

Finally, some unions tend to organize white-collar employees across industrial boundaries *and* irrespective of occupation: for example, the Austrian and Danish white-collar employees' unions. The area of organized white-collar employees in some countries tends to extend to middle and even upper management in the public service – although chiefly through separate occupational unions. In the last years the rise of very particularistic unions (non-affiliated to the confederations) has characterized some important national experiences, like in Italy and France. The trend is more uncertain in the private sector.

C. *Industrial Unions*

7. The second major historical model is the industrial union, organizing all workers of the same branch of the economy, irrespective of occupation. This type of union has developed in most industrialized countries since the turn of the century, along with the rapid growth of mechanization and mass production industry. Recruitment is based mainly on the mass of semi- and unskilled workers, a typical 'product' of this industry.

In some of the first industrialized countries (Britain, the United States) where its growth was strongly resisted by craft unionism, the industrial union developed in those (separate) areas which craft unions had failed to occupy. One of the best examples is the competition and distribution of influence of the AFL and CIO in the United States during the 1930s. In these industrialized countries the two models *co-exist.*

8. Industrial unions developed more easily, soon becoming the dominant structure, particularly among blue-collar workers where strong craft unions had no time to grow, e.g. in most continental European countries (from Sweden, to Germany, to Italy). Most European labour movements also initially endorsed industrial unionism as the ideal type of organization for ideological reasons as well (the promotion of proletarian unity). Industrial unionism was likewise endorsed as the dominant model in planned economies. Pragmatic rather than doctrinal considerations account for the more recent trend – common to most industrialized countries – toward the amalgamation of craft unions into industrial (or general) unions,[2] arising, for example, from the need to enhance the bargaining power and quality of services or to reduce jurisdictional disputes or to save financial resources.

9. The process of amalgamation and the underlying structural changes in modern economies (growing interdependence among sectors, importance of services) tend to blur the distinction between the two models. On the one hand, the growth of occupational unions reduces the total coverage of industrial unions from within; on the other, industrial unions are forced to cover new fields. Thus they are often better defined as multi-industrial or conglomerate (if not general) unions.[3]

---

2. J.P. Windmuller, 'Concentration Trends in Union Structure: An Inter-Trade unionism under collective bargaining, *Industrial and Labour Relations Review*, 1981, p. 54. *See also* J. Waddington et al., 'European trade unionism in transition? a review of the issues', *Transfer*, 1997, pp. 464–497.
3. Windmuller, *op. cit.*, p.93.

10. Whereas the extension of industrial unionism in the earliest industrialized countries was limited by the existence of strong occupational unions, the influence of this model in most newly developing nations has been reduced by the lack of structural preconditions (delayed and limited industrial growth, an industrial labour force smaller than the agricultural one). Even where industrial unions do exist – as in most cases – they are far from dominant, tending to leave room for another model of organization: the territorial type.

D.   General Unions

11. Mass production favoured not only industrial unions but, under given circumstances, a third pattern of organization, i.e. general unions. They can be defined negatively as unions which organize employees irrespective of their occupation and industrial boundaries. This pattern is found first and foremost in countries with a history of strong occupational unions which 'as collective bargaining developed … promoted general unions'.[4] Some of the oldest and most famous general unions originated as such, including the American Teamsters, the British Transport and General Workers' Union (TGWU) and General and Municipal Workers, the Australian Workers' Union. But many originally craft unions have acquired the characteristics of a general union by recruiting in new areas and absorbing other occupational unions (e.g. the International Association of Machinists in the United States).

12. The expansion of the general union is still further reduced among blue-collar workers in countries adopting industrial unionism. But even in these countries, the balance is shifting with the development of private and public services where mostly white-collar employees (the fastest growing manpower group) operate. In these services, the productive identity of the branch and the occupational connotations of the groups tend to be less clear-cut, thereby creating favourable structural conditions for the development of general or multi-occupational unions. Indeed, the same trend has also been noted in some unions organizing mostly blue-collar workers. The former district 50 of the American Mineworkers is one of the first and finest examples.

The above-mentioned elements, especi all he growth of employment in services, explain why general and white-collar unions – more so than the traditionally industrial ones – are strengthening their position as leaders among the largest national unions in many industrialized countries.[5]

E.   Territorial Structures

13. Territorial or horizontal substructures can be found in most main movements, usually not as an exclusive form of organization but together with others, as a way

---

4. Clegg. *op. cit.*, p. 39.
5. *See* the table in Windmuller, *op. cit.*, p. 55. The concentration of trade union structures seems to be a general trend in most developed countries, favoured also by public authorities (*see* below).

of grouping or coordinating them. The importance and functions of the horizontal model of organization – at the decentralized and central level (where the structure is usually called a confederation) – vary in different countries and during different periods within the same country. At one extreme the 'horizontal' structure is only a loose coordinating body with a substantially non-bargaining role and fewer powers than the federated unions. Often it does not even include all the major unions of the country, as has traditionally been the case with the American AFL and later the AFL-CIO. In other countries, horizontal structures and particularly the central confederations have substantial financial and staff resources, a high degree of control over the most important activities of the federated unions (like in the Scandinavian model) and are included in bargaining, sometimes operating as bargaining agents with respect to the employers and public institutions

14. This significant power of the horizontal structure is often correlated with the structural characteristics of the country and its labour movement: the late development of industry and of trade unions in general, the fragmented nature of the economy and of the labour market. Traditionally high unemployment levels and an extreme political orientation of the labour movement stress the importance of the unity of the working class and union pursuit of general goals, of which the horizontal structure is the natural expression. In fact, these factors serve to explain the traditionally central position of these structures in the history of European countries such as France, Spain, Italy, Belgium and, *mutatis mutandis*, may account for the strong territorial basis of trade unions in many developing countries. This form was the most effective means to promote the initiative of a weak and often divided labour movement on both the economic and political fronts.

15. But it would be simplistic to correlate the emergence of the territorial organizational pattern, with the weakness and sometimes the political divisions of the trade union movement. This is particularly true for the role of the central confederations.

In fact, confederations, more than de-centralized territorial structures, prove to have a crucial position in countries with a history of strong, politically united trade union movements, such as Scandinavia, Austria and to, a lesser extent, Germany. The influence of central confederations has grown during the 1970s and early 1980s as a general trend even in countries with a long tradition of organizational complexity and independence of single unions (e.g. Great Britain). Here the correlation can be made and should be more accurately tested, with elements which generally account for the centralization of industrial relations, namely growing state intervention in economic and social affairs and increased union recourse to the political arena, where economic decisions are also made with greater frequency. Both factors favour the role of central horizontal (rather than peripheral) union structures capable of mobilizing large sectors of the labour movement on an interindustrial or interoccupational basis.

16. A further distinction can be made as to whether:

(a) the central horizontal structure, the confederation, groups the entire trade union movement or the vast majority of it (like the British TUC, the German DCB, the Austrian OGB); or

449

(b) there are separate confederations, each grouping mainly white-collar and blue-collar unions (TCO and LO in Sweden, FFF and LO in Denmark, ACSPA and ACTU in Australia); or whether

(c) the pluralism of the confederation basically following political and ideological lines (France, Italy, Spain, Belgium, the Netherlands).

In these latter cases political and ideological elements influence the entire trade union movement, irrespective of other organizational criteria, amounting to a kind of separate principle of organization.

F. Enterprise Unionism

17. Many countries have a history of enterprise unionism (distinguished here from enterprise sections of national unions). Western labour movements looked upon it with diffidence. However, many developing countries have a wide experience of enterprise unions (e.g. Latin America). This is due both to the economic structure (fragmentation of the labour force and concentration in few large enterprises) and to government and employers' action, which was opposed to national union organization for fear of excessive politicization and mass conflictual pressure (general strikes). A significant exception in this respect among developed countries is Japan, where enterprise unionism has been the dominant form of organization since World War II.

The development of this pattern is explained by the peculiar situation of the immediate post-war period when unions were organized within enterprises (and not from the outside as usually occurred in other labour movements), with no resistance either from the government or from the employers. Efforts made by the national trade union centres to overcome enterprise unionism and strengthen industrial unions have been unsuccessful except for a few cases. National unions in Japan are a federation of enterprise unions more than a compact organization, and some enterprise unions are directly affiliated to the national centre. In fact, the most important functions (above all bargaining) are vested at the enterprise level even taking into account the importance acquired by the spring offensive in national wage negotiations. Local or enterprise sections are also highly autonomous in other countries (for example the USA), but the national federations maintain a decisive role in supporting and enlarging union presence in new areas.

The expansion and endurance of enterprise unionism in Japan beyond its origins must be considered in light of the nature of Japanese industrial relations. First of all, the lifetime employment system and the consequent enterprise-wide type of bargaining for which the employees remain tied to the specific enterprise; second, the harmonic relationship which has developed within enterprises between management and employees, based on interests that are common to the well-being of the enterprise.[6]

---

6. For some new features *see* Y. Kuwahara, 'The Future of the Labor Movement in Japan: Experiments and Possibilities', *IIRA 12th World Congress*, Tokyo 2000, proceedings Vol. 3.

III. MEMBERSHIP AND INTERNAL GOVERNMENT

A. Membership

18. Reference has already been made to the different degrees of unionization in different manpower sectors, even in countries with similar economic and political patterns.

The most common features are a rather low trade union density in private white-collar employment with few notable exceptions (such as Sweden and Austria) and a relatively high density in public employment for developed countries, once again with significant exceptions (the US, first and foremost). Private manual employment shows the greatest variation, ranging from very low minima – (France, about 15 per cent, and many developing countries) – to high maxima (over 80 per cent in most Scandinavian countries; nearly total membership in many countries with public or quasi-public unionism: *see* below).[7]

19. An interesting attempt to explain divergencies in union density in six countries linked them to the extent and depth of collective bargaining and to the support of union security from employers or collective agreements.[8] State intervention, in such forms as pressure on employers to recognize unions and protection of organizing rights, played a decisive role, in particular for 'latecomers' in promoting unionization. The high trade union density in the public sector and the apparent trend to expansion in most countries may well be explained by the structural characteristics of public services: high concentration of undertakings, direct government control, bureaucratic organization favouring collective bargaining and control of rulings on employment conditions. Anyway, the impressive privatization drive, with the related process of downsizing, could really lower this density.

20. A positive relationship – not disproving the argument above – has been found in OECD countries between trade union density and (predominant) levels of bargaining, where increasing density goes hand in hand with increasing centralization of the bargaining structure. A somewhat similar relationship has also been ascertained between (the degree of) centralization in the bargaining structure and that of the trade unions and employers' associations, measured by the extent of the union, the number of federations and the control and bargaining powers vested in central union bodies. Sweden, Norway and Austria are among those countries with highly centralized bargaining structures, a prevalence of national bargaining and the highest degree of trade union centralization. Japan, the United States, and Canada lie at the opposite end of the scale.[9]

---

7. On unionization rates *see* the recent and complete B. Ebbinghaus and J. Visser, *Data Handbook on Trade Unions*, London, 2000.
8. Clegg, *op. cit.*, p. 12ff.
9. C. Blyth, 'The Interaction between Collective Bargaining and Government Policies in Selected Member Countries', in *Collective Bargaining and Government Policies*, Paris, 1979, p. 90ff.

B. Government

21. The structure of trade unions appears to point to increasing centralization in many developed countries. Hypotheses have been advanced to the effect that since this trend is related to the predominant bargaining level, it is influenced by the increasing government involvement in industrial relations (income policies in particular). On the contrary, it has also been argued that government intervention and control over bargaining could reduce the bargaining power of central bodies (unions and employers), catalyzing reactions from the rank and file and emphasizing the need for safety valves (i.e. decentralized activities).[10]

22. Another theory (H. Clegg) maintains that the collective bargaining structure, and hence trade union behaviour and organization in general, are under the primary influence of employers' forms of organization (and behaviour). This correlation might well explain the centralization of collective bargaining and trade unions, as well as the internal coherence of organization in countries like Sweden (where employers' associations have been similarly centralized and strong); the territorial (industrial) structure of bargaining in France and Germany (which corresponds to employers' association levels); the fragmented structure of bargaining and trade unions in the United States, Britain and Australia (where large employers' associations are weak or non-existent). But the value of this theory can be questioned in Italy, for example, where the structure and initiatives of employers' organizations have tended to respond to, more than originate, those of the trade union. Moreover, Clegg's basic assumption relating trade union behaviour to collective bargaining needs discussion and specification, particularly when analysing the political action of trade unions and its central role in some countries *(see* below).

23. Internal rules and methods of administration vary not only among countries but within the same system, according to the type of union, its size and degree of centralization. Internal union government in a small highly de-centralized occupational union is likely to be different from that of a large centralized general or industrial union in terms of: the degree of direct member participation in union affairs, the powers of elected bodies and general meetings *vis-à-vis* the bureaucracy, the position and tenure of officers, the degree of autonomy of peripheral bodies, the ratio of officers to members, etc. They may have a few basic principles in common, often deriving from the general rules of representative organs the plurality of decision-making bodies: voting procedures for decision and majority rule; election of governing bodies and officers, although there are many exceptions (probably the most widely adopted method, at least in Europe, is that delegate conferences elect chief officers and governing bodies which in turn appoint and control full-time officers).

24. Financial resources are also differentiated. At one extreme some unions (in many developing countries) can rely only on contributions collected *ad hoc* from members and/or a few occasional contributions, at the other, unions in countries such as Germany, Sweden, and the USA until the 1980s, etc., have strong financial

---

10. Blyth. *op. cit.*, p. 75.

positions, based on stable generalized check-off Systems, and administer considerable funds for various purposes (i.e. pension schemes and strike funds).

25. The predominant influence of collective bargaining patterns and dimensions of union behaviour, analysed by Clegg has also been related to some aspects of union structure, such as the distribution of power and factionalism within the union. The theory maintains that since power is concentrated at the seat of collective bargaining, centralized industry-wide bargaining concentrates power in the centre, promoting integrated bureaucratic government, whereas de-centralized bargaining establishes an independent power centre at a lower level (particularly that of the workshop) which can serve as a basis for factions.[11] Clegg also concedes, however, that the origins of factionalism may not be solely bargaining-structural in nature. The motives may also be political (in European countries such as Italy and France, in Australia, in many developing countries). More generally, the concentration of power at confederate levels in many countries cannot be explained merely on the basis of a bargaining role: it is inevitably concerned with the growing importance of political functions.

IV.   UNIONS AND WORKPLACE ORGANIZATIONS

26. Workplace organizations are considered here in light of their possible relevance to the trade union movement. (Their connection with the problems of workers' participation is covered in chapter 20.)
Four basic situations can be found in principle and in fact:

(a) workplace organizations not directly related to trade unions;
(b) workplace organizations which are formally or in fact an integral part of trade unions (such as plant union sections);
(c) workplace organizations of both types (dual forms of employee representation); and
(d) absence of any substantial form of workplace organization.

27. The oldest labour movements, of Great Britain and the United States, historically took root within the productive units. Workplace organizations in these two countries are still basically integrated in their trade unions and among the most important centres of union power, although British shop stewards have shown greater militancy and autonomy from the external trade union organization. But the same single channel formula also applies to continental Europe, in such different cases as the Italian delegates and factory committees and Swedish plant committees. (Although other forms of specific employee representation have been recognized.) The situation is even more clear-cut in Japan, where enterprise unions have since become the basis of trade unionism and the only form of workers' representation at the enterprise level. The single (union) channel of representation can also be found in Latin American countries for the reasons mentioned above and for different reasons in socialist countries, prevailing until the end of the 1980s in Eastern Europe,

---

11.   Clegg, *op. cit.*, 40ff. On the problem of democracy in trade unions *see* also L. Lewin, *Governing Trade Unions in Sweden*, Cambridge (Mass.), 1980.

where unionism has been organized under public control (a public system of unionism tends to exclude pluralism).

28. Forms of employee representation not directly related to trade unions are traditionally common in continental Europe (France, Germany, Belgium, the Netherlands, Italy until 1970). The origins of these 'works councils', 'enterprise committees' etc. go back to the early history of trade unionism. These origins are linked to the features of the labour movements in these countries: extreme weakness, political orientation and occasional division, centralization, and lack of roots within productive units. In the German experience the principle of works constitution (*Betriebsverfassung*) was very important. And, indeed, this model of (employee) representation (not directly related to unions) is also present in many of the developing countries of Africa, East Asia (India, Singapore) with much the same type of unionism (above a minimum degree of unionization which is a prerequisite for union presence within plants).[12] The model appears to be a more 'diluted' form of collective representation than the plant union section, more acceptable to employers and more easily legitimated by law (for the very fact that it is the representation of all workers and not only of union members).

29. A common characteristic may be that they are a substitute for the remoteness of trade unions from the plant and, in cases of political division, an elementary form of workers' unity as far as the direct relationship with employers is concerned.

Attempts – more successful in Germany and Austria than in other countries – have been made to distinguish their functions of general workers' representation and cooperation with management from the conflictual and bargaining role supposedly typical of unions. On the other hand, this type of representation has survived well beyond the early stages of immaturity and division of the labour movement, acquiring new powers (as in Germany) or being set up (or extended) by law even in countries with no such tradition (such as the developing countries). They indicate the increasing importance of collective forms of action which are different from traditional collective bargaining (participation, information, control and the like), felt to be hand-led better by direct employees' representatives than by union organs. This dual channel formula is in fact rejected by labour movements more directly rooted at the enterprise level and dedicated to collective bargaining (as in Britain, the United States, Italy). Even when they accept forms of participation different from collective bargaining, they tend to use instruments (specialized or mixed committees) composed of union representatives.

30. In European countries where these forms of representation are most firmly established, unions often tend to control them, and thus an important reason of their success. On the other hand works councils are often an important centre of power and can condition union action (e.g. in Germany); so that the relationship is not one-way. In the same countries trade unions have not given up their objective of being directly present at the workshop level in different forms (union trusted persons in

---

12. *See* further information in *Workers' Participation in Decisions within Undertakings*, Geneva, ILO, 1981.

Germany, union plant sections in France, etc.). Results have been almost inconsistent. The success and development of direct employee representative bodies have sometimes hindered the development of effective union plant structures. The growth of the two forms of representation appears to be inversely proportionate. so that a perfect dual channel of representation is never fully implemented, and one form usually prevails. Germany is a clear example, where works councils (*Betriebsräte*), which in fact exercise most important negotiating functions, dominate and where union control over them is still the most effective vehicle of presence in the plant. The opposite is true in the Swedish and Italian system, where union structures are unequivocally dominant. In France the various forms of union and employees' representation are all relatively feeble institutions, because collective action at the plant level is also traditionally weak.

31. In conclusion, the correlation between the type of workplace organization and prevailing forms of trade union organization at the national level and degrees of decentralization is a partial one. It can only be said that the de-centralization of bargaining structures tends to promote the role of workplace organizations within the unions (as in Great Britain, the United States, Japan, and Italy) and favour the single channel formula. The reverse is partially confirmed: centralization leaves room for dual channels of representation (with partial exceptions such as Sweden and, to some extent, Italy). On the other hand, the dual channel may be used to de-centralize collective action and union presence insofar as employees' representative bodies – indirectly linked to unions – serve as important vehicles of such action, including more or less formal collective bargaining.

V. FORMS OF TRADE UNION ACTION AND OBJECTIVES

32. In most developed countries unilateral regulation, originally the basic method of craft unionism, now ranks as a minor form, even for occupational associations (apart from e.g. restrictive practices by some of these unions). Collective bargaining has instead become the dominant instrument for regulating terms of employment *vis-à-vis* the employer. Strikes and other forms of pressure are also fundamental methods of action in 'Western' countries where they are used in different patterns and to different degrees (*see* Chapter 19), and now in late Communist countries of Eastern Europe.

A. *Collective Bargaining and Political Action*

33. At present, probably the most relevant basic variance is not between collective bargaining and unilateral action but, roughly speaking, between bargaining and political action[13] (depending on whether union pressure is exerted on the labour and economic markets or on political institutions such as parties, legislatures etc.). The

---

13. *See* J.H. Goldthorpe (ed.), *Order and Conflict in Contemporary capitalism*, Oxford, 1984, pp. 326–327.

balance or combination of the two methods – which are not alternatives in principle but may be in fact – can be seen as a continuum. At one extreme the unions of some countries have come to rely on collective bargaining as almost the exclusive way to represent members' interests and regulate terms of employment *vis-à-vis* the employer.

34. On the other hand, in many developing nations, particularly when unions are weak in the labour market and form an integrated part of the broader national movement, collective bargaining (as an adversary process with private employers ending in an agreement) is almost unknown and/or hardly accepted.

The regulation of employment terms or other settlement of employees' interests, including broad social reforms, is reached either through legislation or through administrative and political decision making on which unions may exert different degrees of influence. This is also the case, but for different reasons, in centrally planned economy countries (those still existing) where decisions affecting the workers' position and production are made according to publicly directed forms of economic planning rather than according to market evaluations. In both cases, the lack of union market power or the non-existence of a (fully operating) market account for the union's quasi-total reliance on political, legislative or administrative action.

35. Most situations in democratic industrialized countries and in late communist ones fall somewhere in between these two extremes. Political action is used in varying degrees and forms, partly as a substitute but more generally as a complement than an alternative to economic bargaining. Likewise, trade union objectives tend to be broader than those traditionally prevailing in the first group of cases.

36. A change of attitude towards political action and a trend towards a wider use of this method developed early in the majority of these countries, even in those traditionally the most dedicated to pure unionism. Indeed, the most immediate and customary recourse to legislative action points to issues and aims which are clearly compatible with collective bargaining: setting minimum standards for employment conditions, generalizing conditions beyond the areas covered by collective bargaining, providing support and recognition for unions as bargaining agents. Particularly during the 1970s, political action has not only widened but also changed its meaning. The objectives and issues of union political action have extended well beyond the reach of traditional collective bargaining and of possible employers' concessions (even in a broad sense), such as welfare, income distribution, full employment and related policies (industrial labour market policies, etc.), which are coming more and more under direct public influence. On the other hand, the 'complementary' relationship between collective bargaining and state intervention has been altered mainly by a recurring use of the latter, even in countries traditionally dedicated to *laissez-faire*, to control wage bargaining in particular.

37. No simple argument sufficientiy explains this trend. The determinant factors are much the same as those previously mentioned with respect to the growing role within trade union movements of the central confederations, which are also the political centres of unions (section II, E). In the first group of cases, the importance which has always been given to political action is a counterbalance (necessary or believed to be so) to an unfavourable market situation. But the results may differ, depending on the political system itself (in particular, government attitudes toward organized labour). In most of the European and developing countries mentioned here, when this attitude is unfavourable and the labour movement often divided and antagonistic, the use of political action is predominantly 'defensive'.

38. Under different conditions, experiences such as those that Austria and Scandinavian countries have had, show an effective use of political action on reformist targets through strong, united, fully recognized trade union movements. These unions may even be reluctant to use their market power, even for conflicts with employers, preferring political bargaining and trade-offs. Participation in political and economic decisions is the major trade-off made to unions (and employers) by the State as a counterpart to self-restraint in the use of market power.

Some conditions are advisable for this trade-off to work: (in addition to) the reformist attitude of the trade unions themselves, a *pro-labour government* or, generally, a political system in a position to guarantee trade union benefits for the organization and the rank and file; an effective *centralization* of industrial relations, in particular the ability of trade unions to mobilize mass pressure and, at the same time, to control peripheral behaviour in exchange for political benefits.[14] These latter conditions in particular tend to reinforce one another. A decentralized system of industrial relations can hardly bear any weight on political action; centralization is a common feature of trade union movements using both 'defensive' and 'reformist' oriented political action.

B.   Collective Bargaining and Participation

39.   Another basic variance in union methods of action is that between collective bargaining (in a strict sense) and various forms of participation (or control or co-determination, etc.). The meaning and different aspects of participation are discussed in chapter 20. Here the focus will be on trade union attitudes towards the problem. The following types of situation may be identified.

1. Collective Bargaining

40.   Trade unions traditionally more dedicated to collective bargaining (USA, Britain) tend not only to reject the most institutionalized and committing forms of co-determination (such as representation on enterprise managing bodies), but also to resist less binding solutions such as joint or mixed consultation and the like. The reasons are much the same: fear of being involved in responsibilities which limit their autonomy rather than grant them real powers, of interference in the union bargaining role, of a possible reduction in the scope of union representation (where a dual channel exists: *see* section IV above).

---

14.   *See* L. Bordogna and G. Provasi, *Politica, economia e rappresentanza degli interessi*, Bologna, 1984.

41. Trade union movements with a firm, often antagonistic, political orientation and less of a bargaining tradition share this reluctance, partly for the same reasons and partly for ideological motives (France, Italy until the 1970s, some developing countries, but also Australia). Some of the previously mentioned characteristics of these labour movements constitute potential obstacles to institutional participation. In the first group traditional roots in the enterprise, highly de-centralized and effective bargaining; in the second, centralization, weakness at the workshop level, political division and radicalization. In the first case the need for an alternative method to collective bargaining is reduced, and the stress is on adapting or enlarging the latter; in the second effective collective bargaining is yet to be fully practised and recognized.

42. A common argument by most unions in these countries is that – as experience demonstrates – no distinct line can be drawn between what is suitable for collective bargaining and what is suitable for 'participation' – meant here as a non-adversary type of process – on matters of 'common interest' between management and labour or a mere consultative type of union intervention in company 'internal affairs'. The very distinction between the two methods is questioned and all collective dealings between workers and management are seen as a form of trade union activity, and therefore under direct trade union control. According to this position, the best way to promote industrial democracy is to improve the process and enlarge the scope of bargaining.

Interestingly enough, this traditional diffidence towards union participation is less pronounced (beyond the enterprise level) in public bodies, particularly those active in social security and on the labour market.

2. Self-management

43. A different and more drastic approach towards industrial and economic democracy is that of self-management. Among socialist countries Yugoslavia has experimented with self-management, during the past cold war period until the collapse of the regime. It was not only a direct form of workers' participation in company economic decision making, but a means of making the originally rigid method of publicly-planned direction of the economy more flexible and open to the market. Results, however, have been largely negative. Significant, although limited, experiments in self-management are also present in countries with market economies, from the well-known kibbutz of Israel, to the mainly agricultural experiments in newly independent African and South American countries, Algeria and Peru; to trade union self-management in France, Italy, Belgium, Japan and even the United States as a response to the threat of enterprise bankruptcy; to the recent interest shown by some European trade unions in workers' participation in capital formation as a means of shifting power in the economy and among other things, to support industrial co-operatives and self-management.[15]

---

15. *See* J. Rothschild and J. Allen Whitt, *The Cooperative Workplace*, Cambridge, 1986. For a general overview *see* G. Baglioni, *Impossible Democracy? The Progress and Problems of Participation in the Firm*, Avebury, 1996.

3. Institutional Participation

44. The widest application of institutional forms of participation, in particular workers' representation on company supervisory or managing boards that are accepted or even supported by trade unions, can be found in a group of countries originally and still mainly concentrated in continental Western Europe. These systems are characterized by a strong and politically integrated union movement and by centralized bargaining, narrowly practised on specific workshop or internal enterprise matters. Organic participation may be used here as a functional equivalent or substitution for collective bargaining, more so than for the third type of participation (*see* above). It may also be experimental activity, as other forms of participation, in addition to some collective bargaining, particularly in countries where the latter has developed effectively.

45. Apart from variants in forms, the model of workers' representation in managing bodies of the enterprise is slowly expanding to some developing countries (India, Pakistan, Iraq, Congo Republic, and Venezuela) and to those of the first group mentioned above (Britain, France, Belgium), both mostly in public enterprises or the like, where the nature of the enterprise reduces traditional trade union reluctance towards these formulas and, obviously, management resistance.

4. Works Council

46. In almost all these countries, 'intermediate' forms of participation (through works councils or similar consultative committees, specialized joint bodies, etc.) are probably the most widely adopted, fastest growing solutions. They are even accepted by those unions most reluctant to follow patterns of 'organic participation'. Their intermediate and at times ambivalent position may account for their expansion. For unions they are less compromising and risky, yet useful for obtaining information and often for bargaining or establishing bargaining grounds. For management they may serve to channel discussion and consultation on matters of common and crucial interest, such as productivity, mobility, welfare, or the management of industrial re-structuring beyond a strictly adversary process. The economic crisis recurrent in different periods of time tends to stress the importance for both parties of such joint handling of these matters.[16]

VI. POLITICS AND RELATIONS WITH POLITICAL PARTIES

47. Relationships with political parties are crucial for all trade unions. No major union has reached the present day without recognizing the necessity for some sort of party relationship. The two extreme doctrines – complete self-sufficiency of

---

16. *See* D. Sadowski et al., 'Works Council: Barrier or Boots for the Competitiveness of German Firms', *British Journal of Industrial Relations*, No. 3, 1995.

trade unions in an anarchist or quasi-syndicalist perspective, and sheer business unionism – have for the most part been rejected in principle and in practice.

A. No Stable Relationship

48. A practice closer to the second extreme was originally dominant in the United States, where trade unions by tradition not only have no formal allegiance but not even a stable relationship with the national parties (often unstable organizations themselves). But even here political practices of the AFL-CIO very soon showed a preferential link with the Democrats: endorsement of candidates, financial assistance (even though legally restricted), and the voting patterns of members. More than formal relations, influence on single issues is sought according to the traditional political pattern of this country. Some strongly politically oriented labour movements like the French, Italian and Spanish have barely managed to obtain this result, even though the Italian has grown and become more autonomous.

B. Dependence

49. The historical weakness, division and lack of legitimacy, combined with a stronger party organization and presence in public life (plus the division of left-wing parties), have tended to subordinate these European trade union movements to the parties, mainly left-wing but with important exceptions. It is not by chance that they have repeatedly been tempted by syndicalist or quasi-syndicalist behaviour, particularly as a reaction to socialist or communist dominance; nor that they have recently tried to act directly on the political system, bargaining with Parliament and (not necessarily pro-labour) governments.

50. An even more radical position in this direction can be seen in a number of developing countries of Africa and Latin America. As the first organization with a relatively modern, or at least concentrated, working class and an educated leadership, the trade union movements have played a direct and initially dominant role in the push towards political, cultural and economic emancipation of the population (examples range from Algeria, to Kenya, to some Latin-American countries). The growth of national political movements and the relative strengthening of political systems appear to eliminate or restrict the substitution of trade unions for direct party roles in these countries. Indeed, this relationship may change into the opposite model of organic subordination of trade unions to the same national political movements, for reasons similar to those indicated for European countries. These organic ties of subordination may even be stronger or more complete than in the European cases due to the often extremely limited basis and development of trade unions and to the nature of the national political systems.

51. In centrally planned economy countries, mainly under late communist regimes, organic subordination and integration of trade unions with respect to the party is the absolute model, linked to the very basis of the political system. Their subordination is a consequence of the original identity of their basic role with that of the

Party and of the State (in turn identified), all directed to implement the general objectives of socialism, although with specific functions. The fact that trade union and party functionaries are completely interchangeable bears witness to this integration. The specific trade union function is not to represent particular employees' interests, different from or *vis-à-vis* the party, but under Party-State supervision. to help organize the utilization of the labour force and satisfy the basic needs (welfare, education, etc.) to achieve these objectives better.[17]

C. Interdependence

52. The relationship between trade unions and political parties is more balanced in most industrialized countries with market economies compared to the two cases just discussed. More than the formal connection (trade union affiliation or non-affiliation with a political party), the degree of dependence–independence is significant. Independence is never absolute apart from formal affiliations. The best-known cases of direct affiliation with a (labour) party (Britain, Sweden, Australia) involve trade union movements with a long tradition of strong unitary organization, full recognition, reformist orientation, and fruitful relations with a stable political system and a *united* pro-labour political party. In these three cases there are some common characteristics indicative of a relative union predominance in the relationship: namely, union financing of the party, control of votes at the party conference, union officers elected to Parliament. But even here positive union influence may be reduced (the power of veto remains) when the labour party is in government. A tendency to increase interdependence can be seen in other European countries, such as Italy, France and the Netherlands, particularly in cases of non-communist trade unions (but it is very contrasted). A major obstacle to the stability of common trends and relations is the division among left-wing parties which has historically caused a division among trade unions.

VII.   UNIONS AND STATE INTERVENTION IN INDUSTRIAL RELATIONS[18]

53. Historically, the initial attitude of the State and of the law with respect to organized labour has been one of prohibition.

A. Repression

54. In most of the oldest industrialized countries of Europe, coalition and conflict were originally sanctioned as criminal law. This position (also seen in countries where unionism developed later on) was substituted by an attitude of relative

---

17.   *See* B. Grancelli, *Soviet Management and Labour Relations.* London, 1988, and more recently various Eastern European reports in *Economic and Political Changes in Europe: Implication, on Industrial Relations*, proceedings of the III European IIRA Congress, Bari-Naples, September 1991, BariDeventer 1993.
18.   On the same theme *see* L. Bordogna and G.P. cella, 'Admission, exclusion, correction: the changing role of the state in industrial relations', *Transfer*, 1999, pp. 14–33.

tolerance towards organized labour, first in Great Britain and then, during the second half of the nineteenth century, in most European countries. Different factors contributed to this tolerance: the pressure of the rising socialist parties and of the trade union movements themselves, economic growth and the self-confidence of liberalism which allowed governments to extend their basic principles of freedom of initiative to organized labour. It took time, however, for this evolution to be completed. Even after the abolition of general criminal sanctions, collective union actions, in particular conflict, remained unlawful in many respects (e.g. under civil law) and fell under possible limitations by the courts.

The timing and nature of this evolution generally reflect the economic and political development of each country. Economic difficulties, political instability and divisions slowed down the process toward legal tolerance and recognition of trade union action, at times even causing a reversal in trends. The most blatant cases are the Nazi and Fascist periods in Germany, Italy and Spain, where the totalitarian State excluded all sorts of trade union freedom and conflict as a crime against the national economy.

55. Repression or heavy restrictions of trade union action (especially strikes) are the basic attitudes of nations run by authoritarian regimes and, more generally, where trade union movements are considered public bodies or where the direct expression of the State is ruling bureaucracy. Such was the case in some developing countries of Latin America (Chile, Brazil, Colombia) and Africa. In centrally-planned economy countries the important public functions that comprise the trade union's position within the state structure have excluded the possibility and legality of trade union conflictual action.

In the above-mentioned cases legal restrictions correspond to a situation whereby unions are excluded from the decision-making process of the country, while in the latter they reflect the tight integration into state institutions.

B. Tolerance

56. In many developed countries state tolerance towards trade union action has long been a fundamental tenet. This attitude has several implications which are not always coexistent. The most common is that trade unions are considered private voluntary associations, not recognized by law and in principle exempted from direct legal regulation of their internal affairs. In most 'Western' developed countries (but the same is true of Japan and Australia), trade unions have been rather successful in avoiding this type of legal control, more so than public or legal interventions on other aspects of industrial relations, such as collective bargaining and conflict. Even here the immunity is hardly ever total, because some judicial control of most crucial union affairs (discipline, democratic procedures, etc.) has been exerted even in the absence of legislation in order to guarantee minimum standards of fairness and democracy to its members.

57. The *laissez-faire* model in its broadest implications, including lack of special legislation on collective bargaining and strikes, has long prevailed in Great Britain, considered its homeland. It has also been periodically adopted in countries with

different traditions, e.g. Italy from 1960 to 1970. The success, partial or complete, of this model has usually been sustained by a stronger desire for voluntarism and autonomy of the social partners, trade unions and employers, than the need for state assistance. However, a prerequisite (met in a minority of cases) is that the trade union be strong enough to win a minimum bargaining role and recognition from the employers without state intervention.

C. *Intervention*

58. In almost all developed nations, in fact, state abstention from industrial relations has been followed – and substituted – by a period of heightened intervention. A major effect and role of this state action – which in some countries goes back to the early twentieth century – has been to support the formation and growth of trade union movements, through such different measures as support of individual employees on the labour market (protective legislation varied in content), indirect incentives for collective bargaining (e.g. by public conciliation, mediation and arbitration, by union rights to organize at plant level), pressures on employers to make them recognize unions or bargaining agents, and direct imposition on employers of bargaining duties with trade unions on working conditions.

59. Some distinctions may be made according to

(1) the focus or direction of state support; and
(2) the instruments and conditions of support.

Their influence on trade union developments is different. State support may be directed at promoting trade union organization mostly from within the plant and enterprise or from the outside.[19] Trade union rights and protection as stipulated in the USA with the Wagner Act (passed in 1935 during the New Deal) and subsequently adopted by Japan, France, Italy, etc., or in the Australian legislation of 1904 belong to the first type. The promptness and results of such state recognition vary according to same factors influencing union growth: conditions of the labour markets, structure of the economy, attitude and organization of employers.

60. Legal rights which strengthen union organization outside the plant are those to hold funds and property, to use them (also) for political purposes, to designate representatives on public agencies or administrative bodies. They are now part of the legal system of most developed countries. The latter are particularly diffuse in the European experience of the last decades, regarded as evidence of its inclination towards neo-corporatist models.

61. The legal forms of union recognition are important for the relative mix of rights versus restrictions implied therein. In most developed countries unions may receive support without – or with limited – interference in their internal affairs and

---

19. J.S. Valenzuela, 'A Conceptual Framework for the Analysis of Labour Movement Developments', unpublished paper. (Italian translation in *Stato e Mercato*, 1981, no. 3).

activities (*see* above). However, the law usually permits selection among unions, e.g. giving support only to those with certain standards of representativeness (hence it indirectly controls them). This is the case with most continental European systems and also Japan, where representativeness is controlled 'from the outside' on the basis of general criteria (size, activities, etc.).

A much stricter influence is exerted under the USA's legal pattern of exclusive representation. In this country control over trade union and collective bargaining has been further extended – well beyond the limits of most other developed Western countries – by the Taft-Hartley (1947) and Landrum-Griffin (1959) Acts and by court interpretation of the duty to bargain. Somewhat similar controls are granted to federal industrial courts in Australia.

62. A vehicle of direct state control on unions is typically the registration or recognition procedure introduced in some European countries, in spite of union opposition and hence with scarce effectiveness. The British Industrial Relations Act and its subsequent failure in the 1970s have been the most evident case. The widely adopted registration law has given control authorities broad powers of intervention in union life in many developing countries of Latin America, Asia and Africa where they often go back to periods of pre-independence and where the law has usually played an important or decisive role in shaping the trade union movement.

63. The mix of promotion versus restriction depends once again on many factors (*see* above) related to the political system itself. It may be argued that the most lasting and trouble-free recognition processes are granted in either of two ways. By political coalitions, which exclude the labour movement's leadership but are, however, inclined (or forced) to recognize it (e.g. the case of Britain before the Thatcher period but also of Italy); or by pro-labour governments, provided that they are in power for a relatively long period (after recognition), that union leadership is not linked to a Marxist left, and that recognition of leadership is combined with substantial benefits to the rank and file (typical of Northern European countries, excluding Germany, and of the successful state-sponsored unionism of Mexico, Brazil during the last years of the first Vargas period, and Argentina under Peron's first government).[20]

D. Neo-Corporatism

64. As already mentioned, state intervention in industrial relations has grown and changed in most developed countries particularly during the 1970s and early 1980s, becoming more directly involved in the social and economic governing process. Unilateral or authoritative solutions in crisis management are hardly feasible in Western countries. In fact, attempts by the State to impose binding incomes policies on the social parties have only lasted for short periods, usually substituted by the

---

20. For the Latin-American experience *see* R.B. Collier and D. Collier, *Shaping the Political Arena*, Princeton (N.J.), 1991.

search for stabilization through consensual solutions. Again success has been uneven. Even so, restrictions on union bargaining freedom may be quite severe; certainly they are more stringent than traditional instruments such as mere voluntary guidelines or state-oriented mediation in industrial disputes.

65. This trend has often been analysed through conceptual categories, such as 'political trade-off' or 'neo-corporatism'. The debate on their usefulness and meaning is still open.[21] Important distinctions must of course be made among countries where politicization and growing involvement in economic decision-making are under way. A number of elements usually attributed to the corporatist model can be found in countries such as Austria, Sweden and, to a substantial extent, Germany. Trade union involvement in tripartite deals on major economic issues – which substitute in part the traditional political decision-making process – has been widely practised with stabilizing effects. It has been guaranteed by stable links with pro-labour parties and central control of industrial relations, although the degree of institutional and legal constraints differs, being greater in Germany than in Sweden. At the other extreme, in the same period, the model can hardly be applied to cases like Britain and Italy, where any stable institutionalization of tripartism and political trade-off lacks the basic conditions, such as centralization of industrial relations, social and political stability (*see* section V, A). Here the State can win a consensus from trade unions and employers mostly through case-by-case bargaining. Its stabilizing effects are limited and the process of political trade-off is often blocked.

VIII.   MODELS OF NATIONAL TRADE UNION MOVEMENTS

66. In this chapter we have analysed different models of organization, action and relationships in contemporary national trade union movements: the dimensions of union behaviour, using Clegg's terminology, which have been considered above concern: union structure, density, degree of centralization, workshop organization, types of union action, relationship with political parties, plus industrial conflict, and relationship with the State and political system.

The first dimension pertains to the trade union structure (A). Organizational models are the following:

(1) Craft (early period of USA and British unionism, with cases still existing);
(2) Occupational (private and public white-collar unionism in most industrialized countries;
(3) Industrial (predominant model in continental mid-northern Europe);
(4) General (deriving from Craft in USA and Great Britain);
(5) Territorial or horizontal (France, Italy and many 'latecomer' countries);
(6) Enterprise (Japan).

---

21.   *See inter alia* G. Lehmbruch and P.C. Schmitter (eds), *Patterns of Corporatist Policy-Making*, London, 1982; P.J. Williamson, *Corporatism in Perspective*, London, 1989.

67. The second dimension is union density (B). Taking into account union membership as a proportion of the employed labour force, three categories can be considered:

(1) High density (more than 50 per cent: Scandinavian countries, Australia, Austria until the 1980s and the former socialist countries of Eastern Europe);
(2) Medium density (30–50 per cent: Great Britain, Germany, Italy, and Japan);
(3) Low density (less than 30 per cent: USA, France, developing countries).

68. The third dimension is the degree of centralization of union internal government and, given the close correlation with it, of the collective bargaining structure (C). Here too three major models can be identified:

(1) High centralization (Scandinavian countries, Austria);
(2) Bipolar or mixed structures or medium centralization (Germany, Italy);
(3) De-centralization (in decreasing order Japan, Britain, USA).

69. The fourth dimension, more qualitative than the former, has to do with the types of workplace organization (D). The typical models are the following:

(1) No organization (underdeveloped countries and the early periods of most European countries);
(2) Single non-union organization (France and Italy in the fifties);
(3) Single union structure (Britain, USA, Japan, Italy, socialist countries with the possible exception of countries which had experiences of self-management);
(4) Dual channel (Germany, the Netherlands, Austria, and partially Sweden).

70. The fifth dimension indicates types of union action (E). Here the typology is necessarily more complex and corresponds to the following models:

(1) Collective bargaining only (USA and Britain until the First World War);
(2) Collective bargaining and participation at the enterprise level (Japan);
(3) Collective bargaining and occasional partnership, in economic and political decision-making (Britain and Italy);
(4) Collective bargaining, co-determination and institutional partnership (Germany, Scandinavian countries, and Austria);
(5) Institutional partnership (socialist countries of Eastern Europe and other cases of state-sponsored unionism);
(6) Political opposition (early periods of unionism in continental Europe, some underdeveloped countries).

In model E.4 co-determination and partnership reinforce each other, making union action qualitatively different from that prevailing in E.2 and E.3.

71. The sixth dimension is industrial conflict (F), measured on the basis of the number of days lost through strikes yearly per 100,000 workers. Four categories can be considered:

(1) High conflict (over 30,000 days lost in the period 1980–85: Italy, Australia, USA, Britain);

(2) Medium conflict (between 8,000 and 30,000 days lost: Denmark, France, Sweden);
(3) Low conflict (less than 8,000 days lost: Japan, Norway, Germany);
(4) Official conflict non-existent.

72. The seventh dimension concerns the relationship with political parties (G). Three patterns can be identified:

(1) No relationship or no stable organized relationship or 'bargaining' relationship related to specific political circumstances (USA, Italian CISL);
(2) Interdependence with labour parties on an equal basis or with union predominance (Germany, Scandinavian countries, and Britain);
(3) Dependence on communist or nationalist parties (French CGT, Italian CGIL until the 1980s many unions in underdeveloped countries and in socialist countries).

73. The last dimension pertains only indirectly to union behaviour, being related indeed to the context of industrial relations; it indicates the relationship with the State and political system. This dimension (H), which identifies therefore the role of the State, can be seen in four models:

(1) Repression due to exclusion of unions from the system (early period of unionism in industrial countries and also authoritarian conservative political systems);
(2) Repression due to integration (socialist or populist States and also some underdeveloped countries recently independent);
(3) *Laissez-faire* or State abstentionism (an historical pattern of Britain and Italy of the sixties);
(4) Organized or controlled and supported pluralism (Britain under Labour governments, USA until the 1980s, Italy, and Japan);
(5) Neo-corporatism or cooperation (Austria, Sweden, The Netherlands, and FR Germany).

74. On the basis of these dimensions an attempt can be made to identify general models of the trade union movement or typical patterns of union behaviour and industrial relations, which are present in contemporary society. It is not within the purpose of this chapter to expound a general theory of unionism or of union behaviour (for which basic knowledge is still lacking).

We have left in the background the determinants and origins of different models and of the historical experiences of unionism which correspond to them. The table presented on the following page therefore has no definite theoretical value; it is only an instrument for a synthetic appraisal of contemporary unionism.

75. The models of trade union movements which have been identified are the following five: opposition, business (or domestic), competitive, participation, and state-sponsored.

Opposition unionism is typical of the history of some European countries and with a different nature, of some developing countries; it is mainly organized on a territorial basis since its main resource is represented by the general mobilization and organization of the labour force on political grounds and occasions.

Business unionism, originated in the Anglo-American tradition and still characteristic of the North American experience, is identified for its mainly economic

Patterns of Unionism	A Union structure	B Union density	C Collective bargaining and union structure	D Workplace organization	E Union action	F Industrial conflict	G Relations with political parties	H Relations with political systems
Opposition unionism (France: CGT; Italy: CGIL historically; some developing countries)	horizontal	low	bipolar or medium central	none (single) non-union	opposition	medium low	dependence	repression (laissez-faire)
Business unionism (USA)	craft industrial general enterprise	low	de-centralized	single-channel union	coll. barg. (coll. barg. +part.)	high medium	none (or occasional)	laissez-faire
Competitive unionism (Britain, Italy)	all models	medium	bipolar or medium central	single-channel union	coll. barg. +occasional partnership	high medium	inter-dependence	pluralism
Participatory unionism (Germany, Austria, Scandinavia)	occupational industrial territorial	high	centralized (bipolar)	dual-channel	coll. barg. +participation + partnership	low	inter-dependence	neo-corporatism or cooperation
State-sponsored unionism (socialist countries)	(occupational) industrial territorial	high	centralized	single-channel union	partnership	none	dependence	integration

* Models in brackets are not typical

** Japan is in some respects atypical: some characteristics of low conflict, participation and partnership at the enterprise level are typical of the participatory pattern even if de-centralized structure, lack of corporatist relations with political parties and political systems are more typical of business unionism.

objectives, pursued strictly through collective bargaining, outside stable political initiatives, and by relying mostly on direct organization of the workplace.

Competitive unionism has broader objectives which include basic, socio-economic reforms and which are pursued by initiatives both on the economic and political fronts, often highly conflictual, with a close but not necessarily institutionalized relationship with the political system (Britain and Italy being typical cases).

Participatory unionism operates in neo-corporatist or cooperative environments and is an essential actor in the system of economic and political tripartite bargaining which characterizes these environments: this implies high institutional involvement, by means of legislation or collective bargaining, both at the enterprise and labour market level (the clearest cases being countries such as Germany, Austria and the countries of Scandinavia).

State-sponsored unionism is related to a system of industrial relations strictly controlled by the State and operates towards objectives defined at the state level with public or quasi-public functions, which exclude proper bargaining and conflictual action (socialist countries and some developing nations).

76. A final problem is that of ascertaining how the different dimensions influence the general models of unionism, i.e. which dimensions are most decisive or comprehensive. Trade union structure is certainly not decisive. Almost all types of unionism are compatible with different organizational structures. For example, business and competitive unionism are compatible with organizational models 1, 3, 4, and 6. More important is the influence of union density. To each model of unionism there corresponds only one degree of union density, with a positive correlation (increasing density) from opposition to competitive to state-sponsored unionism. Collective bargaining structure (or, more precisely, its degree of centralization) has a more decisive influence than that of union structure on different models. However, the existence of bipolar structures makes it less easy to identify the direction of influence of the bargaining structure. Much the same can be said of the influence of union action, this is likewise due to the complexity of this dimension (moreover, similar types of union action, such as participation, acquire different meanings in different contexts). Levels of industrial conflict do not *per se* define the general model of unionism: more than one level is compatible with one model. Workplace organization, on the contrary, identifies precisely the various models, each model being compatible with only one type of workplace organization.

A definite influence can be attributed to political variables too; to the unions' relationship both with political parties and with the political system as a whole. In conclusion, short of establishing precise cause and effect relationships, it can be said that the most decisive variable affecting general models of unionism are union density, workplace organization, relations with political parties and with the political context of industrial relations. These variables should be mostly considered in comparative analysis of national labour movements.

IX.   TRADE UNIONS AT THE END OF THE XX CENTURY

77. During the last decade, the trade unions in most countries of the world, beginning with the most advanced, have been confronted with particularly serious challenges. Some observers have been inclined to forecast a future of a vertical decline for unions leading to de unionized societies, where labour relations will (again) be governed by market individualism and there will be less and less room for organized collective action. Workers' organizations will lose their traditional strongholds, their blue-collar workers in mass production industries, and have few opportunities to make gains in new sectors of production and new groups of the workforce.

In developing countries – where recession implies a reduction in the production and costs of exported raw material – the economic crisis has affected labour movements, which are generally characterized by weak financial and organizational structures and are not as well equipped to meet the challenge of economic difficulties. In developed societies, national trade union movements will be obsolete, and in developing countries they will be incapable of reaching the threshold of stability.

These forecasts of 'no future' for the labour movement have attracted much attention, particularly at the beginning of the 1980s, but have been significantly reshaped during the decade. While the majority of comparative researchers now reject any deterministic hypothesis of trade union decline, they confirm that the challenges to trade unions both at the national and workplace levels are not transitory.

78. Many indicators of union crisis are visible: the decline of union membership and density, and reduced capacity to mobilize industrial conflict, both reported in many countries; the declining appeal to the public of union ideals: union retrenchment in defensive posture while the employers are more and more often regaining the initiative in industrial relations. The unions themselves publicly acknowledge the seriousness of these indicators.

Different factors (cyclical, structural, institutional)[22] have been considered as possible determinants of such a declining trend in union membership and power. One widely held view points – again – to the *economic and structural changes* occurring over the course of the last decade: recurrent trade imbalances and globalization of markets, accompanied by a reemergence of high unemployment in most industrialized countries and the spread of atypical work;[23] accelerated technological innovations which together with these market developments, have brought about profound modifications in the organization of production (de-industrialization, 'tertiarization', downsizing, outsourcing, de-centralization, and, in general, more flexible productive systems).

These economic developments appear to be reinforced in their impact on union crises by *significant changes in the characteristics of the labour force* such as the increased participation of women, higher levels of education, and a general rise and differentiation in the expectations of workers. The combined influences of these social' changes appear to be a reduction of demand for union representation.

On the other hand, these economic pressures and turbulence have induced *employers and their associations* to become more aggressive in labour relations or more innovative in human resource practices with the convergent aim of reducing union influence, while some changes in worker values seem to favour these new practices.

---

22. B. Ebbinghaus and J. Visser, 'When Institutions Matter: Union Growth and Decline in Western Europe, 1950–1995', *European Sociological Review*, 1999, No. 2, pp. 1–24.
23. *See* D. Meulders, O. Plasman, and R. Plasman, *Atypical Employment in the EC*, Aldershot, 1994.

Finally, *political and institutional factors* are often mentioned as pushing in the same direction, namely, the growing influence of conservative governments (first of all the Thatcher's government in the UK during the 1980s) in some countries and their intervention in labour relations directed to promote extensive de-regulation and maximum flexibility of the labour market: a weakening of the historic alliance between the labour movement and social democratic parties, which appear themselves to be attracted by de-regulatory policies and less firm in promoting the labour cause.

The empirical evidence underlying each of these arguments is far from complete and uneven in different countries. On the whole, it suggests that no single correlation can be found between one given determinant and the trends in unionization. These trends do not follow a uniform boic, but indicate significantly different patterns of 'adjustment' in different countries according to a complex set of variables. Anyway institutional factors can explain cross-national diversities in the European experience better than the cyclical or structural ones.

79. Comparative research conducted in Europe and in the USA converge in indicating that structural and macro-economic changes explain only part of the current decline in union density and power (just as they explained only part of union growth in the past).[24] Other independent or interacting factors must therefore be behind the trend. The explanatory value of business cycle indicators in this respect has also been reconsidered. The cyclical variations appear to have become smaller over time; moreover, they show a very strict correlation with institutional and organizational variables of national systems.[25]

The impact of changes in the demographic profile of the labour force on unionization and workers propensity to unionize is supported by scarce or contradictory evidence. For some aspects in the Nordic countries the gender gap in unionization has disappeared.

The correlation appears to be more complex, i.e. the trends may be indirectly influenced by specific worker attitudes, which affect their propensity to unionize: namely, the degree of job satisfaction, the perception of benefits accruing from union membership and their costs.

Political factors, including the influence of legal institutions and political parties on labour unions, appear to have uneven weight in the various systems: industrial relations dependence on state initiatives has not disappeared as neo-liberal ideologies envisaged or advocated, but has been somewhat loosened and become more ambivalent.[26]

---

24. J. Visser, 'Trade unionism in western Europe', *Labour and Society*, 1988, p. 142 and *Trends in Union Membership*. OCDE, Paris, 1991; T. Kochan, 'The future of worker representation: An American perspective', *Labour and Society*, 1988, p. 188, who points out, among other aspects, the different performances of USA and Canada unions despite comparable structural changes; R.J. Adams, 'Industrial Relations in Europe and North Amenca: Some contemporary themes'. *European Journal of Industrial Relations*, 1995, No. 1. For a general comparative analysis *see* A. Booth et al., *What do Unions do in Europe?*, 2000, A report for Fondazione R. Debenedetti, Milano.
25. J. Visser, *loc. cit.*
26. C. Crouch, 'Future and past of industrial relations', in G. Baglioni and C. Crouch. *op. cit.*

The importance of managerial practices in industrial relations is particularly difficult to evaluate: while it tends to be more frequently stressed in the American context, European research suggests not to overstate it.[27]

The most convincing explanations consider the various factors as interrelated among themselves, and interpret the difficulties/crises of unions as part of broader changes in the institutional structure of industrial relations that are arising in response to long-term changes in the market (mainly due to globalization process and the impact of the information technologies),[28] the technological and political context of employment relations and in actor strategies.

Organizational as well as institutional variables have to be combined in dynamic models, which account for a different *capacity* of labour unions and of the industrial relations systems where they operate to *adjust* to new and often adverse conditions. Indeed, while, according to most observers, the 1970s represented still a period of relative convergence amongst the major developed industrial relations systems, during the 1980s, the elements of divergence seemed to win over those that push toward convergence. As for the European continental experiences, during the 1990s some common trends are again discernible.[29]

The interrelation of this complex set of factors can be usefully explored by analysing their influence on the various dimensions discussed above of union organization and behaviour.

A. Trade Union Structure

80. The process of trade union concentration common to developing and developed countries has continued in the form of a reduction in the number of trade unions affiliated to national labour movements. Mergers are a common feature of many European trade union movements. New big unions take the floor, like UNISON in the UK. But the process has been recently counteracted in some countries (like Italy) by the growth of associations representing some categories of (mainly) professional employees and cadres, with quasi-union status and objectives, and by the reactivated initiative of independent unions, particularly in the service industry. Industrial unionism in some countries remains the dominant type in developed countries. However, it is losing its vitality due to the decline of traditional industrial sectors (e.g. steel) and the reduction of manpower following technological innovations (e.g. automobile).

Industrial unions in some countries are trying to recruit members in different areas that are often quite foreign to their original jurisdiction (*see* UAW in the USA) and thus are behaving more and more like general unions. The most vivacious type seems to be the occupational unions of mainly white-collar employees as a result of the expansion of tertiary industry, both private and public. In almost all developed

---

27. *See* the discussion at the IX IIRA World Congress, Sydney, September 1992, report by A. Purcell.
28. *See* R. Blanpain, 'The impact of the information society on the world of work in developed countries', *IIRA 12th World Congress*, Tokyo 2000, proceedings Vol. 1.
29. *See* A. Ferner and R. Hyman (eds), *Changing Industrial Relations in Europe*, Oxford, 1998.

and developing countries, the only consistently growing or stable unions are those of public employees.

But even in the public sector, the potential of union growth appears to be narrowing due to the financial crisis of the States, which is curbing the expansion of public employment, and to the widespread trend to shift public industries back to the market which consequently exposes labour relations to market-related performance criteria.[30]

These constraints have contributed to foster centrifugal reactions by various groups of employees, particularly those holding key positions in essential services, and dissident forms of organizations (like in Italy and France) which challenge the cohesiveness not only of confederal unions but sometimes also of traditional independent unions.

81. In some European countries, such as Italy, Spain. France and Belgium, which are characterized by multiple unionism due to ideological and political divisions, the processes of trade union concentration also show a decline in the efforts during the 1970s toward unity, and often a reopening of old rivalries and increased competition among different wings of the trade union movement.

A proximate cause of this trend lies in the attitude towards austerity and restriction policies adopted in different degrees by the governments of the countries mentioned above. But even in these countries where workers are traditionally thought to have deep ideological allegiances, the question has been raised whether there is a weakening of the solidarity within the working class due to the diversification of the workforce (and of its values). Ideological and political rivalries continue to fragment and divide the labour movement in many developing countries.

B. *Membership and Internal Government*

82. Unionization and union density. which are good indicators of organizational vitality, present different trends in the various systems. In the majority of countries, since the late 1970s, the long trend toward the development of unionization has been either stopped or reversed. Below this underlying tendency, the scenario varies from cases of dramatic decline like New Zealand to cases of slow shrinking and of relative stability (Scandinavian countries being the clearest example of the latter, with only a light decrease at the end of the 1990s, but also Canada).

The trends in union density continue to be markedly different according to the sectors, the quality of workforce (white, blue-collars), and the size of firm. The decline among blue-collar workers in the private and industrial sectors has been particularly pronounced and has not been contracted by the growth among white-collar workers of the (new) sectors of tertiary industry (with Scandinavia probably the only important exception). In developing countries, too, unionization rates have been

---

30. T. Treu et al., *Public service relations: recent trends and future prospects*, ILO, Geneva, 1987. *See also* S. Bach et al. (eds), *Public Service Employment Relations in Europe: Transformation Modernization or Inertia?*, London, 1999.

affected by economic recession and inflation, even in some trade union movements that had reached a fairly high membership (as in the Brazilian experience).

Two institutional determinants of these cross-national differences in union density are often considered: the degree of centralization within the industrial relation system, i.e. the combination of broadly representative unions in strong peak organizations, which coordinate bargaining with employers; and the degree of *unity* within labour union organization. Here too, however, the evidence is far from uniform.

The positive association of unified unionism with a higher degree of membership stability has been widely tested and is confirmed by the stability of Scandinavian countries (Sweden and Denmark, around 80 per cent). This association is not confirmed for the German experience: since the unification German unions have lost millions of members (the unionization rate from the 36 per cent of 1990 to 27 per cent of 1997).

On the other hand, the Austrian and Dutch cases have been quoted as evidence that monopolistic union systems may set the scene for decline; while competition, of the kind that exists in Sweden and Denmark between different organizations, may favour their positive adjustment to changes.[31]

The impact of centralization is similarly ambiguous. Some trade unions operating in highly de-centralized systems, beginning with the USA and to some extent the UK, have experienced a marked decline in membership (USA below the historical minimum of 15 per cent), but this trend may be attributed to other characteristics of those industrial relations systems and union strategy (*see* below). While a centralized structure of industrial relations is held to be a possible advantage for spreading union recruitment and recognition to new areas, an excessive distance or absence of the union from workplace activities tends to reduce workers' perception of union influence on their conditions and hence their propensity to unionize (evidence in this respect has been submitted with respect to the French and Dutch cases).

Along this line, it has been claimed that a higher level of union stability (and membership) tends to be attained in systems that combine centralized and de-centralized methods of representation and bargaining, in a *mixed* structure of industrial relations with a medium degree of centralization (Germany being the clearest case, and to some extent Italy). In general, the decline in union membership appears to be more pronounced in countries where unionization and union bargaining power has been traditionally weak (France and Spain).[32]

83. It remains a matter of debate whether the stagnation and decline in union membership and organization are a cyclical fluctuation related to the recurrent economic turbulences, possibly reversible under more prosperous conditions, or an indicator of a long-term process of transition of a reversal in trend. As indicated above, the latter hypothesis is gaining ground even among commentators who do not share the view of a definitive decline of unionism.

---

31. J. Visser, 1988 *op. cit.*, p. 151.
32. *See* the various opinions of J. Visser, *op. cit.*, p. 152; T. Treu, *Centralisation and decentralisation in collective bargaining*, Labour, 1987, p. 170ff. For a general overview and the implications for comparative research *see* R. Locke, T. Kochan, and M. Piore, 'Reconceptualizing Comparative Industrial Research', *International Labour Review*, 1995, No. 2.

As to the composition of union membership, there is a relative increase in the number of unionized white-collar workers, due both to their increased presence in industrial unions and to the expansion of occupational unions in the tertiary sector, especially of public services. This trend, not confirmed in the finance sector, is found in countries as different as Belgium, Sweden, and Spain. The growth of unionization among women workers, particularly in northern European countries, is partially related to this phenomenon.

84. As far as forms of trade union Government are concerned, two remarks can be added to the trends already indicated. In the first place, the tendency towards an increase in power of central bodies of trade unions (and employers' associations) seems to have stopped as a result of the growing difficulties in central bilateral or tri-partite neo-corporatist bargaining, even in countries with the longest tradition in this practice (Scandinavia, Germany, and Austria). This phenomenon of de-centraliza-tion, when it does not imply a reduction of union power altogether, has not been counter-balanced by an increased authority of national industrial unions but it seems to favour more de-centralized union structures at the local or enterprise level. Indeed, de-centralization is visible in most aspects of social and economic life and not only in labour relations, again as a response to long-term changes in market conditions.

Significantly, the push toward bargaining de-centralization – favoured by technological change comes predominantly from the employers who have begun to take the initiative in industrial relations as never before. De-centralization goes together with a tendency toward the fragmentation of collective bargaining, even in the German case with the spread of opening clauses,[33] toward the reopening of wage differentials and toward an increasing differentiation of industrial relation patterns.

In the second place, signs of dissent are visible in the attitude of the rank and file towards central leadership, particularly as a reaction to the trade unions' acceptance of wage policies (Italy and Spain), profound industrial restructuring (France, UK) or the practice of concession bargaining (USA). These reactions do not necessarily imply a decreased responsiveness of central union structures, but rather they indicate an obvious problem in the functioning of democratic union procedures and practices.

De-centralization in union (and bargaining) structures may indicate a solution to the problem by increasing the capacity of shop floor members and officers to influ-ence the decision-making process within national unions (as in the Italian case). But it may also reduce the overall cohesiveness of the national organizations and their capacity to control centrifugal factors, in view of solidarity aims. Significantly enough, most labour movements, not only European, are reasserting the importance of keeping or re-gaining some central control in collective action, beginning with collective bargaining. In this effort, they seem still to be supported by some govern-ments and in many countries (like Germany and Italy) also by some sectors of the employers' associations, which appreciate the value of national unions and collec-tive bargaining against an excessive fragmentation of labour relations mainly in industries (like telecommunications and railways) under privatization processes.

---

33. C. Schnabel, 'Collective bargaining under stress: decentralization and opening clauses', *Lavoro e relazioni industriali*, No. 1, 1999.

C. Unions and Workplace Organizations

85. No major structural change has modified the situation of the workplace organization illustrated above. Yet workplace labour relations are more directly affected than other levels of the industrial relations system by the economic and technological challenges. It is precisely at the workplace level that union representation and organization have the most serious problems of initiative and identity.

On the one hand, these difficulties have been related to the reduced scope of economic bargaining, which is a typical 'fuel' for traditional union action at this level; but the re-widening of economic enterprise margins in the last part of the 1980s has not been sufficient to solve the problems; often it has fostered centrifugal trends rather than reinforced the basis of union power within the same enterprises.

Centrifugal pressures have favoured new forms of enterprise unionism or individualism and have fostered divergences between workplace organizations and national unions even in countries with strong central traditions. The increasing factionalism and interunion disputes, mainly in the public sector, recorded in some countries (like Italy and France) have contributed to further weaken union power.

86. On the other hand, management innovative practices in human resources and the increased pressure for greater employee involvement in the joint handling of matters such as industrial re-structuring, organization and technological innovation productivity shares, have found plant union representatives ill-equipped to react.

Management practices and direct employee involvement techniques especially in the European experiences are not *per se* incompatible, according to the research findings on collective action and organization at the plant level; indeed, they may supplement rather than substitute collective labour relations. But much depends on the reaction by the union representatives themselves, beginning precisely at plant level.

It might well be that the dual channel of employee representation proves better able than the single channel to face the diversification of representative tasks within the enterprise, to handle traditional collective bargaining and other forms of worker consultation and participation with different techniques (and people).[34] It is significant that even those countries most dedicated to the single channel, like Italy, are experiencing if not a dual channel at least forms of specialization in union representation at plant level precisely to face new forms of joint consultation and participation which supplement collective bargaining.

D. Forms of Trade Union Actions and Objectives

87. Collective bargaining remains the dominant method of trade union action in developed and some developing countries. However, it faces major obstacles due to the weakening of union organizational power, the resurgence of employers'

---

34. As confirmed by the Report from the Commission on Codetermination of Bertelsmann Foundation and Hans-Böckler Foundation: *The German Model of Codetermination and Cooperative Governance*, Gütersloh, 1998.

initiative, the push to return to market regulation and to allow for a flexible work organization, and the intervention of some governments which tends to limit union bargaining action by some degrees.

The improved economic conditions and consequent opportunities for wage concessions by the enterprises, in the last years, have not restored the effectiveness of collective bargaining to previous levels. It is probable that a period of several decades has now come to an end: the period of continuous development, of collective bargaining based on the acquisition of ever-increasing economic gains for employees and on the rigid regulation of working conditions. Almost everywhere, together with nominal wage flexiblity real wages have stabilized or sometimes decreased (particularly in the first part of the 1980s and early 1990s).

An increasing emphasis is placed on new forms of wages linked in different ways to economic results and therefore, more adaptable to business needs, which is, itself, a challenge to 'normative' collective bargaining.

Similarly, rigid controls on job demarcations and working conditions are either diminishing or being replaced by flexible forms of control, which again test the effectiveness of collective bargaining.

A major innovation has been encouraged by the European unions in collective bargaining objectives: the reduction of working time as a means of defending employment. The major example in this direction is the collective action of Germany's IG Metall to obtain a 35-hour workweek, followed by other unions and also at the European level. The results have been uneven; most often they have been obtained by trading off worktime reduction with flexibility.

88. A second common phenomenon is the slow down or halt, if not the reversal, of a trend towards centralized bargaining, which seemed to be general during the 1970s. In most cases, the pressure for de-centralization comes from the employers, often with government support. Here again, the most obvious signs come from countries which already had a relatively de-centralized bargaining structure: the USA in the first place, and the UK to a large extent. They include the fragmentation of, and increase in, the number of bargaining coordinations or pattern-setting effects.

Difficulties in central bargaining practices due to employer opposition are also reported in countries such as Sweden (1982–1983), which has had the longest tradition in this respect. In Denmark in the 1980s a process of 'centralized decentralization' (took place, favouring the survival of the Nordic model of industrial relations.[35]

This trend toward the de-centralization of bargaining has not cancelled out the role of national collective agreements in most European countries – from Germany and Austria to Italy – where it was firmly established; enterprise bargaining itself has remained largely under the control of national unions. In Japan, which traditionally has a decentralized bargaining system, the practice of setting wage guidelines at the national level, in line with economic prospects, continues to be followed.

Matters like tax reform have been the object of national concern, if not of concerted action, with national trade unions.

---

35. J. Due, J.S. Madsen, C.S. Jensen, and L.K. Petersen, *The Survival of the Danish Model*, Copenhagen, 1994.

The practice and importance of interconfederal bargaining have been more clearly declining during the 1980s. Italy and Spain, two relative latecomers to centralization, are among the few countries where important cases of central bargaining are reported during the 1980s; but it is especially noted in Spain to have reduced content and effectiveness, leading to a general strife between (the then) socialist government and trade unions. But this trend (*see* below) is not so sure in the 1990s. In Italy a very important interconfederal agreement aiming to reform collective bargaining structures was signed in 1993, renewed in 1998. In Spain a tripartite agreement was signed in 1997, under the centre-right government, on the theme of the labour market flexiblity.

89. A decline in the various forms of strike activity, under a general restriction for the essential public services, is also observed everywhere. With the exception of Germany and Belgium the indicator of working days lost is lower for the period 1990–94 than for the previous five years. The difficulties of collective bargaining are not counter-balanced by a renewed vigour of political action or by an increased intensity of various forms of workers' participation.

Whereas in the past decade workers' participation was often intended as a supplement to collective bargaining, now employee consultation and concerted action is often used by management as an alternative to collective bargaining and as a direct form of relationship with the employees outside union channels (USA, Great Britain often following Japanese practices).

Significant exceptions can be found in the Swedish legislation (1983) on worker participation in capital formation (Workers' Funds). The extensive French legislation promoting union rights and worker participation in public and private enterprises have had ambivalent effects.

The present thrust of global competition on 'quality' demands a greater involvement of employees in production and in labour organization.[36] It remains to be seen whether this need will be exploited and interpreted by labour unions or not.

Another critical point is the 'scope' and horizons of labour management participation. A likely prospect is that labour management collaboration will concentrate more and more on the individual enterprise, thereby reducing the links of both parties with their national (or international) constituents.

This possibility, traditionally discarded in the European tradition, has been considered by some commentators[37] as the 'real' alternative to both neoliberalism and neocorporatism. According to these analyses, the basis of new labour relations and social arrangement will be the development of 'community type' commitments within the firm that will foster functional flexibility, productivity and security for the members of this community (outside broader solidarity and social cooperation).

The implications are wide-ranging, not only for the industrial relations systems, but also for the general organization of society and of the welfare state. If the locus of loyalty and solidarity shifts from central entities – nation, region (or class) – to the enterprise, then social and political control over most organizations could be

---

36. D. Sadowski, *op. cit.*
37. R. Dore, *Flexible rigidities: industrial policies and structural adjustment in the Japanese economy*, London, 1986; *Taking Japan Seriously*, London, 1987.

reduced or lost; the unions would change from being actors involved in this control to being junior members of the various firm communities.[38]

E. Politics and Relations with Political Parties

90. In general, the current economic problems have seemed to increase tensions and difficulties in relations between trade unions and pro-labour political parties.

Controversial issues are the attitude towards austerity policies implemented by pro-labour governments and the behaviour with respect to conservative governments. The former is the case, for example, in France at the end of the 1980s and at the beginning of the 1990s and in Italy, where tensions are recurrent among the major confederations originally as consequence of the rapprochement of communist dominated trade unions (CCOO in Spain, CGT in France, CGIL in Italy) with the communist parties (more or less transformed) and the parties' critical attitudes towards the governments, and lately due to the fractionism within the left which has followed the crisis of communism. The latter is the case e.g. of Great Britain and Belgium.

The attempt by the American AFL-CIO to tighten its links with the Democratic Party during the 1984 (and also 1996) presidential campaign does not contradict this trend.

A possible growing influence on or interference by political parties with trade unions is envisaged, parallel to the decline of trade union market power, particularly in those systems where this decline is more pronounced. Moreover, union behaviour and activity are generally more exposed to economic turbulence, which is also due to the reduced protection offered by governments and political actors.

F. Unions and State Intervention in Industrial Relations

91. The types of state intervention in industrial relations basically remain those indicated above (section VII), although a few important changes are noticeable. This does not necessarily hold true in some developing nations where repression of trade union action is the dominant attitude (above VII A).

But a significant exception is the democratic transition of most Latin American countries (Chile, Brazil, Uruguay, etc.) with the consequent democratization of industrial relations.

A most significant and unexpected change has occurred in some centrally planned-economy countries (eastern Europe and the Soviet Union) as part of a general transformation of those political regimes. Beginning with Poland, whose labour movement has also taken the lead in the political arena, the official state-sponsored trade unions of those countries have been first challenged and then substituted by various kinds of autonomous forms of organization. These new unions are also resorting to conflictual action, which was formerly legally excluded. The implication of these changes,

---

38. M. Salvati, *A long cycle on industrial relations or: Regulatory theory and political economy*, Labour 1989, p. 56ff.

although still difficult to evaluate, are wide-ranging and have caused a complete transformation of the labour relations systems of those nations, possibly toward patterns
similar to the Western experience.[39]

Marked changes can be seen in countries corresponding to our models B (Tolerance) and C (Intervention). In Great Britain and the USA, two examples of countries
with a long tradition of *laissez-faire*, the former conservative government and
Republican administration respectively adopted forms of intervention that clearly
restrict trade union action. The Thatcher legislation of the 1980s is the best example.
Something new can be noted with the Clinton Administration and the efforts of the
Labor Department to restore the relations with the trade union movement and also
with the Blair Labour government in Great Britain.

In some countries with a strong tradition of intervention, restriction of control policies tend to prevail over promotion measures. This applies not only to conservative
Governments (Belgium) but also, to some extent, to pro-labour Governments (France,
spain) as well.

Countries with a longer neo-corporatist or cooperative experience seem to be relatively stable. However, the practice of union involvement in tripartite deals on major
economic issues during the 1980s has slowed down[40] on occasion, due either to the
change of political balance in government (Germany, Austria) or to strong employers
opposition (Sweden). Union participation in public administrative institutions remains
solidly entrenched. Remarkable is the favour of the European Union to tripartite practices and policies (confirmed in the Treaty of Amsterdam of 1997). The 'death certifi-
cate' for neo-corporatist agreement was nevertheless prematurely issued: during the
1990s mainly for purposes of adapting national economies to UE Convergence criteria
tripartite agreements came back on the scene (in Ireland, Finland, Spain, Italy, etc.)[41].

92. The models of trade union movements are basically the ones identified in our
conclusions. But the relative positions of the various trade unions with respect to the
most decisive variables (union density, workplace organization, relations with political parties and with the political context) have changed so as more or less to alter
their stability and structure.

Comparative research indicates that the various types of unions have shown a
different capacity of adjustment to the representation crisis of the 1980s, according
to some key variables. The most widely considered are: the mix of centralization and
de-centralization of the industrial relations system and, in particular, of collective bargaining; the capacity of unions to influence and establish alliances with political
actors; and generally the scope of their initiatives with respect both to the employers
and to the political systems.

The unions that have adjusted better are those that have expanded their action
beyond traditional economic and normative negotiation in more than one direction:
toward political action, including some sort of concertation with the State; toward

---

39. *See* various essays on employees' representation in eastern European countries in *Economic and Political Changes in Europe* …, quoted.

40. But was not abandoned: *see* various essays in *Participation in Public Policy-Making*, ed. by T. Treu, Berlin–New York, 1992.

41. J. Grote and P. C. Schmitter, 'The Renaissance of National Corporatism', in *Transfer*, 1999, pp. 34–63.

the enterprise by way of some sort of employee participation, and possibly toward the labour market through participation in manpower policy design and the administration of unemployment benefits (the so-called Ghent system).[42]

This widening of functions helped the unions go beyond the traditional negative motivation in organizing the typical blue-collar industrial workers, and to offer a positive agenda to the expectations of the differentiated and sophisticated working populations of the service industry.

At the same time, it may favour working relations with the State and with the employers by widening the grounds of possible collaboration and trade-off: industrial adjustment, vocational training, smooth introduction of technological innovation, active manpower policies, welfare stabilization, and fiscal policies are some of the grounds on which multifunctional unionism can be a valuable partner for both the State and employers.

These indications seem to confirm that the model of participatory unionism described above may also be better able to face the challenges of the end of the century while more serious difficulties may continue to affect the business unionism models – those heaviest hit by international de-regulation and competition and competitive unionism weakened by the same forces as above; by profound rivalries in the case of organization pluralism; and by restrictive state intervention.

SELECT BIBLIOGRAPHY

R.J. Adams and N.M. Meltz (eds), *Industrial Relations Theory*, Metuchen (N.J.), 1993.

G. Baglioni and C. Crouch (eds), *European Industrial Relations*, London, 1990.

A. Booth, *The Economics of the Trade Union*, Cambridge, 1995.

H.A. Clegg, *Trade Unionism under Collective Bargaining. A Theory Based on the Comparison of Six Countries*, Oxford, 1976.

C. Crouch, *Industrial Relations and European State Traditions*, Oxford, 1993.

J.E. Dølvik, *An Emerging Island? ETUC, Social Dialogue and the Europeanisation of the Trade Unions in the 1990s*, Brussels, 1999.

B. Ebbinghaus and J. Visser, *Trade Unions in Western Europe Since 1945*, London, 2000

A. Ferner and R. Hyman (eds), *Changing Industrial Relations in Europe*, Oxford, 1998.

M. Goldfield, *The Decline of Organized Labour in the United States*, Chigaco (Ill.), 1987

H.C. Katz and O. Darbishire, *Converging Divergences. Worldwide Changes in Employment Systems*, Ithaca (N.Y.), 2000.

---

42. H. Shimada, 'Japanese trade unionism', *Labour and Society*, 1988, p. 220 stresses the need for Japanese unions to expand their capacity of proposal and involvement beyond the level of individual enterprises into the broader area of social policies. For the future R. Hyman suggests four alternative union identities: (i) Unions as service providers; (ii) unions as a partner with firms; (iii) unions as a corporatist partner in social pacts; (iv) the union as a social movement. ('Changing Trade Union Identies and Strategies', in R. Hyman and A. Ferner (eds), *New Frontiers in European Industrial Relations*, Oxford, 1994, pp. 108–139).

M.S. Portella de Castro and A. Wachendorfer (eds), *Sindicalismo y globilización: la dolorosa inserción en un mundo incierto*, Caracas, 1998.

M. Regini (ed.), *The Future of Labour Movements*, London, 1992.

J. Rogers and W. Streeck (eds), *Works Council Consultation, Representation, and Cooperation in Industrial Relations*, Chicago (Ill.), 1995

K. Sisson, *The Management of Collective Bargaining. An International Comparison*, Oxford, 1987.

G. Strauss, D. Gallagher, J. Fiorito (eds), *The State of the Unions*, IRRA Series, Madison (Wis.), 1992.

J. Visser, *In Search of Inclusive Unionism*, Deventer and Boston, 1990.

J. Waddington, R. Hoffman, and J. Lind (eds), *Trade Unions towards The 21st Century*, special issue of 'Transfer' No. 3, 1997.

K.S. Wever and L. Turner (eds), *The Comparative Political Economy of Industrial Relations*, IRRA Series, Madison (Wis.), 1995.

Chapter 20. Forms of Employee Representational Participation

*M. Biagi**

I. INTRODUCTION

1. The subject of this study is a comparative analysis of a number of industrialized market economy countries, with respect to 'representational participation' in the private sector. 'Representational participation' here covers the activities of a variety of councils, committees, sections etc., which share the general function of representing the conflict of interest, real or potential, of workers in their relations with management (and not with other counterparts, e.g. national Governments, local authorities, etc.). This chapter will not discuss direct forms of participation, often initiated by management, ranging from suggestion schemes and team briefings to profit-sharing arrangements, designed basically to improve motivation and efficiency at work. In a broad sense, 'representational participation' refers to the involvement of employees as a collective body in the decision-making process at the workplace or enterprise level, i.e. in micro-economic strategies. Initiatives at Community level, including the 1994 EU directive on European Works Councils, are discussed in chapter 13.

2. The forms of representation found in the different national systems are extremely varied. Moreover, at times, classifications, which are apparently similar (as for example the Italian expression *consigli d'azienda,* an approximate translation of the English 'works councils'), are used to refer to different structures and even to completely divergent functions. All too often in international literature, there are authors who speak of 'works councils' in Germany and in Italy. Apparently, they are unmindful of the fact that linguistic standardization due to universal use of English is not always matched by a similarity of structures and functions, especially where

* The Author wishes to express his gratitude to a number of friends who kindly accepted to offer their views and comments in updating this work: Carmen AGUT GARCIA (University of Castellòn), Marie-France MIALON (University of Paris II), Alan C. NEAL (University of Warwick), Shinya OUCHI (University of Kobe), Marlene SCHMIDT (University of Frankfurt), Michele TIRABOSIRU (University of Modena), Yasuo SUWA (University of Hosei), Manfred WEISS (University of Frankfurt). Needless to say that the Author retains full responsibility for any mistakes or misunderstandings that result from attempting to cover a variety of countries.

prerogatives such as the signing of collective agreements and resorting to industrial action are, in one case ruled out, and in the other, fully legitimate.

3. This complex reality is at times oversimplified, even by the international sources themselves. For example in Article 3 of ILO Convention No. 135, 1971, which relates to the protection of employees' representatives at the level of the undertaking and to the facilities granted to them, the term 'employees' representatives', although defined as 'persons who are recognized as such under national law or practice', is limited to only two forms: trade union representatives, i.e. representatives nominated by trade unions or elected by trade union members, and elected representatives, i.e. freely chosen by rank-and-file workers in an undertaking in accordance with the rules laid down by national legislation or collective agreements and whose functions do not include activities recognized to be the exclusive competence of trade unions in the countries concerned.

4. As well as being oversimplified, the distinction is highly abstract. First of all, it is sometimes difficult to identify functions that are solely and strictly within the competence of the trade unions versus those activities that are reserved for elected representatives. An example is Spain, where both channels of representation (*comités de empresa* and *secciones sindicales*) share bargaining power at the company level. Moreover, the electoral procedures are very often heavily influenced by the trade unions according to legislation or as a matter of practice, as in the French case, where the choice of candidates at the first round of elections for the *comité d'entreprise* is made by the 'representative trade unions'.

5. Workplace representational participation can be analysed from two perspectives, structural and functional. An analysis from the structural perspective focuses upon the structures that operate in the workplace on behalf of the employees, by examining how they are composed and how their members are appointed. The functional analysis focuses upon the type of activity carried out. The analysis will examine the following categories:

(a) bodies directly linked with the trade unions, either because they are an associates (composed of trade union members) or because the selection of a trade union organization results from an electoral procedure. In this case, there is a single-channel system of representation;

(b) bodies which, although in some way linked or affiliated to trade union organizations, operate within a dual channel system of representation;

(c) unitary bodies, i.e. elected by unionized as well as non-unionized workers, and established by law, collective bargaining or practice, at least formally independent of the trade unions, operating in the context of a dualchannel system; and

(d) joint bodies, for the most part not strongly regulated by law, in which there is a combined presence of management and employee representatives.

6. Regarding the functions, that is the type of activity carried out, the analysis will proceed along the following lines:

(a) the right to share information;

(b) the right to be consulted;

(c) the right to decide jointly;
(d) collective bargaining; and
(e) industrial conflict.

7. It should not be overlooked that there may also be specialized forms of shop-floor representational participation. In fact, in various countries, it is possible to observe a certain increase in specialized bodies dealing with productivity, job classification, etc. Among these particular specialized bodies, attention will be given to those appointed, either unilaterally by the workers or on a joint basis together with management representatives, to deal with the protection of the health and safety of employees, also in view of the increasing importance of this matter at EU level.

8. While industry and inter-industry levels of workers' participation are clearly outside the scope of this study, some reference will also be made to the forms of board-level participation, i.e. to models which provide for employee involvement in managerial decision making through the presence of their representatives on managerial bodies.

II. FORMS OF EMPLOYEES GENERAL REPRESENTATION AT THE WORKPLACE:
A STRUCTURAL ANALYSIS

A. *Bodies Directly Linked with Trade Unions in Single-Channel Systems of Representation*

9. Those systems in which the representation of employees in the workplace consists of a single channel linked with trade unions may be placed in this category. Sometimes, however, as for example in Japan, Israel, Denmark and Italy, there are additional joint bodies (i.e. including representatives of the employer), which are regulated by collective bargaining for particular purposes, rather than with general representative functions (see II. D and IV below).

10. The national systems, combining the two elements of the source of the representative power and the effect on the ways in which activities are carried out, may be further subdivided as follows:

(a) a model of selection of trade union representation based on an electoral procedure, where a trade union is recognized as the exclusive agent on the basis of a majority principle (USA, Canada primarily, but also common in the Caribbean, Jamaica, Trinidad, Guyana, and in the Philippines);
(b) a model of selection of trade union representation based on collective bargaining or practice, characterized by a considerable degree of autonomy from the external organization (UK, Denmark, Italy);
(c) a model of enterprise unionism largely independent from external trade union organizations, to which it is formally linked, with designation of representatives on an electoral basis by union members (Japan); and
(d) a model of trade union presence with external appointment of representatives at plant or enterprise level (Sweden, Ireland, and Australia).

11. The first model undoubtedly has certain unique features not to be found, as far as advanced industrialised nations are particularly concerned, outside of North America, with the exception of Israel. But the Israeli system, as will be seen in § 25, the bargaining agent, although selected in ways reminiscent of the North American model, is not the sole agent, thereby, allowing for the presence at the same time of other representative agents with whom the exercise of other functions is shared.

12. It is possible to speak of a North American system, even though the model laid down by US federal legislation, differs in a number of ways from the models accepted by the various Canadian provinces. Characteristic features common to both countries may be listed as follows:

(a) procedure for the certification of the representative agent to avoid the choice being made merely as a result of industrial action;
(b) simultaneous selection of the bargaining agent;
(c) identification of the bargaining unit through an administrative procedure (e.g. the National Labour Relations Board in the United States). In this respect, it should be noted that in Canada the practice of 'agreed-upon-bargaining units' is becoming increasingly common: this means identifying, on a consensual basis, the unit itself. Indeed, for some time now, use has been made of the 'pre-hearing vote', i.e. a ballot which the trade unions are allowed to call before the Labour Board which determines the 'appropriate bargaining unit';
(d) adoption of an electoral mechanism to ascertain whether the majority of workers (employed within the bargaining unit) wish to be represented by a certain trade union;
(e) prohibition of the employer recognizing a minority trade union;
(f) valid elections under the control of administrative bodies (NLRB, Labour Board);
(g) prohibition on recognizing a different representative during the term of a collective agreement, provided that, in the USA, this period is not longer than three years; and
(h) adoption of an electoral mechanism for revoking or at least challenging the position of an exclusive agent (de-certification procedure).

13. The differentiating features must not, however, be overlooked. Among the most important, the following should be mentioned. The first feature relates to the basic prerequisite for the electoral procedure to be set in motion. In the USA, interest must be shown by at least 30 per cent of the workers in the unit, usually in the form of 'authorization cards'. These are declarations signed by individual employees to authorize the trade union to act as their representative. In British Columbia and in Ontario the required number is 40 per cent, in Quebec 35 per cent. Secondly for an election to be valid in Canada, a quorum is required, usually a majority of those, entitled to have vote. Whereas in the USA, valid votes only are taken into consideration, except of the airline and railroad industries. Finally in Canada 'membership evidence' is allowed, i.e. the chance of proving by means of membership that the trade union enjoys a majority status. This is a method generally preferred by the trade unions.

14. This first model is characterized by the fact that once certification as an exclusive agent has been obtained, the trade union acquires a monopoly of representation and an employer who challenges this principle in any way, may be accused of an 'unfair labour practice'. Exceptions are allowed in the USA in the construction industry where, because of the precariousness of employment, employers are permitted to sign collective agreements with trade unions before workers are even hired. The employer may challenge a union's majority status as a bargaining agent by filing a complaint with the NLRB, which may then call an election. In conclusion, one should not forget that primarily as a result of the anti-union managerial culture and also because of this legal framework, over 80 per cent of American employees in the private sector are not represented by a union. As a consequence, their participation is dependent upon the human resource management policies of their employer. Proposals to amend the federal legislation (NLRA) in order at least to provide the establishment of 'employee consultation committees' do not seem to raise any interest outside academic/union circles and may even be unlawful depending on the interpretation of the Wagner Act. In fact, the Dunlop Commission (appointed by President Clinton) recommended that the NLRA be amended to permit the establishment of workplace committees that would participate with manage- ment in the achievement of enhanced productivity and work life quality but would be precluded from engaging in wage and benefit bargaining. The unions did not support this idea but the employers apparently liked it.

15. In the second model, recognition is not necessarily given to a single representative agent but to a body (e.g. a committee) composed by representatives who are possibly linked to different trade unions. In this case, there is usually no legislative framework to regulate the selection process. The rules are, for the most part, determined by the trade unions themselves; otherwise, they may be laid down in collective agreements. It follows that the setting up of this body is voluntary, as the workers may or may not exercise their rights. However, in the case of Denmark, if a collective agreement provides for rules, which can only be applied through an arrangement with shop-stewards, i.e. with the elected representatives, the appointment of these stewards is obligatory. Otherwise, important contractual clauses would be made inoperative, which would contravene the interests of the employer. In this case, it may be said that the trade unions have an obligation to see that representation is set up.

16. Among the various elements, which the three countries in this second group (UK, Denmark, Italy) have in common, perhaps the most important is that shop-floor employee representation is achieved by means of an election, which is then recognized and accredited by the official trade unions. This kind of representation can take a variety of forms and cannot be reduced to a single general model for all three systems. In the case of Denmark, the role of collective bargaining appears to be more important: normally it is stated that the election of the shop-steward will be valid only on condition that a candidate has obtained a qualified majority among those voting. Otherwise, the election has to be held again. In Italy, recent inter-industry-wide arrangements have been concluded by the employers' associations and the three major national union centres to regulate this area (see below § 18).

17. Another common feature is that the *delegates*, in the Italian case, or *shop-stewards*, in the UK, very often drawn from different trade unions, are all active simultaneously at the workplace. In the UK, however, the different unions organize various types of employees. This does not occur in Italy, except in the special case of the *quadri* (middle managerial employees) associations, which have at times obtained employer recognition. This cross-representation is one of the reasons why the number of shop stewards varies greatly. In addition, the number of shop stewards on the size of the groups of workers electing them: they are coordinated in many different ways, depending on the geographical distribution of the company's various work units.

18. In spite of the considerable affinity at a structural level, there is no such standardization from a functional perspective. As regards collective bargaining (see below § 83 on), the Danish *klubber* (in which each shop steward is considered to be in charge) do not in fact have any of the powers exercised by trade unions at local or national level. Similarly, profound differences exist between the British and the Italian situations: in the first case, the whole process of designating representatives is informal, emphasizing the 'dual authority' of the steward as a representative of members at the workplace (actual basis of the steward's power) and also a representative of the external union. In the second case, although no statutory provisions exist for employee participation either at the workplace or board-level, the formal rules are now laid down by collective bargaining. As of 11 June 1995, a national referendum repealed in part the selective mechanism of Art. 19, Act No. 300/1970 (*Statuto dei diritti dei lavoratori*). Previously, RSAs (*rappresentanze sindacali aziendali*, union representatives at the enterprise level) could be established on the initiative of workers in the framework of most representative union confederations at national level. Article 19 survives only in part and presently the status of 'most representative trade union organization' depends only on the fact that it has been able to sign a collective agreement applicable in that work unit. The recognition of the union as bargaining agent by the employer is a pre-condition for the status of most representative trade unions entitled to exercise all rights laid down in Act No. 300/1970 (paid time off, workers' general meetings, etc). In this way, the door is open to enterprise/company unions, which are amicably recognized by employers for bargaining purposes. The destabilizing effect of this solution seems rather obvious. It is equally clear that some criteria for evaluating unions' ability to represent should now be introduced by legislation, but the parliamentary/political debate is still far from reaching a new selective mechanism of trade unions at the workplace level. Nevertheless, it must be underlined that rules on employee representation in the workplace do exist, although provided by agreements binding only the bargaining agents and their membership. In 1993–94, inter-industry-wide 'framework' collective agreements were signed by all employers' associations and the main national union confederations. These agreements now regulate the operation of company-level 'unitary union representation' (*rappresentanze sindacali aziendali* or *RSUs*). RSUs will be elected by secret ballot in the workplace according to a procedure agreed with the employers. All eligible workers will be entitled to vote, including non-union employees. Some 67 per cent of the seats will be assigned proportionately according to the results of the ballot. However, the remaining 33 per cent will be allocated to the above-mentioned union confederations, distributed amongst them on an equal basis to guarantee some form of confederal representation at company level.

19. The Differences between the UK and Italy in this area should not be overestimated. To some extent, the traditional distinction (interventionism vs. voluntarism) in employee representation matters has been superseded by an interesting combination of semi-formal arrangements on which the two systems seem to converge. In particular, in the UK, it is possible to note the contrast between the tradition of employee representation based on the voluntary recognition of trade unions by employers, on one side, and on the other, the legislative provisions recently introduced for the designation of employee representatives for the purposes of information and consultation under two EU directives (i.e. redundancies and transfer of undertakings) where there are no recognized unions. It is true that de-recognition is not a major problem facing the British trade unions. But it is equally clear that new regulations do not require the election of standing employee representatives. In particular, Statutory Instrument 1995, No. 2587 (the response to the European Court of Justice's decision finding the UK in breach of its obligation under the two directives mentioned above, as a result of the failure to provide for the designation of employee representatives where an employer does not agree to it) cannot be considered as a measure effectively promoting employee representational participation. In this context, it is worth stressing the UK Government's reluctance to enact any statutory provision governing the method of election of the employee representatives. The 2000 Employment Relations Act's Statutory trade union recognition procedure, introducing strengthened legal protections against discrimination on the grounds of employee trade union membership or activities, is already influencing employer attitudes. As a consequence, there has been an increase in union recognition agreements. A survey of unions affiliated with the Trade Union Congress (TUC) shows that 34 new union recognition agreements covering 63,500 workers were signed in the period March–November, 1998 – a significant increase on the figures for the previous year's survey when recognition deals covered only 1,383 workers. There were further developments in the area of issue-specific employee representation mechanisms in the absence of union recognition with amendments to the statutory consultation procedure on redundancies and transfers (The Collective Redundancies and Transfer of Undertakings (Protection of Employment) (Amendment) Regulations 1999) and new provision for 'workforce agreements' with non-union employee representatives on parental leave issues (Maternity and Parental Leave Regulations 1999).

20. Among the countries considered, the third model is found in Japan. It is well known under the title of 'enterprise unionism', based on the presence in most cases of a single trade union in the company. This title also means that only workers employed in that company (or in a given internal unit, autonomous enough to have its own separate trade union organization) may join the union. They are associations to which only regular workers (generally employed full-time and for life, under the system of 'life-time employment') may belong, while others (without job security, part-timers, etc.) may not. Enterprise unions ordinarily fulfil two roles: one is to win favourable terms and conditions of employment for their membership through the adversarial process of collective bargaining, the other is to cooperate with employers by participating consultatively in the management of the enterprise to ensure its prosperity and the workers' welfare. It is often the case that a majority of employees are enrolled in the enterprise union, thus achieving a close relationship between the leadership and the members. In a situation in which other trade unions are also present (normally minority unions) they do not share the cooperative attitude of the majority union and adopt a more markedly adversarial ideological approach.

21. The fourth and last model (found in Sweden, Ireland, and Australia) is characterized by a trade union presence in the workplace that is less relevant compared to the preponderant functions carried out by the trade unions outside the enterprise. No electoral machinery is established, but rather there is a sort of hierarchical appointment of representatives within the trade union organization. The choice of trade union representatives in the Swedish case is exclusively in the hands of the respective union. Any union having a member-employee at the workplace has a right to bargain with the employer. The most dominant unions, however, are those, which are signatories to a collective agreement applied to the company (the trade unions are in Swedish called *avtalsbarande*). Such unions are granted a certain privileged status and they benefit from the guarantees laid down by the 1974 Act on the Position of Trade Union Representatives at the Workplace. In Ireland it must be remembered that there are elections for trade unions representatives to the Board of Directors of State and semi-State companies, but no such provision exists for private enterprises.

22. The extremely limited autonomy of trade union activity on the shopfloor, compared to policies decided at a central level, is a feature common also to Australia. The union representative at the shopfloor formally is little more than a link with the trade union structure although in practice sometimes he acts independently (the intensity of unofficial strikes, high in the 1960s and 1970s, then declined markedly in the 1980s and 1990s, is meaningful in this respect). Australian unions have traditionally preferred to use the national industrial tribunals as a method to regulate workplace conditions. However, the expansion of enterprise bargaining during the early 1990s meant that workplace union representatives had greater scope for involvement. Despite this greater scope, not all workplaces were particularly active, and many of the larger unions (e.g. in the metal and building industries) tended to engage in pattern bargaining. Recent surveys conducted in Australia in the early 1990s concluded that there continued to be a low level of union activity in most workplaces and that there was little formal consultation. This feature makes it possible to compare the system with Ireland, but the representative agent is normally elected by unionized employees rather than appointed. However, in Irish State enterprises a ballot of all employees has to be held (on request of at least 15 per cent of the workforce), to determine whether a majority would favour the establishment of sub-board participation. The legislation provides for the drawing up of an agreement between the State enterprise and its employees concerning the specific sub-board participative arrangement to be introduced. Early in 1999, the 'high level group' dealing with the thorny issue of trade union recognition in Ireland formally approved a breakthrough agreement on the issue, which was accepted by the social partners. The agreement retains a voluntarist approach, with the Labour Court issuing legally binding recommendations on recognition only when an employer rejects or deliberately abuses the voluntary process. Consequently, companies have an either/or choice between opting for the voluntary route and rejecting it. In instances where companies reject the voluntary route, a trade union may refer the matter to the Labour Court for a recommendation. Ultimately, the Court cannot issue a legally

490

binding recommendation on employers formally to recognize the union(s) concerned per se, but companies may be compelled to accept the Court's recommendations with respect to pay, procedures and conditions of employment. Further, individual employees will now be entitled to professional representation in instances of disputes or grievances with their employers.

B. Bodies Directly Linked with Trade Unions in Dual Channel Systems of Representation

23. It must be stated at the outset that the expression 'dual-channel systems of representation' used for the purposes of simplification, does not adequately explain the diversity of situations in which employees in a company have more than one representative instrument at their disposal. 'Dual channel' suggests only two means of expression (whereas at times there are more) for carrying out functions perhaps diversified but of equal importance. It is, however, difficult to find a clear division of functions on equal terms between bodies linked with trade unions and those who are directly elected. Even when legislation has tried to achieve this (as in Spain, first with the *Ley del Estatuto de los Trabajadores*, 1980, and later with the *Ley Organica de Libertad Sindical*, 1985), the tendency is still that of the predominance of one form over another, depending on functions and history. A truly 'dual' system does not exist in practice, and it would be better to speak of plural representation consisting of direct forms of trade union presence and employees' representative institutions.

24. The distinction between bodies directly linked with trade unions in the two different contexts (single and dual channel, or single and plural representation) is acceptable because the role they carry out is considerably different. In the first case, the trade unions carry out all the functions and enjoy all the prerogatives granted to employees' representatives. In the second case, they are shared with the elected institutions. In the latter case, the structural analysis must also take the functional factor into account and thus further distinguish between:

(a) trade union bodies performing functions not granted to elected bodies; and
(b) trade union bodies exercising additional functions of assistance or control compared to those granted primarily to elected bodies.

25. Israel, France, Spain, Portugal, and Belgium may be placed in the first group. The situation in Israel has already been mentioned (see § 11 above) in discussing the North American model of exclusive bargaining agent. In the case of Israel, the bargaining agent is exclusive for the purposes of workers' general representation (i.e. without creating a monopoly of representation). However, it is also true that Israeli case law – actually rewriting part of the Act of 1957 on collective bargaining – has introduced the principle that only one organization may represent the workers employed in a particular plant, with certain exceptions. It follows that a 'special' collective agreement (i.e. one signed by just one employer) may be validly agreed on by a trade union authorized to do so by the largest number of employees (but, in any case, not less than one third of those within the scope of application). This authorization may occur taking the number of members into account, or rather the number of

491

authorizations to bargain signed by individuals for this purpose. This arrangement recalls in some ways that of the 'most representative unions' (closer to the Spanish practice than to the French, considering the existence of a mechanism for checking the electoral support enjoyed by the unions). It is by no means a matter of chance that many Acts make reference and assign special powers to the organization representing the largest number of workers in the country, thus, for all intents and purposes, referring to the *Histradrut*, the organization which, in effect, carries out this function also at the company level.

26. In France and Spain, the institutional framework provides for the establishment respectively of the *sections syndicales d'entreprise* (and *délégués syndicaux* if there are more than 50 employees) and of the *secciones sindicales* (and *delegados sindicales* where there are more than 250 employees). They are responsible for workplace bargaining, in a semi-exclusive regime in the first case, and in the second case, together with the *comité de empresa,* and contingent on their ability to rely on a majority of members of the *comisiòn negociadora* (this condition being required for collective agreements binding all workers employed in the plant or enterprise). Both systems grant important powers (including the right to carry out collective bargaining just mentioned) also to trade union sections, even in cases where they can only count on a very small membership. Although with quite different rules, there is a presumption of representativeness in favour of sections affiliated to the (most) representative trade unions. Although the Spanish system, in any case, rewards only those sections set up by unions able to claim an effective electoral *implantaciòn* in the company, giving them the right to trade union delegates who thus retain all the guarantees and privileges granted to the 'unitary institutions' (*comités de empresa, delegados de personal*). In France, many agreements are signed in practice with the elected representatives in the absence of a *sections syndicales d'entreprise*, which is widespread because of the lower rate of unionization (less than 10 per cent). These agreements do not enjoy the status of proper collective agreements, being simply *accords atypiques* governed by the general rules of common law of contracts. It has little consequences in practice, unless they include derogatory provisions. A very strong doubt was cast by an Intersectoral/inter-industry National Collective Agreement of October 31, 1995, which introduced, with the signature of the national unions themselves, a first legally recognized breach in the monopoly of the union delegates to sign collective agreements at the local level in small enterprises. However, this model has been adopted by the French legislation in 1996, 1998 and 2000 in order to support the process of working-time reduction, the transition to a 35-hour week, and in the cases of absence of trade union representation in the workplace. Such negotiation can only take place as a last resort, i.e. where there is no encompassing branch agreement that authorizes the direct application of the worktime reduction, and where there is no labour union representative or authorized employee. The agreement, once signed, must be approved by the majority of the workforce and validated by a labour-management commission at a branch or local level within three months of the approval being given by the workforce. This way of negotiating company agreements reflects the loss of influence, or even distrust, of labour union organizations. This option, to a greater extent even than authorizing employees from the workforce, calls into doubt the role of representative labour union organizations in collective bargaining within companies. In fact, for this hypothesis, the delegated employee is neither appointed as a

labour union representative, nor authorized by a representative labour union organization. It should, however, be remembered that in France delegated employees are proposed by the representative labour union organizations during the first round of the professional elections. During the second round, on the contrary, the elected persons do not necessarily stand as labour unionists. In companies with less than 50 employees, many delegated employees are elected without being labour unionists. It is possible for an agreement relating to work-time reduction to be signed by a delegated employee who was elected during the second round, or at any time in the negotiations, without a representative labour union organization having been involved in any way. Nonetheless, it should be remembered that the agreement negotiated and signed in this way will not become an actual collective work agreement until it has been validated by a labour-management commission at a local or branch level, which is made up of representatives from labour union organizations.

27. While in the Israeli system the mechanism of exclusive representation is accepted (reflecting the semi-institutionalized hegemonic role of *Histadrut*), the French and Spanish systems allow for and encourage trade union pluralism. However, in France, a company-level collective agreement signed even by a 'representative' trade union, automatically binds all the workers (be they non-union or even enrolled in other unions), and thus does not allow for any check on the effective agreement (apart from exceptional cases of 'derogatory' agreements where a right to veto is provided for a dissident trade union organization which, either alone or together with others, obtained more than 50 per cent of the vote in the last trade union election). By comparison, the Spanish legislation is more rigorous in delineating that the *comision negociadora*, at least for the purposes of signing generally binding collective agreements, may indeed consist of a number of trade unions but only when altogether they include the majority of members of the *comité de empresa*. In the case where the *comisiòn* consists of only one trade union delegation, it will not be validly constituted (and the agreement will not have any universally binding effect) if that delegation does not in fact have a sizeable electoral support, including – on its own – the majority of the members of the comité. Whereas the *représentativité d'emprunt* in France works as a *juris et de jure* presumption (indeed, *irréfragable*), in Spain it is undoubtedly much better to speak of a *juris tantum* presumption.

28. In the case of Belgium also, in a framework laid down not by law but by Collective Agreement No. 5, 1971, the 'representative' trade unions (i.e. organizations set up at national level in different sectors of production, represented on the Central Council for the Economy and on the National Labour Council and having at least 50,000 members) have the right to request the setting up of a trade union delegation. Sector/industry-wide agreements will determine the actual conditions for the establishment of a trade union delegation. In the absence of a sector level agreement, conditions can be determined at the level of the individual company. In general, under the No. 5 framework-agreement, to exercise the right to nominate candidates for the appointment or election of the trade union delegation, the 'representative' trade union must be represented on the appropriate Joint Committee of the industry. If this does not occur, the union should at least have representatives who have been elected to the health and safety committee (see below § 101). In the absence of such a committee (if the company employs on average fewer than 50 employees), the 'representative' trade union has to demonstrate that it has recruited at least 10 per cent of unionized employees (the Agreement does not specify how this claim is to be ascertained).

29. The Belgian system is thus very close to those already discussed: it is significant that 10 per cent is the level of *audiencia* required also in Spain (but at national level; 15 per cent at regional level) to qualify as a 'representative' trade union. It must be underlined that, while in Belgium the 10 per cent is related to unionized workers in the enterprise, in Spain the same per centage must be referred to the elected unitary representatives. The Belgian system also requires signs of an effective presence of official trade unions in the company, although it must be stated that the union delegation does not formally represent the trade union (which alone is entitled to sign collective agreements) in relations with the employer. In practice, however, they are closely linked, not only because the delegates are often appointed by the trade union and not elected by the membership as a whole (or in any case selected from lists of candidates chosen by the trade union itself with no place at all for independents), but mainly because revocation of a delegate is allowed during the mandate simply at the request of the sponsoring trade union (i.e. the organization that put forward his/her candidature).

30. In Portugal, it is the Constitution itself (Articles 54–56), which legitimizes a system of dual channel representation, as regulated by law (1975: trade union activity in the company; 1979 *comissoes de trabalhadores*). In spite of this fact, the actual relevance of the *comissoes* is rather limited: out of 150,000 undertakings, only in 380 the *comissoes* have been really set up. In any case, trade unions are increasingly active on matters formally under the competence of the *comissoes*.

31. The second group consists of countries (Germany, Austria, the Netherlands, and Greece) where trade union's presence in the workplace is complementary to the elected institutions (works councils etc.) and takes on functions of initiative and control. The lack of important trade union prerogatives in the workplace was, in the recent past, clear in Germany, where the trade unions could only take the initiative of calling a general meeting of the workers to stimulate the election of a works council. This function, moreover, has not in the past been carried out in a particularly effective way, considering the frequent absence of such councils. Far more important are the so-called control functions at the electoral stage and, in general, the activity of the Betriebsrat, considering above all the right granted to the trade union to make a request to the courts to dissolve the works council if it violates its duties. Furthermore, most of the training courses to which the works council members are entitled (during working time, at the employer's expenses) are offered by trade unions. Thereby, trade unions have a very good opportunity to influence the works council members along their own strategies.

32. The need to resolve (or at least to reduce) this institutional dualism, already reflected in the legislation, emerges above all in day-to-day practice. In Germany, provision is made at the request of at least one-quarter of the members of the *Betriebsrat* or of the majority of a group of workers represented (whether they be blue-collar or white-collar), for an official of a trade union, represented on the council itself, to be able to take part in the meetings. It is necessary, however, to look beyond this formal role to understand the true position of the trade union even when its institutional presence is limited. For example, the German trade unions designate *Vertrauensleute*, 'trusted representatives' or 'trustworthy persons', who are sometimes elected by unionized employees in a particular plant of the company. They serve in the workplace as liaison officers between the membership and the trade union organization as a whole. By contrast, in Austria it is rare to have persons serving this function.

33. In the Netherlands, the absence of organizational forms of trade union activity in the workplace led to a sharp fall in membership and an increase in wildcat strikes in the 1960s. Subsequently, an organizational effort was made to set up and assist groups or units of members in various companies. From the end of the 1960s onwards, trade union activity in companies (*bedrijvenwerk*) was regulated increasingly by collective agreements. More recently (1982), in Greece, the act on the 'democratization of the trade union movement' gave a new stimulus to the workplace level. It is significant, however, that in these countries the trade union presence is not reflected through shop-stewards. The simultaneous presence of works councils elected by non-unionized employees gives rise to a tendency of the trade unions to channel claims and wishes of their membership (and not coming from the rank-and-file). This model also existed in Italy in the 1950s and 60s with the simultaneous presence of *commissioni interne* (elected) and of *sezioni sindacali aziendali* (only associative).

C. Elected Unitary Bodies

34. Dual channel systems are characterized by the coexistence of union representatives with unitary bodies, which may generally be called 'works councils'. These bodies may be classified as 'unitary' because unionized and non-unionized workers elect them. In this way, they obtain a mandate to represent employees across a wide variety of areas and are formally independent of the trade union structure.

35. Historically, this form of representation, – e.g. the German works councils, *Betriebsraete*, which are in many ways the most well-known example – came into being at the instigation of employers to involve the workers in the administration of company welfare institutions, thereby creating a means of cooperation and integration rather than of control over work. Initially, this was a form of representation created as an alternative to the trade union or in any case in competition with it. This, together with the wide representative power (since the right to vote is also given to non-unionized employees), explains the high degree of legal regulation within these councils. They are more often regulated by direct legislative intervention than by recourse to collective agreements, which in general terms, is typical of systems in which the trade union movement is characterized by a rather limited presence in the workplace. Furthermore, this form of representation is rather uncommon in systems where the trade unions are more firmly rooted at the enterprise level (USA, Japan, plus, to some extent, UK and Italy) and where there is greater emphasis on the collective bargaining function than on more directly participatory functions such as

consultation, joint regulation, etc. Moreover, bodies with an electoral basis seem to be favoured under collective bargaining systems, which are centralized or in any case not organized at the level of company bargaining.

36. Even if the works councils' competitive relationship with the trade union form of representation has over time become less intense, and the original anti-trade union plan has practically disappeared, it can still be said in principle that workplace unitary elected bodies have a cooperative relationship with management. This is true also because of a kind of universality of representation, which covers all employees, even those employed in companies that are not large or in any case with a low level of unionisation. Union–employer relations frequently are (e.g. in the United States, but not only there) highly adversarial with the parties often viewing their interests as largely, if not wholly, antagonistic, while works council members (e.g. in Germany) view themselves not so much as adversaries of management, but as co-managers.

37. Industrialized countries with a market economy in which these forms of representation with an electoral basis are present, may be subdivided into two groups, relevant mostly from a legal perspective:

(a) more institutionalized systems, i.e. in which these councils are provided and regulated by law and are often made obligatory; and
(b) less institutionalized systems, in which the setting up of councils is provided and regulated by collective bargaining.

38. The first group includes a number of systems (Germany, Austria, France, Spain, Portugal, Greece, the Netherlands, and Belgium) although there are significant differences between them. The term 'works councils' refers both to bodies in which representatives of management and labour sit together and to committees consisting entirely of employees' representatives. It may be useful at this point of the analysis to consider two countries, France and Belgium, where the two sides are jointly represented. Section II.D (§ 61 et seq.) will be specifically dedicated to joint committees and cover situations with a low degree of legal regulation, sometimes experimental or limited to specific subjects (e.g. new technology, classification of workers, etc.). In other words, in section II.D, single (and not dual) channel systems of representation will be analysed, where these joint committees carry out an ancillary, or even highly specialized role.

39. In the French and the Belgian case, these joint bodies have considerable scope. The French *comités d'entreprise* are chaired by the employer who is part of the committee. In Belgium, however, there is no limit to the number of representatives the employer may nominate (apart from him/herself), as long as the representatives of management in total do not exceed those of the workers. This common feature is directly reflected in the procedure for setting up these bodies on an electoral basis. In fact, in both cases, it is the employer, who is responsible for initiating the establishment of the committee, deciding the date of the election and drawing up the electoral registers. In France, elections have to be called once every two years and, for the particular prerogatives, which the representative unions enjoy, it is the employer who has to invite them to nominate the candidates, at least at the first electoral round. It is still a common characteristic of the two systems that the employer's duty is solely to organize the elections: he is not obliged to guarantee that the representative bodies are actually elected. In fact if the election does not occur, for example, due to the lack of candidates, the employer bears no responsibility but still has not exhausted all his procedural duties. In France, he/she must repeat the procedure after two years or at any request, and in the meantime inform the Labour Inspectorate.

40.   Where the representative body is composed entirely of workers' representatives, the initiative is clearly in their hands. In Greece, Portugal, Spain, and Germany, for example, it is clearly up to the workers to decide whether they want to set up an electoral body: if they decide not to, there are no sanctions against them, even though, in this way, they give up their rights.

41.   With regard to France, the reference made to the *comité d'entreprise* should not underestimate the role played in the workplace by another elected body, the *délégués du personnel*. They act only as employee representatives, presenting individual claims to the employer. The *délégués du personnel* enjoy the powers of the *comité d' enterprise* where it does not exist and where the ceiling of 50 workers is passed. Also, since 1993 in enterprises below 200 employees, the employer may decide, after consulting with the employees that the *délégué du personnel* shall *ex officio* constitute the employee representatives at the *comité d'entreprise*, thus saving an election.

42.   The scope of application of the legislation that regulates the election of these councils, from the point of view of the level of employment required, has been gradually widened in recent years. This may also be noted in the case of legislation regarding single channel systems of representation such as Italy: the limit of 15 employees in each unit of production for setting up *rappresentanze sindacali aziendali* has, on a number of occasions, been lowered by collective bargaining (in the case of artisan firms and the tourist industry, for example, a trade union delegate may be elected even when there are only eight employees). In France, the *délégué de site* is provided for by section L 421-1, § 5, in enterprises under 11 but working together on a same site (even independently and not constituting an economic and social unit).

43.   Whereas Portuguese legislation does not lay down any scope of application with reference to company size, the lowest number for the setting up of a works council is to be found in Austria and Germany. In both cases, just five employees of at least 18 years of age are sufficient. Where there are at least five people below the age of 18, a 'youth delegation' is set up, which in turn nominates a representative to the meetings of the council. Similarly, Spanish law states that in work units between six and ten employees, a delegate may be elected as long as the majority of employees declare that they are in favour of this form of representation. In the Greek case, the 1988 Act distinguishes between situations in which workers are also effectively represented by another body (normally the trade union), and cases in which they are not and the works council is therefore the only form of representation: in the first case, 50 employees are required but in the second (considering the need to ensure representation of some kind) only 20. Perhaps in this respect, Belgium is a case on its own: the comparatively high level of employment required (100 employees) may be explained as a system that, on close inspection, is based on a threefold form of representation. It is significant that where the number of employees falls below 100, the functions of the council are transferred to the health and safety committee, with a kind of merging of representative forms, not therefore depriving the workers of all forms of elected representation.

44. The tendency towards the lowering of the threshold number of employees is well exemplified in the case of the Netherlands, where the 1979 Act was amended in 1981, to set the limit for its application at 35 workers, and in 1986 companies with more than 10 workers were given the right (but not the duty) to set up councils. In any case, at least two meetings a year must be held with management at the request of at least 25 per cent of the employees. Moreover, in France, a *comité d'entreprise* rarely disappears even if the number of employees falls below 50. In fact, not only can collective bargaining provide exceptions to this prerequisite, but also 50 employees for 12 months (not necessarily consecutive) in a three-year period are sufficient to trigger the requirement. This arrangement clarifies a problem (that of the fluctuation over time of the number of employees and of the time period considered in making the calculation) that, in many other systems, is left to occasional and changeable case law.

In addition, even when the number of employees falls below 50, the *comité d'entreprise* does not automatically disappear for that reason. Rather, its survival is guaranteed unless an agreement to abolish it is made between the employer and the representative trade unions present in the company, or unless its abolition is decided by the Director (at a departmental level) of the Office of Labour and Employment, at whose discretion such a decision may be taken for reasons of public order on the grounds of 'important and lasting reductions in the number of workers'. It can be argued that the level of application of 50 employees is not too high since the calculation includes temporary workers, home workers, salespersons, handicapped workers, workers employed abroad and part-timers (as full-time equivalents if they work at least 20 hours a week or 85 hours a month: proportionately to the time worked in other cases). In other countries, the number of workers required is often higher in real terms, because the number of exclusions is greater (typically apprentices and young people working under new contractual forms). The actual number is, therefore, in itself not the significant factor.

45. Another element to bear in mind is that the calculation of the minimum number of employees necessary in the various systems is made with reference to different levels of company organization. For example in France for the election of *the délégués du personnel*, reference is made not to the concept of *entreprise* but to that of *établissement distinct* where at least 11 workers must be employed. In this case, the term 'plant' is relevant from a functional point of view to ensure the greatest possible contact between the delegate and the workers rather than being related to managerial autonomy. This last aspect is, however, decisive for delimiting the enterprise for the election of the *comité*. When the company is subdivided into different technical units (perhaps geographically separate), each of them autonomous, it is in relation to each of these plants (thus defined) that the calculation of 50 employees must take place. Then a *comité central d'entreprise* must parallel at the enterprise level the local *comité d' établissement* in each plant. However, an aggregation of the plants for that purpose may be made through agreement with the representative unions or by order of the departmental Director of Labour and Employment.

46. The French model is particularly interesting for two additional reasons. Firstly legislation has confirmed case law which, in order to avoid artificial and fraudulent subdivision of a company, allows the setting up of a single *comité d'entreprise*, although there may be company units which are legally distinct but part of the same economic and social entity or of the same community of interests. Secondly, a committee must be set up for a group of companies. The importance given to this concept taken from business law has resulted in a different representation of management on the committee: the head of the dominant company (or his/her delegate) and two representatives of the companies in the group, although the latter have a purely consultative role.

47. The refusal to consider the number of employees in relation to the company as a whole is also to be found in the Spanish legislation, which provides for the election of a *comité de empresa* where the *centro de trabajo* employs more than 50 employees. Below this level, but where there are at least between 6 and 10 employees, an election is held for the *delegados de personal*. However, there has to be a single committee when no *centro de trabajo* on its own reaches the threshold of 50 employees but when this number is reached overall in a homogeneous geographical area.

48. Whatever the solution adopted in each country, basing the establishment of employee representation on company size appears to be a common phenomenon that creates a threshold effect within both single and dual channel systems. Employers tend to keep the number of employees below the threshold number, and in any case reduced as much as possible since the level of employment has an influence on the number of members sitting in the representative bodies. This number not only varies considerably from one system to another (in Greece, the maximum is seven representatives, whatever the actual level of employment above 1,000 employees; in the German system, there are 31 between 7,000 and 9,000 employees and there is an increase of two for every 3,000 employees above this figure), but also it is not always permissible for these rules to be modified by collective bargaining, (e.g. in France it is sometimes possible, whereas in Germany this matter cannot be subject of negotiations between the parties). In Spain, the maximum number of members in the *comité de empresa* is 75.

49. One important perspective from which it is possible to infer useful information about relations with trade unions at an institutional level, is concerned with the ways in which workers' representatives are designated. Here again, Belgium and France are the only two countries where the (most) representative unions are granted the exclusive right to choose candidates. In the Belgian system, except in the case of *cadres* (see below § 56), this prerogative is absolute (and, as a consequence, trade union inertia can result in the failure to set up a council), whereas in the French system it applies only to the first electoral round, which is valid when there is a quorum of voters of at least half of those entitled to vote. Otherwise, a second round is held in which candidates may be nominated independently. By contrast, in France, the failure of the trade union to nominate candidates results in calling a single electoral round with candidates independently nominated. In any case the trade union role in France is so decisive that some electoral rules laid down by law may be modified by a pre-electoral agreement (at a company or industry level) signed by the employer and all the 'representative' trade unions.

50. In other countries, there is a mixed system. In Spain and the Netherlands the rules are very similar in the sense that candidates may be nominated by the trade unions or, in the Spanish case, by a group of workers employed in the company at least three times the number of representatives to be elected. In the case of the Netherlands, 30 employees may present lists of candidates or one-third of the total number employed, whichever is lower. The German *Betriebsverfassungsgesetz* has been amended in this respect from 1 January 1989, lowering from ten to five per cent (or from 100 to 50, whichever is lower) the number of signatures necessary for the nomination of candidates. On this point, there are differences both in the Greek legislation (which makes no provisions in this respect) and in the Portuguese one, under which the list must be presented by at least 100 employees or by 10 per cent of permanent workers in the company.

51. Already it may be seen from a structural point of view, how the distinction in the workplace between forms of employees' workplace representation with an electoral basis and those directly connected to trade unions have been overcome because of the control that trade unions are able to exercise over the former. This appears most evident in the systems, where from an historical point of view, there has been the widest experience, Austria, Germany, Belgium, the Netherlands and France. *In the German case, the per centage of unionized members in the Betriebsraete (with reference to the DGB) is around 80 per cent*: a situation not very different from the French, where the independent councillors have reached a level of around 35 per cent. In general, however, relations are far closer than might appear from a consideration of the law itself. Moreover, in Austria an overwhelming majority (98 per cent) of works councillors are union members and they actually represent the union in the company by virtue of rules that are completely internal to the trade union organizations themselves. This does not rule out, however, as in the case of the Netherlands, the possibility that a competitive relationship can develop between the two forms of representational participation.

52. In every system elections are carried out by secret ballot. This standardization is not to be found, however, in relation to the system of electoral constituencies. Whereas in Greece, there is only one electoral unit, in other cases, there is a subdivision (so that each electoral unit elects its own representatives to the works council). In Belgium, blue-collars are separated from white-collars whenever either of the two groups is greater than 25 in a company where the other forms a majority. When the company employs at least 25 young people under the age of 25, there is a separate electoral unit for young employees. This is also the case for *cadres*, where there are at least 15 of them. The Spanish system provides for an analogous subdivision, which allows for the institution of a third electoral unit whenever the particular composition of the employees makes it necessary. In Austria, separate 'section councils' are elected if there are at least five white-collars (*Angestellte*) and five blue-collars (*Arbeiter*). In Germany, however, there is only one council where blue-collar and white-collar workers separately take part in an election of their own representatives in a number reflecting the size of the two groups. However, each of them may decide by majority vote to elect joint representatives. This occurs in over 70 per cent of cases. There is a single electoral unit in France when there are less than 25 employees, whereas two electoral units are formed above this level of employment. In the latter case, there is a new division: on the one hand, *les ouvriers et employés*, on the other, *les ingénieurs, chefs de service, techniciens, agents de maitrise et assimilés* . A third electoral unit may be formed if there are 25 *ingénieurs, chefs de service er cadres administratifs, commerciaux ou techniques assimilés* when the election is called. The French system makes it possible either to increase or to decrease (*college unique*, for instance) the number of electoral units and to modify their composition. The decision is not left to the employees but to an agreement (known as an 'electoral protocol') with all the representative trade unions (any of which may veto the modification of the rules laid down by law).

53. Among the various electoral rules that are significant in this respect, specific mention should be made of two kinds of electoral rights: the right to vote and the right to stand for election. An important element common to all systems (as well as that of giving the right to vote to all workers, even to those not enrolled in a union) consists of a minimum requirement of seniority of service, thus excluding those working intermittently or in any case only for short periods. The French and Belgian systems, for example, both grant the right to vote to workers who have been employed for at least three months (two in the Greek case). In general workers without a permanent job or a full-time contract (often described as 'peripheral employees', an increasing number in all countries) are thus denied certain rights, although not to the same extent in all countries. France excludes temporary workers (i.e. they are not electors in the user company, but are, according to a different count of seniority, in the enterprise of temporary work, which puts them at the disposal of the user). Belgium excludes homeworkers, while Portugal admits only permanent employees. This applies also to the right to stand for election (the minimum length of service required goes up to one year in France and to six months in Spain).

54. The electoral method almost universally adopted is one of proportionality so as to achieve the greatest degree of representativeness. In the Austrian case, according to statutory provisions, the majority vote system is adopted only when fewer than three councillors are to be elected. In Spain too, a modification of the principle of proportionality in its purest form is allowed in that lists of candidates receiving less than five per cent of votes do not obtain any seats. Normally, no exceptions are allowed to these rules. In Greece, however, the law allows a general meeting of the workers to adopt a different system by a two-thirds majority.

55. Works councils are institutions created to ensure stability in relations with the other side, the employer. It is significant that, in some systems, the period for which councillors are elected has been increased to four years as in Austria and Spain. Stability is also ensured, as in the well-tried German system, by the power granted exclusively to the courts to dissolve the council before the end of the period for which it was elected at the request of one-fourth of the workers as well as of the union representatives in the establishment, if the council severely violates its duties. However, some southern European systems provide a much quicker procedure for revocation during the mandate, which is not subject to judicial control. In Spain and Greece, such a decision may be taken simply through a ballot of the workers (by majority vote in an *ad hoc* meeting in the first case, and provided that at least half of those entitled to vote do so in the second). The Austrian staff assembly has the right to discharge the works council from office if half of those entitled to vote are present and a majority of two-thirds is in favour of the dissolution. In the Greek case, the meeting may be called at the request of one-fifth of the workers. France grants significant powers to the representative unions in this case: they have the right to propose the revocation and this is then voted on by secret ballot, not at a general meeting of all the workers but of the electoral unit to which the representatives whose revocation has been requested belong. A majority vote is required for revocation. Obviously, unions can recall only the candidates that they have nominated, not the ones elected at the second ballot or nominated by other unions.

56. It must be mentioned that in at least two countries, Belgium and Germany, there are arrangements to guarantee the representation of particular categories of workers. Since 1990, Germany has a special law guaranteeing a special representative body for the executive staff. Since 1985, the Belgian *cadres* have had the right to elect their own representatives to the works council if there are at least 15 of them. With this innovation, the monopoly of the representative trade unions over the choice of candidates has been broken. Candidates may now be nominated by the *cadres'* own representative unions (as long as at the industry's national level they have at least 10,000 members) or by 10 per cent of the *cadres* employed in the company concerned. Thus, it is possible to nominate independent candidates, even though, in this case, a minimum of five signatures is required to support the nomination, if the overall number of employees in this category is less than 50 (the required number of signatures increases to 10 if there are between 50 and 100 of them). French *cadres*, when they number above 25, may also elect their own representatives.

57. With regard to Germany, mention should be made of the youth representatives, which must be elected if at least five workers below the age of 18 are employed. These youth representatives may call meetings of the young employees, but the relationship with the works councils is predominantly consultative. There is a closer link with the economic committee or *Wirtschaftsausschuss*, provided for in companies with more than 100 employees. All members are nominated by the works council itself. The Betriebsrat also has the right to appoint one of its own councillors as a member of the economic committee. In Germany this committee also has an important role because it meets once a month in the presence of the employer or his/her delegate.

58. The second group identified above (see § 37) includes those countries where the legal regulation of elected bodies is more limited in that it is covered not by legislative intervention (or only to a very small extent) but mainly by collective bargaining. In Israel, Switzerland and Ireland, all employees (unionized or not) elect these bodies by secret ballot according to procedures and rules deriving from agreements at various levels with the employer. These agreements are actually very diverse. For example, the 'workers committees' in Israel have characteristics which make them comparable to British shop-stewards or to Italian delegates, because they represent the trade union in the workplace, although they share that function with other entities identified by the internal statutes of the Histadrut. The same can be said of the Swiss works councils which share the general function of representation with a delegation, which by law industrial workers may set up in the workplace, albeit with extremely limited powers compared to those obtained for the councils through collective bargaining. In Ireland this subject is entirely regulated through collective agreements.

59. It is worth noting, in conclusion, that in the United States, which has a typical single channel system of representation, the exclusive bargaining agent may make an agreement with management for the setting up of bodies as a supplementary channel of information for the workers, e.g. safety committees or quality of working life committees. There are, moreover, case law decisions that have permitted the setting up of alternative forms, such as joint committees in cases where the union has lost certification, as long as these committees do not bargain over wages, hours, terms and conditions of employment. In other words, an agreement between the employer and the employees to set up such a structure, at the initiative of the latter, is not considered an 'unfair labour practice'. Such arrangements, however, are of marginal importance since, for the most part, these committees only concern themselves with shopfloor productivity issues.

60. The panorama of elected unitary bodies is thus not greatly diversified, even considering the structural aspects. The so-called dual system survives by accepting strong control or at least an important influence of an institutional nature by the trade unions over the works council, a way for better fulfilling the indispensable function of representation in a period of union decline. This seems a general tendency, the price paid for an historical evolution, which has led to a differentiation of the two types of representation more at a functional than at a structural level. Although, in countries such as Sweden and Italy this dualism, despite being present for a long period in the post-war years, has been cancelled. Similarly to Italy, Sweden had a type of works council system set up by collective agreement in the late 1940s, but the system was abandoned in the early 1970s after a period of gradual increasing marginalization of the works councils.

D. Joint Bodies

61. Bodies directly linked with trade unions and those with an electoral basis are not the only possible forms of representation in the workplace. The term *works councils* is in fact sometimes used to refer to committees on which both sides sit. Entities of this kind have already been discussed (see § 39 above) with reference to the French and Belgian cases, which were, however, placed in the section dedicated to 'elected unitary bodies' in that they are committees instituted and regulated by law. This section will deal with far less institutionalized systems, where the simultaneous presence of the employer's and of the employees' representatives sometimes takes an experimental form, and at other times is limited to specific subjects (productivity, new technology, classification of workers, etc.). In any case, it does not constitute a characteristic feature of the general system of representation of employees in the workplace.

62. It is significant that these representative forms are not usually to be found in highly institutionalised dual-channel systems of representation (see § 38 above) such as Germany. Or, at least, they are not formalized since the employer and the works council are obliged to meet at least once a month in any case. It is significant that such experiments have occurred where collaboration between the two sides of industry is not institutionalized, as in Ireland and Israel. Whereas in the Irish case the subjects normally dealt with in these bodies do not coincide with those that are issues for collective bargaining, and, certainly not with those that involve questions to do with productivity (partly under the influence of the Irish Productivity Centre). In the Israeli case such a distinction was abandoned after the failure of the 'joint management-labour committees', which were set up by the Hisdadrut in 1957. It must be said, however, that also in this second case, the most active bodies seem to be the 'Joint Production Committees' (introduced in 1952 following an agreement between the Histradrut and the association of industrial manufacturers) whose powers are limited to the improvement of production efficiency without dealing with matters such as wages or working conditions. These committees, consisting of an equal number of representatives on each side, make recommendations (binding since 1967) by majority vote.

63. It seems that systems with representational participation channelled via trade union bodies have favoured this type of experience most, although they are so diversified that it is difficult to compare them. In any case, joint committees of various kinds (but all with essentially consultative functions) tend to emerge as an additional element (with respect to the bargaining function) where the trade unions seem to be deeply rooted in the workplace, yet offer an alternative channel of representation where organization is weak. This remark may be considered relevant to the Danish, British, and Japanese cases even though the first of these differs from the other two in that the 'cooperation committees' derive from a national agreement made on June 9, 1986, between the Confederation of Danish Employers (DA) and the Confederation of Danish Trade Unions (LO), which lays down standard regulations for them. They consist of two groups of representatives (from a minimum of two to a maximum of 12, divided exactly into two parts) designated by management and labour. With regard to this last point, it should be mentioned that the shop-stewards (see § 16 above) are entitled to sit on the committee *ex officio* as full members. This and other aspects (the obligation to hold at least six meetings a year during or outside working hours on full pay) make the Danish case perhaps the closest to the arrangements institutionalized by law which exist in France and Belgium.

64. Also in Italy, collective bargaining is increasingly (but experimentally) producing forms of agreement at company level, which provide for employee participation taking place through joint committees. Highly significant in this respect is the agreement concluded by Zanussi (Italy's second-largest engineering group, employing around 15,000 workers, ultimately owned by Electrolux, the Swedish white goods multinational) and metalworkers' unions. It provides for the establishment of joint bodies (*organismi congiunti*): they will employ majority voting on a wide range of issues previously subject to negotiation, including work organization, new technology, job classifications, health and safety, the working environment, and canteen matters. Joint committees will undertake investigations or enquiries, initiate research, or express views on issues prior to negotiations or formal discussions, but they will be occasionally given 'deliberative functions', i.e. the power to decide. The deal has aroused a great deal of interest as the first agreement on participation in a major private sector corporation, although in (formerly) state owned industry 'bilateral committees' are now an established practice. These bodies may be defined as specialized, distinct but not separate from (so not in opposition to) trade unions generally responsible for collective bargaining, because at company level they are appointed by the *rappresentanze sindacali aziendali* or by the *consigli di fabbrica* themselves.

65. In Japan and the UK, these arrangements are far less regulated. 'Joint consultation committees' perform a particular function which, in the Japanese system of industrial relations, is called *joint consultation*, to distinguish it from collective bargaining. These bodies discuss subjects or questions that employers are reluctant to submit for consideration during bargaining sessions. This is the fundamental reason why such committees are set up, given that they often consist of the same representatives who sit at the bargaining table. The *enterprise union* has the monopoly of the right to choose the employees' representatives but this system is not confined to firms which are organized by trade unions. Furthermore, the joint consultation process, the main type of employee involvement in management decision-making in Japan, has first of all contributed to the smoother introduction of technological innovation and rationalization than management would have been able to achieve without such a process. Secondly (and similarly to the German system of *Mitbestimmung*), unions and managers have been able to gain a better understanding of each other, and so create an atmosphere of cooperation. Finally, management methods have been transformed in recognition of the need for cooperation with the unions, much more aware of the realities of business administration. Also in Britain, *joint consultation committees* can be found, often involved in preliminary (not necessarily alternative) activities to collective bargaining: however such initiatives appear to be superseded by direct communication and involvement (quality circles, briefing sessions, etc.) aimed at providing a relationship between management and individual employees without the mediation of unions (corresponding to a sort of 'temporary derecognition'). This is not surprising since the Japanese experience shows that without mutual trust, joint consultation arrangements cannot work well.

66. In Japan, agreements between management and the enterprise union also often provide for the establishment of works councils. In the majority of cases, councils' members are representatives of the union; in other they are directly elected by employees and in a minority of situations are appointed by the employer. The difference between the two channels tends to be obscure, particularly in cases where works councils are constituted of union representatives. In general, matters concerning working conditions are mainly settled by collective bargaining, while managerial issues, such as new technology or foreign investments, are debated within the works council.

It should be added that board-room participation is not provided by Japanese legislation, but in practice, a great number of former leaders of enterprise unions participate in the managerial organs of enterprises such as boards of directors and auditors.

III. Forms of General Representation of Employees at the Workplace: A Functional Analysis

A. *The Right to Share Information*

67. The analysis of the various functions will be carried out without aiming to deal in full with matters that are dealt with elsewhere in this textbook, but only in order to show the powers that are granted by the different systems to the various bodies which represent workers in the workplace, regardless of their name or composition.

68. In this respect, the Swedish case seems to be indicative of a recent tendency to grant the right to receive information to bodies linked with trade unions, thus progressing beyond an earlier stage in which the main beneficiaries were elected bodies. In fact, the phase beginning with the agreement in 1946 between the two major trade union organizations (LO and TCO) and the employers' organization (SAF) proved to be widely unsatisfactory and not even the new agreements of 1966 and 1975 managed to halt the irreversible decline of elected bodies, although they were the first to have the right to receive information. In 1976 with the passing of the 'Joint regulation of Working Life Act', both sides were placed under an obligation to provide documentation related to bargaining. This obligation to produce documents applies to all those having a general obligation to negotiate, and therefore, extends to trade unions not yet committed to the other side in a contractual relationship, in other words, not qualifying as 'established unions'.

69. Legislation is undoubtedly, the source that most commonly regulates the question of the right to receive information, also specifying which employees' representative bodies may benefit from it. In Great Britain, the Trade Union and Labour Relations (Consolidation) Act 1992 lays down such a right (previously contained in the Employment Protection Act 1975), but it is very narrow in its scope and subject to significant limitations. As already pointed out at § 19, in response to the European Court of Justice's rulings of 1994, the UK Government has issued the Collective Redundancies and Transfer of Undertakings (Protection of Employment) (Amendment) Regulations 1995, which are applicable to dismissals and transfers taking place from 1 March 1996. This instrument has considerably widened information rights in these matters (see also below § 74). Sometimes the legal provision is explained by the fact that information is granted to the representative responsible for collective bargaining, possibly in an exclusive manner as in the USA, and with whom the employer has a duty to negotiate.

70. It is significant that in France the right to share information is not granted solely to the *comité d'entreprise*, a typical form of management – labour collaboration (where, moreover, the information itself concerns not so much the future as the past of

the company), but also to the bargaining agent, the *délégués syndicaux*, who not only has as much right to receive the *bilan social* as the *comité*, but who can utilize additional prerogatives with regard to typical bargaining matters such as working hours and wages. Furthermore, the *comité d'entreprise* has the right to appoint its own expert accountant at the company's expense. Similarly, for work units with 250 or more employees in Spain, the right to share information held by the *comité de empresa* is recognized as equal to that granted to the *delegados sindicales*.

71.   However, in many systems information is made available by the employer to bodies that do not carry out (or only partly carry out) bargaining functions. The German case is one example where, in this matter, the role of the 'committee for economic affairs' appears to be primary, since management must inform it in good time about all economic aspects (the economic and financial situation of the company, production and marketing figures, production and investment programmes, introduction of new production methods, total or partial closure of plants, company transfer, mergers, changes in company organization, etc.). Disclosure of information is also granted to elected bodies in Belgium, the Netherlands and Portugal.

72.   The effectiveness of this function does depend only on whether it is provided for by law. In Italy, where the matter is also covered by collective bargaining, in medium-sized and large companies the exercise of the information function (or the control function, as the unions prefer to call it) is of great importance. It is far less important for smaller companies, for which Italian collective agreements allow negotiations to take place outside the company at a local level between the employers' associations and trade unions.

73.   The success of this function also depends on the subjects dealt with and this in turn gives rise to structures for various purposes. Ranging from social to economic and financial questions, the German system provides for the setting up of a specialized committee in companies with more than 100 employees, with very wide powers. Similarly, companies in France with more than 1000 employees must set up a specialized committee for economic questions, although this committee has fewer powers than the German analogue. The tendency to evolve towards qualitatively different information is also found in more recent systems such as the Spanish, where the law grants both to the *comité de empresa* and to the *delegados de personal* the right to be briefed on company accounts and to receive all the information given to the shareholders of a joint-stock company (identical to the rule existing in Denmark regarding the internal functioning of the 'cooperation committees'). In Portugal too, the 1979 Act has granted employees' representative bodies powers not only concerning social matters but also related to financial issues.

B.   The Right to be Consulted

74.   The scope of this consultative function is so diverse in the various systems that it may be considered simplistic to speak of a single function. It will, therefore, be necessary at least to keep Japanese 'joint consultation' apart from the procedures generally used in European countries. In the Japanese case, it is mainly the enterprise

union that exercises this function, which is often difficult to distinguish from collective bargaining. It is, in any case, by negotiation and not by legislative means that joint consultation bodies are set up, even where there is no trade union organization. Even though, unlike collective bargaining, it is not obligatory, joint consultation has now emerged as the most important channel of communication between management and labour, perhaps constituting the most characteristic feature of the spirit of enterprise unionism. Furthermore, the British case demonstrates that a legislative intervention in the area of consultation does not always correspond to an improvement in terms of cooperation in employer–employee relationships. As already mentioned (see above §§ 19, 65, 69), in response to European Court of Justice's rulings, the UK government has extended information and consultation rights in the event of redundancies and business transfers to workplaces without a recognized trade union. However, the employer may now consult 'employee representatives' even if he recognizes a union. In other words, in situations where no trade union is recognized, the employer must now consult *ad hoc* elected 'employee representatives'. If a union is recognized, it seems to be up to the employer whether to consult representatives of the union, or instead to consult elected 'employee representatives'. A potential 'deregulatory' effect appears to be inherent into new regulation, with a possible detrimental impact on labour–management relations at company level.

75. In other systems, collective bargaining regulates forms of consultation, which trade unions control through the setting up of joint committees. This is the case of Danish 'joint cooperation committees', of analogous committees existing in Ireland and of the advanced forms of participation emerging in former state-controlled companies in Italy over the past few years. In all these cases, these bodies are linked to trade unions, which directly or indirectly appoint their own representatives with highly regulated procedures.

76. In the sense of a formalized procedure provided for by law, consisting of an obligation on the part of the employer to request an opinion before taking certain decisions, the consultative function is generally the concern of representative bodies with an electoral basis. A particularly interesting case in this respect is that of the Netherlands. In this system, it is possible that the employer faces two kinds of consultative obligations: the first, with regard to the trade unions, is laid down by collective agreements negotiated with them, the second is provided by law with regard to works councils. The employer must seriously take into account the opinion of the council, otherwise, the council itself may appeal to the Chamber of Undertakings (*Ondernemingskamer*) of the Court of Justice in Amsterdam. In fact, according to statute, a Dutch employer has the duty to consult the works council on some 'important' economic decisions he/she wishes to take. If, however, such a decision (changes in the organization, takeovers, mergers, financial actions, etc.) leads to the dismissal of more than 20 employees, the employer also has the duty (based again on statute) to consult the trade unions. If there are provisions in collective agreements obliging the employer to inform the trade unions on any economic decisions, he/she has the statutory duty to inform the works council as well as the contractual duty to inform the trade unions. Clearly this system of consultation can represent a considerable burden for the employer and a potential source of confusion caused by the ambiguous term 'important' economic decisions.

77. In countries with dual channel representation, where the consultative function is entrusted exclusively to representative bodies (Germany, France, Greece, and Portugal), this common feature should not obscure the notable differences that exist with regard to the extent of this right. In the Greek case, in fact, the law expressly mentions collective dismissals and makes generic reference to other cases provided for by special laws, whereas consultation regulated by Portuguese legislation concerns matters which in many other systems are dealt with by collective bargaining such as holidays, work organization, the classification of personnel and so on. Portuguese works councils also have a *direito ao exercício de controlo de gestao*, granted to allow them to ensure that the company 'adequately utilizes its technical, financial and human resources (especially in the processes of company reorganization and restructuring), which is essentially of a consultative kind of nature, never developing into a real power of joint regulation or of veto with regard to the employer's decision.

78. Together with the Dutch case referred to above, the systems where the consultative function appears to be most effective are undoubtedly the German and the French ones. Without consulting the *Betriebsrat* beforehand, a German employer cannot, for example, validly dismiss an employee. Moreover, since 1972 the law has strengthened a system of obligatory consultation concerning the implications for working conditions when new technology is introduced: the documentation supplied by the employer must enable the council to express an opinion in time for it to be taken into consideration at a decision-making stage. The *comité d'entreprise* also has a consultative function, which is clearly distinguished both from simple information and from collective bargaining, although it is often formal and little used in SMEs. Moreover, at least in legislative terms, it appears to be the only representative body having a power of what may be called 'active initiative', that *droit d'alerte*, which may be exercised when the committee learns of facts '*de nature à affecter de manière préoccupante la situation économique de l' entreprise*'. This is a prerogative of considerable significance given that, in cases where the justifications used by the employer at the request of the committee (which acts in its capacity of representative of the employees) are insufficient or confirm the state of danger, a report may be written, if necessary, with the help of an expert in business administration: this report is sent to the appropriate judicial authority. This is an interesting example of involvement of employees' representative bodies outside the area of labour law in a sphere typical of company law. In any case, the consultation of the committee is in no way binding for the employer.

C. The Right to Decide Jointly

79. This expression is used to refer not so much to board level participation (see below § 112 on) as to the advanced form of representational participation in the workplace through bodies which in certain matters have prerogatives at their disposal to make management take decisions only with their agreement. The right to this function (which unlike the others is found only in a few of the systems considered) seems for the most part to be held by unitary elected bodies and (in dual channel systems) not by bodies linked with trade unions, which are generally responsible for collective bargaining.

80. The division of forms of representation and correspondingly of functions, is particularly clear in Germany and Austria. The law lists the subjects for which a right of *Mitbestimmung* exists, as long as the specific matter considered has not been regulated by law or by collective agreement. In both cases the prerogatives concerning the management of personnel in a narrow sense are not very great, being covered by the area of collective bargaining, even though the right of *Mitbestimmung* is really advanced in so far as it concerns professional training. Briefly, the joint regulation exercised in the workplace by the *Betriebsrat*, mainly concerns so-called social affairs, meaning the social consequences of economic decisions thus excluding the economic/commercial area. In any case, the catalogue of subjects and matters referring to the right of co-determination is not so important. The mere fact that the co-determination is provided (even if only for a limited number of subject matters) explains the powerful and influential role of the *Betriebsrat*. In view of the mere possibility of co-determination, management tries to establish good relations with the *Betriebsrat*. This means that even in areas where according to the law the position of the *Betriebsrat* is weak, management tends to be generously open, increasing the real power of the works council.

81. In the Dutch case there is an analogous legislative provision that obliges the employer to reach a consensus before taking decisions in what is known as the social policy of the company (pension plans, working hours, health and safety, hiring, dismissals, etc.). The same applies in Greece with reference to internal company regulations, information programmes regarding new technology, continuing and professional training for employees, and other matters including cultural, recreational and social activities. However, in both cases, it is the legislation on works councils which lays down that such powers of joint regulation shall not apply if the matter is already regulated by collective agreement, thus resolving a potential conflict with the trade unions. In the French system there is no risk of such conflict, because the right to joint regulation of the *comité d'entreprise* only regards the choice (and dismissal) of the factory medical officer and the introduction of flexitime, which the committee may veto. The joint regulation rights of the committee also include the mandatory vote on the dismissal of employee representatives (from which the employer must abstain). In Sweden, the 1976 Act provides for a veto right for the established central trade union when the employer contemplates to let outside contract labour perform work in his activity or on his behalf. The veto right may be exercised if the employer's action threatens violation of either the law or the collective agreement. The veto right was abolished by the non-socialist Government in 1993, but was reintroduced by the socialist Government when it returned to power in 1994.

82. Aside from these formalized systems, i.e., regulated by legislation, there are situations where collective bargaining plays a role in establishing rules regarding joint regulation. In this context, the function of the trade unions is far more important. Therefore, there is no standard model, but the rules considered to be most appropriate are agreed upon during each specific occasion depending on the matters to be dealt with and the actual powers exercised. In Sweden, it is the Joint Regulation of Working Life Act, 1976, which assigns the making of such agreements to the trade unions who are thus responsible for operating them. In Switzerland, the most important collective agreements at the national level delegate to the works councils the right to take part in the company decision-making procedure. This participation of the works councils is termed (perhaps in too wide a sense) 'joint regulation'.

D. Collective Bargaining

83. The expression *collective bargaining* does not always refer to the same phenomenon, nor to a function carried out by the same entities in the workplace. In fact, in some systems such as Germany or Greece, where the employer may not take decisions with regard to certain matters except with the prior consent of the works council, agreements are formalised by means of written accords. These, however, are not considered technically to be collective agreements, even if it is clear that bargaining activity takes place, as in the German case, which in this respect precisely expresses the idea of *Mitbestimmung*.

84. Quite a different matter, still with reference to the German case, are *the freiwillige Betriebsvereinbarungen* (voluntary works agreements). While these agreements are not in principle designed to regulate items dealt with in collective agreements (strictly speaking, those items agreed to by unions, primarily at industry level in the various regions) or in statutory provisions, in practice often end up regulating matters closely related to wages and working conditions. Moreover, the *Betriebsrat* may negotiate the *Sozialplan* (social compensation plan) with the employer to minimize the disadvantages, which may be faced by employees as a result of certain important decisions (reduction of productive activity, plant closure, etc.).

85. The growing tendency towards agreements with elected unitary bodies is also to be observed in other systems. In Israel, for example, the 'workers' committees' are not entitled by the constitution of the Histadrut, to make collective agreements, because these committees are not workers' organizations in a technical sense. They do, however, sign documents which are of some importance to relations with management. In France, it is even specified by law that *accords de participation* as well as the *accords d'intéressement à la productivité* may also be made within the *comité d'entreprise*. This is clearly an exceptional provision, even if in case law there has been debate about the validity (at least in certain cases) of *the accords d'entreprise atypiques*, made with unitary elected bodies, contravening the bargaining monopoly of the trade unions (see § 26 above).

86. The informality (and, at least to some extent, the anomaly) of agreements made at the company level also characterises systems with a very weak trade union presence in the workplace. In Australia nevertheless what may be considered bargaining activity does exist. The system of compulsory arbitration works in such a way that the arbitrators simply specify minimum conditions and do not make provision for a maximum, especially in wage matters. Therefore, 'agreements on over-award payments' tend to emerge, clearly showing the complexity of the Australian system of collective bargaining. These agreements are often the outcome of activity coming directly from rank-and-file union members and are aimed at filling the vacuum left by the weak organization of trade unions at company level, which concentrate their energies on legal procedures for the settlement of labour disputes. Such agreements have subsequently been supported by the unions themselves, sometimes, also with the assistance and the blessing (but not the legal recognition) of case law decisions, creating an element of harmonization in labour relations at workplace level. These over-award agreements supplement the arbitrators' award without taking its place. This form of direct collective bargaining often arises from the need to settle company disputes, which are frequently solved by means of arrangements not formally registered or recognized by law partly because they are only rarely put down in writing. In the first half of the 1990s, the bargaining system in Australia has become more complex, especially with the growth of enterprise bargaining. Direct bargaining and formal agreements are now more common.

87.   In order to speak of collective bargaining properly at the workplace level, it seems that the bargaining agent must have the power to resort to industrial conflict. In this sense, this function is generally within the jurisdiction of trade unions or in any case of forms of representation directly linked with them, as occurs, for example in Portugal. While in Germany bargaining activity technically speaking takes place outside the company, in other similar systems with a dual channel of representation, a certain amount of collective bargaining in the workplace is recognized. In France, the *délégués syndicaux* hold a *de jure* monopoly on the power to make agreements that are generally binding on all the workers employed in a company. This power confirms the negotiating competence of the representative trade unions in that they act as their own representatives and not on behalf of the trade union section, which, as such, is not a legal entity. It may be useful to mention, in this respect, that since 1982 the employer has been under a legal obligation to bargain, at least once a year, on wages and working conditions with the trade unions regarded as 'representative' in the enterprise. It should be pointed out that enterprise or plant level agreements dealing with matters other than yearly wage adjustment are few and that the sectoral level remains dominant. However, the recent legislation on working-time reduction (see § 27) has played a decisive role in relaunching the collective bargaining process.

88.   This is not the case, however, in Belgium, where the trade union delegation only represents the members employed in a company and not the (most representative) trade union as an organization, which according to the 1968 Act has the exclusive right to make universally binding collective agreements. Arrangements made by the delegation may, at most, be made binding and effective according to the general rules of civil law, on the basis of custom and practice. This model is not far removed from the Portuguese one, where, in a similar way, trade union delegates do not have the power to conclude collective agreements, granted by the 1979 Act to the trade unions, even though they are increasingly given the right to take part in establishing working conditions, thus bringing them closer to real bargaining power. In both countries, however, trade union delegates have the prerogative to control the application of collective agreements and, more generally, to carry out a function of inspection or control of the rules affecting labour relations.

89.   At times, the bargaining function is placed within a wider right to influence the exercise of the most important management rights, as occurs in the Swedish case within the framework of the system of 'joint regulation', as introduced by the 1976 Act. In this context, two rights to collective bargaining may be distinguished. The

first, which may be defined as a 'general' right to negotiate, is granted to all trade unions having at least one member among the employees. This general right encompasses all matters relating to the employment relationship between the employer and the members of that union. The second right is granted to organizations already having a contractual relationship with the employer and concerns any case in which there is a notable change in the employer's activity or in the organization and conditions of work. Only where there are reasons for particular urgency is the employer allowed to implement decisions of this kind before having satisfied the obligation to negotiate. More generally, the *established unions* have the right to negotiate whenever the employer plans to adopt or implement a decision concerning a member of such organizations, except once again, in particularly urgent cases. Where negotiating activity does not lead to the signing of a 'joint regulation agreement' (*medbestammandeavtal*), the trade union is still granted a 'residual right to direct industrial action'. The employer's primary duty to initiate negotiations of the 1976 Act was amended in 1994 to comply with the requirements set forth in the EC directives 77/187 and 75/129. In essence, if the employer is not bound by any collective agreement, he must initiate negotiations with every trade union having a member employed at the workplace (thus, similar to the general duty to bargain) in relation to redundancies and transfer of undertakings.

90. But perhaps the most important trade union right recognized in Swedish enterprises is the 'priority of interpretation' when a disagreement occurs regarding the meaning to be given to a legislative or collectively agreed provision, provided that these rights arise from the system of 'joint regulation' or from individual workers' duties (e.g. regarding overtime). Disputes of wages are treated in a similar way inasmuch as the employer has the burden to carry the dispute to the Court for final adjudication if the union stand is not unreasonable. In practice, this provision has turned out to be the most useful one for the unions. The 'priority of interpretation' means that, until a dispute is settled definitely, the interpretation supported by the trade union will prevail. A refusal on the part of the employer will make him/her liable to legal action for damages even if the courts rule that the employer's point of view was correct. This arrangement is based on the Swedish legislative policy that the employer should pay for the costs of trade union activity in the workplace and that the 'established unions' carry out an important function in the company. The arrangement seems also to foster the social partners' continuous dialogue, which is the general basis for the joint regulation scheme laid out by the 1976 Act.

91. Aside from the Spanish case, which uniquely allows for the *dualidad de legitimaciòn*, granting bargaining powers both to the elected unitary body (the *comité de empresa*) and to entities with direct trade union affiliation such as the *secciones sindicales*, the bargaining function in the workplace is normally delegated to bodies directly linked to trade unions. Moreover, even in the Spanish case, there does seem to be a difference between the two forms of representation. In fact, when a collective agreement aimed at regulating the conditions of all the workers in a company is under discussion, the law states that the *secciones sindicales* must have a majority of members of the *comité de empresa*. This close intertwining is also to be found, albeit in a different manner, in Austria where the 1973 Act, while stating that the works council must act in agreement with the employees' organizations, requires

that one-quarter of the councillors may at the same time be members of the executive committee of the trade union.

92. In cases in which the bargaining function is carried out by shop-stewards or similar representatives, there is always the problem of the ill-defined relationship with the trade unions. This is the case, for example, in the UK (where the situation is often complicated by the simultaneous presence of a number of unions representing different sectors of the workforce except where *single-union agreements* have been made) and also, in Ireland and in Greece. Similarly, in Italy, collective agreements at the company level are made by the *rappresentanze sindacali unitarie* with the assistance of the relevant trade unions at the provincial level who are, therefore, present with their own representatives in the national delegation. In Denmark the *klubber* do not have the right to make collective agreements even if such agreements are considered to be signed by the trade unions when made, as if the *klubber* (and whoever in turn represents them) had acted on their behalf.

93. Naturally, these problems of identification of the bargaining agent at the company level take a different form in Japan where the enterprise union is granted the right to carry out all the functions (which are often difficult to distinguish), including collective bargaining and joint consultation. The fact that the Constitution itself recognizes the right to collective bargaining sometimes gives rise to the problem of particularly acute 'rival unionism' (a majority enterprise union of a basically cooperative type *vis-à-vis* management challenged by a minority union with radical policies, often having broken away from the majority). However, case law decisions (provided that the employer acted in good faith during negotiations, attempting to persuade the minority union to accept the agreement made by the majority union) allow for different conditions for employees enrolled in different unions as a result of different negotiating strategies. Aside from this, there are also other questions relating to the identification of the bargaining agent in Japan, e.g. the autonomy of different internal units of the company and, therefore, the possibility that bargaining activity may be carried out by rival unions set up in individual units of a company with the power to sign separate agreements. Whether this is actually the case or whether there are different organizational units of the same enterprise is a delicate question that must be resolved on a case by case basis.

94. In terms of entitlement to the bargaining function there can be little doubt in those systems that apply the 'majority rule': the United States and Canada. Rather, in these contexts, the monopoly of representation is so strong and marked as to leave no room for employees to negotiate even at an individual level to obtain better conditions than those laid down by collective agreements. But also in the case of Israel, at least with reference to special collective agreements (i.e. made by only one employer), a sole union agent is appointed to accept the responsibility for this function.

E. Industrial Conflict

95. Obviously, in those systems where the right to strike is held by individuals, the analysis of the conflictual function for the purposes of identifying the forms of employee representational participation in the workplace is rather limited. The functional perspective is considered here only for the purposes of examining the different forms of representation described above within a structural perspective.

96. It should be mentioned, however, that in a system which in other ways is very similar to France and Italy, such as Spain, there is provision for the creation of a special form of representation, the *comité de huelga*. This committee (formed according to legislation limiting it to no more than 12 members), is responsible for activating the means of resolving disputes, including those of a legal – administrative type, as well as having the duty to negotiate with the employer to reach an agreement. Finally, it also has the duty to guarantee the *servicios de seguridad* during strikes.

97. Even in systems (above all in the UK) in which recourse to strike action is not accepted as a positive right, the relevant issue has less to do with forms of representation of employees authorized to call industrial action and more to do with the distinction between 'official action' and 'unofficial strikes'. The official statistics for 1998 indicate that strike activity in the UK remains at its lowest level since records began in 1891. The number of recorded disputes was the smallest ever and the number of workers involved was the fewest for 70 years.

98. There are also systems where the distribution of functions between employees' representative bodies prevents some of them from resorting to industrial action in that they are granted other powers (consultation, joint determination, etc.) which tend to favour the development of a collaborative relationship with the employer. This is true of Germany where the *Betriebsrat* is forbidden to carry out any disruptive activity in the company, even though its members may, as individuals, participate in strikes called legitimately by the unions following a ballot procedure.

99. In Germany, strikes not called by the trade unions are forbidden, and interestingly the conflictual function is, in the same way as the bargaining one, granted only to trade union bodies. Moreover, strikes are legal only in the context of collective bargaining. In Japan trade union monopoly is even more marked. In fact, in order to be able to benefit from legal indemnity, employees (to whom the Constitution grants the 'right to act collectively') must only take part in strikes called by the trade union in which they are enrolled. Japanese case law seems tolerant with a trade union which calls a strike without respecting its own internal statute (e.g. not holding a ballot among its members). However, case law does not appear accept wildcat strikes at all, meaning those made by some of the members without ratification by the trade union, in as much as such a group of employees cannot be considered to be a party to a collective agreement. Despite current case law, the Japanese Supreme Court has not ruled on the issue of wildcat strikes, and scholars are strongly divided on this issue.

100. The North American system (USA and Canada) is not the only one in which 'majority rule' and 'exclusive representation' mean that, in most instances any form of industrial action must be called by the bargaining agent and will have legal protection only if it is approved or later ratified by this agent. It may be noted that in

Portugal, the general rule according to the 1977 Act is that recourse to strike action is the exclusive prerogative of trade unions provided that a majority of employees in a company are represented by them. Otherwise, they loose this monopoly and employees may decide on the matter autonomously during a general meeting called for the purpose at the request of either 20 per cent or 200 of them. In Israel, the 1957 Act provides that 15 days' notice must be given by the trade union that signed the collective agreement (after the employees have expressed their view in a secret ballot). If there is no representation, the workers may appoint an *ad hoc* committee.

IV. 'SPECIALIZED' FORMS OF WORKPLACE EMPLOYEE REPRESENTATION:
HEALTH AND SAFETY AT WORK

101. As already noted (see § 6 above) there are a number of other bodies with specialized functions representing employees in the workplace, particularly joint committees (see § 61 on). Undoubtedly, further attention should be given to those bodies responsible for the health and safety of employees and which often deal more generally with all problems arising from the working environment. In consideration of the EU directives adopted on this matter, the following is an attempt to identify certain models.

102. The first model includes those systems in which general representative bodies of the employees with an electoral basis provided for by law also carry out functions concerning safety. In the case of Germany, important prerogatives in this matter are granted directly to the *Betriebsraete*, although there is also provision for the appointment of workers' representatives on safety matters (*Sicherheitsbeauftragte*) by the employer in consultation with the *Betriebsraete*. In firms where there is a company medical officer or a security expert, a work safety committee (*Arbeitsschutzausschuss*) must be set up including two members of the *Betriebsrat*. Similarly, in Austria a work safety committee (*Arbeitsschtzausschuss*) has to be set up by management in agreement with the *Betriebsrat* when at least 11 workers are employed. However, in companies of up to 50 employees, tasks and responsibilities of the *Arbeitsschutzausschuss* may be transferred to the *Betriebsrat* (actually to one of its members). Similarly, recent legislation in Greece gives power in this matter both to the members of representative councils and to specialized health and safety committees, in both cases elected by the rank-and-file employees. Even more relevant than this first model is the case of the Netherlands, where direct powers in safety matters are granted to employee representative councils, which must be set up in companies where there are at least 100 employees.

103. A second model may be identified with reference to those systems where powers concerning safety at work are devolved to specialized committees even though the creation of such bodies with an electoral basis is provided for by law or by collective agreement. France and Belgium are mainly identified with this model. In both countries, in companies with more than 50 employees, the creation of *comités d' hygiène, de securité et des conditions de travail*, CHSCT in the French abbreviation, is compulsory. Whereas the Belgian system provides for the election of workers' representatives every four years from a list of candidates presented by the representative trade unions, in France, an indirect mechanism is applied in that representatives are designated by the employees' representatives on the *comités d'entreprise* as well as by the *délégués du personnel*. The CHSCT also includes *ex officio* non elected members, such as the company physician, when there is one. In small companies with fewer than 50 employees, the work safety function is carried out by union delegates in Belgium, and by *délégués du personnel* in France, thus, eliminating the division by specialisation of the representative bodies. Spain may also be included in this model, since legislation (Act No. 31/1995) provides for the appointment (amongst the number of the members of the *comité de empresa*) of *delegados de prevenciòn* in enterprises with six or more employees, entitled to receive information. When employment size is over 50, a joint-body called *comités de seguridad y salud* may be set up, having also a consultative function. Members of this committee are representatives identified by either the employer or the *delegados de prevención*.

104. Most countries, however, seem to belong to a third model consisting of systems without legislation of a general nature concerning elected representative bodies, but instead with specific rules for the appointment of safety representatives or committees. These rules are sometimes derived from statutory law and sometimes from collective agreements. Mostly these are single channel systems of representation, consisting of a body linked with a trade union.

105. In this area, the law sometimes requires the setting up of safety committees, even where forms of general representation are not compulsory. This is the case in the UK, where standing representatives are not provided, but only *ad hoc* employee representatives in the event of redundancies and business transfers (see above §§ 19, 69, 74). An analogous situation is found in Japan where the setting up of safety committees is compulsory for employers with more than 100 workers (or with 50 workers if hazardous work is carried out), while health committees are compulsory for employers with 50 or more workers. In Canada, such committees are compulsory in provinces like Ontario above a certain level of employment.

106. In some systems, there is a provision for bodies specializing in this matter, elected by rank-and-file employees even when there is a limited number of workers, as in the case of Scandinavian countries. It is significant that in Sweden, work safety representatives were the first to have their rights recognized by law or by collective agreement. This also explains why there are provisions for the election of such representatives in all workplaces (even where there are no 'established unions') with at least five employees, and in cases of particular necessity, the election must take place even where this minimum numerical requirement is not met. In Denmark, as soon as there are nine employees, a safety steward must be appointed to work with the employer, and when there are at least 19 employees, a safety committee is set up. In Italy, safety representatives must be either elected or designated in each work unit: their number and the procedure for their election or designation are matters to be regulated in collective agreements. It is important to stress the evolution of Italian collective bargaining which frequently provides for the setting up of joint committees, as in the Israeli system. In the USA, collective agreements are the only source allowing trade unions to carry out inquiries relating to health and safety at work, sometimes leading to the creation of joint committees, though recourse to specialized administrative bodies may, by law, result in an investigation in which a union representative is entitled to take part. If there is no recognized bargaining agent, the public investigator has to consult 'a reasonable' number of workers.

107. As regards the powers assigned to those bodies, it may be seen that they most reflect the general model of employees representation of which they are part. Thus the members of the German *Betriebsraete* have the right to *Mitbestimmung* with regard to some subjects relating to health and safety. This means that not only do they have the right to be informed and consulted but also consequent decisions must be taken with their consent. Moreover, they have to sign every written notification of accidents at work sent to the appropriate authorities. The safety representatives (*Sicherheitsbeauftragte*) may themselves inspect workplaces to ensure that safety measures are applied. In the Netherlands, the members of employees' representative committees have joint regulation rights whenever a safety rule has to be introduced or modified, and may even directly request the intervention of the Labour Inspectorate when they consider it necessary. In both systems, elected bodies have quite wide powers (not granted in other systems of specialized committees). The effectiveness of their intervention depends, however, on the degree of priority assigned to safety matters. An exception is Austria, where only information and consultation rights are granted.

108. Among the other systems, perhaps only in Scandinavian countries (especially in Sweden and Norway) do safety representatives have the power to interrupt working activity in certain circumstances. This may occur, according to Swedish law, in the presence of a serious and immediate risk to the life or health of the workers that the employer is not able to or willing to remove immediately, or when, still for safety reasons, it appears necessary for an individual worker to stop working. This power is provisional, until a definitive decision has been taken by the Labour Inspectorate, and bears a close resemblance to the right of priority in the interpretation of collective agreements. In the Spanish case, the right to interrupt working activity, in case of a serious and immediate risk, is given by Act No. 31/1995 to the *comité de empresa*, when the majority of its members so decides.

109. In France, the worker may refuse on an individual basis to continue work if there is a *danger grave et imminent pour la vie ou pour la santé*. Also, the CHSCT (see above § 103) clearly has the right to intervene and may obtain the intervention of the Labour Inspectorate if the employer does not agree to suspend production.

110. The right of representatives to be informed, consulted and even sometimes to take part in inspections in the workplace are widespread. Collective bargaining, in most cases, provides for the granting of additional powers or further specifies those provided by law. This is the case in Italy (with the increasing provision for joint committees where the employees' representatives may sometimes make use of the services of experts paid for by the employer), the United States (where 'shop level safety committees' are becoming more common, albeit on a purely consultative basis) and the UK. However, only in systems where such representatives are provided for by law, as in France and Belgium, is the employer obliged to supply regular reports on potential health and safety hazards. This has been extended in more recent cases, such as in Greece, to the effects on the working environment of the introduction of new working methods, and therefore, also of new technology.

111. Many EU directives now regulate health and safety matters at the workplace. But the EC legislation has not provided any model of 'specialized' representational participation. For instance, Council Directive of 12 June 1989 states (Article 11.1) that 'employers shall consult workers and/or their representatives and allow them to take part in discussions on all questions relating to health and safety at work. This presupposes: – the consultation of workers; – the right of workers and/or their representatives to make proposals; – balanced participation in accordance with national laws and/or practices'. The range of possible interpretations of 'balanced participation' really is very wide and it has been critically as 'back-door participation'. The fear is that an introduction of advanced participatory mechanisms could produce a wide-ranging effect on industrial relations within companies. In other words, the expedient of creating more participatory powers in the area of safety at work might bring in elements of industrial democracy capable of spreading to bargaining over other matters. Future developments in this direction cannot indeed be ruled out.

V.   FORMS OF BOARD-LEVEL EMPLOYEE REPRESENTATION

112. In a number of countries representational participation is institutionalized through two channels: at the workplace, frequently via works councils acting as counterparts of management; and at board-level, i.e. within managerial boards. There arevarious systems where provisions are laid down by statute to regulate employee board-level representation (Germany, Austria, Denmark, France, Sweden, and the Netherlands), but at a closer examination they show deep differences.

113. To start with, the German model is based on the institution of two-tier boards in the major companies. The management board (*Vorstand*) runs the firm, designs long-term policies and implements most decisions. However, the major issues are endorsed by the supervisory board (*Aufsichtsrat*). Although the latter meets only a few times a year and therefore cannot interfere directly with management, it has the power to appoint (or recall) the members of the management board to receive the firm's accounts and is constituted, at least in part, of employee representatives. Since 1951 in the coal and steel industries (*Montanindustrie*), there has been parity of workers' and shareholders' representatives sitting in the supervisory boards. Aside from these industries, in undertakings employing more than 2,000 people, a system has been established since 1976, which provides for countervailing parity. In a deadlock situation, the chairman (chosen by the shareholders' group) is given the casting vote. Furthermore, one workers' representative must be appointed by the senior managerial employees (*Leitende Angestellte*). In smaller companies, employing between 500 and 2000 people, a third model (inaugurated in 1952) operates where one-third of the supervisory board's seats are attributed to employee representatives.

114. In all three models existing in Germany the role played by representatives of workers is the same. The management board is obliged to supply to the supervisory board comprehensive information on all issues related to the running of the company, at least once a year. Additionally, the supervisory board (or any member of it) may at any time request further information on affairs of importance for the enterprise. The management board is under a statutory obligation to meet this request.

115. Although Germany is probably the country where board-level employee participation has reached the most advanced level of development it would be improper to speak of co-management. Indeed workers are represented only on the supervisory board which monitors the activities of the management board but does not perform a management function itself. This does not mean that board-level representation should be underestimated. Firstly one has to remember that employee representatives in the supervisory board are often works council members: that makes it possible to greatly expand the amount of information available to the works council itself. In this way, the employer may monitor the reaction of the labour members of the supervisory board to avoid possible conflict with the works council. Secondly, the integration of workers' representatives in management decision-making has helped to absorb conflicts and to provide legitimacy for difficult economic decisions. Finally workers' participation at different levels establishes a permanent dialogue between the two sides. In particular employee representatives confronted with the details of decision-making get a realistic understanding of the difficulties facing management, which is highly advantageous in times of crisis. The institutionalization of this system is one of the main reasons for the stability and relative harmony of German industrial relations.

116. Also in Austria joint stock companies, limited liability companies (with over 300 employees) and cooperatives all have a two-tier board system. One-third of the supervisory boards' members may be appointed by the works councils, and they enjoy the same rights as those elected by shareholders. The appointment of the board's chair requires majority approval, not only of the entire board but also of the shareholders' representatives.

117. In Denmark the board of directors (*bestyrelsen*) is made up of representatives elected by shareholders at a general meeting and is responsible for the overall management of the company. Companies with share capital exceeding a specific amount must appoint a management team (*direktionen*) to take care of the day-to-day running of the enterprise. In other companies, there is an option of a single- or two-tier board structure. In 1980 the legislation was amended to increase workers' representation on the board of directors. Employees are now entitled to elect one third of the total membership of the board (still with a minimum of two worker directors, if the total size of the board is below six). Employees' representatives have exactly the same rights, obligations and responsibilities as those board members elected by shareholders. They participate directly and on the same terms in company decision-making, but at the same time, they are bound by the identical secrecy requirements which prevent them from informing employees about discussions and decisions on a range of confidential issues.

118. Employees do not always directly elect their representatives on the supervisory board. In the Netherlands, the works council only has the right to recommend persons for membership to the board which decides on the nominations. It is not simply a formal power because the council also has a right to refuse persons whom the supervisory board itself nominates. In fact, such a refusal prevents the person(s) concerned from being appointed unless the board successfully settles the matter in Court. The works councils are, therefore, in the position to have persons of their choice appointed to the top board at least of large companies.

119. In this respect also the Swedish case is relevant since the right to appoint board representatives is conferred on the established local trade unions (having a collective agreement with the company). Such a decision is not compulsory, and it is up to the union(s) whether to choose representatives.

120. Similarly, in French enterprises constituted as limited corporations, *sociétés anonymes*, (which can opt for either type of board structure, depending on the legal status elected by the corporation), employee board representatives are appointed by and from *the comité d'entreprise*. Where there are four seats, two are allocated to the manual and non-manual employees (who constitute a single electoral unit), one to executive and one to supervisory and technical staff. Representatives of the enterprise committee on the board must be invited to all meetings: they have a consultative role and do not vote. However, they are allowed to submit the demands of the enterprise committee to the board which has to provide them with a reasoned answer. Incorporated companies may also voluntarily decide to select the German style of board with an *Aufsichart* and a *Vorstand*. In such a case, they may choose, if they deem it appropriate, that a third of the members of the *Aufsichrat* may consist of employees.

121. Mention also should be made of special arrangements concerning State-sector companies. In some countries statutory requirements for employee board-level representation apply only to this kind of enterprise. In Ireland one-third of the seats on the (unitary) boards of seven State enterprises must be allocated to (non-executive) employee directors, provided that a preliminary poll of the workforce does not result in a majority vote against this kind of board-level representation. In Greece, the State Agency for Industrial Restructuring, established in 1983, assumed the management of over 40 ailing private companies, which were threatened with closure and the loss of almost 40,000 jobs. The Act provides for an eight-member board of directors to run the Agency, one of whom must be a nominee of the General Confederation of Labour (*GSEE*). A *GSEE* nominee also sits on the five-member Technical Advisory Committee to the Agency's secretariat. Finally, the Act allows–but does not require–the appointment of employee representatives to the boards of directors of companies under Agency management. Finally, in Portugal, workers in state-owned companies have the right to elect at least one representative to the board (although this right has never been put into practice).

122. At the end of this comparative overview of forms of board-level representational participation it has to be stressed that practical experience in various national contexts has demonstrated that, in spite of institutional mechanisms, for most private sector employees the nature and the degree of their participation relates primarily to the human resource management policies of their employer. In other words, participation in management decision-making process is less and less brought about by

State intervention and increasingly the outcome of management strategies. But it is equally true that the most interesting experimental programmes seem to be those in which managerial initiatives are carried out in such a way as to succeed in obtaining the trade union consensus indispensable at micro level.

VI. Concluding Remarks

123. The trend in de-collectivization or individualization of labour relations which started in the 1980s has not stopped in the 1990s. Nevertheless, company-wide union de-recognition is absolutely exceptional, although in the US (and, to some extent, in the UK) is increasingly widespread. This phenomenon is also due to the insufficient functioning of various models of employee representational participation, both in the workplace and at board level. De-collectivization of industrial relations can be better explained by looking at the decline of workers' collective identification with trade unions. Additionally, while formal organizational/representational structures may remain intact (at least formally), undoubtedly there is an employers' attempt to undermine workers' collective power through a variety of management-led initiatives (e.g. joint consultation, direct communication and involvement, performance-related pay). This does not amount to an entrepreneurial strategy based on union exclusion measures in every country. In most nations, any decrease in workers' collective solidarity has emphasised their dependence upon management. The consequence is that individuals are stimulated to compete against each other in terms of output and mainly for pay. This is a potentially explosive situation which is difficult for management to keep under control. This is also a consequence which could lead employers to re-think the (positive) role of collective employee representation because of its stabilizing effect.

124. It is by no means surprising that, today, employee participation at the micro-level is increasingly channelled through human resource management initiatives. The essentially 'reactive' attitude of trade unionism (with some notable exceptions, as in Japan) makes it difficult to explore collaborative action over matters to be considered a common interest with the enterprise. Management initiatives to generate trust and cooperation frequently fail because employees and their representatives are excluded from the design and introduction of involvement techniques. For this reason, 'participative management' seems to be a strategic choice without alternatives in the context of total quality projects which inevitably affect industrial relations. This conclusion is not simply a result of the 'new worker', who is more individualistic than in the past, but it is also the result of the awareness that enterprises may only achieve if employees are fully informed, effectively involved and really capable of contributing to decisions.

125. The worldwide process of de-unionization and the opening of new participatory channels are factors which have to be evaluated with particular reference to their potential destabilizing effect on industrial relations systems. On one hand, the comparative experience (e.g. the USA) shows that the establishment of an institutional/collective channel of workers' participation at the plant level appears to be an essential element of a successful cooperative model. On the other hand, there is no empirical evidence that individual/direct relations between the employer and the workers are increasingly an alternative to a reliable, highly representative form of collective representation, able to make commitments on behalf of the entire workforce.

126. Nevertheless, it seems correct to speak in terms of a decline of employee participation, while employee involvement is rising. In the absence of either supportive legislation or strong union power, participation of workers is always exposed to destabilizing pressures of management. The number of employers resorting to employee involvement techniques is constantly increasing. In addition, increasingly, this technique represents the only channel of information and/or communication left to the workforce.

127. It is quite difficult to say whether the rise of human resource management techniques (plus the decline of unionization) will lead towards the end of collective forms of representation. At least in Europe, it would be unthinkable that new forms of participative management could be successfully introduced without the support of collective bargaining. Not by chance, the most interesting experimental programmes seem to be those in which managerial initiatives are carried out in such a way as to succeed in obtaining the trade union consensus indispensable at the micro level. Not only legislation, but also the macroframework of collective bargaining no longer seem to be able to exert a decisive role in shaping models of participation in decision-making, whether they be based on information or consultation or something more.

128. To some extent, management's proactive role in obtaining the involvement of employees requires, workers' representatives to be willing to take on a partnership role, including a closer identification with company values or, at least, with its goals. In other words, marginalization of unions cannot be considered a universal employers' strategy on a global scale. When (and where) this is not the case, it is conceivable that management requests the unions to adopt a position which is more responsible and open to enterprise needs.

129. The continuing importance of collective forms of workers representation from the angle of upward communication should not be underestimated. Senior management regards trade unions and/or works councils as invaluable channels to establish the opinions and obtain input from the workforce, not to mention the stabilizing effect of collective representative bodies in the event of staff reductions.

130. Old forms of employee representation were (and still are) indirect, representative, collective and institutionalized. New models of participation tend to be more direct, individual, and informal. A wide range of different forms of worker representation and participation are now mixed together in many countries. The main question consequently is: What will constitute the effective institution for worker representation in the future? Firstly, it seems clear that this institution must be able to provide representation for individual employees, which is somehow 'portable' throughout the individual's work history, not depending on continuous employment with one employer. Secondly, this institution needs to be more cooperative. Abandoning old adversarial attitudes seems to be inevitable due to the increased global competition: labour and management must find in a cooperative approach to reduce costs by increasing flexibility. Thirdly, this institution has to fulfil a trust-building function, making it possible that industrial relations represent a competitive advantage of the enterprise. Finally, this representative institution must guarantee the legitimacy of management decisions, enhanced by their joint nature, with a favourable impact on their execution.

SELECT BIBLIOGRAPHY

Bertelsmann Foundation/Hans-Boeckler Foundation (ed.), *The German Model of Codetermination and Cooperative Governance*, Guethersloh, 1998.

R. Blanpain and M. Biagi (eds.), 'Participative Management and Industrial relations in a Worldwide Perspective', in *Bulletin of Comparative Labour Relations*, No. 27, 1993.

S. Estreicher (ed.), *Employee Representation in the Emerging Workplace: Alternatives/Supplements to Collective Bargaining*, Proceedings of the New York University 50th Annual Conference on Labor, Kluwer Law International, 1998.

European Commission, *Industrial Relations Report*, Bruxelles, p. 31 et seq.

M. MacNeil, M. Lynk, and P. Angelman, *Trade Union Law in Canada*, Aurora, Ont., Canada Law Book [loose-leaf, release 1999].

National Labor Relations Board, *A Guide to Basic Law and Procedures under the National Labor Relations Act*, U.S. Government Printing Office, Washington, D.C., 1997.

C. W. Summers, 'Exclusive Representation: A Comparative Inquiry into a "Unique" American Principle', *Comparative Labor Law & Policy Journal*, Vol. 20, No. 1, fall 1998, p. 47 et seq.

Lord Wedderburn, 'Collective Bargaining or Legal Enactment: the 1999 Act and Union Recognition', *Industrial Law Journal*, Vol. 29, number 1, March 2000, p. 1 et seq.

Chapter 21. Transnational Information and Consultation: The European Works Council Directive

C. Engels and L. Salas

I. INTRODUCTION

1. The general purpose of the Council Directive on the establishment of a European Works Council or a procedure in Community-scale undertakings and Community-scale groups of undertakings for the purpose of informing and consulting employees[1] (herein referred to as the EWC Directive), as stated in Article 1, 'is to improve the right to information and to consultation of employees with regard to transnational issues'. The preamble of the Directive refers to the current economic reality where 'the functioning of the internal market involves a process of concentration of undertakings, cross-border mergers, take-overs, joint ventures and consequently a transnationalization of undertakings', thus consultation and information on matters which affect employees is necessary, 'if economic activities are to develop in a harmonious fashion'. It is important to note that the Directive cannot be the basis for anything more than the exchange of information and consultation on decision which may affect employees. The Directive characterizes its respect for and deference to managerial prerogative. Management must consult labour, but under this Directive there are no further obligations beyond that. The same also holds with regard to the collective dismissals[2] and transfer of undertakings Directives.[3] The latter two

---

1. Council Directive of 22 September 1994, 94/45/EC, OJ No. L 254/64, 30/09/94, hereinafter 'EWC Directive'.
2. Council Directive of 17 February 1975, 75/129/EEC, on the approximation of the laws of the Member States relating to collective redundancies, OJ L 48/29, 22 February 1975, amended by Directive 92/56/EEC, OJ L 245/3, 26 August 1992. Both Directives were consolidated by Council Directive of 20 July 1998, 98/59 EC, on the approximation of the laws of the Member States relating to collective redundancies, OJ L 225/16, 12 August 1998.
3. Council Directive of 14 February 1977, 77/187 EEC, OJ No. L61/26, 05/03/77, on the approximation of the laws of the Member States relating to the safeguarding of employees' rights in the event of transfers of undertakings, businesses or parts of businesses, amended by Council Directive of 29 June 1998, 98/50/EC, amending Directive 77/187/EEC on the approximation of the laws of the

Directives seem to impose some more duties since they refer to an obligation to consult 'with a view to reaching an agreement'.

2. Another notable feature of the Directive is that it does not expressly provide that trade unions shall be the party representing labour. Through the operation of applicable national law, trade unions will often end up acting on behalf of labour. Trade unions and trade union federations, however, see the EWC Directive as a step towards increased competence and towards the 'Europeanization' of industrial relations. However, their inclusion in European-wide consultation is by no means guaranteed.

3. This Directive introduces a host of new concepts which at first glance appear to be clearly defined, but upon further inspection lead to an extensive debate. Some of these concepts include the following: controlling undertaking, confidential information, employee representatives, and several others. In practice, these concepts are rather malleable and subject to different interpretations. Furthermore, the Directive involves the interplay of several different legal regimes including European law, different national implementing legislation, and international private law. Since experience with the EWC Directive is rather new, case law is very scant. These concepts are still being defined.

The establishment and functioning of an EWC, by its nature, involves people and issues covered by various different legal regimes. The different European States involved have very divergent ways of dealing with (strictly national issues of) information and consultation of employees. In order to avoid a similar divergence from prevailing in the national measures implementing the EWC Directive, a 'Working Party' was founded. The Working Party was established at the request of the Council and is composed of national experts representing the respective Ministries of Employment and Labour and the social affairs counsellors in order to provide a forum for discussing the arrangements for the transposition of the Directive into national law.

4. The ultimate aim of the Working Party was to avoid conflicts in national implementing law by exchanging information and coordinating the transposition work. The observations, comments and conclusions of the Working Party are gathered in Working Papers [herein referred to as WPWP] which will be referred to in this book. The conclusions of the Working Party have been submitted and approved by the Directors General for Industrial Relations of all the countries concerned at a meeting in July 1995 with the indication that the conclusions would be a useful tool in coordinating transposition of the Directive into national law. However, Member States' legislative sovereignty is in no way positively affected.

A. Legal Basis

5. The legal basis of the EWC Directive is the Agreement on Social Policy annexed to Protocol 14 which was agreed upon in Maastricht (herein after referred

---

(*contd.*)
 Member States relating to the safeguarding of employees' rights in the event of transfers of undertakings, businesses or parts of businesses, OJ No. L 201/88, 17/07/98.

to as the Maastricht protocol). Politically the Maastricht protocol was an extremely important legislative act for three main reasons: (1) the extension of EU competencies to social matters; (2) qualified majority voting; and (3) the United Kingdom's opt-out from EU social policy. The EWC Directive is the first piece of social legislation passed under the Maastricht protocol.

The proposal that finally lead to the EWC Directive was addressed to 11 Member States only and thus excluded the UK. In line with the provisions of the Maastricht Social Protocol, the social partners were consulted at European level. They were not able, however, to reach an agreement on the issue. The Commission was of the opinion that Community action was still warranted in this area and introduced the proposal that lead to the present EWC Directive.

6.   The Labour Party's electoral victory in the UK cleared the path for an extension of the EWC Directive to the UK. Since the original Directive came into existence within the frame work of the Maastricht Agreement on Social Policy, a mere extension of the Directive within the same frame work was not possible.

The extension Directive was passed on the basis of article 100 of the Treaty Establishing the European Community, requiring a unanimous vote of all the Member States and necessarily involving an issue directly affecting the common market. The preamble to the extension Directive[4] mentions that the exclusion of the UK from the scope of the original EWC Directive indeed affects the functioning of the internal market.

The extension Directive had to be implemented by the Member States by 15 December 1999. The UK implementing measure itself came into force on 15 January 2000, i.e. one month later than required.

B.   Basic Structure

7.   The subject matter of the Directive is basically divided among three main components:

(1) pre-existing agreements;
(2) establishment of a European Works Council or procedure for informing and consulting employees; and
(3) subsidiary requirements (default provisions).

Either companies will have entered into a voluntary agreement prior to the Directive coming into force, or they will have entered into a (voluntary) agreement negotiated according to the provisions of the Directive(s) and the implementing legislation. In the absence of the above, the subsidiary requirements come into play.

Furthermore, there are also general provisions dealing with applicability, definitions, compliance and the subject matter of the information and consultation.

---

4.   Council Directive of 15 December 1997, 97/74/EC, extending, to the United Kingdom of Great-Britain and Northern Ireland, directive 94/45/EC on the establishment of a European Works Council or a procedure in Community-scale undertakings and Community-scale groups of undertakings for the purposes of informing and consulting employees, OJ L 10/22, 16 January 1998, hereinafter referred to as the EWC extension Directive.

II. GENERAL PROVISIONS

A. Scope

8. The provisions of the Directive apply to Community-scale undertakings and groups of undertakings. The Directive defines the Community-scale undertaking as: any undertaking with at least 1,000 employees within the territorial scope of the directive, and at least 150 employees in at least two Member States.[5] Since the original EWC Directive was not addressed to the UK, the UK workforce was not included in the head count until 15 December 1998 (date of implementation of the EWC Extension Directive). The countries of the European Economic Area (hereinafter EEA) are also subject to the provisions of the Directive. The EEA countries are Iceland, Liechtenstein and Norway.[6] A Community-scale group of undertakings is defined as 'a group of undertakings with

- at least 1,000 employees within the Member States;
- at least two group undertakings in different Member States; and
- at least one group undertaking with at least 150 employees in one Member State and at least one other group undertaking with at least 150 employees in another Member State'.[7]

The definition of the basic concept of undertaking itself remains completely undefined in the Directive. Following the case law of the European Court of Justice dealing with the transfer of undertakings Directive, one of the basic conditions is that the undertaking is engaged in economic activities, whether or not for profit.[8]

9. The Directive does not make a real distinction between public and private undertakings, thus both public and private undertakings will be affected, if they are engaged in economic activities and so far as they satisfy the numerical conditions.

Thus, in order to fall within the scope of the Directive, both a geographical and a numerical criterion have to be satisfied:

- given the fact that the Directive deals with transnational information and consultation, the undertaking needs to have a presence in at least two Member States; and
- the geographical presence in at least two Member States needs to be of a sufficient numerical level.

10. The concept of an employee itself remains undefined in the Directive. It will be up to the Member States to come up with the definition. The same is also true for the collective dismissal and the transfer of undertakings Directives. The Directive itself determines that the prescribed threshold for the size of the workplace needs to be based on the overall number of employees, including part-time employees,

---

5. Article 2, 1(a) EWC Directive.
6. Decision of 22 June 1995 to include a reference to EWC Directive in Annex XVII of the EEA Treaty.
7. Article 2, 1(c), EWC Directive.
8. *See* ECJ, C-382/92, *Commission* v. *UK* (1994), ECR, 2461.

employed during the previous two years.[9] The Working Party suggested part-time workers to be taken into account at least in proportion to the amount of their working time.[10]

B. The Notion of Controlling Undertaking

11. A difficult concept to clearly define is that of a controlling undertaking. As previously stated the Directive applies to Community-scale groups of undertakings, which is defined as a controlling undertaking and its controlled undertakings.[11] The difficulty arises with regard to determining what a controlling undertaking is. Article 3 gives a rather extensive definition, with examples and also provides rules for resolving some conflict of laws situations. Determining which is a controlling undertaking is very important

> 'first of all it determines the existence of a group of undertakings within the meaning of the Directive; it then helps to establish the body responsible for many of the duties in the Directive and is an important factor in determining the level at which the European Works Council should be constituted in the absence of an agreement. It also identifies the national law applicable (where the undertaking is in one of the Member States covered by the Directive)'.[12]

Article 3 of the Directive gives a very general definition of a controlling undertaking as 'an undertaking which can exercise a dominant influence over another undertaking ('the controlled undertaking') by virtue, for example, of ownership, financial participation or the rules which govern it' [emphasis added]. The phrase, for example, is used because the indications of control could be different from or supplemented to those in the Directive, by national rules. Article 3,2 gives three criteria which could be used as indicators of the ability of one undertaking to exercise a dominant influence over another undertaking:

'(a) hold[ing] a majority of that undertaking's subscribed capital;
 (b) control[ling] a majority of the votes attached to that undertaking's issued share capital; or
 (c) [the capacity to] appoint more than half of the members of that undertaking's administrative, management or supervisory body.'

12. The Directive furthermore states that the controlling undertaking's rights as regards voting and appointment include the rights of any other controlled undertaking in this respect.[13]

---

9. Article 2,2 EWC Directive.
10. Working Party 'Information and Consultation', Working Papers, V/9643/95/EN, Conclusion 11.
11. Article 2, 1(b), EWC Directive.
12. WPWP, at 93.
13. Article 3,3, EWC Directive.

This having been stated, paragraph 6 of the Directive puts a kink in this concept by stating that national law will govern the determination of whether an undertaking is a 'controlling undertaking'. According to the Working Party

> '[n]ational legislation on company and tax law provides numerous examples of situations which, from a legal point of view, concern the establishment of a controlling relationship between two companies other than those mentioned in Article 3,2. If the Member States seek inspiration in these other branches of the law to establish a concept of control for purposes of transposition of the Directive into their national law on the basis of criteria other than those of Article 3,2 problems may arise because the Directive does not impose harmonization of national rules in this area.'[14]

If a conflict would arise between the three criteria, according to Article 3,7, criteria (c) then the capacity to appoint more than half of the members of that undertaking's administrative, management or supervisory body should have priority. It is clear that the presumption established in the Directive covers only the 'clear' situations of institutionalized relationships between undertakings.

13. The Working Party addressed this issue and stated that a dominant relationship did not require the numerical ratios of share ownership or board of directors, mentioned in the Directive. A controlling relationship can be established without the numerical majorities explicitly mentioned in the Directive. A minority shareholder can have effective control within a group, such as where the rest of the capital is widely dispersed. Furthermore, dominance can be shown on the basis of purely *de facto* relationships, such as the economic dependence between companies where one is the sole customer of the other company. Certain forms of franchizing and sales distributorships may also establish the dominance of one undertaking over the other.[15]

C. National and Transnational Issues

14. By its nature, the European Works Council involves issues that transcend the national boundaries of any given European Member State. Some provisions of the Directive deal with transnational concepts. However, many are also left up to the national Member States' implementing legislation. Therefore, it is useful to provide an overview of which provisions will be transnational and which are national in nature. According to the Working Party Working Papers:

'To conform with the Directive each Member State will need to adopt two types of provisions:

1. provisions applying to any Community-scale undertaking or Community-scale group of undertakings whose controlling undertaking or central management is

---

14. WPWP, at 95.
15. WPWP, at 95.

situated in the territory of the Member State in question and applying to the whole of the undertaking or group, including establishments or subsidiaries situated in other Member States;

2. provisions applying not to a whole undertaking or group, but solely to those of its units situated in the territory of the Member State in question (and to the employees in those units).'

Provisions of the first type cover most of the measures required for implementing the Directive and most of the obligations on the undertakings and groups concerned. They will therefore be termed 'transnational provisions'.

Provisions of the second type are more instrumental in nature and their scope is confined to the territory of the Member State in question. They will therefore be termed 'national provisions'.

The delegations agree with the following classification which defines transnational and national provisions that each Member State needs to adapt:

1. Transnational Provisions

Art. 1(1 to 4)	Imposition of a general obligation to establish, in certain circumstances, a European Works Council or a procedure informing and consulting employees.
Art. 1.5	Possible exclusion of merchant navy crews
Art. 2.1 (a) to (c)	Concepts of 'Community-scale undertaking' and 'Community scale group of undertakings'.
Art. 3	Concept of 'controlling undertaking'
Art. 4	Responsibility for establishing a European Works Council procedure
Art. 5.1	Obligation to initiate negotiations following a request
Art. 5.2 (b) (c)	Composition of the special negotiating body – Criteria
Art. 5.2. (d)	Obligation on the special negotiating body to inform the central management and local management of its composition
Art. 5.3	Tasks of the special negotiating body
Art. 5.4., first para	Obligation imposed on the central management to convene a meeting with the special negotiating body
Art. 5.4 2nd para	The right of the special negotiating body to be assisted by experts
Art. 5.5	The right of the special negotiating body to decide not to open negotiations or to terminate negotiations – Consequences
Art. 5.6.	Obligation on the central management to fund the special negotiating body
Art. 6	Content of the agreement between the central management and the special negotiating body
Art. 7	Obligatory application of subsidiary requirements
Art. 8.2.	Secrecy clause
Art. 8.3	Tendency clause
Art. 9	The principle of collaboration
Art. 13	Retention of agreements already in force
Annex (except 1.b)	Subsidiary requirements

2. National Provisions

Art. 2.1 (d)	Concept of 'employees' representatives'
Art. 2.2	Method of calculating manpower thresholds
Art. 5.2 (a)	Establishment of a special negotiating body – method of election or appointment
Art. 8.1	Protection of confidentiality[16]
Art. 10	Protection of employees' representatives
Art. 11	Compliance with the Directive[17]
Annex, 1 (b)	Election or appointment of employees' representatives[18]

III. Pre-existing Agreements – Article 13 Agreements

15. Article 13 of the Directive provides that the obligations arising from it shall not apply to Community-scale undertakings and Community-scale groups of undertakings in which, on the date laid down for implementation (which was 22 September 1996) or the date of its transposition in the Member State, where this is earlier, there is already an agreement, covering the entire workforce, providing for the transnational information and consultation of employees. The Directive stipulates that upon termination of the agreement, the parties can renew the agreement, otherwise, the provisions of the Directive will apply. The Community legislator wanted hereby to 'reserve special treatment for undertakings and groups of undertakings which had already taken action in anticipation of the obligations arising from the Directive'.[19]

From a management perspective, Article 13 offers a way to side-step the procedures for establishing an EWC. As long as the following three criteria are met, the agreement will be valid.

1. The agreement needed to be in place on 22 September 1996 or by the date of implementation in the national Member State;
2. The agreement needs to cover the entire workforce; and
3. It needs to provide for transnational information and consultation.

The Directive thus provides an avenue for achieving maximum flexibility between labour and management on this issue.

While the subsidiary requirements to the Directive fill in the necessary details needed to have an operational EWC, Article 13, in contrast, leaves everything open to the parties. The form and title of the agreement and any organ created are open. It

---

16. The *notion* of confidentiality which is defined by the country where the central management is located concerns all the representatives of the group, but the *protection* of the confidentiality is a matter for the national law to define and the definition of the sanctions which will protect the confidentiality depends on national laws.
17. But a distinction has to be made: Article 11 has a national scope, but Article 11.2 has a transnational scope.
18. *See* WPWP, at p. 46.
19. WPWP, at 97.

can be called a council, committee, forum, observatory, European Information Exchange Centre, or whatever. The Directive does not specifically state who the signatory parties must be. The most obvious would be an agreement between the central management of an undertaking and its regular employee representatives, being the trade unions. But this is not expressly stipulated by the Directive.

16. According to the WPWP, the expression 'covering the entire workforce' means that all the workers of the undertaking or group of undertakings in which an Article 13 agreement has been concluded must have been directly or indirectly represented in negotiating and signing this agreement. This is, in fact a question of the representative status of the signatories to the agreement. It should be stressed, however, that Article 13 does not impose any requirement at all with regard to representativity of the signatory parties.

A related issue concerns the question of whether all employees within a given Community-scale undertaking or Community-scale group of undertakings should be covered by the same agreement, or whether it is possible to conclude several agreements, the scope of which together cover the entire workforce of the undertaking concerned. The latter solution is favoured by the Working Party.[20] The requirement that the entire workforce be covered by the Article 13 agreement relates only to those workers covered by the Directive itself. Thus, UK, US and Japanese workers were not to be taken into account for the Article 13 agreements under the original directive.

Other open-ended issues include the duration of the agreement, number of members, meeting times, payment of expenses, etc. The Directive stipulates that upon termination of the agreement, the parties can renew the agreement, otherwise, the provisions of the Directive will apply.

According to the Working Papers, '[i]t is clear that the problem of conformity of [pre-existing] agreements ... will only arise if a request for negotiations under Article 5(1) of the Directive is made in the undertaking or group of undertakings in question. Until such time, the agreement in force is a private agreement and the problem of incorporating it in the legal framework of the national transposition law does not arise.'[21]

17. Article 13, like all other provisions of the Directive, had to be transposed into national law. The Directive lays down the minimum legal standards, which Member States can then augment. The Working Party cautions against Member States adopting more stringent conditions for the application of Article 13 because this would run counter to the basic principle of maintaining the autonomy of workers and employers.[22] It remains to be seen whether Article 13 agreements will be challenged for their validity under national implementing legislation.

18. The EWC extension Directive grants Community-scale undertakings and groups of undertakings that fall within the scope of the EWC Directive solely by virtue of its extension to the UK, the ability to enter into pre-existing agreements,

---

20. WPWP, at Conclusion 5.
21. WPWP, at 107.
22. WPWP.

provided such agreements exist on December 15, 1999[23] or on the date of the implementing legislation, if this happens to be earlier.

Since the UK implementing legislation, to be referred to as the Transnational Information and Consultation of Employees Regulations 1999, came into force on January 15, 2000 only, pre-existing agreements for companies that fall within the scope of the directives merely because of the UK extension, needed to be concluded prior to December 16, 1999.[24]

A.   Article 13 Agreements Analysed

19. The date for signing a voluntary agreement under Article 13 has passed (22 September 1996) at least for those that were already covered by the original Directive. The exact number of voluntary agreements is not known, but it is estimated that one-fifth to one-quarter of all companies affected by the Directive have signed such an agreement.[25]

The Commission report on the implementation of the original EWC directive states that nearly 600 groups with a Community dimension entered into EWC agreements (including also Article 6 agreements).[26]

Companies or groups of companies that fall within the scope of the EWC directives merely because of the extension of the territorial scope to the UK, could enter into valid pre-existing agreements until December 15, 1999 (included), the date mentioned into the extension Directive. The companies aimed at, were companies that did not satisfy the numerical requirements (e.g. 1000 employees in total) until the moment the UK employees were taken into account. Another situation in which a company would be granted an 'extended', prolonged chance to enter into pre-existing agreements was the one in which a group of companies had a sufficiently large presence (more than 150 employees and even more than 1,000) but only in one country or the continent. If the UK work force in such a group would comprise more than 150 workers, the extension directive would grant such a group the possibility to enter into a pre-directive agreement.

It is estimated that about 200 more companies or groups of companies fall within the scope of the EWC directives due to the UK extension.[27]

The European Foundation for the Improvement of Living and Working Conditions has over the years analysed the Article 13 agreements in its possession. In its latest report dealing with Article 13 agreements a total number of 386 agreements were

---

23.   Article 3,1, EWC extension Directive.
24.   Transnational Information and Consultation of Employer Regulations 1999, No 3323, Article 1(1).
25.   *European Works Councils Bulletin*, issue 6, November/December 1996, at 12.
26.   Report from the Commission to the European Parliament and the Council on the application of the Directive on the establishment of a European Works Council or a procedure in Community-scale undertakings and Community-scale groups of undertakings for the purposes of informing and consulting employees (Council Directive 94/45/EC of 22 September 1994), Brussels, 4 April 2000, CUM (2000) 188 final, hereinafter referred to as the 'Commission Report', p. 5.
27.   M. Carley and P. Marginson, *Negotiating EWCs under the Directive: A Comparative Analysis of Article 6 and Article 13 Agreements*, report prepared for the European Foundation for the Improvement of Living and Working Conditions, November 1999, p. 7, hereinafter referred to as the 'European Foundation Report.'

analysed. The full text of these agreements can be consulted on the European Foundations' web site: http://www.eurofond.ie/ewc.

The analysis by the European Foundation show the following results discussed below.

1. Geographical Scope

20. Obviously, most Article 13 agreements will cover those undertakings within the territory of the EU and EEA countries. Although the United Kingdom did formally opt-out of European social policy, this op-out was largely ignored in practice, even before the UK extension directive.

Only seven agreements for companies or groups with a presence in the UK, explicitly excluded UK operations.

In the study conducted by the European Foundation, 26 per cent of the agreements cover non-EU/EEA countries, the most frequently included being Switzerland. Among the most frequently included eastern and central European countries are the Czech Republic, Hungary, and Poland. A few agreements far exceed the boundaries of European countries with world-wide agreements.

2. Nature of the Body Created

21. Within the field of industrial relations, two basic models of national works councils are recognized: (1) the French *comité d'entreprise* which is a joint employee management body, and (2) the German *Betriebsrat* model which is made up solely of employee representatives, meeting bilaterally with management.[28] According to the European Foundation study, 69 per cent of the agreements follow the French joint employee-management model. The German model is in the clear minority.

Regarding the level of the multi-national's business structure at which the EWC is organized, the European Foundation study reports that 78 per cent of the agreements provide for a single structure covering the entire group. Fifteen per cent are established at divisional level, and 7 per cent are integrated structures with EWC's at divisional and group levels.

3. Composition/Number of Members

22. Of the 248 agreements in the European Foundation sample where the number of representatives is specified or can be calculated, the European Foundation reports that over 90 per cent of agreements are in line with the Subsidiary Requirements of the Directive (minimum 3, and maximum 30 representatives).

The distribution of council members among the different undertakings of a multi-national follows a variation on one of two basic methods: a flat-rate allocation of representatives to all operations or countries; or an allocation basis on workforce

---

28. *EWC* Bulletin, issue 6 at 13.

size. Many agreements (44 per cent) set out a minimum workforce size threshold for a country or company to be directly represented on an EWC, such as 100 or 150 employees.

4. Selection of Members

23. Employee representation varies among the EU countries, with a varying degree of trade union representativeness and recognition, and differing relationships between works councils and trade union channels of representation. This lack of uniformity among countries is reflected in the manner in which the members of an EWC are selected under voluntary agreements. According to the European Foundation analysis, about half of the agreements state that selection is to be in accord with national law and/or practice/custom. A combination with a selection to be determined by subsequent agreement or consultation is further specified in 13 per cent of agreements.

Some specific way of electing or appointing employee representatives is applied in one quarter of the cases, for appointing or electing representatives in all countries. Five per cent of agreements do not mention any method for selecting employee representatives.

Many EWC members count non-employees among their ranks, most often being trade union officials, with an equal split between international and national trade union officials. Other members include observers from countries and/or operations not covered by the geographical scope of the agreement.

Thus, it can be seen that trade unions play an important role in voluntary EWC's as either full members, invitees or experts. Their presence reflects the reality of European industrial relations, although the Directive itself does not mention trade unions as participants in EWC's or signatories to voluntary agreements.

5. Competence of the EWC

All agreements with one exception explicitly state that the purpose of the EWC is the provision of information and consultation. The latter concept is most often defined as a 'dialogue' or an 'exchange of views'.

Only 2 per cent of agreements allow for negotiations on certain issues.

The European Foundation reports the following roles for the EWC:

Role of the EWC	%
Information and consultation	99
Giving opinion/comments	7
Making recommendations	4
Negotiations	2

Almost all agreements define the kind of issues for which the EWC is competent. Six agreements do not.

Employment issues and the economic and financial situation of the company are covered in most agreements. Issues likely to create some unrest in the workforce, such as transfers of production, mergers, lay-offs, collective dismissals and plant closures are mentioned in around half of the agreements analysed by the European Foundation.

6. Meetings

Eighty-seven per cent of the Article 13 agreements foresee yearly meetings. The remaining 13 per cent stipulate more frequent meetings (most likely twice a year).

The report states that 81 per cent of all agreements allow for extraordinary meetings to be convened, either when exceptional circumstances have occurred or where both sides believe that extraordinary meetings are necessary and would be beneficial.

The employee side often (85 per cent) has the right to meet without management being present.

IV. ESTABLISHMENT OF EWC OR EMPLOYEE INFORMATION AND CONSULTATION PROCEDURE – ARTICLE 6 AGREEMENTS

25. In companies affected by the Directive which have not signed a voluntary agreement, the procedures for establishing an EWC or procedure for information and consultation as foreseen by the Directive can be followed. This involves first establishing a special negotiating body, which will then be the body that negotiates with central management to establish the actual EWC or procedure. The EWC or procedure will be established in an agreement which must comply with Article 6 of the Directive.

The initiation of negotiations which will lead to the establishment of an EWC or procedure for information and consultation can be taken by central management or upon the written request of 100 employees or representatives in two undertakings/establishments in at least two member States (Article 5,1). The ultimate responsibility for establishing an EWC or procedure rests with central management (Article 4).

A. *Central management and a Representative Agent*

26. A major topic of discussion is the determination of central management. Because of the transnational nature of the subject matter, it is not unlikely that the central management of an undertaking will be located outside of the EU territory. Since central management carries the responsibility for the establishment of an EWC or procedure, and since it is a requisite party for negotiation of an agreement and eventual operation of the EWC or procedure, its identity must be ascertained.

The Directive stipulates that

> 'where the central management is not situated in a Member State, the central management's representative agent in a Member State, to be designated if necessary, shall take on the responsibility [for the establishment of an EWC or procedure].

In the absence of such a representative, the management of the establishment or group undertaking employing the greatest number of employees in any one Member State shall take on this responsibility.'[29]

The question of who can be designated thus arises. The Working Party distinguishes three situations regarding who is responsible for creating an EWC: (1) central management situated within the territory of the EU; (2) a representative agent chosen by central management (if central management is not situated in a Member State); and (3) the establishment or group undertaking employing the greatest number of employees in any Member State (if no representative is designated).[30]

27. The Directive does not give any explicit details on the identity of the representative agent. However, it seems clear that the designated representative agent must have the power to fulfil the obligations imposed upon him by the central management and suffer the consequences in the event of the obligations not being respected. Only an establishment or subsidiary established in one of the affected States fulfils these requirements. This would seem to rule out third persons being designated as representative agents for the purposes of this Directive.

The question arises whether a central management, located outside the EU and EEA, is always allowed to choose its representative agent that will act as central management for the purpose of the EWC. It is, for example, possible that a US multinational corporation with daughter companies within the EU has a European headquarters that is controlling all the European subsidiaries, but that remains subject to US central management. It is clear that the (ultimate) central management is located outside the EU and EEA. However, within the territorial scope of the Directive there is a European central management.

One could wonder whether the US central management should still be able to choose its representative for the purpose of the EWC. The Working Party was of the opinion that no such possibility remained in case one European undertaking was controlling all the others.[31]

B.   Special Negotiating Body

28. Once the process has been initiated, either by central management or by the employees, the next step is the constitution of a Special Negotiating Body (herein referred to as the SNB). Article 5 of the Directive sets out the guidelines to be followed. The SNB shall consist of a minimum of 3 and maximum of 17 members.[32]

As of the implementation of the UK Extension Directive, the maximum number was increased to 18.[33] Member State legislation shall determine the method to be used for the election or appointment of the members of the SNB. This legislation

---

29.   Articles 1, 2 and 4, EWC Directive.
30.   WPWP, at 117.
31.   WPWP, Conclusion 9.
32.   Article 5(b), EWC Directive.
33.   Article 2, EWC Extension Directive.

must provide that employees in an undertaking where there is no employee representative, shall still be able to elect or appoint someone to the SNB, notwithstanding existing national legislation setting thresholds for national employee representative bodies.[34] This means that although a particular undertaking may be too small to have some sort of national employee representative body, they will have to be represented at European level via the SNB.[35]

29. In the election and appointment process of the members of the SNB, it must be ensured that there will be one member representing a Member State in which there is one or more establishments, controlling or controlled undertakings of an affected undertaking. Furthermore, the legislation of the Member State where the central management is located, will establish supplementary members of the SNB in proportion to the number of employees working in the establishments or affected undertakings.[36]

The working group made the following suggestions when dealing with the distribution of additional seats in the SNB, on the basis of the criteria of 'number of employees':

– one additional seat for Member States in which at least 25 per cent of the workforce of the undertaking or group of undertaking is employed;
– two additional seats for Member States where at least 50 per cent of the workforce of the undertaking and groups of undertakings is employed; and
– three additional seats for Member States where at least 75 per cent of the workforce of the undertaking and groups of undertakings is employed.[37]

In its conclusion, the Working Party explicitly stated that the application of these rules may lead to an SNB consisting of more than the maximum number of members in total, especially when the company or group concerned is operating in most of the Member States covered by the Directive. The Member States will determine the method for election or appointment of the members of the SNB to be elected or appointed within their own territory. The Directive does not foresee the election or appointment of replacement members for the situation in which the member of the SNB would lose an essential qualification for membership to the SNB.

Given the fact that the SNB could face negotiations for a period of almost three years, it could well be that a member of the SNB dies, or that the trade union he/she represents loses its representative character that according to a given national law was the condition for its election into the SNB.

30. It is clear that the outcome of any of these questions is determined by the national law of the Member States. However, given the long period of time that may pass between the negotiations and reaching agreement or the establishment of an EWC, it is clear that provisions for the replacement of another member of the SNB may become indispensable. Likewise, what would happen if an undertaking in

---

34. Article 5(a), EWC Directive.
35. Article 5,2(a), 2nd para.
36. Article 5(c), EWC Directive.
37. WPWP, Conclusion No. 13, p. 89

which negotiations with the SNB have started merged with some other undertaking, not in itself satisfying the numerical requirements to set up an EWC? Provisions for the amendment of the SNB seem justified in this context. However, it will again be national law that will have to determine the results of the action described above. The same problems will undoubtedly come up with regard to the composition of the EWC also.

Once the SNB has been established, central management and local management shall be informed of its composition.[38] Thus, the rules on the composition and distribution of seats among Member States will be laid down in national Member State legislation where central management is located.

31. The national law of the Member States may allow the participation of worker representative from a country in which the Directive does not apply (e.g. USA, Japan). The Working Party came to the conclusion, however, that they should not be granted an opportunity to exert a crucial influence on the decision of the SNB. Suggestions are made as to the participation of these worker's representatives as mere observers.[39]

32. The main function of the SNB is to establish an agreement which sets out the details for the European Works Council or procedure for consultation and information. The SNB is the body with which central management will negotiate to come to this agreement. The task of the SNB, together with central management, is to determine the scope, composition, functions and term of office of the European Works Council(s) or the arrangements for implementing a procedure for the information, and consultation of employees.[40] The Directive provides that during this process of negotiation, the SNB may be assisted by experts of its choice.[41] Furthermore, expenses related to the negotiations are to be paid by the central management, but Member States may lay down budgetary rules, and in particular may limit the funding to cover only one expert.[42]

A meeting shall be convened between central management and the SNB with a view to concluding an agreement. The first paragraph of Article 6 states that the SNB and central management must negotiate in a spirit of cooperation with a view to reaching an agreement. The SNB must act by a majority of its members in concluding an agreement.[43] The SNB has the power to decide by at least two-thirds of the votes, not to open negotiations or to terminate negotiations that have already begun. If the SNB takes such a decision, the provisions of the Annex do *not* apply and a new request to convene the SNB can be made at the earliest within 2 years, unless the parties lay down a shorter time period.[44]

---

38. Article 5(d), EWC Directive.
39. WPWP, Conclusion No. 14, 9.
40. Article 5,3 EWC Directive.
41. Article 5,4, EWC Directive.
42. Article 5,6, EWC Directive.
43. Article 6,5, EWC Directive.
44. Article 5,4 and 5, EWC Directive.

C.   Content of the Agreement

33.   The directive grants the parties autonomy to decide upon the details of the agreement establishing an EWC or information and consultation procedure, provided that some items are definitely covered. The agreement must determine the undertakings which are covered; the composition of the EWC, number of members, allocation of seats, and terms of office; the functions and procedure for information/consultation; the venue, frequency, and duration of meetings. It must also discuss the financial and material resources allocated to the EWC, the duration of the agreement and the procedure for re-negotiation.[45] An agreement to establish an EWC or procedure is not subject to the subsidiary requirements of the Annex.[46]

The agreement must also state the manner in which employees' respresentatives shall have the right to meet and discuss the information which is conveyed to them via an EWC or procedure.[47] This information shall relate in particular to transnational questions which significantly affect workers' interests. [48]

D.   Article 6 Agreements Analysed

The European Foundation that had made several analyses of Article 13 agreements, also undertook a comparative analysis of the Article 13 agreements, with 71 Article 6 Agreement.[49] The report states as of November 1999, some 121 Article 6 agreements had been concluded.[50]

1. Geographical Scope

One out of three agreements covers countries beyond the EEA. The Czech Republic, Hungary, and Poland are most commonly covered. The percentage of agreements covering non-EEA countries rose to 30 per cent.[51]

2. Nature of the Body Created

Most Article 6 agreements establish a group-wide EWC (89 per cent). No instances of two tier arrangements are reported and only 11 per cent (i.e. 8 agreements) foresee a single-tier divisional EWC.

Compared to the Article 13 agreements, it can be stated that joint (employer and employee) bodies remain prevalent, but the percentage has gone down to 55 per cent (compared to 69 per cent before).[52]

---

45.   Article 6,2(a)–(f), EWC Directive.
46.   Article 6,4, EWC Directive.
47.   Article 6,3, EWC Directive.
48.   Article 6,3, EWC Directive.
49.   European Foundation Report.
50.   European Foundation Report, p.10
51.   European Foundation Report, p. 20
52.   European Foundation Report, p. 18.

3. Composition/Number of Members

In about three-quarters of the cases (76 per cent, as compared to 69 per cent) the number of employee representatives can be found in the agreement. The other agreements tend to provide a calculation formula only.[53]

EWCs are reported to be slightly smaller, than in Article 13 arrangements.

Both the flate-rate allocation method and the allocation based on the size of the work force are still used. However, there is a big surge in the use of the latter method.[54]

4. Selection of Members

Under Article 6 agreement the reliance on national legislation or practice of the country is even more prevalent as a selection method for the appointment or election of EWC representatives. This reflects the fact that the implementing legislation lays down rules for representatives on SNBs and EWCs according to the subsidiary requirements.[55]

External participation is foreseen in 92 per cent of the agreements. In only 7 per cent of the cases are these external representatives full members (compared to 17 per cent for the Article 13 agreements). All are trade unionists. [56]

E. Competence of the EWC

The Article 6 agreements with the exception of one, state that the purpose for the EWC is to provide information and consultation. There seems to be no difference with Article 13 agreements. More extensive provisions are foreseen only in 11 per cent (as opposed to 14 per cent for the Article 13 agreements) of the Article 6 agreements. While there are slightly more Article 6 agreements that mention a negotiating role for the EWC, also 10 per cent (as opposed to 0 per cent) of the agreements explicitly preclude the EWC from negotiating.

The issues the EWC can deal with and that are mentioned in the agreements are practically the same as for the Article 13 agreements. The contentious issues dealing with transfers, mergers, cutbacks, and closures are more often mentioned.

The number of agreements also mentioning environmental and training issues has increased.

1. Meetings

One meeting a year is the norm, as under Article 13 agreements. A few more agreements (17 per cent) foresee two meetings a year.

---

53. European Foundation Report, p. 28.
54. European Foundation Report, p. 30.
55. European Foundation Report, p. 34.
56. European Foundation Report, p. 35.

Ninety-seven per cent of the Article 6 agreements foresee that meetings can be called in exceptional circumstances.

The right to hold pre-meetings has become an almost universal right, so the European Foundation report states.

Follow-up or debriefing meetings for employee representatives after plenary EWC meetings are less common, but are very much on the increase.

V. SUBSIDIARY REQUIREMENTS

34. Article 7 of the Directive provides for the operation of default provisions in situations where:

– central management and the SNB decide to be covered by them,
– they are unable to conclude an agreement, or
– where central management refuses to commence negotiations within six months after there has been a valid request to do so.[57]

A. *Applicability*

35. The subsidiary requirements are set out in an annex to the Directive. They must also be transposed into the national law of the Member States. The subsidiary requirements basically make up all the basic provisions for an operational European Works Council in the absence of the parties agreement on this issue. As was stated above, if the Special Negotiating Body decides it no longer wants to continue negotiating with central management to reach an agreement and with a two-thirds majority decides to stop negotiating, the subsidiary requirements *do not* apply. This will result in a vacuum within the undertaking. However, if the refusal to negotiate is on the side of central management, there will be a default European Works Council established according to the provisions in the Annex.

B. *Content*

36. The subsidiary requirements make all the necessary provisions for establishing an European Works Council within an undertaking. They establish rules for the composition, the election or appointment procedure for members, frequency of meetings, topics discussed in meetings, the competence of the European Works Council, the right to a pre-meeting for the workers' representatives in order to prepare for the actual meeting with central management, and several other details. Practically speaking, the central management of many companies and workers representatives will look to the subsidiary requirements for some guidance in making their own voluntary agreements.

---

57. Article 7, EWC Directive.

1. Competence

37. According to the subsidiary requirements, the European Works Council will have competence over information and consultation on matters concerning their establishments and undertakings situated within the Member States.[58]

2. Composition

38. The European Works Council shall have a minimum of three members and a maximum of 30, who all must be employees of the Community-scale undertaking or Community-scale group of undertakings.[59] The same provisions are made regarding the distribution of members from different Member States, as those set out for the Special Negotiating Body in Article 5,2(c) of the Directive.[60] Basically, there has to be a representative from each Member State in which there is an establishment of the affected undertaking. Central management needs to be informed of the composition of the workforce. If the size of the EWC warrants, a select committee of at most three shall be elected from its members.[61]

3. Re-evaluation

39. After four years, the EWC shall make a determination of whether to open negotiations to conclude an agreement according to Article 6 of the Directive or whether to continue operating under the subsidiary requirements. If it is decided to negotiate an agreement, the EWC then becomes the Special Negotiating Body for the purposes of negotiating an agreement with central management.[62] National legislation of the Member States in which central management is located, will lay down rules for ensuring that supplementary members are elected or appointed in correspondence with the proportionate representation of the workforce in each Member State, compared to the overall undertaking or group of undertakings.

4. Meetings

40. The Annex provides that the central management and the European Works Council shall meet once a year 'to be informed and consulted, on the basis of a report drawn up by the central management, on the progress of the business'. During the meeting, the following topics shall be addressed: the structure, economic and financial situation, the probable development of the business and of production and sales, the situation and probable trend of employment, investments, and substantial changes concerning organization, introduction of new working methods or production

---

58. Annex 1 (1)(a), EWC Directive.
59. Annex 1 (b), EWC Directive.
60. Annex 1 (d), EWC Directive.
61. Annex 1 (c), EWC Directive.
62. Annex 1 (f), EWC Directive.

processes, transfers of production, mergers, cut-backs or closures of undertakings, establishments or important parts thereof, and collective redundancies.[63]

41. The Annex also makes special provisions for exceptional circumstances, such as relocations, the closure of establishments or undertakings, or collective redundancies, wherein the EWC or the select committee (if one exists) shall have the right to be informed and meet, at its request with the central management.[64] The meeting shall take place as soon as possible on the basis of a report drawn up by the central management, on which an opinion may be delivered at the end of the meeting or within a reasonable time. The meeting shall not affect the prerogatives of the central management.[65] How these meetings should be run, is an issue to be decided by the individual Member States.[66] The EWC or select committee has the right to a pre-meeting without central management being present.

5. Costs and Experts

42. Provisions regarding experts and their funding are the same as in the Directive itself. The Annex goes into more detail by stating that 'the cost of organizing meetings and arranging for interpretation facilities and the accommodation and travelling expenses of members of the European Works Council and its select committee shall be met by the central management, unless otherwise agreed.'[67] Central management has to provide the members of the EWC with the financial and material resources to enable them to satisfy their duties properly.[68]

VI. MISCELLANEOUS PROVISIONS

43. The Directive provides several miscellaneous provisions covering confidential information, the operations of an EWC or procedure, compliance with the Directive, the link between this and other provisions and review by the Commission. Pre-existing agreements are covered by Article 13, which appears as a miscellaneous provision of the Directive.

A. *Confidential and/or Harmful Information*

44. For very practical and obvious reasons, provisions had to be made regarding confidential information. In many instances, the employees and/or undertakings affected by this Directive will have access to information which they did not previously have at national level. This does not take away from the fact that the proper functioning and existence of an undertaking may depend on its most valuable information

---

63. Annex 2, EWC Directive.
64. Annex 3, EWC Directive.
65. Annex 3, EWC Directive.
66. Annex 4, EWC Directive.
67. Annex 7, EWC Directive.
68. Annex 7, EWC Directive.

being kept confidential. To this end, the Directive states that it is up to the Member States to provide that members of SNBs, EWCs, or those involved in an information and consultation procedure and any assisting experts are not authorized to reveal any information which has been expressly provided to them in confidence.[69] This obligation of confidentiality shall apply even after the expiration of their terms of office.

Furthermore, the Directive states that Member States shall provide that central management does not have to transmit information when 'its nature is such that, according to objective criteria, it would seriously harm the functioning of the undertakings concerned or would be prejudicial to them'.

A Member State may make such dispensation to provide/disclose information subject to prior administrative or judicial authorization,[70] with a provision for administrative or judicial appeal procedures for employee representatives to challenge any central management's allegations that information should be kept confidential or where it does not transmit information as it should.[71] On the other hand, administrative or judicial appeal procedures may also be designated to protect the confidentiality of the information in question.[72]

45. Article 8(3) deals particularly with undertakings which pursue ideological guidance regarding information and expression of opinions. This provision is intended for political and professional associations, religious and charitable groups, and educational and scientific groups. Member States may make special provisions for these types of undertakings.

B. *Operation of EWC: Spirit of Cooperation*

46. The phrase 'in a spirit of cooperation' appears once more in the text of the Directive, this time with regard to the operation of the EWC or procedure. 'The central management and the European Works Council shall work in spirit of cooperation with due regard to their reciprocal rights and obligations'. [73]

C. *Protection of Employee Representatives*

47. The Directive provides that the members of SNBs, EWCs and employee representatives exercising their functions under a procedure for information and consultation shall enjoy the same protection and guarantees which employee representatives have under national legislation.[74] This protection includes provisions which will allow members of these bodies to attend meetings and receive wages during periods of absence necessary for the performance of their duties. Such protective measures are necessary to allow these organs to function properly.

---

69. Article 8,1, EWC Directive.
70. Article 8,2 and 3, EWC Directive.
71. Article 11,4, EWC Directive.
72. Article 11,4, EWC Directive.
73. Article 9, EWC Directive.
74. Article 10, EWC Directive.

D. Review by the Commission

48. The Commission had to review the operation of the Directive no later than 22 September 1999. This review had to take place in consultation with the Member States and with management and labour at European level. The review had to focus particularly on whether the workforce size thresholds are appropriate, with a view to proposing amendments to the Council.[75]

The Commission finally came up with a report on April 4, 2000.[76] The report only deals with the status of the transposition law with regard to the original EWC directive.

The major point of the Commission report deals with the national implementing measures of the original directive. The report furthermore highlights some shortcomings, but does not really review the EWCs operation and workforce thresholds with a view to proposing amendments, as requested by Article 15 of the original EWC Directive.

The report notes that the Working Party (see supra) played an important role in the implementation process and states that this method of implementation should be followed more generally.[77]

The commission takes note of a need for further interpretation on a number of issues already identified:

– the concept of 'controlling undertaking';
– the effects of geographical and proportional criteria;
– the conditions for renewing agreements already in force (Article 13);
– changes in the structure of the group;
– the very concept of 'expert'.[78]

The Commission states that these issues were in a significant number of cases resolved by the parties. In other cases courts would be best suited to address the issues.

Other legal issues relate to:

– the legal personality of the EWC;
– the determination of the applicable law;
– the legal status of the EWC agreements; and
– the rules of international jurisdiction.[79]

The report notes that the European social partners highlighted a number of legal and practical problems but that none of them (ETUC, UNICE and CEEP) asked for an immediate revision of the Directive.[80]

---

75. Article 15 EWC Directive.
76. *Report from the Commission to the European Parliament and the Council on the application of the Direc-tive on the establishment of a European Works Council or a procedure in Community-scale undertakings and Community-scale groups of undertakings for the purposes of informing and consulting employees* (Council Directive 94/45/EC of 22 September 1994), Brussels, 4 April 2000, CUM (2000) 188 final, hereinafter referred to as the 'Commission Report'.
77. Commission report, p. 3.
78. Commission report, p. 4.
79. Commission report, p. 4.
80. Commission report, p. 5, e.s.

Chapter 22. Collective Bargaining*

G.J. Bamber and P. Sheldon

I. WHAT IS COLLECTIVE BARGAINING?

1.   Collective bargaining is usually seen as a process of aiming to reach 'collective agreements' (UK), 'labor contracts' (USA) or the equivalent (in other countries) which regulate terms and conditions of employment.[1] The process of collective bargaining requires at least two parties. One, by definition, has to be a collectivity of employees. Usually, the other is an employer, a group of employers or an organization representing employers. Representatives of government may form a third party. The concept was first analysed by the Webbs, who saw it as an alternative to 'individual bargaining' and 'autonomous regulation'. They saw collective bargaining as one of three union strategies; the others were 'mutual insurance' and 'legal enactment'.[2] Research and thinking about the concept developed on both sides of the Atlantic. For example, in the USA, Commons investigated negotiations and compromise among the divergent interests of unions, employers and the public,[3] Slichter et al. saw it as a system of industrial jurisprudence,[4] while Chamberlain analysed collective bargaining in

---

*   We much appreciate the kind assistance of: Linda Dickens, Ken Lovell, Mary Moloney, Peter Ross, Tina Scrine, and several other colleagues, and the helpful comments on earlier drafts from Roy Adams, Oliver Clarke, and Keith Sisson. We are most grateful to Efren Córdova who drafted earlier editions of this chapter.
1.   International Labour Organisation (ILO) instruments deem collective bargaining to be the activity or process leading up to the conclusion of a collective agreement. In ILO Recommendation No. 91, Para. 2, collective agreements are defined as: 'all agreements *in writing* (our emphasis) regarding working conditions and terms of employment concluded between an employer, a group of employers or one or more employers' organisations, on the one hand, and one or more representative workers' organisations, or, in the absence of such organisations, the representatives of the workers duly elected and authorised by them in accordance with national laws and regulations, on the other.' (B. Gernigon, A. Odero and H. Guido, 'ILO principles concerning collective bargaining', *International Labour Review*, 2000, pp. 33–55.) Our working definition of collective bargaining is broader than that of the ILO. In our view, collective bargaining may take place even though it may not lead to the conclusion of a collective agreement *in writing*. On occasion, collective bargaining may take place even though the parties do not conclude a collective agreement. On other occasions, they may conclude an informal collective agreemnent that is not necessarily *in writing*.
2.   S. and B. Webb, *Industrial Democracy*, Longman, London, 1897.
3.   J.R. Commons, *Institutional Economics: Its Place in the Political Economy*, Macmillan, New York, 1934.
4.   S.H. Slichter, J.J. Healy, and E.R. Livernash, *The Impact of Collective Bargaining on Management*, Brookings Institution, Washington D.C. 1960.

terms of three theories: a marketing theory (a means of contracting for the sale of labour); a governmental theory (a form of industrial government); and a managerial theory (a method of management).[5] In the UK, Flanders pointed out that it was misleading to contrast collective bargaining with individual bargaining. He saw collective bargaining as a political process, involving joint rule-making and power relationships which could enhance the dignity of employees.[6] Others examined collective bargaining as an institutionalization of industrial conflict.[7] Subsequent scholars have applied analytical insights into collective bargaining from the fields of economics, organizational behaviour, and human resource management (HRM) whereas most earlier analyses had a more descriptive 'historical-institutional' approach.[8]

2.   There is a wide variety of viewpoints regarding collective bargaining, including broad and narrow descriptive definitions. In its broad sense, collective bargaining is a process of interest accommodation, which includes all sorts of bipartite or tripartite discussions relating to employment and industrial relations that may affect a group of employees directly or indirectly. The notion of bargaining implies that the parties are aiming to reach agreement, if necessary, by competitive negotiation. Consultation is less competitive and a more 'integrative'[9] process, whereby the parties will exchange views but not necessarily reach a formal agreement. For example, before making a decision, an employer may listen to employees' views. Nevertheless, consultation processes may also be included in a broad view of collective bargaining. A narrower but more precise meaning of collective bargaining implies only the bipartite negotiations leading to agreements.

3.   In addition to the more specific negotiations between employers and unions (the two main 'parties'), a broad view of collective bargaining also includes the State as a third party which may be involved in political bargaining and tripartite negotiations at the centralized national (economy-wide) level. Although the broad national types of collective bargaining became more prevalent in some IMEs in the post-1945 period, this contribution focuses mainly on the narrower, less centralized, types in the private sector.

II.   HISTORICAL BACKGROUND

4.   In the early stages of industrialization, collective bargaining began in many countries as a means of regulating pay and a few other conditions of employment.

---

5.   N.W. Chamberlain and J.W. Kuhn, *Collective Bargaining*, 3d ed., McGraw Hill, New York, 1986.
6.   A. Flanders, 'Collective bargaining: A theoretical analysis' in *Management and Unions: The Theory and Reform of Industrial Relations* (ed). A. Flanders, Faber, London, 1975, p. 213ff.
7.   R. Dubin, 'Constructive Aspects of Industrial Conflict', in *Industrial Conflict* (eds), A. Kornhauser, R. Dubin and A.M. Ross, New York: McGraw Hill, 1954, pp. 37–47; A. Fox, *A Sociology of Work in Industry*, Collier-Macmillan, London, 1971, p. 135ff.
8.   T.A. Kochan, *Collective Bargaining and Industrial Relations: From Theory to Practice*, Irwin, Homewood, Ill, 1980, p. viiff; *also see* H.C. Katz and T.A. Kochan, *An Introduction to Collective Bargaining and Industrial Relations*, 2nd ed., McGraw-Hill, New York, 1999.
9.   *See* R.E. Walton and R.B. McKersie, *A Behavioral Theory of Labor Negotiations*, 2nd ed., McGraw Hill, New York, 1991.

Groups of employees and left-wing political groups saw it as a way of replacing unilateral decision-making by the employer and of overcoming the weak bargaining position of individual employees. Usually occurring at enterprise and craft level, but occasionally at industry level – as in the British cotton industry – it also suited the sociological features of manufacturing industries which concentrated sizeable groups of wage earners doing similar tasks into workplaces that were relatively large. Moreover, it gave practical expression to the nascent feelings of solidarity among employees. Union organization channelled such feelings, originally directed in a sporadic fashion towards the declaration of industrial disputes, in a more systematic manner towards the establishment of a common rule in a given craft, district, enterprise, or industry.

5.   In the mid-nineteenth century, as most governments and employers did not recognize unions, collective bargaining rarely played an important role, apart from among select groups of craftsmen. Many negotiations took place in an atmosphere of crisis under the pressure of sanctions (e.g. strikes or lockouts) and collective agreements had only a *de facto* validity. Many of them were the creations of temporary coalitions of employees which subsequently disbanded. When unions grew in strength and were able to obtain recognition (around the end of the nineteenth century in some European countries and Australasia, but a few decades later in most other industrialized countries), the parties developed collective bargaining, which became a key element of nearly all industrial relations systems of IMEs, *albeit* with different styles, patterns and traditions in different contexts. Collective bargaining was by no means always instigated by workers' interests. In many cases it was instigated by employers who wanted to get workers and their unions to agree to a given set of terms and conditions for a specific period. This was against the background that some early workers' collectivities would simply make demands and walk out if the employer did not concede. Such collectivities did not want the nuisance and delays of negotiations.

6.   The British tradition emphasized the voluntary character of negotiations and considerable autonomy for the bargaining parties, with little legal intervention and often a high degree of informality. In a significant divergence from their British heritage, following a wave of industrial strife in the 1890s, Australia and New Zealand experimented with the notion of compulsory and legally binding arbitration which its advocates saw as an effective method of preventing and settling industrial disputes.[10] Although many people assume there is a clear distinction between collective bargaining and arbitration, many such arbitration awards are the outcome of collective bargaining. In continental Europe, the growth of collective bargaining was facilitated by the incorporation of collective agreements in the legal system of various countries as a new source of industrial relations rules. This process started with the Dutch Civil Code (1907) and the Swiss Code of Obligations (1911) and was followed by legislation in Norway (1915), Germany (1918), France (1919), Finland (1924), and (again) the Netherlands (1927). Such laws acknowledged that collective

---

10.   J. Niland, *Collective Bargaining and Compulsory Arbitration in Australia*, New South Wales University Press, Sydney, 1978, p. 25ff.

agreements were a valid way of determining conditions of employment for a collectivity of employees. There were important US developments in 1935 when the National Labor Relations (Wagner) Act introduced novel principles governing the orderly conduct of negotiations and the prohibition of unfair labour practices.

7.   Not only have such influences helped to shape other national models, but they have also been reflected in the conventions and recommendations adopted by the International Labour Organisation (ILO). The continental European model induced most of the provisions on effects, interpretation and extension of agreements included in Recommendation 92 on Collective Agreements 1951. The British influence inspired the reference to 'machinery for voluntary negotiations' in one of the key provisions of Convention 98 on the Right to Organize and to Bargain Collectively 1949. Some elements of the American penchant for regulating collective bargaining procedures appear in Recommendation 130 concerning the Examination of Grievances within Undertakings, as well as in Convention 154 and Recommendation 163 concerning the Promotion of Collective Bargaining, 1981.

8.   Despite the above international influences, national contexts for collective bargaining vary widely. In some European countries, collective agreements bind only affiliated members of the signatory union. In the UK and a few other English-speaking countries, a collective agreement is not legally binding unless specifically requested by the parties (which they rarely do); if such request is not made, the enforcement of the 'voluntary agreement' hinges on the goodwill or relative strength of the parties. Such countries have tended not to regulate negotiations; this reflected the wish of the parties to preserve the autonomy of collective bargaining and avoid government intervention. Nevertheless, the notion of a voluntary agreement is increasingly being challenged and, in practice, agreements come to apply to the generality of employees, even in countries where they are supposed to bind only union affiliates. In the absence of legislative provisions, rules dealing with the negotiations develop as part of a specialized jurisprudence, custom and practice or by an explicit decision of the parties.

9.   Clegg uses discussion of his six 'dimensions' of collective bargaining structures to explain the comparative historical experience of union behaviour.[11] These dimensions are: the 'level' at which bargaining takes place; the 'extent' or inclusiveness of coverage of the process and outcome relative to the potential population of employers and employees; the 'scope' or range of issues bargained; the 'depth' or the degree of involvement of local or plant level union officials in bargaining; 'union security' or support from employers for union recruitment and retention of members; and the 'degree of control', which refers to the extent to which a collective agreement includes obligatory standards and effective grievance procedures. To these can be added the 'form' or type of bargaining structure related to the degree of

---

11. H.A. Clegg, *Trade Unionism Under Collective Bargaining: A Theory Based on Comparisons of Six Countries*, Blackwell, Oxford, 1976, pp. 8–9. Clegg defines union behaviour as: density of membership, external structure, internal government, workplace organization, strikes, attitudes to industrial democracy, and political action.

institutionalization or state involvement in collective bargaining. Focusing on changes to at least some of these dimensions is an effective method for analysing comparatively changes to collective bargaining structures over time and space.[12]

10. Clegg argues that his dimensions of collective bargaining are themselves mainly determined by the structures of management and of employers' organizations; 'but where the law has intervened in the early stages, it may have played an equally important part, or even a more important part, in shaping collective bargaining'. In contrast to the widespread failure to appreciate how the role of employers in collective bargaining varies from country to country, Adams and Sisson seek to examine employer behaviour within the development of collective bargaining cross-nationally.

11. Adams points out that western European employers' behaviour towards unions differs significantly to those in North America.[13] In the former, typically, employers are organized into strong associations that engage in collective bargaining with unions (and with the State). By contrast, in North America, employers have generally not formed strong associations and even where they have, it is much less usual for those associations to engage in collective bargaining. Adams holds that these differences are attributable to the different early political, economic, and organizational strategies of the various labour movements and how these induced differing degrees of state intervention and employer compromise.

12. Sisson compares the role of employers and their organizations in the development of collective bargaining in seven countries.[14] He also concludes that differences between the countries were rooted in historical experience, particularly flowing from the impact of industrialization. In western Europe plus Britain and Australasia, multi-employer bargaining emerged as the predominant pattern largely because employers in the metal working industries were confronted with the challenge of national unions organized along occupational or industrial lines. In contrast, single-employer bargaining emerged in the USA and Japan because the relatively large employers that had emerged at quite an early stage in both countries were able to exert pressure on unions to bargain at the enterprise level.

III. LEVELS OF BARGAINING

13. The level is the most obvious dimension of a bargaining structure and the one which has engendered the most controversy in recent years. In any one country, bargaining can take place at several levels simultaneously (*see* Table 1, p. 566) and

---

12. *See* e.g. L. Thornthwaite and P. Sheldon 'The Metal Trades Industry Association, Bargaining Structures and the Accord', *Journal of Industrial Relations*, 1996, pp. 171–195.
13. R. Adams, 'A Theory of Employer Attitudes and Behaviour towards Trade Unions in Western Europe and North America', in *Management Under Differing Value Systems* (eds), G. Dlugos and K. Weiermair in collaboration with W. Dorow, de Gruyter, Berlin, 1981, pp. 277–293.
14. K. Sisson, *The Management of Collective Bargaining: An International Comparison*, Blackwell, Oxford, 1987.

the connections between these levels may be either systematic or *ad hoc*.[15] Nonetheless, in relation to a particular country, for analytical purposes it is helpful to classify its most important level of bargaining, which is usually at national (or economy-wide), industry (or branch or sectoral) or enterprise (or company) level. Centralized negotiations at the national level were, until the 1980s, a distinguishing feature of Scandinavian countries and Austria and in a more restricted sense through its national arbitration procedures, Australia (but these were more fragmented). Most European countries have traditionally opted for industry-wide bargaining in relation to pay issues. Canada, the USA and Japan (except for the maritime industry) have generally used enterprise bargaining, though there is a clear difference between the Japanese and the North Americans; the former's bargaining can be characterized as cooperative (*'Shunto'* notwithstanding),[16] but the latter's can be traditionally characterized as adversarial, legalistic and as focusing on job control.

14. From Dutch data, Huiskamp suggests that different levels of bargaining among industries in the same country are correlated with the stage of industrial development within which they emerged as well as their size.[17] Older industries (engineering, printing) generally consisting of smaller firms tend to work under industry agreements, newer ones (chemicals, oil refining) under large-corporation enterprise agreements, and the most recently emerging industries (computers, private services) tend towards individual employment contracts at the expense of collective bargaining. As Bean points out, this may relate to employer concerns to regulate the links between labour and product markets. When, in earlier stages of industrial development, these markets were essentially local, multi-employer bargaining was one way to regulate competition. The greater scale and industrial concentration of later industries worked against multi-employer bargaining by undermining the possibility of product market competition within single economies.[18]

15. Apart from the three main levels, bargaining may also be devolved to or fragmented at the level of the establishment and the workplace and may also be limited to specific groups of employees from the same craft or occupation as in the UK. In some countries – Germany, France and Italy – and in the US construction industry, bargaining levels may also include geographic units, with negotiations held at the local and regional, as well the industry levels. While national level bargaining in some cases, for example in the public services, aims at the determination of substantive conditions of employment, it is usually concerned with matters of widespread interest such as pay indexation and retirement benefits, or the establishment

---

15. For an attempt to resolve *ad hoc* articulation via tripartite collective agreement in Italy, *see European Industrial Relations Review* (EIRR), September 1993, p. 15ff.
16. Y. Kuwahara, 'Employment relations in Japan' in *International and Comparative Employment Relations: A Study of Industrialised Market Economies*, 3rd ed., (eds), G.J. Bamber and R.D. Lansbury, Allen & Unwin, Sydney, 1998. On Shunto union bargaining practices, *see Japan Labor Bulletin*, 1 January 1994, p. 4; 1 April 1995, pp. 3–4.
17. R. Huiskamp, 'Collective Bargaining in Transition', in *Comparative Industrial and Employment Relations* (eds), J. V. Ruysseveldt, R. Huiskamp, and J. van Hoof, London, Sage, 1995, pp. 137–138.
18. R. Bean, *Comparative Industrial Relations: An Introduction to Cross-national Perspectives*, 2nd ed., Routledge, London, 1994, pp. 80–83.

of the basic bargaining rules to regulate and facilitate subsequent processes and outcomes of bargaining at lower levels. Substantive standards constitute the minima that underpin lower-level negotiations.

16. Multinational bargaining would be an even higher level of negotiation. This is still an embryonic area of collective bargaining but there are a number of trends becoming apparent. First, there is little intention to use multinational collective bargaining as a way of establishing pay rates across different countries. To the extent that multinational bargaining concerns pay, it is about pay principles rather than outcomes. International Trade (Union) Secretariats such as the International Federation of Chemical, Energy, Mine and General Workers Union, an innovator in such bargaining, have been more concerned with working conditions such as occupational health and safety and with spreading and defending core collective labour rights such as job security across the operations of particular multinational corporations and industry groups.[19]

17. The Social Charter of the European Union (EU) has led to a growth in consultation about social policy between (in the language of the EU) the 'social partners' and it has raised the possibility of collective bargaining leading to agreements at the European level. The first of these resulted in an EU Directive on parental leave. Subsequently, there has been a growing interest in cross-national agreements in the EU. Similarly, the requirements for financial membership of the EURO single-currency area have encouraged collective bargaining within some European Member States explicitly to take into account bargaining outcomes of other states as a way of reducing the size of pay increases. Implicitly, at least, a cross-national bargaining agenda has thus begun to complement national- and industry-level collective bargaining, particularly where this involves tripartite 'social pacts'. Some unions are concerned about the way that this 'competitive corporatism' of the tripartite pacts places downward pressure on pay and occupationally-based social security. This has led the union confederations of Germany and the Benelux countries to establish cross-border coordination of bargaining policy. For their part, the larger multinational corporations have been attempting to diffuse their production, cost and other priorities by using initial bargaining gains as leverage in sequential local-level bargaining across subsidiaries. Unions are even more worried that the larger multinational corporations are spreading pressures on work practices and working conditions by linking subsidiary investment and production decisions to local 'concession bargaining'. Here, the European Metalworkers' Federation has taken the lead on pay and working hours. Much of this has been at industry level although the Federation is also intent on building a cross-national bargaining structure that starts at plant level. As well, the Federation's German affiliate, IG Metall, has begun to develop a series of binational collective bargaining partnerships with other national affiliates.[20] Although European-level works councils are often not supposed to be involved in

19. R. Taylor, *Trade Unions and Transnational Industrial Relations*, Geneva, International Institute for Labour Studies (ILO), 1999, *http://www. ilo. org/public/english/bureau/inst/papers/1999/dp99/ index. htm*, pp. 10–11.

20. 'The Changing Face of Collective Bargaining', EIRR, May 1996, p. 1; P. Marginson and T. Schulten, *The 'Europeanisation' of Collective Bargaining*, Dublin, European Foundation for the

collective bargaining, the 1994 European Works Council Directive offers a range of collective bargaining possibilities at multinational enterprise level for unions and employers. Perhaps, for this reason, international unions have played an important role in negotiations that have established these councils.[21]

IV. The Parties to Collective Bargaining

18. Given the difficulties involved in negotiating and administering an agreement directly with many individual employees, the bargaining agent on the employees' side necessarily implies an organization representing employees, usually a union. Collective bargaining has, in turn, long been one of the main functions of unions in most countries.[22] However, the effectiveness of a union in discharging this function depends on several variables including: the size and density of its membership, its financial resources, the degree of support of its members and their willingness to invoke sanctions. These variables constitute the basis of a union's bargaining power.

19. Typically, then, unions occupy the role of bargaining agent, but in Germany, much of Scandinavia, France and some other European countries, works councils or other enterprise-based organizations perform certain bargaining functions. In many cases, such negotiations are supposed to deal only with non-pay issues or are conducted only on a *de facto* basis, since legislators have tried to separate the bargaining functions of unions from the participative responsibilities of works councils. Nevertheless, in practice, there are often strong links between the unions and works councils. Under the conservative National Government that ruled New Zealand for most of the 1990s, legislative changes encouraged the emergence of non-union bargaining agents such as accounting firms on behalf of employee collectivies.[23] Since 1996, a conservative Australian government has, through legislation, fostered a form of non-union collective bargaining.

20. Particularly where enterprise-level bargaining prevails, employers may conduct negotiations directly, that is without an employers' organization. However, many employers are represented or assisted by an employers' organization, especially where there is industry-wide or national bargaining. Although it is relatively

---

(*Contd.*)

Improvement of Living and Working Conditions, 1999, *http://www/eiro.eurofound.ie/1999/07/study/TN9907201S.html* R. Taylor, *Trade Unions and Transnational Industrial Relations,* Geneva, International Institute for Labour Studies (ILO), 1999, *http://www. ilo.org/public/english/bureau/,* p. 8 For broader discussion of the impacts of capitalist globalization on collective bargaining, *see* ILO, *Your Voice at Work,* ILO, Geneva, 2000.

21. Marginson and Schulten, *The 'Europeanisation'* ...

22. An exception is Taiwan where unions are little involved in collective bargaining. S-J. Chen, 'The Development of HRM Practices in Taiwan' in *Human Resource Management in the Asia Pacific Region: Convergence Questioned* ed, C. Rowley, Frank Cass, London, 1998, p. 158.

23. D. Peetz, D. Quinn, L. Edwards, and P. Riedel, 'Workplace Bargaining in New Zealand: Radical Change at Work', in *Workplace Bargaining in the International Context,* eds. D. Peetz, A. Preston, and J. Docherty, Department of Industrial Relations (Australia), Canberra, Industrial Relations Research Monograph No. 2, 1993. pp. 236–237.

rare, multi-employer bargaining may be conducted without a formal employers' organization. In addition, employers' organizations may act as clearinghouses of information and training, as well as advisers to individual employers in their enterprise-level bargaining. Problems have arisen, however, with regard to the authority of employers' organizations to conclude collective agreements on behalf of their members at the industry level. In some countries, employers' organizations do not engage in industry-wide *negotiations* but are restricted to a *coordinating* role.

21.   Both parties appoint negotiating committees, usually composed of union officers and corporate officials; they may be assisted by lawyers and, in the case of local unions and employers' organizations, by representatives of their parent collectivities and head offices. In certain countries, for example France and Spain, the number of negotiators cannot exceed certain limits. Typically, employers' and employees' negotiators are empowered as real negotiators, not as simple conveyors of proposals and counterproposals. According to ILO Recommendation 163, 'Parties to collective bargaining should provide their respective negotiators with the necessary mandate to conduct and conclude negotiations, subject to any provisions for consultations within their respective organizations'.[24]

V.   BARGAINING UNITS AND THE RECOGNITION OF BARGAINING AGENTS

22.   Identifying an appropriate bargaining unit is an indispensable preliminary step, though the process varies considerably. In some countries, there are no formal established procedures and the determination of the bargaining unit is simply the result of a power struggle, or a tacit understanding between the parties. In a few countries, however, particularly where collective bargaining takes place at the enterprise level, a special agency has the authority to determine the appropriate bargaining unit; criteria are developed to guide its rulings. For instance, the three basic rules used by the US National Labor Relations Board (NLRB) are:

(i)   the desires of the parties;
(ii)   the bargaining history; and
(iii) the commonality of interests.

23.   Another preliminary step is represented by the employers' recognition of the relevant union(s). Such recognition usually depends on proof of representativeness and is a different process to the registration of unions for legal purposes, usually through a government office, upon the fulfilment of minimum requirements. There are at least four major systems of recognition for bargaining purposes:

(i)   exclusive bargaining representation for the majority union (e.g. Canada and the USA);
(ii)   non-exclusive bargaining rights for the most representative unions (e.g. Belgium and the Netherlands);

---

24. ILO, *International Labour Conventions and Recommendations 1919–1981*, ILO, Geneva, 1982, p. 222.

(iii)   multiple representation of various representative unions on the basis of a joint negotiating committee (e.g. Italy,[25] Spain and France); and

(iv)   multiple representation of various unions with no expectation of concurrent bargaining (e.g. the UK).

24.   Multiple representation entails more difficult negotiations and, subsequently, more complications in administering the agreement, not least because, occasionally, different conditions of employment may be adopted even within a similar group of employees. Hence in the UK there there have been moves towards exclusive bargaining rights at enterprise level (single-union recognition) and inward investing foreign firms, especially those from Japan, encourage this trend.[26]

25.   Several mandatory and voluntary procedures have been established to adjudicate in union recognition disputes.[27] Mandatory procedures are established by law, mainly in countries where exclusive bargaining representation or 'most representative systems' have been introduced. They tend to rely on elections by secret ballot or evidence of substantial membership support (usually the majority of employees or voters concerned, although lower and higher percentages are also known). Other criteria may also be used, including an appraisal of the experience, independence and stability of the union. In some countries, independent agencies have been set up to handle union recognition or representation cases, while in others this task is performed by a ministry of labour or by labour courts. These arrangements may be changed reflecting changes in the political complexions of governments. For instance, to adjudicate in disputes about union recognition in Britain, the post-1997 Labour government established a new procedure under the Central Arbitration Committee.[28] Britain had had union recognition mechanisms discontinued following an earlier change of government. According to ILO standards, the determination by public authorities of the union entitled to negotiate should be based on 'pre-established and objective criteria'. Voluntary procedures prescribed in basic agreements or codes of discipline have also been tried by certain countries, but with limited success.

26.   The need for appropriate representation procedures is particularly evident in countries where multi-unionism is acute and bargaining takes place at the enterprise level. While such multiplicity means that employees have a choice between different unions, it may also mean problems of interunion rivalry as well as possible recognition disputes, all of which can detract from enterprise efficiency and effectiveness, as well as from collective bargaining. Enterprise bargaining can entail a more direct challenge to the authority of individual managers, who may consequently be

---

25.   There is a tripartite collective agreement redefining workplace representation rights, EIRR, February 1994, pp. 19–24.

26.   N. Oliver and B. Wilkinson, *The Japanisation of British Industry*, Blackwell, Oxford, 1992; J. Goodman et al., 'Employment relations in Britain', in Bamber and Lansbury, 1998.

27.   On government policies in this field, *see* R. Adams, 'State Regulation of unions and collective bargaining: an international assessment of determinants and consequences' in J. Niland, R. Lansbury, and C. Verevis (eds), *The Future of Industrial Relations*, Sage, London, 1994.

28.   *See* F. Youngson, 'How to handle a union recognition claim', *People Management, 20 July 2000.*

more inclined than employers' organizations to resist the recognition of bargaining rights to unions, to favour the most compliant union or subsequently to engage in union-avoidance tactics.

VI. BARGAINING PROCESSES

27. As collective bargaining spreads, its consequences acquire greater significance, so the parties formulate rules and procedures to govern its processes; these then become more complex and institutionalized. A full sequence of the first round of bargaining usually includes at least six stages:

  (i) the definition of the appropriate bargaining unit;
 (ii) the mutual recognition of the parties;
(iii) the preparation and submission of demands and counter demands;
(iv) the conduct of the negotiations;
 (v) the conclusion of the agreement (and its possible ratification); and
(vi) its registration.

28. Subsequent rounds may omit (i)–(ii). Some of the stages are carefully regulated in many countries by law in an attempt to avoid disputes by ensuring that collective bargaining is orderly. In other countries, there are widely accepted rules established by basic agreement or by tradition.

29. The negotiation stage (iv) alone may include several phases. Increasingly the parties are trying to train their negotiators. Most participants attempt to prepare themselves for bargaining satisfactorily, to analyse background information, and to produce appropriate demands and counter demands. Union demands are usually discussed at general meetings of the local union branch and/or at higher councils of union delegates, then investigated by the officials who are leading the negotiations; they may sometimes decide to resubmit them to a general meeting before presenting them to the employer. Some unions attempt to analyse the employers' economic strength or to make comparisons with key groups. Others approach collective bargaining in a more improvized fashion. For their part, the most sophisticated employers calculate the costs of economic and non-economic demands and possible countermeasures, compare current and projected agreements' costs and devise suitable bargaining strategies.

30. Two institutional models of the bargaining process can be identified from the experience of IMEs. One, from some western European countries with industry-wide bargaining, tends to emphasize the importance of machinery. This approach resulted, for instance, in the creation of permanent bilateral bodies – joint committees in Belgium, employer-labour conferences in Ireland, the Foundation of Labour in the Netherlands and joint industrial councils in the UK. These can settle pay and other conditions of employment and fix their own procedural rules.

31. Another approach is the North American type which pays particular attention to procedures. This model is based on two major pillars: the duty to bargain 'in good faith' and the prohibition of 'unfair labour practices'. While the latter presupposes a

specific identification of certain types of conduct which militate against collective bargaining, the former is a somewhat vaguer notion that usually requires further elaboration by courts or enforcement agencies. As developed by the Wagner Act (1935), Taft-Hartley Act (1947) and NLRB decisions, bargaining in good faith includes four main duties: to meet and confer at reasonable intervals in a mutually convenient place; to engage in meaningful discussions over all negotiable issues; to show the reason why certain demands cannot be accepted; and to make counterproposals. Despite the American labour movement becoming more and more critical of these procedures, elements of the duty to bargain in good faith have been adopted in the legislation of other countries. Paradoxically, while labour in the US suffered the revisions under Taft-Hartley, the postwar US occupation forces in Japan and South Korea adapted only the more pro-union Wagner-type provisions.[29]

32.   The provision of information is an important corollary to the duty to bargain in good faith. What was once regarded as a management prerogative or a procedural matter to be discussed prior to negotiations may be considered as an employer's obligation to disclose and sometimes also as a union's right to obtain. The USA was the first country to introduce the notion that 'good faith' involved the duty to provide the other party with information necessary for meaningful negotiations. However, this applied mostly to the information needed by the union to prepare its pay claims. A more complete definition of this duty appeared in the Civil Service Reform Act 1978 that refers to the information 'which is reasonably available for full and proper discussion, understanding and negotiation of subjects within the scope of collective bargaining'. Legislation to regulate the disclosure of information for collective bargaining purposes has developed furthest in Sweden (Joint Regulation of Working Life Act 1976). German, Belgian, and French employers are obliged to disclose information to works councils rather than to unions. In France, the 1982 law extended this right to the unions engaged in negotiations.

33.   Although the disclosure principle is by no means accepted everywhere, it has reached the international stage through the OECD Guidelines for Multinational Enterprises 1976, ILO Tripartite Declaration of Principles concerning Multinational Enterprises and Social Policy 1977, ILO Recommendation 163 concerning the Promotion of Collective Bargaining 1981 and the EU Directive on European Works Councils 1994. ILO Recommendation 163 indicates that 'public and private employers should, at the request of workers' organizations, make available such information as is necessary on the economic and social situation of the negotiation unit and the undertaking as a whole, as is necessary for meaningful negotiation'.[30] The Recommendation includes *provisos* that if the disclosure of any such information could be prejudicial to the undertaking, the parties may make confidentiality commitments.

---

29. Park Young-ki, 'South Korea', in *Labour Law and Industrial Relations in Asia* (eds), S. J. Deery and R. J. Mitchell, Longman Cheshire, Melbourne, 1993, p. 151; Y. Matsuda, 'Japan', in Deery and Mitchell, pp. 173–174 and 184.
30. ILO, *International Labour Conventions and Recommendations 1919–1981*, ILO, Geneva, 1982, p. 22.

34. Even though unions may not have any legal rights to information, following the maxim that 'knowledge is power', before engaging in collective bargaining, most unions collect as much relevant information as practicable. An employer may disclose a considerable amount of information. To some extent, this can help the employer to shape the expectations of the union (and its members).[31] Even if the employer is not willing to disclose information, the union can usually obtain considerable insight into the employer's activities and finances from the unions' own members, the media, internet, stock exchange and other sources which the better union research departments are adept at tapping.

35. Employers and unions use various negotiating techniques in attempts to minimize their disadvantages and maximize possible advantages. Tactical approaches used by the parties may include bluffing, haggling, formulating inflated demands, hard bargaining, package-deal offers, and splitting the difference. Such practices must, however, be attuned in some countries to a statutory duty to bargain in good faith and to court decisions on the nature and scope of such a duty.

36. Collective bargaining is a complex relationship based on power, reason, tactical skills, and sometimes emotional factors too. Invariably, the threat of sanctions is one of the moving forces behind negotiations. Accordingly, the parties may conduct cost-benefit analyses of the possible concessions and disagreements. Their behaviour is also guided by the degree of trust and the history of the relationship between the parties. When they perceive that they are in a predominantly adversarial position, their reaction differs sharply from that which characterizes more integrative and cooperative relationships.

37. It is not only different parties which experience contrasting styles of bargaining relations. The same parties may experience different styles on various issues. They may enjoy cooperative relations with regard to health and safety, for instance, but be adversarial with regard to economic rewards. Moreover, even on one issue, the bargaining may pass through several stages, with the parties initially displaying adversarial behaviour, but subsequently, having made an agreement, they may be much more cooperative as they implement it.[32] Collective bargaining parties in North America, the UK, and Australia typically start with wider 'ambit' than those in western Europe where final terms will mostly not have moved far from initial claims. Adams explains this in terms of the effects on bargaining expectations engendered by the relatively greater degree of public scrutiny and debate of the more centralized levels of bargaining in Europe.[33]

38. Since most negotiations are initiated by a union, collective bargaining discussions usually start with the union demands and then consider the employer

---

31. This process has been called 'attitudinal structuring', *see* R.E. Walton and R.B. McKersie, *A Behavioral Theory of Labor Negotiations*, 2nd ed., McGraw Hill, New York, 1991, especially ch. VII.
32. Walton and McKersie, especially ch. X.
33. R. Adams, *Industrial Relations under Liberal Democracy*, University of South Carolina Press, Columbia S.C, 1995, pp. 82–83.

responses. These two elements provide the basis for drafting the agreement once an accord is reached. In the USA, a single collective bargaining round includes a wide array of issues and the resulting agreements (contracts) are usually dense documents covering a wide array of dissimilar items. In Europe, it is more usual to have separate collective bargaining rounds dedicated to distinct topic areas so that concurrent agreements emerge, each covering a single theme or topic (e.g. wages or training or pensions or occupational health and safety). According to Adams, the single-round US tradition complicates and protracts the bargaining process and may induce heightened conflict levels. As well, because union negotiators have the tactical option of discarding some of their original list of demands, these issues may remain within the legal province of management prerogative ('reserved rights') rather than being open to joint regulation.[34]

39. Given the scope and complexity of the issues that may be involved, major agreements are normally in writing. Some countries (e.g. Denmark, Japan, and the UK) still permit verbal collective agreements, but they are getting rarer. Many agreements that have a large coverage are published as booklets. Provision is made in some cases for the distribution of copies among the employees concerned and to other interested parties.

40. In certain contexts, an additional step appears towards the end of the bargaining process, but before registration: the ratification of the agreement. In Canada, the UK, Australia, and the USA and to a lesser extent in Japan and other countries, union representatives submit agreements for ratification by their constituents concerned. Ratification is more feasible in countries where enterprise bargaining prevails, therefore it is less typical in continental Europe, though there are cases of negotiations subject to a vote in Belgium (by a national committee of union delegates), Finland, Germany, Norway, and Switzerland. In several countries there has been an increase in the frequency of employees refusing to ratify agreements. This increase appears to reflect the failure of union leaders to communicate effectively the terms of the proposed agreements, union factionalism and dissatisfaction among particular groups of employees, or the inability of union negotiators to deliver on member expectations in more difficult economic times. It may also reflect lobbying by other interest groups either directly or through the media.

41. The process of bargaining may conclude with the registration of the agreement in a government office, labour court, or an industrial relations commission. Registration is in some countries a mere formality for statistical purposes or to facilitate proof of the existence and content of the agreement. Elsewhere, registration has a more substantive implication and depends on a verification of the content of the agreement in the light of legal requirements for the inclusion of certain mandatory clauses and the compatibility of the agreement with public law provisions or the minimum standards of protection. Inflation gave rise to a third type of registration in which government authorities check also on the conformity of the agreement with

---

34. Adams, *Industrial Relations*, p. 82.

incomes policies (discussed later). However, in other countries, including Switzerland and the USA, no registration is required.

42. Bargaining may take place in the presence of third-party governmental (or private) agencies, which may help to mediate, conciliate, or arbitrate, for instance, by ascertaining the views of the other parties, obtaining a concession or suggesting a compromise. Some argue that governments should limit themselves to a role as a neutral third party in collective bargaining and to the establishment of an institutional framework within which the other two parties can operate without too many external constraints. In practice, however, many governments are involved in negotiations because, besides being a third party, they are also the largest employer. Hence, governments may intervene overtly as a party to national agreements, as has happened in Norway (1988 and 1989), Ireland (1996), Italy (1986), Australia (1983 to 1996), and Spain (1985 and 1986), and more frequently in an indirect and informal manner.

VII. THE FUNCTIONS OF COLLECTIVE BARGAINING

43. On the left of the labour movement, assessments have varied as to the functions of collective bargaining. Some revolutionary Marxists and syndicalists have been basically opposed to union involvement in institutionalized collective bargaining, as in their view it merely leads to compromise, class collaboration and the preservation of capitalism. Among some left-wing unions, such as the large French-Communist Party-linked confederation, CGT, collective bargaining has become merely an aspect of the arena for class struggle. Others on the left have accorded more legitimacy to collective bargaining as they have seen it deliver tangible benefits to the unions – by reinforcing their role as permanent organizations – as well as to their members.[35] For such reasons, right-wing managerialist critics, disposed to unitarist values within the world of work, may deny the legitimacy of collective bargaining.

44. Social and liberal democrats tend to see collective bargaining as playing an important role in adjusting and relieving conflicts of interest at work as well as redistributing socially produced wealth. As a means for settling conflict, collective bargaining usually precedes the intervention of third parties and has been developed into an important problem-solving mechanism. One arena for its use is to solve disputes arising from the interpretation or application of existing legal or contractual provisions: 'rights disputes'. Another is deadlocks in the bargaining process: 'interests disputes', as the parties can normally decide at any point in the operation of the dispute-settlement machinery to return to direct negotiations in order to overcome possible areas of disagreement. Collective bargaining also plays an important role regulating relations between the relevant employer or employers' organization and the

---

35. J. Wilczynski, *Comparative Industrial Relations: Ideologies, Institutions, Practices and Problems under Different Social Systems with Special Reference to Socialist Planned Economies*, Macmillan, London, 1983.

unions. As unions became established and as employers intended to retain a certain degree of unilateral power, collective bargaining emerged to clarify the lines of demarcation between management prerogatives and the unions' aspirations. Collective bargaining also provided procedures for the negotiation and administration of agreements.

45. Collective bargaining has many other functions including rulemaking. Collective agreements govern employment relationships in the bargaining unit and thereby create generally applied standards. This indicates the power of groups to provide for their own internal regulation (e.g. by custom and practice) and that there are limits to the sovereign power of an employer. Collective bargaining can thus be regarded as an expression of pluralism. Given that joint regulation takes the place of authoritarian decision making, collective bargaining can be a vehicle for the democratization of industrial life. This comment is as applicable to those societies that have more recently made the transition to greater democracy, such as South Korea, Indonesia, Taiwan, and former Soviet-bloc countries as it was for those IMEs that made such a transition many decades earlier. Collective bargaining has also been heralded as a fundamental human right (similar to protection from forced labour, child labour and discrimination) in several international instruments, for instance, the ILO's Declaration of Fundamental Principles and Rights at Work, 1998.[36]

46. Although collective bargaining is led on the employees' side by union officials or other employees' representatives, the whole bargaining process can entail a wider degree of employee participation. Employees may be involved, for example, in the determination of their conditions of employment, first, when they make suggestions and approve the list of demands in union meetings; second, when they elect the team of officials or negotiators; and, third, if they ratify the agreement entered into by the negotiators. These various forms of participation are particularly visible when negotiations take place at a decentralized level, where employees can exert a more direct influence. Collective bargaining is no longer seen as an alternative to other forms of employee participation (works councils and representation on company boards for instance) and often seen as a complementary means of promoting employee participation. In the Netherlands, sectoral collective agreements increasingly delegate further collective bargaining to works councils.[37] Nevertheless, such participation is generally less prevalent in the case of industry-wide, regional or national negotiations conducted by top officials, usually mandated by delegates or representatives of federations. The lower the level of negotiations, then, the greater the opportunities for direct employee participation.

47. The value of collective bargaining as a form of employee participation should not be exaggerated. Typically, negotiations are conducted only occasionally and both the conclusion of the agreement and its subsequent administration involve

---

36. Information on the implications of such a perspective are available at the web site of the Society for the Promotion of Human Rights in Employment *(http://www.mericleinc.com/sphre)*.
37. EIRR, October 1995, p. 14.

relatively few shop-stewards and union officials.[38] Second, unions themselves are not necessarily democratic and their members may be uninvolved. Third, the coverage of collective bargaining is rather limited in some countries (see Table 1). Fourth, collective bargaining may be a sham and used merely in an attempt to legitimate matters that have already been decided upon by management.[39] In Japan, for example, in theory, unions can represent employees by bargaining about all aspects of managerial decisions affecting conditions of employment in large enterprises. In practice, however, such enterprises in Japan (and elsewhere) have the power to take long-term central initiatives (to open and close establishments at home or overseas, design new products, or to introduce technological change). In contrast, most union power tends to be at the margin and more in the form of delaying. At most, unions may have a limited and short-term power of veto.[40]

VIII. COVERAGE OF BARGAINING

48. As it may be a rule-making and conflict-settlement process or an expression of conflict, a forerunner of legislation, an instrument of peace, a reassertion of pluralism and a means of democratizing industrial life, collective bargaining can have a considerable qualitative impact in society. While most national agreements contain basic principles and industry-wide agreements include minimum rates, enterprise-level agreements usually regulate a wider and more detailed range of issues. The quantitative and qualitative elements are thus interconnected and questions of coverage should be considered along with the level and content of agreements, particularly where agreement making occurs at more than one level.

49. What is the quantitative impact of collective bargaining? What is the significance of its role in industrial relations? Most relevant statistics refer to the number of agreements concluded and the number of employees covered by the agreements. However, the first measure can be misleading because a few industry-wide or national agreements may carry more weight than a relatively high number of enterprise or plant agreements. Because, in recent years, the question of coverage has become increasingly related to debates relating to strategic choice of bargaining level and union representativeness, we combine discussion of these issues below.

50. In IMEs with relatively centralized collective bargaining, for instance, Austria and Sweden, the numbers of national and industry-wide agreements seem modest but the total coverage is very high: 98 per cent of workers in Austria and 85 per cent in Sweden.[41] In the Netherlands 80 per cent of the total workforce have their

---

38. For a critique of the idea that collective bargaining replaces managerial control by industrial democracy, *see* R. Hyman, *Strikes*, Macmillan, London, 1989, p. 100ff.
39. *Cf.* E. Córdova, 'Workers' Participation in Decisions within Enterprises: Recent Trends and Problems', *International Labour Review*, 1982.
40. J. Benson, 'Japanese Unions: Managerial Partner or Worker Challenge?', *Labour & Industry*, 1995, pp. 87–102.
41. F. Fuerstenberg, 'Employment relations in Germany,' in Bamber and Lansbury, 1998; Adams, *Industrial Relations*, p. 78.

Table 1. Collective bargaining coverage, union density and trends in collective bargaining levels in selected IMEs

Country	Coverage (percentage)	Union density. membership as a percentage of wage and salary earners	Bargaining levels over last decade national /sectoral (N/S), company or plant (C)	Dominant levels over past decade: N/S, C	Trends over past decade: Increasing (I), Decreasing (D), Stable (S)	
					N/S	C
Americas						
Argentina	72.9 (1995)	65.6* (1995)	N/S, C	N/S	S	I
Canada	37.0 (1996)	37.4 (1993)	N/S, C	C	D	I
Chile	12.7 (1995)	33.0* (1993)	C	C	—	I
United States	11.7 (1995)	14.2 (1995)	N/S,C	C	D	I
Asia/Oceania						
Australia	65.0 (1995)	35.2 (1995)	N/S, C	C	D	I
Japan	25.0 (1994)	24.0 (1995)	N/S, C	C	S	I
New Zealand	23.1 (1995)	24.3 (1995)	N/S, C	C	D	I
Singapore	18.8 (1996)	15.9 (1995)	N/S, C	C	S	S
Europe						
Czech Repub	55.0 (1995)	42.8 (1995)	N/S, C	C	S	I
Denmark	55.0 (1995)	80.1 (1994)	N/S, C	N/S	S	I
France	90.0 (1995)	9.1 (1995)	N/S, C	N/S	S	I
Germany	90.0 (1996)	28.9 (1995)	N/S, C	N/S	S	I
Ireland	90.0 (1994)	48.9 (1993)	N/S, C	C	I	S
Netherlands	80.0 (1996)	25.6 (1995)	N/S, C	N/S	S	I
Norway	66.0 (1996)	57.7 (1995)	N/S, C	N/S	—	—
Spain	82.0 (1996)	18.6 (1994)	N/S, C	N/S	I	I
Sweden	85.0 (1995)	91.1 (1994)	N/S, C	N/S	S	I
UK	36.5 (1996)	32.9 (1995)	N/S, C	C	D	I

Sources: ILO Task Force on Industrial Relations, World Labour Report 1997–98: Industrial Relations, Democracy and Social Stability, ILO, Geneva, 1999, Tables 1.2, 3.1 and 3.2,
(http://www.ilo.org/public/english/dialogue/govlab/publ/wlr/97/index.htm).

Notes:
Collective bargaining coverage means the % of employees covered by collective agreements in the formal sector.
* As a percentage of wage earners in the formal sector.

jobs regulated by collective agreements, predominantly under the 206 industry-wide agreements.[42] In Switzerland where about half of all employees are covered by collective agreements, just five sectoral agreements cover 25 per cent of all employees while a further 25 per cent come under another 1,226 collective agreements.[43] Turning to IMEs where enterprise bargaining predominates, in the USA, there are a huge number of agreements,[44] but their total coverage is very low (see Table 1).

51. Table 1 displays a general comparison of collective bargaining coverage, trends in collective bargaining levels and union density across selected IMEs. Table 1

---

42. Rood, 'The Netherlands, ' Supplement August 1995, IELL, p. 66.
43. EIRR, February 1996, p. 14.; 12% of employees are covered by enterprise agreements. R. Fulder and B. Hotz-Hart, 'Switzerland: Still as Smooth as Clockwork?' in *Changing Industrial Relations in Europe* eds, A. Ferner and R. Hyman, Blackwell, Oxford, 1998, pp. 275–256.
44. *Statistical Abstract of the United States*, 1995, pp. 443–445.

shows four relevant matters. First, in most IMEs, collective bargaining occurs at more than one level. Second, with France and Spain the most obvious examples, high levels of collective bargaining coverage are more closely correlated with the centralization of collective bargaining than union density. Third, almost invariably, under predominantly decentralized collective bargaining regimes, collective bargaining coverage levels closely approximate union density levels. Notable exceptions, but with opposite patterns, are Denmark and Australia.[45] Fourth, where the use of enterprise bargaining increases within a centralized system, this does not necessarily indicate a decline in the use of collective bargaining at the central level. In European IMEs, much of the increasing decentralized activity reflects organized processes of devolution from within centralized bargaining.[46] Of primary concern for unions, however, is the nature of the institutional or other supports necessary to maintain the primacy of multi-employer bargaining in an environment where employer pressure for greater decentralization signifies an attack on unionism, collective bargaining and employee incomes and conditions.

52. In the German case, there is a clear legal division of labour between collective bargaining and works councils that limits the extent of the recent weakening of the centrality of multi-employer collective bargaining.[47] Other bulwarks for industry-level bargaining include powerful unions, cohesive employer associations intent on a policy of bargaining at that level and legislated 'extension' clauses that pass on the effects of collective agreements to non-union workplaces and to employers that are not members of employers' associations.

53. A survey by Traxler of collective bargaining in OECD countries since 1970 shows a polarization in national patterns according to levels of bargaining: a drive towards enterprise bargaining and then individualization among anglophone countries (apart from Ireland) and Japan; maintenance and sometimes reinforcement of centralized bargaining in mainland Europe and, more recently, Ireland. From this, Traxler developed a model explaining the relationships between multi-employer bargaining, enterprise level collective bargaining, and individual bargaining. Industry level bargaining typically means very high levels of coverage for collective bargaining particularly where extension clauses act to *corrall* employers into cohesive associations committed to bargaining at that level. Where the necessary supports for multi-employer bargaining atrophy sufficiently – for example through legislative changes such as occurred in Britain and New Zealand during the 1980s and 1990s – a shift to an enterprise bargaining regime inevitably means a dramatic decline in the coverage of collective bargaining and the level of union density. Coverage and density then shrink together as coverage comes to directly reflect the unevenness and

---

45. For Denmark, *see* S. Scheuer, 'The Impact of Collective Agreements on Working Time in Denmark', *British Journal of Industrial* Relations, 1999, p. 466. The extensiveness of Australia's collective bargaining coverage is due to the survival of remnants of the old award system as an underpinning for the new enterprise bargaining regime.

46. A. Ferner and R. Hyman, 'Introduction: Towards European Industrial Relations?' in *Changing Industrial Relations in Europe* eds, Ferner and Hyman.

47. A. Hassel, 'The Erosion of the German System of Industrial Relations', *British Journal of Industrial Relations*, 1999, pp. 483–505.

volatility of union membership across sectors and across firms of different sizes, approaches, and locations. The only possible exception would appear to be a situation where the union movement has and can maintain very high levels of density and so avoid the development of a non-union sector. Otherwise, the development of a non-union sector should allow cost advantages to non-union firms to a degree that encourages unionized employers to shake themselves free of collective bargaining and union intervention. A macro-level strategic choice in favour of enterprise bargaining as dominant mode sets in train a dynamic hostile to unions and collective bargaining. The result is that most employees will not be covered by collective agreements. Thus, the successful employer campaigns to install enterprise bargaining in New Zealand and Australia have been Trojan horses to de-unionize and individualize industrial relations.[48]

54. Collective bargaining coverage is generally greater in IMEs than in developing countries and is usually most significant in the public sector and the secondary industry sector. Both observations reflect the proportion of large enterprises, which tend to be high in the public sector and the secondary industry sector of IMEs, as well as the degree of union density. Up to the 1970s, the total coverage of collective bargaining increased in many countries, particularly where collective bargaining grew in the public sector. This pattern is now also occurring in societies, such as South Korea and Indonesia, that have more recently become IMEs.[49] Yet a decrease in total employment in the secondary industry sector of several longer-term IMEs has tended to offset growth in the public sector. As well, a growing trend to privatization of previously public sector functions and organizations has contributed to declines in union density and the coverage of collective bargaining in IMEs with more decentralised bargaining patterns. The coverage of collective bargaining usually expands in periods of prosperity and declines in recessions. In line with Traxler's ideas, the extent of collective bargaining also varies as a result of political vicissitudes which affect unions. In the UK, for instance, successive governments throughout the twentieth century encouraged collective bargaining until the advent of the Thatcher government in 1979. Partly as a consequence of government intervention hostile to unions, the coverage of collective bargaining declined from 71 per cent of a comparable sample of workplaces in 1984 to 54 per cent in 1990, a decline which also reflected structural change from manufacturing to services.[50] By 1996, it had fallen to 37 per cent (see Table 1). An even more dramatic shift occurred in the wake of anti-union legislative change in New Zealand.[51] A similar rate of change in

---

48. F. Traxler, 'Collective Bargaining in the OECD: Developments, Preconditions and Effects', *European Journal of Industrial Relations*, 1998, pp. 207–226.
49. A. Casey, 'Jakarta Breakthrough', *Workers Online*, 14 July 2000, *http://workers.labor.net.au/62/ c_historical* feature_indon.html
50. The sample included establishments with at least 25 employees; *see* N. Millward, M. Stevens, D. Smart, and W.R. Hawes, *Workplace Industrial Relations in Transition*, Dartmouth, Aldershot 1992, p. 91; W. Brown, P. Marginson and J. Walsh, 'Management: Pay Determination and Collective Bargaining', in *Industrial Relations: Theory and Practice in Britain*, ed. P. Edwards, Blackwell, Oxford, 1995, pp. 135–142.
51. R. Harbridge, 'The New Zealand Model – An Assessment: A Late Line in the Sand?', in *Industrial Relations Policy under the Microscope* ed., M. Bryce, ACIRRT Working Paper No. 40, University of Sydney, 1996, p. 100.

the opposite direction can also follow the introduction of union-sympathetic legislation. In France, after a decade's experience of the 1982 *Auroux* laws, an additional 2.5 million employees had come under sectoral collective agreements.[52]

55. Although collective bargaining is often associated with traditional groups of manual workers (e.g. miners and craft-workers), in many IMEs there are various forms of collective bargaining on behalf of so-called 'non-manual' workers including actors, nurses, air traffic controllers, public servants, or employees in state-owned enterprises and even professional staff and managers.[53] Also, there are various forms of negotiation embracing lawyers, medical practitioners, entrepreneurs in farming, fishing, and other self-employed people and these may increase as professions face a loss of occupational autonomy relative to governments and large corporations who determine the shape of their product markets.[54]

56. Another factor influencing the incidence of collective bargaining is size of employing organizations; as firm size decreases, so does collective bargaining coverage. There are a number of reasons for this. In many IMEs, employees of small firms are excluded from general rights to collective representation. Where employees do have these rights in decentralized bargaining systems, many small- and medium-sized employers (SMEs) evade collective bargaining arrangements or seek to do so. It is in the more centralized bargaining systems, particularly where the legal framework mandates collective bargaining outcomes to whole industries, that coverage among SMEs is high. However in recent times, in some of these countries, coordinated groups of SMEs have also sought to break away from or break down industry-level collective bargaining. The results are not surprising. An EU study found that, in general, pay, job security, working conditions, safety, and training possibilities were all worse in SMEs than in larger firms. Yet, SMEs are an increasingly important force as employers in some economies and certain emerging industry sectors.[55]

57. The growth of atypical forms of employment may also affect traditional forms of unionism and collective bargaining. Most atypical types of work (e.g. temporary work, part-time jobs, home work, employment in small sub-contractors and clandestine work) do not easily lend themselves to unionization and collective bargaining, particularly where they occur in smaller SMEs. A further complication in some IMEs is a growing tendency for employers to shift employees into dubious forms of self-employment, the aim of which is to avoid regulation by employment law, collective bargaining, unions, social security, and taxation authorities.[56]

---

52. EIRR, June 1993, p. 31.
53. For an analysis of such developments in the UK, with some international comparisons, *see* G.J. Bamber, *Militant Managers? Managerial Unionism and Industrial Relations*, Gower, Aldershot, 1986.
54. CNN.com, 'AMA debates collective bargaining', 23 June 1999, *wysiwyg://83/http://www. cnn. com/ HEALTH/9906/23/doctors.union.02/*
55. M. Caprile, C. Llore and M. Trentini, *Industrial Relations in SMEs*, European Foundation for the Improvement of Living and Working Conditions, Dublin, May 1999, *http://www.eiro.eurofound. ie/ 1999/05/study/TN9905201S. html*
56. *See* for example, the special 'precarious employment' issue of *Labour & Industry*, April 1998, pp. 1–113; J. Druker and I. Duprè, 'The Posting of Workers Directive and Employment Regulation in

IX. Content of Agreements

58. The content of agreements is determined by the scope of negotiable issues (i.e. the definition by power, law or basic agreement of the areas that can be jointly regulated by the parties). Within those limits, bargaining scope is influenced by various forces. Union pressures to expand the scope of collective bargaining may be countered by employers' resistance and their attachment to management prerogatives. Governments seem to play an ambivalent role (depending partly on their ideological orientation), sometimes favouring an expansion of collective bargaining by providing that certain questions should be the object of negotiations, but at other times, pre-empting the domain of collective bargaining by employment or industrial relations legislation. This latter situation is common in newly industrialized economies where some governments maintain a more authoritarian control over industrial relations.[57]

59. During the 1970s, at the height of union power in several IMEs there was a trend towards the expansion of bargaining scope. Unions challenged many traditional management prerogatives they considered impinged on employment conditions. These included questions of job security, quality of working life, career development, equal opportunity, occupational health and safety, child care, and employee participation. Non-economic benefits and further involvement in management decisions thus gained more attention possibly, but not necessarily, at the expense of more traditional wages and hours issues. Many agreements grew from simple documents specifying a pay scale and hours of work into much more complex documents. In some countries, this surge assumed legislative form, most notably in Sweden, where a 1976 law established a primary duty to bargain which made practically everything negotiable. This represented a dramatic reversal of the traditional shared Swedish institutional understandings which had fiercely isolated personnel and work organization issues from collective bargaining.

60. More acute macro-economic problems since the early 1970s stimulated an expansion of the scope of collective activity at the industry and national levels. Often the result of tripartite bargaining, agreements increasingly dealt with productivity, quality, the organization of the labour market, vocational training, the avoidance and settlement of industrial disputes, and macro-economic tradeoffs, for example, on education, health, employment, and the level of economic rewards.

61. Nevertheless, the scope of issues is typically wider at the enterprise or plant levels where greater specificity is possible. In some leading-edge cases, the parties have striven to simplify agreements in an endeavour to move away from Taylorist

---

(*Contd.*)

the European Construction Industry', *European Journal of Industrial Relations*, 1998, pp. 309-330; A. Broughton, *1999 Annual Review Comparative Overview*, European Foundation for the Improvement of Living and Working Conditions, Dublin, December 1999, pp. 36–38, *http://www. eiro.eurofound.ie/1999/12/features/ tn9912231f.html*

57. C. Leggett, 'Singapore', pp. 99, 109 and Hwang Yueh-chin, 'Taiwan (ROC)', in Deery and Mitchell, 1993.

forms of work organization to more flexible forms of 'lean management'.[58] At the level of the enterprise, collective bargaining may deal with:

(i)   the identification of the parties, the bargaining unit and the groups excluded from the agreement;
(ii)   economic benefits and working conditions dealing with the effort and reward bargain (pay, hours of work, rest periods, vacations, shift work, overtime);
(iii) other terms and conditions directly relevant to the employment relationship (recruitment, job security, staffing levels, seniority, training);
(iv)   management questions indirectly affecting conditions of employment (sub-contracting, investment, changes of technology);
(v)   provision of social services, welfare measures and other matters affecting the employees' conditions of working life (child care, canteens, recreation, transport);
(vi)   social security provisions (sick leave, retirement benefits, maternity/paternity leave);
(vii) other fringe benefits (dependents' allowances, holiday bonuses, medical and dental plans);
(viii) quality of working life matters (safety and health, physical working conditions and employee participation);
(ix)   regulation of relations between the parties (peace obligation, management prerogatives, union security, duration of the agreement); and
(x)   provisions regarding the administration of agreements (grievance procedure and rules concerning the interpretation of their clauses).

62.   Economic factors can also induce the parties to restrict bargaining scope by inducing employers, unions and governments to remove some issues from the bargaining arena. In the USA, for instance, certain 'management function' issues cannot be bargained to impasse. Further, federal employees are not allowed to bargain about pay. Since the 1970s, there has been a significant diminution in the scope of collective bargaining in the UK and USA. This occurred against the background of a decline in union density and of a series of governments hostile to unions and collective bargaining. Further, in the USA in particular, there was a move among numerous employers to initiate 'concession bargaining' where employers demanded that unions accept reduced standards for their members as the price of the continuation of production at certain plants. While this climate of employer intimidation continues, there is some evidence that in the USA large unionized employers have been seeking a more cooperative path, expanding the bargaining scope to include union involvement in some or many areas of the firm's decisionmaking. In exchange, employers expect unions to cooperate with management in its corporate agenda.[59] During the 1990s, in other countries, such as Japan, Italy, Germany, Sweden, France

---

58. *Cf.* J. Womack. , D. Jones, and D. Roos, *The Machine that Changed the World*, Rawson-Macmillan, New York, 1990; G.J. Bamber, 'Flexible work organization: Inferences from Britain and Australia', *Asia-Pacific Human Resource Management*, 1990, pp. 28–44; G.J. Bamber, M.A. Shadur and F. Howell, 'The international transferability of Japanese management strategies: An Australian perspective', *Employee Relations*, 1992, pp. 3–19.
59. *See* H. Wheeler and J.A. McClendon 'Employment relations in the United States', in Bamber and Lansbury, (1998); P.B. Voos, 'An Economic Perspective on Contemporary Trends in Collective Bargaining' in *Contemporary Collective Bargaining in the Private Sector* (ed.) P.B. Voos, Industrial Relations Research Association, Madison, 1994, pp. 2–4; J. Cutcher-Gershenfeld, T.A. Kochan and

and Australia, employers have increasingly sought to seize the initiative over the bargaining agenda.[60] On the other hand, in France, Germany, Belgium, Holland, and Finland, there have been innovations in collective bargaining at a range of levels as part of a quest to reduce unemployment through shorter hours, work-sharing and partial early retirement.[61] Quantitative and qualitative changes in agreements reflect the dynamic nature of collective bargaining and the parties' capacity to develop it according to changing circumstances.

63. Although the variety of subjects dealt with in collective agreements does not lend itself to clear classification, some attempts have been made to group them in distinct categories. We can distinguish between two major groups: normative and contractual (obligatory) clauses. Normative clauses refer to the conditions of employment which must be observed in all the individual employment contracts in the enterprise or industry concerned. Within a bargaining unit, they are the equivalent of substantive legislative provisions at the national level. Their purpose is to provide standards of protection to individual employees. These standards may represent 'minimum' levels open to supplementation through further ('articulated') bargaining at a lower level or they may express actual or ruling rates. Contractual clauses include provisions spelling out rights and duties of the parties to the agreement. They provide stability to labour relations and have acted both as a counter and a stimulus to the expansion of normative clauses.

64. However, contractual provisions, such as union security or 'checkoff' clauses, may also have normative effects as they establish a triangular relationship implying rights and duties for individual employees as well as the contracting parties. There are other clauses found in collective agreements (e.g. protection of the environment, organization of social services, and participation rights) which are neither normative nor contractual. This has prompted some observers to propose new categories of clauses, including institutional clauses (to cover union security and checkoff). In many countries, there is a distinction between substantive and procedural clauses (the former include rates of pay, hours and holidays, while the latter include recognition and grievance procedures and provisions specifying the duration and renegotiation of agreements). Others have tried to distinguish between economic, social, union-related, and general provisions.

65. While new collective agreements have prompted numerous significant changes in substantive labour law, their innovations are just as important in contractual provisions. Two of these provisions have had far-reaching effects: the peace obligation and union security arrangements.

J.C. Wells, 'Report: How do labor and management view collective bargaining?', *Monthly Labor Review Online*, October 1998, *http://www.bls.gov/opub/mlr/1998/10/rpt2full. htm*; G.R. Gray, D.W. Myers, and P.S. Myers, 'Cooperative provisions in labor agreements: a new paradigm?', *Monthly Labor Review*, January 1999, pp. 29–45.

60. *See* e.g. *Japan Labor Bulletin*, 1 February 1996, p. 4; EIRR, March 1993, p. 10; July 1993, pp. 15–16; November 1993, p. 6.
61. EIRR, October 1993, p. 24; December 1993, pp. 8, 15, 17; January 1994, pp. 8, 10, 13–16, 20; October 1995, pp. 16–17; April 1996, pp. 13–17.

66. The peace obligation has been regarded by some as a corollary of collective bargaining agreements of fixed duration which are supposed to bring stability to labour relations and settle for the term of the agreement all the various issues that have arisen between the parties. There are two kinds of peace obligation: first, the absolute one which obliges the parties to refrain from any industrial action during the period of validity of the agreement and, second, the relative one which limits such obligation to the matters dealt with in the agreement. The absolute peace obligation is less usual than the relative one and would require a specific clause to that effect. It has nevertheless been used with considerable success in Switzerland since 1937. The relative peace obligation, included in the law in Austria and Germany and in many collective agreements elsewhere, offers unions the advantage of safeguarding their right to formulate new demands if major changes in the socio-economic environment have taken place. In Sweden, while striking during the currency of agreements is illegal, such strikes do occur.[62] Elsewhere, including France and Italy, peace obligation clauses are seldom included in collective agreements as they are regarded as a breach of the fundamental democratic right to strike.

67. Peace obligation clauses presuppose a measure of internal discipline. Difficulties therefore arise in cases where large groups of employees engage in unauthorized action and the employer or a third party requests the union to initiate disciplinary action against them.

68. Unions seek security arrangements in circumstances where they confront serious difficulties of recognition and survival. They aim to obtain certain guarantees and facilities from the employer and to overcome the reluctance to join among certain employees or in view of the special characteristics of particular labour markets, for instance, where employer or employee turnover was frequent (e.g. actors) or the work force dispersed (e.g. seafarers). Two variants developed: while some clauses sought to strengthen unions by making membership a condition of employment (closed shop or union shop), others provided for a compulsory payment of union contributions (agency shop). These clauses developed mainly in English-speaking countries, but growing anti-unionism among governments and employers in those countries has meant the widespread legislative prohibition of such arrangements in recent years. This has contributed to declining union densities which, in turn, have restricted the extent of collective bargaining. In other countries, union security arrangements are regarded as an infringement of the freedom not to belong to a union and many legal provisions limit or prohibit their use.

X. EFFECTS OF THE AGREEMENT

69. While in some countries the effects of agreements are still limited, at least in theory, to employees affiliated to the union on whose behalf they were concluded, in most IMEs a specific law or established practice has determined that collective

---

62. C. Bratt, *Labour Relations in 18 Countries*, Swedish Employers' Confederation, Stockholm 1996, pp. 117–8.

agreements are applicable to all employees in the bargaining unit. As early as 1951, ILO Recommendation 91 pointed out that the stipulation of a collective agreement 'should apply to all workers of the classes concerned employed in the undertakings covered by the agreement, unless the agreement specifically provides to the contrary'.[63] The general acceptance of this extension effect of collective agreements was due, in part, to the recognition in law of their special nature and also to the realization that if employers were to limit the application of the agreement to union members, they would be indirectly promoting unionization, or fostering the collapse of the union, or discriminating between their employees.

70.   The situation is different with respect to non-signatory employers who are not deemed to be bound by the agreement unless they are members of the employers' organization concerned or voluntarily decide to adhere to the provisions of the agreement. Even if an employer belongs to the contracting employers' organization, there must be a relevant provision in its bylaws or a special authorization empowering the organization to bargain on its behalf. Nevertheless, such countries as Australia, Austria, Belgium, Denmark, France, Germany, Italy, Japan, South Korea, Spain, and Switzerland have devised a range of procedures for the extension of collective agreements, whereby those employers who do not belong to the contracting organizations but who belong to the economic sector covered by the agreement may be bound by its provisions, provided that certain requirements are met. In most cases the original rationale of this procedure was an attempt by employers to avoid unfair competition from non-unionized enterprises; however, there were other considerations including the promotion of collective bargaining and the pursuit of more egalitarian and solidaristic goals.

71.   Such extension procedures generally start with a meeting convened by a relevant state agency on its own initiative as a third party or, as is more customary, on the request of unions. Employers and unions affected by the proposed extension are invited to attend the meeting and to comment on the suitability and implications of the extension. Extension orders usually are issued by the third party only when the agreements in force already cover a substantial proportion of employers and employees in the sector concerned. In some countries, additional proof is required of the difficulties confronted by the employees trying to negotiate an agreement in the enterprises or industries to which the extension would apply (e.g. a large number of SMEs). The practice of 'extension' is particularly significant in France where agreements are often designated as either 'ordinary' or 'extended'.

72.   Thus jointly-regulated rules may become part of all the individual contracts of employment, including, in most countries, those of employees who were not members of the union when the agreement was concluded or who joined the bargaining unit later; then, individual contracts cannot contain any stipulation contrary to the collective agreement. While in most countries individual employees and the employer may improve the standards fixed by collective agreements, in a few others such specific improvements might be regarded as an undue departure from the

---

63.   Article III, 4.

common rule. There is a similar but inverse relationship between collective agreements and statutory provisions. The latter prescribe minimum standards of protection which can be improved for the benefit of the employees by the former. However, collective agreements cannot in turn detract from the level of legislative standards and cannot contravene a public policy provision established by legislation.

73. The rule-making functions of collective bargaining go well beyond the limits of a bargaining unit. Conditions of employment established in collective agreements usually apply indirectly to employees who are excluded from the bargaining unit (e.g. confidential secretaries and supervisors) and sometimes, through extension procedures, to non-signatory and non-unionized enterprises in a given sector. Improvements first introduced in collective agreements may later be incorporated into the law. In view of the flexibility of collective bargaining, then, and its ability to adapt quickly to changing circumstances, it may be an instrument of innovation and social change.

XI. DURATION OF AGREEMENTS

74. Collective agreements can be for a fixed or indefinite duration. Agreements of indefinite duration refer, for the most part, to the basic or procedural kinds of agreements, though there may also be some ordinary substantive agreements of indefinite duration, but usually with a renewal clause. Whatever their nature, most collective agreements of indefinite duration can be terminated by giving a specified notice of termination or if there is no period specified, then a reasonable period.

75. The period of validity of fixed-duration collective agreements is sometimes governed by legal provisions that establish minimum and maximum limits. The former provide a measure of stability in the labour-management relationship. The latter take account of an imbalance of power whereby an employer may try to insist on an excessively long duration to frustrate subsequent collective bargaining. Minimum limits are normally set at one year. Maximum limits range in industrialized countries from four years (Finland) to five years (France, for job classification).

76. While there has been a trend towards longer contracts, the average duration of agreements is likely to change in accordance with economic circumstances. In periods of prosperity, agreements tend to be of shorter duration, as unions seek to exploit more often the employers' greater ability to pay. In periods of recession, unions prefer to obtain longer-term guarantees and protection. Inflation also affects the duration of agreements since it introduces an element of uncertainty and the need to catch up with increases in the cost of living, all of which result in shorter periods of validity. In Belgium where pay is indexed, agreements usually run for a period of 12 to 18 months.

77. The average duration of collective agreements in IMEs is probably no more than two years. Where longer periods prevail, it is customary to insert appropriate clauses for re-opening pay negotiations after one or two years. In a number of IMEs, such as Germany and South Korea, collective agreements on pay are normally for one

year, but of longer duration if they concern other matters. In Japan, 70 per cent of agreements are for one year, and are usually re-negotiated each spring, but there are also two- or three-year agreements. In Switzerland, the duration of agreements varies between two and five years. In the USA, outside the railroad and airline industries, collective agreements are for a specific duration usually ranging from one to three years. While national agreements in Italy were usually for three years, a 1993 tripartite agreement stipulated that, at the national sectoral level, agreements on pay were to last two years, and those over other terms and conditions, four years. Articulated enterprise and workplace agreements were also to last four years.[64] By contrast, in the UK, many collective agreements are open-ended, so that issues may be settled as they arise; there, the multitude of shop stewards, on behalf of their workplace constituents, may negotiate several such agreements each year (many of them informal and even verbal). Nevertheless, there is usually a more formal annual 'pay round', whereby pay negotiations are initiated at approximately annual intervals.

XII. ADMINISTRATION OF THE AGREEMENT

78. Many substantive provisions of agreements hardly require any administration as they are automatically incorporated into individual contracts of employment. But other clauses may provide for the establishment of machinery to regulate jointly, for instance, job classification, safety and health, promotion procedures or the joint administration of social services. Disputes may arise over the interpretation or application of certain clauses, so these necessitate appropriate coping strategies.

79. The British introduced procedures for handling grievances. The North Americans subsequently developed sophisticated approaches; such practices were later adopted by other countries. The ILO's Recommendation 130 (the Examination of Grievances within the Undertakings 1967) contains some general principles. Grievance procedures involve different levels of negotiations in which individual employees and representatives of the parties to the agreement seek to settle disputes. A settlement reached jointly by the employee and employer representatives is generally regarded as final and binding. Failure of the parties to reach agreement at the conciliatory or internal stages of a grievance procedure leads to grievance arbitration (i.e. final and impartial determination by a private arbitrator). The vast majority of all collective agreements in the USA provide for grievance arbitration,[65] 'one of the outstanding success areas of US industrial relations'.[66] Outside Canada and the USA, private arbitration is relatively unusual.

80. Most other countries have followed the European model of enforcement which entrusts the interpretation and implementation of agreements to labour courts

---

64. EIRR, August 1993, p. 9.
65. Wheeler and McClendon, 'Employment Relations in the United States', p. 82.
66. G. Strauss and P. Feuille, 'Industrial relations research in the United States', in *Industrial Relations in International Perspective*, (ed) P.B. Doeringer, Macmillan, London, 1981, p. 114.

or in some instances to ordinary courts. Individual employees and unions can appear at the court and sue for the implementation of normative provisions. Employers and unions are also entitled to claim damages in connection with contractual provisions. Occasionally, an organization may sue its own members for not observing the agreement. The European approach does not prevent the parties themselves from trying to settle disputes directly. In Italy, for instance, nearly all cases arising from the interpretation and implementation of collective agreements are settled through conciliation, either by following a grievance procedure or by the tripartite commissions attached to the labour offices.

XIII. COLLECTIVE BARGAINING AND ECONOMIC PROBLEMS AND POLICIES

81. Collective bargaining is a method of regulating sectional or class interests. While neither employers' nor employees' organizations have direct responsibility for the protection of the 'public interest' (however it is defined), other things being equal, they would probably prefer not to appear to be damaging it, not least because it could harm their public image, which is a 'weapon in their armoury'.[67] Governments may have as high priorities safeguarding macro-economic outcomes, 'investment prospects', and 'public order'. This initial divergence of objectives may lead to conflicts between the outcomes of collective bargaining and the governments' other priorities. Such conflicts become acute when countries experience periods of economic difficulty and may be particularly serious when simultaneously there is high inflation and unemployment.

82. There are at least three ways of reducing the conflicts between collective bargaining and economic policies:

(i) the parties, particularly unions, may be persuaded to moderate their negotiating claims;
(ii) governments take unilateral action using fiscal, monetary or incomes policies. This may include 'a freeze' on pay increases; and
(iii) governments, employers, and unions join forces (bilaterally or trilaterally) and try to devise appropriate responses to their sectoral and national problems.

83. The first solution has often been tried in IMEs and other countries, particularly where the union movement is closely linked to the governing party. In Singapore, it appears to have been the main guiding principle of the officially sanctioned union movement in recent times.[68] The parties may respond to the dual challenge of inflation and government concern for economic stability by, among other things: stipulating pay indexation provisions, exerting moderation and restraint in their pay negotiations, stressing non-economic demands and linking pay cuts to reductions in prices. Responses to unemployment problems have also included a

---

67. For a French example involving public-sector unions, *see* Y. Delamotte, 'France' in *Agenda for Change: An International Analysis of Industrial Relations in Transition*, (eds), J. Niland and O. Clarke, Allen & Unwin, Sydney: 1991, p. 109.
68. Leggett, 1993, pp. 96–136.

variety of formulae including: reduction in hours of work, promotion of early retirement and part-time employment, control of overtime, increases in vacation periods, internal transfers, and re-training. When faced with high inflation and unemployment, these measures generally seem to provide only limited and temporary relief. Moreover, some forms of pay indexation appear to fuel inflation. There are also serious difficulties of implementation and coordination, for instance, when the unions (or employers) are divided ideologically or in terms of other cleavages.

84. Government efforts to reconcile collective bargaining with its own economic policies include a range of approaches. Some are voluntary, such as exhortations, guidelines and using the public sector as a means of setting examples, while others are statutory, like pay ceilings, a pay freeze, pay indexation, or seeking to control pay movements and sometimes other incomes and prices by legislation or executive action. The most important and controversial are the statutory ones and more specifically the incomes policies. Although they have been effective for relatively short periods, the temporary suppression of inflation may be followed by periods of large pay increases. Also, an incomes policy cannot successfully operate for long without the support of employers' and employees' organizations. While unions tend to reject any attempt to impose controls over pay without similar control over other forms of incomes and of prices, most governments have found it even more difficult to operate an effective supervision of prices than of incomes.

85. Also, there is the problem of a possible violation of the principle of 'free' collective bargaining. The ILO Committee on Freedom of Association has considered that 'where intervention by the public authorities is essentially for the purpose of ensuring that the negotiating parties subordinate their interests to the national economic policy pursued by the government, irrespective of whether they agree with that policy or not, this is not compatible with the generally accepted principles in the field of freedom of association.'[69] With regard to government influence on pay determination, the Committee has also observed that: 'if, as part of its stabilization policy, a government considers that pay rates cannot be settled freely through collective bargaining, such a restriction should be enforced as an exceptional measure and only to the extent that is necessary, without exceeding a reasonable period, and it should be accompanied by adequate safeguards to protect employees' living standards.'[70]

86. Between the 1960s and 1980s, the failure of most of the voluntary approaches and the shortcomings of the statutory measures led some governments to seek agreements or understandings with employers and/or unions with a view to limiting the inflationary impact of collective bargaining or to make it more compatible with economic policies in general. The appearance of national bipartite or tripartite agreements has also been prompted by the realization of the potential of joint efforts by the two or three parties when confronting economic problems. The post-1974 Labour Government in Britain and the post-1983 Labor Government in Australia

---

69. ILO, *Freedom of Association: Digest of Decisions of the Freedom of Association Committee of the Governing Body of the ILO*, ILO, Geneva, 1976, para. 284.
70. ILO, *Freedom of Association*, para. 288.

each negotiated novel bilateral agreements with the unions. The British 'Social Contract' was effective for at least two years, while the Australian 'Accord' lasted thirteen years *albeit* with periodic revisions until Labor's electoral defeat in 1996.[71] In Italy, this form of top level 'concertation' has been a regular response to economic crises.[72]

87. Tripartite agreements usually contain a series of tradeoffs intended to avoid unacceptable or uncompensated sacrifices on the part of any of the parties. Some of these agreements limit themselves to the fight against inflation Others have sought broader aims, including increasing employment, combating price rises and helping low-paid employees. For instance, Ireland (1987, 1991, 1994, and 1996) and Norway (1988, 1989, and 1992) embraced policies on issues including employment, pay, taxation, the government, its budget deficit, and housing. The Spanish economic and social agreements of the 1980s included provisions on investment, fiscal policies, job creation and the conduct of industrial relations. As one study puts it: ' … a common denominator of tripartite approaches was the recognition of the need to combine industrial relations and non-industrial relations elements as a means of alleviating or diminishing the economic crisis'.[73]

88. The coordination of collective bargaining and government policies can also take place outside the process of the negotiation of formal agreements, through discussions that are held in tripartite organizations such as the former Concerted Action Mechanism in Germany (which ended in 1977), the Contact Committee in Norway, the Wage and Price Committee in Austria, the Economic Planning Advisory Council in Australia, and the Labour-Management Round Table (*Sanrokon*) in Japan. This approach corresponds to the broad meaning of collective bargaining mentioned at the beginning of this contribution, and represents a relatively mild form of government intervention (particularly in comparison with the practice of some developing countries where, in collective bargaining, the parties are sometimes obliged to follow the specific decrees periodically fixed by government). These developments are examples of tripartism in the conduct of collective bargaining relationships, which involve a degree of government intervention. In these circumstances, the narrow form of collective bargaining (i.e. the negotiation of formal agreements) is strongly influenced by the broad forms of tripartite collective bargaining and discussions about wider economic and social policies.

89. During the 1980s, a combination of monetary, fiscal, incomes and social policies succeeded in lowering the levels of inflation in most IMEs. By the early 1990s, some of them were even approaching a deflationary situation. Nevertheless, in 2000, the level of unemployment is still too high in many of these countries. There have been solidarity contracts in France and Italy and flexibility policies instituted in these and other European countries. Such attempts to reduce unemployment

---

71. *See* Goodman et al. , '*Employment relations in Britain* Australia' in Bamber and Lansbury (1998); E.M. Davis and R. D. Lansbury, 'Employment relations in Australia' in Bamber and Lansbury (1998).
72. *See* e.g. EIRR, September 1993, p. 15ff.
73. ILO, *Collective Bargaining: A Response to the Recession in Industrialised Market Economy Countries*, ILO, Geneva, 1987, p. 3.

through voluntary and statutory approaches have met with relatively little long-term success. In addition, some commentators criticize the results of collective bargaining for inducing patterns of income distribution that lack equity, for instance, whereby women, ethnic minorities, and other minority groups may be disadvantaged in the labour market. Hence governments will continue to be tempted to intervene, so the parties will not always be left alone to engage in 'free' collective bargaining.

XIV. CONCLUSIONS

90. In some countries certain interests are trying to change the prevailing mode of bargaining, so there is a debate about the relative merits of different bargaining levels. An employer exponent of moves away from centralized regulation towards enterprise bargaining cites three supporting rationales: it better suits the bureaucratic needs of complex organizations; it helps them to adapt to specific technologies and tasks; and it is more flexible in terms of internal and external labour markets.[74] Proponents of decentralized bargaining also argue that it facilitates the adaptation of employment arrangements to the specific circumstances of particular enterprises, arguably a crucial consideration in a period of increasing international competition. Further related arguments in favour of decentralization, particularly from the employer side, include its alleged advantages in respect of technological change, the growing preference for greater involvement by line managers in HRM and industrial relations, employee participation, quality considerations, the drive for continuous improvement and an enterprise culture more attuned to customers' preferences. It is also argued that, under enterprise bargaining, the parties are directly responsible for administering the web of rules that they themselves have created; therefore this should lead to more effective implementation and mutual understanding.

91. In the face of such propositions, to what extent can individual parties exercise 'strategic choice' and decide to change, for instance, from industry-level to enterprise bargaining? Many US and UK employers appear to have changed (or even discontinued) their collective bargaining arrangements since the 1980s. The parties can express such preferences, but it is far from straightforward for them simply to implement a strategic choice to change a long-established pattern of bargaining, especially because in such a change there are likely to be winners and losers, with the latter likely to contest the change vigorously.

92. What are the disadvantages of decentralized bargaining? Clegg holds that highly decentralized collective bargaining structures may bring about more industrial disputes because unions can call strikes at much less cost at a local level than if they have to bring out a whole industry, but this argument is contentious and there

---

74. Business Council of Australia, *Enterprise-based Bargaining Units: A Better Way of Working*, Industrial Relations Study Commission, BCA, Melbourne: 1989, p. 43. For the success of BCA arguments in reshaping Australia's bargaining structure, *see* P. Sheldon and L. Thornthwaite, 'The Business Council of Australia', in *Employer Associations and Industrial Relations Change: Catalysts and Captives* (eds), P. Sheldon and L. Thornthwaite, Allen & Unwin, Sydney, 1999.

are other significant variables, including the efficiency of disputes procedures.[75] With fragmented forms of negotiation it is more difficult to bring considerations of general interest into every one of the numerous enterprise bargaining exercises. The higher the level of negotiations, the easier it should be to take account of society-wide economic policies.[76] Under centralized bargaining, union negotiators can pursue more egalitarian objectives and obtain benefits for all employees, including those employed in SMEs. Such a larger coverage may be, however, at the expense of economic rewards, which may be held down by the financial capacity of smaller or marginal enterprises. In the more successful enterprises, this would inevitably result in wage drift or in attempts to supplement industry-wide bargaining with local negotiations or bonuses. Centralized bargaining enables unions to make a more efficient use of their scarce human and financial resources. Further, at an enterprise level unions may feel overpowered by the employer. For employers, centralized bargaining may also provide a range of benefits. It means that the question of pay levels among firms is no longer a factor in their product market competition. Second, by providing them with strength in numbers, centralized bargaining protects individual employers from union'whip sawing'campaigns and the associated costs of standing alone. Third, the multi-employer bargaining process itself brings great economies of scale to individual employers who can delegate much of the time-consuming activities to their employer association officials. Fourth it also reduces uncertainty and unpredictability in operational terms (and therefore transaction costs) by improving levels of information on a range of issues regarding the labour force. Fifth, by generalizing bargaining demands across a sector, multi-employer bargaining necessarily abstracts from the particular issues of any particular workplace. This tends to shift union attention away from questions of control at particular workplaces and thus helps employers to safeguard issues that they seek to claim under managerial prerogative. As such, it may also reduce the degree of personal animosity that can be seen in enterprise bargaining.

93.   Centralized and decentralized bargaining, then, each has advantages and disadvantages, but most parties have strong preferences for one or the other. Their preferences reflect geographic, product- and labour-market circumstances as well as the structure of unions and employers' organizations, and the character of their relationship. Smaller countries and relatively homogeneous sectors may find it convenient to hold negotiations covering their entire economy or whole sectors of economic activity, which would be impracticable in other contexts. Union movements in which the locus of power is at the top of the organization have traditionally sought industry or occupational bargaining, whereas decentralized unions tend to seek enterprise or local negotiations. Employers' preferences have also contributed to influencing bargaining structures, as could be seen in France with the development of multi-occupational agreements, and in Sweden, New Zealand, and Australia where bargaining has become more decentralized since the mid-1980s.

---

75. Clegg, 1976, p. 68ff.
76. Committee of Review into Australian Industrial Relations Law and Systems (Chairman K.J. Hancock), *Report of the Committee of Review*, Australian Government Publishing Service, Canberra, 1985, p. 242.

94. Preferred levels may shift according to the business cycle: in times of prosperity employees and unions favour enterprise or workplace bargaining to maximize their benefits by negotiating directly with prosperous employers, while in periods of adversity they tend to stress solidarity and secure minimum levels of protection at the highest level. The law may influence the level of bargaining by requiring or giving priority to negotiations at a certain level. In France, the establishment in 1982 of a legal obligation to negotiate every year (in all enterprises where there is union representation) induced an increase in the number of enterprise agreements, though the law did not require that negotiations should necessarily conclude with an agreement. Many attempts to change the collective bargaining system by legislation, however, are unlikely to have the intended effect, unless they carefully take into account the parties' wishes.

95. While some analyses seemed to assume that the key features of collective bargaining (whether enterprise or industry-level) were not easily changed except in wars or other such major crisis periods,[77] the results in some IMEs since the mid-1980s suggest otherwise. Recent experiences in the UK, Sweden, Italy, New Zealand, and Australia suggest that fundamental change can occur relatively quickly.[78]

96. Attempts to extend the scope of collective bargaining at the enterprise level in several IMEs in continental Europe have had a mixed record of success. Nonetheless, the parties have devised new forms of enterprise-level negotiations in France, Ireland, Italy, the Netherlands, and Sweden, as well as in Australia, New Zealand and the UK. But other countries with a decentralized system are moving towards some aspects of industry-wide bargaining. Ireland has been a good example of this trend and, in Switzerland where negotiating practices were highly decentralized, some sectoral agreements have acquired great significance. In the USA one trend appears to favour company-wide bargaining and, *albeit* to a lesser extent, even industry-wide bargaining in certain sectors (e.g. transport, glass, aluminium, containers, farm implements). A combination of individual plant negotiations and a type of industry-wide bargaining ('pattern bargaining') has developed in the automobile and steel industries. In other countries there has also been a growth of national-level negotiations, though they may not always lead to formal agreements.

97. Drawing on research in the automotive and telecommunications industries in seven IMEs (Australia, Britain, Germany, Italy, Japan, Sweden, and the USA), Katz and Darbishire find that traditional national systems of employment relations are being challenged by four cross-national patterns.[79] They categorize these patterns as: low-wage, human resource management, Japanese-oriented, and joint team-based

---

77. *See* G.J. Bamber and E. Córdova, 'Collective bargaining', *Comparative Labour Law and Industrial Relations in Industrialized Market Economies*, 5th ed., eds R. Blanpain and C. Engels, Kluwer, Deventer, 1993, pp. 353–82. 1993, p. 373; S.B. Levine, 'Changing Strategies of Unions and Management: Evaluation of Five Industrialised Countries', *British Journal of Industrial Relations*, 1980, p. 80.
78. P. Sheldon and L. Thornthwaite, 'Australian Employer Associations and the International Experience', in *Employer Associations* (eds), Sheldon and Thornthwaite, 1999.
79. H.C. Katz and D. Darbishire, *Converging Divergences: Worldwide Changes in Employment Systems*, Cornell University Press, Ithaca, 2000.

strategies. According to these authors, the four patterns are becoming more prevalent and are closely related to the decline of unions and growing income inequality. They conclude that there are increasing variations in employment relations within countries. However, their findings suggest that the nature and origins of such variations are similar, at least in these key IMEs. Hence, they coin the term 'converging divergences'.

98. Nevertheless it is difficult to detect a general convergence between collective bargaining systems, even though employers may share the motive of seeking to maintain managerial control through collective bargaining. Given that there is a range of such arguments for and against any particular approach to bargaining, it is not surprising that there have been moves towards the diversification of bargaining levels. In Belgium, Finland, Italy, Spain, and several other countries collective bargaining can take place at all or several levels. The trend towards more than one level of bargaining is probably because certain issues lend themselves to specific treatment at different levels. Supplementary social security benefits or national incomes policy, for instance, seem appropriate for national negotiations. Work schedules, productivity or payment by results, on the other hand, seem more appropriately discussed at a decentralized level.

99. If there are various levels of negotiation, there may be problems of coordination between them. There is a need to clarify which issues will be discussed at what levels, to foresee the sequence of negotiations and to provide for various types of safeguards. In the early 1960s, Italy devised a system of articulated bargaining which sought to coordinate the enterprise, industry and national levels; because it failed, in 1993 a tripartite basic agreement established procedures governing the different negotiating levels. Scandinavian countries have also developed some techniques of articulated bargaining which apply mostly to the national and industry levels. Both experiences have relied on successive delegations of authority. Such an objective presupposes a measure of centralization and self-discipline by each party as well as a widespread acceptance of the peace obligation and the criteria for determining which issues are determined at which levels. These conditions are not easy to meet and this may account for the limited success of such experiences. However, alternatives to an effective coordination of bargaining levels include an (authoritarian) imposition of unilateral regulation or one-level bargaining, or an acceptance that any matter can be discussed at any level.

100. In conclusion, at different times, certain parties argue strongly for centralization, while others strongly favour the decentralization of collective bargaining. At other times, their roles are reversed. Clearly, both arguments can have their attractions in certain circumstances. So can a range of other arguments relating to aspects of collective bargaining beyond the question of bargaining level. Rather than necessarily supporting one or other argument in a prescriptive fashion, it is more appropriate to understand particular situations as the result of historical processes, emerging pressures, needs and wants, as well as the parties' relative power, values, priorities and goals. This is because most collective bargaining arrangements have arisen from power struggles of one sort or another. Therefore, it is also important to bear in mind that collective bargaining is all about conflicts of interest and to ask

'who benefits from which bargaining strategies?' There is no 'one best way' in collective bargaining. There will continue to be controversies, so there remains considerable scope for further research, including studies of the above questions and about collective bargaining processes and outcomes. Such research can be especially fruitful if conducted on an international and comparative basis.

SELECT BIBLIOGRAPHY

R.J. Adams, *Industrial Relations under Liberal Democracy*, University of S. Carolina Press, Columbia S.C, 1995.

G.J. Bamber and R.D. Lansbury (eds), *International and Comparative Employment Relations: A Study of Industrialised Market Economies*, 3rd ed., Allen & Unwin, Sydney or Sage, London, 1998.

G.J. Bamber, F. Park, C. Lee, P.K. Ross, and K. Broadbent (eds), *Employment Relations in the Asia-Pacific*, Allen & Unwin, Sydney or Thomson Learning, London, 2000.

A. Flanders, (ed.), *Collective Bargaining: Selected Readings*, Penguin, Harmondsworth, 1969.

E.E. Herman, *Collective Bargaining and Labor Relations*, 4th ed., Prentice Hall, Englewood Cliffs, N.J., 1997.

H.C. Katz, 'The Decentralization of Collective Bargaining; A Literature Review and Comparative Analysis', *Industrial and Labour Relations Review*, 1993, pp. 3–22.

H.C. Katz and D. Darbishire, *Converging Divergences: Worldwide Changes in Employment Systems*, Cornell University Press, Ithaca, 2000.

H.C. Katz and T.A. Kochan, *An Introduction to Collective Bargaining and Industrial Relations*, 2nd ed., McGraw-Hill, New York, 2000.

S.H. Slichter et al., *The Impact of Collective Bargaining on Management*, Brookings Institution, Washington D.C., 1960.

G. Strauss, 'Collective Bargaining', in *International Encyclopedia of Business and Management* (ed.), M. Warner, Routledge, London and New York, 1996.

R.E. Walton and R.B. McKersie, *A Behavioral Theory of Labor Negotiations*, 2nd ed., McGraw Hill, New York, 1991.

J.P. Windmuller et al., *Collective Bargaining in Industrialised Market Economies: A Reappraisal*, ILO, Geneva, 1987.

Chapter 23. The Law of Strikes and Lockouts

A.T.J.M. Jacobs

I. INTRODUCTION

A. *From Crime to Fundamental Right*

1. To 'classic' legal minds the law of strikes is certainly one of the least palatable parts of the law. Those who go on strike seek to impose their stand on the adversary by simply inflicting harm. But resolving a dispute by inflicting harm on the other party runs counter to all notions most dear to lawyers, such as the adagia of '*neminem laedere*', '*nul n'ayant le droit de nuire à autrui*', '*nul ne peut se faire justice à soimême*', etc.

Nevertheless, in the modern welfare state, the practice of collective bargaining is accepted as the most suitable way to settle the conditions of employment. And this method incurs the risk that the parties will not conclude their negotiations successfully. If this occurs, there must be recourse to some method of resolving the impasse, i. e. the parties must be free to mount economic pressures in order to force the opposite party to make concessions.[1] Otherwise collective bargaining would amount to 'collective begging'.[2]

2. The change from the early 'classic' approach towards industrial disputes to the latest 'modern' view has not come overnight. It has taken an evolution of centuries. In virtually all the countries studied, worker organization, collective bargaining, strikes and other collective action were at first suppressed on the grounds of general legal principles or by specific legislation assessing criminal liability, or by the mere showing of police and military muscle. Later, when the repression of worker organization and collective bargaining was lifted, industrial disputes remained curtailed by the employers' right to impose disciplinary sanctions and by the general law of civil liability in the form of damages.[3]

---

1. *See* NLRB v Insurance Agents' International Union, 361 US 477, 1960, pp. 488, 489.
2. Weiss and Schmidt, *IELL* 2000, p. 177; Bundesarbeitsgericht AP No. 64 on Article 9 GG (Arbeitskampf).
3. For an outline of this history in Europe *see* A. Jacobs in B.A. Hepple (ed.), *The Making of Labour Law in Europe*, London, 1986, p. 197.

In the first half of the 20th century the phenomenon of industrial disputes took varying approaches. In *Britain* the worker organizations were exempted from criminal and civil liability for these actions, while in the Netherlands, new prohibitions under criminal law were laid on strikes by civil servants and railway personnel. In Australia, New Zealand, and Canada[4] around 1900 the idea was effectuated to replace the frequent struggle between both sides of industry with a system of compulsory arbitration.

3. A complete ban on industrial action returned under fascism in Italy (1926–1943) and nazism in Germany (1933–1945). The same applied for the countries under corporatist rule, Portugal (1932–1972) and Spain (1936–1975), in the military dictatorship of Greece (1967–1974), and in the countries under communist rule, Russia (1918–1990) and the eastern European states (1945–1989).

On the other hand in some countries of western Europe, the right to strike emerged after the Second World War as one of the shibboleths of a free, democratic order. This right was explicitly mentioned in the Constitutions of France (1946)[5] and Italy (1948).[6] In the 1970s the southern European States – Portugal,[7] Spain,[8] and Greece[9] – followed the examples of France and Italy by inserting the right to strike as a fundamental right in their new democratic constitutions. Sweden[10] and Switzerland[11] too inserted this right in their constitution respectively in 1974 and 1998.

Also in many countries outside Europe, from Japan[12] to Argentina,[13] the Constitution mentions the right to strike.

In the United States, the right to engage in concerted activities has been laid down in the National Labor Relations Act,[14] in Canada, in the federal and provincal laws on labour relations and in New Zealand, in the Employment Contracts Act 1991.[15]

4. On an international level the International Labour Organization failed to include explicitly the right to strike in the standards laid down in its Constitution and

---

4. H.W. Arthurs a.o., *IELL* 1993, p. 267; D.D. Carter, Ch. *Canada* in R. Blanpain and R. Ben-Israel (ed.), Strikes and Lock-outs in Industrialized Market Economies, *Bulletin of Comparative Labour Relations, Deventer*, 1994, p. 47.
5. *Cf.* J. Rojot, Ch. France, in R. Blanpain and R. Ben Israel (eds), Strikes and Lock-outs in Industrialized Market Economies, *Bulletin of Comparative Labour Relations*, Deventer, 1994, p. 55.
6. Article 40 of the Constitution, *see* Treu, *EILL* 1998, pp. 207–209.
7. Article 58 of the Constitution, *see* M. Pinto, *IELL* 1989, p. 215.
8. Article 28.2 of the Constitution, *see* Olea/Rodriguez-Sañuda, *IELL* 1996, p. 142.
9. Article 23 of the Constitution, *see* T.B. Koniaris, *IELL* 1990, p. 180.
10. Article 2:17 of the new Constitution Act, *see* A. Adlercreutz, *IELL* 1997, p. 187; R. Fahlbeck, Ch. Sweden, in R. Blanpain and R. Ben-Israel (ed.), Strikes and Lock-outs in Industrialized Market Economies, *Bulletin of Comparative Labour Relations*, Deventer, 1994, p. 165.
11. *See* EIRR 293/12.
12. Article 28, *see* Hanami and Komiya, *IELL* 1999, p. 161; K. Sugeno, Ch. Japan, in R. Blanpain and R. Ben-Israel (eds), Strikes and Lock-outs in Industrialized Market Economies, *Bulletin of Comparative Labour Relations*, Deventer, 1994, pp. 105, 106.
13. Article 14 bis, *see* M. Ackerman and A. Goldin, *IELL* 1990, p. 221.
14. Sections 7 and 8.
15. *See* G. Anderson, Ch. New Zealand, in R. Blanpain and R. Ben-Israel (eds), Strikes and Lock-outs in Industrialized Market Economies, *Bulletin of Comparative Labour Relations*, Deventer, 1994, p. 126.

its numerous Conventions. However the right to strike was explicitly included in the International Covenant on Economic, Social and Cultural Rights of 1966 (Article 8). At the regional level, the right to strike was recognized in the European Social Charter of the Council of Europe (Articles 4, 6), in the Inter-American Charter of Social Guarantees (Article 27), in the so-called Protocol of San Salvador (Article 8(1)b)[16] and in the Charter of the Organization of American States (Article 43, sub c).[17]

But these international standards cannot claim universal validity and therefore they do not alter the fact, that in many other countries constitutional citations of a right to strike failed to occur. Therefore, for countries like Britain, Austria,[18] and Denmark it is still not possible to speak of a 'right to strike' but only of a freedom to strike.

5.   In part of the doctrine the thesis has been developed, that the right to strike is implicit when constitutions guarantee the right of association and/or the right to collective bargaining. This is also the opinion of the International Labour Organization.[19] Yet, this thesis has not been followed consistently. For example, it has been rejected by the European Court of Human Rights[20] and also by the Supreme Court of Canada.[21]

However, by and by in various countries including Germany,[22] the Benelux-countries,[23] Ireland,[24] and Israel[25] highest judges have made explicit statements of recognition of the right to strike in their jurisdictions as well.

And even if in other countries this basic question is still undecided, it seems to me legitimate to conclude, that at this stage (2000) the right to strike has overwhelmingly acquired the status of a fundamental right in all democratic Western countries.

---

16. *See Report Freedom of Association and Collective Bargaining*, Report III (4B), Geneva, 1994, pp. 62–64.
17. *See* R. Ben-Israel, *International Labour Standards: The Case of Freedom to Strike*, Deventer, 1988, pp. 71–92.
18. *See* R. Strasser, *IELL* 1992, p. 198.
19. *See Report Freedom of Association and Collective Bargaining*, Report III (4B), Geneva, 1994, pp. 65–66; *see* R. Ben-Israel, *op. cit.*, pp. 25–29.
20. Eur. Court H.R., Schmidt and Dahlstrom Case, judgment of 6 February, 1976, Series A, Vol. 21.
21. *See* H.W. Arthurs a.o., *IELL* 1993, p. 276; D.D. Carter, *op. cit.*, p. 41.
22. In Germany initially the judges saw the basis for the recognition of the right to strike in the doctrine of 'Sozialadäquanz' (*see* Bundesarbeitsgericht AP No. 1 on Article 9 GG (Arbeitskampf). In later years the German judges founded the right to strike on Article 9 III of the German Constitition, which recognises the right to trade union association, see Bundesarbeitsgericht AP No. 64 on Article 9 GG (Arbeitskampf), *see* Weiss and Schmidt, *IELL* 2000, pp. 166, 167.
23. In Luxemburg the Cour supérieure de Justice in 1952 deduced the right to strike from the constitutional provision which guarantees the freedom of trade union association, *see* Cass. civ. 24.7.1952; in Belgium the recognition of the right to strike in principle could be read from case law of the Belgium Supreme Court in 1981; *see* Cass. 15.6.1981, *JTT* 1981, p. 329; Cass. 21.12.1981, *JTT* 1982, p. 329; in The Netherlands the Supreme Court in 1986 founded the right to strike on Article 6(4) European Social Charter, *see* Dutch Supreme Court, 30.5.1986, *NJ* 1986, 688, *see* M.G. Rood, *IELL* 1999, p. 76.
24. *See* M. Redmond, *IELL* 1996, p. 193.
25. *See* R. Ben-Israel, *IELL* 1994, p. 173.

B. Crystallization into Distinctive 'Models'

6. For many years, scholars have debated whether it makes a difference if a jurisdiction recognizes a 'freedom to strike' or a 'right to strike'.[26] Now that so many countries have rallied to the recognition of a right to strike either in Constitution, by statute or in case law, one must doubt whether it makes sense to continue to emphasize the legal consequences of the differences between the 'right to strike' and the 'freedom to strike'.

Perhaps, the most important remaining consequence of this difference can be found in the paragraph on the legal effects of the (un)lawful strike in the individual employment contract (para. III.C): in the countries where there is only a 'freedom to strike' the idea that the strike entails a breach of contract is apparently persistent; in the countries where a 'right to strike' is recognized, generally the 'suspension' of the employment contract is seen as the logical corollary of the right to strike.

7. Instead of emphasizing the importance of the difference between the 'right to strike' and the 'freedom to strike' too much, it seems apposite to highlight some other differences between the various systems of the law of strikes and lockouts.

Part of the doctrine in accepting the right to strike of the workers claims at the same time an equivalent right to collective action for the employers – the idea of parity of arms in the industrial dispute, which indeed has largely inspired the law of strikes and lockouts in the United States, Canada, Germany, and the Scandinavian countries. Another part of the doctrine rejects the whole idea of a parity in the right to take collective action on the grounds that workers are thought to be less powerful than employers. This part of the doctrine has heavily inspired the law of strikes and lockouts in the southern European countries.

The most noticeable fruits of the difference between these doctrines figures in the paragraph on lockouts (para. IV.B).[27]

8. Another fundamental difference, which oddly enough runs largely along the same lines, concerns the role of industrial disputes in the system of industrial relations. Part of the doctrine connects the legitimacy of the strike narrowly with the process of collective bargaining. Consequently only the official strike, that is the strike initiated by the recognized trade union can be lawful. Unofficial strikes are in principle unlawful and those who participate in them do not enjoy protection. This is – exceptions apart – the situation in the United States, Canada, Germany and the Scandinavian countries. Another part of the doctrine considers the individual worker (although acting in a collective manner) as bearer of the right to strike. With regard to the question whether a strike is lawful and what effects it entails, it is wholly or largely immaterial whether the strike is an official one or not.

This is the situation in the southern European countries, in Ireland, in Switzerland, and in the Benelux countries (see para. II.B.).

---

26. See for instance M. Goldberg, Ch. Israel, in R. Blanpain and R. Ben-Israel (eds), Strikes and Lock-outs in Industrialized Market Economies, *Bulletin of Comparative Labour Relations*, Deventer, 1994, p. 92.
27. The Committee of Experts on the European Social Charter, noting that the ESC recognises the right of both sides of industry to take industrial action, asserts that this does not necessarily mean full legal equality between strike and lockout, see Conclusions VIII, 95.

II. THE LIMITS OF THE RIGHT TO STRIKE

A. *Ways of Delimiting the Right to Strike*

9. The sanctity of the right to strike is not absolute.[28] For every legislator and judge, it has always been evident that the freedom or the right to strike can only be exercised within certain limits. Whether one is in the legal situation of 'a right to strike' or in the legal situation of 'a freedom to strike', solutions have to be found which prevent harm and losses, especially those inflicted upon society as a whole, from being out of proportion or intolerable.

But who is to draw these limits?

10. High activities of the legislator in delimiting the freedom/right to strike can be detected in the Anglo-American world.

As early as 1906 in Britain a statute delimited the space (circumscribed in the so-called golden formula) in which trade unions can organize strikes without running the risk of being held liable for tort.

The period in which this space was narrowed by case law and statutes (1964–1974), was followed by a period in which the legislator restored it 'to one of West-Europe's most liberal regimes of strike law'[29] (1974–1979), which in turn has been followed by a period in which the legislator has narrowed it again (1979–present). The existing provisions were consolidated in 1992.[30]

Britain's former dominions inherited the classic British approach of the 1906 Act and consequently had to revise it in later years. So, in Ireland, where the legislator kept reshaping statutory strike law until the British 1906 Act was finally replaced by the Industrial Relations Act 1990, and in New Zealand where the statutory provisions on strikes were revised in 1973, in 1987, and finally in 1991.[31]

In Canada, in recent decades, the poor strike record has frequently incited the federal and provincial legislator to impose restrictions on the freedom to strike.[32] And in the United States it is the National Labor Relations Act which in much detail both recognizes and delimits the right to strike.

Outside the Anglo-American world elaborate statutory limitations of the right to strike can be found in Sweden[33], Spain,[34] and Portugal.[35]

---

28. *See Report Freedom of Association and Collective Bargaining*, Report III (4B), Geneva, 1994, p. 66.
29. B.A. Hepple, Ch. United Kingdom, in R. Blanpain and R. Ben-Israel (eds), Strikes and Lockouts in Industrialized Market Economies, *Bulletin of Comparative Labour Relations, Deventer*, 1994, p. 181.
30. In the Trade Unions and Labour Relations Consolidation Act (TULRCA) 1992.
31. *See* J.M. Howells, *IELL* 1996, pp. 221,225; G. Anderson, *op. cit.*, pp. 123–125.
32. *See* H.W. Arthurs a.o., *IELL* 1993, pp. 268–270.
33. In the Codetermination Act of 1974, *see* Adlercreutz, *IELL* 1997, pp. 189–192.
34. In the Labour Relations Decree (RDL) of 1977, *see* Olea and Rodriguez-Sañudo, *IELL* 1996, p. 142. On the basis of a decision of the Constitutional Court, april 1981, several rules of the RDL are abolished, whilst others are maintained in an interpretation in accordance with Article 28 of the Constitution.
35. The Strike Act No. 65/77 of August 26, 1977; *See* M. Pinto, *IELL* 1989, p. 215.

11. In contrast, in most industrial nations in Europe the legislator has failed to mark the borderline between the legal and illegal exercising of the right to strike.[36]

In France[37] and Italy, the legislator assumed only a part of its task leaving much of the job up to the judiciary. In Germany and the Netherlands, the law of strikes and lockouts has been almost completely 'judge-made'.

In jurisdictions, where judges have had to define the limits of the right to strike, they have often looked towards general doctrines, which were mostly to be found in civil law. In France[38] and Spain,[39] the judges have availed themselves of the doctrine of *'abus de droit'*, while the judges in the Netherlands have utilized the concept of 'negligence'. In Austria, industrial disputes should not be *'contra bonos mores'*.[40] The law in Greece considers a strike unlawful if it can be characterized as 'malpractice'.[41]

12. In another group of countries the idea prevails that the rules governing the lawful exercise of the right to industrial action should be decided between the social partners themselves as the most visible expression of their autonomy.

In some countries, like Denmark[42] and Sweden,[43] this work has indeed been accomplished on an all-industry level – the rules of industrial disputes are fixed in Basic Agreements between the confederations of trade unions and employers' associations. These rules are effectively enforced by the courts, and sometimes, also codified by statute. Belgium also embraces the preference for autonomous regulation but an all-industry agreement is absent. The agreements are on industry level and they are considered not to be legally enforceable in court.[44] In Italy, self-regulation by the unions has proved only partially effective[45] so that state intervention has become unavoidable.

B. Official Strikes versus Wild-Cat Strikes

13. In the Introduction, mention has already been made of an important distinction in strike laws between one group of nations and the other, viz. that which centers

---

36. Although the European Social Charter requires that limitations of the right to strike should be laid down by law, the Committee of Independent Experts on this Charter accepts limitations made by case law, provided this case law is bound to the same limits as the legislator, *see Conclusions* I, p. 39.

37. A general statutory regulation was the ambition of the socialist government, 1982, *see* J.-C. Javillier, *Les réformes du droit du travail depuis le 10 mai 1981*, 2e. éd., Paris, 1984, pp. 310–311, 324–325, but it has never been realised; *see also* J. Rojot, *op. cit.*, p. 66.

38. G. Lyon-Caen, J. Pélissier, and A. Supiot, *Droit du Travail*, 18th ed., Paris, 1996, p. 294; J. Rojot, *op. cit.*, pp. 55, 58.

39. This because the RDL, para. 7, expressly alludes to it.

40. *See* A. Strasser, *IELL* 1990, p. 194.

41. *See* T.B. Koniaris, *IELL* 1990, p. 183.

42. First of all in the so-called September-Agreement of 1899 (*see* above) and later in the Standard Rules of Settlement of Trade Disputes, designed by the so-called August-committee in 1910. Initially these rules where free to follow, but since 1934 they have a mandatory-supplementary character: they apply if the social partners omit to make their own rules, *see* Jacobsen and Hasselbalch, *IELL* 1998, p. 26.

43. *See* R. Fahlbeck, *op. cit.*, p. 164.

44. *See* R. Blanpain, *IELL* 1999, p. 302.

45. *See* the initiatives of the trade union confederations to improve the system of self-regulation, *see* T. Treu, *IELL* 1998, p. 212.

around the function of the right to strike and its consequences for the question: who is the bearer of the right to strike?

In various countries, notably Germany, the Scandinavian countries, the United States, and Canada, industrial conflict must be exclusively understood as complementary to collective bargaining. It is seen as a pre-condition for the proper functioning of the process of collective bargaining. To put it differently: industrial action is only allowed in so far as its purpose is the achievement of a collective agreement and the achievement of aims that can be regulated by collective agreements.

It is clear that such a functional approach to the right to strike entails an important limitation on the right to strike: it makes the right to strike a union's right and not an individual right. As a consequence, wild-cat strikes are unlawful, as the workers outside the official trade unions cannot conclude collective agreements. This theoretical difference results not in two, but several 'models'.

14. The preference of the official strike over the unofficial strike entails the heaviest consequences in Germany[46] and the Scandinavian countries,[47] where strikes, which are not organized by the unions, are in principle considered to be unlawful.

In the United States, there is the same preference for the official strike, if workers are represented by a collective bargaining agent. In that case all concerted activity must be channelled through that bargaining representative and is protected only if approved by the representative. However, if a group of workers are not represented by a collective bargaining agent, they have nevertheless a protected right to act in concert.[48] The last mentioned exception does not exist in Canada, where the right to strike is solely attributed to the trade unions in relation with collective bargaining.

Also in Japan an industrial dispute not carried out by a *bona fide* union falls outside the legal immunities for industrial action.[49]

In Israel there is a privilege for union strikes, but only in the public service.[50]

In Britain the workers participating in an official strike are somewhat better protected against the negative effects on their employment relationship than those participating in unofficial strikes.[51]

In Portugal the right to call a strike is enjoyed by trade unions or by workers assemblies in enterprises in which the majority of workers are not unionized.[52]

15. In countries like France,[53] Italy,[54] and Spain[55] the right to strike is essentially conceived as an individual right for each worker (although of course, it can only be

---

46. *See* Bundesarbeitsgericht AP Nos. 34, 37, 41, 43 zu Article 9 III GG (Arbeitskampf); this leaves the possibility open that the strike can be taken over by the trade union and continues as an official strike; *see* Weiss and Schmidt, *IELL* 2000, p. 167.
47. For Sweden *see* R. Fahlbeck, *op. cit.*, p. 165.
48. U.S. Supreme Court in NLRB v Washington Aluminium Co. 370 U.S. 9.15, 1962, *see* A.L. Goldman, *IELL* 1996, p. 371.
49. T. Hanami, *Managing Japanese Workers*, Tokyo, 1991, p. 70; K. Sugeno, *op. cit.*, pp. 106–107.
50. *See* R. Ben-Israel, *IELL* 1996, p. 178.
51. *See* B.A. Hepple, 1994, p. 188.
52. *See Conclusions* XIV-1, p. 662 of the Committee of Independent Experts on the European Social Charter.
53. G. Lyon-Caen a.o., *op. cit.*, p. 927; M. Despax and J. Rojot, *IELL* 1987, p. 295; J. Rojot, *op. cit.*, p. 56. However, an important exception is made for the civil service, *see* para. II.J.
54. *See* T. Treu, *IELL* 1998, p. 209.
55. *See* M.A. Olea and F. Rodrigues-Sanudo, *IELL* 1996, p. 146.

exercised by the workers in common). As a consequence, in these countries wild-cat strikes are not treated any differently to official strikes.

This is also the case in Belgium,[56] The Netherlands, and Switzerland.[57] In a number of countries, the situation is unclear as there is contradictory case law on this point.[58]

Within the orbit of the European Social Charter the restriction of the exercise of the right to strike to trade unions is heavily debated. The Committee of Independent Experts rejects consequently such a restriction,[59] but the Governmental Committee seems to doubt.[60]

C. The Peace Obligation

16. Very often, collective agreements contain a promise that there will be no strike or lockout for the duration of the agreement (no-strike clauses/peace clauses).[61] Peace clauses seldom[62] prohibit all collective disputes before expiration of the collective agreement (absolute peace obligation). Mostly, the peace obligation is only relative. It then leaves space for industrial actions aimed at matters which have not been regulated in the existing collective agreement[63], for example sympathy strikes[64] and actions on other grounds.[65]

17. In many countries, it is the general opinion that even if the collective agreement does not explicitly contain such a clause, a relative duty of peace is nevertheless immanent.[66] This is based on the idea, that it is an expression of a general principle of the law of contracts (*pacta sunt servanda*) and therefore, should be honoured. Thus in countries such as Germany,[67] the Scandinavian countries,[68] the Netherlands,[69]

---

56. *See* Cass. 21.12.1981, *JTT* 1982, p. 329.
57. *See* A. Berenstein, *IELL* 1993, p. 176, contradicted by M. Rehbinder, Schweitzerisches Arbeitsrecht, Bern, Stämpfi Verlag, 1999, p. 250.
58. So in Argentina, *see* M. Ackerman and A. Goldin, *IELL* 1990, p. 222.
59. *See Conclusions* IV, p. 50; Conclusions XIII-4, p. 361.
60. *Conclusions* of the Governmental Committee XIV, p. 94.
61. For Ireland, *see* M. Redmond, *IELL* 1996, p. 199.
62. Although in Canada it comes near to that, *see* D.D. Carter, *op. cit.*, p. 46; rare examples of absolute peace clauses are reported in Switzerland, *see* A. Berenstein, *IELL* 1993, p. 177.
63. Although judges may be inclined to construe this exception narrowly, for Sweden *see* A. Adlercreutz, *IELL* 1997, p. 190.
64. In Sweden, *see* A. Adlercreutz, *IELL* 1997, p. 192; in Denmark *see* Jacobsen and Hasselbalch, *IELL* 1998, p. 265.
65. So in the *United States* judges will not read into broad no stoppage provisions a waiver of the right to respect picket lines, *see* A.L. Goldman, *IELL* 1996, p. 374.
66. For Israel, *see* R. Ben-Israel, *IELL* 1994, p. 177; for Argentina, *see* M. Ackerman and A. Goldin, *IELL* 1990, p. 224.
67. *See* Bundesarbeitsgericht AP Nr. 3 on § 1 TVG (Friedenspflicht); Weiss and Schmidt, *IELL* 2000, p. 170.
68. For Sweden, *see* A. Adlercreutz, *IELL* 1997, p. 189; for Finland, *see* A. Suviranta, *IELL* 1999, p. 191; for Denmark *see* Jacobsen and Hasselbalch, *IELL* 1998, pp. 262, 279; for Norway *see* S. Evju, *Aspects of Norwegian Labour Law*, Oslo, 1991, pp. 86, 94–97.
69. A.T.J.M. Jacobs and G. Heerma van Voss, *Elementair Sociaal Recht*, 6th ed., Alphen and Rijn, 1998, p. 202.

Switzerland,[70] Ireland,[71] New Zealand,[72] Israel,[73] Japan,[74] Canada,[75] and the United States[76] strikes in contravention of collective agreements are in principle unlawful. The logical consequence is, that the aggrieved employer may have recourse against the union in civil court or in arbitration. He can claim that the trade union, which is a party to the collective agreement, is under an obligation to try to prevent their members from taking impermissible industrial action and to try to induce them to stop, if the action is already under way.[77]

In some countries like Germany, the peace obligation only binds the other social partner. In other countries like the Netherlands, Denmark, and Canada[78] both the social partners and the individual employers and employees are bound by it.

18. Another branch of the doctrine sees the peace obligation as being suspect. According to scholars in this area trade unions cannot have the function of restricting the individual workers from exercising their right to strike. So the peace obligation can at most bind the trade unions themselves. However, trade unions may refuse to sign a peace obligation and – failing such an obligation – its existence should not be construed as implicit. This doctrine has mostly influenced strike law in the southern European countries, particularly in Italy.

19. While in France, Belgium,[79] and Spain,[80] the judges consider strikes in contravention of a collective agreement as illegal, the legal consequences differ.

For example in Belgium and Luxembourg, the trade unions are not liable in court (*see* para. III.A.) and by violating the peace obligation they do not risk payment of damages. Yet, they run the risk that the employer may stop complying with the collective agreement with the result that many attractive financial advantages would be lost. In France the collective agreement may contain peace clauses, clauses requiring a cooling-off period etc. although these type of clauses are not widespread. Such clauses cannot bind the individual workers, while the binding of trade unions is very weak.[81]

In Britain peace clauses are rare and if they do figure in a collective agreement they rarely have legal effect.[82]

The consequence is that in the last category of countries strikes in contravention of collective agreements are very well possible or even perfectly lawful.

---

70. *See* A. Berenstein, *IELL* 1993, p. 177; M. Rehbinder, *op. cit.*, pp. 252–254.
71. M. Redmond, *IELL* 1996, p. 199.
72. G. Anderson, *op. cit.*, pp. 127, 129.
73. *See* M. Goldberg, *op. cit.*, p. 90.
74. *See* K. Sugeno, *op. cit.*, pp. 108, 113.
75. H.W. Arthurs a.o., *IELL* 1993, p. 271; D.D. Carter, *op. cit.*, p. 46.
76. *See* A.L. Goldman, *IELL* 1996, p. 373.
77. For Sweden, *see* A. Adlercreutz, *IELL* 1997, p. 194.
78. *See* D.D. Carter, *op. cit.*, p. 46.
79. M. Rigaux, *Staking en Bezetting naar Belgisch Recht*, diss. Antwerpen, 1982, p. 240.
80. *See* Olea and Rodriguez-Sañudo, *IELL* 1996, p. 145.
81. *See* M.Despax and J. Rojot, *IELL* 1987, p. 300; J. Rojot, *op. cit.*, p. 61; G. Lyon-Caen a.o., *op. cit.*, pp. 924, 964.
82. Because collective agreements in Britain are mostly considered not to be legally enforceable, *see* B.A. Hepple, *IELL* 1992, p. 258.

20. Limitations on the right to strike based on collective agreements are in conformity with the European Social Charter, but according to the Committee of Experts of the ILO such restrictions must be compensated by the right to have recourse to impartial and rapid arbitration machinery for individual and collective grievances concerning the interpretation or application of collective agreements.[83]

D. Disputes of Rights and Disputes of Interests

21. Strikes can be about many types of conflicts – to acquire an improvement of wages, to resist a deterioration in working conditions, to fight off an individual dismissal, or the closing down of an entire factory, etc. Often strikes are deployed as a medium for ventilating protests against managerial policies and practices.

The potential variety of purposes of industrial action has led scholars to divide industrial disputes according to their purposes i.e. into *disputes of interests* versus *disputes of rights*. Whereas the latter concern the interpretation and application of existing contractual rights, the former relate to changes in the establishment of collective rules and require conflicting economic interests to be reconciled.

In many countries, the law has tried to make the use of legal remedies in industrial disputes more acceptable. Consequently industrial warfare could be avoided in cases of disputes of rights, since these disputes can be settled by court action. Only disputes of interests are not fit for a judicial decision and it is for these kinds of conflicts that the strike weapon should be reserved.[84]

22. The distinction between disputes of rights and disputes of interests has from the very outset been made in labour law in the Scandinavian countries.[85] In these countries, as well as in Canada,[86] New Zealand,[87] Germany, Luxembourg, Switzerland,[88] Portugal,[89] and to a lesser degree also in the Netherlands,[90] industrial action related to disputes concerning the interpretation, administration or violation of labour laws and collective agreements is unlawful, because legislation provides procedures by which these types of disputes may be adjudicated.[91]

---

83. *See* ILO, *Report Freedom of Association and Collective Bargaining*, Report III (4B), Geneva, 1994, p. 73.
84. Such a limitation of the right to strike is in accordance with the European Social Charter, *see Conclusions* I, p. 39 of the Committee of Experts on the E.S.C.
85. W. Galenson, *The Danish System of Labor Relations*, Cambridge, Mass. 1952, pp. 229–230, 234, 242–244, 246; Jacobsen and Hasselbalch, *IELL* 1998, p. 286; for Norway, *see* S. Evju, *op. cit.*, p. 125; for Sweden *see* A. Adlercreutz, *IELL* 1997, p. 191, who recalls, that an exception is made for a blockade to enforce the payment of undisputed and due demands for wages or other remuneration for work performed.
86. H.W. Arthurs a.o., *IELL* 1993, pp. 276, 295–296.
87. *See* J.M. Howells, *IELL* 1996, pp. 189, 221, 229.
88. M. Rehbinder, *op. cit.*, p. 252.
89. *See* M. Pinto, *IELL* 1989, p. 211.
90. *Cf.* A.T.J.M. Jacobs and G. Heerma van Voss, *op. cit.*, pp. 200, 201.
91. Admittedly, it may easily occur that the parties disagree as to whether the issue is already properly regulated in the law or in collective agreements.

However, in numerous other jurisdictions, like in the United States, Britain,[92] Belgium,[93] Spain, Italy, and France,[94] the distinction between disputes of interests and disputes of rights is (almost) irrelevant.

Some countries occupy a middle position in this area, for example, Ireland,[95] where, since 1990, the immunities no longer apply to disputes concerning one worker where procedures have not been followed.

E. Other Limitations as Regards the Aim of the Strike

23. In Germany[96] and Switzerland[97] a strike is not lawful if its purpose is not fit to be regulated by collective bargaining. In Britain the subject-matter of a 'protected' trade dispute must relate 'wholly or mainly' to one or more specified employment matters.[98] However, in most countries, provided the object of the strike is a *professional* one (in other words, if it is about occupational interests of workers and worker organizations), all manner of claims may be included and they need not be restricted to industrial disputes likely to be solved through the conclusion of collective agreements.[99]

24. In all countries strikes which are purely *political* in nature are in principle considered as unlawful.[100] Yet, the general prohibition of political strikes is somewhat softened by the readiness of the courts in some countries, notably in Scandinavia, to allow manifestations of solidarity for political or trade union purposes in the form of strikes or demonstrations of short duration.[101] For the rest there is the question: what makes a strike a political strike and by consequence: an illegal

---

92. In Britain this is also caused by the fact that collective agreements are not legally enforceable.
93. *See* R. Blanpain, *IELL* 1999, p. 304.
94. *See* G. Lyon-Caen a.o., *op. cit.*, p. 931.
95. *See* M. Redmond, *IELL* 1996, p. 195.
96. *See* Bundesarbeitsgericht AP Nos 2, 52, 58, 64, 82 and 113 on Article 9 GG (Arbeitskampf); Weiss and Schmidt, *IELL* 2000, p. 166; this restriction has been consequently critisised by the Committee of Independent Experts on the European Social Charter, *see* L. Samuel, *Fundamental social rights*, Strassburg, 1997, p. 165.
97. M. Rehbinder, *op. cit.*, p. 251.
98. *See* B.A. Hepple, 1994, p. 185.
99. This is also the opinion of the Freedom of Association Committee of the International Labour Organisation, *see* its 190th *Report*, Case No. 913 (Sri Lanka), para. 450.
100. For France, *see* G. Lyon-Caen a.o., *op. cit.* pp. 439–442; Rojot, *op. cit.*, p. 57; in Britain they, fall outside the 'golden formula' and they are outside the 'immunities', *see* B.A. Hepple, *IELL* 1992, pp. 264–265; for Belgium, R. Blanpain, Ch. Belgium in R. Blanpain and R. Ben-Israel (eds), Strikes and Lockouts in Industrialized Market Economies, *Bulletin of Comparative Labour Relations*, Deventer, 1994, p. 285; for Germany Weiss and Schmidt, *IELL* 2000, pp. 173, 174; for Switzerland, Rehbinder, *op. cit.*, p. 251; for Japan, K. Sugeno, *op. cit.*, p. 106; for Spain, Olea and Rodriguez-Sañudo, *IELL* 1996, p. 144; for Canada, Arthurs a.o., *IELL* 1993, pp. 276–297; this is also the opinion of the Freedom of Association Committee of the International Labour Organisation, *see* its 190th *Report*, Case No. 913 (Sri Lanka), para. 450; the Committee of Experts of the ILO, *see Report Freedom of Association and Collective Bargaining*, Report III (4B), Geneva, 1994, pp. 62–64; the Committee of Independent Experts on the European Social Charter holds the same view, see its *Conclusions*.
101. For Sweden, *see* A. Adlercreutz, *IELL* 1997, p. 193; for Denmark, Jacobsen and Hasselbalch, *IELL* 1998, p. 270; for Norway, *see* S. Evju, *op. cit.*, p. 86.

strike? In many strikes the political and occupational aspects are intertwined. They may be lawful despite the fact that they are against the government policy.[102]

So in the Netherlands the Supreme Court has ruled, that as long as conditions of employment are the reason for a strike it is not to be considered as a political strike even if it is against government policy.[103] Also in Spain the legality of a strike that – for instance – protested against governmental social security policies, was considered lawful. In Italy[104] case law has legalized all sorts of political strikes as long as they are to defend the workers' interests. Only strikes to subvert the constitutional order remain illegal. In France strikes against the State as an employer or against a given social and economic policy of the State, directly influencing wages and working conditions, are lawful.[105] In Israel a strike against the removal of the monopoly of the state-owned telecommunications company was held to be lawful as it aimed at safeguarding employees' rights.[106] On the contrary in Britain industrial action in opposition to government plans to privatize a state-owned corporation has been held to fall outside the immunities.[107]

25. In many countries, such as Belgium,[108] *solidarity strikes (sympathy strikes)* are at risk if they are about non-economic matters, but they enjoy equal protection to that of other strikes as long as they are based on economic matters.

In Greece, there is even a special statutory provision authorizing trade unions to call a strike in sympathy with another trade union of a multinational company which is on strike.[109]

In Finland, the law contains a free right to engage in sympathy action and support strikes with four-day's notice.[110]

At the other end of the spectrum are countries like Canada,[111] New Zealand,[112] Japan,[113] Switzerland,[114] and Britain,[115] where almost every sympathy strike, that has as its objective, putting pressure on a secondary employer, is considered unlawful.

Between these extremes are many countries where, circumstances determine whether solidarity strikes are considered legal.[116] So in Sweden,[117] Denmark,[118]

---

102. This is the situation in Canada, *see* D.D. Carter, *op. cit.*, p. 43 and this is also the opinion of the Freedom of Association Committee of the International Labour Organisation, *see* its 58th *Report*, Case No. 221 (UK/Aden), para. 109.
103. Dutch Supreme Court 30.5.1986, *NJ* 1986, 688; M.G. Rood, *IELL* 1999, p. 76.
104. *See* T. Treu, *IELL* 1998, p. 217.
105. *See* M. Despax and J. Rojot, *IELL* 1987, p. 295.
106. Case No. 1993/4-4 Histadrut v Bezek, *see* R. Ben-Israel, *IELL* 1994, p. 175; M. Goldberg, *op. cit.*, p. 86.
107. Mercury Communications Ltd. v. Scott-Gartner [1984] Industrial Cases Report; *see* Hepple, 1994, p. 185.
108. *See* R. Blanpain, *IELL* 1999, p. 306.
109. *See* T.B. Koniaris, *IELL* 1990, p. 182.
110. *See* EIRR 316, p. 5.
111. H.W. Arthurs a.o., *IELL* 1993, p. 276.
112. G. Anderson, *op. cit.*, pp. 130, 131.
113. *See* K. Sugeno, *op. cit.*, p. 106.
114. *See* M. Rehbinder, *op. cit.*, pp. 251, 252.
115. Now s 244 TULRCA 1992, *see* B.A. Hepple, *IELL* 1992, p. 267.
116. For Argentina, *see* M. Ackerman and A. Goldin, *IELL* 1990, p. 223.
117. *See* Adlercreutz, *IELL* 1997, p. 191.
118. *See* Jacobsen and Hasselbalch, *IELL* 1998, p. 265.

France,[119] and the United States[120] sympathy strikes are permissible if the primary strike is permissible. In Germany a sympathy strike is only lawful, if the employer has not been neutral with regard to the primary action or has economic connections with the employer hit by the primary action.[121] In Italy[122] a sympathy strike is permitted if there is a sufficient community of interests between the two groups of workers concerned. This is also a criterium in Denmark[123] and Spain.[124]

The International Labour Organization, noting that sympathy strikes are becoming increasingly frequent because of the move towards the concentration of enterprises, the globalization of the economy and the delocalization of work centres, warns that a general prohibition on sympathy strikes could lead to abuse.[125]

26.   In some countries *interunion disputes*, such as jurisdictional and demarcation strikes, cannot be lawful.[126]

In Britain disputes between workers and to enforce a closed shop are in some cases illegal.[127]

In Ireland strikes to enforce a closed shop are always unlawful[128] while in New Zealand[129] strikes should not be related to freedom of association matters. By contrast the law in Greece recognizes the right to strike to promote 'syndicalistic interests'.[130]

27.   In most of the countries, *recognition disputes* are in principle lawful.[131] In the United States[132] and Canada,[133] though, these actions are occasionally unlawful, which is to be explained from the fact, that in these countries recognition is to be obtained by statutory procedures. In fact, the desire to avoid industrial action for this purpose was a prime objective of the original labour relations statutes in these countries.

F.   Procedural Restrictions

28.   The right to strike is not only determined by its objective but also by the circumstances in which the strike is initiated.

---

119.   *See* J. Rojot, *op. cit.*, pp. 57, 58.
120.   *See* A.L. Goldman in Ch. United States in R. Blanpain and R. Ben Israel (eds), Strikes and Lockouts in Industrialized Market Economies, *Bulletin of Comparative Labour Relations*, Deventer, 1994, p. 207.
121.   *See* Bundesarbeitsgericht AP No. 85 on Article 9 GG (Arbeitskampf).
122.   *See* T. Treu, *IELL* 1998, p. 217.
123.   *See* Jacobsen and Hasselbalch, *IELL* 1998, pp. 267, 268.
124.   *See* Olea and Rodriguez-Sañudo, *IELL* 1996, p. 145.
125.   *See* Report *Freedom of Association and Collective Bargaining*, Report III (4B), Geneva, 1994, p. 74.
126.   For Canada, see H.W. Arthurs, *IELL* 1993, p. 298; for Britain B.A. Hepple, 1994, p. 71.
127.   s 222(3) TULRCA 1992.
128.   *See* case Education Company of Ireland v Fitzpatrick 2 (1961) IR 345; *see* M. Redmond, *IELL* 1996, p. 194.
129.   J.M. Howells, *IELL* 1996, p. 229; G. Anderson, *op. cit.*, p. 130.
130.   *See* T.B. Koniaris, *IELL* 1990, p. 180.
131.   This is also the opinion of the ILO-Committee on Freedom of Association, *see* B. Gernigon et al., ILO Principles concerning the Right to Strike, *ILR* 1998, pp. 441–481.
132.   *See* A.L. Goldman (1994), p. 208; these actions are unlawful as far as they are directed against third employers, not if they are directed against the own employer.
133.   *See* H.W. Arthurs a.o., *IELL* 1993, pp. 276, 294, 295.

In all countries such procedural restrictions may flow from collective agreements which, for example may require parties to give prior notice of a specific length or to apply for conciliation, mediation or arbitration. Such clauses are common in Belgium, Japan,[134] etc. Yet, as has been observed in a previous section, the binding force of such provisions varies from one country to another.

In a substantial number of countries procedural restrictions on the right to strike are provided for in the laws or regulations. Such restrictions are acceptable, provided that the conditions that have to be fulfilled in order to render a strike lawful are reasonable.[135]

29. In some countries, like Britain,[136] Ireland,[137] Japan,[138] and most jurisdictions in Canada,[139] the law provides that a secret *ballot* among union members must be held prior to the commencement of the strike. Such a provision is designed to protect the interests of individual workers against strikes which are not democratically mandated. Others claim that such provisions increase the formality and complexity of the bargaining process and allow employers to delay or even avoid industrial action.[140] In many other countries like the Scandinavian countries,[141] this requirement is lacking, thus respecting the autonomy of trade unions. In Germany and Switzerland,[142] it is not the law but the standing rules of the unions which often require a strike ballot.

It is submitted that the ballot method, the quorum and the majority required should not be such that the exercise of the right to strike becomes very difficult, or even impossible in practice.[143]

30. Moreover in various countries, like the Scandinavian countries,[144] Britain,[145] Spain,[146] Italy,[147] Portugal,[148] Israel,[149] and the United States,[150] certain

---

134. *See* K. Sugeno, *op. cit.*, pp. 108–114.
135. Such is the opinion of the Freedom of Association Committee of the International Labour Organisation, *see* its 197th *Report*, Case No. 917 (Costa Rica), para. 221.
136. In Britain a strike must have been supported beforehand by a majority of the workers concerned, *see* s 226-234 TULRCA 1992; the law provides for funds to enable trade unions to organise these ballots, *See* B.A. Hepple (1994), pp. 193,194; the relevant articles were somewhat modified by the Employment Relations Act 1999, *see* K.D. Ewing, *ILJ* 1999, p. 293.
137. *See* M. Redmond, *IELL* 1996, p. 195.
138. *See* K. Sugeno, *op. cit.*, p. 108.
139. *See* H.W. Arthurs a.o., *IELL* 1993, p. 299; D.D. Carter, *op. cit.*, p. 47.
140. *See* B.A. Hepple (1994), p. 182.
141. In Denmark three quarters of the members of the competent body of the union have to vote for a strike if it is to be seen as legal, *see* W. Galenson, *op. cit.*, pp. 99, 243; Jacobsen and Hasselbalch, *IELL* 1998, p. 276.
142. *See* M. Rehbinder, *op. cit.*, pp. 255–256.
143. This is the opinion of the Committee of Experts of the ILO, see Gernigon et al., *op. cit.*, p. 457.
144. For Sweden *see* A. Adlercreutz, *IELL* 1997, p. 187 (small amendments are under way, *see* EIRR 311/10); for Denmark *see* W. Galenson, *op. cit.*, p. 99, 243; Jacobsen and Hasselbalch, *IELL* 1998, pp. 275–279; for Norway *see* S. Evju, *op. cit.*, p. 88.
145. *See* s. 234A TULRCA; the relevant articles were somewhat modified by the Employment Relations Act 1999, *see* K.D. Ewing, *ILJ* 1999, p. 295.
146. *See* M.A. Olea and F. Rodriguez-Sañudo, *IELL* 1996, p. 146.
147. In Italy the courts have refused to recognize the legitimacy of strikes effectuated without notice, *see* Cass. 17.10.1961 and Corte Costituzionale 28.12.1962, *see* G. Giugni, *Diritto Sindacale*, 7th ed., Bari, 1984, p. 246.

notice requirements must be met, for example that a certain number of days notice of a strike is given to the employer (and/or to the administrative authorities) prior to the commencement of a strike. Such provisions are designed to protect the employer and/or the public against the effects of precipitate action.

In some countries the obligation to give notice of dispute acts exists under a collective agreement or labour relations custom.[151]

In many other countries such a requirement is absent save perhaps in the public services/essential services sectors (*see* para. II.H.).[152]

In Germany surprise-strikes cannot be legal because of the idea of *ultima ratio* (*ultimum remedium*). Warning-strikes, however, are considered compatible with this principle.[153]

31. Indeed, the idea, that a strike is an *ultima ratio* (*ultimum remedium*) and that it is illegal as long as not all options through which a bargained deal can be made have been exhausted, has often been upheld by judges in Germany,[154] The Netherlands,[155] and Belgium.[156] Also in Sweden industrial peace has to be kept as long as negotiations are in procession.[157]

In other countries, such as Japan, the strike is not regarded as a final weapon.[158] In the United States, a strike can lawfully be called prior to a bargaining impasse.[159]

32. In a number of countries a procedure of previous obligatory conciliation or arbitration has to be observed.[160] For this type of concretization of the *ultima ratio* principle one thinks first of Australia (and New Zealand until 1988),[161] where industrial relations were characterized by this recipe of compulsory arbitration.

In Canada timeliness is the touchstone of the lawfulness of a strike, i.e. whether it follows exhaustion of the negotiating and conciliating procedures prescribed by statute. Indeed Canadian labour legislation generally provides that all lawful strikes must be postponed until various peace-making measures have been exhausted.[162] In

---

148. *See* M. Pinto, *IELL* 1989, p. 218.
149. *See* R. Ben-Israel, *IELL* 1994, p. 176; M. Goldberg, *op. cit.*, pp. 92, 93.
150. But only in case the parties have earlier entered into a collective agreement, *see* A.L.Goldman, *IELL* 1996, p. 371.
151. In Japan, *see* Hamani and Komiya, *IELL* 1999, p. 163.
152. In France no prior notice is required save in cases where the collective agreement requires it explicitly and for the civil service where it is required by statute; *see* G. Lyon-Caen a.o., *op. cit.*, pp. 436, 437; M. Despax and J. Rojot, *IELL* 1987, p. 294.
153. Bundesarbeitsgericht AP No. 51 and 81 zu Article 9 GG (Arbeitskampf); *see* M. Weiss and Schmidt, *IELL* 2000, pp. 171, 172.
154. Bundesarbeitsgericht GS BAGE 23, 292 = AP No. 43 on Article 9 GG Arbeitskampf; also Bundesarbeitsgericht No. 108 on Article 9 GG (Arbeitskampf); *see* M. Weiss and Schmidt, *IELL* 2000, pp. 171, 172.
155. *See* Dutch Supreme Court January 28, 2000; *JAR* 2000/63.
156. Trib. Charleroi, 24.12.1973, *JTT*, 15.3.1974, p. 76.
157. *See* A. Adlercreutz, *IELL* 1997, p. 196.
158. *See* T.A. Hanami and Komiya, *IELL* 1999, p. 163; K. Sugeno, *op. cit.*, p. 108.
159. *See* A.L. Goldman, *IELL* 1996, p. 385.
160. So in Argentina, *see* M. Ackerman and A. Goldin, *IELL* 1990, pp. 220, 225.
161. *See* J.M. Howells, *IELL* 1996, p. 223.
162. H.W. Arthurs a.o., *IELL* 1993, pp. 276, 293–294.

Switzerland a strike should not be started before an attempt of mediation has been made.[163] In Spain the strike committee and the employer are under a statutory duty to negotiate with a view of ending the strike by solving the problems out of which it arose.[164] Greece has for many years been the most noticeable representative of the channelling of the right to strike through the compulsory arbitration procedure. However, in 1992, this system was replaced by a system of voluntary third party intervention which poses only minimal restrictions on the right to strike.[165] In Luxembourg, referring of disputes to conciliation is still obligatory. During concili-ation all industrial action is prohibited. On these grounds surprise-strikes and even warning-strikes cannot be legal.[166]

In Norway, notice of a strike must be given to the State Mediator who may issue a temporary ban on action during mediation. After ten days the parties may terminate mediation procedure and are free to go on with the industrial action. However, in many cases (ca. three each year) the legislator intervenes to settle the dispute by imposing arbitration.[167]

There is international criticism of this system[168] as the substitution of compulsory arbitration for the right to strike by legislative means, as a manner of resolving labour disputes, violates the right to strike, safe exceptional cases.[169]

33. The temporary restriction of the exercise of the right to strike as a sequel of mandatory recourse to procedures of conciliation, mediation, and arbitration is com-patible with the right to strike,[170] provided such machinery should not be so complex or slow that a lawful strike becomes impossible in practice or loses its effectiveness.[171]

G. Principles of Proportionality, Fairness, etc.

34. Another remarkable limitation on strikes is the principle of *proportionality.* Strikes should in length and force be in proportion to the interests at stake. This rule was first developed systematically in Germany by the Bundesarbeitsgericht in

---

163. M. Rehbinder, *op. cit.*, p. 253.
164. *See* Olea and Rodriguez-Sañudo, *IELL* 1996, p. 146.
165. *See EIRR* January 1993, pp. 26, 27.
166. *See* R. Schintgen, *IELL* 1992, pp. 212–217.
167. *See* S. Evju, *op. cit.*, pp. 113, 130, 131.
168. *See* the Committee of Independent Experts on the European Social Charter in its repeated criticism of the situation in Norway, for example in its *Conclusions* XII-1 (1988–89) p. 130; *Conclusions* XIV-1, pp. 620–625. Also the ILO has criticized Norway on this issue, see *EIRR*, January 1994, pp. 10, 11.
169. This is the opinion of the Freedom of Association Committee of the International Labour Organisation, *see* its 226th Report, Case No. 1140 (Columbia), para. 293; as well as of the Committee of Experts, *see* Report Freedom of Association and Collective Bargaining, Report III (4B), Geneva, 1994, pp. 62–64, and of the Committee of Independent Experts on the European Social Charter, *see* its *Conclusions* XIV-1, p. 391.
170. This is the opinion of the Freedom of Association Committee of the International Labour Organisation, *see* its 164th Report, Case No. 845 (Canada), para. 42; *see also* the Comittee of Independent Experts on the European Social Charter, *Conclusions*, I, pp. 38, 39.
171. *See* ILO *Report Freedom of Association and Collective Bargaining*, Report III (4B), Geneva, 1994, p. 75.

1971.[172] It is also applied by the judges in the Netherlands[173] and Switzerland.[174] In many other countries case law has made an incursion into the right to strike by making an appraisal of reasonableness, justice, or moderation of purposes, even of those strikes that are strictly professional.[175] Although this attitude has often been rejected by part of the doctrine, it nevertheless has time and again charmed the courts, even in Belgium[176] and the southern European states.[177] In Italy, the necessity of a certain balance between the sacrifices of the workers on strike and the damages done has been elaborated for this purpose. This not only means that strikes which would completely destroy the productive capacity of the employer are unlawful[178], but this idea also entails that *rotation strikes* (or intermittent strikes, 'estafette strikes', 'grèves tournantes', waves of strikes, 'quickie strikes', hourly strikes, partial and successive strikes in different departments of the same plant or in the same department at short intervals) are at risk of being held unlawful. The same conclusion is often reached in France,[179] Portugal,[180] and Spain.[181]

35. An alternative approach is to consider the lastmentioned types of actions as lawful, but to recognize the employer's right to a proper defense, either by attributing the right to lockout to him (*see* para. IV.B.) or by liberating him from the obligation to pay wages (para III.B.).

36. Another principle, developed by the German judges is the principle of '*Fairness*'.[182] A good application of this principle can be found in cases of *work-to-rule/go slow/go sick/non-cooperation/overtime ban*. Such actions constitute a partial failure to fulfil in good faith the obligations of the labour contract. In most countries[183] they are very much at risk of being declared illegal.

---

172. Bundesarbeitsgericht 1971 = AP No. 43 on Article 9 III GG (Arbeitskampf); also BAG AP Nos. 47 and 62 on Article 9 GG (Arbeitskampf); *see* M. Weiss and Schmidt, *IELL* 2000, p. 170.
173. Dutch Supreme Court, March 21, 1997, *NJ* 1997, 437.
174. *See* M. Rehbinder, *op. cit.*, p. 256.
175. So in Argentina, *see* M. Ackerman and A. Goldin, *IELL* 1990, p. 223.
176. *See* Thonon, *JTT* 1982, pp. 324,325; R. Roels, *JTT* 1979, pp. 229–232; J. Piron, *JTT* 1979, pp. 73–76; *see* for case law in this respect EIRR Report *The Regulation of Industrial Conflict in Europe*, London, 1989, pp. 10, 11.
177. For France *see* G. Lyon-Caen a.o., *op. cit.*, p. 932; G. Lyon-Caen, La recherche des responsabilités dans les conflits du travail, Receuil Dalloz Sirey, 1979, XXXIX *Chron.* pp. 255–258.
178. Cass. 4.3.1952; Cass. 30.1.1980, *see* G. Giugni, *op. cit.*, pp. 247–254; according to T. Treu, *IELL* 1998, p. 218 this doctrine has been somewhat modified recently.
179. *See* G. Lyon-Caen a.o., *op. cit.*, pp. 928, 929; M. Despax and J. Rojot, *IELL* 1988, pp. 296, 297; J. Rojot, *op. cit.*, p. 58, who explains that there does not exist a fixed criterion distinguising a lawful rotation strike from the disorganization of the enterprise. The courts engage in a case by case assessment.
180. *See* M. Pinto, *IELL* 1989, p. 220.
181. *See* Olea and Rodriguez-Sañudo, *IELL* 1996, p. 143.
182. Bundesarbeitsgericht 1971, AP No. 43 on Article 9 GG (Arbeitskampf); *see* M. Weiss and Schmidt, *IELL* 2000, p. 170.
183. For Germany *see* Bundesarbeitsgericht AP No. 61 zu Article 9 GG (Arbeitskampf); for France *see* G. Lyon-Caen a.o., *op. cit.*, pp. 933, 934; M. Despax and J. Rojot, *IELL* 1988, p. 296; J. Rojot, *op. cit.*, p. 57; for Belgium *see* R. Blanpain, *IELL* 1999, pp. 306; for Argentina, *see* M. Ackerman and A. Goldin, *IELL* 1990, p. 224; for the United States *see* A.L. Goldman, *IELL* 1996, p. 380; for Italy *see* T. Treu, *IELL* 1998, p. 219; for Ireland, M. Redmond, *IELL* 1996, p. 198; for Denmark Jacobsen and Hasselbalch, *IELL* 1998, p. 274; for Spain *see* Olea and Rodriguez-Sañudo, *IELL* 1996, p. 143; for Switzerland *see* M. Rehbinder, *op. cit.*, p. 256.

However, in Sweden[184] most forms of partial strikes are lawful per se. In Japan the courts accept that actions which are less than full-fledged strikes such as short-wave strikes or partial strikes, and from which economic damage is minor but may be irritating and even damaging to the normal operation of business, are proper acts of dispute, since they are less damaging than full-fledged strikes. The same approach applies to partial refusal to provide labour such as a go-slow or a work-to-rule. However such action would be regarded as improper if it was in any way malicious or quite unfair.[185]

37. In many countries acts that only destroy the property of the company are unlawful.[186] In all countries the law prohibits any act that endangers human life in the workplace.[187]

In Ireland the system of immunities does not apply if utterly innocent outsiders are hit by the strike.[188]

In Denmark the strike rules lay down that a strike cannot be legal if it is challenging the power of direction of the employer.

The Committee of Independent Experts on the European Social Charter warned that damages caused to third parties and financial losses sustained by the employer could only be taken into consideration in exceptional cases, when justified by a pressing social need.[189]

H. Other Collective Actions of Workers

38. Many scholars assert that the narrow definition of the strike as a work stoppage should be replaced by a wide one, including various means of pressure on the employer, such as *sit-downs, sit-ins, occupations* as well as *work-ins*. Although these forms have become prominent forms of industrial disputes in many countries, they are considered in most countries to be unlawful.[190] They constitute an infringement of various classic civil rights and judges might easily prohibit them for example by requiring the strikers to guarantee free access to the premises and imposing fines in cases where the order is not respected.[191]

However there are exceptions. In some countries the courts have accepted sit-ins in obvious cases of self-defence for example.[192]

---

184. *See* R. Fahlbeck, *op. cit.*, p. 169.
185. T. Hanami, *Managing Japanese Workers*, Tokyo, 1991, p. 71; K. Sugeno, *op. cit.*, pp. 107, 108.
186. *See* Dutch Supreme Court, 19 April 1991, *NJ* 1991, 690 (Elka).
187. In Japan (*see* Article 36 LRAL) there is some contradiction in this area, *see* Hanami and Komiya, *IELL* 1999, pp. 163, 164.
188. *See* the Irish Supreme Court in the case Talbot (Ireland) Ltd vs Merrigan and others, *see* M. Redmond, *IELL* 1996, p. 1996.
189. *See Conclusions* XIII-1 (1990–1991), p. 158.
190. For the United States, *see* A.L. Goldman, *IELL* 1986, pp. 372, 377; for Germany *see* Bundesarbeitsgericht AP No. 58 on Article 9 GG (Arbeitskampf); for Italy *see* T. Treu, *IELL* 1998, p. 218; for France *see* G. Lyon-Caen a.o., *op. cit.*, pp. 943–946; M. Despax and J. Rojot, *IELL* 1988, pp. 297, 298; J. Rojot, *op. cit.*, p. 65; for Ireland, M. Redmond, *IELL* 1996, p. 198; for Belgium *see* R. Blanpain, *IELL* 1999, p. 307.
191. For a Belgian case, *see EIRR* May 1992, p. 4.
192. For Belgium, see R. Blanpain, *IELL* 1999, p. 307; for France, *see* Despax and Rojot, *IELL* 1988, p. 298; J. Rojot, *op. cit.*, pp. 65, 66; for Japan K. Sugeno, *op. cit.*, p. 107.

39. Striking workers might also try to pressure the primary employer by sanctions mounted against third persons.

Boycotts are very common in Sweden[193] to put pressure on employers unwilling to bargain with the unions. Workers of an employer doing business with the primary employer (say a food store catering a restaurant) refuse to have anything to do with the primary employer (to deliver foods and drinks to the restaurant, in the example chosen) if this employer refuses to bargain with the unions. Such actions are utterly lawful in Sweden[194]. They were contested before the European Court of Human Rights of the Council of Europe as being an infringement of the freedom of association of the employer but this was rejected.[195]

In most countries the legal reaction, either in court or by legislature, to secondary disputes has been either to prohibit or to restrict them.[196] But often the *proviso* is made that this holds only when neutral outsiders are involved, i.e. this restriction/prohibition does not cover secondary employers who have close economic relations with the primary employer or have supported him in dispute.[197] (*See also* para. II.E).

I. Picketing

40. In some countries *picketing* is an important component of strike activity. It is a tactic used to support worker's demands during a strike – a means for workers to express their solidarity and their aspirations – and to prevent the employer from keeping his/her business operating.[198] Especially this last function of picketing potentially involves intimidating third parties and infringing the rights and freedoms of such parties in addition to those of employers. So, there is undeniably a tension between the need for organizations like trade unions to show muscle in view of industrial negotiation and the right to work of the non-striking workers.

Historically in all countries ordinary courts, applying the common law to regulate picketing, have tended to condemn the coercive aspects of picketing and to protect third party and employers' rights and interests at the expense of those of the picketers. Nowadays, in most countries[199] the courts consider peaceful picketing *prima facie* as lawful.[200] They consider it to be the exercise of the freedom of speech and they see the physical presence of picketers nearby their own place of work as the exercise of the freedom of assembly and association. In these countries peaceful picketing is presumed lawful when the strike is considered lawful.

---

193. *See* R. Fahlbeck, *op. cit.*, p. 177.
194. Under the Basic Agreement, *see* A. Adlercreutz, *IELL* 1997, p. 196.
195. ECHR April 25, 1996, (Case 18/1995/524/610), Gustaffson v Sweden, *Reports* 1996, p. 637.
196. For the United States *see* A.L. Goldman, *IELL* 1996, p. 381.
197. For Denmark, *see* Jacobsen and Hasselbalch, *IELL* 1998, p. 272.
198. In Sweden, Denmark and the Netherlands called: blockade.
199. *See* for Portugal M. Pinto, *IELL* 1989, p. 220; for Italy, T. Treu, *IELL* 1998, p. 220; for France M. Despax and J. Rojot, *IELL* 1987, p. 298; for Denmark, Jacobsen and Hasselbalch, *IELL* 1998, p. 273; for Norway, S. Evju, *op. cit.*, p. 86; for Canada *see* H.W. Arthurs a.o., *IELL* 1993, p. 288; D.D. Carter, pp. 51, 52; for Switzerland *see* M. Rehbinder, *op. cit.*, p. 256.
200. Such is also the opinion of the Freedom of Association Committee of the International Labour Organisation, *see* its 197th Report, Case No. 923 (Spain), para. 58.

41. However, no court permits picketing which is perceived to interfere with personal security, which entails bodily harm, sequestration of management, breaking and entering, degrading of property or reputation, of either the employer who is its primary target, or other persons to whom appeals for support are directed. Apart from Italy,[201] where it is lawful, in most countries picketing is unlawful if it creates a physical barrier ('human wall') to entering, leaving or using property or is conducted in such a way as to deter workers from performing their work. Such conduct is subject to civil and criminal sanctions under the law of trespass and similar doctrines.[202] In these cases employers may try to obtain a ruling from the judge to lift picketing, backed up by threats of fines.[203]

Yet, the distinction between peaceful picketing and obstructive picketing is blurred as picketing is likely to constitute an offence if it is to achieve its object of hindering or stopping work.

Some countries have seen not only picketing of workers at their own place of work but also picketing of workers on other sites ('flying pickets', secondary picketing). This has brought the legislator in Britain[204] to a more general prohibition of all forms of picketing other than at the worker's own place of work as well as secondary picketing.[205] Secondary picketing is also generally prohibited in Ireland[206] and Canada.[207]

J. *Public Service and Essential Services*

42. A last important limitation on the right to strike concerns strikes in the *public service* or in *essential services*. Such strikes tend to victimize the public and sometimes even threaten the whole economy. Thus in many countries disputes in these areas have for a long time been prohibited under criminal law. And even in cases where the criminal law has been repealed workers in this area have been impeded from striking by forceful hindrances under disciplinary law or by legal powers of the authorities used to limit or neutralize the effects of such actions.[208]

In the United States most jurisdictions by statute or judicial decree prohibit their government employees from striking. A work stoppage by federal government employees can be enjoined. The participants are subject to criminal prosecution, disqualification from further federal government employment and a number of other determents.[209]

---

201. *See* T. Treu, *IELL* 1998, p. 220.
202. For the United States, *see* A.L. Goldman, *IELL* 1996, pp. 382,383; for Denmark *see* Jacobsen and Hasselbalch, *IELL* 1998, p. 273; for Sweden *see* A. Adlercreutz, *IELL* 1997, p. 187; for Japan, Hamani, *Managing Japanese Workers*, Tokyo, 1991, p. 76; for Germany *see* Bundesarbeitsgericht AP Nos. 5, 34 and 108 on Article 9 GG (Arbeitskampf); for Spain, M.A. Olea and F. Rodriguez-Sañudo, *IELL* 1996, pp. 146; for New Zealand G. Anderson, pp. 142, 143.
203. Belgian example in *EIRR* March 1992, p. 4.
204. *See* ss 220 and 224 TULRCA 1992; *see* B.A. Hepple, 1994, p. 197.
205. This is criticized by the Committee of Independent Experts on the European Social Charter. *See Conclusions* XII-1 (1988–1989), p. 131.
206. *See* M. Redmond, *IELL* 1996, p. 194.
207. *See* H.W. Arthurs a.o., *IELL* 1993, p. 291.
208. *See* A. Pankert, The Settlement of Labour Disputes in 'essential services' in industrialised market economies, in Labour Law and Industrial Relations at the turn of the century (*Liber Amicorum R. Blanpain*), Deventer, Kluwer, 1998, p. 537.
209. *See* A.L. Goldman, *IELL* 1996, p. 364.

In Canada some jurisdictions like Ontario completely prohibit strike activity in the public service. Other jurisdictions as well as the federal jurisdiction permit their public servants to strike but even in those jurisdictions strike action has been partially restricted to ensure the provision of essential services.[210]

In Japan collective actions by ordinary civil servants have been prohibited in statutes, made in 1946 and 1948. Despite mounting criticism from unionists, academics, lower courts and the ILO the Japanese Supreme Court upheld these provisions.[211]

In Switzerland strikes are forbidden for members of the federal civil service[212] and, in some cantons, of the cantonal service.

43. Here again it is the recognition of the right to strike as a fundamental right which has brought some changes to the situation. An outright prohibition of the right to strike of the totality of the public service is not in conformity with the right to strike. Only restrictions for certain categories are acceptable.[213]

In France case-law in 1950 concluded that civil servants should enjoy the right to strike and that existing disciplinary sanctions against strikers where to be declared void[214], save in cases of illegal strikes. Since 1982 rotating strikes in the public service have been forbidden.[215]

Also in Italy the judges have concluded that civil servants should enjoy the right to strike and that existing prohibitions under criminal law and their resulting criminal sanctions were to be void.[216]

In The Netherlands the old criminal law prohibition of strikes in the civil service and the railways was repealed in 1979. Case-law subsequently recognized the right to strike of most civil servants, except for a few categories.[217]

In Britain and Sweden,[218] the freedom to resort to industrial action also applies in the public sector, although there are some special restrictions.

In Belgium, despite the fact that there is no explicit case law on this area, it is assumed that the general prohibition on strikes in the public services is no longer valid.[219]

In Spain the right to strike of civil servants is unclear. Presumably, it is enjoyed by the majority of the civil servants but some groups may be deprived of it.[220]

In Germany[221] and Denmark strikes by civil servants are forbidden by disciplinary law. In Denmark this applies to all civil servants employed under the Civil Servants

---

210. *See* D.D. Carter, p. 42.
211. Rulings of 1973 and 1977; *see* Hanami and Komiya, *IELL* 1999, pp. 174, 175; K. Sugeno, *op. cit.*, pp. 116, 118–119.
212. *See* M. Rehbinder, *op. cit.*, p. 257.
213. Such is the opinion of the Committe of Independent Experts on the European Social Charter, *see* Conclusions I, pp. 38, 39 and of the Committee on Freedom of Association and of the Committee of Experts of the ILO, *see* Gernigon et al., *op. cit.*, p. 448.
214. Arrêt-Dehaene, *see* G. Lyon-Caen a.o., *op. cit.*, p. 923.
215. *See* J. Rojot, *op. cit.*, p. 63; G. Lyon-Caen a.o., *op. cit.*, p. 929.
216. *See* T. Treu, *IELL* 1998, p. 211.
217. Central Court of Appeal, 21.10.1982, AB 1983, 35; District Court of Amsterdam, *TAR* 1985, 114.
218. *See* A. Adlercreutz, IELL 1997, p. 188; R. Fahlbeck, *op. cit.*, pp. 174–176.
219. Article 233,236 Penal Code; Article 7, s. 3 Statuut voor het Rijkspersoneel, *see* M. Rigaux, *op. cit.*, pp. 187–194; R. Blanpain, *Grève et Requisition dans le secteur public*, Bruxelles, 1978, pp. 15–18.
220. *See* Olea and Rodriguez-Sañudo, *IELL* 1996, p. 144.
221. *See* Weiss and Schmidt, *IELL* 2000, pp. 174, 176.

Act. In Germany this prohibition does not apply to all workers in the civil service, only to certain 'classes' of civil servants (in Germany: '*Beamte*'). Other 'classes' of civil servants (in Germany the '*Arbeiter*' or '*Angestellte*') do enjoy the right to strike.

Nevertheless the situation in Germany and Denmark is, since many years under attack of the Committee of Independent Experts on the European Social Charter.[222] This Committee considers it acceptable to restrict the right to strike of certain categories of civil servants, in paricular members of the police force and the armed forces, judges and senior civil servants, but it condems the denial of the right to strike to the Public Service as a whole.[223]

In Israel members of the public service enjoy less protection in strikes than employees in private business.[224]

44. Even if nowadays strikes in the public service and essential service sectors are in principle possible, the right to strike is limited to a greater extent in these areas than in other areas. These limitations are of a threefold nature.[225]

A first limitation concerns specific categories of workers in the public service and the essential service sectors.

In various countries the legislator has explicitly denied the right to strike to certain categories, like the police, prison-guards, the army, the firemen, the intelligence services. The same has often happened to workers employed in the production and distribution of gas, electricity, and water, the postal service, public health care, etc.[226] In other countries, such as Greece the legislator has put limitations on the right to strike of civil servants and persons working in bodies of vital importance for society, just falling short of abolishing the right to strike for these categories altogether.[227]

According to the Freedom of Association Committee of the International Labour Organization any prohibition of the right to strike of public servants should be confined to public servants acting in their capacity as agents of the public authority.[228] Moreover, this Committee requires, that adequate guarantees should be provided for these categories of workers to safeguard their interests, such as impartial and speedy conciliation and arbitration procedures, in which the parties can participate at every stage of the procedure and in which the awards are binding on both parties and are applied promptly and to the letter of the law.[229]

---

222. *Conclusions* XIV-1, pp. 183, 300.
223. *Conclusions* I, pp. 38, 39; *conclusions* III, p. 36.
224. *See* M. Goldberg, *op. cit.*, pp. 94, 95.
225. The following types of limitations can all be encountered in various laws of the jurisdictions of Canada.
226. For Britain *see* the Conspiracy and Protection of Property Act 1875, the Emergency Powers Act 1919/1964, the Post Office Act 1908/1953, the Police Act, 1964, etc.; for Italy, *see* T. Treu, *IELL* 1998, pp. 213, 214; for Ireland exception from the immunities as regards the police and the army in the Trade Disputes (Amendment) Act 1982; for Israel, M. Goldberg, *op. cit.*, p. 93; for Norway *see* S. Evju, *op. cit.*, p. 136; for France, *see* G. Lyon-Caen a.o., *op. cit.*, p. 923.
227. *See* T.B. Koniaris, *IELL* 1990, p. 181.
228. *See* its 230th *Report*, Case No. 1173 (Canada), para. 578.
229. *See* for example its 214th *Report*, Case No. 1081 (Peru), para. 265; in Portugal compulsory arbitration may occur in State (financed) corporations, *see* M. Pinto, *IELL* 1989, pp. 213, 221; in New Zealand there is compulsory final offer arbitration for the police, *see* G. Anderson, *op. cit.*, p. 139.

45. A second type of limitation concerns the modalities of the strike. For example, in various countries[230] statutes make it necessary for public employees or employees in essential services to announce a strike a number of days in advance.

In the United States special machinery has been created for delaying or enjoining a work stoppage in certain sensitive sectors, such as the health care, rail and airline industries.[231]

In Finland by law a proclaimed strike can be deferred for a fortnight/three weeks in case where the stoppage is deemed to affect essential functions of the society or to prejudice the general interest to a considerable extent.[232]

In Japan in cases where a stoppage would pose a serious threat to the national economy or the daily life of the nation the government may decide on an emergency adjustment. In such a situation the parties would be forbidden from engaging in any dispute for 50 days.[233]

In some countries judges curtail strikes in essential services by creative restrictions. Thus, in Israel, in a teachers' strike, which was lawful, the Labour Court did not grant an injunction against the strike, but did forbid the teachers from disrupting matriculation examinations.[234] And in The Netherlands a judge only allowed a strike in public transport outside rush hours.[235]

46. A third type of limitation is, that the law often requires that essential services are maintained on a minimal level, particularly in Italy,[236] Spain,[237] Portugal,[238] and France.[239] In Ireland this result is promoted by a Code of Practice[240] and in Sweden by the Basic Agreement between SAF and LO which contains a chapter dealing with the handling of disputes threatening essential societal functions.

---

230. For France see Articles 521, 522 and on of the Code de Travail and Article 8 Code de la Fonction publique; moreover those strikes must last at least one day, *see* J.-C. Javillier, *op. cit.*, pp. 312, 313, and be called by a representative union in order to be lawful, *see* Rojot, *op. cit.*, pp. 62; *see* G. Lyon-Caen a.o., *op. cit.*, p. 927; the French limitations are criticised by the Committee of Independent Experts of the European Social Charter, see *Conclusions* IV, p. 50; *Conclusions* XIV, p. 258; for Greece *see* T.B. Koniaris, *IELL* 1990, pp. 181, 182; for Spain *see* M.A. Olea and F. Rodriguez-Sañudo, *IELL* 1996, p. 146; for Portugal, *see* M. Pinto, *IELL* 1989, p. 218; for Italy, *see* T. Treu, *IELL* 1998, p. 213; for New Zealand, *see* J.M. Howells, *IELL* 1996, p. 229; G. Anderson, pp. 139, 140.
231. *See* A.L. Goldman, *IELL* 1996, p. 371.
232. *See* Suviranta, *IELL* 1999, p. 195; *Conclusions* XIV-1, p. 219 of the Committee on Independent Experts of the European Social Charter.
233. T. Hanami and Komiya, *IELL* 1999, p. 174; K. Sugeno, *op. cit.*, p. 115.
234. M. Goldberg, *op. cit.*, p. 94.
235. Dutch Supreme Court March 21, 1997, *NJ* 1997, 437.
236. In Italy law No. 146 of 1990 on the right to strike in essential services, *see* Treu, *IELL* 1998, pp. 213–215, was tightened up in April 2000 after industrial action in all public sectors in November 1998 had virtually brought the country to a halt, *see* EIRR 299/8, 301/8, 312/8, 315/9-10 and 317/24-26.
237. *See* Olea and Rodriguez-Sañudo, *IELL* 1996, p. 145.
238. Section 8 of the Strike Act No. 65/77, *see Conclusions* XIV-1 pp. 662, 663 of the Committee of Independent Experts on the European Social Charter.
239. In case-law, *see* Rojot, *op. cit.*, p. 63; G. Lyon-Caen a.o., *op. cit.*, pp. 946, 947; as this is not strong enough a regulation by statute was proposed after disturbing strikes in 1999, *see* EIRR 300/p. 5.
240. *See EIRR*, March 1992, pp. 18–19.

It is submitted that the system of guarenteeing minimum services can be legally used in order to avoid a total ban on strikes in essential services,[241] but again it is important, that the minimum service requirement should be restricted to operations necessary to avoid endangering the life, personal safety or health of the whole or part of the population.[242]

In some countries the government has the statutory power of re-quisitioning workers to maintain essential services[243] or it permits the use of the military to secure essential services[244] or it may enact other types of emergency regulations.[245] Although such measures can be justified if they are aimed at maintaining essential services in circumstances of the utmost gravity, they should not be abused, when used as a means of settling labour disputes (in other words: to break a strike of workers defending their occupational interests).[246] So in Germany[247] the Federal Constitutional Court rejected the use of '*Beamte*' (who are not allowed to strike) to replace '*Angestellte*' on strike.

III. The Effects of an (Un)Lawful Strike

47. It is the quintessence of the right to strike that exemptions are granted from criminal and civil liability, that all allegations of non-performance of an obligation and commission of torts are rejected and that there is no room for a discharge or disadvantageous treatment of a worker for engaging in a legal action or dispute. These consequences are not, however unqualified.

A. Liability of Trade Unions

48. In the case of *lawful* collective action the organizers (= trade unions) are exempted from liability for damages. Neither employers nor customers can claim

---

241. Such is the opinion of the Committee of Experts on the application of Conventions and Recommendations, *see* its General Survey, International Labour Conference, 69th Session, Geneva, 1983, para. 215.
242. Such is the opinion of the Freedom of Association Committee of the International Labour Organisation, *see* its 204th *Report*, Case No. 952 (Spain), para. 162; minimum services are limited to the operations which are strictly necessary to meet the basic needs of the population or the minimum requirements of the service, while maintaining the effectiveness of the pressure brought to bear, according to the Committee of Experts, *see Report Freedom of Association and Collective Bargaining*, Report III (4B), Geneva, 1994, p. 71.
243. *See* for France an Act of 1938, prolongued in 1950, *see* J. Royot, *op. cit.*, p. 63; *see* for Belgium an Act of 19 August 1948, amended by the Act of 10 June 1963, *see* R. Blanpain, *IELL* 1999, pp. 308, 309; for Britain the Emergency Powers Act 1919, 1964; for Greece, *see* T.B. Koniaris, *IELL* 1990, p. 182; in Portugal the Industrial Conscription Act, *see* M. Pinto, *IELL* 1989, pp. 219, 220.
244. *See* for New Zealand G. Anderson, *op. cit.*, p. 140.
245. *See* for Israel M. Goldberg, *op. cit.*, p. 99.
246. Such is the opinion of the Freedom of Association Committee of the International Labour Organisation, *see* its 204th *Report*, Case No. 952 (Spain), para. 161 and of the Committee of Experts, *see* Report *Freedom of Association and Collective Bargaining*, Report III (4B), Geneva, 1994, pp. 71, 72.
247. Bundesverfassungsgericht 2.3.1993, *see* Weiss and Schmidt, *IELL* 2000, pp. 178, 179.

indemnity from a trade union or its members for the damages caused by strikes or other acts of dispute which were legal. This also includes the liability of the union in terms of tort.[248]

49. The opposite – viz. that if the strike is *unlawful*, the trade union that organizes or supports the strike can be forced to pay damages – is not universally true.

In France the question of the liability of unions for strikes is a very controversial matter. Some lawyers hold that trade unions can never be held responsible for damages.[249] The French judges have always been very wary in this field. Under French law the funds of a trade union are 'untouchable' and traditionally the judges limit the damages to the one symbolic franc.[250] Also the French trade unions can often (but not always) plead 'not guilty' and argue that they lack an authority over the workers.[251] Nevertheless, in recent years verdicts imposing a more realistic amount of damages are becoming more and more frequent in France.[252] The socialist dominated legislature of 1982 intended to limit the possibility of holding trade unions and individual workers responsible for the damages of a strike (*'immunité civile relative'*), but this has been rejected by the *Conseil Constitutionnel*.[253]

In Belgium and Luxembourg the unions have always refused to seek full legal personality. The judges have respected this choice and thus unions cannot be held responsible for damages caused by a strike nor can they be ordered to withdraw their support for a strike. In these countries only the workers can be sued for participation in an unlawful strike.[254]

Also in Italy only the workers can be sued in the event of an unlawful strike; the judges have turned down all claims for damages for tort that have been directed towards unions.[255] However under the new law on strikes in essential services trade unions which fail to observe agreements on a minimum level of services may be deprived of union dues for a maximum period of one month, during which period such dues are transferred to the National Institute for Social Insurance.

---

248. For Japan by virtue of Article 8 Trade Union Law, *see* T. Hanami, *Managing Japanes Workers*, Tokyo, 1991, pp. 74, 75.
249. H. Sinay, Les Conflits Collectifs et l'argent, in *Tendances du Droit du Travail français contemporain*, Paris 1978, pp. 299–308; M. Cohen, 'Les entraves directes et indirectes à l'exercise du droit syndical et du droit de grève', *Droit Social* 1978, pp. 268–275.
250. *See* Soc. 9 novembre 1978, J.-C. Javillier, *Droit du Travail*, 2e ed., Paris, 1981, p. 576.
251. J. Savatier, La distinction de'la Grève et de l'action syndicale', *Droit Social* 1984, p. 55; G. Lyon-Caen, 'Le grand silence des travailleurs,' *Droit Social* 1981, p. 145.
252. *See* Soc 6 mai 1960; Soc. 8 février 1972; other case law mentionned with J.-C. Javillier, *Droit du Travail*, 2nd ed. 1981, Paris, pp. 574–576; J.-C. Javillier, *Droit du Travail*, Mise à Jour, Paris, 1982, pp. 65–67; J.-C. Javillier, *Les Réformes du droit du travail depuis le 10 mai 1981*, 2nd. ed., Paris, 1984, p. 332; A. Ramin, 'Exercise du droit de grève et responsabilité civile', *Droit Social* 1980, pp. 537–544; J. Savatier, La responsabilité civile des syndicats à l'occasion des grèves, Droit Social 1980, pp. 545–549.
253. C.C. 22.10.1982; 'L. Hamon, Le droit du travail dans la jurisprudence du Conseil constitutionnel', *Droit Social* 1983, pp. 156–163; J.-C. Javillier, *Les Réformes du droit du travail depuis le 10 Mai 1981*, pp. 326–331.
254. *See* R. Blanpain, *IELL* 1999, p. 306; W. Van Eeckhoutte, 'Het stakingsrecht in de privé-sector in België,' *Tijdschrift voor Sociaal Recht*, 1982, pp. 281–284; however, see recent cases is which unions were sued for organising strike *actions EIRR* 313/3–4.
255. *See* T. Treu, *IELL* 1998, pp. 209, 218.

50. In the Scandinavian countries,[256] Greece,[257] Germany,[258] The Netherlands,[259] the United States,[260] Switserland,[261] Canada,[262] and Japan,[263] liability of the trade unions for unlawful strikes has always been taken as a logical consequence of the system.

In Britain and Ireland trade unions since 1906 have virtually had absolute immunity from tort liability in the case of strikes, since every conflict with a professional purpose was considered lawful. But this has changed with time.

In Britain since the 1980s many types of industrial action have been declared unlawful. Unions that organize unlawful actions can be faced with tort liability. However, the British legislator has put a maximum limit on the amount of damages that can be claimed from a union for organizing an illegal strike.[264]

In Ireland, statutes and case law have brought an increasing number of cases outside the protection of immunity. In such 'unprotected' industrial action the trade unions may be sued for damages.[265] Moreover the legislator restricted the system of immunities available to trade unions which have a 'negotiation licence'.[266]

51. Yet, in all countries where the unions can be subject to civil suits only seldom damages are claimed from unions organizing unlawful strikes. In most cases employers are satisfied with a formal declaration from the court, that the strike is illegal. This attitude is encouraged when unions are law-abiding and stop support of a strike as soon as the strike has been declared illegal. Up to this point the strike is assumed to be legal and the unions are not held responsible for damages caused by a strike before the verdict of illegality is pronounced, even if the damaged party (the employer) did seek damages. See further under para. V.

B. The Wages of the Striking Worker

52. It is understood that an *employee* who goes on strike forfeits the right to his/her regular pay unless the strike is provoked by the employer.[267] Even now the

---

256. For Denmark *see* W. Galenson, *op. cit.*, p. 37, 209–210, 219–223; for Sweden *see* A. Adlercreutz, *IELL* 1997, p. 194.
257. *See* T.B. Koniaris, *IELL* 1990, p. 183.
258. *See* for example the metal workers strike in Schleswig-Holstein, 1956 and 1957 and the shoe industry strike in Nürnberg, 1961/1962; *see* Bundesarbeitergericht AP No. 2 on § 1 TVG Friedenspflicht; Bundesarbeitsgericht AP No. 33 zu Article 9 GG Arbeitskampf); claims for damages are founded on § 823 BGB (Recht am Gewerbebetrieb). Constitutional criticism on this possibility has been rejected by the Bundesverfassungsgericht 2.7.1979, *see* R. Richardi, Die Bedeutung des zivilrechtlichen Haftungssystems für den Arbeitskampf, *ZfA* 1985, pp. 102–126.
259. *See* Dutch Supreme Court, 19 April 1991, *NJ* 1991, 690.
260. A.L. Goldman, *IELL* 1996, p. 373.
261. *See* M. Rehbinder, *op. cit.*, pp. 263, 264.
262. *See* H.W. Arthurs a.o., *IELL* 1993, pp. 296, 306; D.D. Carter, p. 46.
263. *See* Hanami/Komiya, *IELL* 1999, p. 169.
264. S 22 TULRCA 1992.
265. *See* for a first case *EIRR*, February 1995, p. 9.
266. Trade Union Act 1941, now the Industrial Relations Act 1990, *see* M. Redmond, *IELL* 1996, pp. 194, 195; this situation is condemned by the Committee of Independent Experts on the European Social Charter, *see Conclusions* XIV-1, p. 422.
267. *See* M. Despax and J. Rojot, *IELL* 1987, p. 300; G. Lyon-Caen a.o., *op. cit.*, pp. 940, 941.

right to strike is recognized as a fundamental right, this consequence is undisputed, at least from a legal point of view.[268]

In fact, if strikes are very short, often the employer will not make deductions from wages for days on which the workers were on strike.[269] At the end of the strike unions and employers normally make arrangements to avoid the forfeiture of wages. But this is not always the case. Hence the employer can use the threat of loss of wages and benefits as a weapon to put pressure on striking employees. Sometimes the employers ask employees to work overtime in compensation for time lost due to the strike.

This is the same in all industrial countries.

However, also the reverse is possible: employers may be tempted to deduct salaries to a larger extent than that corresponding to the length of the strike. In France,[270] this is forbidden and also the Committee of Independent Experts on the European Social Charter is very critical as to such practices as they constitute a form of sanction not compatible with the free exercise of the right to strike.[271]

53. The forfeiture of pay also extends to other 'fringe benefits' rooted in the contract of employment, such as the accrual of paid holidays etc.[272] But normally, it is accepted that participation in a strike does not interrupt the accumulation of seniority, pension rights, health insurance coverage etc. Indeed, it is often seen as a sequel of the 'suspension theory' (see next paragraph) that – upon resumption of work – a worker's service is deemed to be continuous. All rights and benefits resulting from continuous service are retained as if no break in work had occurred.[273] Sometimes this is recognized by case law, sometimes by statutory provisions.[274]

So in Belgium, the days not worked due to strikes are counted as days worked for the purpose of calculating contributions and benefits. In Japan, the deductibility of benefits like family allowances is a matter of contract interpretation.[275]

54. The right to pay is a very delicate issue in situations of a go-slow, work-to-rule, work-in, partial strikes, etc. In Britain, case-law suggests that even if a worker conscientiously performs a number of his or her duties but refuses to perform some other, the employer, provided that he has made it clear that partial performance is not acceptable, may be entitled to deduct the full amount of pay involved for the days on

---

268. This is also the opinion of the ILO-Committee on Freedom of Association, *see* Gernigon et al., *op. cit.*, p. 471.
269. Due to pure salary systems in which the amount of wages is fixed on a monthly basis, *see* K. Sugeno, *op. cit.*, p. 111.
270. Albeit with a small complication in the public sector, see G.Lyon-Caen a.o., *op. cit.*, pp. 939,940, which is critisised by the Committee of Independent Experts on the European Social Charter, *Conclusions* XIV, p. 259.
271. *See Conclusions* XIII-1 (1990–91), p. 154.
272. For France *see* G. Lyon-Caen a.o., *op. cit.*, pp. 938, 941.
273. *See* M. Goldberg, *op. cit.*, p. 88; Weiss and Schmidt, *IELL* 2000, p. 179; M. Rehbinder, *op. cit.*, pp. 260, 261.
274. *See* for Canada H.W. Arthurs a.o., *IELL* 1993, pp. 279, 280; D.D. Carter, pp. 45, 50; also in Britain there is a provision in some labour and social security acts that the 'continuity of employment' required by the act is not broken by a strike or a lockout.
275. *See* K. Sugeno, *op. cit.*, p. 112.

which the worker was on strike.[276] In Israel, in the case of partial strikes case law allows the employer either to stop the payment of wages altogether or to pay the wage only partially.[277]

55. An important difference between the industrial countries is the ability of their respective unions to support striking workers with money from strike funds. The availability of 'healthy' strike funds has always been a characteristic of industrial relations in Germany, Scandinavia, Switzerland,[278] Belgium,[279] and The Netherlands[280].

In other countries such as Britain, Ireland,[281] and Canada,[282] strike funds play a more modest role and in countries like France[283] and Italy,[284] strike funds are almost non-existent.

56. As regards social security it is clear, that if a worker could claim benefits from unemployment benefits schemes or from social assistance while he or she is on strike, the likelihood of a swift settlement of the dispute is lessened.

For this very reason these schemes in all industrial countries contain provisions disqualifying strikers from receiving such benefits for the duration of the labour dispute.[285] Nevertheless some countries provide for some leniency in this respect.[286]

C. Disciplinary Actions against Striking Workers

57. Finally there is the question of whether employers can discipline an employee for going on strike, for example by depriving him or her of certain advantages in his job or by taking more severe measures such as dismissal. This possible consequence of going on strike was as obvious a hundred years ago as was the right of the employer to interrupt the payment of wages. In fact, this weapon of retaliation has often been used by employers to break strikes. Sometimes they have handled this weapon selectively, i.e. only to discipline the militants, not their less aggressive supporters. But it is also evident that the workers have stubbornly resisted the use of this weapon of retaliation. In the negotiations to resume work after a strike, workers' representatives have always insisted that the employers end or redress disciplinary actions against striking workers. But again, whether the employers maintained or ended disciplinary actions against the striking workers was very much dependent on the outcome of the strike.

---

276. *See* B.A. Hepple, *IELL* 1992, p. 258.
277. *See* R. Ben-Israel, *IELL* 1994, p. 182; M. Goldberg, *op. cit.*, p. 89.
278. *See* M. Rehbinder, *op. cit.*, p. 260.
279. *See* R. Blanpain, *IELL* 1999, p. 302.
280. *See* M.G. Rood, *IELL* 1999, p. 77.
281. *See* M. Redmond, *IELL* 1996, p. 200.
282. H.W. Arthurs, *IELL* 1993, p. 281.
283. *See* G. Lyon-Caen a.o., *op. cit.*, p. 941.
284. *See* T. Treu, *IELL* 1998, p. 209.
285. For Britain, *see* B.A. Hepple, *IELL* 1992, p. 278; for Canada *see* H.W. Arthurs a.o., *IELL* 1993, p. 281; for Sweden *see* A. Adlercreutz, *IELL* 1997, p. 188; for Spain *see* Olea and Rodriguez-Sañudo, *IELL* 1996, p. 147; *see also* Article 69, sub i of Convention 102 of the ILO.
286. For Ireland, *see* M. Redmond, *IELL* 1996, p. 200.

58. In this area[287] the law has undergone a large change in the last decades, no doubt as a result of a more moderate attitude of the employers – dismissals or other strike-breaking tactics may easily result in a continuation and widening of the dispute – but also as a result of the recognition of the right to strike as a fundamental right.[288] The Committee of Experts of the ILO sees the maintaining of the employment relationship as a normal legal consequence of recognition of the right to strike.[289]

59. Law in most countries is currently based on the suspension theory. This theory implies that coercive, harmful or discriminatory practices against workers, motivated by their adhesion to a strike, are not allowed. The suspension theory does not sanction the temporary cancelling of all duties of the parties during the strike. Striking workers are required to maintain the safety measures necessary to ensure the protection of people and possessions, the maintenance of premises, machinery and installations, materials, etc.[290]

The suspension theory is nowadays accepted by statute or in case law in the southern European countries,[291] Germany,[292] Luxembourg,[293] Sweden,[294] The Netherlands,[295] Canada,[296] Greece,[297] and many other countries.[298]

In a number of countries the suspension theory is not fully, but only partially applied. Take for example Belgium. There the theory of suspension is accepted[299] but the employer in some cases still has retained the right to dismiss striking workers. This seems to be the case in Switzerland as well.[300]

In Norway a strike terminates the contract of employment, but in practice all workers are reinstated with all acquired rights.[301]

60. In the United States a doctrinal approach is prefered, which differs from the suspension theory, although it comes near to it. In this approach a distinction is made

---

287. *See* X. Blanc-Jouvan, 'The effect of industrial action on the status of the Individual Employee', in B. Aaron and K. Wedderburn, *Industrial Conflict – A Comparative Legal Survey*, London, 1972, p. 175.
288. *See* Committee of Experts on the European Social Charter, *Conclusions* I, p. 39.
289. Report *Freedom of Association and Collective Bargaining*, Report III (4B), 1994, p. 61.
290. Such is the opinion of the Freedom of Association Committee of the International Labour Organisation, *see* its 69th *Report*, Case No. 307 (Somalia), paras 97 and 99.
291. For France: Article L 521-1 CdT, *see* G. Lyon-Caen a.o., *op. cit.*, pp. 935, 936; J. Rojot, *op. cit.*, p. 60; for Italy, *see* G. Giugni, *op. cit.*, pp. 216, 217; for Spain *see* M.A. Olea and F. Rodriguez-Sañudo, *IELL* 1996, p. 143, 147; for Portugal, *see* M. Pinto, *IELL* 1989, p. 218.
292. Bundesarbeitsgericht Nos 58, 59 on Article 9 GG (Arbeitskampf).
293. R. Schintgen, *IELL* 1991, p. 124.
294. R. Fahrbeck, *op. cit.*, pp. 170, 171 who mentions one exception: the employer may lawfully dismiss the strikers if the strike goes on for a very long period of time and jeopardizes the financial health of the company.
295. Dutch Supreme Court 22.4.1988, *NJ* 1988, 952.
296. *See* case Supreme Court of Canada, (1962) 34 O.L.R. (2d) 654 (SCC), C.P.R. Zambri (Royal York Hotel), *see* H.W. Arthurs, *IELL* 1993, p. 277.
297. *See* T.B. Koniaris, *IELL* 1990, p. 183.
298. So in Argentina, *see* M. Ackerman and A. Goldin, *IELL 1990*, p. 227; in Israel, *see* R. Ben-Israel, *IELL* 1988, p. 189; in Japan, *see* T. Hanami, *IELL* 1985, pp. 139, 141; K. Sugeno, *op. cit.*, p. 111.
299. Cour de Cassation, 23.11.1967, 9.10.1970, 14.4.1980, 21.12.1981; *see* R. Blanpain, *IELL* 1999, p. 306.
300. *See* A.L. Berenstein, *IELL* 1993, p. 176; M. Rehbinder, *op. cit.*, p. 260.
301. *See Conclusions* XIV-1, p. 619 of the Committee of Independent Experts on the European Social Charter.

between the employee's contractual and equitable job interests. A strike relieves the employer of his contractual obligations to remunerate the strikers, but their equitable status as employees is preserved. When the strike ends the employees' equitable status entitles them to resume their contractual relationship with the employer. Adverse changes in the striker's tenure or seniority status for example, are treated as unfair labor practices on the theory that the employer is thereby discriminating against those who engaged in concerted activities.[302] Moreover the former striker must be treated as a returning worker and not as a new employee (*see* para IV.B.). Thus the striking employee is protected against dismissals, although this protection is not absolute. The courts have construed this protection to allow employers to terminate strikers under certain circumstances (for example for serious misconduct).[303]

However, the employee's status rights do not preclude the employer from filling their jobs with temporary or even with permanent replacements during a strike.[304] If a worker is not replaced in his job while he is on strike, or if he is only replaced by a temporary worker, the worker has the right to be reinstated in his job upon his abandonment of the strike. If the striker is replaced by a permanently hired person, he has the right to return only when his former position becomes available again.[305]

However, if only some of the workers are replaced, the employers, decision regarding which strikers should be permitted to return to the available jobs cannot be based upon the extent of their participation in, or leadership of, the strike. A distinction based on such union activity is seen as being an 'unfair labour practice'.[306] If the striker accepts permanent employment of a substantially equivalent nature elsewhere, he can lose his protected status as a striking worker.

In Canada however, where the use of replacement labour by an employer during a strike is also considered to be lawful, the judges – or in some jurisdictions, the legislators – went further in protecting the job of the striking worker.[307]

61. In countries like Britain[308] and Denmark[309] the doctrine of suspension has not been accepted as a general rule. It is remarkable that the two countries which have been the first to create a certain 'freedom to strike' are the last to protect the rights of the striking workers. As Elias has put it: 'The organisers are protected, but not the workers.'[310]

In Denmark the system requires all workers to resign from their posts in case of industrial action. At the end of the strike the resulting collective agreements contain a so-called 'contrition clause' which opens the way for the workers to be re-employed if production allows. But the employer can refuse to allow workers to return to their

---

302. A.L. Goldman, *IELL* 1996, p. 369.
303. For the United States A.L. Goldman, *IELL* 1996, p. 376; for France, G. Lyon-Caen, *op. cit.*, pp. 950, 952.
304. A.L. Goldman (1994), *op. cit.*, pp. 212–213.
305. *See* A.L. Goldman, *IELL* 1996, p. 368.
306. Supreme Court NLRB v. Mackay Radio and Telegraph Co. 304 US 333 (1938), *see* A.L. Goldman, *IELL* 1983, p. 367.
307. *See* D.D. Carter, *op. cit.*, p. 49.
308. Workers on strike are protected against tort-responsibility, but not against a breach of contract.
309. Jacobsen and Hasselbalch, *IELL* 1998, pp. 271, 275.
310. P. Elias, *Trade Disputes*, London, 1980, p. 70.

previous jobs after industrial action if they are no longer required. A 1998-ruling of the Labour Court confirmed this system not only for blue-collar workers but also for white-collar workers.[311]

In Ireland[312] even in cases of an official strike, the law allows an employer to dismiss strikers, provided he dismisses all strikers. The workers only regain the right to complain of unfair dismissal, if the employer dismisses or reinstates selectively. In Britain[313] traditionally the employers had the right to dismiss workers taking part of a strike. Only quite recently the actual Labour Government enacted a new law, stating that workers involved in industrial dispute may be dismissed by employers only if the dispute exceeds 8 weeks and the employer has taken all reasonable steps to resolve the dispute.[314]

Over the years the Committee of Independent Experts on the European Social Charter has criticized these three countries on their system which it saw as not in conformity with Article 6, s. 4 ESH.[315]

62. Although in some countries[316] the theory of suspension is applicable to every strike, this is not self-evident. Lawyers easily agree the theory to be applicable to legal strikes, but many lawyers maintain that in the event of an unlawful strike the employer should be able to take disciplinary action. This is the law in Switzerland[317] and Britain[318].

In the United States a worker who participates in an unlawful stoppage is explicitly not protected under the National Labour Relations Act. Accordingly, such a striking worker does not have the normal statutory right to reinstatement upon termination of the strike. The employer can lawfully impose disciplinary sanctions, including discharge.[319] Yet, even in cases where there is participation in an unlawful strike, discharge or other disciplinary action may be deemed too harsh a penalty for employees. In various countries, such as Germany,[320] The Netherlands, Japan,[321] and Canada judges are critical of such penalties and will judge them according to the circumstances of the case.

---

311. *See EIRR* 299/4.
312. *See* M. Redmond, *IELL* 1996, p. 197.
313. *See* ss 237–239 TULRCA 1992; *see* B.A. Hepple, *IELL* 1992, p. 259.
314. New s 238A TULRCA, inserted by Schedule 5 of the Employment Relations Act 1999, *see* K.D. Ewing, ILJ 1999, p. 291; *see also EIRR* 300/13.
315. For Britain *see Conclusions* XII-1 (1988–1989), p. 131 and *Conclusions* XIII-1 (1990–1991), p. 156. For Denmark *see Conclusions* I, p. 39, II, p. 28, III, p. 37, IV, pp. 47, 48; *Conclusions* XIV-1, p. 181; the Danish government defends itself with the remark, that there are in fact arrangements securing the reinstatement of strikers in their previous employment on the termination of the dispute. For Ireland *see Conclusions* XIV-1, p. 422 of the Committee of Independent Experts on the European Social Charter.
316. This is the case in Israel, save for strikes in the public service, *see* R. Ben-Israel, *IELL* 1988, p. 189; M. Goldberg, *op. cit.*, p. 88.
317. *See* A.L. Berenstein, *IELL* 1993, p. 176; M. Rehbinder, *op. cit.*, p. 262.
318. *See* ss. 237 TULR(C)A.
319. A.I. Goldman, *IELL* 1996, p. 374.
320. *See* Bundesarbeitsgericht No. 59 zu Article 9 GG (Arbeitskampf); *see* Weiss/Schmidt, *IELL* 2000, p. 179.
321. *See* K. Sugeno, *op. cit.*, p. 111.

Spain has recently outlawed dismissal as a possible sanction against participation in illegal strikes. Only 'active participation' in illegal strikes and failure to fulfil minimum service provision may result in dismissal.[322]

In many countries these questions have not yet been fully clarified.

In the view of the Committee of Experts of the ILO sanctions in case of unlawful strikes should not be disproportionate to the seriousness of the violations.[323]

D. The Impact of Strikes on Non-striking Workers

63. In some countries, such as the United States, the right of workers to refrain from concerted activities is statutorily protected. It is unlawful for a union or for strikers to coerce or attempt to coerce a worker into joining a strike.[324] The law also recognizes a qualified right of all employees to cross a picket line, even if the picket line is lawful.[325] In most countries such principles are not explicit, but implicit.[326]

64. According to the classic rules of civil law (applied to employment relationships), if employees are willing to work but the employer cannot use their services, the employer is in *mora accipiendi* and must continue to provide pay, despite work not being done. If this rule were to be applied to strikes, the employer would risk extra financial losses due to the strike. Moreover, such a rule could entice the trade unions to organize strikes on a cheap basis: paralysing an entire firm by a strike of only a few 'key' workers while at the same time securing the continuation of payment of the other workers, who are nevertheless to profit of a positive strike result.

This awareness has incited case law in many countries to make an exception of this rule in the case of strikes. In most countries it is accepted that the employer can suspend the payment of wages if he is utterly unable, as a result of strike action, to provide normal work for workers who are not on strike.[327] Although in Germany in 1980 case law in this area was somewhat refined, the result was not much different.[328] In Belgium it is accepted that the strike can be a *force majeure*, an unforeseeable, insurmountable event, preventing the employer from continuing the payment of wages.[329] In The Netherlands in 1976, the Supreme Court made a differentiation. In official strikes the non-striking workers are not entitled to pay if they are implicated by the outcome of the dispute; in wild-cat strikes, the employer

---

322. Mere participation in an illegal strike remains subject to sanctions of a proportional nature, *see* Olea and Rodriguez-Sañudo, *IELL* 1996, p. 148; *EIRR* 1992, December, p. 10.
323. Gernigon et al., *op. cit.*, p. 468.
324. For the United States *see* A.L. Goldman, *IELL* 1996, p. 382, who makes an exception for internal organisatorial sanctions that the union may take versus its own members.
325. For the United States, *see* A.L. Goldman, *IELL* 1996, p. 374, who makes an exception for the case of an explicit waiver in the collective agreement.
326. For Switzerland *see* M. Rehbinder, *op. cit.*, p. 260.
327. For New Zealand, *see* J.M. Howells, *IELL* 1996, p. 222; for France *see* G. Lyon-Caen a.o., *op. cit.*, p. 940; for Switzerland *see* M. Rehbinder, *op. cit.*, p. 260.
328. Bundesarbeitsgericht No. 70 on Article 9 GG (Arbeitskampf); *see* M. Weiss and Schmidt, *IELL* 2000, p. 182.
329. *See* R. Blanpain, *IELL* 1999, p. 307.

must continue the payment of wages to non-striking workers who are not implicated by the outcome of the dispute.[330]

65. An even more delicate issue is that of the right of non-striking workers to unemployment benefits. In Britain[331] the non-striking workers do not have the right to unemployment benefits unless they can prove that they are not implicated by the outcome of the dispute. In Germany a complicated statutory provision has resulted in non-strikers only having the right to unemployment benefits if they are either outside the affected industry or inside the affected industry but not covered by the collective agreement and also not directly implicated by the outcome.[332] In Belgium case law reveals that workers laid off during a strike, but not participating in it, are not entitled to benefits if they belong to the same bargaining unit as the strikers or have an interest in the outcome of the dispute. Other laid-off workers receive benefits.

ILO-Conventions allow the temporary suspension of unemployment benefits where a person has lost his employment as a direct result of a stoppage of work due to a trade dispute.[333]

IV. THE EMPLOYERS' DEFENCE AND RETALIATION

66. Employers confronted with industrial action essentially have two options to face: either to keep their business operating or to close down the unit hit by industrial action (and perhaps of other units as well): the lockout.

A. *The Employers' Right to Keep his Business Operating*

67. Traditionally employers have not hesitated in exercising their right to try to continue operations during a strike, by using non-striking employees, subcontractors or newly-hired replacements.

In the United States the Supreme Court decided that an employer faced with a strike is entitled to try to keep its business operating. To do so the employer is permitted to hire workers on a temporary or permanent basis to replace the strikers.[334] Although this case law was criticized by the ILO[335], it has become a respectable strategy for the US business community to set out to destroy unions by permanently replacing employees who resort to work stoppages.[336] Attemps to override this case law by legislation[337] were not successful. As a palliative in 1995 President Clinton

---

330. Dutch Supreme Court 7.5.1976, *NJ* 1977, 55; *see* M.G. Rood, *IELL* 1999, p. 77.
331. *See* B.A. Hepple, *IELL* 1992, p. 278.
332. *See* former § 116 Arbeitsförderungsgesetz, now s 146 of the Social Security Code Part III; *see* Weiss and Schmidt, *IELL* 2000, pp. 183–185.
333. Convention 102, Article 69, sub (i); Convention 168, Article 20.
334. Supreme Court NLRB v. Mackay Radio and Telegraph Co., 304 *U.S.* 333, 1938, *see* A.L. Goldman (1994), pp. 212, 213.
335. By its Freedom of Association Committee, *see* 278th *Report*, Case No. 1543.
336. *See* A.L. Goldman *IELL* 1994, p. 229.
337. *See* A.L. Goldman, *IELL* 1996, p. 370.

issued Executive Order 12954, authorizing the Secretary of Labor to 'debar' from contracting with the federal government those business units that have permanently replaced lawfully striking employees.[338]

Also in Japan the employer is permitted to mobilize non-members of the union and to hire substitute workers to continue the operations of the firm. Occassionaly unions and employers have concluded 'scab-prohibiting agreements'.[339]

However, in most countries there is no equivalent to Mackay-type counteractions by employers. In many countries[340] the use of 'strike breakers' to replace workers on strike or lockout has not occurred in recent decades.

In other countries, where it did occur, the employers' right to keep his business operating has often been challenged and in Spain,[341] Portugal,[342] Greece,[343] and France,[344] as well as in some jurisdictions in Canada,[345] this right has been restricted by statute.

68. In France the law forbids the employer to entice non-strikers with extra pay.[346] Case law has done the same in the Netherlands.[347] In most countries the law recognizes the right of workers not to undertake work from an establishment on strike (hot cargo).[348] In many countries the law prohibits governmental employment-referral services from referring workers to job vacancies resulting from a strike.[349] Also, the law prohibits private employment agencies or temporary employment companies from supplying workers as replacements for strikers.[350]

B. The Lockout

69. The most forceful weapon with which an employer can react to a strike is the lockout. When an employer conducts a lockout, employees are denied the opportunity to work until the dispute is settled. They forfeit their wages, but the contract of employment is not broken.[351] Two types of lockouts need to be distinguished. The offensive lockout, applied by employers to support their aims in changing employment conditions even though the unions have not resorted to industrial action. The

---

338. *See* A.L. Goldman, *IELL* 1996, p. 367.
339. *See* K. Sugeno, *op. cit.*, p. 109.
340. For Sweden, *see* A. Adlercreutz, *IELL 1997*, p. 186; R. Fahlbeck, *op. cit.*, p. 176; for Denmark, Jacobsen and Hasselbalch, *IELL* 1998, p. 268; for Italy *see* T. Treu, *IELL* 1998, pp. 208, 209.
341. *See* M.A. Olea and F. Rodriguez-Sañudo, *IELL* 1996, p. 147.
342. *See* M. Pinto, *IELL* 1989, pp. 218, 219.
343. *See* T.B. Koniaris, *IELL* 1990, p. 183.
344. *See* G. Lyon-Caen a.o., op. cit., p. 957, 958 for some partial impediments.
345. *See* H.W. Arthurs a.o., IELL 1993, p. 277; D.D. Carter, op. cit., p. 48.
346. *See* M. Despax and J. Rojot, IELL 1987, p. 300; G. Lyon-Caen a.o., op. cit., p. 953.
347. Dutch Supreme Court, January 28, 2000, *JAR* 2000/63.
348. For Germany, *see* Bundesarbeitsgericht AP No. 3 on § 615 BGB, *see* M. Weiss and Schmidt, *IELL* 2000, p. 178.
349. *See* on this issue also Article 12 of the Employment Services Recommendation, No. 83 of 1948 of the ILO; *see* for Britain B.A. Hepple, 1994, p. 195; for the US A.L. Goldman, *IELL* 1996, p. 369.
350. *See* for Britain B.A. Hepple, 1994, p. 195; in the United States only in some states, *see* A.L. Goldman, *IELL* 1996, p. 369; in the Netherlands s 10 of the Act on Labour Contractors.
351. In the past also the lockout, which caused a breach of contract, occurred, but this type of lockout is no longer possible in a democratic state.

defensive lockout, on the other hand, occurs when employers refuse to allow the continuation of work whenever it is made impracticable by industrial action by the same or by other employees, and in doing so legitimates the non-payment of wages.

70. As has been said in the Introduction, the use of the lockout as weapon of retaliation is highly controversial in part of the doctrine and this part of the doctrine has moulded the law, especially in the southern European countries. In these countries the doctrine of parallelism between strike and lockout is rejected.

In Portugal, the lockout is prohibited in the Constitution[352] and in Greece the lockout is prohibited by legislation. Also in France the general principle is that the lockout is unlawful, but case law has created a narrow space for a defensive lockout or a lockout for safety reasons.[353]

In Italy the old fascist prohibition on the lockout is still on the statute book and is applied to all cases of offensive lockouts.[354] However, case law has traditionally regarded the defensive lockout as legal.

In Spain lockouts can only be lawful under a large set of conditions such as that they do not render ineffective the right to strike and that they are necessary to ensure the integrity of persons, goods and equipment.[355]

In some countries, such as Britain, and Ireland, the legislature has purposely maintained the legal space necessary for the lockout, but it is a weapon hardly ever used there. In Belgium, where lockouts are also unusual, the judges have accepted the lockout in certain circumstances.[356]

In some countries, where the lockout is never applied, such as The Netherlands and Luxembourg, its legal status is uncertain.

71. In another part of the doctrine the lockout is considered as a self-evident counter-weapon of the employer, which should be lawful from the principle of equality of arms. In some countries such as Mexico and Sweden, the Constitution explicitly recognizes the lockout.

On the international plane the lockout is not mentioned in the International Covenant on Economic, Social and Cultural Rights, but it is implicitly mentioned in the European Social Charter of the Council of Europe (Articles 6, 4). The Committee of Independent Experts on the European Charter does not raise any objection to the existence of legislation regulating the right to call a lockout, provided that neither legislation nor judicial decisions affect the very existence of the right to lockout.[357]

In countries like Germany, the Scandinavian countries, the United States, and New Zealand the lockout is still used as a weapon of industrial warfare, at times very effectively.

---

352. *See* M. Pinto, *IELL* 1989, pp. 215–222.
353. Cour de Cassation 28.10.1957, 5.5.1959, 2.12.1964, 13.11.1966, *see* M. Despax and J. Rojot, *IELL* 1987, p. 301; J. Rojot, *op. cit.*, p. 59; G. Lyon-Caen a.o., *op. cit.*, pp. 958–962.
354. *See* Cass. 13.2.1978, Cass. 2.11.1978, Cass. 28.7.1983; *see* T. Treu, *IELL* 1998, pp. 220, 221.
355. *See* M.A. Olea and F. Rodriguez-Sañudo, *IELL* 1996, p. 150.
356. Cour de Cassation, 7.5.1984, *see* R. Blanpain, *IELL* 1999, pp. 307, 308.
357. *See* L. Samuel, *op. cit.*, p. 182.

In the United States[358] and New Zealand[359] the lockout is widely permitted.

In the Scandinavian countries industrial action by workers and by employers are judged on a equal footing.[360] The scope of the freedom of industrial action is the same for either party. In Sweden[361] lockouts, like strikes, can be applied as offensive weapons.

This idea of 'formal parity'/'symmetry' is also adhered to in Canada.[362] Other countries, where the law permits the lockout do so on the basis of a rather material concept of parity. In Germany, case law has put a number of more detailed limitations on the use of the lockout[363], departing from the view, that strikes and lockouts need to be treated differently in order to retain the balance of bargaining power. The lockout is only permitted in situations where an uneven balance of power needs to be corrected and after notification and consultation of the social partner. Thus this case law has limited the possibilities of a so-called defensive lockout, while the so-called offensive lockout is almost completely forbidden.

In Israel[364] and Switzerland[365] this is very much the same. To be lawful a lockout must be purely defensive and a necessity.

In Japan the prevailing opinion is that the offensive lockout is unlawful, but the defensive is permitted when the employer is subject to extraordinary disadvantageous pressures.[366]

V. Litigation

72. Since the right to strike is not an unlimited right, employers and third parties have an interest in knowing whether a strike is legal or not. In most countries strikers and/or trade unions can be sued before the ordinary courts. In some countries, such as Germany, Denmark, Norway,[367] Israel,[368] and New Zealand,[369] the judgment on strikes and lockouts is concentrated in specialized courts. Thus, it is guaranteed that the cases are heard by 'industrial relations' judges, who are well aware of the particularities of the labour–management relationship.

Often there is a multiplicity of recourses available – administrative sanctions, prosecution in criminal courts, action for damages or injunctions in the ordinary civil

---

358. *See* the American Shipbuilding Co. v. NLRB case, *see* A.L. Goldman, *IELL* 1996, p. 385.
359. *See* Paul v New Zealand Society for the Intellectually Handicapped case, *see* G. Anderson, *op. cit.*, pp. 132, 133.
360. For Denmark *see* Jacobsen and Hasselbalch, *IELL* 1998, p. 273; for Norway *see* S. Evju, *op. cit.*, p. 87.
361. *See* R. Fahlbeck, *op. cit.*, p. 169.
362. *See* D.D. Carter, *op. cit.*, p. 44.
363. Bundesarbeitsgericht Nos. 64 and 84 on Article 9 GG (Arbeitskampf), *see* Weiss and Schmidt, *IELL* 2000, pp. 176–178.
364. *See* R. Ben-Israel, *IELL* 1994, pp. 178,179.
365. *See* M. Rehbinder, *op. cit.*, p. 243.
366. *See* the Marushima Suimon Com. Case; *see* T. Hanami, *Managing Japanese Workers*, Tokyo, 1991, p. 78; K. Sugeno, *op. cit.*, pp. 109, 110.
367. But only on some aspects of the law on strikes, *see* S. Evju, *op. cit.*, pp. 88, 89.
368. *See* R. Ben-Israel, *IELL* 1994, p. 169.
369. *See* J.M. Howells, *IELL* 1996, p. 229; G. Anderson, *op. cit.*, p. 134.

courts, awards of damages by an arbiter, etc. In cases of occupation and picketing possessory powers may be granted to the employer.

73. The Labour Court of Denmark can impose fines. In Italy criminal sanctions (fines) and disciplinary sanctions are provided for against workers who fail to observe a decision to ensure a minimum level of services in essential industries.

In Canada,[370] unlawful strikes may give rise to possible administrative sanctions by the labour relations tribunals or to prosecution in the criminal courts, but this seldom occurs. However, generally speaking, criminal sanctions are on the wane.

74. Nowadays, preference seems to be for the use of the facilities of procedural law in civil litigations. This is so in Germany,[371] The Netherlands, Austria,[372] Ireland,[373] and Japan.[374] In affording relief to persons injured by unlawful industrial action, the civil courts in most countries ostensibly apply the ordinary law of civil wrongs – tort or delict, and occasionally contract. Although, the usual remedies in civil litigation are money damages, in all countries, cases in which the employer seeks compensation for damages caused by an illegal strike are rare. Often, a mere declaration (unaccompanied by other sanctions) that a strike or lockout is unlawful, brings a strike/lockout to an end because it is a strong indication as to how a court would react to the legality of such conduct in a subsequent proceeding.

75. In one group of countries, like Germany, The Netherlands, Britain,[375] and Israel, the *injunction* with prohibitory and mandatory orders has been by far the most frequently sought remedy for strikes. It has the attraction of being available speedily with relatively little formality with regard to proof or to pleading to stop the illegal action and also reducing the resulting loss or damage, rather than attempting to compensate. Frequently an injunction is sought with the sole purpose of forestalling the action and the employer or third party has no intention of going to a full trial to obtain damages and a permanent injunction. Thus the injunction is a particularly powerful weapon in the hands of the employer or some other affected party.

Clearly this presupposes that if an injunction is given, it is to be respected by the union, which will withdraw its support of the strike. In most countries the vast majority of injunctions are complied with such that there is no need for enforcement proceedings.

In some countries like Britain, the unions in the past were unwilling to bow to such orders, but successful contempt of court proceedings following by sequestration of union assets in some highly publicized cases led to a greater degree of compliance with injunctions. Sometimes the great political and social controversy

---

370. *See* H.W. Arthurs, *IELL* 1993, pp. 301–304; D.D. Carter, p. 51.
371. *See* D. Leipold, 'Die Schutzschrift zur Abwehr einstweiliger Verfügungen gegen Streiks', *Recht der Arbeit* 1983, pp. 164–170.
372. A. Strasser, *IELL* 1990, p. 196.
373. M. Redmond, *IELL* 1996, p. 201.
374. *See* K. Sugeno, *op. cit.*, pp. 112, 113.
375. *See* B.A. Hepple, 1994, p. 182.

arousing from those cases resulted in replacing or radically altering the procedure by which an injunction was obtained.[376]

76. In another group of countries, like France, Belgium,[377] Italy, and Sweden[378] injunctions to stop industrial action are not part of the legal system, but in most countries, employers can and will go to the courts in order to obtain an injunction against blocking of the entrance to enterprises by employees or third parties. The Committee of Independent Experts on the European Social Charter recognizes that an employer may seek an interlocutory injunction in cases where a strike may be unlawful.[379]

77. Employers may also contemplate to sue their striking workers for damages. Obviously no liability can be sought from strikers participating in a lawful strike, although it is possible that unlawful behaviour during a lawful strike can give rise to a suit for damages.[380]

In some countries, like the United States the employer cannot sue employees in an unlawful strike for damages[381] but in many other countries, like Germany[382] they can. However, in countries like Germany, The Netherlands, Britain, Sweden,[383] and Japan[384] in the case of a strike, the employer takes proceedings against the unions in preference to taking them against the individual workers on strike.

The first reason is, that in some countries, like Sweden[385] and The Netherlands, in case of official strikes employees have no personal liability even if the action is unlawful. Hence in these countries individual employee liability may arise only if the employee participates in a wild-cat strike.

The second reason for the unions being the first defendant in various countries is, that personal liability in tort for employees is considered unrealistic as the amounts that the employees can be ordered to pay are very low – in Sweden even if the old limitation of damages on individual members of 200 Swedish crowns was abolished in 1992, it is still a matter-of-course that such damages for taking part in unlawful strikes should be restricted.[386]

78. However, in other jurisdictions such as Belgium and Ontario[387] the individual employees are mostly the first defendant as in these jurisdictions a union is simply an

---

376. For British Columbia and Ontario (Canada), *see* H.W. Arthurs a.o., *IELL* 1993, pp. 313–314; D.D. Carter, p. 50; in Britain s 221 TULRCA has somewhat mitigated disadvantages in the system of labour injunctions concerning industrial disputes, *see* B.A. Hepple, *IELL* 1992, p. 275; for Ireland, *see* M. Redmond, *IELL* 1996, p. 200.
377. *See* R. Blanpain, *IELL* 1999, p. 303.
378. *See* R. Fahlbeck, *op. cit.*, pp. 176, 177.
379. *See Conclusions* XII-1 (1988–1989), p. 131.
380. *See* for Belgium R. Blanpain *IELL* 1999, p. 306.
381. *See* A.L. Goldman, *IELL* 1996, p. 374.
382. *See* Bundesarbeitsgericht No. 32 zu Article 9 GG (Arbeitskampf); *see* Weiss and Schmidt, *IELL* 2000, p. 179.
383. *See* R. Fahlbeck, *op. cit.*, p. 172.
384. *See* K. Sugeno, *op. cit.*, pp. 112, 113.
385. *See* A. Adlercreutz, *IELL* 1997, p. 195.
386. *See* Adlercruetz, *IELL* 1997, p. 195.
387. *See* H.W. Arthurs a.o., *IELL* 1993, p. 306, but this applies only to civils courts. The unions can be sued for damages in arbitral proceedings.

unincorporated collection of individuals with no legal personality; it can neither sue nor defend in its own name in ordinary civil proceedings. Also in Ireland[388] injunctions are issued against people, not unions, safe in cases of a union which does not have a negotiating licence.[389]

In Italy where the unions cannot be held responsible for damages, in recent years employers have used the injunction procedure to summon trade unions in court, just to obtain a verdict on the legality of the strike. If the strike is found to be illegal this decision could influence public opinion and it gives the employer the guarantee, that retaliation measures (dismissals, lockouts) are allowed.[390]

79.   In the United States some jurisdictions have given any local citizen or taxpayer, the right to bring a suit to enforce anti-strike legislation.[391] In Britain in 1993 a newlycreated 'citizens'-right of action was introduced, allowing any individual to apply for an injunction against the organizers of unlawful industrial action.[392]

Also in The Netherlands third parties (for example interest groups) can summon trade unions in the courts to obtain an injunction against a strike. In Israel the injured public has managed to obtain injunctions and damages against striking workers.[393] In the eyes of the ILO Committee of Experts such provisions 'provide yet another obstacle to the exercise of the right to strike by opening the industrial action of trade unions to constant attack from an infinite number of potentially deprived third parties'.[394]

80.   In the past sometimes injunctions were sought requiring strikers to return to work, under astreinte, penalty, or imprisonment.[395] But these types of acts have been declared illegal in numerous industrial countries, notably as a consequence of the recognition of the right to strike as a fundamental right and also supported by the fundamental right which prohibits forced labour.[396]

VI.   EVALUATION AND CONCLUSIONS

81.   This chapter has revealed, that the strike has become a generally accepted weapon in industrial disputes in democratic countries. But this is not the case for all strikes nor for all nations. Many exceptions to the principle can be seen in a variety of nations, each reacting differently to the emergence of strikes.

---

388.   *See* M. Redmond, *IELL* 1996, p. 201.
389.   The Committee of Independent Experts on the European Social Charter is very critical on the Irish system which refuses protection for a trade union not holding a negotiation licence and for its members against a civil action for damages in the event of peaceful incitement to collective action, *see Conclusions* XIII-1 (1990–1991), p. 155.
390.   G. Giugni, *op. cit.*, pp. 247–254.
391.   *See* A.L. Goldman, *IELL* 1996, p. 366.
392.   *See* s. 235A–C *TULRCA* 1992.
393.   *See* R. Ben-Israel, *IELL* 1988, p. 184.
394.   Quoted by the Committee of Independent Experts on the European Social Charter, *Conclusions* XIII-3 (1996), p. 144.
395.   For Canada, *see* H.W. Arthurs a.o., *IELL* 1993, p. 313.
396.   In Germany as contradictory to Article 12 Constitution; in Britain by s. 236 TULRCA; in the Netherlands by an Act of 14.12.1979; in the United States the 13th Amendment to the Constitution, *see* Goldman, *Bulletin*, pp. 199, 200.

It is tempting to compare the law on strikes in different nations with the varying pattern of industrial action in each. In fact the strike statistics of many countries over a long period of time reveal that there is a large difference in the incidence of strikes in various countries, the incidence varying over time and also over the various economic sectors within a single national economy. At the moment a downward trend in industrial action is recorded from a number of countries.[397]

The reasons for the fluctuations are complex but a particular factor which stands out is that of the level of employment. In times of high unemployment it is difficult for trade unions to motivate their members to go on strike.

82.   However, it seems almost impossible to establish a relationship between the strike pattern and the legal system. Denmark has an elaborate, largely autonomous system of strike law and nevertheless many strikes. The Netherlands has a rudimentary system of heteronomous case law and few strikes. New Zealand has had a coercive system and many strikes. Germany has no coercive system and a low strike frequency.

In some countries there are many micro-conflicts which influence the industrial relations process but they are often beyond the control of the trade unions.[398] In other countries, there are few but influential conflicts which are under the control of the unions.[399]

From all this we might infer that the strike pattern is to a large extent determined by non-legal factors such as the position and the political orientation of the trade union movement, the character of the employer–employee relationship, the availability of redress via courts, intervention of labour inspectors, grievance procedures, etc. This has led part of the doctrine to doubt whether industrial conflict can be controlled by strict legal regulation. It considers legal norms and sanctions as blunt instruments in shaping labour–management relations. In the two decades, up to about 1980 strikes seemed to be regarded as an unavoidable incident of industrial relations.[400]

83.   Nevertheless continuous discussions on the rules of strikes occur on the issue of how to get a better grip on the phenomenon. Even though modern democratic societies have accepted either the right or the freedom to take industrial action, among all responsible persons the feeling prevails that the protracted use of industrial sanctions threatens the interests of the public. Even if the right to strike is recognized, many people in government, in the judiciary, in the general public, and among the employers, feel reluctant to accept this recognition wholeheartedly. They argue that resorting to industrial action is an immature, unconstructive and damaging way of dealing with industrial problems and that strikes are wasteful, expensive, and disruptive for workers, employers, and society. Interruptions of the production process are generally perceived to reduce the well-being of the national economy as a whole and to divide workers and employers.

---

397.   For Ireland *see EIRR* 304/8; for France *see EIRR* 305/6; for Spain *see EIRR* 307/12.
398.   *See* for example Israel, *see* R. Ben-Israel, *IELL* 1994, p. 169.
399.   For example Canada, *see* D.D. Carter, p. 42.
400.   J.M. Howells, *IELL* 1996, p. 199.

84. Although most democracies now accept industrial conflicts as being a 'necessary wrong', they still remain a 'wrong'. In reality even minor strikes can cause enormous damages in industrialized countries. This may lead to small key groups creating difficulties in society as a whole. Interdependencies within societies often result in the actions of these small groups harming innocent third parties. Consequently, scholars and politicians have looked at other methods of resolving conflict. In Christian Social teaching there has always been a certain understanding in support of the strike. But it has also recognized the darker side of the strike and has a preference for peaceful conflict solutions.[401] Nowadays Social–Democratic thinking also often comes to the same conclusion: for example President Kekkonen of Finland in 1977 said that strikes were by then considered to be an outmoded weapon in industrial relations.[402]

85. One should not overlook the sociological dimension of strike action, which, like any other social phenomenon, is affected by economic, social, technological and other changes to which it has to adapt.[403] To name only a few examples. The more industry wide-collective bargaining gives way to enterprise bargaining, the more strikes will be confined to smaller groups of workers and to a single employer. While most strikes used to support demands for improved pay or other working conditions, strikes have recently been held for the protection of employment, against de-localization, etc. [404]

Moreover technological advances, increasing globalization and the development of multinational enterprises – all factors profoundly affecting the conditions in which goods and services are produced and their relationship with work – cannot but influence the issue of strike action.

Practice does show that the 'classic' strike is increasingly losing its adequacy and its effectiveness. New technology combined with multinationalization of business helps employers to circumvent the pressures of a strike. They can transfer production to units of production abroad. This requires the trade union movement to react with international collective action. But such international action is difficult to organize and the legal obstacles to it are quite considerable.[405]

86. Another relevant phenomenon is the change in the character of the working population. The male full-time industrial worker is increasingly accompanied by the female part-time service worker, the latter less likely to be unionized and less likely to go on strike than the former category. Furthermore wages are nowadays so high, that the strike funds of the trade unions are quickly exhausted when a major strike does occur. Workers nowadays have more to lose than chains. If a worker has an obligation towards a family then a strike may hold less incentive for him or her.

---

401. *See* the papal encyclics Rerum Novarum paras. 16/29/31, Laborem Excercens, paras 11–15, 20 and Centesimus Annus, para. 14; also the constitution text Gauda et Spes, para. 68 of Vaticanum II.
402. *See* A. Suviranta, *IELL* 1999, p. 195.
403. *See* R. Ben-Israel, Introduction to Strikes and Lockouts: A Comparative Perspective, in R. Blanpain and R. Ben-Israel (ed.), Strikes and Lockouts in Industrialized Market Economies, *Bulletin of Comparative Labour Relations*, Deventer, 1994, pp. 2–5.
404. Report *Freedom of Association and Collective Bargaining*, Report III (4B), 1994, p. 61.
405. *See* A. Jacobs, Towards Community Action on Strike Law?, *Common Market Law Review* 1978, pp. 133–155.

Thus unions in all nations have adopted forms of action, which tend to produce maximum loss of production with minimum loss of wages. Instead of a full curtailment of work, the workers nowadays content themselves with disturbing the smooth functioning of their work. In doing so they have increasingly resorted to rotating strikes (intermittent strikes, *grèves tournantes*), affecting different groups of workers successively.[406] The law, increasingly has to address the legal aspects of strike patterns, which fall short of work stoppage or do not consist of a cessation of work of any kind. And as we have seen these forms of action are more at risk of being considered unlawful than the traditional strike.

As the 'classic' ways of industrial conflict are no longer successful, more violent action methods are emerging, like lorry drivers blocking roads.[407] This type of action does not only violate national law, but also the EU rules on free movement, and this has prompted the EU to adopt a regulation on this issue.[408]

Moreover, employers, as a reaction to these forms of industrial action, have developed strategies like partial lockouts or non-payment of wages during the intervals of intermittent strikes or to workers made idle by the strikes of others. These are strategies towards which judges are often sympathic.

The right to strike, raises special difficulties in the public and semi-public sectors, where the concept of employer is not without ambiguities and where the problem of essential services arises more frequently than in other sectors, since the exercise of this right inevitably affects third parties who sometimes feel that they are the victims in disputes in which they have no particle

87. In many countries, legal measures to curtail the freedom of industrial action have been discussed publicly from time to time, especially after actions which caused much inconvenience and even danger to the general public.[409] In this context it is often contended that 'small key groups' should not be allowed to create difficulties to the society at large. Moreover, especially when threats of general strikes during depression times are held or considered to prevent governments from taking economic measures, the legality of political strikes is questioned.

People may then ask that it should be possible to enjoin industrial actions by referring disputes to conciliation, mediation and arbitration before strike action takes place. Consequently, policymakers time and time again envisage measures to canalize strike action and to promote recourse to the services of mediators, conciliators or arbiters. Such an approach was considered in Sweden, where in 1998 a State Commission drew up a list of proposals to overhaul the right to strike. In the end of the day the present Social–Democratic government renounced of most of the proposals and tabled only some minor amendments.[410] Yet, in Italy in 2000 the law on the maintenance of essential services at a minimum level was tightened up by the

---

406. For example in Israel, *see* R. Ben-Israel, *IELL* 1994, p. 169.
407. *See* R. Blanpain, *IELL* 1999, p. 302.
408. *See* Regulation of the Council of December 7, 1998, *OJ L* 337/887, which under the recognition of the right to strike (Article 2) obliges the EU Member States to take all necessary action when 'obstacles' are disrupting the free movement of goods.
409. *See* for Finland Suviranta, *IELL* 1999, p. 195; for France, EIRR 300/5.
410. *See EIRR* 301/12 and 311/10.

actual centre-left majority, after industrial action in all public sectors in November 1998 had virtually brought the country to a halt.

It was especially the ideological approach to labour law and industrial relations of the so-called New Right, which was in power in Britain (1979–1997) and New Zealand (1991–1998) that saw unions as an impediment to an efficient labour market and thought they therefore should be restricted in their functions. These objectives necessarily involved restrictions in the right to strike. In those countries, the reform of labour law was primarily concerned with enhancing the power of employers and reducing the power of organized labour.

88. Part of the doctrine rejects such limitations as contravening the rights of association and free collective bargaining and the right to strike. This part of the doctrine sees methods of self-regulation by the social partners as by far the most preferable way to solve industrial conflict. But if the social partners do not satisfy the public, pressure on the legislature and the courts may mount.

In my view reasonable limitations on the right to strike are not in contradiction to the right to strike as a fundamental right. No right, even if it is a fundamental right, has an absolute character. It has to bear limitations. This is also the view of the Committee of Experts on the European Social Charter, which considers a 'cooling-off' period compatible with the right to strike.[411]

I will not be amazed if the decades to come see a growing interest in the development of new techniques, e.g. final offer arbitration, for the peaceful solution of interest conflicts in the labour market.

I think the aim of every civilized society should not be to outlaw strikes altogether but to stimulate as much as possible the replacement of the use of this weapon in the resolution of industrial conflict by other less harmful techniques.

SELECT BIBLIOGRAPHY

B. Aaron/K. Wedderburn, *Industrial Conflict – A Comparative Legal Survey*, London, 1972.

T. Hanami and R. Blanpain, *Industrial Conflict in Market Economies*, Deventer, 1984.

R. Ben-Israel, *International Labour Standards: The Case of Freedom to Strike*, Deventer, 1988.

R. Blanpain and R. Ben-Israel (ed.), Strikes and lockouts in Industrialized Market Economies, *Bulletin of Comparative Labour Relations*, Deventer, 1994.

R. Ben-Israel, Chapter 15, Strikes, Lockouts and other kinds of Hostile Actions, in B.A. Hepple (ed.), Vol. XV (Labour Law) of the *International Encyclopedia of Comparative Law*, 1994.

J. Bernier (red.), *Grèves et services essentiels/strikes and essential services*, Sainte-Foy, 1994.

B. Gernigon, A. Odero, and H. Guido, ILO principles concerning the right to strike, International Labour Review, 1998, pp. 441–481.

---

411. *See Conclusions* I, p. 39.

Chapter 24. Settlement of Disputes over Rights

A. Gladstone

I. CLASSIFICATION AND CATEGORIES OF DISPUTES AND OF SYSTEMS FOR THEIR RESOLUTION

1.   The manner in which labour disputes are classified differs in various national industrial relations systems. In a very few, but sometimes significant, systems, labour disputes are not classified at all. Nevertheless, the intrinsic nature of one or another labour dispute is such that the dispute will inevitably fall into a certain category, whether intended or not. And this regardless of the procedures and mechanisms foreseen for its resolution. However, the choice of procedures and mechanisms employed to resolve the dispute will, in most industrial relations systems, be dictated by the classification of the labour dispute into a given category.

2.   The most common sets of classifications are first, 'interest' disputes (sometimes referred to as 'bargaining' or 'economic' disputes) as opposed to 'rights' disputes (sometimes referred to as 'legal' or 'juridical' disputes); and, secondly, 'collective' disputes as opposed to 'individual' disputes. Interest disputes arise out of a failure of the parties (normally a trade union or other organ for workers' representation, and an employer or employers' grouping) to agree in collective bargaining on the establishment of new, or on the renewal or modification of existing, norms. Interest disputes will not be dealt with further in this chapter[1] except to say that there is often a close affinity, if not identity, between interest disputes and collective disputes on the one hand, and between rights disputes and individual disputes, on the other.

3.   In regard to disputes over rights, one may envision a limited (and probably not exhaustive) number of general or specific grounds that give rise to such disputes. These include, from the point of view of an aggrieved worker, claimed violation or non-application of legislative or regulatory norms, of the provisions of a collective agreement, of the provisions of works rules or, perhaps, unilateral enterprise policies – including disciplinary rules, and of provisions of an individual contract of employment. All of these grounds involve an assertion by or on behalf of the aggrieved worker that he/she

---

1.   *See* chapter 25. *See also* A. Gladstone, *Voluntary Arbitration of Interest Disputes*, ILO, Geneva, 1984.

has suffered from a violation or non-application of legally enforceable standards applicable to that worker. In other words, he/she has not been treated in accordance with what is due to him/her; that his/her rights or entitlements have not been respected. There may also be some situations in which the employer or employers groupings may claim that their *rights* have not been respected, particularly in the collective employment situation.

4. It would be helpful to look more closely at some of the grounds resulting in disputes over rights. Examples of complaints by workers concerning violations or non-application of statutory or regulatory norms fall largely into three groups: (a) non-respect of statutory obligations regarding terms and conditions of employment (e.g. minimum wages, maximum hours, leave and holidays, safety and health, etc.); (b) violation of legal norms concerning workers' freedom of association where these are inscribed in legislation (e.g. discriminatory dismissal for reasons of trade union membership or activity); (c) employer violation of other statutory rules respecting various types of discriminatory treatment in the employment situation (e.g. race, religion, gender, age, sexual orientation, disability, etc.).

Similarly, where collective agreements are legally binding (the usual rule in the vast majority of the industrialized market economies), the worker may seek to vindicate his/her *rights* under the agreement through legal, or legally recognized, procedures. For instance, if the worker concerned believes that he/she has not been paid wages in accordance with the applicable scales of the collective agreement, he/she would have a legally recognized remedy to pursue. Complaints for breach of a legally binding collective agreement can also be brought by the employer. This is not infrequently the case where the trade unions party to an agreement strike in violation of a 'no-strike' clause in the agreement.[2]

Rights disputes may also arise concerning individual contracts of employment where the worker maintains that the employer with whom he/she has a contract has not met the employer's obligations under that contract. (The employer may of course also bring an action for the alleged breach of the contract, but the more common employer reaction is to take disciplinary action against the worker concerned.) It may be noted in passing that the contract of employment need not necessarily be a written one, and that such contract will normally exist, explicitly or implicitly, in all employment relationships.[3]

The non-application of employer-promulgated (and not mutually agreed or bargained) works rules, or similar directives, as valid grounds for a dispute over rights may give rise to some debate, specifically regarding whether such rules confer *rights* on employees. Employee rights arising out of works rules might depend on whether the rules are considered to be, by implication, a part of the individual contract of employment, or otherwise considered to have achieved the status of 'acquired rights'.

---

2. An employer may also claim that its rights have been violated in a strike situation where the strike may have been called in violation of statutory restrictions applying at the time of the strike (e.g. notice requirements, non-exhaustion of prescribed procedures, etc.).
3. There may be a question of the existence of an employment relationship or another type of work relationship such as an independent contractor relationship where a contract of employment (of 'service') does not exist and will not be implied.

However, a more likely scenario regarding works rules is disciplinary action by the employer against workers for alleged breach of such rules.

5. It should be reiterated that the above descriptions of various types of disputes over rights and their causes are meant to serve as illustrations of the varied nature and characteristics of such disputes.

It may further be emphasized that, in general, we are concerned with rights disputes and methods for their resolution in the private sector of industrialized market economies. The public sector or, more narrowly, the public service may have a substantially different regime in dealing with rights disputes.

6. As regards the mechanisms for resolving disputes over rights, these generally fall into four categories: the regular court system, labour courts, quasi-judicial administrative agencies, and arbitration. Each of these will be treated below.

7. However, mention should also be made of mediation and conciliation procedures. These are means of assisting the parties to the dispute, through neutral third party intervention, to reach a mutually agreed settlement of the conflict.[4] These terms and such intervention do *not* refer to or reflect procedures whereby a *decision* resolving the dispute is taken by the third party neutral. While mediation and conciliation are more commonly identified with disputes over interests (see chapter 25) than with disputes over rights, these procedures are nevertheless frequently resorted to in the latter as a precursor to adjudication or arbitration. This is effected either in the guise of an independent mechanism or as a part of the adjudicatory or arbitral process. Sometimes this is done quite informally and as an *ad hoc* measure, and sometimes it is an obligatory feature of the system for resolution of rights disputes.

8. There has in the past been some controversy regarding the use of formal or informal conciliation or mediation in rights disputes. These procedures are often identified with compromise and, in the view of certain commentators, there is no room for compromise as between the parties in a question concerning rights. One either has an entitlement or does not have it. This, however, seems to be a rather short-sighted view for two reasons. First, there are certainly many issues, particularly of a collective nature, which may well be subject to a compromise. An example would be the interpretation of a vague clause in a collective agreement to which the parties, in good faith, attribute different meanings. Secondly, the conciliation/mediation process may well serve the purpose of better informing the parties of their respective rights and obligations and thereby obviate the need for litigation. An example would be the existence, applicability or interpretation of the relevant statutory provisions.

9. In addition to conciliation/mediation as a possible precursor to adjudication or arbitration, mention should also be made of internal (usually) bilateral procedures within the enterprise or, possibly, the industry which may be utilized in efforts to resolve rights disputes typically, but not necessarily, of an individual nature. Such

---

4. Although a distinction is sometimes made between mediation and conciliation, the two terms are used here interchangeably.

grievance procedures, implicitly or explicitly, reserve to the employer the decision prior to possible recourse to adjudication or arbitration. At times the exhaustion of grievance procedures (as may be the case with conciliation/mediation) may be a pre-requisite to resolution through adjudication or arbitration.

10. In the discussion below, we shall group together labour courts and those administrative agencies of a quasi-judicial nature found chiefly in the United States, Great Britain, Japan and Canada, although these administrative agencies frequently exercise a quite limited jurisdiction limited to specific types of rights disputes. The administrative agencies may also be subject to a wider degree of judicial review by the regular courts than would be the case in respect of labour courts. And we group together, under the heading of regular or ordinary courts both those courts where absolutely no provision is made for any kind of special handling of labour disputes over rights, and those in which there is, within the regular court system, some measure of special dealing such as special 'social' chambers at the baseline or appellate level.[5] No effort is made to draw any distinctions with regard to the various fora on the basis of their place within or outside of the regular judiciary, or on the basis of hierarchical or administrative reporting or financing arrangements within a given system.

II.   ORDINARY COURTS

A.   *In General*

11. In a number of those countries concerned there is no special juridical or quasi-judicial procedure or institution to which a complaint may be taken when a dispute over rights arises. Such conflicts are treated in exactly the same manner and by exactly the same judicial bodies as any legal dispute under civil law. After all, it is argued, a contract dispute is no different depending on whether it concerns an employment contract, or a collective labour contract, or a commercial or other con-tract. And a generally trained judge is competent to apply the law – statutory or com-mon law – regardless of the situational context. This line of thinking is of course directly contrary to the very idea on which labour court (and, indeed, other special-ized court) systems are grounded. And, as we shall see later, one of the criticisms of certain labour court (and arbitration) systems is precisely that they overly rely on procedures and attitudes reminiscent of the regular courts. This being said, there are only a small number of those countries with which we are concerned (Germany and Israel, for example) in which the labour courts have a general or wide competence and in which the regular courts are not involved in any significant labour cases.

12. Countries in which ordinary courts play the major (and often exclusive) role in the resolution of disputes over rights include the Netherlands and Italy. And even within this very limited number of countries, Italy, as we shall see, does accord a

---

5.   However, where such 'social' chambers and similar organs (particular at the lower levels) are of a per-manent character (e.g. judges who sit exclusively or regularly in the social chambers), they may be assimilated to specialized labour courts.

degree of special treatment to cases relating to labour disputes over rights. Japan may also be included among those countries where competence over rights disputes lies almost exclusively with the regular judiciary, although disputes relating to unfair labour practices will be heard by special commissions under a system somewhat similar to that in the United States. This being said, it is worth noting that traditionally in Japan rights disputes have not frequently found their way to the courts.

13. Furthermore, even those countries with labour court or arbitration systems, as alluded to above, may still rely on the regular courts to handle many labour disputes over rights. Thus, for example, in the Nordic countries, the labour courts are competent only in cases involving alleged non-compliance with collective agreements (including wildcat or unofficial strikes). All other rights disputes are heard by the regular courts. Similarly, in the United States, the regular civil courts will deal with breaches of individual contracts of employment (and can be involved in damage actions based on certain breaches of collective agreements). And it must be remembered that in the US the 'grievance/arbitration' system applies only to that part of the workforce covered by collective agreements[6] (some 95 per cent of which contain arbitration clauses). In Great Britain, apart from the specialized tribunals handling complaints under the laws concerning termination of employment and employment discrimination, breaches of individual employment contracts and of certain other legislated protection for workers would be heard by the regular courts.

14. Thus, in the vast majority of the countries with which we are dealing, the regular courts continue to play a significant role in one way or another in the resolution of labour disputes over rights. Given the fact that Italy and the Netherlands reflect the predominant role of the ordinary courts, and that Italy presents a somewhat unusual case in this context, while the Netherlands represents a traditional approach, we shall take a somewhat closer look at these two countries, as well as Japan.[7]

B.   *Specific Countries*

1. Italy

15. Company grievance procedures are quite prevalent, for both individual and collective rights disputes, under collective agreements in Italy. These (mostly national, sometimes regional) agreements also provide for higher level discussions, particularly where the dispute concerns the application of national or territorial collective agreements. While the law recognizes the possibility of a form of seemingly

---

6. While less than 15 per cent of the workforce is unionized, collective agreements will cover non-members of the union as well as members within the same 'bargaining unit'.
7. A passing reference may be made to the Court of Justice of the European Communities (Union) and the European Court of Human Rights which, at European level, deal, *inter alia*, with labour cases arising out of the application of the relevant directives, conventions and related international instruments. *See* e.g. A. Gladstone (ed.), *International Labour Law Reports*, Vol. 19, Martinus Nijhoff, The Hague, 2001.

non-binding private arbitration for 'individual' disputes under collective agreements, this possibility is virtually never used.[8] On the other hand, many rights disputes are settled through the intervention of state labour officers. This being said, it would appear that the bulk of cases coming before the regular courts mainly concern, not unexpectedly, dismissals contrary to legislated norms, as well as cases concerning payment of wages and job classification.

16. While such cases find their place in the context of the regular courts, there is nonetheless an element of special treatment involved. As mentioned there are no labour courts as such. However, labour disputes over rights are usually subjected to a procedure more rapid than that for other cases and they can be heard by judges who have a special competence in labour matters, the so-called *pretore*. One can note here that the Italian system does in fact bear some aspects of a labour court system.[9]

17. The expedited, simplified and somewhat informal procedure before the *pretore* (usually younger judges who have demonstrated an appreciation for issues in labour cases) sitting alone can rely more on oral evidence and presentations than would be true of other civil proceedings. At the conclusion of the hearing, the decision of the judge is announced immediately. It may be noted that the *pretore* also hear cases of anti-union activity proscribed by the 'Statute of Workers' Rights'.

18. Appeals from the judgments of the *pretore* may be taken to three-judge appellate courts – the *tribunale*. This appellate jurisdiction also specializes in labour matters. Finally, questions of law only may be appealed to a special section of the Supreme Court (*Corte di cassazione*) which exclusively deals with labour cases.

19. Unlike normal civil cases, the above system is free of costs to the parties, other than lawyers' fees which may be levied against the losing party. It would appear that cases, particularly those involving dismissal, are handled rather expeditiously in northern Italy where the courts are better staffed than elsewhere in the country. Problems of undue delay, in spite of the specialized nature of the system, are however, the rule in the southern area of the country, including Rome.

20. Finally, it may be pointed out that demands in Italy for a completely separate and distinct labour court system, which were heard prior to the enactment of the 1973 legislation instituting the procedures described, are no longer being pressed. Thus the *pretore* arrangements seem to be giving some substantial degree of satisfaction to the litigants in labour disputes concerning rights.

---

8. *See* T. Treu, 'Conflict Resolution in Industrial Relations' in T. Hanami and R. Blanpain, ed., *Industrial Conflict Resolution in Market Economies*, 2nd ed., Deventer, 1989, p. 159.
9. Labour courts as such are prohibited by Article 102 of the Italian Constitution, which, nevertheless, permits the establishment of 'specialized sections' of the ordinary courts. However, the pretore system is not considered a 'specialized section' under the constitutional provisions.

2. The Netherlands

21. As mentioned above the Netherlands, perhaps more than any other country of those with which we are concerned, represents a system where there is essentially no distinction made as between the handling of labour and other civil cases. The ordinary courts are competent in respect of alleged breaches of both individual contracts of employment and collective agreements (which are legally enforceable except as mentioned below in connection with arbitration agreements). Neither are there any special administrative agencies or boards to deal with breaches of statutory duties of any kind in the labour field. It may also be noted that the law does not recognize or enforce private voluntary arbitration arrangements.

22. There being no significant particularities as regards legal procedures, it should suffice to make reference to some features of the general judicial system. Decisions of a court of first instance, the 'lower court', are appealable to a three-judge district court and ultimately, on questions of law (the facts as determined by the lower courts are not reviewed), to the Supreme Court. Should the Supreme Court disagree with the decision of the lower court it either remands the case for judgment in accordance with its ruling, or renders final judgment itself.

23. It is difficult to evaluate the efficacy of the Dutch system as opposed to those of countries with labour courts. Nevertheless, the fact that it could take over five years to ultimately decide a dismissal case (where recourse is had to the full appeals procedure) indicates that rapidity in rendering industrial justice is not a keystone of the Dutch system.[10] Moreover, a Dutch scholar has commented 'The absence of an informal, quick-working labour court … is a serious drawback of the Dutch labour law system'.[11]

3. Japan

24. Grievance procedures exist in Japan but these or other formalized procedures are not frequently utilized. This may reflect to some extent a certain cultural dislike of face-to-face conflictual confrontation that appears to be prevalent not only in Japan, but in many Asian cultures. This of course does not mean that collective confrontation is not usual, as evidenced, among other things, by the annual Spring Wage Offensive and, indeed, (although to a lesser extent) by enterprise collective bargaining itself. Nor does it mean that individual (and group) grievances do not exist; they do indeed, and seem to be settled in a quite informal manner by colleagues and foremen. This in spite of the fact that formal grievance procedures may be found, as suggested above, in a fair number of Japanese collective agreements.[12]

---

10. H. Bakels, 'The Netherlands', in R. Blanpain, ed., *International Encyclopaedia for Labour Law and Industrial Relations*, 1987, p. 28.
11. *Ibid.*
12. *See* Hanami in Hanami and Blanpain, *op. cit.*, p. 212.

25. Probably for the same cultural reasons, and as alluded to above, recourse to the courts for the resolution of rights disputes would not appear to be as frequent in Japan as in other countries with or without specialized labour jurisdictions. Nevertheless, the statistics indicate that in the last half of the 1990s, Japan was experiencing a very significant increase in employment litigation. Indeed this development has been partially spurred by the recent judicially created doctrine of abusive dismissal, in addition to the increased enforcement of anti-discrimination legislation. We should briefly examine the practice in Japan for the handling of such disputes, while recalling that, as opposed to Italy and the Netherlands, special procedures and fora do exist in Japan to treat cases of alleged unfair labour practices.

26. While Hanami speaks of the difficulty, certainly not unique to Japan, of distinguishing between rights and interest disputes (as well as between collective and individual dispute),[13] there is nonetheless a distinction that must be made – as mentioned in part I of this chapter – for the dispute in question to be receivable by the regular courts. The fact is that such distinction may not be apparent or even relevant at the pre-litigation stages, but *only* a dispute involving the breach of a claimed legal right will be justiciable. On the other hand, it seems not unusual for rights disputes, particularly of a collective nature, to be absorbed into those informal and formal (e.g. Labour Relations Commissions) mechanisms and procedures that are available for what are basically interest disputes.[14] In this respect it may be noted that 'rights' deriving from collective agreements may not be 'rights' in the law. Hanami states that collective agreements are merely gentlemen's agreements[15] which suggests the non-enforceability of their provisions. Sugeno, without citing Japanese jurisprudence, argues for a clear normative effect for collective agreements.[16]

27. In classifying Japan as one of the countries in which the regular courts have jurisdiction of labour disputes over rights, it might be placed somewhere between the Netherlands and Italy. This is because it is not unheard of, particularly in the bigger urban centres, for rights disputes that come before the district courts to be assigned to certain judges that are frequently called upon to handle labour law cases; but it would appear that even these judges are frequently rotated. Finally, it has been commented that procedures before the courts, in labour as well as other cases, is painfully slow. In the mid-90s, the average time for a district court to dispose of a case was more than 15 months.

---

13. *Ibid.*, p. 204.
14. *Ibid.*
15. T. Hanami, IELL (Japan), 1978, p. 140.
16. K. Sugeno, *Japanese Labor Law*, Seattle, 1992, pp. 512–515 (provided they do not involve more disadvantageous conditions than are otherwise accorded). This view seems to be shared in an older study by the Japan Institute of Labor which cites cases. (Report of the Research Commission on Labor Relations Law, 1967, Ministry of Labor.)

III. Labour Courts and Similar Institutions

A. In General

28. In the industrialized market economies, labour courts and similar institutions which serve as vehicles for adjudicating labour disputes over rights, have become quite prevalent. At the same time it is clear that the range of competence and the types of cases treated by the various fora are often quite different. Indeed, interest in the administration of industrial justice through instituting systems of labour courts has heightened in recent years. It has become increasingly evident, in certain of those remaining countries where rights disputes are referred to the ordinary courts, that these courts are not always in a position to render such justice in an adequate manner. But it should also be noted that much of the pressure for introducing a system of labour courts in countries where such system does not exist comes from academic circles, and rarely from members of the judiciary.[17] There is still the belief among many judges that, as mentioned earlier in this chapter, any competent judge is qualified to deal with any legal dispute or, at least, any contractual or torts dispute. Moreover, there is also the residual idea among certain jurists that labour court systems 'usurp' the powers and functions of the regular judiciary. This 'proprietary' attitude of jurists can particularly be noted in a transitional period when a labour court system is being introduced. This was the case, for example, in the 1990s in New Zealand where a growing tension developed between the ordinary courts and the new Employment Court.[18]

29. Why labour courts? Traditional theory holds that the resolution of industrial disputes, in this case rights disputes, requires, in order to ensure social justice, that cases be heard and decided rapidly, at no or with a minimum of cost to the litigants, with a relative lack of formality and judicial trappings, and by bodies with a specialized capability in labour matters. Whether in the present situation labour courts in all of the industrialized market economies in which such courts exist substantially meet these criteria is an open question. However, it is generally recognized that in respect of most of the elements mentioned, labour courts are more user-friendly than the ordinary courts. This is so in spite of the fact that complaints are quite widely heard that labour courts, in their operation if not in theory, have become too formal, particularly in terms of legal procedures (e.g. rules of evidence), use of lawyers, and the atmosphere of hearings. Complaints are also heard that, from a substantive point of view, there may be too much reliance on precedents. It would be in order to have a closer look at certain of the criteria mentioned above.

---

17. *See* Lord Wedderburn, 'Labour Law: From Here to Autonomy?', 16 *Industrial Law Journal*, 1, 1987; W.E.J. (Lord) McCarthy, 'The Case for Labour Courts', 21 *Industrial Relations Journal*, 1990, pp. 98 ff. At the 10th World Congress of the International Industrial Relations Association, held in Washington D.C. in May–June 1995, a special seminar devoted to Labour Courts and Labour Judges drew an overflow attendance.
18. *See* M. Vranken, 'The Role of Specialist Labour Courts in an Environment of Substantive Labour Law Deregulation: A New Zealand Case Study', 15 *International Journal of Comparative Labour Law*, 1999, p. 303 ff.

30. Rapidity in deciding cases is of importance in adjudication, in any area of law, but can often be crucial in respect of labour law. Let us take two types of cases as examples, cases which in certain jurisdictions constitute significant percentages of the work load of labour courts (and which will be discussed further below).

First, that of a challenge by an employee (or his/her union) to his/her dismissal. In virtually all of the countries with which we are concerned, a dismissal can be contested on the grounds of insufficient cause. Such protection is most often based on legislative standards or, less frequently, on provisions of collective agreements barring unjustified dismissals. Dismissal being industrial capital punishment, it would be unconscionable to require, particularly in a situation of a tight employment market or, worse, massive unemployment, that a dismissed employee suffer the delays that are common to ordinary court procedures, delays which can run into years. The repercussions of such delay on the employee and his family's well-being are patent. The importance of relative rapidity in resolving conflicts is often reflected in cases involving the application or interpretation of collective agreements. Here, the possible negative impact on the individual and, particularly, the collective labour–management relationship, and the decline in morale resulting from the frustrations of the parties where decisions in cases involving important personnel and labour relations matters are not forthcoming in a timely manner, may compromise the economic well-being of the enterprise (or industry).

31. Labour courts differ from each other in many respects in the many industrialized market economies where they have been established. As already noted, they differ in their competence, i.e. the types of cases over which they exercise jurisdiction. They also differ in their composition (tripartite, bipartite or unipartite[19]), the choice and role of lay judges or assessors in tripartite courts, the use of pre-trial procedures (conciliation of one sort or another), remedial powers and in a host of other characteristics. To have a better idea of these differences between, as well as of the functioning of, labour courts, a number of examples are described briefly hereafter.

B. Specific Countries

1. France

32. Although a quite atypical institution,[20] we might start this brief survey by examining the French labour court (*conseil des prud'hommes*), inasmuch as the French system is the oldest, dating back to the early nineteenth century. There are some 300 courts each serving a distinct district of the country.

33. A unique feature of the courts are that they are bipartite (rather than tripartite), comprising equal numbers of members elected periodically by workers and

---

19. In Europe the only 'unipartite' labour courts are found in Spain. In that country the labour courts of various types and at various levels are composed exclusively of 'professional' judges. *See* W. Blenk (ed.), *European Labour Courts: Current Issues*, Geneva, 1989, pp. 47–48.
20. The French-speaking Swiss canton of Geneva has a somewhat similar system.

employers from lists initially submitted by 'representative' trade union and employers' organizations for each district. They hear only 'individual' disputes arising out of (individual) contracts of employment (for which they enjoy exclusive jurisdiction) and which would include disputes concerning termination of employment. In effect, and in practice, this means rights disputes. Moreover, any distinction between individual and collective rights disputes that might have existed has broken down. The French High Court (*Cour de cassation*) has in fact ruled that a collection of individual claims arising out of a collective agreement is to be considered as an individual dispute and hence subject to the jurisdiction of the labour court.[21]

The bipartite court, being a judicial body, in spite of the fact that its members are not necessarily (or usually) lawyers, is assisted by a legally-trained secretary whose role is purely advisory.

34. On the question of limitation of jurisdiction, it may be noted that the French labour courts, as a number of others and in particular the Scandinavian labour courts, do not deal with rights disputes involving alleged breaches of labour legislation. These are left to the ordinary courts and certain other bodies.

It is also important to note that the concept of 'exclusive' jurisdiction means that, in addition to exclusivity within the judicial system, no other rights dispute resolution procedure, agreed or otherwise, can supplant the labour court, should the worker concerned attempt to avail him/herself of adjudication by the court. Incidentally, it is probably, at least in part, this reason, as well as the inviolable and non-waivable constitutional right of workers to strike, that contributes to an explanation for the virtual absence of arbitration arrangements in rights (and indeed in interest) disputes in France. 'Final' arbitration could never really be final in these circumstances since the unsuccessful party could then have recourse to the courts (or to a strike).

35. There is an official and compulsory conciliation procedure before a partial panel of the court itself. It is only if this fails that the case comes before the full panel. It is reported that there is a fair measure of success in achieving settlements at the conciliation stage. During the hearings, which are quite informal, the parties may be represented by legal counsel, but this is in no way obligatory. Workers are frequently represented by trade union representatives or by fellow workers.

36. While majority or even unanimous decisions are not at all uncommon, the bipartite nature of the courts does in fact lead to stalemates which then must be decided at a subsequent stage of the proceedings. In the event of such stalemate, further sessions are held in which the court is joined by a regular judge of the base-line court who will decide. Another characteristic of the French system is that appeals can be taken from a decision of the labour court on questions of fact in addition to questions of law. Thus, the whole case may be heard *de novo* by the ordinary courts. This does not appear, in practice, to be unusual. And further appeals may be taken to the court of appeal, again on the facts as well as the law, in cases where the monetary amount in question is greater than a given figure (relatively low). On appeal to

---

21.   J. Rojot, 'France', 9 *Comparative Labor Law Journal*, 1987, p. 71.

the highest level court, the *Cour de cassation*, only questions of law can be advanced. The appeals from the base-line courts are heard by a 'social chamber' of the court of appeals and of the *Cour de cassation*, but this does not mean that the judges concerned have unique or deep experience of labour questions or of labour-management relations.

Without being too severe, it would seem that the French labour court system suffers from at least two basic features which give rise to delays in disposing of cases. Both relate to the appeal procedure (which is abundantly used). First is the feature that the facts can be re-tried on appeal; secondly, the very low level of the threshold monetary amount required for appeal to the court of appeal and beyond. The experience of other labour court systems in severely restricting appeals is relevant in this regard.

2. Germany

37. The labour court system with the greatest range of jurisdictional competence is probably the German system. The labour courts in that country are exclusively competent to deal with virtually all legal disputes arising out of the employment relationship (with the exception of those concerning social security for which there is another specialized judicial forum).[22] The German system has come to be considered a model. The labour courts of Israel, among others, were fairly closely modeled on the German system.[23] And a number of the east and central European countries, in restructuring their industrial relations systems, adopted aspects of the German labour court system as they moved to a market economy.

38. As opposed to the French *conseil des prud'hommes*, and in common with almost all labour court systems, the German labour courts are tripartite. The system comprises three levels: those of first instance and appellate labour courts, both at the state (*Länder*) level, and the Federal Labour Court. Since the reunification of Germany, the 94 labour courts of first instance have grown in number as additional courts have been established in the eastern region.

39. Both at the lower labour court and appellate labour court levels, the courts comprise two lay judges, one each from employers' and trade union circles, and a 'professional' judge as chairperson. At the Federal Labour Court level, three professional judges sit with the two lay judges. The lay judges are selected at all levels from lists submitted by the trade unions and employers' associations but are not answerable to those organizations in the performance of their judicial duties as members of the court. Professional judges at the labour court and appellate labour court levels are appointed with the participation of a tripartite advisory committee on which representatives of the trade unions and the employers' associations sit. At the

---

22. The labour courts also have exclusive competence to deal with certain disputes in connection with the Works Constitution Act, including most disputes arising out of enterprise-level co-determination.
23. In Israel, the labour court system has even wider competence than in Germany in that social security rights also come with its purview.

federal level the trade unions and employers' organizations do not officially play any role in the designation of the professional judges.[24]

All judges, lay or professional, have a decision-making role, and all decisions are by a majority. This means that it is possible at the *Länder* level for the lay judges to out-vote the professional judge. However, in practice, the professional judge normally dominates the procedure and the decision-making process. The parties may represent themselves or be represented by a representative or an attorney at the first two levels. At the Federal Labour Court level an attorney is required.[25]

40. As in the French system, there is normally an initial effort at conciliation made by the court.[26] This is done by the chairperson alone at a preliminary hearing. If conciliation proves unsuccessful, the case continues before the full court, usually several months later. The procedures in the labour court are somewhat simplified as compared with those before the ordinary courts, and efforts are made to finish the hearing in one sitting. Further, in response to the criterion of due dispatch, the decisions are in principle announced immediately following the completion of hearings before the court.[27] On an average, some two thirds of the cases submitted to the lower level labour courts are disposed of within three months (at that level, and including those resolved by conciliation).[28]

41. Appeals to the appellate labour court are allowed on matters of law and fact. The relative ease of appeal means that some one fourth of all decisions of the labour courts are appealed to and heard by the appellate labour courts.[29] Appeals to the Federal Labour Court are only permitted by leave of the Court, which in principle must be granted if the appellate court decision is counter to the *stare decisis* of the Federal Court. The Federal Labour Court limits its review to the legal issues, relying on the findings of fact of the lower courts.[30] Obviously, as cases go through the appeals stages, the length of time for final decision increases. Estimates indicate that the great bulk of cases that reach the Federal Labour Court take more than one year to decide. And a total time lapse of over three years for a case going through all the echelons would not at all be unusual.[31]

42. While grievance procedures within the enterprise (which may involve the works council) are not unknown and, indeed, are sanctioned by the Works Constitution Act, formal procedures do not seem to be very much in evidence in

---

24. *See generally* M. Weiss, *Labour Law and Industrial Relations in the Federal Republic of Germany*, Deventer, 1987, pp. 96–101.
25. *Ibid.* at p. 98.
26. Indeed, conciliation is obligatory under the law. *See* D. Neumann, 'Federal Republic of Germany' in W. Blenk (ed.), *European Labour Courts: Current Issues*, Geneva, 1989, p. 19.
27. *Ibid.*, p. 20. In exceptional cases the decision, under the law, may be announced 'within a very short time after the hearing.' *Ibid.*
28. *See* O. Sköllerholm, 'Sweden', in Blenk, *op. cit.*, p. 75.
29. *See* M. Weiss, S. Simitis and W. Rydzy, 'The Settlement of labour Disputes in the Federal Republic of Germany', in Hanami and Blanpain, *op. cit.*, p. 104.
30. *Ibid.*
31. *Ibid.*, 105.

Germany. In any event, their existence would not preclude an aggrieved worker complaining of a denial of his or her rights from bringing the case directly before the labour court. The labour court cannot in any event be deprived of its jurisdiction by any privately negotiated arrangements. As a practical matter, rights disputes arising within the enterprise, if not settled through informal and *ad hoc* arrangements, will virtually always go to the labour courts.

3. Sweden

43. Our third and final example of a labour court system is that of Sweden, which is fairly representative of the Nordic countries in general. The Swedish court, as that in Norway and Denmark, is competent to deal only with disputes arising out of the application and interpretation of collective agreements and matters touching on the legality of industrial action. Other rights disputes are brought before the ordinary courts. In all of these countries (which of course are far smaller than France or Germany) there is, territorially, a single labour court. (Although in Norway there is provision for local county or city courts to act as labour courts in cases of local disputes, the provision is rarely utilized in view of the national reach of collective agreements.) There are certain cases in which, the Swedish court hears appeals from lower echelons of the ordinary courts, but generally the system is one of a single instance.

44. Given the jurisdictional competence of the labour court in Sweden, and as opposed to the situation in France and Germany, only the trade unions and employer associations (or individual employers) who are signatory parties to the collective agreement involved in the dispute can bring suit before the court. It is also possible, in the rare cases where the employee concerned is covered by the relevant collective agreement, but not a member of the signatory union, but rather a 'minority' union, for the latter union to bring suit in the labour court on behalf of that employee.[32]

45. As in Germany, and the bulk of the countries concerned, the Swedish court is tripartite. The lay members of the court are chosen on the recommendation of the trade unions and employers' associations (including those in the public service). All members, lay and professional, have a vote in taking decisions (which require a simple majority). Typically, the court sits with seven members. Four members represent equally the labour market parties (although not acting in a partisan capacity) and the three remaining judges are 'independents', comprising two professional judges and – a rather unique feature – one non-lawyer who is particularly knowledgeable of labour market conditions. The judge-like quality of all members of the court is reflected in the fact that unanimous decisions are reached in some three quarters of the cases before the court.[33]

---

32. *See* O. Sköllerholm, 'Sweden', in Blenk, *op. cit.,* p. 75.
33. R. Fahlbeck, 'Sweden' in 9 *Comparative Labor Law Journal*, 1987, p. 190.

46. In pre-trial action, the court can attempt conciliation where it thinks agreement with regard to the subject of litigation is possible. It can also instruct the parties to negotiate, or continue negotiations outside of the court, where it thinks that these have been insufficient, the parties having the right to return to the court if they are unsuccessful.[34] Procedures during the trial follow closely those of the ordinary courts, and it would seem that there is somewhat less flexibility and informality in procedures than is found in the practice of labour courts elsewhere. At the conclusion of the hearings the court sets a date for the decision, usually four to eight weeks later.[35]

47. As noted above, certain cases, for example where the union fails to press a case before the labour court on behalf of an employee, can be brought before the lower ordinary courts by the aggrieved employee himself. An individual employee covered by the relevant collective agreement who is not a member of any union may also bring his case before the lower ordinary courts.[36] In such cases, the labour court can exercise appellate jurisdiction. Otherwise the labour court is one of original and final jurisdiction.

48. Agreed final and binding arbitration of rights disputes arising out of collective agreements is countenanced by the law in Sweden and the labour court (or other courts) will not entertain cases subject to resolution through such arbitration.[37] Nevertheless (and even though bilateral grievance procedures are common) arbitration is very rarely resorted to.[38] This may indeed reflect the status of the labour court and the high esteem in which it is held by the social partners.

IV. HIGHLY SPECIALIZED TRIBUNALS AND BOARDS

A. *In General*

49. This review of the various judicial and quasi-judicial bodies dealing with labour disputes concerning rights would not be complete without a reference to those bodies constituted to ensure the application of a limited area of specific legislation. Under this heading, and as examples, we may examine the British system of industrial tribunals, as well as the United States and, incidentally, the Canadian and the Japanese labour relations boards, which examine complaints of unlawful unfair labour practices. In all these cases, an important distinction from the labour courts and ordinary court systems for the adjudication of rights disputes is that the bodies concerned exist to enforce specific measures of legislative protection for the industrial relations parties.

---

34. *See* A. Bouvin, 'The Court Procedure in Labour Disputes in Sweden' in Essenberg, ed., *Labour Courts in Europe*, Geneva, 1986, pp. 55,56.
35. Sköllerholm, *op. cit.*, p. 36. In dismissal cases four to six months seem to be the norm. *Ibid.*,p. 76.
36. Bouvin, *op. cit.*, p. 53.
37. Bouvin, *op. cit.*, p. 53.
38. Fahlbeck, *op. cit.*, p. 97.

B. Specific Countries

1. Great Britain

50. The industrial tribunals in Britain were originally established in the 1960s to assume exclusive jurisdiction with respect to complaints under new legislation concerning mainly termination of employment – redundancy payments and unfair dismissals (the latter being by far the great majority of cases to come before the tribunals). Later, with the adoption of legislation on equal pay and sex and race discrimination, the tribunals were given competence in these areas as well. They also have competence with regard to a limited number of other statutory rights (constituting less than two per cent of the caseload).[39]

51. The some 70 industrial tribunals, which form part of the British administrative law system, exist throughout the country. They are composed of the chairperson, who is an experienced barrister or solicitor, assisted by two lay persons. The latter were traditionally appointed from lists submitted by the leading trade union (TUC) and employers' (CBI, at the time) organizations, although more recently the government was to make selections for the lay members of the tribunals from a wider field, while adhering to the principle that members had to be representative of the two sides of industry and experienced in industrial relations.[40] All members have an equal voice; it is interesting that, as noted with regard to other tripartite labour court systems and in spite of the partisan background of the lay members, they nevertheless show great impartiality, with over 90 per cent of decisions being unanimous.[41]

52. The industrial tribunals have an official conciliation function. However, conciliation may be provided prior to tribunal proceedings by the state Advisory Conciliation and Arbitration Service.[42] Proceedings before the industrial tribunals were conceived as being informal, with no need for lawyers in what were thought of as peoples' courts. Over the years there has been an increase in representation, including by lawyers. In any event, the tribunals are masters of their own procedures and these procedures remain far more relaxed and simple than those obtaining in the ordinary courts in Britain.[43]

---

39. *See* Lord McDonald, 'Industrial Tribunals in the United Kingdom' in Essenberg, *op. cit.*, pp. 60–62.
40. Sir John Wood, 'Procedural Aspects – United Kingdom' in W. Blenk, ed., *European Labour Courts: Industrial Action and Procedural Aspects*, Geneva, 1993, pp. 101,102.
41. *See* J. Wood, B.A. Hepple and T.L. Johnson, 'United Kingdom' in *Comparative Labor Law Journal*, Vol. 9, No. 1, 1987, p. 204.
42. *See* R. Singh, 'Dispute Resolution in Britain: Contemporary Trends, in 16 *International Journal of Manpower*, No. 9, 1995, pp. 45–47. Singh notes that individual conciliation under ACAS auspices was had in over 65,000 cases in 1994. *See also* K. Mumford, 'Arbitration and ACAS in Britain: a Historical Perspective, in 34 *British Journal of Industrial Relations*, 1996, pp. 287 ff.
43. Wood, Hepple and Johnson, *loc. cit.* 'However, recent reports on the functioning of the Industrial Court system indicate a systematic failure to fully achieve its objectives of cheapness, accessibility and, particularly, speed'. Singh, *op. cit.*, p. 49, referring to a report of 1993 and a 'Green paper' of 1994.

53. Appeals may be taken from the industrial tribunals, on questions of law only, to the Employment Appeals Tribunal (EAT). The EAT, like the tribunals, is tripartite, with the lay members selected in the same manner as described above for the tribunals. The President of the EAT is a High Court judge. The other 'legal' members are also High Court judges or their Scottish equivalent. The EAT having the status of a High Court, further appeal (on questions of law) could lie to the Court of Appeal and the House of Lords.

2. United States

54. In the United States the National Labor Relations Board (NLRB), in addition to certain other functions,[44] is a quasi-judicial agency which rules on actions brought by trade unions or employers in the limited field of alleged violations of the opposite parties' legal obligations under the National Labor Relations Act (as amended). These involve essentially what are termed unfair labour practices, which may be committed by employers or unions, proscribed by the Act. These include employer practices that operate to deny workers the right to organize and bargain collectively. Examples are dismissals for union membership or activity, employer support of workers' organizations with a view to dominate such organizations, and failure to bargain collectively in good faith, to state just a few in a very simplified manner. Employer allegations of unfair labour practices might also cover refusal to bargain in good faith as well as a number of types of industrial action, and union restraint or coercion of employees in various domains. Action before the NLRB in respect of unfair labour practices can be initiated by a union, employee or employer.

55. The NLRB consists of five members, all 'independent', appointed by the President for a fixed term. Thus, as opposed to the composition of the labour courts we have examined, there is neither a statutory nor other requirement to maintain any form of tripartite structure. In fact, appointments to the NLRB are viewed as highly political although the appointees are usually lawyers with some grounding in labour matters. The NLRB acts mainly as an appellate body in unfair labour practice cases, hearing appeals from administrative law judges, sitting alone, who serve under the aegis of the NLRB and as part of the system under the National Labor Relations Act. It is generally acknowledged that the processing of unfair labour practice complaints is unduly slow, a contributing factor undoubtedly being the legalistic and formal nature of the procedures. Even with a decline in case load during the 1980s and 1990s, the median time for processing cases was well over one and a half years. This does not include the additional time involved in possible further appeals to the courts.

56. Decisions of the NLRB may be appealed to the federal courts of appeal and, eventually, to the US Supreme Court; in both cases on questions of law. Moreover, the NLRB cannot enforce its own decisions. It must apply to the courts for enforcement

---

44. E.g., the NLRB plays a key role in supervising the election of employee representatives (i.e. the choice of trade union).

orders (which constitutes a limited avenue of appeal for dissatisfied litigants) if voluntary compliance is not had.[45]

3. Canada and Japan

57. The treatment of statutory unfair labour practices by specialized quasi-judicial bodies whose operations are largely limited to this area is found in Canada (federal and provincial levels) and Japan (in the form of local labour commissions and the Central Labour Commission)[46] as well. While there are many similarities in the three countries, there are also quite significant differences in both substance and procedure.

V. ARBITRATION

58. Arbitration as used here is understood to mean a procedure and mechanism for settling disputes through a final and binding decision or award made by an independent and neutral third party.

59. We have already noted that in a number of countries, alongside the ordinary courts and the labour courts, private arbitration of labour dispute concerning rights are countenanced and sometimes utilized. But in none of the countries does it constitute a major vehicle for resolution of rights disputes. On the other hand, in the United States and Canada, private and voluntary arbitration is the overwhelmingly principal means of resolving disputes arising out of the interpretation, application or violation of collective agreements. (The province of Quebec does have a labour court system, but arbitration is still the institution preferred for settling rights disputes arising out of collective agreements.)[47] It is the practice of these two countries that will be discussed below.

60. In both countries arbitration is closely linked with and viewed as the culmination, or subsequent, or the final stage, of the grievance procedures contained in virtually all collective agreements. These in-plant procedures are normally bilateral and end, within the enterprise, with a managerial determination which an aggrieved worker, through his trade union, can bring to arbitration.

As regards the grievance procedure proper, there is no single definition of the term. 'Grievance' could have a wide meaning in a given collective agreement, encompassing any question relating to the employment situation about which the

---

45. For a detailed examination of the NLRB and its functioning with regard to unfair labour practices, *see*, e.g. B.J. Taylor and F. Witney, *Labor Relations Law*, Englewood Cliffs, 1987, pp. 171–186, 216–218, 221–228.
46. For the operation of the Japanese commissions *see* Sugeno, *op. cit.* and particularly, chapter 5.
47. In Canada, at the Federal and provincial (with one exception) levels, the parties to a collective agreement are required to include in the agreement a clause providing for arbitration without work stoppages of disputes arising out the interpretation or application of that agreement; in the absence of such clause and in the event of a dispute, the government can designate, or require the parties to select, an arbitrator. It should be noted that disputes not based on collective agreements, and excluding illegal unfair labour practices, will be heard by the regular courts (as in the US) except in the province of Quebec.

employee or trade union is unhappy. More commonly, the term connotes a complaint of treatment inconsistent with the provisions of the collective agreement. In any case, it is only the latter type of grievance, being based on a definite and definable right emanating from the collective agreement which, in normal practice, could be carried to arbitration.

61. An understanding of the functioning of the arbitration systems requires an examination of the role of the trade unions. In both Canada and the United States, the trade union chosen by a majority of the workers concerned exercises exclusive representation rights for all of those workers in the given bargaining unit. Bargaining by the employer or employers with any other union, or directly with the employees concerned, would be unlawful. The union thus has control of the bargaining process and hence of the grievance and arbitration procedure in the collective agreement that it negotiates. As long as the union acts in good faith with its members – the duty of fair representation – the union can decide whether or not to process a grievance through its final stages and, more particularly, whether to submit an unresolved grievance to arbitration.

62. The linkage between work stoppages, the collective agreement, and the arbitration process is also of prime importance. In Canada, strikes (or lockouts) concerning the application, interpretation or violation of a collective agreement during the term of that agreement are forbidden by law. In the United States well over 90 per cent of collective agreements contain clauses prohibiting strikes (or lockouts) during the currency of the agreement. Some one-half of these provide for an absolute 'peace' obligation while others call for a more 'relative' peace obligation (meaning, for example, that while the agreement is in force strikes would not be permissible on issues that are already part of the agreement). It is clear that arbitration clauses are a sort of *quid pro quo* for the peace agreement.[48] Indeed, a final and binding arbitration clause in a collective agreement will be deemed to imply a no-strike (and no lockout) agreement.[49]

63. Arbitration may take many forms. It may be *ad hoc* in the sense that the parties will choose an arbitrator, as necessary, in particular cases. Somewhat less prevalent is the case where a permanent arbitrator (often called an 'umpire' or 'impartial chairperson') is named in the collective agreement. Arbitration of rights disputes may be in the hands of a single arbitrator or, less frequently (at least in the US), of an arbitration panel which is usually, but not necessarily, tripartite. In essence, the parties are free to choose whatever procedures and features they wish and can agree upon.

64. The use of pre-agreed umpires or impartial chairpersons is more frequent in the very large enterprises or in the case of industry-wide agreements. And it must be recalled that permanency is relative. Just as the parties by mutual agreement can reopen their collective agreement prior to its expiration, so can they decide to change

---

48. This view has been expressed by the US Supreme Court. *Textile Workers* v. *Lincoln Mills*, 353 U.S. 455 (1957).
49. Local 174, *Teamsters Union* v. *Lucas Flour Co.*, 369 U.S. 95 (1962).

the agreement's provision which designates by name or quality a particular arbitrator. This being said, an advantage of the permanent named arbitrator is that he/she acquires an in depth knowledge of, and familiarity with, the parties and particularly of the operation and problems of the enterprise or industry he/she is serving. The quality of decision making may be thereby enhanced. Moreover, it is not unusual for the permanent arbitrator to act, unofficially, in a mediatory role favouring an agreed settlement of the issue in arbitration. Also, where there are recurrent cases, consistency of treatment can be enhanced. And such arrangements can be more economical of time and energy since otherwise the selection process and the scheduling of the arbitrator can be arduous and long.

65. As indicated above, the majority of arbitration arrangements in US collective agreements provide for *ad hoc* arbitration. Arbitrators are chosen on a case-by-case basis. They may be less familiar with the parties and their problems and thus rely more on a strict interpretation of the language of the agreement provisions underlying the issue or issues being arbitrated. As a corollary, *ad hoc* arbitrators rarely would attempt to conciliate the parties and, indeed, such attempts might well be resented.

66. Whether *ad hoc* or permanent arrangements are opted for, the parties must decide if they wish to have a single arbitrator or a panel or board hear and decide the case. Where the latter obtains, there is normally a neutral chairperson and one or more persons representing or named by each side. The 'partisan' members usually have voting rights, and decisions of the board is normally by majority vote. The role and attitude of the partisan members varies from one of purely judicial to one of advocacy. They may play an active role in the hearings, or defer to the chairperson in questioning witnesses and ordering the proceedings. The role of preparing the written decision is normally that of the chairperson, the partisan members usually being free to dissent, sometimes giving their reasons and commenting.

67. Under US practice, in cases where the parties must choose an *ad hoc* arbitrator, recourse is generally had to the assistance of the Federal Mediation and Conciliation Service or the American Arbitration Association (a private institution), both of which keep carefully screened rosters of qualified arbitrators. A typical practice is for the parties to receive a list with an odd number of names from one of these services; each party may strike a name from the list alternatively until only one name is left. One or the other side might wish to strike a name in view of past arbitral awards made by that person with which the striking party is familiar and disagrees, or for other reasons which need not be expressed. If both parties agree that no name on the list is appropriate (which would be quite unusual), a new list of names may be requested.[50]

68. In Canada, the parties choose to submit some seventy-five per cent of their cases to arbitration by *tripartite boards*. Pursuant to the statutory base for rights

---

50. For a discussion of arbitrator selection, *see* E.E. Herman, A. Kuhn, and R.L. Seeber, *Collective Bargaining and Labor Relations*, 2nd ed., 1987, pp. 396–397. *See also* F. Bairstow, 'Grievance arbitration in Canada and the US', in W. Kaplan, J. Sacka, and M. Gunderson (eds), *Labor Arbitration Yearbook*, Toronto 1993, pp. 86–88.

arbitration in Canada, and unlike the US, the decision of the chairperson will become the decision of the board if there is no majority view, unless the parties have expressly agreed otherwise. But it should be recalled that the provisions agreed by the parties must, under most of the applicable law, involve a final decision.

69. Agreements to arbitrate, as well as the arbitral awards, are final, binding and enforceable in the US. But recourse must be had to the courts for such enforcement if one of the party refuses to comply with its contractual obligation to arbitrate, or with the award. The arbitrator has absolutely no legal powers of his or her own to enforce the awards he or she renders.

On the basis of a line of Supreme Court decisions over the years, the federal or state courts must refrain from intervening in the substance of the arbitral process provided for by collective agreements. Any doubts regarding the issue of 'arbitrability' are resolved in favour of the arbitral process. And the courts can never substitute its own judgment for that of the arbitrator. Judicial review, usually when enforcement of the arbitral award is sought, is limited to the question of whether the arbitrator has exceeded his jurisdiction, i.e. the mandate given to him by the parties. The courts may not reverse an award on the basis of what it may believe to be an error of fact or law.[51]

70. Canadian judicial practice seems to be somewhat different. In principle, and statutorily, arbitral awards are final and binding but the courts appear to hold to their traditional practice of intervention and non-deference to the arbitration process. The courts tend to exercise what they consider to be their inherent jurisdiction to look into the substance and merits of the case, sometimes in the name of natural justice (among other perhaps more understandable grounds such as fraud, bias, excess of jurisdiction, and the like).[52]

71. As regards the actual conduct of arbitration proceedings, there are of course no stated rules. As opposed to the manner in which most of the labour courts operate, the arbitration hearing, particularly in the US, is normally a fairly informal affair, the parties and the arbitrator(s) sitting around a table. Of course formal rules of procedure, including rules of evidence need not apply, although there are certain requisites for ensuring decorum, a proper development of the evidence and a general logic of case presentation. Thus, there will always be a certain analogy with courtroom procedures. These are all in the arbitrators' hands. And it must be remembered that there are many arbitrators who are not lawyers and who do not have legal training.[53] While the arbitrator normally has no power to *subpoena* witnesses or documentary evidence,

---

51. For a review of the question of the role of the courts, *see* M. Berger, 'Judicial Review of Arbitration Awards' in *Hofstra Labor Law Journal*, Vol. 10, No. 1, Fall, 1992, p. 245 ff. and particularly pp. 295–297.
52. *See* (with some special reference to Quebec) R. Gagnon, L. Lebel, and P. Verge, *Droit du Travail*, 2nd ed., Ste. Foy 1991, pp. 712–716.
53. In the United States, while there are many full-time professional arbitrators, there are probably more who are actively exercising other professions. Generally, we find that arbitrators are university professors from economics and other faculties, perhaps more so than from law faculties. Retired public officials (not necessarily lawyers) and clergymen are two other sources from which arbitrators are drawn.

it is clear that the recalcitrance of party to provide evidence will work against the interests of that party in the arbitral decision-making process.

72.   There are heard complaints of a 'developing excess' in formalism, sometimes referred to as 'creeping legalism' encroaching on the process of arbitration. While this is probably true, it nevertheless is uncontested that grievance and arbitration processes under collective bargaining – as a most prominent feature of industrial relations in the US and Canada – are widely appreciated by the parties and are regarded as one of the more successful aspects of industrial relations in the two countries.

73.   There is another aspect of arbitration to which reference should be made. In the process of collective bargaining, it sometimes happens that vague or ambiguous language is deliberately used to cloud over an issue on which the parties are unable to reach real agreement, but which they do not consider so vital as to risk a breakdown in negotiations and a possible work stoppage. They are willing to rely on an arbitrator's decision at a later date, should the issue result in a grievance. Here, we detect a limited example of the convergence of rights and interest arbitration. But more than that we see a constructive role for the arbitrator who, by attempting under the guise of seeking the parties' original intent as to the meaning of the provision, may actually function as a mediator in effecting an agreement on an issue that the parties were unable to agree upon in collective bargaining.

74.   In spite of the fact that the union 'owns' the grievance, under the statutory duty of fair representation, the union must not unreasonably refuse to bring an unresolved grievance to arbitration (even if the aggrieved employee is not a member of the union). However, the aggrieved employee's fate remains largely in the hands of the union, as an allegation of breach of the union's duty of fair representation is not easy to establish and, moreover, the costs to the employee could be considerable. And, of course, should the arbitration lead to an award unfavourable to the employee concerned, owing to the inefficacity of the union's representation or otherwise, there is no recourse as the award of the arbitrator is final and binding.

There have been a number of recent cases in the United States on the question of whether grievances or other complaints that are based both on alleged violations of statutes (particularly anti-discrimination legislation) at both state and federal levels, and involve the interpretation, application or violation of collective bargaining provisions, are to be subjected to the arbitration procedure or to the normal statutory procedures before the courts or agencies established to administer such statutes. An example would be a dismissal, allegedly based on race contrary to both the 'just cause' provisions of the collective agreement and to anti-discrimination legislation. It would appear, although many sub-issues are still in doubt (with conflicting court decisions) that subjection to arbitration (and even an arbitral decision) would not preclude recourse by the concerned employee to the statutory redress provided, i.e. before the courts or specialized quasi-judicial bodies.[54]

---

54.   For a recent review of this question, *see* M. Delikat and R. Kathawaler, 'Arbitration of Employment Discrimination Claims under Pre-Dispute Agreements: Will Gilman Survive?' 16 *Hofstra Labour and Employment Law Journal*, 1998, p. 83 ff.

75.   There are certainly other problems with the system of arbitration of unresolved grievances. One, that of increased formalism, has already been noted. But on another level, and not concerning the system as such but rather the industrial relations situation in the US and to a lesser degree in Canada, arbitration is by definition relevant only to those covered by collective bargaining.[55] Given the low ratio of workers covered by collective agreements – less than 20 per cent in the US – most employees enjoy less protection against economic risks and unfair treatment than do workers in most industrialized countries. Nevertheless, the system of arbitration of disputes concerning rights under collective agreements, in addition to being considered worthwhile by the parties, seems to fit well with the economic, political and social environment of the US. And it is rather surprising that in a country with a traditionally high level of adversarialism in its industrial relations, as well as strong disagreement as between organized labour and management as to basic principles of social protection (long accepted by all parties in other industrialized market economies), nevertheless there is a common consensus that collective agreements should be for a fixed term and legally binding, that industrial action during the term of a collective agreement should not take place, and that unresolved grievances should be referred to final and binding arbitration.[56]

VI.   REMEDIES IN RIGHTS DISPUTES: TWO EXAMPLE

76.   This chapter is meant to deal generally with procedures and mechanisms for resolving conflicts of rights. However, there are two areas of particular substantive interest when considering the handling of rights disputes through certain, if not all, of the procedures and institutions discussed in this chapter. These are remedies in cases of unjustified termination of employment of workers at the initiative of the employer and, secondly, remedies, particularly temporary or interim relief, for employers in cases of allegedly unlawful strikes. In the case of termination of employment, it will be noted that, for a great many of the courts, boards, tribunals, commissions, etc., this is the preponderant item on their case load. Moreover, dismissals can involve situations that threaten either the morale of the workplace or the possibility of evolving or maintaining sound labour–management relations. At the same time the need to adjust the size and composition of the workforce in the face of a changing and increasingly competitive economy is widely recognized. In the case of the delicate area of strikes, the economic implications for the enterprise or industry are apparent.[57]

---

55.   It should be noted however that there has been a thus far small but significant trend towards grievance arbitration in a non-union setting. This is normally employer-initiated and permits grievances under works rules and disciplinary procedures to be carried to arbitration. *See* e.g. R. Bales and R. Burch, 'The future of employment arbitration in the non-union sector' in *Labor Law Journal*, Oct. 1994, pp. 627–635. *See also* R. Heenan, *Wrongful Dismissal of Non-Union Employees*, (current issues series) IRC Press, Kingston, 1992. A voluntary 'due process protocol' was developed in the mid-1990s in the United States which seeks to ensure fair procedures in respect of this type of alternate dispute settlement and, in particular, cases involving alleged statutory violations. See A. Zack, 'Can ADR Help Resolve Employment Disputes?' in 136 *International Labour Review*, 1997, p. 95 ff.

56.   *See* B. Aaron in the fourth edition of this volume, 1990, pp. 256–257.

57.   The issues of racial, gender and other discriminatory practices, as well as more recently sexual harassment have lately become very significant in the domain of (statutory) rights disputes. *See*, e.g. special issue of the *Canadian Labor and Employment Law Journal*, Vol. 3, No. 1, Dec. 1994.

A. Termination of Employment

77. Either legislative or collectively bargained protection, against unjust dismissal is provided in virtually all industrialized economies. Where this protection results from the provisions of collective agreements, then protection is obviously limited to those employees covered by the agreement.[58] A major point of contention has been the nature of the remedy for unjust dismissals, particularly, since the remedy must serve the double purpose of indemnifying the employee concerned and deterring such dismissals. Criminal penalties excluded, the two remedies available are re-instatement with back pay or compensation.

78. In Germany, Sweden (as well as in Denmark and Norway), and the United Kingdom, for example, the judges have a certain discretion as between the two possible remedies. However, in some of these countries, such as Sweden, the re-instatement remedy will not be awarded if the employer objects or, as in the case of Germany, if the labour court finds that it is unreasonable to assume that the parties can cooperate in the future. In Britain re-instatement will be awarded unless it is 'inappropriate'. In such cases, compensation will be awarded. In other countries, save in exceptional cases, compensation would be the rule. Where re-instatement is granted, it is usually accompanied by a monetary award to make up for lost wages and, where appropriate, restoration of seniority is ordered.

79. Arbitral practice in North America, as well as that of the NLRB and the Japanese labour relations commissions, is to award re-instatement almost automatically in cases where the dismissal is found to be unjustified or an unfair labour practice. Even in the European context where compensation might be the more usual remedy, it is common to award re-instatement in cases of dismissal for reasons of trade union membership or activity. In these cases the concern is to preserve the integrity of trade union centred industrial relations and to prevent employers from ridding themselves, for a price, of trade union elements they find annoying.[59] In the eyes of many commentators, the existence and utilization of the re-instatement remedy is key to a real protection of workers against unjust dismissal.

---

58. In the US there is no federal system (other than in cases of discrimination defined in statutes), and only one state affords general statutory protection, concerning unjustified dismissals. Virtually all collective agreements accord such protection but, as noted earlier, collective agreements cover a relatively limited portion of the workforce. In this context the doctrine of 'employment at will' still predominates. Nevertheless, some limited inroads on the doctrine have been made by courts, basing their decisions on contract (implied) or tort theory. In the US there is a 'model uniform Employment Termination Act' published in 1991 by the National Conference of Commissioners on uniform state laws. Both the model law and that of the state of Montana give preference to arbitration to resolve such termination disputes. In Canada there is recent legislation protecting employees against unjust dismissal at the federal and provincial levels. In both cases disputes arising under the legislated protection are subjected to arbitration (as opposed to labour courts or ordinary courts as is largely the case elsewhere). See Kaplan et al., op. cit., pp. 103–114.
59. For a more detailed review of the question of re-instatement, and the wider question of the treatment of termination cases by labour courts, see Blenk, op. cit., 1989, p. 47 ff.

B. Remedial Measures for Illegal or Unlawful Strikes

80. In some industrialized market economies no strike would be illegal, unlawful or enjoinable, because of either constitutional or legislative dispositions. However, in most of the countries concerned, resorting to strike action contrary to the provisions of industrial peace obligations (dictated by agreement, legislation or jurisprudence) or without fulfilling prior procedural requirements (e.g. notice periods, exhaustion of conciliation procedures, etc.) would be illegal or unlawful. Here we will limit our consideration to the role of labour courts and their jurisdiction to rule in questions of strikes,[60] and we will stress the use of interim or provisional measures, i.e. temporary injunctions. This is a vital but problematical sphere of action since the courts (or other bodies) can determine, by the position they take, the ultimate outcome of what is essentially an economic and not a juridical conflict. This is because where even temporary relief is granted and the strike is later found to be lawful or legal, the injunction may well have broken the strike by stifling the momentum that had built up and discouraging the workers concerned. It is very difficult in most cases to simply resume the strike at a later stage. Thus judges generally do, or should, approach applications for injunctions with caution and circumspection.

81. Interim measures may be applied for in many countries. This would not be the case for Finland where the labour court is barred from entertaining such applications. However, in practice, the court will hear the case expeditiously and finally decide on the legality of the strike in a question of four to six days. Given that many strikes last only a few days and can be effective in that limited period, there is some discussion in Finland aimed at reviewing the ban on interim injunction orders.[61] The situation is not dissimilar in Norway where it is felt that interim measures may be superfluous since the labour court will deal with the matter definitively within 48 hours.[62] In other countries, as a matter of judicial policy, temporary injunctions are available but, for the reasons mentioned above, are rarely used.

82. Where they are used, the court will normally make its decision balancing the various interests at stake. This would mean, in particular, weighing the degree of damage to the employer, enterprise or industry in question (including, possibly, a consideration of the capacity of the trade union to respond in damages should the strike be illegal) if the preliminary injunction is refused, as against the effect on the position of the trade union and the workers involved should the injunction be granted and the strike later be found legal. This is frequently a very delicate balancing act, made more difficult for the court by the fact that a decision must be taken almost immediately.

---

60. In some countries with labour court or similar systems, it is nonetheless the ordinary courts which are competent to deal with injunctive relief in case of strikes. This is the case for example in Britain where industrial action is explicitly excluded from the jurisdiction of the industrial tribunals.

61. *See* Blenk, 1993, *op. cit.*, p. 11. However it would not seem that any legislative changes have yet been made in this area. *See* J. Pelkonen and P. Orasmaa, 'Finland' in Trebilcock, *European Labourt Courts: Remedies and Sanctions in Industrial Action; Preliminary Relief* (Geneva), ILO, 1995, p. 14.

62. Blenk, 1993, *Ibid.*

83. The above examination of labour disputes concerning rights can only be considered cursory at best. The differences in treatment of such disputes both in terms of the fora available (often multiple) and the conceptual limits and diversity itself of the notion of rights disputes, not to mention the substantive treatment of such disputes in legislation and by the various courts, tribunals, boards, commissions, etc. which deal with them, are certainly the subject of a far longer and more comprehensive comparative effort than is reflected in this chapter.

SELECT BIBLIOGRAPHY

B. Aaron (ed.), *Labor Courts and Grievance Settlement in Western Europe*, Los Angeles, 1971.

American Arbitration Ass'n, *The Future of Labor Arbitration in America*, New York, 1976.

R. Blanpain (ed.), *International Encyclopaedia for Labour Law and Industrial Relations*, (loose leaf), Vols 1–24.

W. Blenk (ed.), *European Labour Courts: Industrial Action and Procedural Aspects*, Geneva, 1993.

A. Bronstein and C. Thomas (eds), *European Labour Courts: International and European labour standards in labour court decisions, and jurisprudence in sex-discrimination*, Geneva, 1995.

T. Hanami and R. Blanpain, (eds), *Industrial Conflict Resolution in Market Economies*, 2nd ed., Deventer, 1989.

B. Hepple, 'Labour Courts: Some Comparative Perspectives', University College London, Faculty of Laws, *Working Papers*, No. 6, 1987.

Chapter 25. Settlement of Disputes Over Interests

A. Goldman

I. Overview of Models for Interests Disputes Settlement

1. Employment interests[1] disputes involve differences concerning what obligations the parties should have toward each other or to third parties as a result of the employment relationship. To a considerable degree, the processes of employee representational participation, discussed earlier in this book, serve to avoid disputes over interests. This chapter examines and compares eight basic models for the resolution of such disputes when they do arise. These models are:

(a) Acquiescence in Unilateral Action;
(b) Governmental Fiat;
(c) Political Discipline;
(d) Adjudication;
(e) Voting;
(f) Negotiation;
(g) Conciliated Negotiation; and
(h) Prestigious Exhortation.

Each of these dispute resolution models has variations in structure. Though each model at times is used independently to resolve an interests dispute, at other times two or more are involved either simultaneously or sequentially in dispute settlement. In broad terms, these models can be described as follows.

A. *Acquiescence in Unilateral Action*

2. Some would argue that Acquiescence in Unilateral Action is not a model for interests dispute settlement but rather represents the absence of such disputes. However, the failure of a party to assert displeasure concerning employment interests

---

1. Although many writers use 'interest' in the singular to describe such conflicts, the plural is used here to avoid confusing the term with the alternative meaning of 'interest' – a rent paid for use of capital. Also, the plural reflects the reality that the obligations of an employment relationship are multifaceted.

does not necessarily mean that that party is satisfied with the nature, level, or distribution of those interests. Acquiescence in Unilateral Action occurs if the acquiescing party either does not have a way to influence the resolution of those differences, or does not wish to expend the time, energy or resources required to alter the result. Accordingly, the differences do not go unresolved; they are resolved, but the resolution results from one side submitting to the other's dominance, or accepting the other's initiative.

B. Governmental Fiat

3.   An essential characteristic of every social unit is the ability to establish, alter, and enforce behavioural norms. Societal units have greater ability than do individuals or informal groups to achieve adherence to norms because, in addition to inducements, social units generally can legitimately resort to a variety of coercive techniques including manipulating psychological ties of group loyalty. When all members of a social unit are committed to conformity with a particular behavioural norm, we can speak of that norm as a law or a rule of governance.

4.   The norms established and maintained by social units sometimes are the product of prior exercises of individual autonomy to which others have acquiesced and which have developed into a generally imitated pattern of behavior. Such patterns are known as customs or tradition. Other norms are determined at the discretion of those who control the prerogatives of the societal unit. For our purposes, when imposed by those responsible for exercising the social unit's prerogatives (e.g. the legislature or the executive branch of government), establishing or modifying a social unit's behavioural norms is the exercise of the Governmental Fiat model for conflict resolution.

C. Political Discipline

5.   In some political systems, the coercive power of the state treats nonconformity with the controlling political party's doctrine as a crime against the state itself. The political party, thereby, wields the power of Governmental Fiat. Even in pluralist political systems, a prevailing political party asserts tangible influence to the extent that it can offer economic opportunities. Generally, such patronage benefits are available to the party in power with respect to at least some government jobs. Also, often some employment opportunities with government owned, controlled or influenced enterprises are reserved for members of the dominant political party. Opportunities to do business with the government similarly may be reserved for loyal supporters of the party in power. Generally, beneficiaries of such patronage are expected to comply with the dictates of those who control the party. The party's influence over its members also may be enhanced by the psychological and ideological ties of the alliance. Whatever the source of that influence, the party's ability to control its members' conduct constitutes its power of Political Discipline.

D.   Adjudication

6.   Adjudication is the model by which one or more independent individuals having no direct personal interest in a dispute rely on settled principles to impose a resolution upon the interested parties. Employment disputes over interests are adjudicated by a variety of entities including courts of justice, specially structured labour courts, administrative agencies, and arbitrators. The latter term refers to a process in which, typically, the impartial tribunal that decides the dispute is selected either by or with the participation of the disputing parties.

E.   Voting

7.   Voting is a format for collective self-determination by which each interested participant makes an unequivocal choice from among specific alternatives. Essentially, it is a fact-finding method for recording individual preferences. Because Voting requires that the issue be defined before the choices are made, it almost always is utilized in conjunction with other models of interests dispute resolution.

F.   Negotiation

8.   Negotiation is the process by which two or more parties through some form of explicit or implicit communication mutually resolve to alter, or refrain from altering, the relationship between or among themselves, or with others, or their relationship with respect to an object or group of objects. The process involves clarifying issues, exchanging information, exploring alternative settlements, examining the consequences of not settling, persuasion and mutual accommodation. It covers a broad range of formats. In Germany, for example, the term 'bargaining' is used to connote a settlement reached under pressure of a work stoppage. Clearly, though, this process is Negotiation. The term 'co-determination' is used in Germany to connote settlements reached through the deliberations of works councils, and of supervisory boards having joint representation. However, applying our description of the dispute resolution model, it is clear that these institutions, too, largely rely on Negotiation in reaching their decisions.

9.   As previously noted in this book, there is an uncertain line between consultation and Negotiation. In its pure form, consultation aims at dispute avoidance. It accomplishes this through the exchange of information and persuasion that results in unilateral acts of accommodation. However, if that exploration fails to avoid the dispute, and if the issue is not reserved for unilateral resolution, consultation is readily transformed into Negotiation.

G.   Conciliated Negotiation

10.   When negotiating parties are unable to agree, impartial third parties sometimes try to assist the negotiators in reaching a settlement. The resulting Conciliated

Negotiation can involve the third party serving as a communications conduit or may serve in the more active third party role of making fact findings or suggesting formulas for agreement. In the area of disputes concerning employment interests, government agencies often offer or mandate the aid of mediators or conciliators.[2]

H.   Prestigious Exhortation

11. Determinative guidance for conflict resolution sometimes is provided when highly respected persons or institutions offer hortatory suasion; that is, urging, encouraging, and earnestly recommending conduct that is regarded as laudable. Such exhortations succeed because the decision makers wish to adhere to a predictable, normative course of conduct or a course of conduct that will be perceived as wise, responsible, and equitable by the decision makers or those to whom the decision makers are responsible.

II.   ACQUIESCENCE IN UNILATERAL ACTION

12. Market enthusiasts argue that the ultimate determination of employment interests should be regulated by the law of supply and demand operating in a free market. The underlying assumption is that, in the absence of interference with the movement of workers, those who seek to labour will move to jobs offering more favourable employment benefits and that management will provide those benefits necessary to attract and retain a workforce of the size and ability that will result in it profiting from the employment of its least productive worker. As the supply of labour increases in relation to the demand, competition for jobs enables management to reduce employment remuneration; when the supply decreases in relation to the demand, competition for workers forces management to increase employment remuneration. In the first instance, the market places management in the dominant position so that workers must acquiesce; in the second situation, labour is in the dominant position and it is management that must acquiesce. Thus, to the extent that there is a competitive market system for establishing work benefits, it is an example of Acquiescence in Unilateral Action.

13. Most market theorists recognize that, at least in industrially advanced societies, considerable economic effort is directed toward avoiding the free play of market forces. One reason is that a free market generates a good deal of waste through duplication, another is that the risk of miscalculating future market fluctuations increases, in a wholly competitive system, and that increased risk impairs investment

---

2.   The terms 'mediation' and 'conciliation' are used interchangeably in many countries and are so used here. Some national systems, however, distinguish between the terms. In Britain and Japan, for example, 'conciliation' refers only to efforts to assist in communications while 'mediation' refers to the additional effort of formulating and proposing suitable settlement terms. In contrast, in Denmark conciliation is used for the more intrusive, rather than the less intrusive, third party role. *See also* A. Roo and R. Jagtenberg, *Settling Labour Disputes in Europe*, Deventer, 1994, pp. 24–28.

in research, development, and capital re-allocation. Still another reason is that market competition for labour often produces results that do not satisfy the community's concepts of social justice. Although those who find ethical virtue in the law of natural evolution (survival of those most fit to survive) may take some comfort from the impact of the free market upon those who labour, even the theory of evolution recognizes that the best can fall victim to random or idiosyncratic events. In contrast, those who adhere to competing concepts of social justice often seek to alter, control, or eliminate the competitive market for labour. As Harry Arthurs has observed: '[A]ll complex relationships – not the least those concerned with work – give rise to explicit and implicit systems of governance ... which make life more tolerable to those who live within them.'[3]

14. In some economies, Acquiescence in Unilateral Action resolves many interests disputes, despite the attempted imposition of settlements by Governmental Fiat. Thus, it has been observed that in developing countries, 'violations of the minimum wage rate are very frequent, especially in those areas, where, because of budget limitations, inspection of the Labour Department is almost impossible as in the cases of small businesses or employment of ... domestic workers.'[4] This problem exists in developed economies as well. For example, in the USA and elsewhere, illegal aliens in particular often acquiesce in accepting wages below the rate required by law or by the employer's collective agreement.[5]

Privileged workers, too, often acquiesce in accepting terms of employment other than those officially established by law or by contract. An example is the employee who, in conformity with the norms of the establishment, demonstrates personal dedication and industriousness by not scheduling allotted paid annual leave time.[6]

15. Many labour relations systems exclude various classes of employees from collective bargaining. In such situations, differences respecting employment interests often are settled using the model of Acquiescence in Unilateral Action. Thus, in Canada and the United States, those exercising managerial decision-making authority, including shop floor supervisors, and persons who work directly under those who formulate the enterprise's labour relations policies, are excluded from collective bargaining. As a result, generally such workers acquiesce in the benefits unilaterally bestowed from above or seek other employment.[7]

Similarly, as a result of being excluded from minimum wage standards adopted by Governmental Fiat, many domestic and agricultural workers in countries as diverse

---

3. H. Arthurs, 'The Collective Labour Law of a Global Economy' in *Labour Law and Industrial Relations at the Turn of the Century: Liber Amicorum in Honour of Roger Blanpain* at 143, 161–62, 1998.
4. R. Alburquerque, 'Minimum Wage Administration in Latin America', 6 *Comp. Lab. L.J.* 57, 65, 1984.
5. R. Alburquerque, 'Minimum Wage Administration in Latin America', 6 *Comp. Lab. L.J.* 57, 65, 1984.
6. *See* for example, K. Sugeno, *Japanese Labor Law* (L. Kanowitz, trans.), Seattle/Tokyo, 1992, pp. 277, 278, 280, 281 for discussion of efforts to combat this pattern among Japanese workers.
7. In the US, at top levels of management of large corporations, compensation levels have become absurdly inflated. This indicates that in such instances acquiescence is by the shareholders, not the managers. To date, legal efforts to curb these excesses have had little success. *See* discussion at A. Goldman, 'Potential Refinements of Employment Relations Law in the 21st Century', 3 *Employee Rights & Employment Pol. J.* 269, 286–89, 1999.

as the USA and the Dominican Republic, among other nations, can be expected to settle interests disputes largely by Acquiescence in Unilateral Action.

16. The Acquiescence in Unilateral Action model is available, too, in situations in which workers are collectively represented. Legal rules may impose the requirement of Acquiescence in Unilateral Action with respect to some types of decisions. Although labour law systems differ respecting which decisions are recognized as areas of unilateral managerial authority, such 'managerial prerogatives' typically involve matters of finance, investment, pricing, and marketing.[8]

Acquiescence in Unilateral Action also functions as a method of resolving interests differences where the law allocates bilateral decision making authority. To illustrate, shop floor workers through informal collective action frequently set a work pace which goes unchallenged by management. With the passage of time, such unilaterally established practices may come to be regarded as customs recognized by the common law of the shop and, therefore, are subject to modification only through contractually negotiated changes or a new pattern of unilaterally adopted conduct in which there is acquiescence.[9] In a like manner, in a country in which shop floor rules must be co-determined by management and a works council, often, a new work assignment policy is discussed with the works council and is then instituted in the absence of the council's opposition, or in the absence of its emphatic opposition.

17. In those labour relations situations in which one side plays a wholly dominant role, whether as a result of the structure of the legal relationship, the great imbalance in economic positions, or through physical or psychological coercion, the model of Acquiescence in Unilateral Action constitutes the principal method for resolving interests disputes. At most, the dominated party's participation in the outcome is limited to calling attention to the existence of its desires concerning the particular employment interest. In law or effect the worker in such a subservient position is in a property type relationship with the employer.

When labour is treated as property, the subservient employee is unlikely to seek legal relief by resorting to the Adjudication model, even if such relief is available in theory. He is unlikely to seek enforcement of any applicable Governmental Fiat because he lacks the bargaining leverage to enter into Negotiations. Thus, the subservient worker can merely plead his differences and accede to the unilateral solutions imposed by a dominating employer.

18. Either through internal law, ratification of international conventions, or both, most nations have outlawed slavery. However, the most complete property-type employment relationship, the system of owned workers, has not been totally eradicated. The dowry system practiced in parts of the Asia, Africa and the Indian subcontinent has been characterized as a slavery-like system, and exploitation of prostitutes in developed as well as developing economies has been similarly characterized. Debt

---

8. T. Hanami and R. Blanpain, *Industrial Conflict Resolution in Market Economies*, Deventer, 1984, pp. 11–12.
9. L. Haiven, 'Past Practice and Custom and Practice: Adjustment and Industrial Conflict in North America and the United Kingdom', 12 *Comp. Lab. L.J.* 300, 314–17, 1991.

bondage, or peonage, and caste bondage, though outlawed, still exists in India and other countries. In South Africa, for several decades the system known as Apartheid severely limited the economic opportunities of non-whites and thereby converted their market position into what was characterized as a 'collective form of slavery'.[10]

19. Although penal labour is rationalized as rehabilitative or an extension of the wrongdoer's social responsibility, often it is contracted out and becomes an exploitive substitute for paying below legally established minimum or market influenced wages.[11]

20. Because of their reduced ability to resist domination, children are ready victims of imposed subservience including activities involving sexual exploitation. Legislation at the international as well as national levels designed to protect young workers are not always enforced, generally do not attempt to provide protection beyond the early stages of puberty, and frequently make exceptions for employment within family enterprises.[12]

21. For the most part, rules of substantive law prohibit workers from placing management in a subservient position. Accordingly, as a general rule workers who seize the authority for determining the operations of a seagoing vessel, can anticipate severe punishment for the crime of mutiny. Similarly, seizing control of a business establishment in the form of a sit-in, sit-down, or work-in action is an illegal trespass in Belgium, France, Italy, and the USA, among other nations, and is unlawful under some circumstances even in Japan, where an especially broad range of industrial actions is tolerated.[13] Nevertheless, there are situations in which employees can, through the exercise of economic dominance, dictate a settlement of differences regarding employment interests and anticipate employer acquiescence in the result.

Examples of employee dominance are sometimes encountered in the rules of conduct adopted by professional organizations or craft rules adopted by a trade union as an internal regulation of its membership. A very different form of worker domination is the Indian tactic of gheraos in which a human blockade of workers isolates the managers from all amenities and sustenance until they accede to the workers' demands. Although illegal, the tactic apparently persists.[14]

22. In every labour relations system one can find evidence of some reliance upon Acquiescence in Unilateral Action for settling interests disputes. As a method of dispute resolution, this model has the virtue of efficiency. The result is reached promptly with a minimum of resources required to permit the model to function. Also, it can be tailored to meet the needs of the particular situation; at least as perceived by the

---

10. L. Betten, *International Labour Law: Selected Issues*, Deventer, 1993, pp. 135–44 provides an overview. Also, C. Johri, IELL (India), 1998, paragraphs 124, 689–94 and D. Ziskind, 'Forced Labor in the Law of Nations', 3 *Comp. Lab. L.* 253, 1980.

11. L. Betten, *above*, at pp. 151–55.

12. L. Betten, *above*, at pp. 301–11.

13. *See* K. Sugeno, *Japanese Labor Law* (L. Kanowitz, trans.) Seattle/Tokyo, 1992, pp. 559–67 for a description of the range of tolerated industrial actions.

14. C. Johri, *IELL* (India), 1998, at paras 649–51.

dominant party. One drawback is that the level of the underlying discontent is likely to remain undisclosed until such time as the dominated party is prepared to sever the relationship or resort to violence in an effort to reverse the roles. Another drawback is that the unilaterally imposed solution, while tolerable, may not be the most advantageous settlement for either side because it is unlikely that there has been full utilization of the process of deliberation, rationalization, and information exchange by all affected or informed parties.

III. GOVERNMENTAL FIAT

23. Governments often stand ready to enforce norms established by custom and tradition. The Anglo-American systems refer to this as common law, but the practice is found in other legal systems as well. To illustrate, in France the period of required dismissal notice beyond the statutory minimum, if not specified by collective agreement, is determined by the customs of the locality or the industry. In Israel an employee's right to receive advance notice of discharge is wholly derived from custom. And, Treu explains that in Italy 'custom can be applied when legislation and collective agreements are lacking and, if it is more favorable to the workers, it can prevail over non-imperative provisions of law (not over provisions of collective agreements).'[15] Thus, as a form of unwritten law, custom often prevails as a surrogate for the active exercise of Governmental Fiat.

24. Governmental Fiat normally takes the form of a formal document such as a statute, decree, or regulation. As is illustrated by the above reference to custom in Italian labour law, Governmental Fiat does not always preclude a different settlement by means of some other model for settling interests disputes. Even when Governmental Fiat is supposed to prevail over all other determinations, the parties may find ways to evade or avoid the law or may be guided by some other norm of conduct as a result of lack of knowledge of the law.

25. Often Governmental Fiat is used to structure the relationship between workers' representatives and enterprise management. For example, in the USA the collective bargaining system is structured largely by statute. In Belgium, the collective bargaining structure under which workers' interests are represented by the 'most representative organizations' (the Christian, the Socialist and Liberal union organizations) is recognized by a legislative act. In contrast, the Danish system of collective bargaining operates without legislative management of its structuring. Both in the case of Belgium and the USA, the legislative enactments formalized and expanded approaches that largely had become customary. Similarly, Governmental Fiat often provides the structure and procedural rules for other dimensions of the industrial relationship such as works councils, grievance, machinery, and co-determination.[16]

---

15. T. Treu, *IELL* (Italy), 1998, para. 50.
16. *See*, for example, F. van Waarden, 'Government Intervention in Industrial Relations' in *Comparative Industrial & Employment Relations*, London, 1995, at pp. 116–125 (J. Van Ruysseveldt, R. Huiskamp and J. van Hoof, eds).

26. Perhaps the most characteristic of all employment interests disputes are those concerning remuneration. The role played by Governmental Fiat in settling such disputes in any particular nation provides considerable revelation concerning the nature of that labour relations system. Compare, for example, the legal requirement that workers receive a minimum of five or more weeks of paid annual leave in countries such as Austria, Denmark, Finland, France, Spain, and Sweden, with the absence of any mandated paid annual leave in the United States.

27. Minimum wage laws and laws requiring overtime differentials are common. The underlying dispute resolved by such laws is the competition between management's goal of higher profits and the collective interest of workers in being shielded from market forces that might otherwise drive wage levels down to or below survival standards. In more prosperous nations minimum wage laws usually leave actual wage adjustment to the Negotiation and Acquiescence in Unilateral Action processes so long as the result is no less advantageous than the minimum standards established by the government. In some instances, such as Germany, there is legislative authority to establish minimum wages but, with the exception of the construction industry, that authority has not been exercised. Still other prosperous nations rely on minimum wage legislation to protect workers who lack union representation or to reshape wealth and employment distribution. Thus, minimum wage and overtime differential legislation is pervasive in the USA, where the federal standard is sometimes supplemented by even more protective state regulations. Although the minimum wage level sets the pay for only a small portion of the American workforce, overtime pay requirements have a direct impact on most non-managerial employees. Similarly, in France Governmental Fiat imposes restraints on the amount of overtime that can be worked, and socially conscious adjustments in the minimum standard have affected national wealth distribution.

28. One might expect to find government imposed minimum wage standards prevalent in developing countries inasmuch as other interests dispute settlement models are unlikely to provide an effective barrier to exploitation of large numbers of desperate workers. On the other hand, the presence of those same large numbers of desperate workers leads to wide evasion of government standards. As a result of these conflicting forces, the extent to which Governmental Fiat has been used to establish minimum wage standards in developing economies is quite varied. For example, in India minimum pay standards have been established by judicial decree as well as by state administered regulations which vary according to job, industry and region. However, often workers are unaware of the existence of such protections. In addition, the enforcement machinery is inadequate, especially in rural areas.

29. As an interests dispute settlement model, Governmental Fiat holds out the promise that the result will accurately reflect society's notions of moral and economic justice. In addition, if the government functions efficiently and honestly, its prestige and power in support of the settlement provides economic stability and predictability respecting anticipated costs of labour. Also, because the governmental decision makers often have no personal stake in the interests dispute, there is enhanced opportunity for an objective, rational result that serves the needs of the total community, not just those of the interested parties.

On the other hand, Governmental Fiat is a cumbersome process if carried out with responsibility, objectivity and reason; too cumbersome to deal with more than a small fraction of the interests disputes that arise in the course of a nation's employment relations. Also, Governmental Fiat can become arbitrary or corrupt. Even when operating in a reasoned, honest manner, government decisions typically are most responsive to those elites that are strategically best positioned as a result of superior organizational skill, special knowledge, or happenstance.[17] In addition, it is a relatively inflexible device that is unable to adjust to special or momentary needs. Often it can deal effectively with questions of broad principle but not with problems requiring responsiveness to minute detail or frequent variation. And, settlement imposed by Governmental Fiat is unlikely to satisfy either side if the authorities do not enjoy the disputing parties' trust. Moreover, globalization has placed substantial constraints on political willingness to disadvantage local competitiveness through regulations and standards aimed at social welfare improvements. Finally, a settlement imposed by Governmental Fiat does not add to the parties' skill in developing or sustaining a harmonious relationship.

IV. POLITICAL DISCIPLINE

30. The Political Discipline model for conflict resolution is not confined to political entities. It is available to other partisan alliances whose foundations are ideological, emotional, economic or opportunistic. Labour and business entities can use Political Discipline to gain their goals within a political party as can partisan factions functioning within a labour or business organization. In addition, Political Discipline is an especially important model for interests dispute resolution in those nations in which a single political or religious alliance is the exclusive reservoir of collective authority. (Such nations, however, are beyond the scope of this book's examination.)

31. In many countries there is a strong link between one or more political parties and various labour organizations. In Denmark the Social Democratic Party and the major federation of national unions are closely related. Each organization has representatives on the other's governing bodies. The link between the Labour Party and the central union federation in Britain is less formal than in Denmark, but a regular liaison is maintained. About half of the member unions of the British Federation are affiliated with the Labour Party and constitute a critical voting block in determining party policies. The link between the New Democratic Party in Canada and Canadian unions is perhaps even stronger and comparable links generally are found in European countries.

A different sort of interrelationship is found in Israel where, in much the same way as they compete for election to the national legislature, the numerous political organizations vie for their candidates' election to the National Convention of the Histadrut, the dominant labour federation.

---

17. L. Betten, 'The Role of Social Partners in the Community's Social Policy Law-Making' in *Labour Law and Industrial Relations at the Turn of the Century: Liber Amicorum in Honour of Roger Blanpain* at 239, 1999.

32. Employer and managerial organizations also have the potential for exercising the Political Discipline model. Members often share common ideological and economic ties and can wield patronage power in the form of willingness or unwillingness to engage in business with one another or alert each other to business opportunities with others. These organizations are likely to carry influence within the more conservative political parties, and are prone to be more cooperative in carrying forward the programs of such parties when they are in power.

33. Political Discipline can also influence seemingly bilateral employment relations decisions. Thus, it has been observed that the representatives of supervisory personnel, a component of the employee delegation on supervisory boards in Germany, are far more inclined to share the views of management than are other employee representatives.

34. The most obvious opportunity for Political Discipline to serve as a model for interests dispute settlement is in shaping employment and labour relations policies imposed through Governmental Fiat. To illustrate, the Industrial Relations Act adopted in Britain in 1971 sought to modify the very structure of labour–management relations as well as alter, to some degree, the parties' respective power positions. The Act had the support of employers organizations and the Conservative Party, which was in power. However, it was opposed and resisted by most unions. The Trade Union and Labour Relations Act, adopted by the Labour Government when it had regained power in 1974, repealed most of the 1971 reforms.

35. A different sort of example of the Political Discipline model for settling interests disputes is found in the employment of some local government workers in the United States. By working diligently in the campaigns for the election of local officials, and soliciting the votes of relatives and friends, government workers in many localities have made their support an essential element in any serious candidate's election effort. These 'loyal' supporters then have special claims upon the elected officials' highly sympathetic consideration of the workers' position respecting their employment interests.[18]

36. Similarly, the choice of bargaining demands, which a labour or employer organization makes, can reflect the dispute settlement model of Political Discipline. Thus, if the goal of the partisan group, whether allied with labour or with management, is to create an atmosphere of harmony, controversial issues might be avoided, or dealt with in vague or incomplete ways. Whereas, if the goal is to create or aggravate an atmosphere of crisis or a sense of ineffectiveness, then positions can be adjusted to serve that purpose. This is illustrated by the posture taken by Australian unions in connection with the 1983 federal election. The government imposed a wage-freeze several months prior to the election. Although the labour unions

---

18. Such activity often violates statutory and constitutional prohibitions against political favoritism in government employment or statutory regulation of government worker contributions to political candidates. *See* Rutan v. Republican Party of Illinois, 497 *US* 62, 1990, and US Civil Service Commission v. National Association of Letter Carriers, 413 *US* 548, 1973.

opposed the freeze, they refrained from industrial actions so as to avoid creating an issue that would weaken the Australian Labour Party's campaign prospects. When the Labour Party prevailed at the polls, the union continued to exercise restraint; this time, in order to give their political allies breathing space in establishing the new government.

37. Another example of Political Discipline as a method of settling interests disputes is the impact of the Zaikai in Japan's economy including the resolution of labour–management disputes. Zaikai is a group representing the leaders of Japan's financial institutions, employer associations and other business organizations. It is said that together 'with several informal clubs of influential business leaders they are believed to make and break governments.'[19] Through the Zaikai, employers influence government as well as employer representatives in the tripartite deliberations that shape economic planning and public–employee relations. Japanese employer associations additionally have had some success in closing ranks and coordinating employer responses to Shunto, the labour movement's annual coordinated 'Spring Offensive' collective bargaining demand for higher wage levels in enterprise and industry collective agreements.

38. At the plant level, Political Discipline is likely to play an important role in those labour law systems that require the establishment of elected employee representation on a works council. For example, in Germany, where the works council has significant authority and influence over the quality of work life, unions expend considerable effort to ensure that the elected councilors are union members. Only with the presence of that alliance can the unions coordinate their collective bargaining and co-determination efforts to maximize the prospects of implementing their policies.

39. Depending upon the respective political influence of the parties, and the strength of a political party within the economic and social system, Political Discipline can be a central or an inconsequential model for settling employment disputes. It can have the virtue of expediency and of promoting social harmony. But it can as easily have the vice of confusing employment interests with other social and economic concerns, and can promote settlements that lack economic or social rationality, that are inflexible, and that give too little consideration to the needs of affected persons who are not part of the controlling alliance.

V. ADJUDICATION

40. One distinguishing feature of interests dispute settlement through Adjudication is the assumption that the result will be a principled decision. A variable in the adjudicative process, therefore, is the nature and source of the guiding principles. Should they reflect only the goals of the disputing parties or should they reflect the broader concerns of social and economic policy? The answer in some

---

19. S. Levine, 'Employer Associations in Japan', in *Employer Associations and Industrial Relations*, J. Windmuller and A. Gladstone (eds), 1984, pp. 318, 324, 326–27, 343–45, 353.

countries is to attempt to provide public policy oriented guidelines. For example, in Israel, an arbitral decision is supposed to be guided by 'fairness' and 'justice'.[20]

41. Another variable in the Adjudication model is the structure and source of the impartial members of the tribunal. Frequently such people are professors or retired high ranking civil servants. Often they have had legal training. In some systems, such as Australia and some Canadian provinces, the adjudicators are full-time government employees who are specifically assigned this responsibility. In Germany, where appointment is made by the parties, most commonly, the impartial adjudicators are labour court judges.

42. When discussing Adjudication of interests disputes, one must begin with the foremost example of Australia and New Zealand where for most of the 20th Century Adjudication was a central mechanism for resolving interests disputes. New Zealand's system of comprehensive interests arbitration was abandoned in large measure in 1984 and totally abandoned in 1991. During the early 1990s a majority of Australian States and the Federal Parliament significantly reduced the role of Adjudication of interests disputes and by 1996 the remaining states had similar changes under consideration. Perhaps most significant, in early 1996 national elections were won by a political coalition committed to further reduction of the role of Adjudication in resolving employment interests disputes.[21] Although compulsory interest arbitration may soon be a relic of 'down-under' history, it continues to warrant examination both because rejuvenation remains a possibility and because this unique structure endured longer than most other legal structures regulating labour-management interests disputes resolution in advanced economic systems.

43. In Australia, because of its federated structure and the significant role that state governments play in much of the employment relations area, the available Adjudication machinery varies depending upon which set of laws control a particular employment relationship. Yerbury and Isaac divide the various arbitral tribunal structures into three classes: curial types, tripartite boards, and a mixture of the two.[22] The curial type bodies are presided over by legally trained judges assisted by lay members called commissioners. These tribunals operate with greater formality than the tripartite boards which consist of equal representatives from each side and are presided over by a neutral. Whatever the tribunal, its awards are enforceable in the manner of legislative enactments.

Up to the early 1990s, interests disputes could be brought to an arbitral tribunal either on the initiative of a party or through the tribunal's own intervention. Once the

---

20. R. Ben-Israel, *IELL* (Israel), 1994, para. 521.
21. For a sketch of these historic changes *see* R. McCallum, 'The New Millenium and the Higgins Heritage: Australian Industrial Relations in the Twenty-First Century', keynote address, 8th Nat'l Convention, Indus. Rel. Soc'y of Australia, 16 Feb. 1996; B. Brooks, 'De-regulating the Labour Market: Reflections on the New Zealand Experience' and M. Vranken, 'Labour Law Deregulation and the Australian Workplace Relations Act of 1996', in *Labour Law and Industrial Relations at the Turn of the Century: Liber Amicorum in Honour of Roger Blanpain* at 651, 823, 1999.
22. D. Yerbury and J. Isaac, 'Recent Trends in Collective Bargaining in Australia', in II *Collective Bargaining in Industrial Market Economies*, 1973, pp. 173, 176.

arbitral process was initiated, the parties generally negotiated a settlement, with or without the aid of government conciliators. However, negotiated settlements often were submitted for award certification since only certified arbitration awards were judicially enforceable. Applications for such consent awards were rejected if the Commission found that they would be contrary to the public interest. Arbitration awards of the Industrial Relations Commission were binding on all employees and employers in the classification defined by the award regardless of whether their representative organization, if any, was a party to the dispute. At various times the Commission defined the public interest as requiring consideration of labour market flexibility, employment growth, comparative worth, monetary stability, price stability, and foreign competition.

Changes introduced in the early to mid-1990s vary by jurisdiction but included allowing collective agreements to be enforced without tribunal approval, restricting the subject matter scope of tribunal authority, and confining awards to the enterprise. In the case of a couple of states and employment that comes within federal jurisdiction, subject to commission oversight designed to ensure against bargaining away employee advantages, the amended laws permit employers to enter directly into 'workplace agreements' with individual employees or with the workforce. That is, to establish agreements without negotiating with a union.

44. In Canada, several provincial governments as well as the federal government require parties when they reach an impasse to submit to binding third party resolution in the negotiation of an initial collective agreement. In a couple of provinces the administrative agency that supervises labour–management relations serves as the Adjudication tribunal. Specially selected tripartite boards or single arbitrators serve this function in the other jurisdictions.[23]

With respect to its own workers, the federal government in Canada requires the representative union to elect, prior to commencing negotiations, whether impasses will be resolved by conciliation, subject to an ultimate right to strike, or by compulsory arbitration by a tribunal consisting of a labour and a management representative, plus an impartial member drawn from permanent panels. About half of all provincial government workers in Canada are subject to arbitration mechanisms in the event of collective bargaining impasses.

45. Bargaining impasses in Greece may be resolved by Adjudication by an Administrative Arbitration Court consisting of judges together with employer and union representatives. The dispute initially is heard and decided by a First Level Administrative Arbitration Court whose decision is subject to review by a Second Level Administrative Arbitration Court.

46. In the US interests arbitration was encouraged and sometimes required in the railroad industry early in the 20th Century. Since then it has played a minor role in

---

23. Assessments of the limited effectiveness of first contract impasse arbitration in Canada as a means of developing a long term collective bargaining relationship are summarized in S. Estreicher, 'The Dunlop Report and the Future of Labor law Reform', 12 *The Lab. Lawyer* 117, 128–29, 1996.

non government labour relations. At times it has been available by contractual arrangement in a few industries, including steel, and is used to resolve impasses concerning the individual compensation rates for athletes in some professional sports. In contrast, interests arbitration is widely used in the employment relations of government workers. Impasses in collective bargaining for American postal workers, for example, must be submitted to arbitration if fact finding and conciliation efforts fail. The mandated arbitration procedure requires each side to designate an arbiter with a third selected by those two arbitrators. The parties equally share the costs and have the right to adopt an alternative procedure by mutual consent.

A variety of interests arbitration formats have been adopted as mandatory settlement procedures for state and local government workers in the USA. A few state courts reject such legislation on the ground that it violates the constitutional prerogatives and responsibilities of executive and legislative officers. Where it has survived judicial scrutiny, mandatory arbitration, sometimes, is limited to certain groups such as police and fire fighters. A few states use a tripartite format while others provide for an award by a single arbiter. In some instances the tribunal must choose between each side's final bargaining offer package, while in other jurisdictions, the tribunal must separately choose between each side's last offer with respect to each disputed issue. A format used in some states requires the arbiter to select from among the parties' last offers or the fact finder's recommendation to the parties. (Fact finding and conciliation generally are earlier mandated stages of the procedure under these state laws.) Other American states allow the arbitrator to shape the award without restriction respecting the parties' bargaining positions but often subject to a statutory list of criteria to be weighed as the basis for decision.

Several studies attempt to assess the impact of interests arbitration upon government employee labour relations in the USA. One observation is that while collective bargaining continues to be the dominant model for resolving such disputes, even when arbitration is available, some parties become dependent upon arbitration if available. An explanation for this dependence is the presence of special problems regarding the parties' respective power positions and political or personal pressures. In any event, the difference in results between negotiated settlements and arbitral awards does not appear to be very great.[24]

47. Collective agreements in Switzerland often provide for arbitral resolution of impasses concerning interests disputes that arise during the life of the agreement and are not covered by the terms of the agreement. In some cases this includes wage rates or inflation adjustments. Typically, both the employers' organization and the labour organization select arbitrators who in turn select an impartial presiding arbitrator. The impartial tribunal member is a judge. Awards are subject to judicial review only if they suffer from serious arbitrariness.

48. Many nations have policies that give preference to Adjudication machinery that is established by the disputing parties. For example, in Germany the parties shape the mechanism for resolving works council disputes and make every effort to

---

24. P. Feuille, 'Selected Benefits and Costs of Compulsory Arbitration', 33 *Indus. & Lab. Rel. Rev.*, 64, 74–76, 1979.

reach a settlement even when the mechanism for adjudicative resolution has been initiated.

49. In most national systems, Adjudication is seldom or never used to resolve interests disputes. Even when it is available, its greatest impact is not in its actual use but in the impetus it gives the parties to find their own solutions rather than become the victim of the third party's 'wisdom'. This is illustrated by the Swedish newspaper industry where, for over fifty years, by agreement the parties were required to submit deadlocked negotiations to arbitration. Nevertheless, they managed to reach mutual agreement on all but one occasion.

50. Acceptance of the Adjudication model for settling interests disputes largely results either from a desire to avoid an alternative of prolonged economic warfare, or avoid work stoppages by those who provide important public services. The Adjudication model, even when applied through the generally informal processes of arbitration, is relatively time consuming because the arbiters need to be appointed, or at least notified, the issues must be framed, and the decision makers must be educated concerning the competing contentions and considerations. In addition, to the extent that there are neutral principles to be applied, at best they are vague. There is always the danger, too, that the 'impartial' party will harbor secret biases or will reach an impractical solution.

On the other hand, because social or economic justice is not a precise science, no particular dispute resolution mechanism is innately superior to the rest. Therefore, the benefit of having a method available to definitively resolve the parties' differences often outweighs the disadvantages and dangers of relying upon an impartial third party's imposed decision. Unresolved interests differences are costly when they create open economic warfare; they are costly, as well, when they fester in the form of uncertainties or repressed discontent.

VI. VOTING

51. Although Voting is a fact finding process, the facts that are found can be influenced by the choice of procedural variables for structuring the process. One such variable is the choice of those who will participate: the electors. Another structural variable is the degree of secrecy of the ballot. Still another is the choice of the time and place for balloting. The result can be influenced, too, by the manner of phrasing the question to be decided, by the number or proportion of votes needed to resolve the question or selection, and by whether the ballot is open or secret. Finally, the method of counting and weighing ballots are additional variables that can affect the outcome.

The most obvious use of voting to settle interests disputes is in the determination of who will represent those interests. Representatives to works councils, safety and health committees, shop-stewards, negotiating committees, and the like, often are selected by a majority vote of the workers whose interests are affected by the conduct of those representatives.

52. In the less formal structures of shop level joint committees and autonomous work groups, Voting is likely to serve as the model for settling differences when the participants are unable to resolve them through Negotiation and are unwilling to allow them to be resolved through Acquiescence in Unilateral Action. Voting often is used in determining whether to resort to work stoppages and other actions respecting unresolved differences. For example, in the USA, a strike vote must be taken before a stoppage is allowed in a dispute found to pose danger of a national emergency.

53. When Negotiation is the principal model used for resolving an interests dispute, frequently the result is subject to a ratifying vote by the affected workers. This is the practice in Germany where rejection of the negotiated agreement is rare. Rejection is less rare in the USA where ratification votes generally are required under the labour organization's constitution or by laws. Finnish labour organizations, too, often condition their collective agreements upon approval by the membership. Conciliated settlements in Denmark can be submitted to the parties' membership for a ratification vote.

54. Voting provides an efficient means for ascertaining the preferences of interested parties and for enabling groups to be self-governing. Also, Voting gives every affected member a chance to participate in determining the outcome and in this way provides a sense of personal identification with the settlement. That personal identification can be expected to promote individual commitment to carrying out whatever settlement has been reached.

On the other hand, Voting involves regulation based upon power differences rather than the balanced, reasoned accommodation of competing and conflicting goals. Often minority interests are ignored, and the process is subject to manipulation by those who structure the balloting or the propositions to be decided. Also, it can be manipulated by controlling the information available to electors or by a well-organized, energetic minority that takes advantage of a complacent or poorly motivated, inadequately organized majority that fails to fully exercise the ballot or gives insufficient attention to the implications of how they vote. In the latter situations, Voting can be but a facade for the resolution of disputes through Political Discipline.

VII. NEGOTIATION

55. At the shop floor level, it is probably impossible to wholly eliminate at least some resort to Negotiation as a method of interests dispute settlement. In many systems, Negotiation is used frequently at all levels and the determination of whether and when to bargain and the subject matter of bargaining is left entirely to the parties' discretion. This essentially is the situation in Germany, Italy, Sweden, and Denmark, among other countries.

In the USA, in contrast, important details concerning bargaining procedure are regulated under the duty to bargain provisions of the National Labour Relations Act, and the potential subjects of bargaining have been classified by the courts into the categories of mandatory (either side may compel good faith discussion), permissive, and illegal.

56. Interests disputes can be divided into three classes: integrative, distributive, and mixed. Integrative disputes are those in which the parties' interests are not in conflict.

The dispute is of a problem solving nature: how can the mutual interests of the parties be best satisfied. Shop floor issues within a work group – such as how do we eliminate unnecessary effort, how do we avoid getting injured, how do we coordinate rest breaks, and the like – generally involve integrative interests. In contrast, distributive issues involve those situations in which the parties' interests conflict: one side's gain is the other's loss. Examples include: how much of an enterprise's income will be distributed in wages, how much will be reinvested, how much will be distributed to the owners, how much to the managers, and how much to the workers. The mixed category of interests disputes covers those situations in which there are both distributive and integrative elements. An example would be the issue of how to schedule annual paid leave days for each employee without shutting down operations.

57. The choice between settling a dispute by Political Discipline, by Governmental Fiat, or by Negotiation, may at times be affected by whether the nature of the dispute is integrative or distributive. As between the parties immediately involved, an integrative dispute is not likely to concern questions of economic or moral justice. Hence, there is little motivation for, and no principles to guide, settlement by Adjudication, Political Discipline or by Governmental Fiat. If the parties' efforts in Negotiation are unfruitful, however, there may be resort to an alternative means of settlement in order to allow them to resume a constructive relationship. Distributive issues, in contrast, largely involve questions of moral and economic justice. Therefore, if the labour relations system exists in a society which accepts non–*laissez faire* concepts of morality and community responsibility, intervention in settling those differences is more likely to be imposed by governmental or political authorities. Alternatively, as can be seen in many developing nations, those same authorities are likely to intervene, when influence over their conduct is concentrated in the hands of a small group with common interests who have no desire to make accommodations required in Negotiation.

58. The attitude of the parties toward the Negotiation process affects both the outcome and the availability of the method as a means of resolving interests disputes. In some nations there is a tradition of looking upon negotiating as an opportunity for the parties to accommodate their differences in a conciliatory and harmonious way. Among the advanced industrial nations, Japan probably is the prime example of such an attitude. Accordingly, many of the 'acts of dispute' utilized by Japanese workers in support of their bargaining demands are designed not so much to place economic or political pressure on the enterprise as to emphatically communicate the absence of harmony and need for further exploration and mutual adjustment.

In the USA, in contrast, there is a tradition of adversarial approach to the bargaining table. Although the intensity of that adversity probably is less today than it was 60 years ago, a common concern of the parties' representatives is that their constituents will question their integrity and dedication if the relationship begins to reflect too much accommodation and trust. Many observers have suggested that the US type adversarial approach at the bargaining table often is counterproductive.[25]

---

25. For example, T. Canova, 'Monologue or Dialogue in Management Decisions: A Comparison of Mandatory Bargaining Duties in the United States and Sweden', 12 *Comp. Lab. L.J.* 257, 1991.

59. Attitudes toward Negotiation can change with political and social trends. Thus, in Belgium for a long period after the Second World War, negotiations were approached with a considerable degree of mutual trust and willingness to compromise, but in recent years a more adversarial tone has come to characterize the relationship.

VIII. CONCILIATED NEGOTIATION

60. When negotiating parties have difficulty in adjusting differences through their own efforts, it often helps to introduce an outsider whose goal is to facilitate reaching agreement. At the least intrusive level of such intervention, a private outside party is invited by the negotiators to assist in efforts to communicate. More intrusive are those situations in which the third party is a government official whose presence is mandated. Still more intrusive is the third party whose assigned task is to make findings of fact respecting the matters at issue and report those findings to the parties or even to the public. Finally, there is third party intervention in the form of one whose responsibilities include proposing terms of settlement and who has the potential authority to impose those terms or invoke penalties if they are rejected. In the latter situations the process is more accurately described as 'leveraged mediation'.

Negotiated settlements ultimately turn on the parties' respective perceptions of the benefits of each side's offer, the benefits of the alternatives to agreement, the costs of past and future negotiating and the risks of error in assessing those costs, benefits, and prospects of performing what is promised.[26] Because mediation normally involves impartial intervention, observers often overlook the fact that its success is dependent upon altering the parties' perceptions and, thereby, altering their relative bargaining power. Leveraged mediation differs in that the intervener has the ability to alter the elements affecting bargaining strength and not merely the parties' perceptions of those elements.[27]

61. Mediation formats are quite varied. In Belgium, collective bargaining is carried on through a joint committee chaired by a civil servant. If joint negotiations fail, the parties convene in the form of a conciliation committee. The parties are equally represented and again are chaired by a civil servant but at this stage the latter's role is to actively seek agreement.

62. Denmark has a Public Conciliation Service consisting of three conciliators and an alternate. Each conciliator has responsibility for a particular bargaining sector. The Danish conciliator's role is very influential because the conciliator can propose a solution and require that the proposal be submitted for vote by the negotiating parties' memberships. Normally a conciliator does not submit questions to a

---

26. A. Goldman, *Settling for More: Mastering Negotiating Strategies and Techniques*, Washington, DC, 1991, pp. 6–25.
27. A. Goldman, 'Comparative Analysis of Labor Mediation Using a Bargaining Strength Model', 82 *Ky. L.J.* 939, 1994.

membership vote unless the parties' representatives have requested this action. The Service must be informed of bargaining disputes and the appropriate conciliator can intervene by request of a party. The conciliators are assisted by a corps of mediators who are assigned to aid the parties in negotiating differences of local interest. If unsuccessful, the mediator submits a written report to the conciliator who can then elect to intervene personally. The parties must jointly consent to the participation of a mediator, but this consent is rarely withheld if requested by the conciliator. Another feature of the Danish system that is encountered in some other countries (for example, Norway) is the prohibition against lawyers presenting the parties' positions to conciliators.

63.   In some countries, mediation is a product of contractual arrangements. Thus, in Germany in most industries the parties have established conciliation arrangements for dealing with impasses in industry-wide bargaining. Although there are a few examples of state sponsored conciliation in Germany, as a practical matter the only significant conciliation carried out is the unofficial intervention of high government officials in major industrial disputes.

Conciliation by political mediators is a significant institution in Italy where local government officials, including judges of prefect courts, as well as the Labour Ministry, intervene in local, national and enterprise bargaining by offering highly publicized settlement proposals. The accompanying public pressure, as well as the parties' frequent reliance upon government sponsored programs that aid economic and industrial adjustment, often forces acceptance of these third party proposals.

Similar, though less pervasive, examples of leveraged mediation by government officials acting through informal processes can be found also in systems as diverse as the USA, Sweden, and Israel.

64.   At the formal level, however, more typically mediation is a structure for making impartial assistance available at the parties' election. Ireland provides government conciliators to assist the parties if they desire. Similarly, voluntary conciliation by government mediators generally is available in the USA, Sweden, Australia, and elsewhere. Often, though, in particular categories of disputes, or at the discretion of a high ranking government official, the parties are compelled to submit to mediation efforts. In the USA one such situation is where the dispute involves a health care institution.

Conciliation is also compulsory in the USA for the railroad and airline industries, in government employee collective bargaining, and in situations in which a court, upon Presidential request, has issued a decree temporarily halting a strike found to threaten national health or safety.

Conciliation, normally by a member of the Labour Commission or its staff, is available in Japan at the initiative of the chairman of the Labour Commission or the request of either party. Most often it is requested by a union.

In India conciliation officers are entitled to intervene if there is a threat to industrial peace. They must intervene if a notice of strike or lockout is given and the dispute involves a public utility. Similarly, in Israel government conciliation may be imposed at the discretion of the Chief Labour Relations Officer if the parties resort to work stoppages. Once appointed, an Israeli conciliator is given some investigatory authority. Investigatory power is given to conciliators as well in Finland, Sweden,

Denmark, and India among other countries. Generally, information thereby obtained must be treated as confidential.

65. Formal structures for mediation sometimes include the possibility of leveraged mediation. Until recently, Australia provided a prime example because the legal enforceability of the parties' agreement was dependent upon its acceptance by the Conciliation and Arbitration Commission as being consistent with the public interest. Under the circumstances, recommendations of the government mediator carried significant weight. A similar situation exists in France where the Minister of Labour has the authority to decide whether to extend or enlarge a collective agreement to others who are beyond the scope of the occupations or region covered by the collective agreement. Because the mediator reports to the Minister respecting any rejected recommendations, the parties are likely to think twice before discarding mediatory recommendations.

In Japan, the term 'mediation' is reserved for a process established by joint agreement by the parties or by order of the Labour Commission in a dispute seriously affecting the public welfare. Under the Japanese system, a tripartite panel proposes a specific settlement and, if necessary, uses publicity to help pressure the parties to accept.

66. Both the Negotiation and Conciliated Negotiation models provide disputing parties with a goal directed opportunity to gain a better understanding of each other's needs, values and alternative opportunities. If they are amenable to improving the harmony of their interrelationship, these models provide a means with which this can be achieved. Moreover, these models allow the flexibility needed to examine complex, multifaceted problems and adjust competing values and goals in such a way that the dignity and worth of all participants are acknowledged and the result is tailored to meet their unique needs. In addition, negotiated solutions can be innovative; they can explore previously untried adjustments of differences. Finally, Negotiation can take account of unofficial norms (for example, deference to the interests of longer term workers) and can accommodate competing norms (for example, promotion based on ability versus promotion opportunities for loyal, long-term workers.)

On the negative side, Negotiation and Conciliated Negotiation pose an opportunity for sacrificing the interests of the weak and for reaching expedient settlements that satisfy the desires of the participants but ignore the demands of social and economic interests (including official norms) not represented at the bargaining table. However, where the role of the conciliator is mandatory and the conciliator occupies a governmental position, there is an opportunity to introduce larger concerns of national need and principles of justice into the deliberations. This is especially true if the process involves leveraged mediation.

67. Intervention by impartial parties seeking to mediate often adds to the time and effort that must be expended by the negotiating parties. The cost of that additional time and effort assists both sides if the respective benefits of settlement are enhanced beyond those added costs. However, it is possible for those costs to exceed such enhancement, even if the intervention produces a settlement more valuable to both sides. Moreover, if one side is significantly better equipped to bear added costs of negotiating, or if maintenance of the *status quo* during mediation significantly aids one party, the intervention mechanism will itself alter the parties' relative bargaining power.'[28]

IX. PRESTIGIOUS EXHORTATION

68. Much of the effort of legal scholars in preparing publications and delivering speeches is based on the assumption that those who make important decisions often are influenced by the exhortations of high status individuals and institutions. That this assumption is more than the wishful thinking of mere academicians finds support in the frequency with which Adjudication takes guidance from, or at least, attempts to explain its results by reference to, authorities such as treatises and scholarly journals. In the exercise of Governmental Fiat, too, justification often cites to similar 'authoritative sources'. Whether by means of a Papal Encyclical On Work or a specially convened council of experts, such as President Clinton's Commission on the Future of Worker–Management Relations, persons in high office often invest substantial resources in an effort to utilize Prestigious Exhortation as a method of interests dispute resolution.

69. A considerable range of techniques is used in an effort to engage in Prestigious Exhortation as a method for resolving employment interests disputes. At the international level, Recommendations of the International Labour Organization provide the prime example of reliance upon Prestigious Exhortation as a method of resolving interests disputes. A comparable international instrument of more limited scope is the OECD's Guidelines for Multinational Enterprises. In both cases the source of recommendation carries the prestige of being a product of deliberation by representatives selected by member governments as well as by the leading organizations representing employer and worker interests.

Multilateral treaties such as the European Communities' Charter of Fundamental Social Rights for Workers also rely on authoritative persuasiveness to influence decisions by those who shape Governmental Fiat, Adjudication and, perhaps, Negotiation. In time, such exercises in non-binding Prestigious Exhortation sometimes are converted into binding codes of conduct imposed through Governmental Fiat. However, as noted by more than one respected observer, in the absence of external monitoring and enforcement sanctions, often exhortations by public and private international bodies have been 'rich in principle, but weak in enforcement.'[29] Efforts such as the OEDC Guidelines and the corporate codes of conduct adopted by many merchandizing companies whose goods are produced in Third World countries, in large measure have been designed to deter government regulation (Governmental Fiat) and boycotts of consumers, labour organizations, and investors (Acquiescence

---

28. H. Collins, Justice is Dismissal: The Law of Termination of Employment, Oxford, 1992, pp. 137–139; A. Goldman, above at 82 *Ky. L.J.* 939, 1994.
29. B. Hepple, 'A Race to the Top? International Investment Guidelines and Corporate Codes of Conduct', 20 *Comp. Lab. L. & Pol. J.* 347, 354, 1999.

in Unilateral Action). Here, again, the rhetoric generally exceeds the impact due to inadequate independent monitoring.[30]

70. Some efforts to utilize the mechanism of Prestigious Exhortation are institutionalized within a national system. For example, in the United States the National Conference of Commissioners on Uniform State Laws is a body of lawyers, judges, legislators, and law professors appointed from each state, usually by the State's Governor, for three-year terms. The responsibility of the Conference is to develop, in consultation with the appropriate committee of the American Bar Association, proposed legislative codes so as to harmonize and improve state laws. In 1991 the Conference approved a Model Employment Termination Act.

Other efforts to utilize Prestigious Exhortation are organized *ad hoc* as was the case of the proposed amendments to the Treaty of the European Union on the subject of Fundamental Social Rights. That proposal, developed in 1996 by Professors Roger Blanpain, Bob Hepple, Silvana Sciarra, and Manfred Weiss, was endorsed by well over a hundred labour and employment law scholars throughout Europe.

71. Prestigious Exhortation is used not only to urge adoption of specific standards for balancing competing interests involved in the employment relationship, but also to obtain adherence to recognized standards. In such instances the process relies on the desire of the parties to maintain a good reputation either with the highly respected persons in particular or with the public in general. The latter approach sometimes is referred to as the 'sunshine effect'. (The reference is to the cleansing effect that often results from exposure to sunshine.)

72. An example of the ILO's use of Prestigious Exhortation as a means of attaining compliance with recognized standards is found in the activities of the Committee of Experts which annually publishes observations noting discrepancies between the reports respecting the state of affairs in a nation's employment relations and the applicable standard established by an ILO Convention. Similarly, the Committee of Experts exerts such pressure of public opinion when it issues requests for additional information concerning a nation's compliance with a Convention.

Still another example of Prestigious Exhortation as a means of encouraging parties to settle labour relations interests disputes by adhering to established norms of behaviour has begun to develop under the North American Agreement on Labour Cooperation which was adopted as an adjunct to the North American Free Trade Agreement (NAFTA). This treaty among Canada, Mexico and the US does not establish new labour standards but rather calls for the member nations to meaningfully enforce their own laws. In the event a party asserts that there is a deficiency in such enforcement, it can request establishment of a tri-national Evaluation Committee of Experts to examine the enforcement practices in question. A finding of persistent failure of enforcement respecting minimum wage, child labour or safety and health laws can eventually be resolved by Adjudication by a five member arbitral panel. However, the inquiry by the Evaluation Committee of Experts, whose approach is

---

30. B. Hepple, above, 20 *Comp. Lab. L. & Pol. J.* 347, 355, 359–60.

that of Prestigious Exhortation, is the final step respecting all other labour relations interests disputes.

73. Although cynics might assert that Prestigious Exhortation is nothing more than wishful thinking or even window dressing to placate the public, there is some evidence of its effectiveness. Certainly the extent to which such sources are cited by courts, administrators, and other adjudicative bodies demonstrates that this approach has at least some impact on conflict resolution. Similarly, the ILO Committee of Experts reports show a pattern of progress that indicates that its process of inquiry has generated greater compliance with ILO Conventions.[31] And, informal reports from the early NAFTA Evaluation Committee of Experts experience suggests that, there too, some impact is being made through the public exposure of deficiencies.

74. One problem with Prestigious Exhortation is that its effectiveness often is lost if the pronouncement is ill-timed.[32] Another inherent weakness is the danger that frequent use diminishes its effectiveness both because the prestige of the institution or the individuals may tarnish with use and because the public and the parties may become numbed and cease to give much attention to the urgings.[33] Also, it has been observed that the prestigious institutions themselves can become administratively overwhelmed, attempt to accomplish more than is feasible, become mired in institutionally narrow thinking, and lose effectiveness.

SELECT BIBLIOGRAPHY

R. Ben-Israel, R. Fahlbeck, A. Goldman, J. Isaac, R. McCallum, M. Mironi, J. Rojot, A. Suviranta, T. Treu, and J. Wood, 'Comparative Study of the Role of Third Party Intervention in Resolving Interests Disputes', 10 *Comp. Lab. L.J.* 271, 1989.

R. Blanpain (ed.), *International Encyclopaedia for Labour Law and Industrial Relations*, Deventer.

EEC, *Prevention and Settlement of Industrial Conflict in EEC Countries*, Brussels, 1982.

A. Goldman, *Settling for More: Mastering Negotiating Strategies and Techniques*, Washington, DC, 1991.

---

31. N. Valticos and G. von Potobsky, *IELL* (Int'l Lab. L.), 1994, para. 698. However, there are alternative assessments that question whether the ILO has had a material impact on the lives of workers. S. Cooney, 'Testing Times for the ILO: Institutional Reform for the New International Political Economy', 20 *Comp. Lab. L. & Pol. J.* 365, 1999.

32. Political or economic events can quickly overshadow carefully orchestrated efforts to utilize the device of Prestigious Exhortation. For reports of such an experience, *see* S. Estreicher, 'The Dunlop Report and the Future of Labor Law Reform', 12 *The Lab. Lawyer* 117, 1996 and P. Leibold, 'Labor Legislation in the 104th Congress: Follow the Money', 12 *The Lab. Lawyer* 137, 1996.

33. S. Cooney, 'Testing Times for the ILO: Institutional Reform for the New International Political Economy', 20 *Comp. Lab. L. & Pol. J.* 365, 1999; E. Córdova, 'Some Reflections on the Overproduction of International Labor Standards', 14 *Comp. Lab. L. J.* 138, 1993.

T. Hanami, 'The Settlement of Labour Disputes in Worldwide Perspective', *Int'l Soc. Sci. J.*, 1980, p. 490.

T. Hanami and R. Blanpain, *Industrial Conflict Resolution in Market Economies*, Deventer, 1984.

ILO, *Conciliation and Arbitration Procedures in Labour Disputes*, Geneva, 1980.

Japan Institute of Labor, *The Future of Dispute Resolution in Labour and Employment Law*, Tokyo, 1996.

J. Isaac, J. Loewenberg, R. McCallum, J. Rojot. A. Suvirenta, T. Toriendl, T. Treu, M. Weiss and J. Wood, 'The Neutral and Public Interests in Resolving Disputes', 13 *Comp. Lab. L. J.*, 371, 1992.

J. Rojot, *Negotiation: From Theory to Practice*, London, 1991.

J. Schregle, *Negotiating Development: Labour Relations in Southern Asia*, Geneva, 1987.

Index

685

687

697